A GREEK - ENGLISH LEXICON

OF THE SEPTUAGINT

A Greek - English Lexicon

of the Septuagint

Part I

A - I

Compiled by

J. Lust
E. Eynikel
K. Hauspie

with the collaboration of

G. Chamberlain

Deutsche Bibelgesellschaft

1992

ISBN 3-438-05125-7
A Greek-English Lexicon of the Septuagint, Part I
© 1992 Deutsche Bibelgesellschaft, Stuttgart
Printed in Germany

5. 2000

CONTENTS

Introduction

Abbreviations

Bibliography

Contents

PREFACE

The present lexicon is a companion to the edition of the Septuagint edited by A.Rahlfs published by the Würtembergische Bibelanstalt, now Deutsche Bibelgesellschaft in Stuttgart. The authors would like to thank Dr. E.W. Tuinstra, Translation Supervisor of the Dutch Bible Society (Nederlands Bijbelgenootschap), J. de Waard, Regional Translation Coordinator of the United Bible Societies, and Dr. S. Meurer, General Secretary of the German Bible Society (Deutsche Bibelgesellschaft), for having made this publication possible.

In composing this lexicon we have benefited from the advice and assistance of many others. First of all we are indebted to E. Tov (Jerusalem), R. Kraft and J. Abercrombie (Pennsylvania) who aroused our interest in the lexicography of the Septuagint and who encouraged us to start the project supporting us with their "Computer Assisted Tools for Septuagint Studies". C.C. Caragounis (Lund) corrected the first print-outs and made valuable suggestions. The much appreciated cooperation of G. Chamberlain (Champaign, IL) is explained in the introduction. In our own university we were fortunate to have understanding collegues who have offered constructive criticism. We are especially indebted to W. Clarysse of the Department of Ancient History, a specialist in papyrology, who offered helpful advice and provided us with useful complements to our own findings. In seminars several students assisted us with the initial efforts. Others helped with the typing of the manuscript: especially F. Van Gerven, G. Hauspie, E. Joris. Special mention should be made of B. Doyle who corrected the English, W. Bouciqué, and V. Vandermeersch, specialists in classical Greek and the first regular collaborators to the project, and M. van Rooij an occasional collaborator.

The present team consists of J. Lust, Professor of Old Testament Exegesis and Septuagintal Studies in Leuven (Belgium), E. Eynikel, Professor of Old Testament Exegesis in Nijmegen and Heerlen (The Netherlands), K. Hauspie, specialist in Classical and Koine Greek, trained at the K.U. Leuven (Belgium). The team is assisted by A. Claes (theologian and biblicist of the K.U. Leuven) who took care of the CATSS data-base, and D. D'huyvetters (classicist of the K.U. Leuven) responsible for the final lay-out.

The research for this work was facilitated by the availability of the excellent library of the Faculty of Theology and its helpful staff, and the library of the Departments of Classical and Oriental Studies. The project is supported by the Faculty of Theology and the "Onderzoeksfonds" of the K.U. Leuven, the Belgian "Nationaal Fonds voor Wetenschappelijk Onderzoek", the Faculty of Theology of the K.U. Nijmegen, the Abbay of Westmalle, and the Dutch and German Bible Societies.

Leuven, May, 1992   J. Lust

INTRODUCTION

I. IN GENERAL

Background and Need

The last lexicon specifically geared to the requirements of the Septuagint is now more than a century and a half old: J.F. Schleusner's *Novus thesaurus philologico criticus, sive lexicon in LXX et reliquos interpretes graecos ac scriptores apocryphos veteris testamenti*, Leipzig, 1820-1821. Re-editions of its five impressive volumes were published in Glasgow, in 1822, and in London in 1829.[1] Notwithstanding these reprints, surviving copies are rare. While it was and remains a good tool, it is, nevertheless, antiquated. Since its appearance many new papyri have been found, the vocabulary of which sheds a new light on several terms of the Septuagint, and numerous lexicographic studies have been published which have refined our knowledge of biblical and Koine Greek. It should also be observed that Schleusner did not produce a lexicon of biblical Greek in the strict sense of the word, but rather a lexicon of biblical Hebrew.[2]

The lack of an up-to-date lexicon of the LXX was partly compensated for by the production of several good lexica in related fields. Reference should be made to G. Lampe's dictionary of Patristic Greek, W. Bauer's lexicon of the NT, the UBS lexicon of the NT based on semantic domains, and Moulton-Milligan's vocabulary illustrated from the papyri, to be complemented with Preisigke-Kiessling's lexicon of the Greek papyri. Septuagint scholars may also have recourse to Liddell-Scott-Jones' excellent comprehensive Greek dictionary.[3] It is the best general source of information concerning the Greek language. Its supplement issued in 1968 palliates some of its deficiencies in the area of the Septuagint. Nevertheless many shortcomings remain in this particular area. They are clearly indicated in the reviews by W. Baars and J. Lee, and in E. Tov's 1976-report on a lexicon of the Septuagint.[4]

---

1. The reprints are bound up into three volumes.
2. See our contribution on *J.F. Schleusner and the Lexicon of the Septuagint*, in *ZAW* 102 (1990) 256-262.
3. G.W.H. LAMPE, *A Patristic Greek Lexicon*, Oxford, 1968; W. BAUER, *Griechisch-deutsches Wörterbuch zu den Schriften des Neuen Testaments und der frühchristlichen Literatur*, 6., völlig neu bearbeitete Auflage von Kurt und Barbara Aland, Berlin, 1988, compare with *A Greek-English Lexicon of the New Testament and Other Early Christian Literature*. A Translation and adaptation of the fourth revised and augmented edition of W. BAUER's Griechisch-deutsches Wörterbuch by W.F. ARNDT - F.W. GINGRICH, second edition, revised and augmented from W. Bauer's fifth edition, Chicago, 1979; J.H. MOULTON -G. MILLIGAN, *The Vocabulary of the Greek Testament*, London, 1930; J.P. LOUW, E.A. NIDA, *Greek English Lexicon of the New Testament, Based on Semantic Domains*, 2 vols., New York, UBS, 1988; H.G. LIDDELL - R. SCOTT - H.S. JONES, *A Greek-English Lexicon, with a Supplement*, Oxford, ⁹1968 (= LSJ); M.A. BAILLY, *Dictionnaire Grec-Français*, éd. rev. par L. SÉCHAN et P. CHANTRAINE, Paris, 1984; F. PREISIGKE - E. KIESSLING, *Wörterbuch der griechischen Papyrusurkunden* Band 1, Berlin, 1925; Band 2, Berlin, 1927; Band 3, Berlin, 1931; Band 4, fasc.1-4, Marburg, 1944-1971.
4. W. BAARS, *Review of "The Greek English Lexicon. A Supplement"*, in *VT* 20 (1970) 371-379 = SCS,1, ed. R. KRAFT, Missoula MT, 1972, p.11-12; E. TOV, *Some Remarks on a Lexicon of the Septuagint*, in *BIOSCS* 9 (1976) 14-46; J.A. LEE, *A Note on Septuagint Material in the Supplement to Liddell and Scott*, in *Glotta* 47 (1969) 234-242; see also G.B. CAIRD, *Towards a Lexicon of the Septuagint*, in *JTS* 19 (1968) 453-475 = SCS,1, ed. R. KRAFT, Missoula MT, 1972, p.110-132. More supplements to LSJ can be found in R. RENEHAN, *Greek Lexicographical Notes*

The need for a new lexicon of Septuagintal Greek has long been felt. In his *Introduction to the OT in Greek*, H.B. Swete mentions that already in 1895, a Cambridge committee drew up a plan for a new LXX lexicon.[5] A decade later, A. Deissmann and M. Margolis independently expressed the need for such a research tool. The latter provided us with some fine probes and sample approaches related to Septuagintal lexicography. His major preoccupation was the refinement of the Hatch and Redpath concordance, which according to him, was deficient in many respects. More recently, H. Gehman was asked to prepare a LXX-dictionary. When he was halfway through the work on the first letter of the alphabet, the plan was abandoned. In a variety of ways, scholars like J.E. Gates, G.B. Caird, and G.D. Kilpatrick have been working on various aspects of LXX lexicography. Samples of their work and their proposals were collected by R. Kraft in the first volume of Septuagint and Cognate Studies. Following the initiative of its first president Sidney Jellicoe, the International Organisation for the Septuagint and Cognate Studies (IOSCS), founded in 1968, agreed to sponsor a project to create a lexicon of the Septuagint. The dynamic forces chosen to steer the project were R. Kraft and E. Tov. They were convinced that the only efficient and realistic way in which to approach the problems of the undertaking was to establish a computer generated base from which the necessary work of concordancing and sorting could be done. This resulted in the CATSS (Computer Assisted Tools for Septuagint Studies) enterprise. The lexicon project proper, however, did not get off the ground and seems to be dormant. In the sections on Septuagint Lexicography in his recent survey of studies on the Septuagint, E. Tov does not even mention the project any more.[6] Recently T. Muraoka launched his pilot plan intending to explore the concrete problems connected with Septuagintal lexicography. His endeavour is confined to the Minor Prophets.[7] Meanwhile, F. Rehkopf completed a Vocabulary of the Septuagint.[8] It is a simple tool, intended as a help for students. It offers a one-word translation of all terms occurring in the edition of Rahlfs. Approximate information is added concerning the frequency of each word in the Old Testament and the New. Simultaneously and independently, a similar project was launched by G. Chamberlain in the U.S. His concise dictionary was to comprise only those words that are not included in Bauer's New Testament Lexicon. Around the same time, we started our work on a Septuagint lexicon in Leuven. In a meeting with G. Chamberlain at the SBL convention in Kansas (November 1991) we decided to make a joint venture. The basic pattern to be followed was the one of the Leuven project.

(Hypomnemata, 45), Göttingen, 1975, and (Hypomnemata, 74), Göttingen, 1982 (reprint of material which originally appeared in *Glotta*, in a series of articles published between 1968 and 1972); see also T. DREW-BEAR, *Some Greek Words*, in *Glotta* 50 (1972) 61-96 and 182-228; S. TIGNER, *Some LSJ Addenda and Corrigenda* in *Glotta* 52 (1974) 192-206.

5. Cambridge, 1900, p.290, n.1. For the following survey, see R. KRAFT (ed.), *Septuagintal Lexicography* (SCS,1), Montana, Missoula, 1972.

6. See e.g. *Die griechischen Bibelübersetzungen*, in ANRW, vol.20.1, Berlin, New York, 1987, p.170.

7. T. MURAOKA, *Towards a Septuagint Lexicon*, in C. COX (ed.), *VI.Congress of the International Organisation for Septuagint and Cognate Studies: Jerusalem 1986* (SCS, 23), Atlanta, G., 1987, pp.255-276; ID., *Septuagintal Lexicography: Some General Issues*, in ID. (ed.), *Melbourne Symposium on Septuagint Lexicography* (SCS, 28), Atlanta, G., 1990, pp.17-48; ID., *Hebrew Hapax Legomena and Septuagint Lexicography*, in C. COX, *VII Congress of the International Organisation for Septuagint and Cognate Studies. Leuven 1989* (SCS, 31), Atlanta, G., 1991, 205-222.

8. *Septuaginta-Vokabular*, Göttingen, 1989.

Contents

The Leuven lexicon project is associated with the CATSS project and uses its computer-readable files. With the exception of proper names, the lexicon covers all the words in Rahlfs' edition of the Septuagint.[9] For practical reasons, words occurring in the critical apparatus, as well as the variants attested in the critical editions from Cambridge and Göttingen, are not systematically incorporated. They should be fully added in a later version. Proper names are included only when they are a transliteration of Hebrew words that are common nouns. Thus it is noted that, for instance in 1 Kgs 9,13, Βαμα stands for Hebrew במה *high place*.

Each word is provided with morphological tagging. The grammatical abbreviations in this section are an adaptation of those used in the CATSS files.[10] See "Abbreviations. II. Morphological Codes".

Drawing from the same CATSS files, the lexicon provides statistics telling the reader how often a word occurs in the respective books of the Greek Bible. For this purpose we classified those books in five groups of approximately the same size: the Torah, the Early Prophets including 1 and 2 Chronicles, the Later Prophets, the Writings without Chronicles, and those books which do not occur in the Hebrew Bible. A sixth figure gives the total.

These statistics should offer a double improvement on X. JACQUES, *Index des mots apparentés dans la Septante* (Subsidia biblica, 1), Rome, 1972. First, X. Jacques subdivides the Biblical books into four groups, following their sequence in Rahlfs' edition. In so doing, he mixes the Deuterocanonial books with the Protocanonical. Most of the Deuterocanonical writings were composed in Greek, not in Hebrew. The Greek vocabulary used in these books differs from that employed in the translation of the others. For statistical purposes it is better to keep them apart. Secondly, while X. Jacques indicates whether or not a given Greek word is attested in one or more of his categories of biblical books, he omits to give figures.

No attempt was made to separate the deuterocanonical sections from the protocanonical books such as Esther and Daniel, nor to distinguish between those deuterocanonical books that are, and those that are not based on Semitic originals.

The Lexicon further supplies up to five references to biblical texts in which a given word occurs, in the order of their appearance.

These data are followed by one or more translations rather than by a description of the meaning. For each translation implying a new meaning, a reference is given to an example. In addition to the translation, four categories of special cases may be indicated. First, expressions which can be labeled as classical Greek, and verb forms deserving a special tranlation. Second, expressions which are less common or suitable in classical Greek but which are literal renderings of Hebrew idioms. Third, passages in which the Greek text may be corrupt. These cases are rare since Rahlfs most often printed the corrected version. Fourth, passages in which the LXX differs from the MT, having misread the Hebrew, or read it differently, or having used a slightly divergent text. In categories three and four, the beginning of the discussion is marked with

---

9. First edition: Stuttgart, 1935; several anastatic reprints.
10. R.A. KRAFT, E. TOV, *Computer Assisted Tools for Septuagint Studies (CATSS). Volume 1, Ruth* (SCS, 20), Atlanta, G., 1986, p.73.

an asterisk (*) and a reference to the biblical passage. Exhaustiveness is not intended. For a further discussion of this approach, see the second part of this introduction.

When a word appears to be proper to the Septuagint and the literature depending on it, it is characterized as a neologism. When it occurs in the Septuagint as well as in the contemporary papyri and in the literature from the period of Polybius onwards, it is also labeled as a neologism but a question mark is added. The label suggests that the word in question was probably not used before the time of the composition of the Septuagint. It should be noted that this suggestion is rather tentative. Indeed, we do not know exactly when the respective books of the Septuagint were written. Moreover, it is hard to define the exact date of some other texts, especially of the inscriptions. These and other pitfalls make it difficult to decide which of the septuagintal words should be called neologisms with or without a question mark.

At the end of the treatment of each lemma, bibliographical information is provided. For each word, abbreviated references are given to lexicographical bibliography, when available. The fuller references are listed in the bibliographical list following upon the present introduction. Selections had to be made. With the exception of some publications that are exceptionally relevant for the OT, most of the works mentioned in TWNT are not included. Special attention has been given to authors such as G.B. Caird who seek to offer systematic corrections to the treatment of the Septuagint in Liddell-Scott-Jones. Numerous lexicographical contributions have been published in a diversity of periodicals, monographs, commentaries and volumes of collective essays. Our bibliographical list may help to save some of them from oblivion. Its compilation has been made possible thanks to the help of P.-M. Bogaert.[11]

Finally, compound verbs are referred to under the simple form. When the simple form is not used in the LXX, it is listed without translation and statistics, but with its prefixes. This should facilitate the finding of etymologically connected verb-clusters.

The work will be complemented with a separate volume listing all the verb forms and their lemmata. This should help beginners to determine under which lemma they should look for the translation of a difficult form.

Lay-out

The lay-out can best be explained with some examples:

γαβιν   N 0-1-0-0-0-1   Gn 38,8; Dt 7,3
2 Kgs 25,12   A: *to form connexions by marriage* [πρός τινα] Dt
=נבין (Aram.?) for MT יגבים farmers, cpr.   7,3; M: *to marry* sb [τινα] Gn 38,8; neol.
γεωργοί Jer 39(52),16   Cf. HARL 1986, 265; HELBING 1928, 251-252
γαβις   N 0-0-0-1-0-1   (→ ἐπι-)
Jb 28,18   γάρ[+]   X 294-32-190-371-641-1528
=נביש *crystal*   Gn 2,5; 3,5; 4,25; 7,4; 9,5
γαμβρεύω   V 2-0-0-0-0-2   conjunction used to express cause, inference,

---

11. P.-M. Bogaert graciously gave us a copy of his rich card index. Use was also made of E. TOV, *Lexical and Grammatical Studies on the Language of the Septuagint*, Jerusalem, 1975 (internal publication). To these data we added our own findings.

continuation, or to explain; *for, since, as* (cause) Gn 2,5; *for* (explanation) Gn 9,5; γάρ ... γάρ ... (introducing several arguments for the same assertion) Sir 37,13; γὰρ ... γάρ ... (one clause confirming another clause) Jdt 7,27; with other particles and conjunctions: ἰδοὺ γάρ *for, behold* Jdt 5,23; καὶ γάρ *for* 2 Mc 1,19; οὔτε γὰρ ... οὔτε ... *for neither ... nor ...* Wis 12,13; *Jb 9,24 γάρ corr.? γῆ or γαῖ for MT ארץ *land* or *lands*
Cf. AEJMELAEUS 1982, 64-66; LE BOULLUEC 1989, 31

γένημα,-ατος⁺   N3N 35-5-14-9-14-77

Gn 41,34; 47,24; 49,21; Ex 22,4; 23,10
that which is begotten or *born, offspring, product, fruit* Gn 41,34; *Gn 49,21 γενήματι -אמירי *branches* or -אמרי *fawns* for MT אמרי *words*
Cf. LE BOULLUEC 1989, 224-225; LEE 1983, 99; WALTERS 1973, 115

γεώργιον,-ου⁺   N2N 1-0-1-5-1-8
Gn 26,14; Jer 28(51),23; Prv 6,7; 9,12; 24,5
tilled land, field Gn 26,14; *farming* Jer 28(51),23; *crop* Prv 24,5; *Prv 6,7 γεωργίου -◊ קצר *harvest* for MT קצין *chief, ruler*

- A supralinear ⁺ added to the lemma signals that the word occurs also in the New Testament.
- The lemma is always followed by a code indicating its **grammatical form**. It defines the "kind of word" (e.g. N for noun), the class (1, 2, or 3), the gender (M, F, N, respectively for masculine, feminine, or neuter). When the noun is a transliteration of the Hebrew, only the kind of word is mentioned. See General Abbreviations. Also, for nouns the genitive is indicated, and for adjectives the masculine, feminine, and neuter forms.
- The same line gives the **statistical information** explained above. The figures are divided by a hyphen. The sixth figure represents the total. For some biblical books -Judges, Tobit, Daniel with its Greek appendices, and for parts of Joshua-Rahlfs' edition gives two versions based on different manuscripts. A word occurring in both of these versions is counted twice in the statistics.
- The second line provides the references to the **first five occurrences**, when available.
- The text starting on the third line may exceptionally begin with an **equals sign** (=) followed by a Hebrew word. This indicates that the Greek is a transliteration. As a rule, the third line renders the translation of the lemma in *italics*. When the word in question has more than one meaning, several translations are offered, each of them with a reference to an example.
- The **asterisk** (*) indicates that the following case deals with a passage in which the Greek differs from the Hebrew and in which the difference can be explained on the level of the writing, reading, or hearing of the Hebrew word, or as an error in the transmission of the Greek text.
- The abbreviation "**corr.**" suggests that the Greek word found in the manuscripts printed in Rahlfs may be corrupt. It may have to be replaced by the following Greek word which gives a better rendition of the Hebrew.
- The **hyphen** (-) before a Hebrew word indicates that the translator probably read or wished to read that word instead of the term given by the MT.
- The **diamond** (◊) before a Hebrew word designates it as a "root" rather than the form in which it occurs in the text.
- The **slash** (/) in a Hebrew word indicates prefixed and attached elements. As a rule, prefixes and suffixes are marked only when useful for the argument.
- The qualifier **neol.** at the end of a lemma indicates that the word in question is a neologism. It occurs only in the LXX and in the literature based on it. When a question-mark is added (neol.?) the suggestion is that the word does not occur before Polybius.
The abbreviations in the bibliography are explained in the fuller bibliography given in the introduction to the lexicon.

Methods and Justification

In the composition of a lexicon several options are taken and certain methods are followed. For practical reasons we opted in favour of a dictionary offering translation-equivalents rather than descriptions of meanings. Also, it was decided to present the lemmata according to their alphabetical order rather than to group them according to their meaning. This may not be the best approach for the composition of a more complete and final lexicon of the Septuagint. However, in the case of a more succinct lexicon the arrangement adopted allows the user the fastest access to the meanings of the words found in the biblical text. Also, without this approach, the realisation of the project, within reasonable time limits and with restricted resources, seemed to be impossible.

The limitation of the scope of the lexicon, covering the vocabulary of the Septuagint in Rahlfs' edition, was again guided by practical considerations. With E. Tov we are convinced that the choice is justifiable.[12] It certainly offers the advantage of a clear demarcation. Moreover, its computerised form facilitates the generation of statistical data. Also, it involves a project of a reasonable size. In future editions, the vocabulary should be added of the variants attested in the manuscripts of the LXX.

The question of the inclusion of the vocabulary of Aquila, Symmachus, and Theodotion is more complicated. First of all it should be noted that they do not belong to the canon of the Septuagint. Furthermore, it is not always easy to define which words belong to the "Three". Also, it is difficult to provide an adequate lexicographical description of the words used by Aquila and καίγε-Theodotion since these two revisers did not intend to give a translation in the traditional sense of the word.[13]

The detection and classification of the respective translations of each Greek word has been done by an expert in classical and Koine Greek. This procedure helped us to avoid the pitfalls of Schleusner's lexicon in which all too quickly the meaning of the underlying Hebrew was given rather than that of the Greek. As a rule, each occurrence of a word has been checked in its immediate context with the help of the concordance of Hatch and Redpath and the text of Rahlf's edition.[14] Most often, the work of Liddell-Scott-Jones was the immediate guide. Its slightly archaic English has been updated. Special attention has been given to works providing information on the papyri, such as the lexicon of Preisigke - Kiessling, Lee's standard work on the Pentateuch, and Horsley's studies.[15] This procedure has been strictly observed in the treatment of words that do not occur in the New Testament. Exceptions have been made for some very common words that are also attested in the New Testament, such as θεός. In these cases the lemma was construed with the help of the lexicon of Bauer and the other lexica listed above.[16]

Special cases were detected while checking the words in their context and with the help of the existing tools. They were divided into the four categories mentioned above. Much attention has been given to the instances in which the Greek seemed to differ from the Hebrew of the

---

12. E. TOV, *Some Thoughts on a Lexicon of the LXX*, in *BIOSCS* 9 (1976) 25-26.30-33.
13. TOV 1976 (A), 31.
14. E.HATCH-H.A.REDPATH, *A Concordance to the Septuagint and the Other Greek Versions of the Old Testament*, Oxford, 1897.
15. See note 3, as well as the bibliographical list.
16. See note 2.

Masoretic Text. Septuagint Greek is first of all translation Greek. Therefore, a lexicon of the Septuagint should refer to the Semitic original, at least in those cases where the deviations between a Greek word and its Semitic equivalent can be explained on the level of the morphemes, but also when the Greek words are incomprehensible because they are transliterations or because they adopted the meaning of the underlying Hebrew or Aramaic. A fuller justification of this procedure can be found in the next chapter of this introduction entitled: *Translation Greek*. The treatment of the cases in question is largely based on a series of commentaries with good philological notes. The ones that were consulted most frequently are listed in the section entitled "Bibliography. II. Commentaries". Only rarely an explicit reference to one of them has been given *in situ*. The same holds good for most of the lexica, such as Schleusner's *Thesaurus* and MM. On the other hand, references have been given systematically to TWNT and NIDNTT when these works appear to provide more or less substantial information on the use of a word in the OT.

The Target Group

In view of the lack of a contemporary lexicon of the Septuagint, the present work is aimed at a large group of scholars in many disciplines: students and specialists in the Old Testament and more specifically in the Septuagint, the New Testament, Intertestamental Literature, Patristics, Jewish Hellenism, and Greek linguistics. Its limited scope and its practical features make it more directly useful for students in these fields. On the other hand, its treatment of special cases as well as its bibliography should be of interest for more advanced scholars. The ideal user of the lexicon should have some knowledge of both Greek and Hebrew in order to understand the compact presentations of the cases in which the Greek differs or seems to differ from the Hebrew of the Masoretic text.

J. Lust

When preparing a lexicon of the Septuagint, one is faced with several basic questions related to the fact that most of the books of the LXX are translations. The lexicon is supposed to give the meaning of the words used in the Septuagint. However, which meaning should be given, the one intended by the translator or the one understood by the readers for whom it was intended? Is reference to be made to the underlying Hebrew or Aramaic, or is the search for meaning to be confined to the Greek? These questions are interrelated and connected with the special character of Septuagint Greek.

A. The Greek of the Septuagint

1. Which Type of Greek?

An impressive series of recent publications tries to define the special character of the Greek of the Septuagint.[17] Most of the authors are agreed that it reflects the Koine language and not a Jewish-Greek dialect nor a supernatural "language of the Holy Spirit". Especially the argumentation of J. Lee appears to be convincing. He and many others are the spiritual inheritors of the thoughts and views of A. Deissmann[18] who drew attention to the correspondences between the vocabulary of the papyri and that of biblical Greek. It should not be forgotten though that Deissmann's attention was focused on the Greek of the New Testament. However, when he dealt with the Septuagint he did not fail to notice the Semitic influence. It is of course most pronounced in those books that were not originally written in Greek but translated from a Hebrew or Aramaic original. When in the following pages we discuss the nature of "Septuagint Greek" and "translation Greek", we refer to the typical characteristics of the Greek used in that category of books.

Although it may be based on it, Septuagint Greek cannot simply be characterized as Koine Greek. It is first of all translation Greek.[19] This is most obvious on the level of syntax and style. The order of the words in the translation most often closely sticks to that of the Hebrew original. In fact, in many passages, the Hebrew and the Greek can be put in parallel columns,

---

17. S. OLOFSSON, *The LXX Version. A Guide to the Translation Technique of the Septuagint* (CBOT, 30), Stockholm, 1990, p.33-36; M. HARL, G. DORIVAL, O. MUNICH e.a., *La Bible grecque des Septante* (Init. au christianisme ancien), Paris, Cerf, 1988, p.233-241; E. TOV, *Die griechischen Bibelübersetzungen*, in ANRW II,20,1 (1987) 121-189, esp. 151-152; G.H.R. HORSLEY, *Divergent Views on the nature of the Greek of the Bible*, in Biblica 65 (1984) 393-403; J.A. LEE, *A Lexical Study of the Septuagint Version of the Pentateuch* (SCS,14), Chico, California, 1983, p.11-30; M. SILVA, *Bilingualism and the Character of Palestinian Greek*, in Biblica 61 (1980) 198-219 with a discussion of the views of J. VERGOTE, *Grec biblique*, in DBSuppl. 3 (1938) 1321-1396; C.H. RABIN, *The Translation Process and the Character of the Septuagint*, in Textus 6 (1968) 1-26.
18. A. DEISSMANN, *Biblische Studien. Beiträge, zumeist aus den Papyri und Inschriften, zur Geschichte der Sprache, des Schrifttums und der Religion des hellenistischen Judentums und des Urchristentums*, Marburg, 1895, and *Neue Bibelstudien. Sprachgeschichtliche Beiträge, zumeist aus den Papyri und Inschriften zur Erklärung des Neuen Testaments*, Marburg, 1897.
19. TOV 1987, 151; R. SOLLAMO, *Renderings of Hebrew Semiprepositions in the Septuagint* (Annales Acad. Sc. Fennicae, Diss. Hum. Litt., 19), Helsinki, 1979, p.6-8; R.A. MARTIN, *Some Syntactical Criteria of Translation Greek*, in VT 10 (1960) 295-310 and *Syntactical Evidence of Semitic Sources in Greek Documents* (SCS, 3), Missoula, Montana, 1974.

word by word.[20] The result is that the syntax of the Septuagint is Hebrew rather than Greek. No classical author and hardly any author using Koine Greek would have written sentences the way they are composed in the first Bible translation. Obviously, the translators payed more attention to the Semitic source language than to the Greek target language. They did not try to create an artistic Greek literary composition, but chose to stay as closely as possible with the Semitic original. This led to what is usually called "Hebraisms" or "semitisms" and which should probably better be called "translationisms".[21]

Of course, these remarks do not apply equally to all parts of the Septuagint. The first Bible translation displays a great variety in style and vocabulary and in the translation technique adopted. The typical traits of translation Greek are to be found especially in those books that are translated in a literal way.

2. Translation Greek and Vocabulary

Although less blatant, the translation character of the Greek of the Septuagint can also be detected on the level of the vocabulary. Admittedly, the translators appear to have most often carefully selected Greek terms whose semantic range covered more or less that of the Hebrew equivalent. They did not coin a new dialect nor did they use a Jewish-Greek jargon. Pure neologisms are not abundant. When some terms of the Septuagint seem rarely or not to be used in classical Greek, they are often attested in the Koine language of the papyri. Sometimes the translators had problems finding an adequate equivalent. In several instances they appear to have forged new words. For this purpose they often added prefixes to existing words, or they simply transliterated the Hebrew. On other occasions they chose a purely mechanical translation, or a "translation of embarrassment" using a colourless Greek word, such as διάστημα, when rendering a variety of techical Hebrew expressions.[22]

For some Hebrew words, the translators employed a stereotyped Greek equivalent, disregarding the context and semantic nuances. Thus שלום was as a rule translated by εἰρήνη although the semantic field covered by the Greek word does not coincide with that of the Hebrew. It is well known that this led to Greek sentences which must have been hard to understand for native Greek speakers, e.g. when in 2 Sam 11,7 David informs about εἰρήνην τοῦ πολέμου (the peace of the war).[23]

This leads us to an other observation which is usually overlooked in this context. When the Greek of the LXX is translation Greek, then the deviations between the Hebrew and the Greek are remarkable. The translators tried to render the Semitic text as faithfully as possible. When their translation deviates from it, this should be explained. It may be due to a series of facts. We confine ourselves here to the level of the vocabulary. The translators may have worked with a *Vorlage* which differed from the MT. Or they may have misunderstood the Hebrew, or understood it in a way differing from that of the masoretes. One should not forget that they worked with unvocalised texts. The identification of the root of some Hebrew word forms

---

20. This is demonstrated very clearly in the CATSS computer-readable aligned Hebrew and Greek Bible. See E. TOV, *A Computerized Data Base for Septuagint Studies. The Parallel Aligned Text of the Greek and Hebrew Bible* (Computer Assisted Tools for Septuagint Studies (CATSS) 2), Stellenbosch, 1986.

21. For a good classification of these "Hebraisms", see SOLLAMO 1979, 6-7.

22. Thus in the final vision of Ezekiel the translator uses διάστημα when translating several architectural terms: Ez 41,6.8; 42,5.12.13; 45,2; 48,15.17, see ZIMMERLI 1969, 1030, cpr. M. FLASHAR, *Exegetische Studien zum LXX-Psalter*, in *ZAW* 32 (1912) 94-95; RABIN 1968, 23-24.

23. See TOV 1987, 151.

may have caused problems. It should be added that the masoretes had to deal with similar difficulties. Their solution is not necessarily the best. Other differences between the Greek and the Hebrew may be due to the tendency of the translator to adapt the text to his public and its cultural environment. Or he may have wished to bring in his own theological views. Or the Greek may have been corrupted in the process of copying.

What implications does this have for the public using the translation? Were they aware of the translation character of its Greek and of its deviations from the original?

3. The Public and Their Language[24]

We do not know much about the public for which the translation was created. If one believes the letter of Aristeas, the Greek Pentateuch was made by Palestinian Jews for a scholarly purpose: for the library of the Ptolemaic king. In fact it was probably made for the Jews living in Egypt in the 3rd century B.C. Which language did they speak and write? The papyri suggest that they used the Greek of the Koine type. Some may have had a certain knowledge of Hebrew or Aramaic or both.[25] The translation may have helped them in their understanding of the Scriptures written in Hebrew and Aramaic.

However, there is a good chance that most of the early users read the Septuagint as a Greek text, without any knowledge of the Hebrew original. This is certainly the case when one turns to the members of the early christian church for whom the Septuagint became their canonical writings.

The Septuagint was also used by the Jews in Palestine. The scrolls found in Qumran are a final witness to that. They appear to have read it in the light of the Hebrew text and revised it accordingly.[26]

Some people maintain that the Jews in Egypt spoke a Jewish-Greek jargon. The evidence is usually taken from the Septuagint. We already suggested that no proof can be found for this. One of the strongest arguments against the existence of a Jewish-Greek dialect and its current use is the fluent Greek in the original Greek writings of the Bible. The Jews who wrote these books and who probably lived in Egypt, do not seem to have been influenced by a special Jewish-Greek dialect nor by a hebraising style or vocabulary.

When we study the Greek Bible, we are an entirely new public. Do we have to search for its meaning with the eyes and ears of 3rd century Jews in Egypt, or in Palestine, or of the early Christians? Or do we have to try to find out what the translator meant? Or should we read the Greek Bible as a timeless literary work in its own right, disregarding the author and its original public?

One possibility does not necessarily exclude the others. It may be interesting first to try to trace the intentions of the translator, comparing his Greek version with the Hebrew text,[27]

---

24. See especially HARL 1988, 224-228 and OLOFSSON 1990,36-39.
25. About the question of bilingualism, see VERGOTE 1945 and SILVA 1980.
26. See D. BARTHÉLEMY, *Les devanciers d'Aquila* (VTS, 10), Leiden, 1963 and E. TOV, *The Greek Minor Scroll from Naḥal ḥever* (DJD, 8), Oxford, 1990, esp. p.103-106.
27. In this process one is to be aware of the fact that the Hebrew of the MT is not necessarily the Hebrew text the translator worked with.

and then to study the interpretation given by the early christian authors.[28] In another step
one may approach the Septuagint from the point of view of the Jews in Palestine or in Egypt
in the early christian era and in the period immediately before it, comparing the Greek translation
with the targumim and the rabbinic interpretations of the Scriptures.[29] Or one may read the
Greek Bible as a classicist, noting the parallels and differences with classical Greek authors.
All these approaches can be labeled as diachronic. Alongside with or in contradiction to these
options one may prefer a synchronic reading. This possibility is much in favour in the realm
of the study of the Hebrew Bible and its modern translations. They are read as artistic compo-
sitions with rhetorical critical or structuralistic or wholistic or similar methods. Why would it
not be possible to do the same with the Septuagint?

4. The Septuagint, a Literary Work?

There is a tendency to take the Septuagint more seriously than it used to be.[30] However, this
does not necessarily mean that scholars who support this tendency defend the LXX as a literary
work in its own right. They first of all react against those who tend to use it as "a grab-bag
for conjectures and for rewriting the MT".[31] In many instances, it is the earliest commentary
of the Hebrew Scriptures. Moreover, it contains the canonic Scriptures of the early christian
church. Whether it can or should be considered as a literary work which should be studied
without reference to its historic situation is a different question.[32] Its artistic value differs from
book to book. In many cases it has its own message. The special characteristics of that message
are most clearly pronounced in those books which are translated in a rather free way, such
as Isaiah, and in books that were originally written in Greek. Studies of the Septuagint as an
independent literary work are not numerous. For Isaiah, reference can be made to J. Coste's
study of Is 25,1-5, for Hosea to those of T. Muraoka, and for Job to those of C. Cox.[33] However,
both Coste and Muraoka admit that the specificity of the contents of the LXX is best recognized
in a comparison with the MT. This practically means that, even when the Septuagint is studied
for its own sake, it still should not be forgotten that it is a translation.

B. The Lexicon and the Meanings of the Greek words of the Septuagint

Armed with these considerations on the specific character of the Septuagint and its translation
Greek, we now return to our questions about the typical features of a lexicon intended as a

---

28. See M. HARL, *Traduire la Septante en français*: pourquoi et comment? in *Lalies* 3 (1984) 83-93 and HARL
1988, 8-14.269-320.
29. See M.A.ZIPOR *Notes sur les chapitres XIX à XXII du Lévitique dans la Bible d'Alexandrie*, in *ETL* 67 (1991)
328-337
30. HARL 1988, 259; C. COX, *Methodological Issues in the Exegesis of LXX Job*, in C.Cox (ed.), *VI Congress of
the IOSCS* (SCS, 23), Atlanta, Georgia, 1987, p.79-89; J.W. WEVERS, *An Apologia for Septuagint Studies*, in *BIOSCS*
18 (1985) 16-38; A. PIETERSMA, *Septuagint Research: A Plea for a Return to Basic Issues*, in *VT* 35 (1985) 296-311;
T. MURAOKA, *Hosea IV in the Septuagint Version*, in *AJBI* 9 (1983) 24-64; ID., *Hosea V in the Septuagint Version*,
in *Abr-Nahrain* 24 (1986) 120-138; ID., *Introduction by the Editor*, in *Melbourne Symposium on Septuagint Lexicography*
(SCS, 28), Atlanta, Georgia, 1990, p.7-14; J. COSTE, *Le texte grec d'Isaïe XXV,1-5*, in *RB* 61 (1954) 36-66.
31. WEVERS 1985, 38. Compare with PIETERSMA 1985, 297 who reacts in a similar way and states that the primary
aim of LXX research is the recovery of the Old Greek text.
32. The strongest advocate of this approach seems to be C. Cox. See COX 1987, 79-89 and his paper read in
the IOSCS congress Leuven 1989. T.Muraoka (1982, 25) also strongly affirms that the Septuagint should be
studied as an independent work in its own right, however, he immediately adds: "of course with constant reference
to the original work".
33. See note 12.

tool for the study of that work. A good guide for such thoughts is offered by the proceedings of the symposium on Septuagint Lexicography in Melbourne.[34]

It is amazing that several leading authorities, who seem to accept that a lexicon of the LXX should first of all give the meaning intended by the translator, nevertheless hold that it should not, or rarely, refer to the Semitic text. Let us have a closer look at the problem.

If one decides that such a lexicon is to render the meaning of the words as they were read and understood by a public that had no knowledge whatsoever of the Semitic text underlying the Greek, perhaps no reference should be made to the Hebrew. However, if one opts for the other approach which seeks for the meaning intended by the translator, then this view can hardly be adopted. Indeed, the translator appears to have first of all wished to render his *Vorlage* as faithfully as possible. He wanted his translation to communicate the same message as that intended by the original text. When deviations occur, it seems reasonable that they should be signaled in the lexicon.

That does not mean that the lexicon should follow the example of its illustrious predecessor composed by Schleusner, or his source, the *Novus thesaurus philologicus* of J. Biel.[35] These works are Hebrew lexica rather than Greek ones. First of all, attention is to be given to the meaning of the Greek word in its context. However, when deviations from the Hebrew occur, and when these can be explained on the level of the morpheme, this should be noted. We opted for a non-directive indication, showing how the deviations could be explained, but not pointing at the party responsible for them. For instance, when a metathesis appears to have occurred between a ר and a ד, this is indicated without saying which direction the metathesis went.

A distinction can be made between several types of cases. Before we try to summarize them, it should be noted that the distinctions are sometimes rather artificial, and that several types may occur simultaneously.

1. In a first series of cases, the translator appears to have read in his *Vorlage* the same unvocalised word or morpheme which we can find in our printed Hebrew Bibles, but he gave it an interpretation differing from that found in the vocalized Masoretic Text.

1.a. He had to identify the root from which a noun or verb was derived. Thus when he found וירא he had to decide whether this form was a derivation of the verb ירא (to fear) or from ראה (to see). Many of these cases were caused by verb forms derived from weak verbs the root of which was hard to identify in an unvocalised text. Often only two consonants were easily recognisable. The editors of the MT and the translators made a different guess at the third consonant. In this rubric we may place the so called etymologising renderings.[36]

1.b. The translator also had to decide how the morpheme was composed. Indeed, in some cases, prefixes and suffixes were confused with parts of the root or of the main word: thus Nah 2,2 ἐκ θλίψεως -מ/צרה *from affliction* for MT מצורה *fortification*.

---

34. T. MURAOKA (ed). *Melbourne Symposium on Septuagint Lexicography* (SCS, 28). Atlanta, G., Scholars, 1990, XVI + 136 p.
35. See our contribution on *J.F. Schleusner and the Lexicon of the Septuagint*, in *ZAW* 102 (1990) 256-262.
36. TOV 1987, 138.

1.c. Similarly he had to decide how the words were split. In the handwritten texts, the blanks between the respective words were not always equally clear. One or more letters which in the MT are written at the end of a word are reflected in the translation as belonging to the beginning of the following word, or *vice versa*.[37] An example may be found in Gn 49,19-20 where the translator read the Hebrew *mem* as a suffix at the end of the last word of verse 19, whereas the MT understood it as a prefix at the beginning of the first word of a new verse. The LXX has: αὐτῶν κατὰ ποδάς. Ασηρ, rendering עקבם אשר *their heel. Asher*. The MT reads: עקב מאשר *heel. Of Asher*.

1.d. Even when the translator read the same vocalisation as the redactor or copyist of the MT, he had to decide which semantic interpretation he wished to give to each word. Some words had a wide range of meanings which could hardly be covered by one and the same Greek equivalent. Of course, the context could help him. However, in some cases he seems to have understood the context in a way differing from that found in the MT. This could lead to the choice of a translation which does not agree with the MT. We may refer to Jer 2,36 where τοῦ δευτερῶσαι *to repeat* is a correct translation of the Hebrew infinitive לשנות when taken out of its context. Another meaning of the same word fits the context of the MT much better: *to change (one's ways)*. It is often difficult to decide whether or not these cases should be taken up among the lexicographical differences between the LXX and the MT.

2. In a second series of cases, the translator may have read or heard a morpheme that slightly differed from that in the unvocalised MT.[38] This may be due to a mistake. It is not always clear to whom the mistake is to be attributed. It may have been caused by the translator or by a copyist of the Hebrew text. Some instances may not have to be evaluated as mistakes but rather as interpretative changes caused by the translator or by the redactor of the Semitic version he was working with.

2.a. One or more Hebrew characters could easily be interchanged in the copying or in the reading process.[39] The classical example is that of the confusion between ד and ר. This explains why the MT in Ez 17,7 mentions *one eagle* נשר אחד whereas the LXX has ἀετὸς ἕτερος - נשר אחר.[40]

2.b. In a similar way a metathesis could occur. This seems to have happened in Jb 36,15 where חלץ (MT: to set free) and לחץ (LXX: to afflict) were confused.

2.c. *Matres lectionis* could be added or dropped which could lead to different vocalisations and interpretations.

Several of these phenomena could occur simultaneously in the same word or context. For an example we may refer to Nah 2,12: τοῦ εἰσελθεῖν - ל/בוא *to go* for MT לביא *lion*. Whereas the MT read one word, the translator split it into a prefix and a verb. Moreover he seems to have

---

37. Tov 1981, 175.

38. For a good survey, see E. Tov, *The Text-critical Use of the Septuagint in Biblical Research* (JBS, 3), Jerusalem, 1981, 195-205, and *Interchanges of Consonants between the TM and the* Vorlage *of the Septuagint*, in *FS S. Talmon*, Winona Lake, IN, 1990.

39. A good survey is given in Tov 1981, 195-212.

40. Another well known example: in Gn 22,13 the LXX reads κριὸς εἷς - איל אחד *one ram* for MT איל אחר *a ram behind (him)*.

read a ו where the MT has a י. An other example is to be found in Hos 11,4. The end of the verse is perhaps most illustrative. The LXX has: δυνήσομαι αὐτῷ corresponding to Hebrew: אוכל לו, in which the verb is derived from יכל. The meaning is: *I shall prevail over him*. The MT however has: אוכיל : לא, deriving the same verb from אכל and splitting the expression over two sentences. In translation this can be rendered as follows: *I fed. Not...* In this case the words and even the sentences are split differently in the MT and in the Greek. Moreover, the MT seems to have read one more *mater lectionis* than the Hebrew. Also, the translator appears to have interpreted the words differently.

3. A third series of differences may be due to inner Greek corruptions. One Greek word was replaced by a another similar word through metathesis, or through the confusion of characters, or through another mechanism. Often the corruption occasioned a deviation from the Hebrew. In a lexicon based on the edition of Rahlfs, examples of this kind will be rare. Indeed, in his eclectic text, Rahlfs frequently corrected the Greek. Nevertheless the examples are not all together absent. Thus in 2 Chr 30,8 δότε δόξαν *give glory* probably originally read δότε δεξιᾶν as a translation of Hebrew תנו יד *give a hand, yield yourselves*. A similar case can be found in the older Greek manuscripts of Is 62,8 reading κατὰ τῆς δόξης αὐτοῦ *for his glory* for Hebrew בימינו *by his right hand*. However, in this case Rahlfs as well as Ziegler prefer the version of the hexaplaric manuscripts which corrected the text towards the MT and read κατὰ τὴν δεξιᾶν *by his right hand*.

4. Not only the differences should be noted. Incomprehensible Greek words which are in fact transliterations should also be signalled. Thus γαβις = נביש *crystal* in Jb 28,18. Moreover, in several instances, a well known Greek word does not seem to make sense in its context. A comparison with the Hebrew or Aramaic reveals that the translator used a stereotype rendering of the Semitic equivalent. The semantic range of that equivalent was larger or simply not completely coinciding with the chosen Greek term. E. Tov treated these instances in a balanced way.[41] Somehow they should be taken care of in the lexicon. In our succinct version we often simply give the meaning of the Hebrew, all or not adding the Hebrew term, and refer to the literature dealing with the case.

Furthermore, we observe that the translators sometimes created new expressions in order to render the Hebrew.[42] Often these neologisms were derived from existing words: thus ἀβατόω from ἄβατος. Information concerning these neologisms certainly fits very well into a lexicon of Septuagint Greek. However, it is not always easy to reach certainty in these matters. A word which may seem to be a neologism in the Septuagint may in fact be attested in the Koine Greek of earlier papyri.[43] In the present lexicon we indicate the neologisms without trying to be exhaustive. More important is that an adequate translation or interpretation is given. Similar problems exist in the area of "semitisms" or "translationisms". They are not always easy to identify unambiguously. Moreover, they are more current on the level of syntax and expressions then on that of the individual words. We already dealt briefly above with those phenomena. In our

---

41. E. Tov, *Greek Words and Hebrew Meanings*, in T.Muraoka (ed.), *Melbourne Symposium on Septuagint Lexicography* (SCS, 28), Atlanta, Georgia, 1990, p.83-126.
42. Lists of such words can be found in H.St John Thackeray, *A Grammar of the Old Testament Greek according to the Septuagint*, Cambridge, 1909, 104-105.299 and more extensively in H. Swete, *An Introduction to the Old Testament in Greek*, Cambridge, 1900, p.452-453. See also J. Lee 1983, 50-52.85-117, and LSJ *passim*.
43. See O. Montevecchi, *La Papirologia*, Turino, 1973 and the warnings of J.Lee 1983, 32-50. For the distinction between the labels "neol." and "neol.?" see the first part of this introduction.

lexicon some of the most pregnant ones are indicated as Greek expressions giving a literal rendition of the Hebrew. This is done e.g., by the abbreviation "semit.", or by means of a reference to the Hebrew: thus θανάτῳ ἀποθανεῖσθε for MT מות תמות *you shall surely die* Gn 2,17.

Conclusion

Septuagint Greek is first of all translation Greek. Therefore, a lexicon of the Septuagint should refer to the Semitic original, at least in those cases where the deviations between a Greek word and its Semitic equivalent can be explained on the level of the morphemes, but also when the Greek words as such are incomprehensible because they are transliterations or because they adopted the meaning of the underlying Hebrew or Aramaic. It may also be useful to note neologisms and expressions which can be labelled as "translationisms" or "semitisms".

J. Lust

ABBREVIATIONS

I. MORPHOLOGICAL CODES

This list contains the codes used in the morphological tagging of each word. The information is given on the first line, immediately before the statistical data.

V = verb
N = noun 1 = first declension
             2 = second declension
             3 = third declension
                           M = masculine
                           F = feminine
                           N = neuter
A = adjective
M = numeral
P = preposition
D = adverb
X = particle
I = interjection
C = conjunction
R = pronoun

II. BOOKS OF THE BIBLE

The following list includes the full and the abbreviated forms of all the biblical books. For statistical purposes they are subdivided into five groups of approximately the same size. The first four contain the books of the Hebrew Bible: the Torah, the Early Prophets including 1 and 2 Chronicles, the Later Prophets, the Writings without Chronicles. The fifth group contains the books of the Greek Bible which do not occur in the Masoretic Text.

Some books, or parts of books, occur twice. The reason for this is that Rahlfs' edition comprises two versions of these texts. An example may be useful. At εἴσοδος the abbreviation "Jgs^A 1,24" in the list of the first five occurrences indicates that the word in question occurs in the text of manuscript A of Judges. "Jgs 1,24" in the description of the lemma indicates that the word occurs both in ms A and in ms B. The word is counted twice in the statistics. In Joshua 15,22-62 and 18,22 - 19,45 the respective abbreviations "Jos^A" and "Jos^B" indicate that a word occurs respectively in ms A or in ms B, whereas "Jos^{BA}" means that it occurs both in ms A and in ms B. In the latter case, the word is counted twice.

1.	Genesis	Gn	4.	Psalms	Ps
	Exodus	Ex		Job	Jb
	Leviticus	Lv		Proverbs	Prv
	Numbers	Nm		Ruth	Ru
	Deuteronomy	Dt		Canticle (Song of Solom.)	Ct
2.	Joshua	Jos		Ecclesiastes (Preacher)	Eccl
	Joshua^B (15,22-62; 18,22-19,45)	Jos^B		Lamentations (Threni)	Lam
	Joshua^A (15,22-62; 18,22-19,45)	Jos^A		Esther	Est
	Judges^A	Jgs^A		Daniel^{LXX}	Dn^{LXX}
	Judges^B	Jgs^B		DanielTh	DnTh
	1 Samuel (1 Kingdoms)	1 Sm		Ezra (Esdras II)	Ezr
	2 Samuel (2 Kingdoms)	2 Sm		Nehemiah	Neh
	1 Kings (3 Kingdoms)	1 Kgs	5.	Esdras a (Esdras I)	1 Ezr
	2 Kings (4 Kingdoms)	2 Kgs		Judith	Jdt
	1 Chronicles	1 Chr		Tobit^{BA}	Tob^{BA}
	2 Chronicles	2 Chr		Tobit^S	Tob^S
3.	Isaiah	Is		I Maccabees	1 Mc
	Jeremiah	Jer		II Maccabees	2 Mc
	Ezekiel	Ez		III Maccabees	3 Mc
	Hosea	Hos		IV Maccabees	4 Mc
	Joel	Jl		Psalm 151	Ps 151
	Amos	Am		Odes	Od
	Obadiah	Ob		Wisdom of Solomon	Wis
	Jonah	Jon		Wisdom of Sirach	Sir
	Micah	Mi		Psalms of Solomon	PSal
	Nahum	Na		Baruch	Bar
	Habakkuk	Hab		Epistle of Jeremiah	LtJ
	Zephaniah	Zph		Susannah^{LXX}	Sus^{LXX}
	Haggai	Hag		SusannahTh	SusTh
	Zechariah	Zech		Bel^{LXX}	Bel^{LXX}
	Malachi	Mal		BelTh	BelTh

A:	active	LXX	Septuagint
abbrev.	abbreviation	M:	medium, middle
abs.	absolute	metaph.	metaphorical
acc.	accusative	metath.	metathesis
act	active	meton.	metonymical
adj.	adjective	metonym.	metonymically
adv.	adverb	mil.	military
aff.	affirmative	mss	manuscripts
affirm.	affirmative	MT	masoretic text
aor.	aorist	n.	note
Aram.	Aramaic	neg.	negative
Cf.	Confer (bibl.)	neol.	neologism
cl.	clause	neutr.	neutral
cogn.	cognate	nom.	nominative
coll.	collective	opp.	opposite
comp.	comparative	opt.	optative
corr.	correction for	P:	passive
cpr.	compare	pass.	passive
dat.	dative	pers.	person
dim.	diminutive	pft.	perfect tense
dir.	direct	pi.	piel
e.g.	*exempli gratia*	pl.	plural
epith.	epitheton	pos.	positive
esp.	especially	pred.	predicate
etym.	etymological	pres.	present tense
euph.	euphemism	prob.	probably
fem.	feminine	prol.	prologue
fut.	future	pron.	pronoun
gen.	genitive	ptc.	participle
gen.abs.	*genetivus absolutus*	1QIsᵃ	Qumran scroll, Isaiahᵃ
haplogr	halography	Sam.Pent.	Samaritan Pentateuch
Hebr.	Hebrew	sb	somebody
hist.	historical	sc.	*scilicet*
id.	idem	semit.	semitism
i.e.	*id est*	sg.	singular
imper.	imperative	sth	something
impers.	impersonal	subj.	subjunctive
impft.	imperfect	subst.	substantive
ind.	indicative	sup.	superlative
indir.	indirect	tit.	title
inf.	infinitive	transl.	translation
instr.	instrumental	usu.	usually
intrans.	intransitive	var.	variant
l.	litre(s)	vl.	*varians lectio*
Lat.	Latin	verb. adj.	verbal adjective
LH.	Late Hebrew	voc.	vocative
lit.	literally		

AASF	= Annales Academiae Scientiarum Fennicae
Aeg	= *Aegyptus*
AGJU	= Arbeiten zur Geschichte des Antiken Judentums und des Urchristentums
AEcR	= *American Ecclesiastical Review*
AJSL	= *American Journal of Semitic Languages and Literatures*
AnBib	= Analecta Biblica
AncB	= Anchor Bible
AnCl	= *Antiquité classique*
ANRW	= Aufstieg und Niedergang der Römischen Welt
AThR	= *Anglican Theological Review*
BeO	= *Bibbia e oriente*
BETL	= Bibliotheca ephemeridum theologicarum Lovaniensium
Bib	= *Biblica*
BibOr	= Biblica et orientalia
BiTr	= *Bible Translator*
BKAT	= Biblischer Kommentar. Altes Testament
BZ	= *Biblische Zeitschrift*
CB.OT	= Coniectanea biblica
CBLa	= Collectanea biblica Latina
CÉg	= *Chronique d'Egypte*
ÉeC	= Etudes et commentaires
Est Bib	= *Estudios Biblicos*
ET	= *Expository times*
EtB	= Etudes bibliques
ETL	= *Ephemerides theologicae Lovanienses*
Glotta	= *Glotta*
HSM	= Harvard Semitic Monographs
Hyp	= Hypomnemata. Untersuchungen zur Antike und zu ihrem Nachleben
ICC	= The International Critical Commentary
IEJ	= *Israel Exploration Journal*
IJT	= *Indian Journal of Theology*
IP	= Instrumenta patristica
JBL	= *Journal of Biblical Literature*
JJP	= *Journal of Juristic Papyrology*
JQR	= *Jewish Quarterly Review*
JSJ	= *Journal for the Study of Judaism in the Persian, Hellenistic and Roman Period*
JSSt	= *Journal of Semitic Studies*
JTS	= *Journal of Theological Studies*
KAT	= Kommentar zum Alten Testament
Klio	= *Klio*
LeDiv	= Lectio Divina
Mar.	= *Marianum*
MSS	= Münchener Studien zur Sprachwissenschaft
MSSNTS	= Monograph series. Society for New Testament studies

MSU	=	Mitteilungen des Septuaginta-Unternehmens
Muséon	=	*Le Muséon. Revue d'études Orientales*
NT	=	*Novum Testamentum*
NTS	=	*New Testament Studies*
OBO	=	Orbis Biblicus et Orientalis
OLA	=	Orientalia Lovaniensia Analecta
Or	=	*Orientalia*
OTL	=	Old Testament Library
OTS	=	Oudtestamentische Studiën
RB	=	*Revue Biblique*
RdÉ	=	*Revue d'égyptologie*
RÉAug	=	*Revue des études augustiniennes*
RÉByz	=	*Revue des études byzantines*
RechSR	=	*Recherches de Science Religieuse*
RÉG	=	*Revue des études grecques*
RCatalana Teo	=	*Revista Catalana de Teologia*
RFIC	=	*Rivista di filologia e d'istruzione classica*
RSPhTh	=	*Revue des sciences philosophiques et théologiques*
SBFLA	=	*Studium Biblicum Franciscanum. Liber Annuus*
SCS	=	Septuagint and Cognate Studies
SO	=	*Symbolae Osloenses*
StHell	=	Studia Hellenistica
SVT	=	Supplements to Vetus Testamentum
SVTG	=	Septuaginta. Vetus Testamentum Graecum
Textus	=	*Textus*
ThLZ	=	*Theologische Literaturzeitung*
TU	=	Texte und Untersuchungen zur Geschichte der altchristlichen Literatur
UUA	=	Uppsala universitets arsskrift
VetChr	=	*Vetera Christianorum*
VT	=	*Vetus Testamentum*
ZAW	=	*Zeitschrift für die alttestamentliche Wissenschaft*
ZNW	=	*Zeitschrift für die neutestamentliche Wissenschaft*
ZPE	=	*Zeitschrift für Papyrologie und Epigraphik*

BIBLIOGRAPHY

I. GENERAL

The following list includes in alphabetical order the abbreviations and the full titles of all the works referred to in the description of the lemmata, and of the most frequently used commentaries (see also Bibliography: II. Commentaries). The lexica are mentioned in the Introduction: I. General, note 4).

ABEL 1949
F.M. ABEL, *Les livres des Maccabées* (ÉtB), Paris, 1949.

AEJMELAEUS 1982
A. AEJMELAEUS, *Parataxis in the Septuagint: A Study of the Renderings of the Hebrew Coordinate Clauses in the Greek Pentateuch* (AASF Diss. Hum. Litt., 31), Helsinki, 1982.

AEJMELAEUS 1991
A. AEJMELAEUS, *Translation Technique and the Intention of the Translator*, in COX 1991, pp. 23-36.

AERTS 1965
W.J. AERTS, *Periphrastica. An Investigation into the Use of* εἶναι *and* ἔχειν *as Auxiliaries or Pseudo-auxiliaries in Greek from Homer up to the Present Day* (Publications Issued under the Auspices of the Byzantine-New Greek Seminary of the University of Amsterdam, 2), Amsterdam, 1965, pp. 52-209.

ALBREKTSON 1963
B. ALBREKTSON, *Studies in the Text and Theology of the Book of Lamentations* (Stud. Theol. Lundensia, 21), Lund, 1963.

ALFRINK 1959
B. ALFRINK, *L'idée de résurrection d'après Dan. , XII,1.2* in *Bib* 40 (1959) 355-371.

ALLEN 1974[I]
L.C. ALLEN, *The Greek Chronicles. The Relation of I and II Chronicles to the Massoretic Text. Part I, The Translator's Craft* (SVT, 25), Leiden, 1974.

ALLEN 1974[II]
L.C. ALLEN, *The Greek Chronicles. The Relation of I and II Chronicles to the Massoretic Text, Part II, Textual Criticism* (SVT, 27), Leiden, 1974.

AMSTUTZ 1968

J. AMSTUTZ, Ἁπλότης. *Eine begriffsgeschichtliche Studie zum jüdisch-christlichen Griechisch* (Theophaneia. Beiträge zur Religions- und Kirchengeschichte des Altertums, 19), Bonn, 1968.

AVALOS 1989

H. AVALOS, δεῦρο/δεῦτε *and the Imperatives of* הלך. *New Criteria for the "Kaige" Recension of Reigns*, in *Est Bib* 47 (1989) 165-176.

AUBIN 1963

P. AUBIN, *Le problème de la "Conversion". Etude sur un terme commun à l'hellénisme et au christianisme des trois premiers siècles* (Théologie historique, 1), Paris, 1963.

BARBER 1968

E.A. BARBER, *Greek-English Lexicon. A Supplement*, Oxford, 1968, see Liddell-Scott.

BARDTKE 1963

H. BARDTKE, *Das Buch Esther* (KAT, 17,5), Gütersloh, 1963

BARDY 1910

G. BARDY, Δεσπότης, in *RechSR* 1 (1910) 373-379.

BARDY 1911

G. BARDY, *Le plus ancien usage de* δεσπότης, in *RechSR* 2 (1911) 458-459.

BARR 1961

J. BARR, *The Semantics of Biblical Language*, Oxford, 1961.

BARR 1968

J. BARR, *Seeing the Wood for the Trees? An Enigmatic Ancient Translation*, in *JSS* 13 (1968) 11-20.

BARR 1974

J. BARR, ἐρίζω *and* ἐρείδω *in the Septuagint: A Note Principally on Gen. XLIX. 6*, in *JSSt* 19 (1974) 198-215.

BARR 1979

J. BARR, *The Typology of Literalism in Ancient Biblical Translations* (MSU, 15), Göttingen, 1979, pp. 279-325.

BARR 1980

J. BARR, *The Meaning of* ἐπακούω *and Cognates in the LXX*, in *JTS* 31 (1980) 67-72.

BARR 1987

J. BARR, *Words for Love in Biblical Greek*, in L. D. HURST & N. T. WRIGHT (eds.), *The Glory of Christ in the New Testament*, Oxford, 1987, pp. 3-18.

BARTHÉLEMY 1963

D. BARTHÉLEMY, *Les Devanciers d'Aquila. Première publication intégrale du texte des fragments du Dodécaprophéton* (SVT, 10), Leiden, 1963.

BARTHÉLEMY 1978
D. BARTHÉLEMY, *Etudes d'Histoire du Texte de l'Ancien Testament* (OBO, 21), Fribourg/Suisse - Göttingen, 1978.

BARTHÉLEMY 1978
D. BARTHÉLEMY, *Eusèbe, la Septante et "les autres"*, in BARTHÉLEMY 1978, 179-193.

BARUCQ 1964
A. BARUCQ, *Le livre des Porverbes* (Sources Bibliques), Paris, 1964.

BATTAGLIA 1989
E. BATTAGLIA, *'Artos': Il lessico della panificazione nei papiri greci* (Bibl. Aevum Antiquum, 2), Milan, 1989.

BAUMGARTEN 1984
J. M. BAUMGARTEN, *On the Non-literal Use of* Ma'aser/Dekatè, in *JBL* 103 (1984) 245-251.

BEEK 1950
M.A. BEEK, *Das Problem des aramäischen Stammvaters (Deut. XXVI 5)*, in OTS 8 (1950) 192-212.

BERENGUER SANCHEZ 1989
J.A. BERENGUER SANCHEZ, Ἀρνόν *en PGurob 22 y el empleo del término* ἀρνίον *en los papiros documentales,* in *Emerita* 57 (1989) 277-288.

BERGMANS 1979
M. BERGMANS, *Théores argiens au Fayoum (P. Lond. VII 1973)*, in *CÉg* 54 (1979) 127-130.

BERTRAM 1958
G. BERTRAM, Ἱκανός *in den griechischen Übersetzungen des ATs als Wiedergabe von* schaddaj, in *ZAW* 70 (1958) 20-31.

BICKERMAN 1976
E. BICKERMAN, *Studies in Jewish and Christian History. Part One* (AGJU, 9), Leiden, 1976.

BICKERMAN 1980
E. BICKERMAN, *Studies in Jewish and Christian History. Part Two* (AGJU, 9), Leiden, 1980.

BICKERMAN 1986
E. BICKERMAN, *Studies in Jewish and Christian History. Part Three* (AGJU, 9), Leiden, 1986.

BISCARDI 1979
A. BISCARDI, *Ossercaziono critiche sulla terminologia* διαθήκη - διατίθημαι, in *Symposium 1979,* Köln - Wien, 1983, pp. 21-36.

BISSOLI 1983
G. BISSOLI, *MAKON* - ἕτοιμος, *A proposito di Esodo 15,17*, in *SBFLA* 33 (1983) 53-56.

BOGAERT 1981
P.-M. BOGAERT, *L'orientation du parvis du sanctuaire dans la version grecque de l'Exode (Ex., 27,9-13 LXX)*, in *AnCl* 50 (1981) 79-85.

BONNEAU 1985
D. BONNEAU, *Aigialos* (αἰγιαλός), *la "terre riveraine" en Egypte, d'après la documentation papyrologique*, in N. LEWIS (ed.), *Papyrology* (Yale Classical Studies, 28), Cambridge, 1985, pp. 131-143.

BRAUNERT 1971
H. BRAUNERT, ἀγοραστής, in *ZPE* 8 (1971) 118-122.

BRENT SANDY 1984
D. BRENT SANDY, *Oil Specification in the Papiri: What is* ἔλαιον, in *Atti XVII Congr. Int. Pap.*, Napoli, 1984, III, pp. 1317-1323.

BROCKINGTON 1951
L. H. BROCKINGTON, *The Greek Translator of Isaiah and His Interest in* δόξα, in *VT* 1 (1951) 23-32.

BRUNET 1966
G. BRUNET, *La Vision de l'étain: réinterprétation d'Amos VII 7-9*, in *VT* 16 (1966) 387-395.

BUSCEMI 1983
M. BUSCEMI, Ἐξαιρέομαι, *verbo di Liberazione*, in *SBFLA* 29 (1979) 293-314.

BUTLER 1983
T.C. BUTLER, *Joshua* (Word Biblical Commentary, 7), Waco, Texas, 1983.

CADELL 1984
H. CADELL, *Sur un hapax grec connu par le Code Théodosien*, in *Atti XVII Congr. Int. Pap.*, Napoli, 1984, pp. 1279-1285.

CAIRD 1968
G.B. CAIRD, *The Glory of God in the Fourth Gospel: An Exercise in Biblical Semantics*, in *NTS* 15 (1968) 265-77.

CAIRD 1972
G.B. CAIRD, *Towards a Lexicon of the Septuagint. I*, in KRAFT (ed.) 1972, pp. 110-152; = *JTS NS* 19 (1968) 453-475 and 20 (1969) 21-40.

CAQUOT 1980
A. CAQUOT, *Ben Porat (Genèse 49,22)*, in *Semitica* 30 (1980) 43-56.

CASANOVA 1982

G. CASANOVA, *Le parole dell'amore nei papiri: ossercazioni su* ἐράω *e corradicali*, in *Anagennesis* 2 (1982) 213-226.

CASARICO 1984
L. CASARICO, ἑορτή *e* πᾶνηγῦρις *nei papiri,* in *Aeg.* 64 (1984) 135-162.

CERESA-GASTALDO 1953
A. CERESA-GASTALDO, ἀγάπη *nei documenti estranei all' influsso biblico*, in *RFIC* 31 (1953) 347-355.

CHANTRAINE 1955
P. CHANTRAINE, *Les noms de l'agneau*, in H. KRAHE (a.o.), *Corolla Linguistica. Festschrift Ferdinand Sommer zum 80. Geburtstag am 4. mai 1955*, Berlin, 1955, pp. 12-19.

CHANTRAINE 1964
P. CHANTRAINE, *Grec* αἴθριον, in *Rech. de Pap.* 3 (1964) 7-15.

CIFOLETTI 1974
G. CIFOLETTI, ἀποδέχομαι *nella diplomazia imperiale (a proposito di P. Ned. 70. 01)*, in *Incontri linguistici* 1, Trieste, 1974, pp. 55-60.

CIMOSA 1985
M. CIMOSA, *Il vocabolario di preghiera nel pentateuco greco dei LXX* (Quaderni di Salesianum, 10), Rome, 1985.

CLARK 1972
K.W. CLARK, *The Meaning of* APA, in E. H. BARTH (ed.), *Festschrift to honor F. Wilbur Gingrich, Lexicographer, Scholar, Teacher and Committed Layman*, Leiden, 1972, pp. 70-84.

CLARYSSE 1990
W. CLARYSSE, *Abbreviations and Lexicography*, in *Ancient Society* 21 (1990) 33-44.

CLERMONT-GANNEAU 1905
C. CLERMONT-GANNEAU, *Recueil d'Archéologie Orientale (6),* Paris, 1905, pp. 357-359

COLEMAN 1927
W.D. COLEMAN, *Some Noteworthy Uses of* εἰ *or* εἶ *in Hellenistic Greek, with a Note on St. Mark VIII 12*, in *JTS* 28 (1927) 159-167.

CONNOLLY 1924
R.H. CONNOLLY, *The meaning of* "ἐπίκλησις": *A Reply*, in *JTS* 25 (1924) 337-364.

CONYBEARE 1980
F.C. CONYBEARE, ST.-G. STOCK, *A Grammar of Septuagint Greek*, Boston, Massachussets, 1980 (Reprint of p. 25-100 of *Selections from the Septuagint, According to the Text of Swete*, 1905).

COOK 1991

J. COOK, *Hellenistic Influence in the Septuagint Book of Proverbs,* in COX 1991, pp. 341-353.

COX 1981
C.E. COX, Εἰσακούω *and* Ἐπακούω *in the Greek Psalter,* in *Bib* 62 (1981) 251-258.

COX 1990
C.E. COX, *Vocabulary for Wrongdoing and Forgiveness in the Greek Translations of Job,* in *Textus* 15 (1990) 119-130.

COX 1991
C.E. COX (ed.), *VII Congress of the International Organization for Septuagint and Cognate Studies, Leuven 1989,* Atlanta, GA, 1991.

CUSS 1974
D. CUSS, *Imperial Cult and Honorary Terms in the New Testament* (Paradosis, 23), Fribourg, 1974.

DA FONSECA 1927-1928
L.G. DA FONSECA, διαθήκη - *Foedus an Testamentum?,* in *Bib* 8 (1927) 31-50, 161-181, 290-319, 418-441; 9 (1928) 26-40, 143-160.

DANIEL 1966
S. DANIEL, *Recherches sur le vocabulaire du Culte dans la Septante* (ÉeC, 61), Paris, 1966.

DANIEL 1971
C. DANIEL, *Trois noms égyptiens de chefs en grec:* βασιλεύς, ἥρος *et* τίταξ, in *Studia et Acta Orientalia* 8 (1971) 59-69.

DARIS 1983
S. DARIS, *Ricerche di papirologia documentaria II: Nota lessicale* (Ἀργια/σχολή), in *Aeg* 63 (1983) 158-161.

DAVID 1943
M. DAVID, *Deux anciens termes bibliques pour le gage* (OTS, 2), 1943, pp. 79-86.

DAVISON 1985
J.E. DAVISON, ἀνόμια *and the Question of the Antinomian Polemic in Matthew,* in *JBL* 104 (1985) 617-635.

DEISSMANN 1901
A. DEISSMANN, *Anathema,* in *ZNW* 2 (1901) 342.

DEISSMANN 1903
A. DEISSMANN, ἰλαστήτιος *und* ἰλαστήριον. *Eine lexikalische Studie,* in *ZNW* 4 (1903) 93-212.

DE LA POTTERIE 1974
I. DE LA POTTERIE, *La parole de Jésus "Voici ta Mère" et l'accueil du Disciple (Jn 19,27b),* in *Mar* 36 (1974) 1-39.

DELCOR 1967
  M. DELCOR, *Le livre de Judith et l'époque grecque*, in *Klio* 49 (1967) 151-179.

DELLING 1970
  G. DELLING, *Studien zum Neuen Testament und zum hellenistischen Judentum. Gesammelte Aufsätze 1950-1968*. Herausgegeben von F. HAHN, T. HOLTZ, N. WALTER, Göttingen, 1970.

DELLING 1977
  G. DELLING, *Das* ἀγαθόν *der Hebräer bei den griechischen christlichen Schriftstellern*, in TU 120 (1977) 151-172.

DEPUYDT 1985
  L. DEPUYDT, *"Voir" et "regarder" en Copte: étude synchronique et diachronique*, in *RdÉ* 36 (1985) 35-42.

DESCAMPS 1948
  A. DESCAMPS, *La justice de Dieu dans la Bible grecque*, in StHell 5 (1948) 69-92.

DES PLACES 1975
  E. DES PLACES, *Un terme biblique et platonicien:* ἀκοινώνητος, in M. PELLEGRINO (a.o), *Forma Futuri. Studi in Onore del Cardinale Michele Pellegrino*, Torino, 1975, pp. 154-158.

DHORME 1926
  P. DHORME, *Le livre de Job* (ÉtB), Paris, 1926.

DHORME 1910
  P. DHORME, *Les livres des Samuel* (ÉtB), Paris, 1910.

DIETHART 1982
  J.M. DIETHART, Κύριε βοήθει *in byzantinischen Notarunterschriften*, in *ZPE* 49 (1982) 79-82.

DIHLE 1988
  A. DIHLE, *Heilig*, in *Reallexikon für Antike und Christentum, 14*, Stuttgart, 1988, 2-66.

DIMANT 1981
  D. DIMANT, *A Cultic Term in the Psalms of Solomon in the light of the Septuagint*, in *Textus* 9 (Hebrew) (1981), כא כח, 136.

DODD 1930
  C.H. DODD, Ἱλάσκεσθαι *Its Cognates, Derivates, and Synonyms in the Septuagint*, in *JTS* 32 (1930-1931) 352-360.

DONAT 1911
  H. DONAT, *Mich 2,6-9*, in *BZ* 9 (1911) 350-366.

DRESCHER 1970
  J. DRESCHER, *Graeco-coptica II*, in *Muséon* 83 (1970) 139-155.

DRESCHER 1976
   J. DRESCHER, *Graeco-coptica. Postscript*, in *Muséon* 89 (1976) 307-321.

DRESSLER 1947
   H. DRESSLER, *The usage of* ἀσκόω *and its Cognates in Greek Documents to 200 A. D.* (Cathol.
   Univers. of America, 78), Washington, 1947.

DREW-BEAR 1972
   T. DREW-BEAR, *Some Greek Words: Part I*, in *Glotta* 50 (1972) 61-96.

DRIVER 1902
   S.R. DRIVER, *A Critical and Exegetical Commentary on Deuteronomy* (ICC), Edinburgh, 1902.

DRIVER 1940
   G.R. DRIVER, *Hebrew Notes on Prophets and Proverbs*, in *JTS* 41 (1940) 162-175.

DRIVER 1954
   G.R. DRIVER, *Problems and Solutions*, in *VT* 4 (1954) 225-245.

DUBARLE 1955
   A.M. DUBARLE, δράξασθε παιδείας *(Ps. , II, 12)*, in *RB* 62 (1955) 511-512.

ENGEL 1985
   H. ENGEL, *Die Susanna-erzählung: Einleitung, Übersetzung und Kommentar zum Septuaginta-Text
   und zur Theodotion-Bearbeitung* (OBO, 61), Fribourg/Suisse - Göttingen, 1985.

EYNIKEL-LUST 1991
   E. EYNIKEL, J. LUST, *The Use of* δεῦρο *and* δεῦτε *in the LXX*, in *ETL* 67 (1991) 57-68.

FASCHER 1954
   E. FASCHER, *Theologische Beobachtungen zu* δεῖ *im Alten Testament*, in *ZNW* 45 (1954)
   244-252.

FERNANDEZ MARCOS 1980
   N. FERNANDEZ MARCOS, Ἐλπίζειν *or* ἐγγίζειν? *in Prophetarum Vitae Fabulosae 12,9 and
   in the Septuagint*, in *VT* 30 (1980) 357-360.

FIEDLER 1970
   M.J. FIEDLER, Δικαιοσύνη *in der diaspora-jüdischen und intertestamentarischen Literatur*, in
   JSJ 1 (1970) 120-143.

FISCHER 1958-59
   J.B. FISCHER, *The Term* δεσπότης *in Josephus*, in *JQR* 49 (1958-59) 132-138.

FLASHAR 1912
   H. FLASHAR, *Exegetische Studien zum Septuagintapsalter*, in *ZAW* 32 (1912) 241-268.

FORSTER 1929

A.H. FORSTER, *The meaning of* δόξα *in the Greek Bible*, in *AThR* 12 (1929-30) 311-316.

FRAADE 1984
S.D. FRAADE, *Enosh and His Generation. Pre-Israelite Hero and History in Postbiblical Interpretation*, California 1984

FRANKEL 1841
Z. FRANKEL, *Historisch-kritische Studien zu der Septuaginta. Vorstudien zu der Septuaginta I/1*, Leipzig, 1841.

FREY 1952
J. FREY, *Corpus Inscriptionum Iudaicarum II*, Rome, 1952, pp. 218-219.

FRIDRICHSEN 1916
A. FRIDRICHSEN, *Hagios-qados. Ein Beitrag zu den Voruntersuchungen zur christlichen Begriffs-geschichte*, Kristiana, 1916.

FRIDRICHSEN 1938
A. FRIDRICHSEN, ἰσόψυχος = *ebenbürtig, solidarisch*, in *SO* 18 (1938) 42-49.

GEHMAN 1953
H.S. GEHMAN, *Hebraisms of the Old Greek Version of Genesis*, in *VT* 3 (1953) 141-148.

GEHMAN 1954
H.S. GEHMAN, Ἅγιος *in the Septuagint, and Its Relation to the Hebrew Original*, in *VT* 4 (1954) 337-348.

GEHMAN 1972
H.S. GEHMAN, *Adventures in Septuagint Lexicography*, in KRAFT (ed.) 1972, pp. 102-109 = *Textus* 5 (1966) 125-132.

GEHMAN 1972
H.S. GEHMAN, Ἐπισκέπομαι, ἐπίσκεψις, ἐπίσκοπος, *and* ἐπισκοπή *in the Septuagint in Relation to* פקד *and other Hebrew Roots - A Case of Semantic Development Similar to that of Hebrew*, in *VT* 22 (1972) 197-207.

GEHMAN 1972 (A)
H.S. GEHMAN, *The Hebraic Character of Septuagint Greek*, in KRAFT (ed.) 1972, pp. 92-101 = *VT* 1 (1951) 81-90.

GERMAIN 1984
L.R.F. GERMAIN, *Apothesis ou ekthesis. Problème de terminologie en matière d'exposition d'enfants*, in *MNHMH Georges A Petropoulos*, I, Athenes, 1984, pp. 389-399.

GHEDINI 1935
G. GHEDINI, *Note di sintassi greca*, in *Aeg* 15 (1935) 230-238.

GILBERT 1973

M. GILBERT, *La critique des dieux dans le Livre de la Sagesse (Sg 13-15)* (AnBib, 53), Roma, 1973.

GILMORE 1890
G.W. GILMORE, ἕος *in Hellenistic Greek*, in *JBL* 9 (1890) 153-160.

GLOMBITZA 1958
O. GLOMBITZA, *Die Titel* διδάσκαλος *und* ἐπιστάτης *für Jesus bei Lukas*, in *ZNW* 49 (1958) 275-278.

GÖTTSBERGER 1906
J. GÖTTSBERGER, *Zu "*εἰρήνη*" bei Hatch-Redpath*, in *BZ* 4 (1906) 246.

GOLDSTEIN 1976
J. GOLDSTEIN, *I Maccabees. A New Translation with Introduction and Commentary* (AncB, 41), New York, 1976.

GOLDSTEIN 1983
J. GOLDSTEIN, *II Maccabees. A New Translation with Introduction and Commentary* (AncB, 41 A), New York, 1983.

GÖRG 1991
M. GÖRG & B. LANG, *Neues Bibel-Lexikon, Band I,* Zürich, 1991.

GRAYSTON 1981
K. GRAYSTON, Ἱλάσκεσθαι *and Related Words in LXX*, in *NTS* 27 (1981) 640-656.

GRIBOMONT - THIBAUT 1959
J. GRIBOMONT & A. THIBAUT, *Méthode et esprit des traducteurs du Psautier grec*, in P. SALMON (ed.), *Richesses et Déficiences des Anciens Psautiers Latins* (CBLa, 13), Roma, 1959, pp. 51-105.

GROSSFELD 1984
B. GROSSFELD, *The Translation of Biblical Hebrew* פקד *in the Targum, Peshitta, Vulgate and Septuagint*, in *ZAW* 96 (1984) 83-101.

GRUNDMANN 1932
W. GRUNDMANN, *Der Begriff der Kraft in der neutestamentlichen Gedankenwelt* (BWANT, 60), Stuttgart, 1932.

GUILLAND 1959
R. GUILLAND, *Études sur l'histoire administrative de l'empire byzantin: le despote,* δεσπότης, in *REByz* 17 (1959) 52-89.

GUINOT 1989
J.N. GUINOT, *Sur le vêtement du grand prêtre: le* δῆλος *était-il une pierre divinatoire?*, in *VetChr* 26 (1989) 23-48.

HABERMANN 1988

W. HABERMANN, *Lexikalische und Semantische Untersuchung am griechischen Begriff* βύρσα, in *Glotta* 66 (1988) 93-99.

HALLEUX 1973

R. HALLEUX, *Le sens d'*ἄσημος *dans le papyrus chimique de Leyde et dans l'alchimie gréco-égyptienne,* in *CÉg* 48 (1973) 370-380.

HARL 1984

M. HARL, *Un groupe de mots grecs dans le judaïsme hellénistique: à propos d'*ἐμπαιγμός *dans le Psaume 37,8 de la Septante,* in E. LUCCHESI & H.D. SAFFREY, *Mémorial André-Jean Festugière, Antiquité païenne et chrétienne* (Cahiers d'Orientalisme, 10), Genève, 1984, pp. 89-105.

HARL 1986

M. HARL & M. ALEXANDRE & C. DOIGNIEZ, *La Bible d'Alexandrie I. La Genèse,* Paris, 1986.

HARL 1986 (A)

M. HARL, *Les origines grecques du mot et de la notion de "componction" dans la Septante et chez les commentateurs (KATANUSSESTHAI),* in *RÉAug* 32 (1986) 3-21.

HARL 1987

M. HARL, *Le nom de l'"arche" de Noé dans la Septante,* in C. MONDESERT (a.o.), Αλεχανδρινα, *Hellénisme, judaïsme et christianisme à Alexandrie. Mélanges offerts au P. Claude Mondésert,* Paris, 1987, pp. 18. 31-35.

HARL 1988

M. HARL & G. DORIVAL & O. MUNICH, *La bible grecque des Septante. Du judaïsme hellénistique au christianisme ancien* (Initiations au christianisme ancien), Paris, 1988.

HARL 1991

M. HARL, *Le renouvellement du lexique des "Septante" d'après le témoignage des recensions, révisions et commentaires grecs anciens,* in COX 1991, 239-259.

HARLÉ 1988

P. HARLÉ & D. PRALON, *La Bible d'Alexandrie III. Le Lévitique,* Paris, 1988.

HATCH 1889

E. HATCH, *Essays in Biblical Greek,* Oxford, 1889.

HEDLEY 1933

P.L. HEDLEY, διαβουλία, in *JTS* (1933) 270.

HELBING 1907

R. HELBING, *Grammatik der Septuaginta. Laut- und Worthlehre,* Göttingen, 1907.

HELBING 1928

R. HELBING, *Die Kasussyntax der Verba bei den Septuaginta. Ein Beitrag zur Hebraismenfrage und zur Syntax der* Κοινή, Göttingen, 1928.

HERTZBERG 1963
H.W. HERTZBERG, *Der Prediger* (KAT, 17,4), Gütersloh, 1963.

HILHORST 1989
A. HILHORST, *"Servir Dieu" dans la terminologie du judaïsme hellénistique et des premières générations chrétiennes de langue grecque* (IP, 19), 1989, p. 176-192.

HILL 1967
D. HILL, *Greek Words and Hebrew Meanings: Studies in the Semantics of Soteriological Terms* (MSSNTS, 5), Cambridge, 1967.

HINDLEY 1961
J.C. HINDLEY, *The Translation of Words for Covenant*, in *IJT* 10 (1961) 13-24.

HOFFMEIER 1985
J.K. HOFFMEIER, *"Sacred" in the Vocabulary of Ancient Egypt. The Term "dsr" with Special Reference to Dynasties I-XX* (OBO, 59), Fribourg/Suisse - Göttingen, 1985.

HOLLADAY 1958
W.L. HOLLADAY, *The Root šûbh in the Old Testament with Particular Reference to Its Usages in Covenantal Contexts*, Leiden, 1958.

HOLLADAY 1986
W.L. HOLLADAY, *Jeremiah 1: A Commentary on the Book of the Prophet Jeremiah Chapters 1-25* (Hermeneia), Philadelphia, 1986.

HOLLADAY 1989
W.L. HOLLADAY, *Jeremiah 2: A Commentary on the Book of the Prophet Jeremiah Chapters 26-52* (Hermeneia), Minneapolis, 1989.

HORSLEY 1981
G.H.R. HORSLEY, *New Documents Illustrating Early Christianity. Vol 1. A Review of the Greek Inscriptions and Papyri Published in 1976*, North Ryde, 1981.

HORSLEY 1982
G.H.R. HORSLEY, *New Documents Illustrating Early Christianity. Vol 2. A Review of the Greek Inscriptions and Papyri Published in 1977*, Alexandria, 1982.

HORSLEY 1983
G.H.R. HORSLEY, *New Documents Illustrating Early Christianity. Vol 3. A Review of the Greek Inscriptions and Papyri Published in 1978*, Alexandria, 1983.

HORSLEY 1987
G.H.R. HORSLEY, *New Documents Illustrating Early Christianity. Vol 4. A Review of the Greek Inscriptions and Papyri Published in 1979*, Marrickville, 1987.

HORSLEY 1989
  G.H.R. HORSLEY, *New Documents Illustrating Early Christianity. Vol 5. Linguistic Essays*, Marrickville, 1989.

HUMBACH 1968
  H. HUMBACH, *Die Feminina von* ἱερεύς, in (MSS, 24) 1968 10-25.

HUSSON 1983
  G. HUSSON, *Oikia. Le vocabulaire de la maison privée en Égypte d'après les papyrus grecs* (Papyrologie, 2), Paris, 1983.

HUSSON 1983 (A)
  G. HUSSON, *Un sens méconnu de* θυρίς *et de* fenestra, in *JJP* 19 (1983) 155-162.

HUYS 1989
  M. HUYS, ἔκθεσις *and* ἀποθεσις: *The Terminology of Infant Exposure in Greek Antiquity*, in *AnCl* 58 (1989) 190-197.

JEANSONNE 1988
  S.P. JEANSONNE, *The Old Greek Translation of Daniel 7-12* (CBQ MS, 19), Washington, 1988.

JOHNSON 1938
  A.C. JOHNSON & H.S. GEHMAN & E.H. KASE, *The John H. Scheide Biblical Papyri: Ezekiel* (Princeton University Studies in Papyrology, 3), Princeton, 1938.

JONES 1955
  D. JONES, ἀνάμνησις *in the LXX and the Interpretation of I Cor. XI. 25*, in *JTS NS* 6 (1955) 183-191.

KAHANE 1987
  H.&R. KAHANE, *Religious Key Terms in Hellenism and Byzantium; Three Facets*, in *Illinois Classical Studies* 12 (1987) 243-263.

KASE 1938
  E.H. KASE, *The nomen sacrum of Ezekiel*, in JOHNSON 1938, pp. 48-51.

KATZ 1938
  P. KATZ, *Biblia Hebraica*, in *ThLZ* 2 (1938) 32-34.

KATZ 1946
  P. KATZ, *Notes on the Septuagint: IV.* ἐα δέ *"Let alone" in Job*, in *JTS* 47 (1946) 168-169.

KATZ 1950
  P. KATZ, *Philo's Bible. The Aberrant Text of Bible Quotations in Some Philonic Writings and Its Place in the Textual History of the Greek Bible*, Cambridge, 1950, esp. pp. 141-154.

KERR 1988

A.J. KERR, ἀρραβών, in *JTS* 39 (1988) 92-97.

KIESSLING 1927

E. KIESSLING, *Die Aposkeuai und die prozessrechtliche Stellung der Ehefrauen im ptolemäischen Ägypten*, in *Archiv für Papyrusforschung und verwandte Gebiete* 8 (1927) 240-249.

KIESSLING

F. PREISIGKE - E. KIESSLING, *Wörterbuch der griechischen Papyrusurkunden, mit Einschluss der griechischen Inschriften, Ausschriften, Ostraka, Mumienschilder usw. aus Ägypten* Band 1, Berlin, 1925; Band 2, Berlin, 1927; Band 3, Berlin, 1931; Band 4 (KIESSLING), fasc.1-4, Marburg, 1944-1971.

KILPATRICK 1942

G.D. KILPATRICK, *A Theme of the Lucan Passion Story and Luke 23,47*, in *JTS* 63 (1942) 34-36; = (BETL, 96), Leuven, 1990, 327-329.

KILPATRICK 1961

G.D. KILPATRICK, *The Meaning of Thuein in the New Testament*, in *BiTr* 12 (1961) 130-132.

KILPATRICK 1963

G.D. KILPATRICK, *Atticism and the Text of the Greek New Testament*, in J. BLINZLER (ed.), *Neutestamentliche Aufsätze. Festschrift für Professor Josef Schmid*, Regensburg, 1963, pp. 125-137; = (BETL, 96), Leuven, 1990, 14-32.

KILPATRICK 1967

G.D. KILPATRICK, *The Aorist of* γαμεῖν *in the New Testament*, in *JTS* NS 18 (1967) 139-140.

KILPATRICK 1969

G.D. KILPATRICK, *Some Problems in New Testament Text and Language*, in E.E. ELLIS & M. WILCOX (eds.) *Neotestamentica et Semitica* (Festschrift for M. Black), Edinburgh, 1969, 198-208; = (BETL, 96), Leuven, 1990, 327-329.

KILPATRICK 1975

G.D. KILPATRICK, *Anamnesis*, in *Liturg. Review* 5 (1975) 35-40.

KILPATRICK 1977

G.D. KILPATRICK, *Eclectism and Atticism*, in *ETL* 53 (1977) 107-112.

KILPATRICK 1979

G.D. KILPATRICK, *Three Problems of New Testament Text*, in *NT* 21 (1979) 289-292.

KILPATRICK 1983

G.D. KILPATRICK, *Atticism and the Future of* Ζῆν, in *NT* 25 (1983) 146-151.

KILPATRICK 1983 (A)

G.D. KILPATRICK, Ἐπιθύειν *and* ἐπικρίνειν *in the Greek Bible*, in *ZNW* 74 (1983) 151-153.

KLAUCK 1980

H.J. KLAUCK, Θυσιαστήριον - *eine Berichtigung*, in *ZNW* 71 (1980) 274-277.

KOEHLER - BAUMGARTNER 1990
L. KOEHLER & W. BAUMGARTNER & J.J. STAMM, *Hebräisches und aramäisches Lexikon zum Alten Testament*, Dritte Auflage, Leiden, 1990.

KOENIG 1982
J. KOENIG, *L'herméneutique analogique du Judaïsme antique d'après les témoins textuels d'Isaïe*, Leiden, 1982.

KOONCE 1988
K. KOONCE, Ἄγαλμα *and* εἰκών, in *American Journal of Philology* 109 (1988) 108-110.

KORN 1937
J.H. KORN, Πειρασμός. *Die Versuchung des Gläubigen in der griechischen Bibel* (BWANT, 72), Stuttgart, 1937.

KRAFT 1972
R.A. KRAFT, *Prefatory Remarks to the Lexical "Probes". Towards a Lexicon of Jewish translation Greek*, in KRAFT (ed.) 1972, pp. 157-178.

KRAFT (ed.) 1972
R.A. KRAFT (ed.), *Septuagintal Lexicography* (SCS, 1), Montana, 1972.

LABERGE 1978
L. LABERGE, *La Septante d'Isaïe 28-33. Etude de tradition textuelle*, Ottawa, 1978.

LACHS 1978
S.T. LACHS, *A Note on the Original Language of Susanna*, in *JQR* 69 (1978) 52-54.

LARCHER 1969
C. LARCHER, *Etudes sur le Livre de la Sagesse* (ÉtB), Paris, 1969.

LARCHER 1983
C. LARCHER, *Le Livre de la Sagesse ou la Sagesse de Salomon I* (ÉtB NS 1), Paris, 1983.

LARCHER 1984
C. LARCHER, *Le Livre de la Sagesse ou la Sagesse de Salomon II* (ÉtB NS 3), Paris, 1984.

LARCHER 1985
C. LARCHER, *Le Livre de la Sagesse ou la Sagesse de Salomon III* (ÉtB NS 5), Paris, 1985.

LE BOULLUEC 1989
A. LE BOULLUEC, P. SANDEVOIR, *La Bible d'Alexandrie II. L'Exode*, Paris, 1989.

LE DÉAUT 1984
R. LE DÉAUT, *La Septante, un Targum?* (LeDiv, 119), Paris, 1984, 147-195.

LEDOGAR 1967
   R.J. LEDOGAR, *Verbs of Praise in the LXX Translation of the Hebrew Canon*, in *Bib* 48 (1967) 29-56.

LEE 1969
   J.A.L. LEE, *A Note on Septuagint Material in the Supplement to Liddell and Scott*, in *Glotta* 47 (1969) 234-242.

LEE 1980
   J.A.L. LEE, *The future of* Ζῆν *in Late Greek*, in *NT* 22 (1980) 289-298.

LEE 1983
   J.A.L. LEE, *A Lexical Study of the Septuagint Version of the Pentateuch* (SCS, 14), Chico, California, 1983.

LEFORT 1935
   L.T. LEFORT, *Un passage obscur des hymnes à Chenoute*, in *Or* 4 (1935) 411-415.

LEWIS 1989
   N. LEWIS, *The Documents from the Bar Kokhba Period in the Cave of Letters: Greek Papyri*, Jerusalem, 1989.

LIEBERMAN 1946
   S. LIEBERMAN, *Two Lexicographical Notes*, in *JBL* 65 (1946) 67-72.

LIEBERMANN 1950
   S. LIEBERMANN, *Hellenism in Jewish Palestine*, New York, 1950, 1962², p. 205, n.23.

LIFSHITZ 1961
   B. LIFSHITZ, *The Greek Documents from Nahal Seelim and Nahal Mishmar*, in *IEJ* 11 (1961) 52-63.

LIFSHITZ 1962
   B. LIFSHITZ, *Papyrus Grecs du désert de Juda*, in *Aeg* 42 (1962) 240-256.

LINDHAGEN 1950
   C. LINDHAGEN, ἐργάζεσθαι. *Die Wurzel* σαπ *in NT und AT. Zwei Beiträge zur Lexikographie der Griechischen Bibel* (UUA, 5), Uppsala, 1950.

LIPINSKI 1970
   E. LIPINSKI, *Recherches sur le livre de Zacharie*, in *VT* 20 (1970) 25-55.

LOUW 1988
   P. LOUW & A. NIDA, *Greek-English Lexicon of the New Testament (Vol 1 & 2)*, New York, 1988.

LUCCHESI 1978
   E. LUCCHESI, *Un terme inconnu de l'Evangile de Vérité,* in *Or.* 47 (1978) 483-484.

LÜHRMANN 1971
D. LÜHRMANN, Ἐπιφάνεια. Zur Bedeutungsgeschichte eines griechischen Wortes, in G. JEREMIAS, H-W. KUHN & H. STEGEMAN (eds.) Traditions und Glaube, Göttingen, 1971, pp. 185-199.

LUST 1990
J. LUST, J. F. Schleusner and the Lexicon of the Septuagint, in ZAW 102 (1990) 256-262

LUST 1991
J. LUST, Molek and ἄρχων, in Studia Phoenicia 11 (OLA, 44), Leuven, 1991, pp. 193-208.

LUST 1991 (A)
J. LUST, Messianism and the Greek Version of Jeremiah, in C.E. COX (ed.), VII Congress of the International Organisation for Septuagint and Cognate Studies 1989, Leuven, Atlanta, 1991, pp. 87-122.

LUST 1992
J. LUST, Cult ans Sacrifice in Daniel. The Tamid and the Abomination of Desolation in Ritual and Sacrifice in the Ancien Near East (OLA, 14) (forthcoming Proceedings of the Leuven Colloquium, 1991)

LUST 1992 (A)
J. LUST, Ἕδρα and the Philistine Plague, in The Septuagint and its Relations to the Dead Sea Scrolls and other Writings (forthcoming Proceedings of the Manchester Colloquium, 1990).

LUST 1993
J. LUST, The Septuagint Version of Daniel 4-5, in A.S. VAN DER WOUDE (ed.), The Book of Daniel in Light of New Findings (BETL) (forthcoming Proceedings of the Colloquium Biblicum, Leuven, 1991).

MANSON 1945
T.W. MANSON, "ἱλαστήριον", in JTS 46 (1945) 1-10.

MARGOLIS 1970
B. MARGOLIS, The Psalm of Habakkuk: A Reconstruction and Interpretation, in ZAW 82 (1970) 409-442.

MARGOLIS 1907
M.L. MARGOLIS, Studien im griechischen alten Testament, in ZAW 27 (1907) 212-270.

MARGOLIS 1909
M.L. MARGOLIS, The Particle ἤ in Old Testament Greek, in AJSL 25 (1908-1909) 257-275

MARGOLIS 1911
M.L. MARGOLIS, ἡνία, χαλινός, in ZAW 31 (1911) 314.

MARGOLIS 1972
M.L. MARGOLIS, λαμβάνειν (Including Compounds and Derivatives) and its Hebrew-Aramaic Equivalents in Old Testament Greek, in KRAFT (ed.) 1972 70-79; = AJSL 22 (1906) 110-119.

MARGOLIS 1972 (A)
M.L. MARGOLIS, *Specimen Article for a Revised Edition of the Hebrew-Aramic Equivalents in the Oxford Concordance to the Septuagint and the other Greek Versions of the Old Testament,* in KRAFT (ed.) 1972 52-69; = *ZAW* 25 (1905) 311-319.

MARTIN 1960
R.A. MARTIN, *Some Syntactical Criteria of Translation Greek,* in *VT* 10 (1960) 295-310.

MARTIN 1974
R.A. MARTIN, *Syntactical Evidence of Semitic Sources in Greek Documents* (SCS, 3), Missoula, Montana, 1974.

MARTINI 1980
C.M. MARTINI, *Eclectism and Atticism in the Textual Criticism of the Greek New Testament,* in ID., *La parola di Dio alle origini della Chiesa* (AnBib, 93), Roma, 1980, pp. 145-152.

MAYSER 1970
E. MAYSER & H. SCHMOLL, *Grammatik der Griechischen Papyri aus der Ptolemäerzeit. Mit Einschluss der Gleichzeitigen Ostraka und der in Ägypten verfassten Inschriften. Band I: Laut- und Wortlehre. I. Teil: Einleitung und Lautlehre,* Berlin, 1970.

MCKANE 1970
W. MCKANE, *Proverbs* (OTL), London, 1970.

MCKANE 1986
W. MCKANE, *A Critical and Exegetical Commentary on Jeremiah. Volume I* (ICC), Edinburgh, 1986.

MENESTRINA 1979
G. MENESTRINA, *Nota,* in *BeO* 21 (1979) 12.

MERCATI 1943
G. MERCATI, *Una singolare versione di Deut. XXVI, 17 e 18 e l'originale di essa,* in *Bib* 24 (1943) 201-204.

MEYERS 1971
E. M. MEYERS, *Jewish Ossuaries: Reburial and Rebirth* (BibOr, 24), Roma, 1971.

MILLIGAN 1980
G. MILLIGAN (ed.), *Selections from the Greek Papyri,* Chicago, 1980.

MM
J.H. MOULTON & G. MILLIGAN, *The Vocabulary of the Greek Testament,* London, 1949.

MOHRMANN 1953
C. MOHRMANN, *Epiphania,* in *RSPhTh* 37 (1953) 644-670.

MOHRMANN 1954

C. MOHRMANN, *Note sur doxa*, in *Sprachgeschichte und Wortbedeutung. Festschrift A. Debrunner*, Bern, 1954, pp. 321-328.

MONSENGWO-PASINYA 1980
L. MONSENGWO-PASINYA, *Deux textes messianiques de la Septante: Gn 49,10 et Ez 21,32*, in *Bib* 61 (1980) 357-376.

MONTEVECCHI 1957
O. MONTEVECCHI, *Dal Paganesimo al Cristianesima: aspetti dell' evoluzione della lingua greca nei papiri dell' Egitto*, in *Aeg* 37 (1957) 41-59.

MONTGOMERY 1927
J.A. MONTGOMERY, *A Critical and Exegetical Commentary on the Book of Daniel* (ICC), Edinburgh, 1927.

MONTGOMERY 1951
J.A. MONTGOMERY & H.S. GEHMAN, *A Critical and Exegetical Commentary on the Books of Kings* (ICC), Edinburgh, 1951.

MONTGOMERY 1951
J.A. MONTGOMERY & H.S. GEHMAN, *A Critical and Exegetical Commentary on the Books of Kings* (ICC), Edinburgh, 1951.

MORENZ 1964
S. MORENZ, *Ägyptische Spuren in der Septuaginta*, in *Jahrbuch für Antike und Christentum* 1 (1964) 250-258.

MOORE 1977
C.A. MOORE, *Daniel, Esther and Jeremiah: The Additions. A New Translation with Introduction and Commentary*, New York, 1977.

MORRIS 1955
L. MORRIS, *The Meaning of* ἱλαστήριον *in Romans III, 25*, in *NTS* 2 (1955-1956) 33-43.

MOULTON 1910
J.H. MOULTON, *A Grammar of the Septuagint*, in *JTS* 11 (1910) 293-300.

MULDER 1987
M.J. MULDER, *Koningen* (Commentaar op het Oude Testament), Dl 1, Kampen, 1987.

MUNNICH 1983
O. MUNNICH, *La Septante des Psaumes et le groupe* καιγε, in *VT* 23 (1983) 75-89.

MURAOKA 1984
T. MURAOKA, *On Septuagint Lexicography and Patristics*, in *JTS* NS 35 (1984) 441-448.

MURAOKA 1989
T. MURAOKA, *Hebrew Hapax Legomena and Septuagint Lexicography,* in COX 1991 205-222.

MURAOKA 1990
T. MURAOKA (ed.), *Melbourne Symposium on Septuagint Lexicography* (SCS, 28), Atlanta, 1990.

MURPHY 1958
J.L. MURPHY, *"Ekklesia" and the Septuagint*, in *AEcR* 139 (1958) 381-390.

NEIRYNCK 1982
F. NEIRYNCK, παρακύψας βλέπει: *Lc 24,12 et Jn 20,5*, in F. VAN SEGBROECK (ed.), *Evangelica I* (BETL, 60), Leuven, 1982, 400-440.

NEIRYNCK 1982 (A)
F. NEIRYNCK, εἰς τὰ ἴδια: *Jn 19,27 (et 16,32)*, in F. VAN SEGBROECK (ed.), *Evangelica I* (BETL, 60), Leuven, 1982, 456-464.

NESTLÉ 1895
E. NESTLÉ, חבר = ἔθνος, in *ZAW* 15 (1895) 288-290.

NESTLÉ 1904
E. NESTLÉ, *Zur aramäischen Bezeichnung der Proselyten*, in *ZNW* 5 (1904) 263-264.

NIDNTT
The New International Dictionary of New Testament Theology, 3 vol., Grand Rapids, Michigan, 1976-1978.

NIEDDU 1988
G.F. NIEDDU, *Sulla nozione di 'leggere' in greco; decifrare* [ἀνανέμω, ἐπιλέγομαι, ἀναγιγνώσκω]. *. . percorrere* [διέρχομαι], in *Giornale Italiano di Filologia* 40 (1988) 17-37.

NOCK 1972
A.D. NOCK, *Soter and Euergetes. Essays on Religion and the Ancient World 2*, 1972, pp. 720-735.

NORTH 1973
J.L. NORTH, Ακηδία *and* ἀκηδιᾶν *in the Greek and Latin Biblical Tradition*, in TU 112 (1973) 387-392.

NORTON 1908
F.O. NORTON, *A Lexicographical and Historical Study of* διαθήκη, Chicago, 1908.

O'CALLAGHAN 1971
J. O'CALLAGHAN, *El vocativo singular de* ἀδελφός *en el griego biblico*, in *Bib* 52 (1971) 217-225.

O'CALLAGHAN 1980
J. O'CALLAGHAN, *Il termine* θυσία *nei papiri* in *Sangue e Antropologia Biblica a cura di Francesco Vattioni* (Centro Studi Sanguis Christi, 1), Roma, 1980, pp. 325-330.

O'CALLAGHAN 1986
J. O'CALLAGHAN, ¿*Ἀγάπη como titulo de trato en el siglo VP?*, in *Aeg* 66 (1986) 169-173.

OLLEY 1978

J.W. OLLEY, *'Righteousness' in the Septuagint of Isaiah: A Contextual Study* (SCS, 8), Montana, 1978.

OLOFSSON 1990

S. OLOFSSON, *The LXX Version. A Guide to the Translation Technique of the Septuagint* (CB. OT, 30), Stockholm, 1990.

OLOFSSON 1990

S. OLOFSSON, *God is my Rock. A Study of Translation Technique and Theological Exegesis of the Septuagint* (CB. OT, 31), Stockholm, 1990.

ORLINSKY 1937

H.M. ORLINSKY, Ἀποβαίνω *and* ἐπιβαίνω *in the Septuagint of Job*, in *JBL* 56 (1937) 361-367.

ORLINSKY 1948

H.M. ORLINSKY, *Book Reviews: Studies in the Septuagint: I. Book of Job; II Chronicles*, in *JBL* 67 (1948) 381-390.

OTTLEY 1906

R.R. OTTLEY, *The Book of Isaiah According to the Septuagint*, Cambridge, 1906.

OTTO 1949

W. OTTO, *Beiträge zur Hierodulie im hellenistischen Ägypten*, in *Bayerische Akademie der Wissenschaften* N. F. 29 (1949) 9-12

OWEN 1929

E.C.E. OWEN, ἀποτυμπανίζω, ἀποτυμπανισμός (τυμπανισμός), τυμπανίζω, τύμπανον (τυπανον), in *JTS* 30 (1929) 259-266.

PAESLACK 1954

M. PAESLACK, *Zur Bedeutungsgeschichte der Wörter* φιλεῖν *'lieben'*, φιλία, *'Liebe'*, *Freundschaft*, φίλος, *'Freund' in der Septuaginta und im Neuen Testament (unter Berücksichtigung ihrer Beziehungen zu* ἀγαπᾶν, ἀγάπη, ἀγαπητός), in *Theologia Viatorum, Jahrbuch der Kirchlichen Hochschule Berlin* 5 (1953-54) 51-142.

PASSONI DELL'ACQUA 1976

A. PASSONI DELL'ACQUA, *Euergetes*, in *Aeg* 56 (1976) 177-191.

PASSONI DELL'ACQUA 1982

A. PASSONI DELL'ACQUA, *Ricerche sulla versione dei LXX e i papiri*, in *Aeg* 62 (1982) 173-194.

PASSONI DELL'ACQUA 1982 (A)

A. PASCONI DELL'ACQUA, *Precisazione sul valore di* δῆμος *nella versione dei LXX*, in *Rivista Biblica* 30 (1982) 197-214.

PASSONI DELL'ACQUA 1983

A. PASCONI DELL'ACQUA, *Indagine lessicale su* ἐπευναω *e composti. Dall'età classica a quella moderna,* in *Anagennesis* 3 (1983) 201-326.

PAX 1955
E. PAX, ἐπιφάνεια: *Ein religionsgeschichtlicher Beitrag zur biblischen Theologie* (Münchener Theologische Studien, I Hist. Abt. 10), München, 1955.

PELLETIER 1954
A. PELLETIER, *L'attentat au droit du pauvre dans le Pentateuque des LXX,* in *RechSR* 42 (1954) 523-527.

PELLETIER 1962
A. PELLETIER, *Flavius Josèphe adaptateur de la Lettre d'Aristée. Une réaction atticisante contre la Koine,* Paris, 1962, p. 25.

PELLETIER 1967
A. PELLETIER, *Note sur les mots:* ἱερόν, διάδεσις *dans P. Gen. , inv. 108,* in *Recherches de Papyrologie* 4 (1967) 5-86.

PELLETIER 1967
A. PELLETIER, *Une Particularité du Rituel des "pains d'oblation" conservée par la Septante (Lev. xxiv 8 & Ex. xxv 30),* in *VT* 17 (1967) 364-367.

PELLETIER 1982
A. PELLETIER, *L'autorité divine d'après le Pentateuque grec,* in *VT* 32 (1982) 236-242.

PELLETIER 1984
A. PELLETIER, *De la culture sémitique à la culture hellénique: rencontre, affrontement, pénétration,* in *RÉG* 97 (1984) 403-418.

PENNA 1965
A. PENNA, Διαθήκη *e* συνθήκη *nei libri dei Maccabei,* in *Bib* 46 (1965) 149-180.

PETERSEN 1986
H. PETERSEN, *Wörter zusammengesetzt mit* αμφί, in *Glotta* 64 (1986) 193-213.

PIETERSMA 1985
A. PIETERSMA, *Septuagint Research: A Plea for a Return to Basic Issues,* in *VT* 35 (1985) 296-311.

PODECHARD 1912
E. PODECHARD, *L'ecclesiaste* (ÉtB), Paris, 1912.

PODECHARD 1949
E. PODECHARD, *Le Psautier: notes critiques, Psaumes 1-75,* Lyon, 1949.

PODECHARD 1954

E. PODECHARD, *Le Psautier: traduction littérale, explication historique et notes critiques, Psaumes 76-100 et 110,* Lyon, 1954.

PREISIGKE
F. PREISIGKE - E. KIESSLING, *Wörterbuch der griechischen Papyrusurkunden, mit Einschluss der griechischen Inschriften, Ausschriften, Ostraka, Mumienschilder usw. aus Ägypten* Band 1, Berlin, 1925; Band 2, Berlin, 1927; Band 3, Berlin, 1931; Band 4 (KIESSLING), fasc.1-4, Marburg, 1944-1971.

PRIJS 1948
L. PRIJS, *Jüdische Tradition in der Septuaginta,* Leiden, 1948.

QUAST 1990
U. QUAST, *Der rezenstonelle Charakter einiger Wortvarianten im Buche Numeri,* in D. FRAENKEL (ed.), Studien zur Septuaginta (MSU, 20), Göttingen, 1990, pp. 230-252.

RABINOWITZ 1958
J.J. RABINOWITZ, *Grecisms and Greek Terms in the Aramaic Papyri,* in *Bib* 39 (1958) 77-82.

RAC 1981
Reallexikon für Antike und Christentum, Band 5, Stuttgart, 1981.

RAHLFS 1911
A. RAHLFS, *Septuaginta-Studien 3. Heft. Lucians Rezension der Königsbücher,* Göttingen, 1911.

RAURELL 1979
F. RAURELL, *Significat antropologic de "doxa" en Job-LXX,* in *RCatalana Teo* 9 (1984) 1-33.

RAURELL 1979
F. RAURELL, *The Religious Meaning of "Doxa" in the Book of Wisdom,* in M. GILBERT (ed.), *La Sagesse de l'Ancien Testament* (BETL, 51), Leuven, 1979, 370-383.

RAURELL 1980
F. RAURELL, *"Doxa" i particularisme nacionalista en Ba 4,5-5,9,* in *RCatalana Teo* 5 (1980) 265-269.

RAURELL 1982
F. RAURELL, *LXX-Is 26: la "Doxa" com a participacio en la vida escatologica,* in *RCatalana Teo* 7 (1982) 57-89.

RAURELL 1984
F. RAURELL, *"Doxa Kyriou" in Ez-LXX: Between Nationalism and Universalism,* in *Estudios Franciscanos,* 85 (1984), 287-311.

RAURELL 1985
F. RAURELL, *Lloc i signifcat de "Doxa" en Jer-LXX,* in *RCatalana Teo* 10 (1985) 1-30.

RAURELL 1986
    F. RAURELL, *The Polemic Role of the* ἄρχοντες *and* ἀφηγούμενοι *in Ez LXX*, in J. LUST (ed.), *Ezekiel and his Book* (BETL, 74), Leuven, 1986, pp. 85-89.

REDPATH 1906
    H.A. REDPATH, *A Contribution towards Settling the Dates of the Translation of the Various Books of the Septuagint*, in *JTS* 7 (1906) 606-615.

REEKMANS 1985
    T. REEKMANS, Ἀργός *and its Derivatives in the Papyri*, in *CÉg* 60 (1985) 275-291.

RENEHAN 1972
    R. RENEHAN, *Greek Lexicographical Notes: Fifth Series*, in *Glotta* 50 (1972) 38-60.

RENEHAN 1975
    R. RENEHAN, *Greek Lexicographical Notes. A Critical Supplement to the Greek-English Lexicon of Liddell-Scott-Jones* (Hyp, 45), Göttingen, 1975.

RENEHAN 1982
    R. RENEHAN, *Greek Lexicographical Notes. A Critical Supplement to the Greek-English Lexicon of Liddell-Scott-Jones. Second Series* (Hyp, 74), Göttingen, 1982.

RIESENFELD 1941
    H. RIESENFELD, *Etude bibliographique sur la notion d'*ἀγάπη, in *Coniectanea Neotestamentica* 5 (1941) 1-27.

ROBERT 1938
    L. ROBERT, *Etudes épigraphiques et philologiques* (Bibliothèque de l'école des hautes études. Sciences historiques et philologiques, 272), Paris, 1938.

ROBERT 1950
    L. ROBERT (ed.), *Hellenica. Recueil d'épigraphie, de numismatique et d'antiquités grecques* 11, Paris, 1940-1965.

ROBERT 1958
    J. & L. ROBERT, *Bulletin épigraphique*, in *RÉG* 71 (1958) 208.

ROBERT 1989
    L. ROBERT, *Le Serpent Glycon d'Abônouteichos à Athènes et Artémis d'Ephèse à Rome*, in ID. *Opera minora Selecta. Epigraphie et antiquités grecques*, Amsterdam, 1989, pp. 747-769.

RONCHI 1975
    G. RONCHI, *Lexicon theonymon rerumque sacrarum et divinarum ad Aegyptum pertinentium quae in papyris ostracis titulis Graecis Latinisque in Aegypto repertis laudantur*. II: Διοσκούρειος - Θεός, Milano, 1974; III: Θεός - μέγας μέγας, Milano, 1975.

ROUSSEL 1927

P. ROUSSEL, *Les mystères de Panamara*, in *Bulletin de Correspondance Hellénique* 51 (1927) 123-137.

ROQUET 1988
G. ROQUET, *Chenoute critique d'une étymologie du Cratyle:* δαιμόνιον, in *Zeitschrift für ägyptische Sprache und Altertumskunde* 115 (1988) 153-156.

RUDOLPH 1962
W. RUDOLPH, *Das Buch Ruth, Das Hohe Lied, Die Klage Lieder* (KAT, 17,1-3), Gütersloh, 1962.

RUDOLPH 1966
W. RUDOLPH, *Hosea* (KAT, 13,1), Gütersloh, 1966.

RUDOLPH 1971
W. RUDOLPH *Joel, Amos, Obadja, Jona* (KAT, 13,3), Gütersloh, 1971.

RUDOLPH 1975
W. RUDOLPH, *Micha, Nahum, Habakuk, Zephanja* (KAT, 13,3), Gütersloh, 1975.

RUDOLPH 1976
W. RUDOLPH, *Haggai, Sacharja 1-8/9-14, Maleachi* (KAT, 13,4), Gütersloh, 1976.

RUOZZI SALA 1974
S.M. RUOZZI SALA, *Lexicon nominum semiticorum quae in papyris graecis in Aegypto repertis at anno 323 a. Chr. n. usque ad annum 70 p. Chr. n. laudata reperiuntur* (Testi e Docum. per lo studio dell' Antichità, 46), Milano, 1974.

SANTI AMANTINI 1979-1980
L. SANTI AMANTINI, *Sulla terminologia relativa alla pace nelle epigrafi greche fino all'avvento della 'Koiné Eiréne',* in Atti dell'Istituto Veneto di Scienze, Lettere ed Arti. Classe di scienze morali, lettere ed arti, 138, Venezia, 1979-1980, pp. 467-495.

SCHERMANN 1910
T. SCHERMANN, Εὐχαριστία *und* εὐχαριστέω *in ihrem Bedeutungswandel bis 200 n. Chr.* , in Philologus 69 (1910) 375-410.

SCHLEUSNER 1820
J.F. SCHLEUSNER, *Novus Thesaurus Philologico-Criticus, sive Lexicon in LXX et reliquos interpretes graecos ac scriptores apocryphos veteris testamenti*, Leipzig, 1820-21.

SCHMIDT 1927
K.L. SCHMIDT, *Die Kirche des Urchristentums. Eine lexikographische und biblisch-theologische Studie*, in A. DEISSMANN (a.o.), *Festgabe für Adolf Deissmann zum 60. Geburtstag, 7. November 1926*, Tübingen, 1927, pp. 258-319.

SCHMITT 1974
A. SCHMITT, *Interpretation der Genesis aus hellenistischem Geist*, in *ZAW* 86 (1974) 137-163.

SCHREINER 1957
   J. SCHREINER, *Septuaginta-Massora des Buches der Richter; eine textkritische Studie* (AnBib, 7), Rome, 1957.

SCHREINER 1961
   J. SCHREINER, *Zum B-Text des griechischen Canticum Deborae*, in *Bib* 42 (1961) 333-358.

SCHREINER 1972
   J. SCHREINER, ἀντί *in der Septuaginta*, in J. SCHREINER (ed.), *Wort, Lied und Gottespruch. Beiträge zur Septuaginta. Festschrift für Joseph Ziegler* (Forschung zur Bibel, 1), Würzburg, 1972, pp. 171-176.

SEELIGMANN 1940
   I. L. SEELIGMANN, *Problemen en perspectieven in het moderne Septuaginta-onderzoek*, in *JEOL* 7 (1940) 395-390e, 763-766.

SEELIGMANN 1948
   I. L. SEELIGMANN, *The Septuagint Version of Isaiah: A discussion of its problems* (Mededelingen en Verhandelingen aan het Voorazïatisch-Egyptisch Genootschap "Ex Oriente Lux", 9), Leiden, 1948.

SEGALLO 1965
   G. SEGALLO, *La voluntà di Dio nei LXX in rapporto al TM:* θέλημα, *rasôn, hefes*, in *Rivista Biblica* 13 (1965) 121-143.

SETTIS 1973
   S. SETTIS, *'Esedra' e 'ninfeo' nella terminologia architettonica del mondo romano. Dall'età republicana alla tarda antichità*, in ANRW, 1,4 Text, Berlin, 1973, 661-745.

SHENKEL 1968
   J. D. SHENKEL, *Chronology and Recensional Development in the Greek Text of Kings* (HSM, 1), Cambridge, 1968.

SHIPP 1979
   G.P. SHIPP, *Modern Greek Evidence for the Ancient Greek Vocabulary*, Sydney, 1979.

SIJPESTEIJN 1987
   P.J. SIJPESTEIJN, *On the meaning of* ὁ δεῖνα (δεύτερος), in *ZPE* 68 (1987) 138-141.

SILVA 1980
   M. SILVA, *Bilingualism and the Character of Palestinian Greek*, in *Biblica* 61 (1980) 198-219.

SIMOTA 1968
   N. SIMOTA = N. ΣΙΜΩΤΑ, αι αμεταφραστοι λεξις εν τω, κειμενω, των Ο', Tessalonika, 1968.

SKEHAN 1987
   P. W. SKEHAN & A. A. DI LELLA, *The Wisdom of Ben Sira* (The Anchor Bible), New York, 1987.

SNAITH 1944
   N.H. SNAITH, *The Distinctive Ideas of the Old Testament*, London, 1944.

SOISALON-SOININEN 1975
   I. SOISALON-SOININEN, *Septuaginta, Vetus Testamentum*, in *Theologische Revue* 71 (1975)
   col. 367-369.

SOISALON-SOININEN 1978
   I. SOISALON-SOININEN, *Der Gebrauch des Verbes ἔχειν in der Septuaginta*, in *VT* 28 (1978)
   92-99.

SOISALON-SOININEN 1982
   I. SOISALON-SOININEN, *ἐν für εἰς in der Septuaginta*, in *VT* 32 (1982) 190-200.

SOLLAMO 1975
   R. SOLLAMO, *Some "improper" Prepositions such as ἐνώπιον, ἐναντίον, ἔναντι, etc. , in the
   Septuagint and Early Koine Greek*, in *VT* 25 (1975) 773-782.

SOLLAMO 1979
   R. SOLLAMO, *Renderings of Hebrew Semiprepositions in the Septuagint* (AASF, Diss. Hum.
   Litt. 19), Helsinki, 1979.

SOLLAMO 1991
   R. SOLLAMO, *The Pleonastic Use of the Pronoun in Connection with the Relative Pronoun
   in the Greek Pentateuch*, in COX 1991, pp. 75-85.

SOUTER 1926-1927
   A. SOUTER, ἀγαπητός, in *JTS* 28 (1926-1927) 59-60.

SPARKS 1972
   I.A. SPARKS, *A Fragment of Sapientia Salomonis from Oxyrhynchus*, in *Journal of the Study
   of Judaism in the Persian, Hellenistic and Roman Period* 3 (1972) 149-152.

SPICQ 1957
   C. SPICQ, Ἐπιποθεῖν, *désirer ou chérir?*, in *RB* 64 (1957) 184-195.

SPICQ 1978
   C. SPICQ, *Notes de Lexicographie néo-testamentaire. Tome I/II* (OBO, 22/1 and 2), Fribourg
   (Suisse) - Göttingen, 1978.

SPICQ 1981
   C. SPICQ, *Religion (Vertu de)*, in *Supplément au Dictionnaire de la Bible*, X, fasc. 54, Paris,
   1981, col. 210-240.

SPICQ 1982
   C. SPICQ, *Notes de Lexicographie néo-testamentaire. Supplément* (OBO, 22/3), Fribourg/Suisse -
   Göttingen, 1982.

STERENBERG 1908
   J. STERENBERG, *The Use of Conditional Sentences in the Alexandrian Version of the Pentateuch*, Munich, 1908.

STEINMÜLLER 1951
   J. E. STEINMÜLLER, Ἐρᾶν, φιλεῖν, ἀγαπᾶν *in extra-Biblical and Biblical Sources,* in *Misc. Bibl. et Or.* A. Miller, Oblata, 1951, pp. 404-423.

STEUERNAGEL 1898
   C. STEUERNAGEL, *Das Deuteronomium* (HAT), Göttingen, 1898.

STEUERNAGEL 1899
   C. STEUERNAGEL, *Das Buch Josua* (HAT), Göttingen, 1899.

STIEB 1939
   R. STIEB, *Die Versdubletten des Psalters,* in *ZAW* 57 (1939) 102-110.

SWETNAM 1966
   J. SWETNAM, *Diatheke in the Septuagint Account of Sinai: A Suggestion,* in *Bib* 47 (1966) 438-444.

SWINN 1990
   S.P. SWINN, ἀγαπαν *in the Septuagint,* in MURAOKA 1990, pp. 49-81.

TABACHOVITZ 1956
   D. TABACHOVITZ, *Die Septuaginta und das Neue Testament,* Lund, 1956.

TALMON-TOV 1981
   S. TALMON - E. TOV, *A Commentary on the Text of Jeremiah. I The LXX of Jeremiah 1:1-7,* in *Textus* 9 (1981) 1-15.

TARELLI 1950
   C.C. TARELLI, ἀγάπη, in *JTS* NS 1 (1950) 64-67.

THACKERAY 1909
   H.J. THACKERAY, *A Grammar of the Old Testament in Greek according to the Septuagint,* Cambridge, 1909.

THACKERY 1923
   H.J. THACKERAY, *The Septuagint and Jewish Worship. The Schweich Lectures 1920,* Londen, 1923 (2nd ed.).

THIBAUT 1988
   A. THIBAUT, *L'Infidilité du peuple élu:* ἀπειθος *entre la Bible hébraïque et la Bible latine* (CBLa, 17), 1988, 336.

THOMAS 1939/40
   D.W. THOMAS, *A Note on the Meaning of* מתנהם *in Gen xxvii, 42,* in *ET* 51 (1939/40) 252.

TOSATO 1982
A. TOSATO, *Sulle origini del termine* ἀκροβυστία *(prepuzio, incirconcisione)*, in *BeO* 24 (1982) 43-49.

TOV 1976
E. TOV, *Three Dimensions of LXX Words*, in *RB* 83 (1976) 529-544.

TOV 1976 (A)
E. TOV, *The Septuagint Translation of Jeremiah and Baruch* (HSM, 8), Missoula, Montana, 1976.

TOV 1977
E. TOV, *Compound Words in the LXX Representing Two or More Hebrew Words*, in *Bib* 58 (1977) 189-212.

TOV 1981
E. TOV, *The Text-critical Use of the Septuagint in Biblical Research* (Jerusalem Biblical Studies, 3), Jerusalem, 1981.

TOV 1984
E. TOV, *The LXX Additions (Miscellanies) in 1 Kings 2 (3 Reigns 2)*, in *Textus* 11 (1984) 89-118.

TOV 1987
E. TOV, *Die griechischen Bibelübersetzungen*, in ANRW II, 20,1, Berlin - New York, 1987, pp. 121-189.

TOV 1990
E. TOV, *Greek Words and Hebrew Meanings*, in T. MURAOKA (ed.), *Melbourne Symposium on Septuagint Lexicography*, Atlanta, 1990, pp. 83-125.

TURNER 1926
C.H. TURNER, ὁ υἱός μου ὁ ἀγαπητός, in *JTS* 27 (1926) 113-129.

TURNER 1977
P.D.M. TURNER, ἀνοικοδομειν *and Intra-septuagintal Borrowing*, in *VT* 27 (1977) 492-493.

TWAT
G.J. BOTTERWECK & H. RINGGREN (eds.), *Theologisches Wörterbuch zum alten Testament*, Stuttgart, 1970-; = *Theological Dictionary of the Old Testament*, Michigan, 1977-.

TWNT
G. KITTEL (ed.), *Theologisches Wörterbuch zum neuen Testament*, Stuttgart, 1933-1979.

TYRER 1924
J.W. TYRER, *The Meaning of* ἐπίκλησις, in *JTS* 25 (1924) 139-150.

VAN HOONACKER 1905

A. VAN HOONACKER, *Un nom grec* (ᾅδης) *dans le livre de Jonas (II,7)*, in *RB* NS 2 (1905) 398-399.

VAN LEEUWEN 1940

W.S. VAN LEEUWEN, *Eirene in het Nieuwe Testament. Een semasiologische, exegetische bijdrage op grond van de Septuaginta en de Joodsche Literatuur*, Wageningen, 1940.

VAN MENXEL 1983

F. VAN MENXEL, Ἐλπίς. *Espoir. Espérance. Etudes sémantiques et théologiques du vocabulaire de l'espérance dans l'Hellénisme et le Judaïsme avant le Nouveau Testament* (Europäische Hochschulschriften Reihe 23 Theologie, Bd 213), Frankfurt am Main - Bern - New York, 1983.

VAN 'T DACK 1988

VAN 'T DACK, *Ptolemaïca Selecta* (StHell, 25) 1988 96-102

VAN UNNIK 1973

W.C. VAN UNNIK, *Jesus: Anathema or Kurios (I Cor. 12:3)*, in B. LINDARS (ed.), *Christ and Spirit in the New Testament. Studies in Honour of C. F. D. Moule*, London, 1973, pp. 113-126.

VATTIONI 1980

F. VATTIONI, *La lessicografia dei LXX nei papiri*, in *Studia Papyrologica* 19 (1980) 39-59.

VERGOTE 1938

J. VERGOTE, *Grec biblique*, in DBSuppl. 3 (1938) 1321-1396.

VERMES 1961

G. VERMES, *Scripture and Tradition in Judaism. Hagadic Studies* (Studia Post-Biblica, 4), Leiden, 1961.

VYCICHL 1983

W. VYCICHL, *Dictionnaire étymologique de la Langue Copte*, Leuven, 1983.

UMBERTO 1986

M. UMBERTO, ἀσθένεια, ἀνδρεία; *aspetti della femminilità nella letteratura classica, biblica e cristiana antica*, in *Univ. Parma, Ist. lat.* 9, 1983.

WALTERS 1973

P. WALTERS, *The Text of the Septuagint. Its Corruptions and their Emendation*, Cambridge, 1973.

WAMBACQ 1959

B.N. WAMBACQ, *L'unité littéraire de Bar.*, *I-III,8*, in J. COPPENS (ed.), *Sacra Pagina. Miscellanea Biblica Congressus Internationalis Catholici de Re Biblica, I* (BETL, 12), Leuven, 1959, pp. 455-460.

WEBER 1950

R. WEBER, *La traduction primitive de* βάρις *dans les anciens psautiers latins*, in *VetChr* 4 (1950) 20-32.

WEINFELD 1980
    M. WEINFELD, *The Royal Guard According to the Temple Scroll*, in *RB* 87 (1980) 394-396.

WELCH 1918
    A.C. WELCH, *The Septuagint Version of Leviticus*, in *ET* 30 (1918-1919) 277-278.

WESTERMANN 1974
    C. WESTERMANN, *Genesis 1-11* (BKAT, 1,1), Neukirchen-Vluyn, 1974.

WESTERMANN 1981
    C. WESTERMANN, *Genesis 12-36* (BKAT, 1,2), Neukirchen-Vluyn, 1981.

WESTERMANN 1982
    C. WESTERMANN, *Genesis 37-50* (BKAT, 1,3), Neukirchen-Vluyn, 1982.

WEVERS 1950
    J.W. WEVERS, *Exegetical Principles underlying the Septuagint Text of 1 Kings ii 12 - xxi 43*, in OTS 8 (1950) 300-322.

WEVERS 1985
    J.W. WEVERS, *An Apologia for Septuagint Studies*, in *BIOSCS* 18 (1985) 16-38.

WEVERS 1990
    J.W. WEVERS, *Notes on the Greek Text of Exodus* (SCS, 30), Atlanta, 1990.

WEVERS 1991
    J.W. WEVERS, *The Göttingen Pentateuch: Some Post-partem Reflections*, in COX 1991, pp. 51-60.

WIKENHAUSER 1910
    A. WIKENHAUSER, Ἐνώπιος-ἐνώπιον-κατενώπιον, in *BZ* 8 (1910) 263-270.

WILLIAMSON 1985
    H.G.M. WILLIAMSON, *Ezra, Nehemiah* (WBC, 16), Waco, Tx, 1985.

WILLIGER 1922
    E. WILLIGER, Hagios. *Untersuchungen zur Terminologie des Heiligen in den hellenisch-hellenistischen Religionen* (Religionsgeschichtliche Versuche und Vorarbeiten, 19,1), Giessen, 1922.

WILLIS 1970
    J.T. WILLIS, *Micah 2:6-8 and the "People of God" in Micah*, in *BZ* 14 (1970) 72-87.

WOLFSON 1947
    H.A. WOLFSON, *On the Septuagint Use of* τὸ ἅγιον *for the Temple*, in *JQR* NS 38 (1947) 109-110.

WOSCHITZ 1979
    K.M. WOSCHITZ, *Elpis Hoffnung. Geschichte, Philosophie, Exegese, Theologie eines Schlüssel-
    begriffs*, Wien - Freiburg - Basel, 1979.

WOSCHITZ 1988
    K.M. WOSCHITZ, αἰων, in *Neues Bibel Lexikon, 1,* (1988) 52-54.

X 1982
    'Απογραφή *censimento*, in *BeO* 24 (1982) 206.

YOUTIE 1975
    H.C. YOUTIE, *Commentary,* in *ZPE* 18 (1975) 149-154.

YOUTIE 1978
    H.C. YOUTIE, *Wörterbuch I, s. v.* βρέχω, in *ZPE* 30 (1978) 191-192.

ZIEGLER 1934
    J. ZIEGLER, *Untersuchungen zur Septuaginta des Buches Isaias* (Alttestamentliche Abhandlungen
    12,3), Münster, 1934.

ZIEGLER 1939
    J. ZIEGLER, *Isaias* (SVTG, 14), Göttingen, 1939.

ZIEGLER 1962
    J. ZIEGLER, *Sapientia Salomonis* (SVTG, 12,1), Göttingen, 1962.

ZIEGLER 1965
    J. ZIEGLER, *Sapientia Jesu Filii Sirach* (SVTG, 12,2), Göttingen, 1965.

ZIMMERLI 1969
    W. ZIMMERLI, *Ezechiel,* I, 1-24 (BKAT, 13,1), Neukirchen-Vluyn, 1969 = (Hermeneia),
    Philadelphia, 1979; *Ezechiel,* II, 25-48 (BKAT, 13,2), Neukirchen-Vluyn, 1969 = (Hermeneia),
    Philadelphia, 1983

ZORELL 1927
    F. ZORELL, *Der Gottesname "Saddai" in den alten Übersetzungen,* in *Bib* 8 (1927) 215-219.

ZUNTZ 1956
    G. ZUNTZ, *Greek words in Talmud,* in *JSSt* 1 (1956) 129-140.

ZUNTZ 1959
    G. ZUNTZ, *Aristeas Studies II: Aristeas on the Translation of the Tora,* in *JSSt* 4 (1959) 109-126.

II. COMMENTARIES

The following list includes the abbreviated references to commentaries providing lexicographical and text-critical information frequently used in the lexicon. With the exception of the commentaries to the Septuagint they are not, or only exceptionally, explicitly referred to at the lemmata.

Genesis: C.WESTERMANN 1974; 1981; 1982; HARL 1986
Exodus: LE BOULLUEC 1989; WEVERS 1990
Leviticus: HARLÉ 1988
Deuteronomy: DRIVER 1902

Joshua: STEUERNAGEL 1899; BUTLER 1983
Judges: SCHREINER 1957
Ruth: RUDOLPH 1962
Samuel: DHORME 1910
Kings: MONTGOMERY 1951; MULDER 1987
Chronicles: ALLEN 1974[I&II]

Isaiah: OTTLEY 1906; KOENIG 1982; SEELIGMANN 1948; ZIEGLER 1934
Jeremiah: MCKANE 1986; HOLLADAY 1986; 1989
Ezekiel: ZIMMERLI 1969
Minor Prophets: RUDOLPH 1966; 1971; 1975; 1976

Psalms: PODECHARD 1949; 1954
Job: DHORME 1926
Proverbs: MCKANE 1970; BARUCQ 1964
Canticle: RUDOLPH 1962
Ecclesiastes: PODECHARD 1912; HERTZBERG 1963
Lamentations: ALBREKTSON 1963
Esther: BARDTKE 1963
Daniel: MONTGOMERY 1951
Ezra & Nehemiah: WILLIAMSON 1985

Maccabees: ABEL 1919
Wisdom: LARCHER 1969; 1983; 1984; 1985
Sirach: SKEHAN 1987

ἄ I 0-6-0-0-0-6
Jgs 6,22(bis); Jgs^B 11,35(bis)
ah, alas!
Cf. KRAFT 1972, 160-162; WALTERS 1973, 341

ααρ N 0-0-0-2-0-2
Neh 7,33.34
=אחר/*other*; *Neh 7,33 Ναβι-ααρ *Nabiar* for MT
נבו אחר *the other Nebo*, cpr. Neh 7,34

αβακ N 0-1-0-0-0-1
1 Chr 4,21
=הבץ/*the byssus, fine white linen*
Cf. ALLEN 1974^II, 62

Αβαμα N 0-0-2-0-0-2
Ez 20,29(bis)
=הבמה/*the cultic highplace* (interpreted as a proper noun)

αβαρκηνιν N 0-1-0-0-0-1
Jgs^B 8,7
=ברקנין/ה for MT ברכנים/ה *the thornbushes*; see
βαρκοννιμ

ἀβασίλευτος,-ος,-ον A 0-0-0-1-0-1
Prv 30,27
without king

ἀβατόομαι V 0-0-1-0-0-1
Jer 30,14(49,20)
to be laid waste; neol.

ἄβατος,-ος,-ον A 1-0-17-4-6-28
Lv 16,22; Jer 2,6; 6,8; 12,10; 28(51),43
untrodden Jb 38,27; *inaccessible* Est 8,12x;
impassable Am 5,24; *desolate* Jer 6,8; *not to be trodden* 3 Mc 5,43; ἄβατον (sc. γῆν) *waste lands, desert* Jer 33,18

αβεδηριν N 0-1-0-0-0-1
1 Chr 4,22
=הברדין for MT רברים/ה *the words, records*

αβιρα N 0-0-0-1-0-1
Neh 1,1
=הבירה/ה *the fortified town, the citadel*
Cf. WALTERS 1973, 304-305

ἀβλαβής,-ής,-ές A 0-0-0-0-2-2
Wis 18,3; 19,6
harmless Wis 18,3; *unhurt* Wis 19,6

ἀβοηθησία,-ας N1F 0-0-0-0-1-1
Sir 51,10
helplessness

ἀβοήθητος,-ος,-ον A 0-0-0-1-2-3
Ps 87(88),5; 2 Mc 3,28; Wis 12,6
helpless Wis 12,6; *unhelpful* 2 Mc 3,28; neol.?

ἀβουλεύτως D 0-0-0-0-1-1
1 Mc 5,67

recklessly, inconsiderately

ἀβουλία,-ας N1F 0-0-0-1-1-2
Prv 14,17; Bar 3,28
recklessness, irresolution, indecision

ἄβρα,-ας N1F 3-0-0-5-7-15
Gn 24,61; Ex 2,5(bis); Est 2,9; 4,4
favourite, faithful or *devoted slave*; neol.?
Cf. HARL 1986, 204; WALTERS 1990, 13

ἀβροχία,-ας N1F 0-0-2-0-1-3
Jer 14,1; 17,8; Sir 35,24
lack of rain, drought

ἄβρωτος,-ος,-ον A 0-0-0-1-0-1
Prv 24,22e
inedible

ἄβυσσος,-ος,-ον^+ A 5-0-9-23-12-49
Gn 1,2; 7,11; 8,2; Dt 8,7; 33,13
bottomless, deep Dt 33,13; ἡ ἄβυσσος *the sea* Is
44,27; *the (cosmic) deep, the abyss* Gn 1,2
Cf. HARL 1986, 87; LARCHER 1984, 644-645; SCHMITT
1974, 149-150; →TWNT

ἀγαθοποιέω^+ V 1-1-1-0-2-5
Nm 10,32; Jgs^A 17,13; Zph 1,12; Tob^BA 12,13; 2
Mc 1,2
to do good [abs.] Zph 1,12; *to do good to* [τινα]
Jgs^A 17,13; *to do good to sb in sth* [τί τινα] Nm
10,32
Cf. HELBING 1928, 9; SPICQ 1978, 11

ἀγαθοποιός,-ός,-όν^+ A 0-0-0-0-1-1
Sir 42,14
beneficent
Cf. SPICQ 1978, 13, n.1

ἀγαθός,-ή,-όν^+ A 39-133-52-223-152-599
Gn 24,10; 45,18.20.23; 50,20
well-born, gentle Tob 7,6; *good* (in moral sense,
of pers.) 1 Sm 25,15; *fair* Dn^Th 1,25; *good* (of
things) Ex 3,8; *fine* (of metals) Ezr 8,27; τὰ
ἀγαθά *goods* Gn 24,10; εἰς ἀγαθά *for good* Gn
50,20; πολιὰ ἀγαθή *blessed age* Jgs^A 8,32;
εὐαγγελία ἀγαθή *glad tidings* 2 Sm 18,27;
ἀγαθὸς δρομεὺς *a swift courier* Prv 6,11; ἀγαθὸν
ὅτι [+ind.] *it is well that* 2 Sm 18,3; ἀγαθώτερος
better Jgs^B 11,25; see ἄριστος, βελτίων and
βέλτιστος
Cf. DELLING 1977, 152-172; →NIDNTT; TWNT

ἀγαθότης,-ητος N3F 0-0-0-0-4-4
Wis 1,1; 7,26; 12,22; Sir 45,23
goodness, friendly disposition; neol.
Cf. LARCHER 1983, 165-166

ἀγαθόω V 0-2-2-0-1-5
1 Sm 25,31(bis); Jer 39(32),41; 51(44),27; Sir

49,9
to benefit, to do good to sb [τινι] 1 Sm 25,31;
[τινα] Sir 49,9; neol.
Cf. HELBING 1928, 9

ἀγαθύνω   V 0-15-0-12-1-28
Jgs 16,25; Jgs^B 17,13; Jgs 18,20
A: to honour, to magnify [τινα] 1 Kgs 1,47; to
adorn [τι] 2 Kgs 9,30; to comfort, to cheer Jgs^B
19,22; to do good to, to do well to [τινι] Jgs^B
17,13; to do well Ps 35,4; P: to be of good cheer,
to rejoice greatly, to be merry Jgs 16,25; to find
favour Neh 2,5; to seem good Ezr 7,18; neol.
Cf. HELBING 1928, 10-11

ἀγαθῶς   D 0-2-0-0-1-3
1 Sm 20,7; 2 Kgs 11,18; Tob^BA 13,11
well, completely 2 Kgs 11,18; well (as
interjection) 1 Sm 20,7

ἀγαθωσύνη,-ης^+   N1F 0-3-0-11-1-15
Jgs^A 8,35; Jgs^B 9,16; 2 Chr 24,16; Ps 51(52),5;
Eccl 4,8
goodness, kindness Neh 9,25; εἰς ἀγαθωσύνην
for good Neh 13,31; ἀγαθωσύνην ποιέω μετά
τινος to deal well with Jgs^B 9,16; neol.
Cf. SPICQ 1978, 13-14

ἀγαλλίαμα,-ατος   N3N 0-0-9-4-10-23
Is 16,10; 22,13; 35,10; 51,3.11
joy, rejoicing Is 16,10; religious joy, joyful worship
Is 35,10; neol.

ἀγαλλιάομαι^+   V 0-2-12-53-7-74
2 Sm 1,20; 1 Chr 16,31; Is 12,6; 25,9; 29,19
to rejoice (exceedingly), to exult [abs.] 2 Sm 1,20;
to declare joyfully [τι] Tob^BA 13,9; to rejoice in
[τινι] Ps 80,2; [τι] Ps 58,17; *Ps 74(75),10
ἀγαλλιάσομαι -אניל I will·exult for MT אניר I
will declare; neol.
Cf. HELBING 1928, 255-257; →NIDNTT; TWNT

ἀγαλλίασις,-εως^+   N3F 0-0-1-16-2-19
Is 51,11; Ps 29(30),6; 41(42),5; 44(45),8.16
great joy, exultation Ps 29,6; προσευχή
ἀγαλλίασις prayer of rejoicing Tob^BA 13,1; neol.

ἄγαλμα,-ατος   N3N 0-0-2-0-1-3
Is 19,3; 21,9; 2 Mc 2,2
idol, statue, image
Cf. KOONCE 1988, 108-110

ἄγαμος,-ος,-ον^+   A 0-0-0-0-1-1
4 Mc 16,9
unmarried

ἄγαν   D 0-0-0-0-1-1
3 Mc 4,11
very (much)

ἀγανακτέω^+   V 0-0-0-0-4-4
4 Mc 4,21; Wis 5,22; 12,27; Bel^Th 28
to be displeased, to be vexed, to show indignation
Wis 12,27; to rage Wis 5,22
Cf. SPICQ 1982, 5-7

ἀγαπάω^+   V 42-37-49-89-66-283
Gn 22,2; 24,67; 25,28(bis); 29,18
to love (among men, the love of God for man
and of man for God) Gn 22,2; to love, to prize
[τι] 1 Chr 29,17; to be content with [τι] Eccl 5,9;
to be fond of doing, to love to do [+inf.] Prv
20,13; ἠγαπημένος beloved Is 44,2; τὴν ἀγάπην,
ἣν ἠγάπησεν αὐτήν the love with which he had
loved her 2 Sm 13,15; *2 Chr 18,2 ἠγάπα he
desired corr.? ἥπατα for MT ◊ סות he compelled,
cpr. Ps 77(78),36; *2 Sm 7,18 ἠγάπηκάς με
-אהבתני you loved me for MT הביאתני you brought
me; *Prv 30,15 ἀγαπήσει ἀγαπώμεναι -◊ אהב or
◊ חבב dearly loved for MT הבהב?, cpr. Hos 8,13;
Hab 3,4; *Ps 28(29),6 ὁ ἠγαπημένος ישרון- the
beloved for MT שריון Sirion
Cf. SWINN 1990, 49-79; →NIDNTT; TWNT

ἀγάπη,-ης^+   N1F 0-1-1-13-4-19
2 Sm 13,15; Jer 2,2; Ct 2,4.5.7
love
Cf. BARR 1987, 3-18; CERESA-GASTALDO 1953, 347-355;
HORSLEY 1987, 258-259; KAHANE 1987, 243-263;
PAESLACK 1954, 51-142; RIESENFELD 1941, 1-27; SPICQ
1978, 15-30; SWINN 1990, 80-81; TARELLI 1950, 64-67;
WEST 1967, 142-143; 1969, 228-230; WITT 1968, 209-211

ἀγάπησις,-εως   N3F 0-2-5-1-4-12
2 Sm 1,26(bis); Jer 2,33; 38(31),3; Hos 11,4
affection, love 2 Sm 1,26; *Hab 3,4 ἀγάπησιν
-◊ חבב love for MT חבה חביון ◊ veil, see also
ἀγαπάω

ἀγαπητός,-ή,-όν^+   A 3-1-7-6-7-24
Gn 22.2.12.16; Jgs^A 11,34; Is 5,1
desirable, amiable Ps 83(84),2; beloved Gn 22,2;
ἐστιν ἀγαπητόν τινι it is loved by, he loves Sir
15,13; *Ps 67(68),13 τοῦ ἀγαπητοῦ ירד- the
beloved for MT ידרון נרד ◊ they flee?
Cf. ENGEL 1985, 132-133; HARL 1986, 192-193; HORSLEY
1987, 254-255; PAESLACK 1954, 51-142; SOUTER 1926-
1927, 59-60; SWINN, 1990, 81; TURNER 1926, 113-129

ἀγαυρίαμα,-ατος   N3N 0-0-2-1-1-4
Is 62,7; Jer 31(48),2; Jb 13,12; Bar 4,34
pride, insolence; neol.

ἀγαυριάομαι   V 0-0-0-1-0-1
Jb 3,14
to be insolent; neol.

Cf. HELBING 1928, 261-262

ἀγγεῖον,-ον⁺   N2N 6-3-9-2-4-24
Gn 42,25; 43,11; Lv 11,34; 14,5; Nm 4,9
vessel, container
Cf. HARL 1986, 280-281

ἀγγελία,-ας⁺   N1F 0-3-6-3-1-13
1 Sm 4,19; 2 Sm 4,4; 2 Kgs 19,7; Is 28,9; 37,7
message, tidings, news, report
Cf. LARCHER 1984, 371 (Wis 5,9); →NIDNTT; TWNT

ἀγγέλλω
(·· ἀν-, ἀφ-, δι-, ἐξ-, ἐπ-, καθ-, παρ-, προαπ-,
προσ-)

ἄγγελος,-ου⁺   N2M 42-150-43-51-64-350
Gn 16,7.8.9.10.11
messenger Gn 32,4; *angel* Gn 16,7; *2 Kgs 7,17
τὸν ἄγγελον -המלאך *the messenger* for MT המלך
the king; *Jgsᴮ 5,16 ἀγγέλων -עירין (Aram.)
angels for MT עדרים *flocks;* *Jb 36,14 ὑπὸ
ἀγγέλων -ב/קרושים *by messengers* for MT בקרשים
by male prostitutes?
Cf. HARL 1986, 53-54; HORSLEY 1989, 72-73; LE
BOULLUEC 1989, 103 (Ex 4,24); WALTERS 1973, 225.279
(Jgs 5,16); WEVERS 1990, 54.369.540; →NIDNTT; TWNT

ἄγγος,-ους⁺   N3N 1-1-4-0-0-6
Dt 23,26(25); 1 Kgs 17,10; Jer 19,11; Ez 4,9; Am
8,1
vessel, vat Dt 23,26; *basket* Am 8,1

ἄγε⁺   D 0-1-0-0-0-1
2 Kgs 4,24
come on (imper. of ἄγω used as adv.)

ἀγελαῖος,-α,-ον   A 0-0-0-0-1-1
2 Mc 14,23
in group, flocking

ἀγελάζω
(·· συν-)

ἀγέλη,-ης⁺   N1F 0-2-1-6-1-10
1 Sm 17,34; 24,4; Is 60,6; Prv 27,23; Ct 1,7
herd, flock 1 Sm 17,34; *company, assembly* 4 Mc
5,4
Cf. WALTERS 1973, 279 (Jgs 5,16)

ἀγεληδόν   D 0-0-0-0-2-2
2 Mc 3,18; 14,14
in companies, by flocks

ἀγερωχία,-ας   N1F 0-0-0-0-3-3
2 Mc 9,7; 3 Mc 2,3; Wis 2,9
arrogance 2 Mc 9,7; *revelry* Wis 2,9; neol.?

ἀγέρωχος,-ος,-ον   A 0-0-0-0-1-1
3 Mc 1,25
arrogant, haughty

ἁγιάζω⁺   V 88-36-34-11-27-196

Gn 2,3; Ex 13,2.12; 19,14.22
A: *to hallow, to make sacred, to sanctify* [τι] Gn
2,3; *to consecrate to* [τί τινι] Neh 12,47; P: *to be
sanctified, to be holy* Ex 29,21; ἡγιασμένος
sanctified, sacred (of pers.) 2 Chr 26,18; *sacred
one, nazirite* Am 2,12; *sacred* (of places) 1 Sm
7,16
Cf. GEHMAN 1972, 98 (Lv 25,11); HARL 1986, 99; HARLÉ
1988, 29.114-115.178-181
(→ καθ-)

ἁγίασμα,-ατος   N3N 9-7-11-14-26-67
Ex 15,17; 25,8; 28,36; 29,6.34
sanctuary Ex 15,17; *holy object* Ez 20,40;
holiness Ex 28,36; *Zech 7,3 τὸ ἁγίασμα -ה/נזר?
the holy (offering)? for MT הנזר (inf. niphal)
keeping abstentions; *Lv 25,5 σταφυλὴν τοῦ
ἁγιάσματος -ענבי נזרך *grapes of your holy
offering?* for MT ענבי נזירך *grapes singled out,
withheld from cultivation?* or *grapes of your
nazir?;* neol.?
Cf. HARLÉ 1988, 178-181.197 (Lv 25,5)

ἁγιασμός,-οῦ⁺   N2M 0-1-2-0-6-9
Jgsᴬ 17,3; Ez 45,4; Am 2,11; 2 Mc 2,17; 14,36
consecration, sanctification Jgsᴬ 17,3; *Am 2,11
εἰς ἁγιασμόν -ל/נזר? *for consecration* for MT
ל/נזרים *for nazirites;* neol.

ἁγιαστήριον,-ου   N2N 1-0-0-3-0-4
Lv 12,4; Ps 72(73),17; 73(74),7; 82(83),13
holy place, sanctuary; neol.
Cf. LEE 1983, 52

ἁγιαστία,-ας   N1F 0-0-0-0-1-1
4 Mc 7,9
corr. ἁγιστεία *ritual, service*
Cf. WALTERS 1973, 38

ἅγιος,-α,-ον⁺   A 260-76-186-146-164-832
Ex 3,5; Ex 12,16(bis); 15,11.13
sacred, holy (of things) Ex 3,5; *holy, pure* (of
pers.) Ex 19,6; τὸ ἅγιον *holy place, sanctuary,
temple* Ex 26,33; τὸ ἅγιον τῶν ἁγίων *Holy of
Holies* Ex 26,34; ὁ ἅγιος *the Holy One* Ps 77,41;
*Ex 35,5 τοῦ ἁγίου -קרש *of the sanctuary* for
MT חרש *of a craftsman;* *Is 27,1 ἁγίαν -קרשה
holy for MT קשה *hard*
Cf. BARR 1961, 282-286; DIHLE 1988, 1-63; DIMANT 1981,
136; FRIDRICHSEN 1916; GEHMAN 1954, 337-348; HARLÉ
1988, 30.114-115.123.132-133.178-181; MOTTE 1987, 135-
152; NUCHELMANS 1989, 239-258; WILLIGER 1922, 85-88;
WOLFSON 1947, 109-110; →NIDNTT; TWNT

ἁγιότης,-ητος⁺   N3F 0-0-0-0-1-1
2 Mc 15,2

holiness, sanctity

ἁγιωσύνη,-ης⁺   N1F 0-0-0-4-1-5
Ps 29(30),5; 95(96),6; 96(97),12; 144(145),5; 2
Mc 3,12
holiness, sanctity; neol.

ἀγκάλη,-ης   N1F 0-1-0-2-0-3
1 Kgs 3,20; Prv 5,20; Est 5,1
(bent) arm, embrace, lap

ἀγκαλίζομαι
(→ ἐν-)

ἀγκαλίς,-ίδος⁺   N3F 0-0-0-1-0-1
Jb 24,19
arm; ἀγκαλίδα ὀρφανῶν ἥρπασαν *they have
taken away from the fatherless even the smallest
portions (even an armful?)* (combination of
Hebr. Jb 24,9a.10b)

ἄγκιστρον,-ου⁺   N2N 0-1-3-1-0-5
2 Kgs 19,28; Is 19,8; Ez 32,3; Hab 1,15; Jb 40,25
hook 2 Kgs 19,28; ἄγω τι ἐν ἀγκίστρῳ *to catch
with a hook* Jb 40,25

ἀγκύλη,-ης   N1F 9-0-0-0-0-9
Ex 26,4.5(bis).10(bis)
loop Ex 26,4; *hook* Ex 37,15
Cf. LE BOULLUEC 1989, 361; WEVERS 1990, 615

ἀγκών,-ῶνος   N3M 0-2-1-1-2-6
2 Chr 9,18(bis); Ez 13,18; Jb 31,22; 4 Mc 10,6
elbow Jb 31,22; *arm* (of a throne) 2 Chr 9,18

ἀγκωνίζω
(→ περι-)

ἀγκωνίσκος,-ου   N2M 1-0-0-0-0-1
Ex 26,17
dim. of ἀγκών; *anything which is bent* or *curved,
joint*; neol.
Cf. WEVERS 1990, 420-421

ἀγνεία,-ας⁺   N1F 2-1-0-0-1-4
Nm 6,2.21; 2 Chr 30,19; 1 Mc 14,36
chastity, purity (of the Nazirite) Nm 6,2; *purity*
(of the temple) 1 Mc 14,36

ἁγνίζω⁺   V 7-20-2-0-5-34
Ex 19,10; Nm 6,3; 8,21; 11,18; 19,12
A: *to cleanse, to purify* [τινα] Ex 19,10; *to
sanctify* [τι] 2 Chr 29,5; M: *to purify oneself* Ex
8,21
Cf. WEVERS 1990, 298; →TWNT
(→ ἀφ-)

ἅγνισμα,-ατος   N3N 1-0-0-0-0-1
Nm 19,9
purification, expiation
Cf. DANIEL 1966, 306

ἁγνισμός,-οῦ⁺   N2M 5-0-1-0-0-6

Nm 6,5; 8,7(bis); 19,17; 31,23
purification, expiation
Cf. DANIEL 1966, 306

ἀγνοέω⁺   V 4-3-1-1-12-21
Gn 20,4; Lv 4,13; 5,18; Nm 12,11; 1 Sm 14,24
*not to discern, to be ignorant of, to fail to
understand* [τι] Gn 5,18; *not to know that* [ὅτι
+ind.] Nm 12,11; [+inf.] Wis 7,12; *to be
ignorant of what is right, to act amiss* [abs.] (in
moral sense) Lv 4,13; οὐκ ἀγνοέω *to know well*
Wis 12,10; ἀγνοῶν *ignorantly, by mistake* Gn
20,4; *Wis 19,14 τοὺς ἀγνοοῦντας *those who
did not know* corr.? τοὺς ἀγνῶτας *those
unknown*
Cf. LARCHER 1985, 1074-1075 (Wis 19,14); WALTERS 1973,
108 (Wis 19,14); →TWNT

ἀγνόημα,-ατος⁺   N3N 1-0-0-0-6-7
Gn 43,12; Jdt 5,20; Tob 3,3; 1 Mc 13,39
fault of ignorance, oversight, mistake Gn 43,12;
sinful ignorance, mistake Tob 3,3
Cf. DANIEL 1966, 323-324; HARL 1986, 283 (Gn 43,12);
→TWNT

ἄγνοια,-ας⁺   N1F 3-2-4-8-11-28
Gn 26,10; Lv 5,18; 22,14; 1 Sm 14,24; 2 Chr
28,13
ignorance Wis 17,13; *sin of ignorance* Gn 26,10;
sin, mistake 1 Ezr 9,20
Cf. DANIEL 1966, 321-326; HARL 1986, 211; LARCHER
1985, 825 (Wis 14,22); →TWNT

ἁγνός,-ή,-όν⁺   A 0-0-0-6-5-11
Ps 11(12),7; 18(19),10; Prv 15,26; 19,13; 20,9
pure, chaste, holy (of things) Ps 11,7; *undefiled,
chaste* (of a maiden) 4 Mc 18,7; *pure, upright*
(generally of pers.) Prv 15,26; τὰ ἁγνὰ τῆς
παρθενίας *chaste virginity* 4 Mc 18,8
→TWNT

ἄγνος,-ου   N2F 1-0-0-1-0-2
Lv 23,40; Jb 40,22
willow, chaste-tree

ἄγνυμι
(→ καθ-)

ἀγνωσία,-ας⁺   N1F 0-0-0-1-2-3
Jb 35,16; 3 Mc 5,27; Wis 13,1
ignorance
Cf. GILBERT 1973, 42; LARCHER 1985, 751-752

ἄγνωστος,-ος,-ον⁺   A 0-0-0-0-4-4
2 Mc 1,19; 2,7; Wis 11,18; 18,3
unknown

ἄγονος,-ος,-ον   A 2-0-0-1-0-3
Ex 23,26; Dt 7,14; Jb 30,3

impotent, sterile, childless
Cf. Le Boulluec 1989, 240

ἀγορά,-ᾶς⁺   N1F 0-0-5-3-4-12
Ez 27,12.14.16.19.22
marketplace 1 Ezr 2,18; *market* Ez 27,14;
δίδωμί τι εἰς τὴν ἀγοράν *to supply the market
with* Ez 27,12

ἀγοράζω⁺   V 8-4-3-1-8-24
Gn 41,57; 42,5.7; 43,4.22
to buy Gn 41,57; *Jer 44(37),12 τοῦ ἀγοράσαι
-ל/לקח *to buy* for MT ל/לכת *to go?*
Cf. Spicq 1978, 34-36; NIDNTT
(· ἐξ-)

ἀγορανομία,-ας   N1F 0-0-0-0-1-1
2 Mc 3,4
office of the clerk of the market

ἀγορασμός,-οῦ   N2M 2-0-0-2-3-7
Gn 42,19.33; Prv 23,20; Neh 10,32; 2 Mc 8,11
purchasing Sir 27,2; *purchase* Gn 42,19; *sale* 2
Mc 8,11; *merchandise* Neh 10,32
Cf. Harl 1986, 280; Lee 1983, 100

ἀγοραστής,-οῦ   N1M 0-0-0-0-1-1
Tob^BA 1,13
*the slave who had to buy provisions for the
house, purveyor*
Cf. Braunert 1971, 119-122

ἀγορεύω
(– ἀν-, ἀπ-, δι-, ἐξ-, προσ-, ὑπ-)

ἀγρεύω⁺   V 0-0-1-4-0-5
Hos 5,2; Jb 10,16; Prv 5,22; 6,25.26
to hunt, to catch [τινα] Jb 10,16; *to ensnare*
[τινα] (metaph.) Prv 5,22; *to hunt for* [τι]
(metaph.) Prv 6,26

ἀγριαίνομαι   V 0-0-0-1-0-1
Dn^Th 11,11
to be angry or *inflamed*
(· ἐξ-)

ἀγριομυρίκη,-ης   N1F 0-0-1-0-0-1
Jer 17,6
tamarisk

ἀγριόομαι   V 0-0-0-0-1-1
3 Mc 5,2
to grow wild

ἄγριος,-α,-ον⁺   A 5-2-4-12-5-28
Ex 23,11; Lv 21,20; 26,22; Dt 7,22; 28,27
wild (of animals) Ex 23,11; *wild* (of plants)
2 Kgs 4,39; *savage, fierce* (in moral sense) 3 Mc
7,5; *wild, raging* Wis 14,1; *malignant* Lv 21,20;
*Jer 31(48),6 ὄνος ἄγριος - ערוד *a wild ass* for
MT ערוער *a naked thing*

Cf. Wevers 1990, 363

ἀγριότης,-ητος   N3F 0-0-0-0-1-1
2 Mc 15,21
savageness, wildness

ἀγρίως   D 0-0-0-0-1-1
2 Mc 15,2
cruelly

ἄγροικος,-ος,-ον   A 2-0-0-0-1-3
Gn 16,12; 25,27; 2 Mc 14,30
dwelling in the country or *fields* Gn 25,27; *rude,
rough* Gn 16,12

ἀγρός,-οῦ⁺   N2M 64-79-52-43-8-246
Gn 2,5(bis).19.20; 3,18
field, land Gn 2,5; *country* (opp. of city) 1 Kgs
12,24m; οἱ ἀγροί *the fields, the lands* Nm 20,17;
land, territory, nation (semit.?) 1 Sm 6,1
Cf. Laberge 1978, 105 (Is 33,12)

ἀγρυπνέω⁺   V 0-1-0-7-3-11
2 Sm 12,21; Ps 101(102),8; 126(127),1; Jb 21,32;
Prv 8,34
to lie awake, to pass sleepless nights Ct 5,2; *to be
watchful* [abs.] 2 Nm 12,21; [ἐπί τι] Dn^LXX 9,14;
[ἐπί τινι] Jb 21,32

ἀγρυπνία,-ας⁺   N1F 0-0-0-0-10-10
2 Mc 2,26; Sir prol.,31; 31,1.2.20
sleeplessness, wakefulness Sir 31,1; *watchfulness*
Sir prol., 31; *wakeful care* (metaph.) Sir 42,9

ἄγρωστις,-ιδος   N3F 1-0-4-0-1-6
Dt 32,2; Is 9,17; 37,27; Hos 10,4; Mi 5,6
grass, weed

ἀγυιά,-ᾶς   N1F 0-0-0-0-2-2
3 Mc 1,20; 4,3
street

ἀγυρόω
(··· περι-)

ἀγχιστεία,-ας   N1F 0-0-0-5-0-5
Ru 4,6.7(bis).8; Neh 13,29
duty of redeeming, right or *responsibility of next
of kin* Ru 4,7; *Neh 13,29 ἐπὶ ἀγχιστείᾳ
-נאל ◊ על נאלי *right of inheritance of* for MT
נאל ◊ על נאלי^II *for the defilement of*
Cf. Walters 1973, 149

ἀγχιστεύς,-έως   N3M 0-1-0-7-0-8
2 Sm 14,11; Ru 3,9.12(bis); 4,3
near relation, kinsman, relative Ru 3,9; *redeemer*
Ru 4,14; ἀγχιστεὺς τοῦ αἵματος *avenger of
blood* (semit.) 2 Sm 14,11
Cf. Walters 1973, 149

ἀγχιστευτής,-οῦ   N1M 0-0-0-1-0-1
Ru 4,1

near-kinsman, redeemer; neol.

ἀγχιστεύω V 14-2-0-16-0-32
Lv 25,25.26; Nm 5,8; 35,12.19
to be next of kin [τινα] Ru 2,20; *to exercise the rights and responsibilities of a kinsman, to redeem* [abs.] (semit.) Ru 4,4; *to marry the widow of a kinsman* [τινα] (semit.) Ru 3,13; ὁ ἀγχιστεύων *kinsman* Lv 25,25; ὁ ἀγχιστεύων τὸ αἷμα *avenger of blood* (semit.) Nm 35,12; ἀγχιστεύω κληρονομίαν *to enter upon an inheritance* Nm 36,8; *Ezr 2,62 ἠγχιστεύθησαν -נאל◊ גֹּאַל they were made next of kin? for MT נֹאַליֹ גֹּאַל◊ᴵᴵ they were disqualified (from)*, see also Neh 7,64
Cf. GEHMAN 1972, 106; HARL 1991, 245; HELBING 1928, 321; WALTERS 1973, 149-150 (Ezr 2,62)

ἄγχω V 0-0-0-1-3-4
Ps 31(32),9; 4 Mc 9,17; 10,7; 11,11
to squeeze (the jaws) [τι] Ps 31(32),9; *to strangle* [τινα] 4 Mc 10,7; ἄγχω τὸν λογισμόν *to stifle the reasoning* 4 Mc 9,17
(⁻ ἀπ-)

ἄγω⁺ V 28-38-67-39-102-274
Gn 2,19.22; 38,25; 42,34.37
A: *to bring (towards), to lead (on)* [τινα] Gn 2,19; *to bring, to lead* [τι] Is 31,2; *to bring up, to educate* [τινα] 1 Mc 6,15; *to take forcibly, to catch* [τι] (of animals) Jb 40,25; *to drive (a waggon)* [τι] 1 Chr 13,7; *to gather (a force)* [τι] 1 Chr 20,1; *to hold, to keep, to celebrate* [τι] Tobᴮᴬ 11,19; *to keep, to observe* [τι] Prv 11,12; *to esteem* [τί τι] 3 Mc 7,15; *to treat* [τινα] Sir 33,32; *to pass* [τι] (of time) Ez 22,4; M: *to take with oneself, for oneself* [τινα] Wis 8,9; ἄγω μετοικεσίαν τινά *to carry someone captive* 2 Kgs 24,16; ἐπὶ τέλος τι ἄγω *to accomplish* 1 Chr 29,19; ἄγω τὴν ἡμέραν *to keep the day, to celebrate the day* 1 Mc 7,48; ἄγω τὸ πάσχα *to hold the feast of the passover* 1 Ezr 1,1; νύμφην ἄγομαι ἐμαυτῷ *to make someone my spouse* Wis 8,2; ἄγε (δή) *come on* Nm 5,1
⁻ SCHLEUSNER (Ez 28,16)
(⁻ ἀν-, ἀντιπαρ-, ἀπ-, ἀποσυν-, δι-, διεξ-, εἰσ-, ἐξ-, ἐπ-, ἐπαν-, ἐπισυν-, καθ-, μετ-, παρ-, περι-, προ-, προσ-, συν-, συναπ-, ὑπ-, ὑπερ-)

ἀγωγή,-ῆς⁺ N1F 0-0-0-2-4-6
Est 2,20; 10,3; 2 Mc 4,16; 6,8; 11,24
way of life, conduct, custom Est 2,20; *policy* 2 Mc 6,8; *treatment* 3 Mc 4,10; διηγέομαι τὴν ἀγωγήν *to pass one's life* Est 10,3
Cf. SPICQ 1978, 38

ἀγών,-ῶνος⁺ N3M 0-0-2-1-13-16
Is 7,13(bis); Est 4,17; 2 Mc 4,18; 10,28
struggle, battle Est 4,17; *contest* 4 Mc 17,11; *game* 2 Mc 4,18
⁻ ⁻ NIDNTT; TWNT

ἀγωνία,-ας⁺ N1F 0-0-0-0-3-3
2 Mc 3,14.16; 15,19
conflict 2 Mc 3,14; *agony* (of mind) 2 Mc 3,16

ἀγωνιάω V 0-0-0-2-1-3
Est 5,1; Dnᴸˣˣ 1,10; 2 Mc 3,21
to be distressed, to be in anguish Est 5,1; *to fear* [τινα] Dnᴸˣˣ 1,10
Cf. HELBING 1928, 34

ἀγωνίζομαι⁺ V 0-0-0-2-6-8
Dnᵀʰ 6,15(bis); 1 Mc 7,21; 2 Mc 8,16; 13,14
to fight 2 Mc 8,16; *to contend* 1 Mc 7,21; *to exert* [+inf.] Dnᵀʰ 6,15
Cf. MARGOLIS 1907, 248.256
(⁻ ἀντ-, ἐν-, προ-)

ἀγωνιστής,-οῦ N1M 0-0-0-0-1-1
4 Mc 12,14
competitor, champion [τινος]

ἀδαμάντινος,-η,-ον A 0-0-1-0-1-2
Am 7,7; 4 Mc 16,13
adamantine, unbreakable, of steel Am 7,7; *adamantine* (metaph.) 4 Mc 16,13
Cf. BRUNET 1966, 387-395

ἀδάμας,-αντος N2M 0-0-3-0-0-3
Am 7,7.8(bis)
adamant, i.e. hardest metal, prob. *steel*
Cf. BRUNET 1966, 387-395

ἀδάμαστος,-ος,-ον A 0-0-0-0-2-2
4 Mc 15,13; Sir 30,8
unsubdued 4 Mc 15,13; *untamed, unbroken* Sir 30,8

ἄδεια,-ας N1F 0-0-0-0-3-3
2 Mc 11,30; 3 Mc 7,12; Wis 12,11
freedom from fear, safe conduct 2 Mc 11,30; *license, permission* 3 Mc 7,12; δίδωμι ἄδειαν *to give pardon* Wis 12,11
Cf. LARCHER 1985, 719-720

ἄδειπνος,-ος,-ον A 0-0-0-1-0-1
Dnᵀʰ 6,19
without the evening meal, supperless

ἀδελφή,-ῆς⁺ N1F 45-27-21-11-18-122
Gn 4,22; 12,13.19; 20,2.5
sister Ex 6,20; *kinswoman* Jb 42,11; *dear, beloved* (term of endearment) Ct 4,9; δίδωμι ἀδελφήν τινι *to give one's sister in marriage* Gn 34,14
Cf. ENGEL 1986, 129

ἀδελφιδός,-οῦ N2M 0-0-0-34-0-34
Ct 1,13.14.16; 2,3.8
kinsman Ct 5,16; *beloved one* Ct 2,3; neol.
ἀδελφικῶς D 0-0-0-0-1-1
4 Mc 13,9
brotherly
ἀδελφοκτόνος,-ος,-ον A 0-0-0-0-1-1
Wis 10,3
murdering a brother or *a sister, fratricidal*
ἀδελφοπρεπῶς D 0-0-0-0-1-1
4 Mc 10,12
as befits a brother; neol.
ἀδελφός,-οῦ⁺ N2M 295-269-45-68-247-924
Gn 4,2.8(bis).9(bis)
brother Gn 4,2; *brother* (metaph.) Jb 30,29; *kinsman* Gn 13,8; *other, fellow-man* Lv 19,17; (metaph.) Jb 41,9; *neighbour, friend* Gn 43,33; *son in
law* (as term of affection in family relations)
Tob 10,13; ἀδελφοί *brothers* (term of address)
Jdt 7,30; *Jgs 5,14 ἀδελφοῦ σου -אחיך *your
brother* for MT אחריך *after you;* *Neh 12,12
ἀδελφοὶ αὐτοῦ -אחיו *his brothers* for MT היו *were*
Cf. LIFSHITZ 1962, 252-253; O'CALLAGHAN 1971, 217-225;
WALTERS 1973, 94; →NIDNTT
ἀδελφότης,-ητος⁺ N3F 0-0-0-0-7-7
1 Mc 12,10.17; 4 Mc 9,23; 10,3.15
brotherhood; neol.
ἀδεῶς D 0-0-0-0-1-1
3 Mc 2,32
without fear
ἄδηλος,-ος,-ον⁺ A 0-0-0-1-3-4
Ps 50(51),8; 2 Mc 7,34; 3 Mc 1,17; 4,4
unknown, obscure, secret Ps 50,8; *uncertain* 2 Mc
7,34
ᾅδης,-ου⁺ N1M 7-4-20-43-37-111
Gn 37,35; 42,38; 44,29.31; Nm 16,30
Hades, netherworld, hell Gn 37,35; *grave* 3 Mc
4,8; *death* Wis 1,14; εἰς ᾅδου (sc. οἶκον or
δόμον) *to Hades* Gn 42,38; most often
equivalent of Hebrew שאול *she'ol, netherworld*
Cf. LARCHER 1983, 204-205 (Wis 1,14); VAN HOONACKER
1905, 398-399; →NIDNTT; TWNT
ἀδιάκριτος,-ος,-ον⁺ A 0-0-0-1-0-1
Prv 25,1
mixed
ἀδιαλείπτως⁺ D 0-0-0-0-6-6
1 Mc 12,11; 2 Mc 3,26; 9,4; 13,12; 15,7
unintermittently, without ceasing, continually
ἀδιάλυτος,-ος,-ον A 1-0-0-0-0-1
Ex 36,30(39,23)

untearable
ἀδιάπτωτος,-ος,-ον A 0-0-0-0-1-1
Wis 3,15
infallible
ἀδιάστροφος,-ος,-ον A 0-0-0-0-1-1
3 Mc 3,3
unswerving, undeterred
ἀδιάτρεπτος,-ος,-ον A 0-0-0-0-2-2
Sir 26,10; 42,11
headstrong; neol.
ἀδιεξέταστος,-ος,-ον A 0-0-0-0-1-1
Sir 21,18
*that will not stand up to examination,
unconsidered*
ἀδικέω⁺ V 11-7-16-20-16-70
Gn 16,5; 21,23; 26,20; 42,22; Ex 2,13
A: *to be* ἄδικος *to do wrong, to act unjustly*
1 Kgs 8,47; *to wrong, to injure* [τινα] Gn 21,23;
to wrong sb in sth [τινά τι] Prv 24,29; *to sin
against* [ἔν τινι] (semit.) 2 Chr 26,16; P: *to be
injured, to be wronged* Gn 16,5; *Ps 61(62),9(10)
τοῦ ἀδικῆσαι -עול *to act unjustly, to be
deceitful* for MT לעלות עלה *to go up*
Cf. HELBING 1928, 11; LE BOULLUEC 1989, 84; →NIDNTT;
TWNT
(→ ἀπ-, προ-)
ἀδίκημα,-ατος⁺ N3N 4-3-8-1-3-19
Gn 31,36; Ex 22,8; Lv 5,23; 16,16; 1 Sm 20,1
injustice, trespass, intentional wrong
Cf. DANIEL 1966, 309-312; →TWNT
ἀδικία,-ας⁺ N1F 14-20-100-52-42-228
Gn 6,11.13; 26,20; 44,16; 49,5
wrongdoing, injustice Gn 6,11; *wrongful act,
offence* Ex 34,7; Ἀδικία *Injustice* Gn 26,20;
*DnᴸˣˣX 12,4 ἀδικίας -רעה *injustice* for MT רעת
wisdom; *Mal 3,7 ἀπὸ τῶν ἀδικιῶν -ל/מומי *from
the wrongful acts* for MT ל/מ/ימי *from the days;*
*Ps 72(73),7 ἀδικία αὐτῶν -עונמו *their injustice*
for MT עינמו *their eyes,* see also Hos 10,10; Zech
5,6; *Jb 36,33 περὶ ἀδικίας -על עולה *for unrighteousness* for MT על עלה *of (his) coming?*
Cf. DANIEL 1966, 309.312; HARL 1986, 63.213 (Gn 26,20);
→NIDNTT; TWNT
ἄδικος,-ος,-ον⁺ A 11-4-22-49-39-125
Gn 19,8; Ex 23,1(bis).7; Lv 19,12
unrighteous, wrongdoing, unjust (of pers.) Ex
23,1; *unjust, unrighteous* (of things) Gn 19,8; ἐπ'
ἀδίκῳ *unjustly, falsely* Lv 19,12; ποιέω ζυγὸν
ἄδικον *to make the balance unfair* Am 8,5
Cf. LE BOULLUEC 1989, 33.232 (Ex 23,1); WEVERS 1990,

358; →NIDNTT; TWNT

ἀδίκως⁺   D 2-0-2-16-6-26
Lv 5,22.24; Is 49,24; Ez 13,22; Ps 34(35),19
unjustly, wrongfully Jb 20,15; *unjustly, falsely* Lv
5,22; *without reason* Ps 34,19

ἀδόκητος,-ος,-ον   A 0-0-0-0-1-1
Wis 18,17
unexpected

ἀδόκιμος,-ος,-ον⁺   A 0-0-1-1-0-2
Is 1,22; Prv 25,4
not approved, without value, drossy (of silver)
Cf. LEE 1969, 239; SPICQ 1982, 165

ἀδολεσχέω   V 1-0-0-9-2-12
Gn 24,63; Ps 68(69),13; 76(77),4.7.13
to talk idly, to chatter Sir 7,14; *to talk* (generally)
Ps 68(69),13; *to meditate* Gn 24,63; *to complain*
Ps 76(77),4
Cf. HARL 1986, 204-205
(· κατ-)

ἀδολεσχία,-ας   N1F 0-3-0-2-0-5
1 Sm 1,16; 1 Kgs 18,27; 2 Kgs 9,11; Ps 54(55),3;
118(119),85
idle tales Ps 118(119),85; *conversation, talk*
2 Kgs 9,11; *meditation* 1 Kgs 18,27; ἐκ πλήθους
ἀδολεσχίας *from the abundance of talk* 1 Sm
1,16
Cf. HARL 1986, 204-205

ἀδόλως   D 0-0-0-0-1-1
Wis 7,13
guilelessly, honestly

ἀδοξέω   V 0-0-1-0-0-1
Is 52,14
*to be held in no esteem, to be of ill repute, to be
despicable*

ἀδοξία,-ας   N1F 0-0-0-0-1-1
Sir 3,11
ill repute

ἄδοξος,-ος,-ον   A 0-0-0-0-2-2
1 Mc 2,8; Sir 10,31
inglorious, dishonourable

ἀδρανέστατος,-η,-ον   A 0-0-0-0-1-1
Wis 13,19
sup. of ἀδρανής; *utterly impotent*; neol.

ἁδρός,-ά,-όν   A 0-4-2-2-0-8
2 Sm 15,18; 1 Kgs 1,9; 2 Kgs 10,6.11; Is 34,7
adult 1 Kgs 1,9; οἱ ἁδροί *the men of might,
chiefs, princes* 2 Sm 15,18
Cf. WALTERS 1973, 86

ἀδρύνομαι   V 1-5-0-2-1-9
Ex 2,10; Jgs^A 11,2; Jgs^B 11,2; 13,24; 2 Sm 12,3

to come to maturity Ex 2,10; *to be magnified*
(metaph.) 1 Mc 8,14
Cf. LE BOULLUEC 1989, 82-83; WALTERS 1973, 86;
WEVERS 1990, 16

ἀδυναμέω   V 0-0-0-0-1-1
Sir prol.,20
to be incapable; neol.

ἀδυναμία,-ας   N1F 0-0-1-0-1-2
Am 2,2; 3 Mc 2,13
lack of strength, debility Am 2,2; ἀδυναμίαι
inability, incapacity 3 Mc 2,13

ἀδυνατέω⁺   V 3-1-3-5-2-14
Gn 18,14; Lv 25,35; Dt 17,8; 2 Chr 14,10; Is 8,15
to be unable (of pers.) Wis 12,9; *to be weak* Is
8,15; *to be without strength* Lv 25,35; *to be
impossible* (of things) Gn 18,14; ἀδυνατεῖ
[+inf.] *it is impossible* Wis 13,16
Cf. HARL 1986, 176 (Gn 18,14)

ἀδύνατος,-ος,-ον⁺   A 0-0-1-15-11-27
Jl 4,10; Jb 5,15.16; 20,19; 24,4
without strength, powerless, weak (of pers.) Jb
5,15; *helpless* Jb 30,25; *impossible* (of things) Prv
30,18; *intolerable* (of things) Wis 17,13;
ἀδύνατοι *the poor* Jb 31,20; ἀδύνατος τοῖς
ὀφθαλμοῖς *blind* Tob^S 2,10; *Jb 24,22
ἀδυνάτους -אבירים? *the helpless* for MT אבירים
the mighty, see also Jb 5,15 or ἀδυνάτους corr.
δυνατούς?
Cf. SPICQ 1978, 44

ᾄδω⁺   V 4-13-4-49-3-73
Ex 15,1(bis).21; Nm 21,17; Jgs^A 5,1
to sing (a song) [abs.] 1 Chr 16,9; *to sing of, to
chant* [τι] Ps 88(89),2; *to sing with* [ἕν τινι]
(semit.) 2 Chr 23,13; ᾄδω ἐν ταῖς ὁδοῖς ὅτι *to
sing in the ways that* or *to sing of* for MT
וישירו בדרכי *they sung of the ways* Ps 137(138),5;
ᾄδω τὴν ᾠδήν *to sing a song* Ex 15,1
Cf. HELBING 1928, 69; →NIDNTT; TWNT
(→ ἐπ-, συν-)

αδων   N 0-0-1-0-0-1
Jer 41(34),5
=ארון *Lord*

αδωναι   N 0-1-0-0-0-1
1 Sm 1,11
=ארני *Lord, God*
Cf. KASE 1938, 48-51

αδωναιε   N 0-2-0-0-0-2
Jgs^B 13,8; 16,28
=ארני *Lord* (addressing God)

αδωρημεμ   N 0-0-0-1-0-1

Neh 3,5

=אדיריהם *their nobility*

ἀεί⁺   D 0-1-2-4-7-14

Jgs^ 16,20; Is 42,14; 51,13; Ps 94(95),10; Est 3,13
always, ever Jgs^ 16,20; *everlasting* (as adj.) 3 Mc
3,21; ὁ ἀεὶ χρόνος *eternity* 3 Mc 3,29

ἀέναος,-ος,-ον   A 3-0-0-1-3-7

Gn 49,26; Dt 33,15.27; Jb 19,25; 2 Mc 7,36
everflowing Wis 11,6; *everlasting* Gn 49,26;
eternal Jb 19,25

ἀεργός,-ός,-όν   A 0-0-0-3-0-3

Prv 13,4; 15,19; 19,15
idle Prv 13,4; *not working, idle* Prv 19,15

Cf. SHIPP 1979, 44

ἀετός,-οῦ⁺   N2M 5-1-11-11-1-29

Ex 19,4; Lv 11,13; Dt 14,12; 28,49; 32,11
eagle

Cf. SHIPP 1979, 44

ἄζυμος,-ος,-ον⁺   A 35-17-1-1-3-57

Gn 19,3; Ex 12,8.15.18.20
unleavened (of bread, cakes) Ex 12,39; (τὰ)
ἄζυμα *unleavened bread* Ex 12,8; ἄζυμοι (sc.
ἄρτοι) *unleavened bread* Gn 19,3

Cf. HARL 1986, 68.179; HARLÉ 1988, 188

ἀηδία,-ας   N1F 0-0-0-1-0-1

Prv 23,29
unpleasantness

ἀήρ, ἀέρος⁺   N3M 0-1-0-1-8-10

2 Sm 22,12; Ps 17(18),12; 2 Mc 5,2; Wis 2,3;
5,11
air, sky

ἀθανασία,-ας⁺   N1F 0-0-0-0-7-7

4 Mc 14,5; 16,13; Wis 3,4; 4,1; 8,13
immortality

·TWNT

ἀθάνατος,-ος,-ον   A 0-0-0-0-5-5

4 Mc 7,3; 14,6; 18,23; Wis 1,15; Sir 17,30
immortal

ἀθέμιτος,-ος,-ον⁺   A 0-0-0-0-4-4

2 Mc 6,5; 7,1; 10,34; 3 Mc 5,20
unlawful, against the law 2 Mc 6,5; *godless* 3 Mc
5,20

ἀθεσία,-ας   N1F 0-0-1-1-2-4

Jer 20,8; Dn^Th 9,7; 1 Mc 16,17; 2 Mc 15,10
faithlessness; neol.?

ἄθεσμος,-ος,-ον⁺   A 0-0-0-0-1-1

3 Mc 5,12
unlawful

ἀθέσμως   D 0-0-0-0-1-1

3 Mc 6,26

unlawfully

ἀθετέω⁺   V 2-21-22-9-10-64

Ex 21,8; Dt 21,14; Jgs 9,23; 1 Sm 2,17
to set at naught [τι] 1 Sm 2,17; *to reject (the law)*
[τι] Ez 22,26; *to deal treacherously with, to break
faith with* [τινα] Dt 21,14; [εἴς τινα] 1 Kgs
12,19; [ἔν τινι] (semit.) Ex 21,8; *to revolt* [abs.]
2 Kgs 8,20; *Is 27,4 ἠθέτηκα -◊פשע? *I have set
(rebelliously)* for MT ◊פשע *I will step*

Cf. HELBING 1928, 92-93; LE BOULLUEC 1989, 216 (Ex
21,8); LEE 1969, 239; SPICQ 1978, 47-48; WALTERS 1973,
256-257

ἀθέτημα,-ατος   N3N 0-2-1-0-0-3

1 Kgs 8,50; 2 Chr 36,14; Jer 12,1
a breach of faith, transgression; neol.?

ἀθέτησις,-εως⁺   N3F 0-1-0-0-0-1

1 Sm 24,12
breach of faith

Cf. SPICQ 1978, 47

ἀθεώρητος,-ος,-ον   A 0-0-0-0-1-1

Wis 17,18
not seen, not to be seen

ἀθλέω

(→ ἐν-)

ἀθλητής,-οῦ   N1M 0-0-0-0-3-3

4 Mc 6,10; 4 Mc 17,15.16
athlete 4 Mc 6,10; *athlete, champion* (metaph.)
17,15; *master of, champion in* [τινος] 4 Mc 17,16

ἀθλιώτατος,-η,-ον   A 0-0-0-0-2-2

3 Mc 5,37.49
sup. of ἄθλιος; *most miserable*

Cf. SHIPP 1979, 45

ἀθλοθετέω   V 0-0-0-0-1-1

4 Mc 17,12
to offer a prize, to offer rewards; neol.

ἆθλον,-ου   N2N 0-0-0-0-2-2

4 Mc 9,8; Wis 4,2
prize

ἀθλοφόρος,-ος,-ον   A 0-0-0-0-2-2

4 Mc 15,29; 18,23
victorious, carrying off the prize

αθουκιν   N 0-1-0-0-0-1

1 Chr 4,22
personal name for MT עתיקים *ancient*

ἀθροίζω⁺   V 2-2-2-0-9-15

Gn 49,2; Nm 20,2; 1 Sm 7,5; 2 Kgs 6,24; Jer
18,21
A: *to gather together, to collect* [τινα] 1 Sm 7,5;
M: *to assemble together in* 3 Mc 1,20; P: *to be
gathered together in* Gn 49,2; *Jer 18,21 καὶ

ἄθροισον -והאנרם ◊ אנר and gather them together for MT והגרם ◊ נגר and deliver them to (the sword)?

(· συν-)

ἄθροισμα,-ατος   N3N 0-0-0-0-1-1
1 Mc 3,13
multitude, gathering, assembly

ἀθρόος,-η,-ον   A 0-0-0-0-1-1
3 Mc 5,14
in crowds, gathered

ἀθυμέω⁺   V 1-4-1-0-2-8
Dt 28,65; 1 Sm 1,6.7; 15,11; 1 Chr 13,11
to be disheartened

ἀθυμία,-ας   N1F 0-1-0-1-0-2
1 Sm 1,6; Ps 118(119),53
despondency, discouragement

ἄθυτος,-ος,-ον   A 1-0-0-0-0-1
Lv 19,7
not fit to be offered
Cf. BICKERMAN 1980, 98 n.71

ἄθῷος,-ος,-ον⁺   A 11-15-8-15-8-57
Gn 24,41(bis); Ex 21,19.28; 23,7
unpunished Sir 7,8; innocent, guiltless Ex 23,7; free from [ἀπό τινος] Jb 10,14; αἷμα ἀθῷον innocent blood 1 Sm 19,5; ἀθῷος ὅρκῳ free of an oath Jos 2,17; ἀθῷος ἔσται ἐν τῇ οἰκίᾳ αὐτοῦ he shall stay at home without being liable to military service Dt 24,5; ἀθῷος χερσί one with innocent hands Ps 23(24),4
Cf. LE BOULLUEC 1989, 218-219; WALTERS 1973, 75.293

ἀθῷόω   V 0-4-8-3-3-18
JgsᴮB 15,3; 1 Sm 26,9; 1 Kgs 2,9.35o; Jer 15,15
A: to let go unpunished [τινα] 1 Kgs 2,9; to leave unavenged [τι] Jl 3,21; to take revenge on sb's life on someone else [τινα ἀπό τινος] Jer 15,15; P: to remain unpunished 1 Sm 26,9; to be guiltless Jgsᴮ 15,3; ἀθῷόν τινα ἀθῷόω to hold entirely guiltless Jer 26(46),28; neol.
Cf. WALTERS 1973, 75.293-294

αἴγειος,-α,-ον⁺   A 4-0-0-0-0-4
Ex 25,4; 35,6.26; Nm 31,20
of a goat

αἰγιαλός,-οῦ⁺   N2M 0-1-0-0-0-1
Jgsᴬ 5,17
sea-shore, beach
Cf. BONNEAU 1985, 131-143

αἰγίδιον,-ου   N2N 0-1-0-0-0-1
1 Sm 10,3
kid, young goat

αιδαδ   N 0-0-2-0-0-2

Jer 31(48),33; 32(25),30
=הידד shouting in harvest

αἰδέομαι   V 0-0-0-1-5-6
Prv 24,23; Jdt 9,3; 2 Mc 4,34; 4 Mc 5,7; 12,11
to be ashamed to [+inf.] 4 Mc 12,11; to have respect for [τι] 4 Mc 5,7; αἰδέομαι πρόσωπον to be partial (in judgement) Prv 24,23
Cf. HELBING 1928, 24

(→ κατ-)

αἰδήμων,-ων,-ον   A 0-0-0-0-2-2
2 Mc 15,12; 4 Mc 8,3
modest

ἀίδιος,-α,-ον⁺   A 0-0-0-0-2-2
4 Mc 10,15; Wis 7,26
everlasting, eternal
Cf. WALTERS 1973, 93

ἀιδιότης,-ητος   N3F 0-0-0-0-1-1
Wis 2,23
eternity
Cf. LARCHER 1983, 268; WALTERS 1973, 93

αἰδοῖον,-ου   N2N 0-0-2-0-0-2
Ez 23,20(bis)
private parts; *Ez 23,20 τὰ αἰδοῖα male sexorgan -◊ זמורה shoot, twig for MT זרמת זרם heavy rain, thunder

αἰδώς,-οῦς⁺   N3F 0-0-0-0-2-2
3 Mc 1,19; 4,5
shame, modesty, reserve
Cf. SHIPP 1979, 45-47; →TWNT

αἰθάλη,-ης   N1F 2-0-0-0-0-2
Ex 9,8.10
soot
Cf. LE BOULLUEC 1989, 130

αἴθριον,-ου   N2N 0-0-8-0-0-8
Ez 9,3; 10,4; 40,14.15(bis)
inner-court giving light to the adjacent rooms
Cf. CHANTRAINE 1964, 7-15; HUSSON 1983, 29-36

αἴθριος,-ος,-ον   A 0-0-0-1-1-2
Jb 2,9; 1 Ezr 9,11
kept in the open air (of pers.)

αἰκία,-ας   N1F 0-0-0-0-3-3
2 Mc 7,42; 3 Mc 4,14; 6,26
torture
Cf. WALTERS 1973, 44-45

αἰκίζομαι   V 0-0-0-0-8-8
2 Mc 7,1.13.15; 8,28.30
M: to maltreat, to torture [abs.] 2 Mc 7,13; P: to be tortured 2 Mc 7,1; οἱ αἰκισάμενοι the torturers 4 Mc 1,11
Cf. WALTERS 1973, 45

(→ κατ-)

αἰκισμός,-οῦ N2M 0-0-0-0-5-5
2 Mc 8,17; 4 Mc 6,9; 7,4; 14,1; 15,19
maltreatment, torture
Cf. WALTERS 1973, 45

αιλ N 0-0-2-0-0-2
Ez 40,48; 41,3
=איל *door-post*

αιλαμ N 0-12-29-0-0-41
1 Kgs 6,3.36; 7,43(6)(bis).43(7)
=אולם / אלם / אילם *porch* Ez 40,9; *Ez 40,25 τοῦ
αιλαμ -האלם *of the porch* for MT האלה *these*;
*Ez 40,49 ἐπὶ τὸ αιλαμ -האילם *by the porch*
for MT האילים אל *by the door-posts*; *Ez 41,1 τοῦ
αιλαμ -האלם? *the porch* for MT האהל *the tent*

αιλαμμω N 0-0-16-0-0-16
Ez 40,21.22(bis).24.25
=אילמו or אלמו *its porch* Ez 40,24; *Ez 40,37
καὶ τὰ αιλαμμω -ואלמו *and its porch* for MT
ואילו *and its door-post*, see also Ez 40,38

αιλευ N 0-0-10-0-0-10
Ez 40,9.21.24.26.29
=אילו *its door-post*

αἴλουρος,-ου N2M 0-0-0-0-1-1
LtJ 1,21
cat
Cf. WALTERS 1973, 297

αἷμα,-ατος+ N3N 156-69-91-36-49-401
Gn 4,10.11; 9,4.5.6
blood Ex 12,7; *anything like blood, wine* Gn
49,11; *blood relationship, kin* Nm 35,11; *blood,
life* Ez 16,36; αἵματα *bloodshed, murder* 1 Sm
25,33; κρίνω αἵματι *to punish with death* Ez
38,22; ἀνὴρ αἱμάτων *cruel man* 2 Sm 16,7;
ἐπιτίθημι τὸ αἷμά τινος ἐπί τινος *to count sb
guilty for the death of sb* 2 Sm 1,16; αἷμα
ἀναίτιον *innocent blood* Sus 62; αἷμα ἐκχέω *to
shed blood, to kill* Gn 9,6; πηγὴ αἵματος
fountain of blood, menstrual flow Lv 12,7; ῥύσις
αἵματος *menstrual flow* Lv 15,25; *Ez 24,17
αἵματος -רם *blood*? for MT דם ◊רממם *silence*?;
*Ez 32,5 ἀπὸ τοῦ αἵματός σου -מ/רמך *with
your blood* for MT רמותיך *(with) your rubble*?
Cf. ENGEL 1985, 131; HARL 1986, 61; HARLÉ 1988, 34; LE
BOULLUEC 1989, 45; →NIDNTT

αἱμάσσω V 0-0-0-0-1-1
Sir 42,5
to make bloody, to make to bleed [τι]

αἱμοβόρος,-ος,-ον A 0-0-0-0-1-1
4 Mc 10,17

bloodthursty

αἱμορροέω+ V 1-0-0-0-0-1
Lv 15,33
to lose blood

αἱμωδιάω V 0-0-2-0-0-2
Jer 38(31),29.30
to become dumb or *tingly* (of teeth)

αιν N 0-0-0-1-0-1
Neh 12,37
=עין *spring*

αἴνεσις,-εως+ N3F 4-6-9-37-9-65
Lv 7,12(bis).13.15; 1 Chr 16,35
praise 7,13; *Is 42,21 αἴνεσιν -תורה *praise* for
MT תורה *law*; neol.
Cf. HARLÉ 1988, 108

αἰνετός,-ή,-όν A 1-3-0-9-6-19
Lv 19,24; 2 Sm 14,25; 22,4; 1 Chr 16,25; Ps
47(48),2
praiseworthy, be praised

αἰνέω+ V 1-21-7-78-37-144
Gn 49,8; Jgs^ 16,24; 1 Chr 16,4.7.10
to praise [τι] Gn 49,8; [τινι] 1 Chr 16,36; *to
glorify* [τινα] (esp. in religious sense of God)
1 Chr 16,4; *Jer 38(31),5 αἰνέσατε -הללו *praise*
for MT חללו *begin to use, treat as common*?, cpr.
Jb 35,14
Cf. ENGEL 1985, 174; HELBING 1928, 15-17; LEDOGAR
1967, 34-36; →NIDNTT

(→ ἐπ-, παρ-, συν-)

αἴνιγμα,-ατος+ N3N 2-2-0-2-3-9
Nm 12,8; Dt 28,37; 1 Kgs 10,1; 2 Chr 9,1; Prv
1,6
obscure saying, riddle
→TWNT

αἰνιγματιστής,-οῦ N1M 1-0-0-0-0-1
Nm 21,27
one who speaks riddles; neol.

αἶνος,-ου+ N2M 0-1-0-5-5-11
2 Chr 23,13; Ps 8,3; 90(91),1; 92(93),1; 94(95),1
praise 2 Chr 23,13; αἶνος ᾠδῆς *sung praise, song
of praise* Ps 90(91),1

αἴξ, αἰγός N3M/F 54-17-2-9-2-84
Gn 15,9; 30,32.33.35; 31,10
goat Gn 15,9; *2 Chr 31,6 ἐπιδέκατα αἰγῶν
tithes of goats corr. ἐπιδέκατα ἁγίων for MT
מעשר קרשם *tithes of holy things*

αἰπόλιον,-ου N2N 0-0-0-1-0-1
Prv 30,31
flock of goats

αἰπόλος,-ου N2M 0-0-1-0-0-1

Am 7,14
goatherd
αἵρεσις,-εως⁺   N3F 3-0-0-0-1-4
Gn 49,5; Lv 22,18.21; 1 Mc 8,30
free choice 1 Mc 8,30 *freewill offering* Lv 22,18;
ἐξ αἱρέσεως *by choice, at one's own discretion*
Gn 49,5

Cf. HARLÉ 1988, 185; →TWNT

αἱρετίζω⁺   V 2-7-7-5-8-29
Gn 30,20; Nm 14,8; Jgsᴬ 5,8; 1 Sm 25,35; 1 Chr 28,4
A: *to choose* Gn 30,20; M: *to choose* Ps 24(25),12; αἱρετίζω πρόσωπόν τινος *to act in favour of sb, to accept the petition of* 1 Sm 25,35; αἱρετίζω ἐν τινι *to choose sb* 2 Chr 29,11

Cf. HORSLEY 1983, 25; WALTERS 1973, 142-143

αἱρετίς,-ίδος   N3F 0-0-0-0-1-1
Wis 8,4
one who chooses
Cf. LARCHER 1984, 524

αἱρετός,-ή,-όν   A 0-0-0-3-4-7
Prv 16,16(bis); 22,1; 2 Mc 7,14; Sir 11,31
to be choosen, eligible Prv 16,16; *elected* Sir 11,31

αἱρέω⁺   V 2-4-3-1-3-13
Dt 26,17.18; Jos 24,15; 1 Sm 19,1; 2 Sm 15,15
A: *to take, to select* [τι] 1 Chr 21,10; M: *to choose* [τι] 2 Sm 15,15; *to prefer* [τι] Jer 8,3; *to take to oneself, to be fond of* [τινα] 1 Sm 19,1; *to prefer* [+inf.] 2 Mc 11,25

Cf. HELBING 1928, 60

(→ ἀν-, ἀνθυφ-, ἀνταν-, ἀφ-, δι-, ἐξ-, ἐπαν-, ἐπιδι-, καθ-, καταδι-, παρ-, περι-, προ-, ὑφ-, ὑπεξ-)

αἴρω⁺   V 41-106-68-40-34-289
Gn 35,2; 40,16; 43,34; 44,1; 45,23
A: *to lift, to take up* [τινα] Gn 46,5; *to take up and carry* [τι] Gn 43,34; *to remove, to take away* [τινα] Gn 35,2; *to kill* [τινα] 1 Mc 16,19; *to wear* [τι] 1 Sm 2,28; *to excite* [τι] 1 Mc 13,17; P: *to be lifted up, to be carried* Ex 25,28; *to be removed, to be taken away* Jer 38(31),24; *to be eliminated, to be destroyed* Est 4,1; αἴρω τοὺς ὀφθαλμούς *to raise the eyes* Ps 120(121),1; αἴρω κεφαλήν *to raise the head* (as a sign of pride) Jgs 8,28; αἴρω τὴν χεῖρα *to raise the hand* (for an oath) Dt 32,40; αἴρω τὸ πρόσωπον πρός τινα *to look honestly into the eyes of* 2 Sm 2,22; αἴρω τὸν θηλάζοντα *to take a baby to the breast* Nm 11,12; αἴρω χεῖρας ἐναντίον τινός

to lift the hand against Jb 15,25; ἀρθήσεται ἡ σκήνη *the tabernacle shall be carried further, set forward* Nm 2,17; αἴρω ἐπί τινα *to select and put before sb* 2 Sm 24,12

(→ ἀντ-, ἀπ-, ἐξ-, ἐπ-, μετ-, ὑπερ-)

αἰσθάνομαι⁺   V 0-0-2-4-5-11
Is 33,11; 49,26; Jb 23,5; 40,23; Prv 17,10
to perceive [abs.] Jb 40,23; *to feel* [τι] LtJ 19; *to understand* [τι] Jb 23,5; *to take notice of, to have perception of, to have feeling of* [τινος] Wis 11,13; *Is 33,11 αἰσθηθήσεσθε - חשׁשׁ (Aram.)? *you will perceive* for MT חשׁשׁ *dried grass, stubble*

Cf. ZIEGLER 1934, 9-10 (Is 33,11); →TWNT

αἴσθησις,-εως⁺   N3F 1-0-0-22-4-27
Ex 28,3; Prv 1,4.7.22; 2,3
perception Ex 28,3; *knowledge* Prv 1,7; *feeling* 1 Ezr 1,22

Cf. LE BOULLUEC 1989, 281-282 (Ex 28,3); WEVERS 1990, 445

αἰσθητήριον,-ου⁺   N2N 0-0-1-0-1-2
Jer 4,19; 4 Mc 2,22
senses, sensitive powers

αἰσθητικός,-ή,-όν   A 0-0-0-2-0-2
Prv 14,10.30
sensitive

αἰσχρός,-ά,-όν⁺   A 6-0-0-0-5-11
Gn 41,3.4.19(bis).20
ugly, ill-favoured Gn 41,3; *ugly, horrible* 3 Mc 3,27; *shameful* [+inf.] 4 Mc 16,17

αἰσχρῶς   D 0-0-0-1-1-2
Prv 15,10; 2 Mc 11,12
shamefully

αἰσχύνη,-ης⁺   N1F 0-7-29-25-23-84
1 Sm 20,30(bis); 2 Sm 23,7; 1 Kgs 18,19.25
shame, dishonour 1 Sm 20,30; *shame, sense of honour* Sir 4,21; *shame for* [τινος] 2 Mc 5,7; *pudenda, sexual parts* Na 3,5; ποιέω αἰσχύνην εἴς τι *to bring shame upon* Jdt 14,18; *1 Sm 18,25 τῆς αἰσχύνης -בשׁת *of shame* for MT בעל *Baal* (contemptuous defamation of name); *2 Sm 23,7 αἰσχύνην -בשׁת *shame* for MT בשׁבת ◊ ישׁב *in the sitting?*; *Is 47,10 σοι αἰσχύνη -בושׁתך *shame for you* for MT שׁובבתך *led you astray*

Cf. SHIPP 1979, 49; →TWNT

αἰσχυντηρός,-ά,-όν   A 0-0-0-0-3-3
Sir 26,15; 32,10; 41,27
modest, shamefaced

αἰσχύνω⁺   V 1-10-34-30-19-94
Gn 2,25; Jgs 3,25; 5,28; 1 Sm 13,4

A: *to dishonour, to shame* [τινα] Sir 13,7; *to disfigure* [τι] (metaph.) Jl 1,12; P: *to be ashamed, to feel shame* Gn 2,25; *to be ashamed at doing* [+ptc.] Wis 13,17; *to be ashamed to do* [+inf.] Ezr 8,22; *to feel shame before* [τινα] Jb 32,21; *to have respect for, to reverence, to stand in awe of* [τινα] Prv 22,26; *Is 24,9 ᾐσχύνθησαν -יבֹשׁוּ *they are ashamed* for MT בשׁיר *with a song;* *Eccl 10,17 αἰσχυνθήσονται -בשׁת *they shall be ashamed* for MT בשׁתי/ל *for drinking*

Cf. HELBING 1928, 24.262; SHIPP 1979, 49; →NIDNTT; TWNT

(·ἀπαν-, ἐπ-, κατ-)

αἰτέω⁺ V 6-47-5-21-15-94
Ex 3,22; 11,2; 12,35; 22,13; Dt 10,12
A: *to ask for, to demand* [τι] Ex 3,22; *to beg of, to demand of* [τί τινα] Jb 6,22; [τι παρά τινος] Jb 6,22; M: *to claim* [τι] Dt 10,12; *to ask a person for a thing, to ask sth of a person* [τινά τι] Jos 14,12; P: *to be required* 2 Mc 7,10

Cf. HELBING 1928, 41; →NIDNTT; TWNT

(·ἀπ-, δι-, ἐπ-, παρ-, προσ-)

αἴτημα,-ατος⁺ N3N 0-5-0-9-1-15
Jgs^B 8,24; 1 Sm 1,17.27; 1 Kgs 3,5; 12,24
request, demand

αἴτησις,-εως N3F 0-3-0-1-0-4
Jgs^A 8,24; 1 Kgs 2,16.20; Jb 6,8
request, demand

αἰτία,-ας⁺ N1F 1-0-0-2-18-21
Gn 4,13; Jb 18,14; Prv 28,17; 1 Ezr 2,17; 1 Mc 9,10
guilt Gn 4,13; *blame* 1 Mc 9,10; *accusation* Prv 28,17; *charge* 3 Mc 7,7; *cause* 1 Ezr 2,17; αἰτία βασιλικῇ *by royal responsibility, by royal decision which cannot be disobeyed*? Jb 18,14

Cf. BICKERMAN 1980, 215-219; HARL 1986, 63.115-116 (Gn 4,13); RABINOWITZ 1958, 80; SCHLEUSNER (Jb 18,14)

αἰτιάομαι V 0-0-0-1-2-3
Prv 19,3; 4 Mc 2,19; Sir 29,5
to blame, to accuse [τινα] Prv 19,3; *to allege as the cause* [τι] Sir 29,5

Cf. BICKERMAN 1980, 216-219

αἴτιος,-ος/-α,-ον⁺ A 0-1-0-0-7-8
1 Sm 22,22; 2 Mc 4,47; 13,4; 4 Mc 1,11; PSal 9,5
responsible for, guilty of [τινος] 1 Sm 22,22; ὁ αἴτιος *the accused, the culprit* Sus^Th 53; [τινος] Bel 42

αἰφνίδιος,-ος,-ον⁺ A 0-0-0-0-3-3
2 Mc 14,17; 3 Mc 3,24; Wis 17,14
unforeseen, sudden

Cf. SPICQ 1982, 8

αἰφνιδίως D 0-0-0-0-2-2
2 Mc 5,5; 14,22
suddenly

Cf. SPICQ 1982, 8

αἰχμαλωσία,-ας⁺ N1F 7-11-45-35-40-138
Nm 21,1; 31,12.19.26; Dt 21,13
captivity Dt 28,41; *body of captives* Nm 31,12; *a band of prisoners* 2 Chr 28,5; ἀποστρέφω τὴν αἰχμαλωσίαν *to turn back the captivity, to bring back the captives* Ez 39,25; ἐπιστρέφω τὴν αἰχμαλωσίαν Ps 13(14),7; *Ez 11,15 τῆς αἰχμαλωσίας σου -גולתך *your captivity, your group of captives* for MT גאלתך *of your kindred;* *Is 1,27 αἰχμαλωσία αὐτῆς שׁביה ◊ שׁבה *her captives* for MT שׁביה ◊ שׁוב *those in her (Sion) who repent;* *Ezr 5,5 αἰχμαλωσίαν שׁבי- ◊ שׁבה *captivity* for MT שׁבי ◊ שׁיב *elders;* *Jl 4,8 εἰς αἰχμαλωσίαν לשׁבים- *into captivity* for MT לשׁבאים *to the Sabeans;* *Ez 32,9 αἰχμαλωσίαν σου שׁביך- *your captivity* for MT שׁברך *your destruction*

→NIDNTT

αἰχμαλωτεύω⁺ V 3-12-13-7-4-39
Gn 14,14; 34,29; Nm 24,22; 1 Sm 30,2.3
A: *to take prisoner, to take captive* [τινα] Gn 34,29; *to capture* [τι] 1 Chr 5,21; P: *to be taken captive* Gn 14,14; αἰχμαλωτεύω τινὰ εἴς τι *to lead captive into* Jdt 5,18; *Jb 1,15 οἱ αἰχμαλωτεύοντες -שׁבה *the captives* for MT שׁבא *Saba, the Sabeans*

αἰχμαλωτίζω⁺ V 0-8-0-3-13-24
Jgs 5,12; 1 Kgs 8,46(bis); 2 Kgs 24,14
to take prisoner, to take captive [τινα] Jgs 5,12; *to take, to capture* [τι] Tob^S 14,15

αἰχμαλωτίς,-ίδος N3F 2-0-0-0-0-2
Gn 31,26; Ex 12,29
captive(-maid)

Cf. LE BOULLUEC 1989,151

αἰχμάλωτος,-ος,-ον⁺ A 3-0-12-4-7-26
Ex 22,9.13; Nm 21,29; Is 5,13; 14,2
captive, prisoner, prisoner of war Nm 21,29; *taken away, stolen* Ex 22,9(10); *Jb 41,24 αἰχμάλωτον -שׁבה *captive* for MT שׁיבה *a hoary head*

Cf. LE BOULLUEC 1989, 227 (Ez 22,9(10)); →NIDNTT

αἰών,-ῶνος⁺ N3M 25-72-74-348-231-750
Gn 3,22; 6,3.4; 13,15; Ex 12,24
often stereotyped rendition of עולם; *lifetime, life* Tob^S 14,7; *age, generation* 1 Ezr 4,40; *long space of time, age* Ezr 4,15; *eternity* Tob^S 14,6; *world*? Wis 14,6; αἰῶνες *the ages, eternity* Tob 13,4; ἀπ'

αἰῶνος *of old* Gn 6,4; ἀπὸ τοῦ αἰῶνος καὶ ἕως τοῦ αἰῶνος *from age to age* 1 Chr 16,36; δι'αἰῶνος *for ever* Dt 12,28; εἰς τὸν αἰῶνα *for ever* Gn 3,22; ἐξ αἰῶνος *of old* Jer 7,7; εἰς τὸν αἰῶνα χρόνον *for ever* Jdt 15,10; εἰς αἰῶνα αἰῶνος *for ever and ever* Ps 18(19),10; ἕως (τοῦ) αἰῶνος *for ever* Gn 13,15; ἕως αἰῶνος οὐκ *never* Ps 48(49),19; πρὸ τῶν αἰώνων *from eternity* Ps 54(55),20; τὸν αἰῶνα *Aïon, a cosmic deity?* or *world?* Wis 13,9; *Est 9,32 εἰς τὸν αἰῶνα הלאה- הָאֵלֶּה *onwards, for ever* for MT האלה *these;* *Ps 89(90),8 ὁ αἰὼν ἡμῶν עלמינו- ◊ עולם *our age* for MT עלמנו ◊ עלם *our hidden things, secret sins;* *Ez 32,27 ἀπὸ αἰῶνος מעולם- *of old* for MT מערלים *of the uncircumcised;* *Is 19,20 εἰς τὸν αἰῶνα לעד- *for ever* for MT לעד *as a witness;* *Jb 19,18 εἰς τὸν αἰῶνα עולם- *for ever* for MT עוילים *young children;* *Is 17,2 καταλελειμμένη εἰς τὸν αἰῶνα עזבת ער- *abandonned for ever* for MT עזבות ערי *deserted cities*
Cf. GILBERT 1973, 34-35 (Wis 13,9); LARCHER 1985, 771-772 (Wis 13,9; 14,9); LE BOULLUEC 1989, 176 (Ex 15,18); WOSCHITZ 1991, 52-54; →NIDNTT; TWNT

αἰώνιος,-ος,-ον⁺ A 45-2-45-30-41-163
Gn 9,12.16; 17,7.8.13
often stereotyped rendition of עולם, עלם; *without beginning* or *end, eternal* Gn 21,33; *everlasting* Jb 40,23; ὁ αἰώνος *eternal, Lord of the world?* Sus^LXX 35a; *Jb 33,12 αἰώνιος עולם- *eternal* for MT מ(אנש) אלוה *God than (man);* *Ps 75(76),5 ἀπὸ ὀρέων αἰωνίων טרם- מהררי *from the eternal mountains* for MT טרף מהררי *from the mountains of prey?;* *Jb 21,11 αἰώνια עולם- *eternal* for MT עויליהם *their infants;* *Is 54,4 αἰώνιον עולמי(ך)- ? *eternal* for MT עלומיך *your youth*
Cf. ENGEL 1985, 107; HILL 1973, 186; LE BOULLUEC 1989, 93; WALTERS 1973, 316; →TWNT

ἀκαθαρσία,-ας⁺ N1F 24-4-16-5-14-63
Lv 5,3(bis); 7,20.21; 15,3
physical and ritual impurity Lv 7,20.21; *moral impurity* Wis 2,16; *cultic impurity caused by idolatry* Dt 7,25

ἀκάθαρτος,-ος,-ον⁺ A 125-6-16-8-5-160
Lv 5,2(quater); 7,19
impure, moraly unclean Jdt 13,7; *impure in the cultic sense* Lv 11,4
Cf. HARLÉ 1988, 31

ἄκαιρος,-ος,-ον⁺ A 0-0-0-0-2-2
Sir 20,19; 22,6

unseasonable, unsuitable

ἀκαίρως⁺ D 0-0-0-0-1-1
Sir 32,4
at unseasonable time, unsuitably

ἀκακία,-ας N1F 0-0-0-12-2-14
Ps 7,9; 25(26),1.11; 36(37),37; 40(41),13
guilelessness, innocence, integrity

ἄκακος,-ος,-ον⁺ A 0-0-1-12-4-17
Jer 11,19; Ps 24(25),21; Jb 2,3; 8,20; 36,5
innocent Jer 11,19; *simple* Prv 1,4
Cf. SPICQ 1982, 13-16

ἀκάλυπτος,-ος,-ον A 0-0-0-0-2-2
Tob^BA 2,9; LtJ 1,30
uncovered, unveiled

ἀκαλύπτως D 0-0-0-0-1-1
3 Mc 4,6
unveiled, in unveiled manner

ἄκαν,-ανος N3M 0-2-0-0-0-2
2 Kgs 14,9(bis)
thistle; see ἄκανθα; neol.
Cf. WALTERS 1973, 101

ἄκανθα,-ης⁺ N1F 2-5-13-7-4-31
Gn 3,18; Ex 22,5; Jgs^A 8,7.16; Jgs^B 8,7
thorny plant Gn 3,18; *Ps 31(32),4 ἄκανθαν קוץ- *thorn* for MT קיץ *summer*

ἀκάνθινος,-η,-ον A 0-0-1-0-0-1
Is 34,13
thorny

ἀκάρδιος,-ος,-ον A 0-0-1-2-1-4
Jer 5,21; Prv 10,13; 17,16; Sir 6,20
heartless, foolish Prv 10,13; *senseless* Jer 5,21; ἀκάρδιος *foolish person* Sir 6,20

ἀκαριαῖος,-α,-ον A 0-0-0-0-1-1
2 Mc 6,25
brief

ἀκαρπία,-ας N1F 0-0-0-1-0-1
Prv 9,12
unfruitfulness, barrenness

ἄκαρπος,-ος,-ον⁺ A 0-0-1-0-2-3
Jer 2,6; 4 Mc 16,7; Wis 15,4
barren, without fruit Jer 2,6; *sterile, unproductive* Wis 15,4

ἀκατάγνωστος,-ος,-ον⁺ A 0-0-0-0-1-1
2 Mc 4,47
not to be condemned, innocent

ἀκατακάλυπτος,-ος,-ον⁺ A 1-0-0-0-0-1
Lv 13,45
uncovered

ἀκατάλυτος,-ος,-ον⁺ A 0-0-0-0-1-1
4 Mc 10,11

perpetual

ἀκαταμάχητος,-ος,-ον   A 0-0-0-0-1-1
Wis 5,19
unconquerable; neol.

ἀκατάποτος,-ος,-ον   A 0-0-0-1-0-1
Jb 20,18
not to be swallowed; neol.

ἀκατασκεύαστος,-ος,-ον   A 1-0-0-0-0-1
Gn 1,2
unwrought, unformed
Cf. HARL 1986, 87; SCHMITT 1974, 137-163

ἀκαταστασία,-ας⁺   N1F 0-0-0-1-1-2
Prv 26,28; Tob^BA 4,13
instability, confusion

ἀκαταστατέω⁺   V 0-0-0-0-1-1
Tob^BA 1,15
to be unstable

ἀκατάστατος,-ος,-ον⁺   A 0-0-1-0-0-1
Is 54,11
unstable

ἀκατάσχετος,-ος,-ον   A 0-0-0-1-1-2
Jb 31,11; 3 Mc 6,17
uncontrollable

ἀκατέργαστος,-ος,-ον   A 0-0-0-1-0-1
Ps 138(139),16
not worked up, unformed

ἄκαυστος,-ος,-ον   A 0-0-0-1-0-1
Jb 20,26
unquenchable

ἀκέραιος,-ος,-ον   A 0-0-0-1-0-1
Est 8,12
inviolate, unshattered

ἀκηδία,-ας   N1F 0-0-1-1-2-4
Is 61,3; Ps 118(119),28; Sir 29,5; Bar 3,1
apathy, indifference Sir 29,5; *weariness,
exhaustion* Ps 118,26
Cf. NORTH 1973, 387-392; WALTERS 1973, 40

ἀκηδιάω   V 0-0-0-4-1-5
Ps 60(61),3; 101(102),1; 142(143),4; Dn^LXX 7,15;
Sir 22,13
to be exhausted, to be weary Ps 60(61),3; *to be in
anguish* Ps 142(143),4; neol.
Cf. HARL 1991, 250-251

ἀκηλίδωτος,-ος,-ον   A 0-0-0-0-2-2
Wis 4,9; 7,26
spotless; neol.

ἀκιδωτός,-ή,-όν   A 0-0-0-1-0-1
Prv 25,18
pointed; neol.?

ἀκινάκης,-ου   N1M 0-0-0-0-2-2

Jdt 13,6; 16,9
short, straight sword

ἀκίνητος,-ος,-ον   A 1-0-0-1-1-3
Ex 25,15; Jb 39,26; 3 Mc 6,19
unmoved, motionless Jb 39,26; *immovable, hard
to move* Ex 25,15

ἀκίς,-ίδος   N3F 0-0-0-1-0-1
Jb 16,10(9)
arrow, dart (metaph. of the eyes)

ἀκλεής,-ής,-ές   A 0-0-0-0-1-1
3 Mc 4,12
without fame, inglorious, ignominious

ἀκλεῶς   D 0-0-0-0-1-1
3 Mc 6,34
ingloriously

ἀκληρέω   V 0-0-0-0-1-1
2 Mc 14,8
to be unfortunate

ἄκλητος,-ος,-ον   A 0-0-0-1-0-1
Est 4,11
uncalled, unbidden

ἀκλινής,-ής,-ές⁺   A 0-0-0-0-2-2
4 Mc 6,7; 17,3
bending to neither side without swaying 4 Mc
17,3; *unbending* (metaph.) 4 Mc 6,7
Cf. SPICQ 1978, 60

ἀκμάζω⁺   V 0-0-0-0-1-1
4 Mc 2,3
to be in full bloom, to be ripe
(→ παρ-)

ἀκμαῖος,-α,-ον   A 0-0-0-0-1-1
3 Mc 4,8
in full bloom, at prime, rigorous

ἀκμή,-ῆς   N1F 0-0-0-1-4-5
Est 5,1; 2 Mc 1,7; 4,13; 12,22; 4 Mc 18,8
point 2 Mc 12,22; *fullest* or *highest expression,
prime, flower* Est 5,1b; *culminating point* 2 Mc
1,7; *best* or *most fulfilling* (of time) 4 Mc 18,9

ἄκμων,-ονος   N3M 0-0-0-1-1-2
Jb 41,16; Sir 38,28
anvil

ἀκοή,-ῆς⁺   N1F 11-9-16-6-9-51
Ex 15,26; 19,5; 22,22; 23,1.22
sound Wis 1,9; *report, tiding* Ex 23,1; *ear* 2 Mc
15,39; *obedience* 1 Sm 15,22; ἐὰν ἀκοῇ ἀκούσῃς
if you really listen (semit.) Ex 15,26; *Na 1,12 ἡ
ἀκοή σου -◊ ‏ענה‎ᴵᴵ *your report* for MT ‏ענתך‎ ◊ ‏ענה‎ᴵᴵ *I
have afflicted you*
Cf. HORSLEY 1983, 61

ἀκοίμητος,-ος,-ον   A 0-0-0-0-1-1

Wis 7,10
sleepless, unresting, never leaving
ἀκοινώνητος,-ος,-ον   A 0-0-0-0-1-1
Wis 14,21
incommunicable
Cf. DES PLACES 1975, 154-158
ἀκολασία,-ας   N1F 0-0-0-0-1-1
4 Mc 13,7
intemperance, wantoness, debauchery
ἀκόλαστος,-ος,-ον   A 0-0-0-3-0-3
Prv 19,29; 20,1; 21,11
licentious, intemperate, wanton Prv 19,29; *con-
ducive to licentiousness* (of wine) Prv 20,1
ἀκολουθέω⁺   V 1-2-3-1-6-13
Nm 22,20; 1 Sm 25,42; 1 Kgs 19,20; Is 45,14; Ez
29,16
to follow, to go after or *with* [τινι] Nm 22,20; *to
follow* (metaph.) [abs.] Jdt 12,2; *to obey* [τινι]
Jdt 2,3
→NIDNTT; TWNT
(– ἐξ-, ἐπ-, κατ-, παρ-, συν-, συνεπ-)
ἀκολουθία,-ας   N1F 0-0-0-0-1-1
4 Mc 1,21
sequence
ἀκόλουθος,-ος,-ον   A 0-0-0-0-2-2
1 Ezr 8,14; 2 Mc 4,17
following 2 Mc 4,17; *appropriate to, belonging to*
[τινι] 1 Ezr 8,14
ἀκολούθως   D 0-0-0-0-6-6
1 Ezr 5,48.68; 7,6.9; 8,12
according to [τινι] 1 Ezr 5,18; *accordingly* 2 Mc
6,23
ἀκονάω   V 0-0-0-6-0-6
Ps 44(45),6; 51(52),4; 63(64),4; 119(120),4;
139(140),4
to sharpen [τι] Ps 44(45),6; *to sharpen* [τι]
(metaph. of tongues) Ps 63(64),4
(→ ἐξ-)
ἀκοντίζω   V 0-4-0-0-0-4
1 Sm 20,20.36(bis).37
to hurl, to strike (with a javelin)
(κατ-)
ἀκοντιστής,-οῦ   N1F 0-1-0-0-0-1
1 Sm 31,3
javelin-thrower
ἀκοπιάτως   D 0-0-0-0-1-1
Wis 16,20
untiringly, not getting tired, free from fatigue, or
without labour
Cf. LARCHER 1985, 924-925

ἄκοσμος,-ος,-ον   A 0-0-0-1-0-1
Prv 25,26
disordered; ἄκοσμον [+inf.] *it is unseemly that*
ἀκόσμως   D 0-0-0-0-1-1
2 Mc 9,1
in dishonour
ἀκουσιάζομαι   V 1-0-0-0-0-1
Nm 15,28
to sin inadvertently or *through ignorance*; neol.
ἀκούσιος,-ος,-ον   A 3-0-0-1-0-4
Nm 15,25(bis).26; Eccl 10,5
against the will, involuntary, constrained Nm
15,25; ἀκούσιον *involuntary* or *inadvertent
offense, error* Eccl 10,5
ἀκουσίως   D 12-2-0-1-1-16
Lv 4,2.13.22.27; 5,15
involuntarily
ἀκουστής,-οῦ   N1M 0-0-0-0-1-1
Wis 1,6
hearer, listener
ἀκουστός,-ή,-όν   A 4-2-12-2-3-23
Gn 45,2; Ex 28,35; Dt 4,36; 30,13; Jgsᴬ 13,23
heard, audible Gn 45,2; ποιέω τι ἀκουστόν *to
cause to be heard, to proclaim* Jgsᴬ 13,23
ἀκουτίζω   V 0-1-1-4-1-7
Jgsᴮ 13,23; Jer 30(49),18(2); Ps 50(51),10;
65(66),8; Ct 2,14
to make to hear [τινά τι] (Hebr. hiphil, semit.)
Jgsᴮ 13,23; [τινά τινος] Sir 45,5; neol.
Cf. HELBING 1928, 49
ἀκούω⁺   V 151-264-296-182-176-1069
Gn 3,8.10.17; 4,23; 11,7
to hear [τί τινος] Gn 3,8; *to hear (of)* [τινος]
Gn 3,17; *to hear* [τι] 1 Chr 14,15; *to hearken, to
give ear* [abs.] Gn 37,27; *to listen to, to give ear
to* [τινος] Gn 27,8; [εἴς τι] (semit.) Jer 36(29),8;
to obey [abs.] Ex 19,8; *to comply with* [ἐπί τινι]
2 Kgs 17,40; *to hear, to understand* [τι] 1 Sm
2,24; *to hear, to answer (a prayer)* [τινος] 2 Chr
6,21; [τι] Nm 30,4; *to hear that* [ὅτι +ind.] Gn
42,2; *to hear* [+indir. question] Jgs 7,11; ἀκήκοα
λεγόντων *I heard men saying* Gn 41,15
Cf. HELBING 1928, 150-153; →NIDNTT; TWNT
(– ἀντ-, δι-, εἰσ-, ἐν-, ἐπ-, παρ-, ὑπ-)
ἄκρα,-ας   N1F 0-3-0-0-24-27
Dt 3,11; 2 Sm 5,9; 1 Kgs 10,22a(9,15); 11,27;
12,24b
hill-top, height 4 Mc 7,5; *citadel, tower* Dt 3,11;
end, extremity Sir 13,19; *top* 4 Mc 14,16
ἀκρασία,-ας⁺   N1F 0-0-0-0-1-1

PSal 4,3

incontinence, want of self-control

ἀκρατής,-ής,-ές⁺ A 0-0-0-1-0-1
Prv 27,20a
intemperate

ἄκρατος,-ος,-ον⁺ A 0-0-1-1-2-4
Jer 32(25),15; Ps 74(75),9; 3 Mc 5,2; PSal 8,14
unmixed, very strong (of wine)

ἀκριβάζομαι V 0-0-0-0-1-1
Sir 46,15
to be proved accurate, reliable; neol.

Cf. CAIRD 1972, 113; WALTERS 1973, 206
(· δι-, ἐξ-)

ἀκριβασμός,-οῦ N2M 0-1-0-0-0-1
Jgs^A 5,15
careful investigation of sth, commandment;
ἀκριβασμοὶ καρδίας *searchings of the heart*
Jgs^A 5,15, see also 1 Kgs 11,34 vl.; neol.

Cf. CAIRD 1972, 113; WALTERS 173.205-206

ἀκρίβεια,-ας⁺ N1F 0-0-0-3-3-6
Dn^LXX 7,16; Dn^Th 7,16(bis); Wis 12,21; Sir 16,25
exactness, precision Wis 12,21; *precise meaning*
Dn 7,16

Cf. WALTERS 1973, 44.205-209

ἀκριβής,-ής,-ές⁺ A 0-0-0-4-4-8
Est 4,5; Dn^LXX 2,45; 4,27(24); 6,13; Sir 18,29
exact, precise, accurate Sir 31(34),24; τὸ ἀκριβές
the precise meaning Est 4,5

Cf. WALTERS 1973, 44.205-210

ἀκριβόω
(– · δι-)

ἀκριβῶς D 1-0-0-1-1-3
Dt 19,18; Dn^Th 7,19; Wis 19,18
accurately, precisely, diligently Dt 19,18; *carefully*
Dn^Th 7,19

Cf. WALTERS 1973, 208

ἀκρίς,-ίδος⁺ N3F 9-6-12-5-3-35
Ex 10,4.12.13.14.19
locust Ex 10,19; *a swarm of locusts* (coll. sg.) Ex
10,4; *Hos 13,3 ἀπὸ ἀκρίδων -מֵאֲרֻבָּה *of the
locusts* for MT מֵאֲרֻבָּה *out of the window*

Cf. WEVERS 1990, 146

ἀκρίτως D 0-0-0-0-2-2
1 Mc 2,37; 15,33
without trial, unjustly 1 Mc 2,37; *illegitimately*
1 Mc 15,33

ἀκρόαμα,-ατος N3N 0-0-0-0-1-1
Sir 32,4
a piece recited or *sung*

ἀκροάομαι V 0-0-1-0-4-5

Is 21,7; Wis 1,10; Sir 6,35; 14,23; 21,24
to listen to [τι] Wis 1,10; *to listen* [abs.] Sir 14,23

ἀκρόασις,-εως N3F 0-2-1-1-1-5
1 Kgs 18,26; 2 Kgs 4,31; Is 21,7; Eccl 1,8; Sir
5,11
hearing, listening 1 Kgs 18,26; *obedience* 1 Sm
15,22; ἀκροάομαι ἀκρόασιν πολλὴν *to listen
attentively* (semit.) Is 21,7

ἀκροατής,-οῦ⁺ N1M 0-0-1-0-1-2
Is 3,3; Sir 3,29
hearer Is 3,3; *disciple, pupil* Sir 3,29

ἀκροβυστία,-ας⁺ N1F 9-4-1-0-2-16
Gn 17,11.14.23.24.25
=ἄκρο +בֹּשֶׁת deformation of ἀκροποσθία *foreskin* Gn 17,11; ἐποίησαν ἑαυτοῖς ἀκρο-
βυστίας *they made themselves uncircumcised,
they had their foreskin remade* 1 Mc 1,15; neol.

Cf. HARL 1986, 170; TOSATO 1982, 43-49; WALTERS 1973,
165; →TWNT

ἀκρογωνιαῖος,-α,-ον⁺ A 0-0-1-0-0-1
Is 28,16
at the extreme angle; λίθος ἀκρογωνιαῖος
corner-stone, foundation-stone; neol.

ἀκρόδρυα,-ων N2N 0-0-0-3-2-5
Ct 4,13.16; 7,14; Tob^S 1,7; 1 Mc 11,34
fruit (esp. with hard, wooden shell) Tob^S 1,7;
fruit-trees 1 Mc 11,34

Cf. HARL 1991, 243-244

ἀκρόπολις,-εως N3F 0-0-0-0-3-3
2 Mc 4,12.28; 5,5
citadel, castle

ἄκρος,-α,-ον⁺ A 37-24-21-9-16-107
Gn 47,21(bis).31; Ex 29,20(bis)
utmost Is 13,5; τὸ ἄκρον *top* Gn 28,18; *end,
extremity* Gn 47,21; *skirt* (*of a garment*) Hag
2,13; ἄκρα *heights* Prv 8,26; ἐπὶ τὸ ἄκρον τῆς
δεξιᾶς χειρός *on the thumb of his right hand* Ex
29,20

Cf. WEVERS 1990, 474.605

ἀκρότομος,-ος,-ον A 1-3-0-4-3-11
Dt 8,15; Jos 5,2.3; 1 Kgs 6,7; Ps 113(114),8
cut off, rough quarried (of building stone) 1 Kgs
6,7; *sharp* Jos 5,2; *steep* Jb 40,20; *hard, sharp
edged* (of stones) Dt 8,15; *flinty ground* Ps
113(114),8; neol.?

Cf. LARCHER 1985, 656 (Dt 8,15; Wis 11,4)

ἀκροφύλαξ,-ακος N3M 0-0-0-0-1-1
4 Mc 3,13
governor of the citadel, guardian; neol.?

ἀκρωτηριάζω V 0-0-0-0-2-2

2 Mc 7,4; 4 Mc 10,20
to cut off hands and feet, to mutilate

ἀκρωτήριον,-ου   N2N 1-2-1-1-0-5
Lv 4,11; 1 Sm 14,4(bis); Ez 25,9; Jb 37,9
mountain peak Jb 37,9; ἀκρωτήρια *the
extremities of the body, members* Lv 4,11; ἀπὸ
πόλεων ἀκρωτηρίων *from the frontier cities* Ez
25,9; ἀκρωτήριον πέτρας *hill* 1 Sm 14,4

ἀκτίς,-ῖνος   N3F 0-0-0-0-3-3
Wis 2,4; 16,27; Sir 43,4
beam, ray (of sun)

ἀκύματος,-ος,-ον   A 0-0-0-1-0-1
Est 3,13
waveless, calm (metaph.)

ἄκυρος,-ος,-ον   A 0-0-0-2-0-2
Prv 1,25; 5,7
invalid

ἀκυρόω⁺   V 0-0-0-0-7-7
1 Ezr 6,31; 4 Mc 2,1.3.18; 5,18
to set at naught, to treat as of no effect Ezr 6,31;
to destroy 4 Mc 17,2; *to render powerless* 4 Mc
2,1

ἀκώλυτος,-ος,-ον   A 0-0-0-0-1-1
Wis 7,23
unhindered, independent; neol.?
Cf. LARCHER 1984, 478

ἄκων,-ουσα,-ον⁺   A 0-0-0-1-1-2
Jb 14,17; 4 Mc 11,12
involuntary, constrained

ἀλάβαστρος,-ου⁺   N2M 0-1-0-0-0-1
2 Kgs 21,13
round vase without handles, (for holding
perfumes; often made of alabaster), *jar*

ἀλαζονεία,-ας⁺   N1F 0-0-0-0-7-7
2 Mc 9,8; 15,6; 4 Mc 1,26; 2,15; 8,19
boastfulness
Cf. LARCHER 1984, 369-370; SPICQ 1978, 64-65

ἀλαζονεύομαι   V 0-0-0-1-1-2
Prv 25,6; Wis 2,16
to brag, to be boastful Prv 25,6; [τινά τινα] Wis
2,16

ἀλαζών,-όνος⁺   N3M 0-0-1-2-0-3
Hab 2,5; Jb 28,8; Prv 21,24
boaster Jb 28,8; *boastful, pretentious, insolent* (as
adj.) Prv 21,24
Cf. SPICQ 1978, 64-65

αλαιμωθ   N 0-1-0-0-0-1
1 Chr 15,20
=עלמות *unidentified musical instruments*

ἀλαλαγμός,-οῦ   N2M 0-1-2-5-1-9

Jos 6,20; Jer 20,16; 32(25),36; Ps 26(27),6;
32(33),3
shout, cry Jos 6,20; *loud voice, loud sound* Ps
150,5; *bleating* (of sheep, goats) Jer 32(25),36

ἀλαλάζω⁺   V 0-4-5-8-2-19
Jos 6,20; Jgs 15,14; 1 Sm 17,52; Jer 4,8
to raise the war-cry 1 Sm 17,52; *to cry, to shout
aloud* Jos 6,20; *to cry with pain* Jer 4,8

ἄλαλος,-ος,-ον⁺   A 0-0-0-2-0-2
Ps 30(31),19; 37(38),14
speechless Ps 30(31),19; *dumb* Ps 37(38),13
Cf. HORSLEY 1987, 149

ἀλάστωρ,-ορος   N3M 0-0-0-0-4-4
2 Mc 7,9; 4 Mc 9,24; 11,23; 18,22
he who does deeds which merit vengeance
4 Mc 9,24; *avenger, avenging angel, demon* 4 Mc
11,23;

ἀλγέω   V 0-1-1-4-1-7
2 Sm 1,26; Jer 4,19; Ps 68(69),30; Jb 5,18; 14,22
to feel bodily pain, to suffer [τι] Jb 16,7; *to suffer
hardship* [abs.] Ps 68(69),30; *to feel pain of
mind, to feel grief* [ἐπί τινι] 2 Sm 1,26; *to be
pained at* [τινι] 4 Mc 14,17
Cf. HELBING 1928, 260
(→ συν-)

ἀλγηδών,-όνος   N3F 0-0-0-1-15-16
Ps 37(38),18; 2 Mc 6,30; 7,12; 9,5.9
pain, suffering 2 Mc 6,30; *grief* Ps 37(38),18

ἄλγημα,-ατος   N3N 0-0-0-3-0-3
Ps 38(39),3; Eccl 1,18; 2,23
pain, grief

ἀλγηρός,-ά,-όν   A 0-0-3-0-0-3
Jer 10,19; 37(30),12.13
painful; neol.

ἄλγος,-ους   N3N 0-0-0-4-2-6
Ps 68(69),27; Lam 1,12(bis).18; 2 Mc 3,17
pain (of body) Ps 68(69),27; *grief* Sir 26,6

ἀλεεύς,-έως   N3M 0-0-3-0-0-3
Is 19,8; Jer 16,16; Ez 47,10
see ἁλιεύς

ἄλειμμα,-ατος   N3N 1-0-1-1-0-3
Ex 30,31; Is 61,3; Dnᵀʰ 10,3
anything used for anointing, unguent
Cf. LE BOULLUEC 1989, 311

ἀλείφω⁺   V 4-4-8-4-1-21
Gn 31,13; Ex 40,15(bis); Nm 3,3; 2 Sm 12,20
to anoint [τι] Gn 31,13; [τινα] Ex 40,15;
ἀλείφομαι ἔλαιον *to anoint oneself with oil*
2 Sm 14,2
→NIDNTT; TWNT

(— ἀπ-, ἐξ-)

ἀλεκτρυών,-όνος N3M 0-0-0-0-1-1
· 3 Mc 5,23
cock

ἀλέκτωρ,-ορος⁺ N3M 0-0-0-1-0-1
Prv 30,31
cock

ἄλευρον,-ου⁺ N2N 1-11-2-0-0-14
Nm 5,15; Jgs 6,19; 1 Sm 28,24; 2 Sm 17,28
meal (of grain) (often pl.)

ἀλέω V 0-1-1-0-0-2
Jgsᴮ 16,21; Is 47,2
to grind
(— κατ-)

ἀλήθεια,-ας⁺ N1F 8-19-24-94-61-206
Gn 24,27.48; 32,11; 47,29; Ex 28,30
truth Gn 24,27; truthfulness Prv 28,6; symbol of
truth (of the Thummim) Lv 8,8; fidelity,
faithfulness Gn 47,29; ποιέω μετά τινος
ἀλήθειαν to deal truthfully with sb 2 Sm 15,20
Cf. BARR 1961, 187-200; CAIRD 1972, 124 (Lv 8,8; Dt
33,8); HARL 1986, 301 (Gn 47,29); LARCHER 1983, 290;
1984, 365; SPICQ 1982, 17-19; —NIDNTT; TWNT

ἀληθεύω V 2-0-1-1-1-5
Gn 20,16; 42,16; Is 44,26; Prv 21,3; Sir 34,4
to speak the truth [abs.] Gn 42,16; to prove true,
to verify [τι] Is 44,26; ἀληθεύω πάντα to speak
the truth in all things Gn 20,16
Cf. SPICQ 1982, 31-32

ἀληθής,-ής,-ές A 2-0-2-9-9-22
Gn 41,32; Dt 13,15; Is 41,26; 43,9; Jb 5,12
true Gn 41,32; truthful, honest (of pers.) Neh
7,2; genuine Wis 6,17; τἀληθές truly 3 Mc 7,12
Cf. SPICQ 1982, 33-34

ἀληθινός,-ή,-όν⁺ A 5-5-9-22-9-50
Ex 34,6; Nm 14,18; Dt 25,15(bis); 32,4
truthful, trusty (of pers.) Ex 34,6; true Dt 25,15;
true, genuine Is 38,3
Cf. SPICQ 1982, 34-35

ἀληθινῶς D 2-0-0-0-5-7
Nm 24,3.15; Tob 14,6; Tobˢ 3,5
truly, really

ἀλήθω V 1-1-0-2-0-4
Nm 11,8; Jgsᴬ 16,21; Eccl 12,3.4
to grind

ἀληθῶς⁺ D 4-5-2-4-5-20
Gn 18,13; 20,12; Ex 33,16; Dt 17,4; Jos 7,20
truly, really, indeed Gn 18,13; actually 2 Mc 3,38;
ὡς ἀληθῶς in a true way, really 4 Mc 6,5; *Jer
28(51),13 ἀληθῶς -אֱמֶת verily for MT אַמָּה extent,

measure
Cf. SPICQ 1982, 36

ἄληκτος,-ος,-ον A 0-0-0-0-1-1
3 Mc 4,2
unceasing

ἁλιαίετος,-ου N2M 2-0-0-0-0-2
Lv 11,13; Dt 14,12
sea-eagle
Cf. WALTERS 1973, 80-81

ἁλιεύς,-έως⁺ N3M 0-0-0-1-0-1
Jb 40,31
fisher, fisherman Ez 47,10; *Jb 40,31(26) ἁλιέων
-רִיגִים fishermen for MT דגים fishes
Cf. HORSLEY 1983, 18-19; MILLIGAN 1980, 34

ἁλιεύω⁺ V 0-0-1-0-0-1
Jer 16,16
to catch fish (metaph. of avenger)

ἁλίζω⁺ V 1-0-1-0-1-3
Lv 2,13; Ez 16,4; Tobˢ 6,5
to salt

ἅλιμα,-ων N2N 0-0-1-2-0-3
Jer 17,6; Jb 30,4(bis)
sea-side, salt places Jer 17,6; salty plants, sea
oraches Jb 30,4; neol.?

ἀλισγέω V 0-0-3-3-1-7
Mal 1,7(bis).12; Dn 1,8
to pollute
Cf. WALTERS 1973, 149.319

ἁλίσκομαι V 2-0-24-5-5-36
Ex 22,8; Dt 24,7; Is 8,15; 13,15; 14,10
to be taken, to be conquered, to fall into an
enemy's hand Zech 14,2; to be convicted Ex
22,8(9); to be taken (metaph.) Sir 9,4; to be
caught or detected doing a thing [+ptc.] Dt 24,7
Cf. LEE 1983, 35

ἀλιτήριος,-ου A 0-0-0-0-4-4
2 Mc 12,23; 13,4; 14,42; 3 Mc 3,16
wretch, horrid wicked person, sinner

ἀλκή,-ῆς N1F 0-0-0-1-3-4
Dnᴸˣˣ 11,4; 2 Mc 12,28; 3 Mc 3,18; 6,12
strength (of pers.) 2 Mc 12,28; force, might Dnᴸˣˣ
11,4

ἀλλά⁺ C 86-109-97-101-194-587
Gn 15,4; 17,5.15; 18,15; 19,2
but 2 Chr 1,4; but, surely, certainly Jb 32,8; but,
except Nm 10,30; but, yet 1 Sm 15,30; come on
(with imper.) 1 Mc 10,56; ἀλλ' ἤ but, except Is
42,19(bis); ὅτι ἀλλ' ἤ nevertheless, only 2 Chr
19,3; but (only) 2 Chr 28,22(21); but, except Est
5,12; οὐχί, ὅτι ἀλλά no, but, not only, but 2 Sm

24,24

ἀλλαγή,-ῆς   N1F 0-0-0-0-1-1
Wis 7,18
change

ἄλλαγμα,-ατος   N2N 3-2-2-3-2-12
Lv 27,10.33; Dt 23,19(18); 2 Sm 24,24; 1 Kgs
10,28
that which is changed Lv 27,10; *that which is
given in exchange, ransom* Is 43,3; *reward, price*
Dt 23,19(18); λαμβάνω τι ἐν ἀλλάγματι *to
receive at a price* 1 Kgs 10,28
Cf. CAIRD 1972, 114

ἀλλάσσω⁺   V 12-8-7-9-6-42
Gn 31,7; 35,2; 41,14; Ex 13,13(bis)
A: *to make other than it is, to change, to alter*
[τι] Gn 35,2; *to give in exchange for, to change
for* [τί τινος] Gn 31,7; *to exchange with* [τί τινι]
Lv 27,10; [τι ἔν τινι] (semit.) Ps 105(106),20; *to
gain, to take in return* [τι] Is 40,31; M: *to take in
exchange* [τι ἀντί τινος] 3 Mc 1,29;
ἀλλασσόμενοι *in turns* 1 Kgs 5,28(14)
Cf. HELBING 1928, 246-247; HORSLEY 1982, 63
(→ἀντ-, ἀντικατ-, ἀπ-, δι-, ἐξ-, κατ-, μετ-, παρ-)

ἀλλαχῇ   D 0-0-0-0-2-2
2 Mc 12,22; Wis 18,18
elsewhere, in another place; ἄλλος ἀλλαχῇ *one
here, another there*

ἀλλαχόθεν⁺   D 0-0-0-0-1-1
4 Mc 1,7
from another place

αλληλουια⁺   I 0-0-0-20-3-23
Ps 104(105),1; 105(106),1; 106,1(48); 110(111),1;
111(112),1
הללו יה= *hallelu-jah, praise the Lord* Ps
104(105),1; τὸ αλληλουια *the (hymn called)
Hallelujah* 3 Mc 7,13
→NIDNTT

ἀλλήλους,-ας,-α⁺   A 10-2-4-7-26-49
Gn 15,10; 42,28; Ex 4,27; 14,20; 18,7
of one another, to one another, one another
(only gen., acc., dat.) Ex 18,7; ἀπ' ἀλλήλων *the
one from the other* Sus^{LXX} 13; εἰς ἀλλήλους *one
to another* Ex 25,20(19); πρός ἀλλήλους Gn
42,28; ἐξ ἀλλήλων *one to the other* Ex 26,3; ἐπ'
ἀλλήλων *one upon another* Wis 18,23
Cf. WALTERS 1973, 216.338

ἀλλογενής,-ής,-ές⁺   A 14-0-13-3-17-47
Gn 17,27; Ex 12,43; 29,33; 30,33; Lv 22,10
of another race, foreign Gn 17,27; ἄλλογενής
stranger Ex 30,33; *layman* Ex 29,33; *Mal 3,19

ἀλλογενεῖς -זרים *strangers* for MT זרים *the
proud, arrogant,* cpr. Mal 3,15
Cf. BICKERMAN 1980, 215; LE BOULLUEC 1989, 312

ἀλλόγλωσσος,-ος,-ον   A 0-0-1-0-1-2
Ez 3,6; Bar 4,15
speaking a foreign language

ἀλλοεθνής,-ής,-ές   A 0-0-0-0-1-1
3 Mc 4,6
of a foreign nation, outlandish
Cf. BICKERMAN 1980, 91.215

ἄλλοθεν   D 0-0-0-1-0-1
Est 4,14
from another place

ἀλλοιόω   V 0-2-1-35-12-50
1 Sm 21,14; 2 Kgs 25,29; Mal 3,6; Ps 33(34),1;
44(45),1
A: *to change, to alter* [τι] 1 Sm 21,14; M: *to
change* Sir 27,11; P: *to be changed, to be altered*
Jdt 10,7; *to be changed, to be scorched* Dn
3,94(27); *to be changed for the worse* Lam 4,1;
*Ps 44(45),1 τῶν ἀλλοιωθησομέ νων -שׁנים/שׁשׁנים
those who will be changed, made different for MT
שׁשׁנים/ שׁושׁן *lilies,* see also 59(60),1; 68(69),1;
79(80),1; *Ps 72(73),21 ἠλλοιώθησαν -השׁתנו
שׁנה/ *were changed* for MT שׁנן /אשׁתונן *to be
pierced?*
(→ ἐξ-)

ἀλλοίωσις,-εως   N3F 0-0-0-1-2-3
Ps 76(77),11; Sir 37,17; 43,8
alteration, change, changing Sir 37,17; *Ps
76(77),11 ἀλλοίωσις - שׁנה *change* for MT שׁנות
years

ἄλλομαι⁺   V 0-5-1-2-2-10
Jgs^B 14,6.19; 15,14; 1 Sm 10,2.10
to spring, to leap upon Jgs^B 14,6; *to jump about*
Jb 41,17(16); *1 Sm 10,2 ἀλλομένους -צלח
exulting, jumping about, in ecstatic behaviour for
MT צלצח *Zelzah*
Cf. LIEBERMAN 1946, 67-72
(→ ἀφ-, δι-, ἐν-, ἐξ-, ἐφ-, ὑπερ-)

ἄλλος,-η,-ον⁺   A 12-19-10-22-45-108
Gn 19,12; 41,3.6.23; Ex 4,13
(an)other Gn 41,3; ἄλλος τις *any other* Gn
19,12; ἄλλος *another* (without subst.) Ex 4,13;
ἄλλος ἀλλαχῇ *one here, another there* Wis
18,18; *2 Sm 7,23 ἄλλο -אחר *other* for MT אחר
one, see also 1 Sm 14,4; 1 Kgs 18,6.23; Ez 19,5;
Mal 2,15
Cf. SHIPP 1979, 58.61; WALTERS 1973, 215

ἄλλοτε   D 0-0-0-0-1-1

2 Mc 13,10
at another time; εἴ ποτε καὶ ἄλλοτε, καὶ νῦν
if ever, then now
ἀλλοτριόομαι　　　　　　　　　　　V 1-0-0-0-4-5
Gn 42,7; 1 Ezr 9,4; 1 Mc 6,24; 11,53; 15,27
M: *to estrange oneself from* [ἀπό τινος] Gn 42,7;
[τινι] 1 Mc 11,53; P: *to become estranged, to be
made enemy* [ἀπό τινος] 1 Ezr 9,4
Cf. HARL 1986, 279 (Gn 42,7); HELBING 1928, 159-160
(　ἀπ-, ἐξ-)
ἀλλότριος,-α,-ον⁺　　　　　Λ 22-22-39-45-36-164
Gn 17,12; 31,15; 35,2; 35,4; Ex 2,22
of or *belonging to another* Gn 17,12; *foreign,
strange* Gn 31,15; *hostile, unfavourable disposed*
[τινος] 2 Mc 14,26; ἀλλότριος οἶκος *a house of
harlotry* Prv 23,27; τὰ ἀλλότρια *what belongs to
others, not one's own* Prv 27,13; ἀλλότριος
stranger Ez 31,12; *Jb 19,17 ἀλλοτρίους זרים
strangers for MT זרו *they turn away*; *Ps
18(19),14 ἀλλοτρίων זרים- *strangers* for MT זרים
arrogant (sins), see also Mal 3,15, cpr. Mal 3,19
Cf. WALTERS 1973, 215.345
ἀλλοτριότης,-τητος　　　　　　N3F 0-0-0-0-1-1
PSal 17,13
fact of being alien
ἀλλοτρίως　　　　　　　　　　　D 0-0-1-0-0-1
Is 28,21
strangely, hostilely
ἀλλοτρίωσις,-εως　　　　　　　N3F 0-0-1-1-0-2
Jer 17,17; Neh 13,30
estrangement Neh 13,30; μὴ γενηθῇς μοι εἰς
ἀλλοτρίωσιν *do not be a hostile stranger to me*
Jer 17,17
ἀλλοφυλέω　　　　　　　　　　　V 0-0-0-0-1-1
4 Mc 18,5
to adopt foreign customs or *religions*; neol.
ἀλλοφυλισμός,-οῦ　　　　　　　N2M 0-0-0-0-2-2
2 Mc 4,13; 6,24
adoption of foreign customs or *religions*; neol.
ἀλλόφυλος,-ος,-ον⁺　　　　Λ 1-275-20-5-16-317
Ex 34,15; JgsᴬΑ 3,3.31; 10,6.7
of another tribe, foreign Is 61,5; (οἱ) ἀλλόφυλοι
Philistines (mostly) Jgs 3,3; ἀλλόφυλοι *Syrians*
2 Kgs 8,28
Cf. BICKERMAN 1980, 90-91
ἀλλόφωνος,-ος,-ον　　　　　　Α 0-0-1-0-0-1
Ez 3,6
speaking a foreign language; neol.
ἄλλως⁺　　　　　　　　　　　　D 0-0-0-4-6-10
Jb 11,12; 40,8; Est 1,19; 9,27; 3 Mc 1,20

otherwise, in another way Jb 40,8; *especially,
above all* 4 Mc 1,2; *differently* Est 1,19; *in vain*
Jb 11,12; *otherwise than right, wrongly* 4 Mc 5,18;
ἄλλως καὶ ἄλλως *(some) here, (some) there*
3 Mc 1,20
ἄλμα,-ατος　　　　　　　　　　N3N 0-0-0-1-0-1
Jb 39,25
spring, leap
ἄλμη,-ης　　　　　　　　　　　N1F 0-0-0-1-1-2
Ps 106(107),34; Sir 39,23
saltness Ps 106(107),34; *salt marsh* Sir 39,23
ἁλμυρίς,-ίδος　　　　　　　　　N3F 0-0-0-1-0-1
Jb 39,6
salt land
ἁλμυρός,-ά,-όν　　　　　　　　Α 0-0-1-0-0-1
Jer 17,6
salt
ἀλοάω⁺　　　　　　　　　　　　V 1-3-5-0-0-9
Dt 25,4; Jgsᴮ 8,7.16; 1 Chr 21,20; Is 41,15
to tread Dt 25,4; *to thresh* 1 Chr 21,20; *to thresh,
to tear* Jgsᴮ 8,7; *Jgsᴮ 8,16 καὶ ἠλόησεν -שׁ וידשׁ
and he tread for MT וידע *and he taught*?
Cf. CAIRD 1972, 114-115; WALTERS 1973, 129
(　συν-)
ἀλογέομαι　　　　　　　　　　　V 0-0-0-0-1-1
2 Mc 12,24
to be disregarded
ἀλογιστία,-ας　　　　　　　　　N1F 0-0-0-0-2-2
2 Mc 14,8; 3 Mc 5,42
thoughtlessness, recklessness
ἀλόγιστος,-ος,-ον　　　　　　　Α 0-0-0-0-5-5
3 Mc 6,12; 4 Mc 3,11; 6,18; 16,23; Wis 12,25
thoughtless Wis 12,25; *unreasonable, irrational*
3 Mc 6,12
ἀλογίστως　　　　　　　　　　　D 0-0-0-0-1-1
4 Mc 6,14
unreasonably
ἄλογος,-ος,-ον⁺　　　　　　　　Α 2-0-0-0-6-8
Ex 6,12; Nm 6,12; 3 Mc 5,40; 4 Mc 14,14.18
lacking in eloquence Ex 6,12; *unreasoning,
unreasonable* Wis 11,15; *not counted, null and
void* Nm 6,12
Cf. LE BOULLUEC 1989, 113; LEE 1983, 50 (Nm 6,12)
ἀλόγως　　　　　　　　　　　　D 0-0-0-0-1-1
3 Mc 6,25
unreasonably
ἀλοητός,-οῦ　　　　　　　　　　N2M 1-0-1-0-0-2
Lv 26,5; Am 9,13
threshing (-season); neol.?
Cf. WALTERS 1973, 226

ἀλοιφή,-ῆς N1F 1-0-2-1-0-4
Ex 17,14; Ez 13,12; Mi 7,11; Jb 33,24
*anything with which one can smear, anoint,
plaster, paint* Jb 33,24; *wiping out, erasure* Ex
17,14; *plastering* or *painting* Mi 7,11

ἅλς, ἁλός⁺ N3M 8-11-3-4-8-34
Gn 14,3; 19,26; Lv 2,13(ter)
salt (also pl.)
Cf. HARL 1986, 157 (Gn 14,3); WALTERS 1973, 137

ἄλσος,-ους N3N 4-39-4-0-1-48
Ex 34,13; Dt 7,5; 12,3; 16,21; Jgs^ 3,7
grove, sacred grove Ex 34,13; *1 Sm 7,3 τὰ ἄλση
-הָאֲשֵׁרוֹת *the sacred groves* for MT הָעַשְׁתָּרוֹת *the
Ashtaroth,* see also 1 Sm 7,4; 12,10; *2 Sm 5,24
τοῦ ἄλσους -אֲשֵׁרֵי *the grove* for MT רֹאשׁ *the tops*
Cf. WEVERS 1990, 561

ἀλσώδης,-ης,-ες A 0-3-4-0-0-7
2 Kgs 16,4; 17,10; 2 Chr 28,4; Jer 3,6.13
of wood Ez 27,6; *growing in woods* 2 Kgs 16,4;
shady Jer 17,8

ἁλυκός,-ή,-όν⁺ A 6-2-0-0-0-8
Gn 14,3.8.10; Nm 34,3.12
salt Gn 14,3; ἡ θάλασσα ἡ ἁλυκή *the Salt Sea*
Nm 34,3

ἁλυσιδωτός,-ή,-όν A 2-1-0-0-1-4
Ex 28,22.29; 1 Sm 17,5; 1 Mc 6,35
wrought in chain-fashion, of chainmail 1 Sm
17,5; ἔργον ἁλυσιδωτόν *chainwork* Ex 28,22
Cf. LE BOULLUEC 1989, 287.288 (Ex 28,22.29); WEVERS
1990, 455.457 (Ex 28,22.29)

ἅλυσις,-εως⁺ N3F 0-0-0-0-1-1
Wis 17,16
chain

ἄλφιτον,-ου N2N 0-2-0-1-1-4
1 Sm 25,18; 2 Sm 17,28; Ru 2,14; Jdt 10,5
groats, grain

ἀλφός,-οῦ N2M 1-0-0-0-0-1
Lv 13,39
eczema, skin disease
Cf. HARLÉ 1988, 45.139

αλωθ N 0-0-0-1-0-1
Ct 4,14
=אֲהָלוֹת *aloes*

ἅλων,-ωνος⁺ N3F/M 5-11-8-6-0-30
Gn 50,10.11; Ex 22,5.28; Dt 16,13
threshing-floor Gn 50,10; *1 Kgs 20(21),1 ἅλῳ
threshing floor corr. ναῷ for MT הֵיכַל *temple,
palace;* *Zph 2,9 ἅλωνος *on the threshing floor*
corr. ἁλός for MT מֶלַח *sal;* *1 Sm 19,22 τοῦ
ἅλου -גֹּרֶן *of the threshing floor* for MT גָּדוֹל *great*

Cf. SHIPP 1979, 62; WALTERS 1973, 129.137.290

ἀλώπηξ,-εκος⁺ N3F 0-5-1-4-0-10
Jgs 1,35; 15,4; 1 Kgs 21(20),10
fox Jgs 15,4; *Jgs 1,35 ἀλώπεκες -שַׁעַלְבִים *foxes* for
MT שַׁעַלְבִים *Shaalbim;* *1 Kgs 21(20),10 ταῖς
ἀλώπεξιν -לִשְׁעָלִים *for foxes* for MT לִשְׁעָלִים *for
handfuls*

ἅλως N 3-7-0-2-0-12
Nm 15,20; 18,27.30; 2 Sm 6,6; 1 Kgs 20(21),1
see ἅλων

ἅλωσις,-εως⁺ N3F 0-0-1-0-0-1
Jer 27(50),46
capture

ἅμα⁺ D 14-13-50-18-29-124
Gn 13,6(bis); 14,5; 19,4; 22,6
at once Gn 19,4; *at the same time* Sir 45,15;
together, both Gn 13,6; ἅμα πάντες *all together*
Jos 9,2; [τινι]: *at the same time with* 1 Mc 4,6;
together with Gn 14,5; ἕως ἅμα τῷ ἡλίῳ *till
sunrise* Neh 7,3; *Dt 32,43 ἅμα αὐτῷ -עַמּוֹ *with
him* for MT עַמּוֹ *his people*

αμαδαρωθ N 0-1-0-0-0-1
Jgs^ 5,22
=מֵרֻהֲרוֹת *from galloping*

ἀμαθία,-ας N1F 0-0-0-0-1-1
PSal 18,4
ignorance, stupidity

ἅμαξα,-ης N1F 9-12-4-0-2-27
Gn 45,19.21.27; 46,5; Nm 7,3
waggon Gn 45,19; *Is 25,10 ἐν ἁμάξαις
-בְּמֶרְכָּבָה *with chariots* for MT בְּמֵי מַדְמֵנָה *in the
water of Madmenah, in the dung-pit*?

ἀμάραντος,-ος,-ον⁺ A 0-0-0-0-1-1
Wis 6,12
unfading (metaph.)

ἁμαρία sic. ἁμαρτία
Dt 23,22

ἁμαρτάνω⁺ V 59-55-31-61-64-270
Gn 4,7; 20,6.9; 39,9; 40,1
to do wrong, to err, to sin [abs.] Gn 4,7; [τινι]
Jgs 10,10; [εἴς τινα] Gn 20,6; [πρός τινα] Ex
23,33; *to do wrong in sth* [περί τινος] Lv 5,5; *to
offend with* [ἔν τινι] Sir 19,16; *to fail* [abs.] Jb
5,24; ἁμαρτάνω ἁμαρτίαν μεγάλην *to sin
greatly* (semit.) Ex 32,30; ἀδικίας ἁμαρτάνω *to
commit sins* Hos 12,9(8); ἡμαρτηκὼς ἔσομαι *to
be guilty* Gn 43,9; ἁμαρτάνω ἀκουσίως *to sin
through ignorance* Lv 5,15; ποιέω ἁμαρτάνειν *to
cause to sin* Ex 23,33; ὁ ἁμαρτάνων *the sinner*
Sir 2,26

Cf. DANIEL 1966, 308-310; HARL 1986, 62-63; HARLÉ
1988, 33; HELBING 1928, 215-217; →TWNT
(→ δι-, ἐξ-, ἐφ-)

ἁμάρτημα,-ατος⁺   N3N 8-4-6-1-17-36
Gn 31,36; Ex 28,38; Lv 4,29; Nm 1,53; 18,23
sin Gn 31,36; *offence* 1 Mc 13,39; *sin-offering* Lv
4,29; ἁμάρτημα θανάτου *sin worthy of death* Dt
22,26
Cf. DANIEL 1966, 304.308-313; →TWNT

ἁμαρτία,-ας⁺   N1F 186-54-94-92-119-545
Gn 15,16; 18,20; 20,9; 41,9; 42,21
guilt, sin Gn 15,16; *sin-offering* Lv 4,33
Cf. COX 1990, 119-130; DANIEL 1966, 301-328; HARL
1986, 62.63; HARLÉ 1988, 33; LE BOULLUEC 1989, 294.297;
-TWNT

ἁμαρτωλός,-ός,-όν⁺   A 4-2-10-75-87-178
Gn 13,13; Nm 17,3; 32,14; Dt 29,18; 1 Kgs 1,21
sinning, sinful Gn 13,13; ὁ ἁμαρτωλός *sinner*
Nm 17,3; *Dt 29,18 ὁ ἁμαρτωλός -הרע the
sinner for MT הרוה ?; *Ps 140(141),5 ἁμαρτωλοῦ
-רשע *of a sinner* for MT -ראש *of first quality*
--TWNT

αμασενιθ   N 0-1-0-0-0-1
1 Chr 15,21
=השמינית (metath.) *the sheminith, the eighth,
octave?* (musical term?)

ἁμάσητος,-ος,-ον   A 0-0-0-1-0-1
Jb 20,18
unchewed; neol.

αματταρι   N 0-1-0-0-0-1
1 Sm 20,20
=מטרה *mark, target*

ἀμαυρός,-ά,-όν   A 6-0-0-0-1-7
Lv 13,4.6.21.26.28
dark(-coloured), dim

ἀμαυρόω   V 1-0-0-1-1-3
Dt 34,7; Lam 4,1; Sir 43,4
A: *to make dim (the eyes)* [τι] Sir 43,4; *to make
obscure* [τι] Wis 4,12; P: *to be dimmed* (of eyes)
Dt 34,7; *to be tarnished* (of metals) Lam 4,1
(→ ἀπ-)

αμαφεθ   N 0-1-0-0-0-1
1 Sm 5,4
=המפתן *the threshold*

ἀμάω⁺   V 2-0-3-0-0-5
Lv 25,11; Dt 24,19; Is 17,5; 37,30; Mi 6,15
to reap
Cf. SHIPP 1979, 63

ἀμβλάκημα,-ατος   N3N 0-0-0-1-0-1
Dnᵀʰ 6,5

error, fault

ἀμβλύνομαι   V 1-0-0-0-0-1
Gn 27,1
to be dim (of eyes), *to become blind*

ἀμβλυωπέω   V 0-1-0-0-0-1
1 Kgs 12,24i
to be dim-sighted; ἀμβλυωπέω τοῦ βλέπειν *to
become dim-sighted*

ἀμβρόσιος,-α,-ον   A 0-0-0-0-1-1
Wis 19,21
divine, heavenly
Cf. LARCHER 1985, 1092

ἀμέθυστος,-ου⁺   N2M 2-0-1-0-0-3
Ex 28,19; 36,19(39,12); Ez 28,13
amethyst

ἀμείδητος,-ος,-ον   A 0-0-0-0-1-1
Wis 17,4
gloomy; neol.?

ἀμειξία,-ας   N1F 0-0-0-0-2-2
2 Mc 14,3.38
social or *political disturbance, state of war*
Cf. BICKERMAN 1980, 155

ἀμέλγω   V 0-0-0-2-0-2
Jb 10,10; Prv 30,33
to milk out Prv 30,33; *to squeeze out like milk, to
pour out like milk* (metaph.) Jb 10,10

ἀμελέω⁺   V 0-0-2-0-2-4
Jer 4,17; 38(31),32; 2 Mc 4,14; Wis 3,10
to neglect, to be neglectful Wis 3,10; *Jer
38(31),32 ἠμέλησα αὐτῶν -בם בחלתי *I neglected
them* for MT בעלתיבם *I was their husband* or *I
lorded over them*, cpr. Zech 11,8
Cf. HELBING 1928, 112-113; HORSLEY 1981, 62; 1982, 176;
SPICQ 1978, 67; →KOEHLER בחל

ἄμελξις,-εως   N3F 0-0-0-1-0-1
Jb 20,17
milking

ἀμελῶς   D 0-0-1-0-0-1
Jer 31(48),10
carelessly

ἄμεμπτος,-ος,-ον⁺   A 1-0-0-13-3-17
Gn 17,1; Jb 1,1.8; 2,3; 4,17
blameless, without reproach

ἀμέμπτως   D 0-0-0-1-0-1
Est 3,13
blamelessly
Cf. HORSLEY 1987, 141

ἀμερής,-ής,-ές   A 0-0-0-0-2-2
3 Mc 5,25; 6,29
momentary (of time)

ἀμέριμνος,-ος,-ον⁺   A 0-0-0-0-2-2
Wis 6,15; 7,23
free from care

ἀμετάθετος,-ος,-ον⁺   A 0-0-0-0-2-2
3 Mc 5,1.12
inalterable

ἀμέτρητος,-ος,-ον   A 0-0-1-0-7-8
Is 22,18; 3 Mc 2,4.9; 3 Mc 4,17; Od 12,6
immeasureable, immense

αμην⁺   D 0-1-0-2-9-12
1 Chr 16,36; Neh 5,13; 8,6; 1 Ezr 9,47; Tob^BA 8,8
=אמן *truly, surely*
Cf. BARR 1961, 168; →NIDNTT; TWNT

ἄμητος,-ου   N2M 6-1-8-7-1-23
Gn 45,6; Ex 34,21; Dt 16,9; 23,25(26)(bis)
harvest Prv 6,8; *reaping* 2 Kgs 19,29
Cf. WALTERS 1973, 95.226-227

ἀμήχανος,-ος,-ον   A 0-0-0-0-1-1
2 Mc 3,12
impossible

ἀμίαντος,-ος,-ον⁺   A 0-0-0-0-5-5
2 Mc 14,36; 15,34; Wis 3,13; 4,2; 8,20
undefiled

ἀμισθί   D 0-0-0-1-0-1
Jb 24,6
without reward

ἄμμος,-ου⁺   N2F 7-9-7-6-6-35
Gn 13,16(bis); 22,17; 28,14; 32,13
sand Gn 13,16; *Jer 26(46),22 ἐν ἄμμῳ -בחול *on
the sand* for MT בחיל *with power*

ἀμμώδης,-ης,-ες   A 0-0-0-0-1-1
Sir 25,20
sandy

ἀμνάς,-άδος   N3F 19-4-0-1-0-24
Gn 21,28.29.30; 31,41; Lv 5,6
(ewe)lamb Gn 21,28; *Gn 31,41 δέκα ἀμνάσιν
ten lambs corr.? δέκαμναις -מנים עשרת *ten
mines* for MT מנים עשרת *ten times*, cpr. Gn 31,7;
neol.
Cf. GEHMAN 1953, 146; LEE 1983, 108; WALTERS 1973,
193-194 (Gn 31,7.41)

ἀμνημονέω   V 0-0-0-0-1-1
Sir 37,6
to forget, to be unmindful of [τινος]

ἀμνησία,-ας   N1F 0-0-0-0-1-1
Sir 11,25
forgetting, forgetfulness

ἀμνησικακία,-ας   N1F 0-0-0-0-1-1
3 Mc 3,21
forgivingness; neol.

ἀμνήστευτος,-ου   N2F 1-0-0-0-0-1
Ex 22,15
not yet engaged, not get betrothed

ἀμνηστία,-ας   N1F 0-0-0-0-2-2
Wis 14,26; 19,4
forgetting, forgetfulness

ἀμνός,-οῦ⁺   N2M 77-5-11-5-3-101
Gn 30,40(bis); 31,7; 33,19; Ex 29,38
(he-)lamb Gn 30,40; *sacrificial he-lamb* (mostly)
Ex 29,39; *Gn 33,19 ἑκατὸν ἀμνῶν -קשׂיטה מאה
(Aram.) *hundred lambs* for MT קשׂיטה מאה
hundred pieces of money, see also Jos 24,32; Jb
42,11; see ἀμνάς
Cf. CHANTRAINE 1955, 12-19; TOV 1987, 137; →NIDNTT

ἄμοιρος,-ος,-ον   A 0-0-0-0-1-1
Wis 2,9
without share in [τινος]; neol.

ἀμόλυντος,-ος,-ον   A 0-0-0-0-1-1
Wis 7,22
undefiled; neol.?

ἀμόρα,-ας   N1F 0-0-0-1-0-1
Ct 2,5
sweet cake

ἀμορίτης,-ου   N1M 0-1-0-0-0-1
1 Chr 16,3
cake; neol.

ἄμορφος,-ος,-ον   A 0-0-0-0-1-1
Wis 11,17
without form, shapeless
Cf. LARCHER 1985, 676-680

ἄμπελος,-ου⁺   N2F 11-10-33-11-6-71
Gn 40,9.10; 49,11; Lv 25,3.4
vine Gn 49,11; *grape* Ct 2,15; *vineyard* Gn 40,9;
wine (meton.) 2 Kgs 18,31; ἄμπελος σωρηχ
(σωρηχ =שׂרק) *choice vine* Is 5,2
→NIDNTT

ἀμπελουργός,-οῦ⁺   N2M 0-2-2-0-0-4
2 Kgs 25,12; 2 Chr 26,10; Is 61,5; Jer 52,16
vine-dresser

ἀμπελών,-ῶνος⁺   N3M 18-29-27-18-10-102
Gn 9,20; Ex 22,4(bis); 23,11; Lv 19,10
vineyard Gn 9,20; *1 Sm 15,9 τῶν ἀμπελώνων
-הכרמים *the vineyards* for MT הכרים *the rams*
Cf. LEE 1983, 107

ἀμπλακία,-ας   N1F 0-0-0-0-1-1
3 Mc 2,19
error, fault

ἀμύγδαλον,-ου   N2N 0-0-0-1-0-1
Eccl 12,5
almond-tree

Cf. Shipp 1979, 66

ἀμύθητος,-ος,-ον   A 0-0-0-3-2-5
Jb 8,7; 36,28; 41,22; 2 Mc 3,6; 12,16
unspeakably great Jb 8,7; *innumerable* Jb 36,28

ἄμυνα,-ης   N1F 0-0-0-0-1-1
Wis 5,17
vengeance, revenge of or *defense, protection from*
[τινος]
Cf. Larcher 1984, 388

ἀμύνομαι⁺   V 0-1-1-5-3-10
Jos 10,13; Is 59,16; Ps 117(118),10.11.12
to keep off, to ward off oneself [τινα] Ps
117(118),10; *to defend oneself against* [τινα] Est
8,12s; *to avenge oneself on, to execute vengeance
on* [τινα] Jos 10,13
Cf. Helbing 1928, 36
(-ἀπ-, ἐπ-)

ἀμφιάζω⁺   V 0-0-0-2-0-2
Jb 29,14; 31,19
A: *to clothe* [τινα] Jb 31,19; M: *to clothe oneself*
(metaph.) Jb 29,14; neol.?

ἀμφίασις,-εως   N3F 0-0-0-3-0-3
Jb 22,6; 24,7; 38,9
garment, clothing; neol.

ἀμφιβάλλω⁺   V 0-0-1-0-0-1
Hab 1,17
to cast, to throw round

ἀμφίβληστρον,-ου⁺   N2N 0-0-3-2-0-5
Hab 1,15.16.17; Ps 140(141),10; Eccl 9,12
(casting-)net
Cf. Petersen 1986, 198

ἀμφιβολεύς,-έως   N3M 0-0-1-0-0-1
Is 19,8
fisherman, angler; neol.

ἀμφιέννυμαι   V 0-1-0-1-0-2
2 Kgs 17,9; Jb 40,10
to clothe oneself with [τινα] (metaph.) Jb 40,10;
[τι]: ἀμφιέννυμαι λόγους *to clothe one's words,
to conceal one's plans, to act secretly* or *to
embellish one's words* 2 Kgs 17,9

ἀμφιλαφής,-ής,-ές   A 0-0-0-0-1-1
Wis 17,17
wide-spreading

ἀμφίταπος,-ου   N2M 0-1-0-1-0-2
2 Sm 17,28; Prv 7,16
double-sided rug 2 Sm 17,28; *tapestry* Prv 7,16;
neol.?

ἄμφοδον,-ου⁺   N2N 0-0-2-0-0-2
Jer 17,27; 30,33(49,27)
block of houses surrounded by streets

Cf. Milligan 1980, 81; Tov 1976, 530-531

ἀμφοτεροδέξιος,-ος,-ον   A 0-4-0-0-0-4
Jgs 3,15; 20,16
ambidextrous; neol.

ἀμφότεροι,-αι,-α⁺   R 50-37-3-14-35-139
Gn 21,27.31; 22,8; 33,4; 40,5
both 1 Sm 3,11; *on both accounts* Wis 14,30

ἄμωμος,-ος,-ον⁺   A 47-3-12-17-4-83
Ex 29,1.38; Lv 1,3.10; 3,1
blameless, without blemish 2 Sm 22,24; *un-
blemished* (of victims) Ex 29,1; *spotless, perfect*
Ps 18(19),8

ἄν⁺   X 273-85-78-129-87-652
Gn 2,17; 3,5; 6,4; 11,6; 12,1
modal particle used with verbs to indicate that
the action is limited by circumstances or defined
by conditions. Incapable of translation by a
simple English word; the effect of ἄν upon the
meaning of its cl. depends on the mood and
tense of the verb with which it is used. In simple
sentences: *(I) would (have destroyed)* [ἄν +ind.
hist. tenses] (irreality) Jb 42,8; *(How) should (we
steal)* [+opt.] (wish in questions) Gn 44,8; *(I)
would (advise)* [ἄν +opt.] (potential, in
apodosis; often in dir. question) 4 Mc 1,1; in
dependent cl.: *(as it) may (please you)* [ἄν
+subj.] (fut. or general condition in comp. cl.)
Gn 19,8; *each time (you hear)* [ὅταν +subj.] (in
temporal cl.) Dnᴸˣˣ 3,5; *(in) whatsoever (day)
you eat* [ἄν +subj.] (in relative cl.) Gn 2,17; *(if
he) offers* [κἄν = καὶ ἐάν] (in conditional cl.)
Lv 7,16(6); *whosoever shall not* [ἄν μή +subj.]
Dnᵀʰ 3,6
Cf. Wevers 1991, 53

ἀνά⁺   P 125-142-64-27-19-377
Gn 1,4(bis).6.7(bis)
[τι]: *up, from bottom to top* (of place, motion
upwards); *by, in bodies of* (distributively with
numerals) 1 Kgs 18,13; *each of* Gn 24,22; ἀνὰ
χεῖρα *by the side of* 2 Sm 15,2; ἀνὰ μέσον
τινός *between* Gn 1,4
Cf. Sollamo 1979, 254-255.342-343.347-348; Walters
1973, 200 (Mal 3,18)

ἀναβαθμίς,-ίδος   N3F 1-0-0-0-0-1
Ex 20,26
step, stair; neol.

ἀναβαθμός,-οῦ⁺   N2M 0-6-6-15-0-27
1 Kgs 10,19.20; 2 Kgs 9,13; 20,11; 2 Chr 9,18
stair

ἀναβαίνω   V 117-340-112-60-57-686

Gn 2,6; 13,1; 17,22; 19,28.30

to go up, to mount to [τι] Nm 21,33; [εἴς τι] Nm
14,44; [ἐπί τι] Ex 17,10; [ἐπί τινα] Gn 38,12;
[πρός τινα] Gn 44,17; *to go up (out of)* Gn 13,1;
to rise out of, to flow from (of rivers, fontains)
Gn 2,6; *to shoot up* (of plants) Is 11,1; *to dawn*
(of morning) Gn 32,27(26); *to mount, to cover*
Gn 31,10; *to arise* (of anger, feelings) 2 Sm
11,20; *to advance* Neh 4,1(7); *to go away, to be
removed* Jon 2,7; *to enter into* [ἐπί τι] 2 Kgs
12,5(4); *to go up* (metaph.) Ex 2,23; τὰ
βαίνοντα *the produce* Lv 25,5; ἀναβαίνω εἰς
πόλεμον *to go to war, to battle* 1 Kgs 22,15;
ἀναβαίνει ἐν τοῖς ὠσί *it comes to one's ear*
2 Kgs 19,28; ἀναβαίνει ἡ θυσία *the sacrifice is
offered* 1 Kgs 18,29; *1 Sm 2,10 ἀνέβη -עלה *has
gone up* for MT עלו *against him;* *2 Kgs 1,11
καὶ ἀνέβη -ויעל *and he went up* for MT ויען *and
he answered*

Cf. HORSLEY 1981, 55.131; 1982,62 (ἀναβαίνω πρός
τινα); MURAOKA 1990, 37.40

ἀναβάλλω							V 0-1-0-3-2-6
1 Sm 28,14; Ps 77(78),21; 88(89),39; 103(104),2;
Tob^BA 6,3

A: *to throw onto* [τι ἐπί τι] Tob^BA 6,3; *to lay*
[τινα ἐπί τι] 4 Mc 9,12; M: *to throw over the
shoulder, to be clothed with* [τι] 1 Sm 28,14; *Ps
88(89)39 ἀνεβάλου -◊עבר *you rejected* for MT
התעברת◊עבר^II *you are infuriated,* cpr. Ps
77(78),21

ἀνάβασις,-εως						N3F 1-17-4-8-9-39
Nm 34,4; Jos 10,10; 18,17; Jgs^A 8,13; 11,13
ascent Nm 34,4; *going up* Jgs^A 11,13; *road, path,
passage* Jdt 4,7; *Jgs^A 8,13 ἀπὸ ἀναβάσεως
-מ/מעלה *from the ascent* for MT מלמעלה *from
above;* *Ez 47,12 ἀνάβασις -◊עלה *ascent* for MT
עלה *foliage*

ἀναβαστάζω						V 0-2-0-0-0-2
Jgs 16,3
to lift up; neol.

ἀναβάτης,-ου						N1M 8-0-16-0-6-30
Ex 14,23.26.28; 15,1.4
one who mounts, horseman, rider Ex 14,23;
mounted, riding (as adj.) Is 21,7

ἀναβιβάζω⁺						V 17-11-6-3-2-39
Gn 37,28; 41,43; 46,4; Ex 4,20; 8,2
to bring up, to guide up [τινα εἴς τι] Gn 46,4; *to
take up, to mount up* [τινα ἐπί τι] Ex 4,20; *to
make to go up, to help to come up* [τινα] Gn
37,28; *to offer* [τι] (on an altar) Ex 32,6; *to bring*

up against, to instigate against [τινα ἐπί τι] Jer
28,27; ἀναβιβάζω χοῦν ἐπὶ τὴν κεφαλήν μου
to cast dust on one's (own) head Lam 2,10
Cf. DANIEL 1966, 36

ἀναβίωσις,-εως						N3F 0-0-0-0-1-1
2 Mc 7,9
return to life, resurrection; neol.

ἀναβλαστάνω						V 0-0-0-2-0-2
Jb 5,6; 8,19
to shoot up, to sprout

ἀναβλέπω⁺						V 16-3-7-3-6-35
Gn 13,14; 15,5; 18,2; 22,4.13
to look up Dt 4,19; ἀναβλέπω τοῖς ὀφθαλμοῖς
to lift up the eyes, to look up Gn 13,14;
ἀναβλέπω τοὺς ὀφθαλμούς *to lift up the eyes, to
look up* Is 40,26; ἀνέβλεψαν οἱ ὀφθαλμοὶ
αὐτοῦ *his eyes looked up, he saw* 1 Sm 14,27
Cf. DEPUYDT 1985, 39; WEVERS 1990, 213

ἀνάβλεψις,-εως⁺					N3F 0-0-1-0-0-1
Is 61,1
recovery of sight; neol.?

ἀναβοάω⁺						V 7-16-8-4-13-48
Gn 21,16; 27,34.38; Ex 2,23; 14,10
to shout aloud, to cry out

ἀναβολή,-ῆς⁺						N1F 0-1-1-1-0-3
1 Chr 19,4; Ez 5,3; Neh 5,13
mantle, garment Ez 5,3; *mound* (euph. for
buttock) 1 Chr 19,4
Cf. GEHMAN 1972, 106 (1 Chr 19,4)

ἀναβράσσω						V 0-0-2-0-1-3
Ez 21,26; Na 3,2; Wis 10,19
to throw up, to reject [τινα] Wis 10,19; *to cast*
[τι] (of a stick for divination) Ez 21,26; *to bound*
[abs.] (of a chariot) Na 3,2
Cf. LARCHER 1984, 645 (Wis 10,19)

ἀναγγέλλω⁺						V 40-59-73-63-25-260
Gn 3,11; 9,22; 21,7; 22,20; 24,23
A: *to report, to recount, to announce, to declare*
[τινι ὅτι +ind.] Gn 3,11; *to reveal to* [τινι]
2 Kgs 4,27; *to proclaim, to publicize* [τι] Ps 9,12;
to teach [τινι ὅτι +ind.] Dt 8,3; *to confess, to
avow* [τι] Ps 37(38),19; P: *to be reported, to be
announced, to be declared* Gn 22,20; *Is
33,14(2x) τίς ἀναγγελεῖ -מי יניר *who reports* for
MT מי יגור *who stays with;* *Jb 13,17 ἀναγγελῶ
γάρ -ואחוה *and I report* for MT ואחוי *my
exposition, my report;* *Dt 13,10 ἀναγγέλων
ἀναγγελεῖς -הגד תגירנו *you shall surely report
concerning him* for MT הרג תהרגנו *you shall surely
kill him;* *Is 30,10 ἀναγγέλλετε -◊חוה *report* for

MT ◊ חוה see?; *Is 38,16 ἀνηγγέλη -◊ חוה report
for MT ◊ חיה live
Cf. HARL 1986, 282; KILPATRICK 1963, 134-135

ἀναγινώσκω⁺   V 3-8-23-14-14-62
Ex 24,7; Dt 17,19; 31,11; Jos 9,2(8,34).2(8,35)
to read Ex 24,7; to read aloud Jer 39(32),11;
*Am 4,5 καὶ ἀνέγνωσαν -ויקראו and they read
publicly for MT וקטרו and offer
Cf. NIEDDU 1988, 17-37

ἀναγκάζω⁺   V 0-0-0-1-19-20
Prv 6,7; 1 Ezr 3,24; 4,6; Jdt 8,30; 1 Mc 2,25
to compel to [+inf.] 1 Ezr 3,24; to constrain
[τινι] 1 Ezr 4,6
Cf. BARR 1961, 223
(→ κατ-)

ἀναγκαῖος,-α,-ον⁺   A 0-0-0-0-5-5
2 Mc 4,23; 9,21; 4 Mc 1,2; Wis 16,3; Sir prol.,30
necessary Sir prol.,30; ἀναγκαία ὄρεξις
elementary appetite Wis 16,3
Cf. SPICQ 1978, 77-80

ἀνάγκη,-ης⁺   N1F 0-1-3-17-22-43
1 Sm 22,2; Jer 9,14; 15,4; Zph 1,15; Ps 24(25),17
necessity 4 Mc 8,24; destiny Wis 19,4;
compulsion, pressure 4 Mc 3,17; tribulation,
punishment Wis 17,16; distress 1 Sm 22,2; κατ'
ἀνάγκην forcibly, by force 2 Mc 15,2; δι'
ἀνάγκην through compulsion 4 Mc 5,13;
σιδηροδέσμοις ἀνάγκαις with unyielding chains
3 Mc 4,9
Cf. BARR 1961, 223

ἀναγκεία,-ας   N1F 0-0-0-0-1-1
2 Mc 4,13
abominable wickedness

ἀναγνωρίζομαι   V 1-0-0-0-0-1
Gn 45,1
to make yourself known

ἀνάγνωσις,-εως⁺   N3F 0-0-0-1-3-4
Neh 8,8; 1 Ezr 9,48; Sir prol.,10.17
(public) reading Neh 8,8; recognition 1 Ezr 9,48;
τὴν ἀνάγνωσιν ποιέομαι to read Sir prol.,17
Cf. SPICQ 1978, 81-82

ἀναγνώστης,-ου   N1M 0-0-0-0-6-6
1 Ezr 8,8.9.19; 9,39.42
(public) reader
Cf. SPICQ 1978, 81-82

ἀναγορεύομαι   V 0-0-0-1-0-1
Est 8,12
to be called, to be publicly proclaimed

ἀναγραφή,-ῆς   N1F 0-0-0-0-1-1
2 Mc 2,13

record, writing

ἀναγράφω⁺   V 0-0-0-0-6-6
1 Ezr 1,22.31.40; 1 Mc 14,22; 2 Mc 4,9
to engrave [τι] 4 Mc 17,8; to inscribe, to enter in
a public register [τινα] 2 Mc 4,9; to register [τι]
1 Mc 14,22; to write [τι] 1 Ezr 1,22

ἀνάγω⁺   V 22-42-32-7-11-114
Gn 42,37; 50,24; Ex 8,1.2.3
to bring up [τι] Ex 8,5; to raise up [τινα] Ez
26,3; to lead up to, to bring to [τινα] Jos 7,24; to
bring up (from grave) 1 Sm 2,6; to offer [τινα]
2 Kgs 10,24; to guide [τινα] Ps 77(78),52; P: to
retire to [πρός τινα] 2 Mc 5,9; ἀνάγω
μηρυκισμόν to bring up, to chew the cud Lv 11,3
Cf. LE BOULLUEC 1989, 90-91

ἀναγώγως   D 0-0-0-0-1-1
2 Mc 12,14
ill-bred, rudely

ἀναδείκνυμι⁺   V 0-0-1-2-16-19
Hab 3,2; Dn^LXX 1,11.20; 1 Ezr 1,32.35
A: to show, to reveal [τι] 2 Mc 2,8; to proclaim,
to appoint [τινα] 1 Ezr 8,23; P: to be manifested
Hab 3,2; to be dedicated, to be consecrated 3 Mc
2,14; ἀναδείκνυμί τινα βασιλέα to make sb
king 1 Ezr 1,35
Cf. HELBING 1928, 60; SPICQ 1982, 38-39

ἀνάδειξις,-εως⁺   N3F 0-0-0-0-1-1
Sir 43,6
declaration
Cf. BICKERMAN 1980, 1-6; SPICQ 1982, 38-39

ἀναδενδράς,-άδος   N3F 0-0-1-1-0-2
Ez 17,6; Ps 79(80),11
vine that grows up trees

ἀναδέχομαι⁺   V 0-0-0-0-2-2
2 Mc 6,19; 8,36
to accept [τι] 2 Mc 6,19; to ondertake to [+inf.]
2 Mc 8,36
Cf. SPICQ 1978, 83-84

ἀναδίδωμι⁺   V 0-0-0-0-2-2
2 Mc 13,15; Sir 1,23
to give [τί τινι] 2 Mc 13,15; to burst, to issue
forth [τινι] (metaph.) Sir 1,23

ἀνάδυσις,-εως   N3F 0-0-0-0-1-1
Wis 19,7
emergence (of land from water)

ἀναζεύγνυμι   V 3-0-0-0-14-17
Ex 14,15; 40,36.37; 1 Ezr 2,25; 8,60
to break up, to shift one's quarters [abs.] Ex
14,15; to break up a camp and move towards
[ἐπί τι] Jdt 7,1; to return to [εἰς τι] Jdt 16,21

Cf. QUAST 1990, 230-252 (esp. 250-251)

ἀναζέω   V 2-0-0-1-1-4
Ex 9,9.10; Jb 41,23; 2 Mc 9,9
to break out (of sores) Ex 9,9; *to make to boil*
[τι] Jb 41,23

ἀναζητέω⁺   V 0-0-0-2-1-3
Jb 3,4; 10,6; 2 Mc 13,21
to investigate, to search out, to discover [τι] Jb
10,6; *to search for* [τι] Jb 3,4

ἀναζυγή,-ῆς   N1F 1-0-0-0-2-3
Ex 40,38; 2 Mc 9,2; 13,26
*breaking up one's quarters, marching forth, return
home* 2 Mc 9,2; *journey* Ex 40,38; neol.?
Cf. LEE 1983, 101

ἀναζώννυμι⁺   V 0-1-0-1-0-2
Jgsᴮ 18,16; Prv 31,17
to gird

ἀναζωπυρέω⁺   V 1-0-0-0-1-2
Gn 45,27; 1 Mc 13,7
to rekindle, to revive (metaph.)

ἀναθάλλω⁺   V 0-0-2-1-6-9
Ez 17,24; Hos 8,9; Ps 27(28),7; Wis 4,4; Sir 1,18
to sprout afresh, to flourish Wis 4,4; *to sprout
afresh, to revive* (metaph.) Ps 27(28),7; *to make
to flourish, to revive* [τι] Sir 1,18
Cf. WALTERS 1973, 307

ἀνάθεμα,-ατος⁺   N3N 6-13-1-0-1-22
Nm 21,3; Lv 27,28(bis); Dt 13,16.18
anything devoted to destruction, an accursed thing
(semit.) Dt 13,18; ἀναθέματι ἀναθεματίζω
τινά *to devote to evil* or *destruction, to curse* Dt
13,16; ἀναθέματι ἀνατίθημί τινι *to devote a
dedicated thing to destruction to* Lv 27,28;
᾿Ανάθεμα *Anathema* (name of a city) Nm 21,3;
see ἀνάθημα
Cf. DEISSMANN 1901, 342; HARLÉ 1988, 214; MENESTRINA
1979, 12; VAN UNNIK 1973, 113-126; →NIDNTT; TWNT

ἀναθεματίζω⁺   V 5-7-0-2-1-15
Nm 18,14; 21,2.3; Dt 13,16; 20,17
A: *to devote* Nm 21,2; P: *to be devoted* Nm
18,14; *to be accursed* Ezr 10,8; ἀναθέματι ἀναθεματίζω τινά *to devote to evil* or *destruction, to
curse* Dt 13,16
→NIDNTT; TWNT

ἀνάθημα,-ατος⁺   N3N 2-0-0-0-3-5
Dt 7,26(bis); Jdt 16,19; 2 Mc 9,16; 3 Mc 3,17
votive offering, gift 2 Mc 9,16; *anything devoted
to destruction, accursed thing* Dt 7,26; see
ἀνάθεμα
→NIDNTT; TWNT

ἀναίδεια,-ας+   N1F 0-0-0-0-1-1
Sir 25,22
shamelessness, impudence
Cf. SPICQ 1973, 49-52

ἀναιδής,-ής,-ές   A 1-1-2-6-4-14
Dt 28,50; 1 Sm 2,29; Is 56,11; Jer 8,5; Prv 7,13
shameless 1 Sm 2,29; *bold* Dt 28,50; *hard,
peremptory* Dnᵀʰ 2,15; *1 Sm 2,29 ἀναιδεῖ
ὀφθαλμῷ -מָעֹין ◊ עין *with an evil eye* for MT מָעֹון
place, temple?

ἀναιδῶς   D 0-0-0-1-0-1
Prv 21,29
impudently, ungodly
(→ ἀπ-)

ἀναίρεσις,-εως⁺   N3F 1-1-0-0-2-4
Nm 11,15; Jgsᴮ 15,17; Jdt 15,4; 2 Mc 5,13
destruction, slaying, putting to death Nm 11,15;
taking up, elevation Jgsᴮ 15,17

ἀναιρέω⁺   V 14-14-27-10-25-90
Gn 4,15; Ex 2,5.10.14(bis)
A: *to destroy* [τι] 2 Sm 10,18; *to destroy, to kill,
to slay* [τινα] Gn 4,15; M: *to take up, to carry
off, to adopt* [τι] Ex 2,5; *to take away* [τι] Dnᵀʰ
1,16; *Ex 15,9 ἀνελῶ (τῇ μαχαίρῃ μου)
-(בחרבי) אהרג? ◊ הרג *I shall kill (by my sword)* for
MT (חרבי) אריק ◊ ריק *I shall draw (my sword)*

ἀναίτιος,-ος/-α,-ον⁺   A 4-0-0-0-2-6
Dt 19,10.13; 21,8.9; Susᴸˣˣ 60
innocent

ἀναιτίως   D 0-0-0-0-1-1
4 Mc 12,14
having no cause

ἀνακαινίζω⁺   V 0-0-0-4-1-5
Ps 38(39),3; 102(103),5; 103(104),30; Lam 5,21;
1 Mc 6,9
to renew

ἀνακαίω   V 0-0-4-0-3-7
Ez 5,2; 24,10; Hos 7,6(bis); Jdt 7,5
to kindle, to light up Jdt 7,5; *to kindle* (metaph.)
Sir 9,8

ἀνακαλέω   V 5-1-0-0-1-7
Ex 31,2; 35,30; Lv 1,1; Nm 1,17; 10,2
A: *to call* [τινα] Ex 35,30; *to call* [τι] (an
assembly) Nm 10,2; M: *to call* [τινα] Ex 31,2; *to
call out* [abs.] 4 Mc 14,17

ἀνακαλύπτω⁺   V 0-0-11-8-9-28
Dt 23,1; Is 20,4; 22,8.9.14
to uncover Dt 23,1; *to discover, to disclose* 1 Ezr
8,76; *to reveal* Tob 12,7; *Jb 28,11 ἀνεκάλυψεν
-חפש *explored* for MT חבש *bound?*; *Is 24,1 καὶ

ἀνακαλύψει -וערה he will expose, he will lay
bare for MT וערה and he will twist, pervert
ἀνακάμπτω⁺   V 1-5-5-1-3-15
Ex 32,27; Jgs^ 11,39; 2 Sm 1,22; 8,13; 1 Kgs
12,20
to return Ex 32,27; to turn back 2 Sm 1,22
Cf. HORSLEY 1987, 141
ἀνάκειμαι⁺   V 0-0-0-0-2-2
1 Ezr 4,11; Tobˢ 9,6
to lie at table, to recline
ἀνακηρύσσω   V 0-0-0-0-1-1
4 Mc 17,23
to proclaim
ἀνακλάω   V 0-0-0-0-1-1
4 Mc 11,10
to bend back
ἀνακλίνω⁺   V 0-0-0-0-1-1
3 Mc 5,16
to lean back, to recline
Cf. MARGOLIS 1907, 247
ἀνάκλισις,-εως   N3F 0-0-0-1-0-1
Ct 1,12
lying or leaning back; *Ct 1,12 ἐν ἀνακλίσει at
table or corr.? ἀνακυκλήσει for MT במסבו while
he was in the surroundings (of Jerusalem, cpr.
2 Kgs 23,5)
Cf. KATZ 1938, 34
ἀνάκλιτον,-ου   N2N 0-0-0-1-0-1
Ct 3,10
sth to recline on, back of a chair
ἀνακοινόομαι   V 0-0-0-0-1-1
2 Mc 14,20
to communicate with, to take counsel with [τινι]
ἀνακομίζομαι   V 0-0-0-0-3-3
2 Mc 2,22; 12,39; 3 Mc 1,1
M: to carry up, to take up, to take away with one
[τι] 2 Mc 12,39; to recover [τι] 2 Mc 2,22; P: to
return, to come back 3 Mc 1,1
ἀνακόπτω   V 0-0-0-0-3-3
4 Mc 1,35; 13,6; Wis 18,23
A: to push back, to break [τι] 4 Mc 13,6; to stop,
to still (an anger) [τι] Wis 18,23; P: to be driven
back, to be restrained 4 Mc 1,35
ἀνακράζω⁺   V 0-7-5-0-3-15
Jos 6,5(bis); Jgs 7,20; 1 Sm 4,5
A: to cry out, to lift up the voice, to shout Jos
6,5; M: Jl 3,16
ἀνακρίνω⁺   V 0-1-0-0-5-6
1 Sm 20,12; Sus^LXX 13.48.52; Sus^Th 49
to examine [abs.] Sus^LXX 48; to examine closely,

to interrogate [τινα] Sus^LXX 13; to sound [τινα]
1 Sm 20,12
Cf. ENGEL 1985, 98.118
ἀνάκρισις,-εως⁺   N3F 0-0-0-0-1-1
3 Mc 7,5
inquiry, examination
Cf. BICKERMANN 1986, 110-111
ἀνακρούομαι   V 0-6-1-0-0-7
Jgs 5,11; 2 Sm 6,14.16; 1 Chr 25,3
to strike up, to touch (the strings) [ἔν τινι] 2 Sm
6,14; to prophesy with music? 1 Chr 25,3.5; *Jgs
5,11 ἀνακρουομένων -מ/חזים ◊ חזה of music
making prophets? for MT מחצצים ?
ἀνακύπτω⁺   V 0-0-0-1-1-2
Jb 10,15; Sus^LXX 35
to keep one's head up
Cf. ENGEL 1985, 103-104; NEIRYNCK 1982, 409-410
ἀναλαμβάνω⁺   V 24-5-24-19-27-99
Gn 24,61; 45,19.27; 46,5.6
A: to take up, to take into one's hands [τινα] Gn
24,61; to take up into heaven [τινα] 2 Kgs 2,9; to
take with me [τι] Ex 10,13; to take away [τι] Tob
3,6; to take over, to adopt [τι] Nm 23,7; to take
upon oneself, to assume [τι] Jb 40,10(5); to raise,
to lift up [τι] Lam 3,41; to raise, to gather [τι] (of
an army) 2 Mc 12,38; to lift up one's voice Nm
14,1; to regain, to get back [τι] Jb 36,3; to take
up [τι] (metaph.) Jb 17,9; to take [τινα] Jb
27,21; to carry [τι] Ex 28,12; ἀναλαβών τι or
τινα with Gn 48,1; ἀναλαμβάνω ὀφθαλμούς to
lift up the eyes Jer 13,20
Cf. BICKERMAN 1980, 51 n.28, 171 n.86; MARGOLIS 1907
247-248; 1972, 75
ἀναλάμπω   V 0-0-1-1-1-3
Am 5,6; Jb 11,15; Wis 3,7
to shine out 2 Mc 1,22; to flame up, to catch fire
Am 5,6; to shine out (metaph.) Jb 11,15
ἀνάληπτος,-ος,-ον   A 0-0-0-1-0-1
Prv 14,23
fool
ἀναλέγω   V 0-2-0-0-1-3
1 Sm 20,38; 1 Kgs 21(20),33; 3 Mc 2,24
to pick up, to gather up [τι] 1 Sm 20,38; to note,
to seize upon [τι] 1 Kgs 21(20),33;
ἀναλεξάμενος ἑαυτόν when he had come to
himself 3 Mc 2,24
ἀνάλημμα,-ατος   N3N 0-1-0-0-1-2
2 Chr 32,5; Sir 50,2
fortified wall, fortification, fortress
ἀναλημπτέος,-α,-ον   A 0-0-0-0-1-1

2 Mc 3,13
must be taken up, must be brought
ἀναλημπτήρ,-ῆρος   N3M 0-1-0-0-0-1
2 Chr 4,16
bucket, ladle, bowl; neol.

ἀνάλημψις,-εως⁺   N3F 0-0-0-0-1-1
PSal 4,18
taking up, taking away, removal
ἀναλίσκω⁺   V 2-0-8-3-7-20
Gn 41,30; Nm 14,33; Is 32,10; 66,17; Ez 5,12
A: *to spend* [τι] Wis 13,12; *to consume* [τι] Gn
41,30; *to kill, to destroy* [τινα] Prv 24,22d; P: *to
be consumed* Nm 14,33; *to be wasted* (metaph.)
1 Ezr 6,29; *to be cut off* Is 32,10; *Prv 23,28
ἀναλωθήσεται -פה‎ *shall perish, shall be cut off*
for MT תוסיף‎ ◊ סוף‎ *shall add*
(→ ἐξ-, κατ-, παρ-)

ἀναλογίζομαι⁺   V 0-0-1-0-2-3
Is 44,19; 3 Mc 7,7; PSal 8,7
to consider, to take into consideration

ἀναλόγως   D 0-0-0-0-1-1
Wis 13,5
proportionally
Cf. GILBERT 1973, 25-30; LARCHER 1985, 763-764

ἀναλύω⁺   V 0-0-0-0-18-18
1 Ezr 3,3(bis); Jdt 13,1; TobᴮA 2,9; 2 Mc 8,25
A: *to set free* [τι] Wis 16,14; *to cancel* [τι] 3 Mc
5,40; *to depart, to go away* [intrans.] 1 Ezr 3,3; *to
return* [intrans.] Wis 2,1; P: *to melt away* Sir
3,15; εἰς ἑαυτὸν ἀναλύομαι *to come together
again* Wis 5,12
Cf. LARCHER 1983, 214 (Wis 2,1)

ἀνάλωσις,-εως   N3F 1-0-3-0-0-4
Dt 28,20; Ez 15,4.6; 16,20
consumption, wasting

ἀναμάρτητος,-ος,-ον⁺   A 1-0-0-0-3-4
Dt 29,18; 2 Mc 8,4; 12,42; Od 14,33
sinless Dt 29,18; *innocent* 2 Mc 8,4

ἀνάμειξις,-εως   N3F 0-0-0-0-1-1
PSal 2,13
mingling, sexual intercourse
ἀναμένω⁺   V 0-0-2-2-6-10
Is 59,11; Jer 13,16; Jb 2,9; 7,2; Jdt 7,12
to wait for, to await [τι] Jdt 8,17; *to wait, to stay,
to remain* [abs.] Jdt 7,12; *to tarry* [+inf.] Sir 5,7
Cf. MARGOLIS 1972 (A), 60

ἀναμίγνυμι   V 0-0-3-6-0-9
Ez 22,18(bis); 46,14; Est 3,13d; Dnᴸˣˣ 2,41
A: *to mix up, to mix together* [τι] Ez 46,14; P: *to
be mixed with* [ἔν τινι] (of pers.) Est 3,13d;

[τινι] (of things) Ez 22,18
Cf. HELBING 1928, 250

ἀναμιμνήσκω⁺   V 4-6-8-2-2-22
Gn 41,9; Ex 23,13; Nm 5,15; 10,9; 2 Sm 18,18
A: *to recall to memory, to make mention* [τι] Gn
41,9; P: *to remember, to recall to mind* [τινος]
Neh 9,17; [τι] Ex 23,13; *to be brought to
remember* Jb 24,20; ἀναμιμνήσκων *recorder*
2 Sm 20,24
Cf. HELBING 1928, 49; →NIDNTT

ἀνάμνησις,-εως⁺   N3F 2-0-0-2-1-5
Lv 24,7; Nm 10,10; Ps 37(38),1; 69(70),1; Wis
16,6
calling to mind, reminiscence, remembrance
Cf. CAIRD 1972, 115; DANIEL 1966, 160-161.226.235-237;
JONES 1955, 183-191; KILPATRICK 1975, 35-40; →NIDNTT

ἀναμοχλεύω   V 0-0-0-0-1-1
4 Mc 10,5
to wrench

ἀναμφισβητήτως   D 0-0-0-0-1-1
1 Ezr 6,29
without further question, indisputably

ἄνανδρος,-ος,-ον   A 0-0-0-0-3-3
4 Mc 5,31; 6,21; 8,16
wanting in manhood, weak 4 Mc 5,31; *wanting in
manhood, cowardly* 4 Mc 6,21

ἀνανεάζω   V 0-0-0-0-1-1
4 Mc 7,13
to become young again

ἀνανεόω⁺   V 0-0-0-2-8-10
Jb 33,24; Est 3,13b; 1 Mc 12,1.3.10
A: *to restore* Jb 33,24; M: *to renew* 1 Mc 12,1; *to
restore* Est 3,13b
Cf. HORSLEY 1983, 61-62

ἀνάνευσις,-εως   N3F 0-0-0-1-0-1
Ps 72(73),4
rejection, refusal; neol.?
Cf. CAIRD 1972, 115

ἀνανεύω   V 9-0-0-1-1-11
Ex 22,16(bis); Nm 30,6(ter)
to make signs of refusal, to refuse Ex 22,16; *to
disclaim* Nm 30,6
Cf. CAIRD 1972, 115

ἀνανέωσις,-εως   N3F 0-0-0-0-1-1
1 Mc 12,17
renewing

ἀναντλέω   V 0-0-0-1-0-1
Prv 9,12
to go through (troubles) [τι] (metaph.)

ἀναξηραίνω   V 0-0-2-0-2-4

Jer 27(50),27; Hos 13,15; Sir 14,9; 43,3
to dry up [τι] Hos 13,15; *to consume, to exhaust*
[τι] (metaph.) Sir 14,9

ἀνάξιος,-α,-ον⁺   A 0-0-1-1-2-4
Jer 15,19; Est 8,12g; Od 12,14; Sir 25,8
unworthy (of pers.) Sir 25,8; *worthless* Est 8,12g

ἀναξις,-εως   N3F 0-0-0-0-1-1
PSal 18,5
bringing up, raising up

ἀναξίως⁺   D 0-0-0-0-1-1
2 Mc 14,42
worthlessly

ἀνάπαλιν   D 0-0-0-0-1-1
Wis 19,21
on the opposite side, on the other side

ἀνάπαυμα,-ατος   N3N 0-0-1-1-0-2
Is 28,12; Jb 3,23
repose, rest Jb 3,23; *fallow land* Is 28,12
Cf. HELBING 1907, 113; SHIPP 1979, 69

ἀνάπαυσις,-εως⁺   N3F 15-2-13-13-18-61
Gn 8,9; 49,15; Ex 16,23; 23,12; 31,15
repose, rest (sometimes pl.) Gn 8,9; *resting place*
Gn 49,15; *a day of rest (Sabbat)* Lv 16,31; *Jb
7,18 εἰς ἀνάπαυσιν -רגע לרגעים (moment)
until the (time of) rest? for MT רגע לרגעים
(moment) *every moment*
Cf. DANIEL 1966, 198; HARLÉ 1988, 155-156 (Lv 16,31);
LE BOULLUEC 1989, 57.186.236.317; WALTERS 1973,
160.161.308.320.329.342; WEVERS 1990, 255.514.575;
→NIDNTT

ἀναπαύω⁺   V 8-6-30-20-8-72
Gn 29,2; 49,14; Ex 23,12; Lv 25,2; Nm 24,9
A: *to give rest from* [τινα ἀπό τινος] 2 Sm 7,11;
to give rest [τινι] 1 Kgs 5,18; *to give rest* [τινα]
1 Chr 22,18; *to quiet, to calm* [τι] Zech 6,8; *to
refresh* [τι] 1 Sm 16,16; *to give respite* [τι] Sir
18,16; M: *to take rest* Gn 49,14; *to halt, to rest*
(of troops) Gn 29,2; *to sleep with* [μετά τινος]
Susᴸˣˣ 37; *to rest, to settle upon* [ἐπί τι] Is 11,2;
to cease from [ἐπί τινι] Jer 49,10; *to die* Sir
22,11; P: *to have a rest* Lam 5,5; *Jgsᴬ 4,11
ἀναπαυομένων -◊צעה? *of the resting (flocks?)*
for MT ב/צענים *in Zaannim;* *Prv 21,20
ἀναπαύσεται -ישכון *will rest* for MT ושמן *and oil*
Cf. HELBING 1928, 168-169; WALTERS 1973, 320.342;
→NIDNTT

ἀναπείθω⁺   V 0-0-2-0-1-3
Jer 36(29),8(bis); 1 Mc 1,11
to persuade, to convince (deceptively) [τινα]

ἀνάπειρος,-ος,-ον⁺   A 0-0-0-0-2-2

Tobˢ 14,2; 2 Mc 8,24
maimed, mutilated

ἀναπείρω   V 0-0-0-0-1-1
2 Mc 12,22
to pierce through

ἀναπετάννυμι   V 0-0-0-1-0-1
Jb 39,26
to spread out, to unfold

ἀναπηδάω⁺   V 0-2-0-1-7-10
1 Sm 20,34; 25,9; Est 5,1; Tob 2,4
to start up, to spring up, to leap up [abs.] Tob
2,4; *to leap up from* [ἀπό τινος] 1 Sm 20,34

ἀναπηδύω   V 0-0-0-1-0-1
Prv 18,4
to spring up
Cf. WALTERS 1973, 66

ἀναπίπτω⁺   V 1-0-0-0-7-8
Gn 49,9; Jdt 12,16; Tob 2,1; 7,9
to fall back, to sit down Jdt 12,16; *to lay oneself
back, to lay* Gn 49,9; *to recline* Tob 2,1

ἀναπλάσσομαι   V 0-0-0-0-1-1
Wis 15,7
to model, to mould, to shape [τι]

ἀναπληρόω⁺   V 6-1-1-4-1-13
Gn 2,21; 15,16; 29,28; Ex 7,25; 23,26
A: *to fill up* [τι] Gn 2,21; *to complete* [τι] (a
time span) Ex 23,26; *to finish* [τι] (a work)
1 Kgs 7,37(51); P: *to be made complete* Gn
15,16

ἀναπλήρωσις,-εως   N3F 0-0-0-3-1-4
Dnᴸˣˣ 9,2; Dn 12,13; 1 Ezr 1,54
fulfilment

ἀναπνέω   V 0-0-0-1-0-1
Jb 9,18
to recover one's breath, to recover

ἀναποδίζω   V 0-0-0-0-2-2
2 Mc 14,44; Sir 48,23
to step back, to return

ἀναποδισμός,-οῦ   N2M 0-0-0-0-1-1
Wis 2,5
return; neol.

ἀναποιέω   V 31-0-1-0-0-32
Lv 7,10(bis).12; 23,13; Nm 6,15
to make up, to prepare

ἀναπτερόω   V 0-0-0-2-1-3
Prv 7,11; Ct 6,5; Sir 34,1
A: *to excite* [τινα] Ct 6,5; P: *to be capricious,
flighty, fickle* Prv 7,11

ἀναπτέρωσις,-εως   N3F 0-0-0-0-1-1
PSal 4,12

clamour; λόγοι ἀναπτερώσεως *clamorous words*

ἀναπτύσσω⁺   V 1-3-2-0-0-6
Dt 22,17; Jgs 8,25; 2 Kgs 19,14; Ez 41,16
A: *to unfold, to spread out* Dt 22,17; P: *to be folded back* (of doors) Ez 41,16; *to be opened* Ez 41,21

ἀνάπτω⁺   V 0-2-13-5-4-24
Jgsᴬ 6,21; 2 Chr 13,11; Jer 9,11; 11,16; 17,27
A: *to light up, to kindle* [abs.] 2 Chr 13,11; *to set on fire* [τινα] Mal 3,19; P: *to be kindled, to be lighted up* Jgsᴬ 6,21; *to be ravaged by fire* Jer 9,11

ἀναρίθμητος,-ος,-ον⁺   A 0-1-1-4-7-13
1 Kgs 8,5; Jl 1,6; Jb 21,33; 22,5; 31,25
not to be counted, countless, immeasurable

ἀναρπάζω   V 0-1-0-0-0-1
Jgsᴬ 9,25
to snatch away, to rob

ἀναρρήγνυμι   V 0-3-0-0-0-3
2 Kgs 2,24; 8,12; 15,16
to tear open, to rip up

ἀνασκάπτω   V 0-0-0-2-0-2
Ps 7,16; 79(80),17
to dig up

ἀνασπάω⁺   V 0-0-2-1-1-4
Am 9,2; Hab 1,15; Dnᴸˣˣ 6,18; Belᵀʰ 42
to draw back, to pull down violently Am 9,2; *to draw, to pull up* Hab 1,15

ἀνάστασις,-εως⁺   N3F 0-0-1-2-2-5
Zph 3,8; Ps 65(66),1; Lam 3,63; Dnᴸˣˣ 11,20; 2 Mc 7,14
rising up, standing up Lam 3,63; *rising up, resurrection* Ps 65(66),1; *Dnᴸˣˣ 11,20 εἰς ἀνάστασιν* -לעמר/ *to resurrection* for MT מעביר *one who causes to pass through*

ἀναστατόω⁺   V 0-0-0-1-0-1
Dnᴸˣˣ 7,23
to unsettle, to upset; ncol.?

ἀναστέλλομαι   V 0-0-1-0-1-2
Na 1,5; 1 Mc 7,24
to draw back, to recoil [ἀπό τινος] Na 1,5; *to draw back from, to renounce* [τινος] 1 Mc 7,24

ἀνάστεμα,-ατος   N3N 0-0-0-0-1-1
Jdt 9,10
height, majesty; see ἀνάστημα

ἀναστενάζω⁺   V 0-0-0-1-3-4
Lam 1,4; 2 Mc 6,30; Sir 25,18; Susᵀʰ 23
to groan aloud

ἀναστεύω
(· μετ-)

ἀνάστημα,-ατος   N3N 1-1-2-0-1-5
Gn 7,23; 1 Sm 10,5; Zph 2,14; Zech 9,8; Jdt 12,8
height Zph 2,14; *erection, encampment* 1 Sm 10,5; *raising up* Jdt 12,8; πᾶν τὸ ἀνάστημα *everything that had been rising* Gn 7,23
Cf. GEHMAN 1972, 99.106; LEE 1983, 51; TOV 1984 (A), 68 (Gn 7,23)

ἀναστρατοπεδεύω   V 0-0-0-0-1-1
2 Mc 3,35
to move camp, to move one's camp; neol.?

ἀναστρέφω⁺   V 10-57-19-7-20-113
Gn 8,11; 14,7.17; 18,14; 22,5
A: *to turn upside down, to upset* [τι] Jgsᴮ 7,13; *to turn back, to return* [abs.] Gn 8,11; *to return (in conversion)* Jer 3,7; *to send away* [τινα] Jdt 1,11; P: *to dwell* Ez 3,15; *to be engaged in, to be conversant* [ἔν τινι] Wis 13,7; *to behave* Ez 22,7; *to wander in* [ἔν τινι] Jos 5,6; *Gn 49,22 ἀνάστρεψον -◊שוב *turn* for MT שור *wall*; *Ez 22,29 οὐκ ἀναστρεφόμενοι μετὰ κρίματος- עשו בלא משפט? *they do not act justly* for MT עשקו בלא משפט *they have oppressed*
Cf. LEE 1983, 82; SPICQ 1978, 85

ἀναστροφή,-ῆς⁺   N1F 0-0-0-0-2-2
Tobᴮᴬ 4,14; 2 Mc 6,23
way of life, behaviour
Cf. SPICQ 1978, 85

ἀνασύρω   V 0-0-1-0-0-1
Is 47,2
to expose, to lay bare, to uncover

ἀνασχίζω   V 0-0-1-0-2-3
Am 1,13; Tobˢ 6,4.5
to rip up

ἀνασῴζω   V 1-2-20-1-2-26
Gn 14,13; 2 Kgs 19,31; 2 Chr 30,6; Jer 26(46),6; 27(50),28
A: *to rescue* [τινα] Zech 8,7; M: *to escape (from)* [ἔκ τινος] 2 Kgs 19,31; P: *to be rescued, to be delivered (from)* Gn 14,13; *to be preserved* 3 Mc 7,20
Cf. HORSLEY 1987, 142

ἀνατείνω   V 0-0-0-0-3-3
2 Mc 15,21; 4 Mc 6,6.26
to lift up, to raise 4 Mc 6,6; *to stretch out* 2 Mc 15,21

ἀνατέλλω⁺   V 9-10-22-13-5-59
Gn 2,5; 3,18; 19,25; 32,32; Ex 22,2
to make to rise up [τι] Gn 3,18; *to cause to spring forth* [τι] Is 61,11; *to rise, to appear above*

the horizon (of the sun) Gn 32,32; *to grow* (of hair) Jgs^A 16,22; *to spring up* (of plants) Gn 2,5; *to break out* Lv 14,43; *to arise* Jb 11,17; *to appear* Sir 37,17; *Hab 2,3 καὶ ἀνατελεῖ -ויפרח and it shall spring forth* for MT ויפח *and it hastens?*

Cf. HELBING 1928, 78; →TWNT

ἀνατέμνω V 0-0-0-0-1-1
Tob^BA 6,4
to cut open

ἀνατίθημι⁺ V 2-2-2-0-3-9
Lv 27,28.29; 1 Sm 31,10; 2 Sm 6,17; Mi 4,13
A: *to set up and leave (in a place)* [τι] 1 Sm 31,10; M: *to lay upon, to communicate* [τί τινι] Mi 7,5; *to refer* [περί τινος] 2 Mc 3,9; ἀνάθεμα ἀνατίθημί τινι *to dedicate to destruction* (semit.) Lv 27,28; see ἀνάθεμα

Cf. HELBING 1928, 220

ἀνατίκτω V 0-0-0-0-1-1
4 Mc 16,13
to bring forth again; neol.

ἀνατιναγμός,-οῦ N2M 0-0-1-0-0-1
Na 2,11
shaking violently; neol.

ἀνατολή,-ῆς⁺ N1F 31-63-71-15-12-192
Gn 2,8; 10,30; 11,2; 12,8(bis)
east Nm 3,38; *morning* 2 Mc 10,28; ἀνατολαί *rising* Nm 21,11; *east* Gn 2,8; *growing, branch, sprout* (messianic title?) Jer 23,5; πρὸς ἀνατολὴν φωτός *at dayspring* Wis 16,28; κατὰ ἀνατολάς *eastward(s)* Jos 11,8; πρὸς ἀνατολάς *eastward(s)* Nm 35,5; πρὸς ἀνατολὴν φωτός *at dayspring* Wis 16,28; *Is 11,11 ἀπὸ ἡλίου ἀνατολῶν -מ/חמה *from the rising of the sun* for MT מ/חמת/from Hamath*; *Ez 8,5 πρὸς ἀνατολάς -המזרח *toward the east* for MT המזבח *the altar*

Cf. GEHMAN 1972, 99.106; HARL 1986, 64.101.148; LUST 1991(A), 98-99 (Jer 23,5)

ἀνατρέπω⁺ V 0-0-0-4-6-10
Ps 117(118),13; Prv 10,3; 21,14; Eccl 12,6; Jdt 16,11
A: *to overthrow, to ruin* [τι] Tob^S 13,14; *to throw* [τινα] Sir 12,16; *to calm* [τι] Prv 21,14; P: *to be overthrown, to be ruined* Jdt 16,11; *to be upset, to be disheartened* Ps 117(118),13; *to be diverted from* 2 Mc 5,18; *Eccl 12,6 ἀνατραπῇ -ירחק (qere) *is removed* for MT ירתק (ketib) *is bound*

ἀνατρέφομαι⁺ V 0-0-0-0-3-3
4 Mc 10,2; 11,15; Wis 7,4
to be brought up, to be educated

Cf. SPICQ 1978, 89-90

ἀνατρέχω V 0-0-0-0-3-3
Tob^S 11,9; 2 Mc 9,25; 14,43
to run (back)

ἀνατροπή,-ῆς N1F 0-0-1-0-1-2
Hab 2,15; 3 Mc 4,5
overthrow, ruin 3 Mc 4,5; *pouring out (of drink)* Hab 2,15

ἀνατροφή,-ῆς N1F 0-0-0-0-1-1
4 Mc 16,8
education, rearing

ἀνατυπόομαι V 0-0-0-0-1-1
Wis 14,17
to form an image of, to imagine [τι]; neol.

ἀναφαίνομαι⁺ V 0-0-0-5-1-6
Ct 6,5; Jb 11,18; 13,18; 24,19; 40,8
to appear, to dawn Jb 11,18; *to appear* [+pred.] Jb 13,18; *to appear* [+inf.] 4 Mc 1,4

ἀναφάλαντος,-ος,-ον A 1-0-0-0-0-1
Lv 13,41
bald on the forehead; neol.?

Cf. LEE 1983, 111

ἀναφαλάντωμα,-ατος N3N 3-0-0-0-0-3
Lv 13,42(bis).43
baldness on the forehead; neol.

Cf. HELBING 1907, 117

ἀναφέρω⁺ V 51-81-10-10-18-170
Gn 8,20; 22,2.13; 31,39; 40,10
to bring (up), to bring (back) [τι] Jgs 16,8; *to raise up* [τι] Lv 23,11; *to uphold, to take upon one, to bear* [τι] Is 53,12; *to offer* [τι] Gn 8,20; *to bear, to pay* [τι] Nm 14,33; *to bring back to, to report to* [τι πρός τινα] Ex 18,19; *to shoot forth, to produce* [τι] Gn 40,10; *to send up* [τι] Jgs 20,38; *to add to* [τι ἐπί τι] 2 Sm 1,24; *to pay (a tribute) to* [τινι] 1 Ezr 4,6; ἀναφέρω πρὸς ἐμαυτὸν λόγον *to take counsel with myself* Jb 7,13; ἀναφέρω ὀρθά *to speak the truth* Prv 8,6; ἀναφέρω θυμόν *to inflame* 1 Mc 2,24; ἀναφέρω τινὶ χάριν *to be grateful to sb* Sir 8,19; *1 Sm 20,13 ἀνοίσω -אביא? *I will bring* for MT אבי *my father*

Cf. DANIEL 1966, 240-255.258.266; SPICQ 1978, 91-93

ἀναφορά,-ᾶς N1F 1-0-0-1-0-2
Nm 4,19; Ps 50(51),21
offering Ps 50(51), 21; *office of* ἀναφορεύς Nm 4,19

Cf. CAIRD 1972, 116; DANIEL 1966, 78.79.219.269.270

ἀναφορεύς,-έως N3M 14-4-0-0-0-18
Ex 25,13.14.15.27.28

bearer, carrying-pole, stave; neol.
Cf. DANIEL 1966,79; LE BOULLUEC 1989, 256

ἀναφράσσομαι V 0-0-0-1-0-1
Neh 4,1
to be barricaded against, to be blocked up; neol.?

ἀναφύω V 2-1-1-2-0-6
Gn 41,6.23; 1 Sm 5,6; Is 34,13; Dn^LXX 7,8
A: *to produce vegetation, to grow* [abs.] Is 34,13;
P: *to grow up* Gn 41,6; *to arise, to spring up*
1 Sm 5,6
Cf. HELBING 1907, 96

ἀναφωνέω⁺ V 0-5-0-0-0-5
1 Chr 15,28; 16,4.5.42; 2 Chr 5,13
to call aloud, to shout, to lift the voice 1 Chr
16,4; *to play loudly* 1 Chr 15,28

ἀναχαίνω V 0-0-0-0-2-2
2 Mc 6,18(bis)
to open the mouth

ἀναχωρέω⁺ V 2-5-2-2-3-14
Ex 2,15; Nm 16,24; Jos 8,15; Jgs^A 4,17; 1 Sm
19,10
to depart, to withdraw [ἀπό τινος] Ex 2,15; [abs.]
1 Sm 19,10; *to flee* [ἐκ τινος] 1 Sm 25,10; *to
recoil from* [ἀπό τινος] Jer 4,29; *Prv 25,9
ἀναχώρει εἰς τὰ ὀπίσω -סור אחר‎ *retreat
backward* for MT סור אחר‎ *another's secret*
Cf. LE BOULLUEC 1989, 84-85

ἀνάψυξις,-εως⁺ N3F 1-0-0-0-0-1
Ex 8,11
relief, respite
Cf. HORSLEY 1987, 262; LE BOULLUEC 1989, 125

ἀναψυχή,-ῆς N1F 0-0-2-1-0-3
Jer 30(49),26(31); Hos 12,9; Ps 65(66),12
relief, refreshment

ἀναψύχω⁺ V 1-3-0-1-2-7
Ex 23,12; Jgs^A 15,19; 1 Sm 16,23; 2 Sm 16,14; Ps
38(39),14
to recover, to revive, to refresh [intrans.] Ex
23,12; *to breathe* [intrans.] (metaph.) 2 Mc 13,11
Cf. SPICQ 1978, 94

ἀνδραγαθέω V 0-0-0-0-4-4
1 Mc 5,61.67; 16,23; 2 Mc 2,21
*to behave in a manly, upright manner, to act
heroically;* neol.?

ἀνδραγαθία,-ας N1F 0-0-0-1-6-7
Est 10,2; 1 Mc 5,56; 8,2; 9,22; 10,15
bravery, manly virtue, heroism Est 10,2;
ἀνδραγαθίαι *manly acts* 1 Mc 5,56

ἀνδράποδον,-ου N2N 0-0-0-0-1-1
3 Mc 7,5

slave

ἀνδρεία,-ας N1F 0-0-0-12-12-24
Ps 67(68),7; Prv 21,30; Eccl 2,21; 4,4; 5,10
manliness, courage, virtue Prv 21,30; *skill* Eccl
4,4; ἐν ἀνδρείᾳ *mightily, manfully* Ps 67(68),7
Cf. MATTIOLI 1983

ἀνδρεῖος,-α,-ον A 0-0-0-1-6-7
Prv 10,4; 11,16; 12,4; 13,4; 15,19
manly, masculine, courageous 4 Mc 2,23;
courageous, virtuous, brave (also of women)
Tob^S 6,12; *bold* Prv 28,3; *strong, vigorous* Prv
10,4; *diligent* Prv 15,19

ἀνδρειόω V 0-0-0-0-1-1
4 Mc 15,23
to fill with courage; neol.?

ἀνδρείως D 0-0-0-0-1-1
2 Mc 6,27
manfully

ἀνδρίζομαι⁺ V 3-11-4-5-2-25
Dt 31,6.7.23; Jos 1,6.7
to play the man, to be valiant Dt 31,6; *to
strengthen oneself* Sir 31,25; *Jer 2,25
ἀνδριοῦμαι -◊ אישׁ‎ *I will strenghten myself* for MT
נואשׁ‎ ◊ יאשׁ‎ *it is hopeless,* see also Jer 18,12
Cf. PASSONI DELL'ACQUA 1982, 178-191

ἀνδρογύναιος,-ος,-ον A 0-0-0-1-0-1
Prv 19,15
like an effeminate man; neol.
Cf. WALTERS 1973, 122

ἀνδρόγυνος,-ου N2M 0-0-0-1-0-1
Prv 18,8
womanish man, effeminate person
Cf. WALTERS 1973, 121-122

ἀνδρολογία,-ας N1F 0-0-0-0-1-1
2 Mc 12,43
gathering or *list of soldiers;* neol.
Cf. WALTERS 1973, 41

ἀνδροφονέω V 0-0-0-0-1-1
4 Mc 9,15
to murder

ἀνδροφόνος,-ου⁺ N2M 0-0-0-0-1-1
2 Mc 9,28
murderer

ἀνδρόομαι V 0-0-0-2-0-2
Jb 27,14; 33,25
to become man, to reach manhood
(→ ἐπ-)

ἀνδρωδῶς D 0-0-0-0-2-2
1 Mc 6,31; 2 Mc 14,43
manly

ἀνεγείρω   V 0-0-0-0-1-1
Sir 49,13
to raise up again [τι]

ἀνέγκλητος,-ος,-ον⁺   A 0-0-0-0-1-1
3 Mc 5,31
blameless, without reproach, innocent

ἀνείκαστος,-ος,-ον   A 0-0-0-0-1-1
3 Mc 1,28
immense

ἀνειλέω   V 0-0-1-0-0-1
Ez 2,10
to unroll

ἄνεμι (ἀνιέναι)   V 0-0-0-0-1-1
4 Mc 4,10
to go up; fut. of ἀνέρχομαι

ἀνεκλιπής,-ής,-ές   A 0-0-0-0-2-2
Wis 7,14; 8,18
unfailing; neol.

ἀνελεημόνως   D 0-0-0-2-0-2
Jb 6,21; 30,21
without mercy, without pity

ἀνελεήμων,-ων,-ον⁺   A 0-0-0-6-5-11
Jb 19,13; Prv 5,9; 11,17; 12,10; 17,11
merciless, without mercy Prv 5,9; *Jb 19,13
ἀνελεήμονες γεγόνασιν -אכזרו (Aram.?) *they
have become merciless* for MT זרו אך *they are
wholly estranged*

ἀνέλπιστος,-ος,-ον   A 0-0-1-0-0-1
Is 18,2
unexpected, unhoped for; *Is 18,2 ἀνέλπιστον
קוה לוא קו- *unexpected, unhoped for* for MT
קו קו *line, line*?

ἀνελπίστως   D 0-0-0-0-1-1
Wis 11,7
unexpectedly

ἄνεμος,-ου⁺   N2M 4-2-22-28-11-67
Ex 10,13(bis).19; 14,21; 2 Sm 22,11
wind Ex 10,13; *cardinal point, quarter* 1 Chr
9,24; εἰς ἄνεμον *vainly, in vain* Eccl 5,15; *Jer
18,14 ἀνέμῳ -קרים? *(east)wind* for MT קרים *cold*
Cf. MORENZ 1964, 255-256

ἀνεμοφθορία,-ας   N1F 1-1-1-0-0-3
Dt 28,22; 2 Chr 6,28; Hag 2,17
blasting, blight; neol.?
Cf. BICKERMAN 1976, 183 n.41; ROBERT 1950, 63

ἀνεμόφθορος,-ος,-ον   A 5-0-2-1-0-8
Gn 41,6.7.23.24.27
blasted by the wind; neol.
Cf. HARL 1986, 273

ἀνεμπόδιστος,-ος,-ον   A 0-0-0-0-2-2

Wis 17,19; 19,7
unhindered Wis 17,19; *without impediment, easy*
Wis 19,7

ἀνεξέλεγκτος,-ος,-ον   A 0-0-0-2-0-2
Prv 10,17; 25,3
incapable of disproof or *criticism*

ἀνεξικακία,-ας   N1F 0-0-0-0-1-1
Wis 2,19
forbearance, patient endurance; neol.

ἀνεξιχνίαστος,-ος,-ον⁺   A 0-0-0-3-1-4
Jb 5,9; 9,10; 34,24; Od 12,6
unsearchable, inscrutable; neol.

ἀνεπιεικής,-ής,-ές   A 0-0-0-1-0-1
Prv 12,26
without consideration, unreasonable

ἀνεπιστρέπτως   D 0-0-0-0-1-1
3 Mc 1,20
without turning round, indifferently (metaph.);
neol.?

ἀνερευνάομαι   V 0-0-0-0-1-1
4 Mc 3,13
to search out, to examine, to investigate

ἀνέρχομαι⁺   V 0-1-0-0-0-1
1 Kgs 13,12
to depart, to return

ἄνεσις,-εως⁺   N3F 0-1-0-1-4-6
2 Chr 23,15; Ezr 4,22; 1 Ezr 4,62; Od 12,10; Sir
15,20
indulgence, licence 2 Chr 23,15; *relaxing, liberty*
1 Ezr 4,62

ἀνετάζω⁺   V 0-1-0-0-1-2
Jgs^A 6,29; Sus^Th 14
to inquire of [τινά τι] Sus^Th 14; *to examine* [abs.]
Jgs^A 6,29; neol.?
Cf. ENGEL 1985, 157

ἀνέτλην   V 0-0-0-1-0-1
Jb 19,26
to bear up against, to endure [τι] (only aor.)

ἄνευ⁺   D 3-2-9-17-17-48
Gn 41,16.44; Ex 21,11; 1 Sm 6,7; 2 Kgs 18,25
without [τινος] Gn 41,16; τινος ἄνευ *without*
3 Mc 4,5; *away from, far from* Jb 34,32

ἀνευρίσκω⁺   V 0-0-0-0-1-1
4 Mc 3,14
to discover

ἀνέφικτος,-ος,-ον   A 0-0-0-0-1-1
3 Mc 2,15
out of reach, unattainable; neol.

ἀνέχω⁺   V 1-1-7-2-5-16
Gn 45,1; 1 Kgs 12,24; Is 1,13; 42,14; 46,4

A: *to hold up, to withhold* [τι] Sir 48,3; *to cease from* [ἀπό τινος] Hag 1,10; M: *to hold oneself up, to bear up* Jb 6, 11; *to tolerate (the presence of)* [τινος] Gn 45,1; *to bear* [τι] 3 Mc 1,22; *to be content with, to abide* [τινος] Is 46,4; P: *to be held back, to be checked* 4 Mc 1,35

Cf. HARL 1986, 289-290 (Gn 45,1); HELBING 1928, 131; →TWNT

ἀνεψιός,-οῦ⁺   N2M 1-0-0-0-2-3
Nm 36,11; TobᴮᴬА 7,2; Tobˢ 9,6
cousin
Cf. SHIPP 1979, 72

ἄνηβος,-ος,-ον   A 0-0-0-0-1-1
2 Mc 5,13
young, not yet grown up; neol.?

ἀνήκεστος,-ος,-ον   A 0-0-0-1-2-3
Est 8,12e; 2 Mc 9,5; 3 Mc 3,25
irremediable, fatal, cruel

ἀνήκοος,-ος,-ον   A 1-0-2-2-0-5
Nm 17,25; Jer 5,23; 6,28; Jb 36,12; Prv 13,1
not willing to hear, disobedient

ἀνήκω⁺   V 0-2-0-0-7-9
Jos 23,14; 1 Sm 27,8; 1 Mc 10,40.42; 11,35
to belong, to appertain [abs.] 1 Mc 10,40; [τινι]
Jos 23,14; [εἴς τι] Sir prol.,10; *to be due to* [τινι]
1 Mc 11,35; *1 Sm 27,8 ἀνηκόντων -בוֹאוּ? *who come up to* for MT בֹאֲךָ *your going*
Cf. WALTERS 1973, 88 (1 Sm 27,8)

ἀνήλατος,-ος,-ον   A 0-0-0-1-0-1
Jb 41,16
not malleable, not struck with a hammer; neol.

ἀνηλεής,-ής,-ές   A 0-0-0-0-1-1
3 Mc 5,10
without pity, merciless

ἀνήνυτος,-ος,-ον   A 0-0-0-0-1-1
3 Mc 4,15
endless, never-ending, remaining incomplete;
ἀνήνυτον λαμβάνουσα τὸ τέλος *it was not brought to an end*

ἀνήρ, ἀνδρός⁺   N3M 175-940-154-332-317-1918
Gn 2,23; 3,6.16; 4,23; 12,20
man Gn 4,23; *husband* Gn 23,2; *(the) men* Jgs 20,17; *a man, any man* 1 Sm 2,25; *each* (as ἕκαστος, semit.) Jgs 8,24; ἀνὴρ ἀνήρ (semit.) *anyone* Lv 15,2; κατ' ἄνδρα *man by man* Jos 7,14; ἀνὴρ εἷς *a man* 2 Sm 18,10; ἀνὴρ γεωργός *farmer* (often ἀνήρ +subst.) Gn 49,15; *Am 7,7 ἀνὴρ -אדם *a man* for MT אֲדֹנָי *the Lord*, cpr. 1 Sm 17,32; *Ez 8,2 ἀνδρός -אִישׁ *a man* for MT אֵשׁ *fire*

Cf. GEHMAN 1972, 103; HARL 1986, 59.105-106; WALTERS 1973, 231.232; →TWNT

ἀνθαιρέομαι   V 0-0-0-1-0-1
Prv 8,10
to choose rather [τί τινος]

ἀνθέμιον,-ου   N2N 0-0-0-1-0-1
Eccl 12,6
flower
Cf. CAIRD 1972, 116; WALTERS 1973, 50-51.286

ἀνθέω   V 0-0-4-9-1-14
Is 18,5; 35,1; Ez 7,10; Hos 14,6; Ps 89(90),6
to blossom, to bloom Jb 14,2; *to flourish* (metaph.) Jb 20,21; *to flourish, to be popular* (of pers.) Ps 91(92),13; *Eccl 12,5 καὶ ἀνθήσῃ -יניץ *and he shall blossom* for MT וינאץ *and he shall contemn*
Cf. HELBING 1928, 78
(→ ἐξ-, ἐπ-)

ἄνθινος,-η,-ον   A 1-0-0-0-0-1
Ex 28,34
like flowers
Cf. LE BOULLUEC 1989, 291; WEVERS 1990, 460

ἀνθίσταμαι⁺   V 11-11-15-10-25-72
Lv 26,37; Nm 10,9; 22,23.31.34
to outweigh [τι] Sir 8,2; *to stand against, to stand in opposition to, to withstand, to resist* [abs.]
2 Sm 5,6; [τινι] Lv 26,37; [ἔναντί τινος] Sir 46,7; [κατά τινος] Dt 19,18; [κατὰ πρόσωπόν τινος] Dt 7,24; [κατενώπιόν τινος] Jos 1,5; [πρός τινα] 2 Chr 20,6; ἀνθέστηκα *to stand in opposition* Nm 22,34
Cf. HELBING 1928, 313

ἀνθίζω
(→ δι-)

ἀνθομολογέομαι⁺   V 0-0-0-3-3-6
Ps 78(79),13; Dnᴸˣˣ 4,37(34)(bis); 1 Ezr 8,88;
3 Mc 6,33
to confess freely and openly [abs.] 1 Ezr 8,88; *to admit fault* [abs.] Sir 20,3; *to give thanks to* [τινι]
Ps 78(79),13
Cf. HELBING 1928, 244-245; TOV 1990, 98.100.106-110

ἀνθομολόγησις,-εως   N3F 0-0-0-1-1-2
Ezr 3,11; Sir 17,27
thanksgiving; neol.?
Cf. TOV 1990, 99.110

ἄνθος,-ους⁺   N3N 3-0-11-7-6-27
Ex 28,14; 30,23; Nm 17,23; Is 5,24; 11,1
blossom, flower Ex 28,14; *shoot* Is 11,1; *Zph 2,2
ὡς ἄνθος -כמו ציץ *as a flower* for MT כמוץ/כ *like chaff*; *Jb 15,30 αὐτοῦ τὸ ἄνθος -פרחו *his*

blossom for MT פיו *his mouth*
Cf. LE BOULLUEC 1989, 285.311

ἀνθρακιά,-ᾶς⁺   N1F 0-0-0-0-2-2
4 Mc 9,20; Sir 11,32
burning charcoals, hot embers

ἀνθράκινος,-η,-ον   A 0-0-0-1-0-1
Est 1,7
of carbuncle; neol.?

ἄνθραξ,-ακος⁺   N3M 4-3-11-9-4-31
Gn 2,12; Ex 28,18; 36,18; Lv 16,12; 2 Sm 14,7
coal Lv 16,12; *precious stone of dark-red colour
including the carbuncle, ruby and garnet,
carbuncle* Gn 2,12

ἀνθρωπάρεσκος,-ου⁺   N2M 0-0-0-1-4-5
Ps 52(53),6; PSal 4,0.7.8.19
men-pleaser

ἀνθρώπινος,-η,-ον⁺   A 3-0-3-4-4-14
Nm 5,6; 19,16.18; Ez 4,12.15
of, from, belonging to man, human Nm 19,16;
human, suited to man Jb 10,5; *venial* (of sins)
Nm 5,6

ἄνθρωπος,-ου⁺   N2M 313-146-351-335-285-1430
Gn 1,26.27; 2,5.7(bis)
man Gn 1,26; *the men, people* (of Judah) Bar
1,15; *man* (opp. γυνή) Dt 22,29; *a man, one*
(semit.) Lv 27,28; ἄνθρωποι *mankind* Jgsᴬ 9,9;
ἄνθρωπος ἄνθρωπος *any one* (semit.) Lv 17,3;
ἄνθρωπος ἀνθρώπῳ *one man to another* Sir 25,3;
ἄνθρωποι ἀδελφοί *men, brothers* (often
ἄνθρωπος +subst.) Gn 13,8; *Nm 24,17
ἄνθρωπος corr. ἄνθος? influenced by Is 11,1?,
see also Nm 24,7; *Ez 27,16 ἀνθρώπους -אדם
men for MT ארם *Aram*; *Na 2,4 ἐξ ἀνθρώπων
-מ/אדם *from among men* for MT מאדם *dyed red*;
*Am 9,12 τῶν ἀνθρώπων -אדם *of mankind* for
MT אדום *Edom*; *Jer 17,9 ἄνθρωπος -אנוש *a man*
for MT אנש *corrupt*, see also Is 17,11; Jer 17,16;
*Dnᴸˣˣ 11,17 ἀνθρώπου -אנשים *men* for MT
הנשים/ה *the women*; *Is 25,4 ἀπὸ ἀνθρώπων
πονηρῶν -מ/זרים? *from wicked men, from
strangers* for MT מ/זרם *from the storm*; *Is 32,3
ἀνθρώποις -אדם? *men* for MT ראים *they that see*
Cf. BICKERMAN 1986, 160; HARL 1986, 59.95-96.104-105;
VERMES 1961, 59-60.159-166 (Nm 24); →NIDNTT; TWNT

ἀνθυφαιρέομαι   V 1-0-0-0-0-1
Lv 27,18
to be taken in return, to be deducted; neol.?
Cf. HARLÉ 1988, 212

ἀνίατος,-ος,-ον   A 2-0-3-3-3-11
Dt 32,24.33; Is 13,9; 14,6; Jer 8,18

incurable Dt 32,33; *irremediable* Dt 32,24;
incurable (moral sense) Lam 4,3; ἡμέρα ...
ἀνίατος *day which cannot be averted* Is 13,9;
*Jb 24,20 ἀνιάτῳ -עול *rotten* (of wood) for MT
עולה *unrighteousness*; *Jer 8,18 ἀνίατα
-מבלי נהת *incurable, without cure* for MT מבליגיתי
I suffer from desolation?

ἀνιερόω   V 0-0-0-0-2-2
1 Ezr 9,4; 3 Mc 7,20
to dedicate, to devote [τι] (as a sacrifice)

ἀνίημι⁺   V 5-11-16-4-7-43
Gn 18,24; 49,21; Ex 23,11; Dt 31,6.8
A: *to spread forth* [τι] Is 25,11; *to lift up the
voice* [abs.] Is 42,2; *to let go, to leave* [τι] 1 Sm
9,5; *to leave* [τι] Ex 23,11; *to leave, to forsake*
[τινα] Dt 31,6; *to leave unpunished* [τι] Gn
18,24; *to loosen, to unfasten* [τι] Mal 3,20; *to
loosen, to withhold* [τι] 1 Chr 21,15; *to ease*
[abs.] 2 Chr 10,9; *to forgive* [τι] Jos 24,19; *to
allow to* [τί τινι] 1 Sm 11,3; *to cease from* [τί
τινος] 1 Sm 12,23; M: *to relax* Wis 16,24; P: *to
be left to oneself* Sir 30,8; *to be ruined* Is 3,8; *to
be calmed* Jgsᴮ 8,3; *to be allowed to run wild* Gn
49,21; φλὸξ ἀνειμένη *violent flame* Is 5,24

ἀνίκητος,-ος,-ον   A 0-0-0-0-6-6
2 Mc 11,13; 3 Mc 4,21; 6,13; 4 Mc 9,18; 11,21
unconquerable 2 Mc 11,13; *unconquered* 4 Mc
11,27

ἀνίπταμαι   V 0-0-1-0-0-1
Is 16,2
to fly up, to fly away

ἀνίστημι⁺   V 81-215-74-102-67-539
Gn 4,8; 9,9; 13,17; 19,14.15
A: *to make to stand up, to raise up* [τινα] Dt
18,15; *to set up* [τι] Ex 26,30; *to build, to rear up*
[τι] Lv 26,1; *to establish* [τι] Gn 9,9; *to stand up
against, to resist* [πρός τινα] Hos 14,1; *to
confirm* [τι] 2 Chr 6,10; *to restore* [τι] Ezr 9,9; *to
re-establish* [τι] 2 Chr 23,18; M: *to stand up, to
rise* Gn 4,8; *to rise from the dead* Is 26,19; *to
stand* (up) Gn 37,7; *to stand* [+pred.] Dnᵀʰ
10,11; *to arise, to rise* (metaph.) Dnᵀʰ 11,7; *to
rise to go* Jer 30,8(49,14); ἀνίστημι χεῖρα *to set
up a monument* 1 Sm 15,12; *Jer 37(30),12
ἀνέστησα -אנש *I established* for MT אנוש
incurable; *Am 7,2 τίς ἀναστήσει מי יקים *who
shall raise up* (Jacob) for MT מי יקום *how shall
(Jacob) stand*
Cf. HARL 1986, 73.141; SHIPP 1979, 75-80; WALTERS 1973,
151; →TWNT

ἄνισχυς,-υς,-υ   A 0-0-1-0-0-1
Is 40,30
without strength; neol.

ἀνόητος,-ος,-ον⁺   A 1-0-0-4-6-11
Dt 32,31; Ps 48(49),13.21; Prv 15,21; 17,28
*not understanding, unintelligent, senseless, devoid
of understanding* Ps 48(49),13; ἀνόητος *fool* Prv
15,21; *Dt 32,31 ἀνόητοι -אוילים *fools* for MT
פלילים *judges?*

ἄνοια,-ας⁺   N1F 0-0-0-5-8-13
Ps 21(22),3; Jb 33,23; Prv 14,8; 22,15; Eccl 11,10
folly, stupidity Jb 33,23; *Ps 21(22),3 εἰς ἄνοιαν
for folly corr.? εἰς ἄνεσιν for MT רומיה *(leading)
to indulgence*

ἀνοίγω⁺   V 24-33-36-51-38-182
Gn 7,11; 8,6; 21,19; 29,31; 30,22
A: *to open* [τι] Gn 8,6; *to open, to spread out*
[τι] (of the hands) Dt 15,8; *to disclose* [τι] Jb
7,11; P: *to be open(ed)* Gn 7,11;
to be open(ed), to lie open Dnᴸˣˣ 7,10; ἀνοίγω
τὴν μήτραν *to open the womb, to make fruitful*
Gn 29,31; *Is 13,2 ἀνοίξατε -פתחו *open up* for
MT פתחי *gates*

ἀνοικοδομέω⁺   V 1-0-10-9-0-20
Dt 13,17; Jer 1,10; 18,9; 24,6; Hos 2,8
A: *to build up* [τι] (a city) Ezr 4,13; *to rebuild, to
restore* [τι] (ruins, desolate places) Mal 1,4; *to
rebuild, to restore* [τινα] (metaph.) Jer 24,6; P:
to be exalted Mal 3,15; *Mi 1,10 μὴ
ἀνοικοδομεῖτε -אל תבנו *do not rebuild* for MT
אל תבכו *do not cry*; *Dnᴸˣˣ 11,14 καὶ
ἀνοικοδομήσει -ויבנה *and he shall rebuild* for
MT ובני *and the sons*
Cf. TURNER 1977, 492-493

ἄνοικτος,-ος,-ον   A 0-0-0-0-1-1
3 Mc 4,4
pitiless, ruthless

ἀνομβρέω   V 0-0-0-0-3-3
Sir 18,29; 39,6; 50,27
to gush out, to pour forth (metaph.); neol.?

ἀνομέω   V 6-5-9-11-3-34
Ex 32,7; Nm 32,15; Dt 4,16.25; 9,12
A: *to be* ἄνομος, *to act lawlessly* Ex 32,7; *to be
corrupted by sins* Is 24,5; P: *to be considered
lawless, to be condemned* 1 Kgs 8,32
Cf. HELBING 1928, 12; LE BOULLUEC 1989, 320; WALTERS
1973, 117-118.312

ἀνόμημα,-ατος   N3N 3-3-4-2-3-15
Lv 17,16; 20,14; Dt 15,9; Jos 7,15; 24,19
transgression of the law, iniquity, wicked(ness);

neol.?
Cf. DANIEL 1966, 311.312

ἀνομία,-ας⁺   N1F 11-8-80-101-28-228
Gn 19,15; Ex 34,7(bis).9; Lv 16,21
*transgression, evil, evil conduct, iniquity,
wickedness* Gn 19,15; *Ps 49(50),21 ἀνομίαν
-הוות? *wicked(ly)* for MT היות *to be*; *Mal 3,6-7
ἀπὸ τῶν ἀδικιῶν -ל/מומי *from the transgressions*
for MT ל/מימי *from the days*; *Ez 37,23 τῶν
ἀνομιῶν αὐτῶν -משובתיהם *their transgressions*
for MT מושבתיהם *their habitations?*; *Ps
128(129),3 τὴν ἀνομίαν αὐτῶν - עון *their
iniquity* for MT מעננתם *their furrows*
Cf. COX 1990, 119-130; DANIEL 1966, 309.311.312;
DAVISON 1985, 619-623; ENGEL 1985, 89-90; ·TWNT

ἀνόμοιος,-ος,-ον   A 0-0-0-0-1-1
Wis 2,15
unlike, dissimilar

ἄνομος,-ος,-ον   A 0-4-47-27-28-106
1 Sm 24,14; 1 Kgs 8,32; 2 Chr 6,23; 24,7; Is 1,4
evil, wicked (of pers.) 1 Sm 24,14; *evil* (of
things) Jb 11,14; *Jb 34,17 ἄνομα -משפח
wickedness for MT משפט *justice*; *Is 57,3 υἱοὶ
ἄνομοι בני עון *wicked sons* for MT בני עננה *sons
of the sorceress*; *Ez 3,19 ὁ ἄνομος ἐκεῖνος
-הרשע ההוא or הוא רשע *that wicked man* for MT
הרשעה הוא *(the) bad (way), he ...*
Cf. DAVISON 1985, 619-623

ἀνόμως   D 0-0-0-0-1-1
2 Mc 8,17
wickedly

ἀνόνητος,-ος,-ον   A 0-0-0-0-3-3
4 Mc 16,7.9; Wis 3,11
unprofitable

ἀνορθόω⁺   V 0-6-3-5-2-16
2 Sm 7,13.16; 1 Chr 17,12.14.24
to set up again, to restore, to rebuild [τι] 2 Sm
7,13; *to make stand upright* [τι] Sir 27,14; *to set
up, to establish* [τι] Jer 10,12; *to set straight
again, to set right, to correct* [τινα] Ps 17(18),36;
οἱ μαστοὶ ἀνορθοῦνται *the breasts grow firm*
Ez 16,7

ἀνορύσσω   V 0-0-0-2-0-2
Jb 3,21; 39,21
to dig up, to dig for Jb 3,21; *to paw* (of animals)
Jb 39,21

ἀνόσιος,-ος,-ον   A 0-0-1-0-6-7
Ez 22,9; 2 Mc 7,34; 8,32; 3 Mc 2,2; 5,8
unholy, profane (of things) Wis 12,4; *evil* 3 Mc
5,8; *godless* 2 Mc 7,34

ἀνοσίως   D 0-0-0-1-1-2
Est 8,12g; 3 Mc 1,21
in an unholy manner

ἄνους,-ους,-ουν   A 0-0-1-2-1-4
Hos 7,11; Ps 48(49),11; Prv 13,14; 2 Mc 11,13
without understanding, senseless Ps 48(49),11;
silly Hos 7,11

ἀνοχή,-ῆς⁺   N1F 0-0-0-0-1-1
1 Mc 12,25
relief, respite, pause

ἀνταγωνίζομαι⁺   V 0-0-0-0-1-1
4 Mc 17,14
to be the opponent

ἀνταγωνιστής,-οῦ   N1M 0-0-0-0-1-1
4 Mc 3,5
opponent, antagonist

ἀνταίρω   V 0-0-1-0-0-1
Mi 4,3
to lift up against, to rise up against [ἐπί τι]

ἀντακούω   V 0-0-0-1-0-1
Jb 11,2
to listen in turn

ἀντάλλαγμα,-ατος⁺   N3N 0-1-1-4-3-9
1 Kgs 20(21),2; Jer 15,13; Ps 54(55),20;
88(89),52; Jb 28,15
that which is given or *taken in exchange, price*
1 Kgs 20(21),2; *bargain* Ru 4,7; *change* Ps
54(55),20; *Ps 88(89),52 ἀντάλλαγμα -עֵקֶב
reward for MT עקבות עֵקֶב ◊ *footsteps*
··TWNT

ἀνταλλάσσομαι   V 0-0-0-2-0-2
Jb 37,4; Prv 6,35
to give in exchange [τί τινος] Prv 6,35; *Jb 37,4
ἀνταλλάξει -יערב? *he shall exchange* for MT
יעקב *he shall restrain*
Cf. MERCATI 1943, 201-204

ἀντάμειψις,-εως   N3F 0-0-0-1-0-1
Ps 118(119),112
exchanging, requital; neol.
Cf. HELBING 1907, 113

ἀνταναιρέω   V 0-0-0-11-0-11
Ps 9(10),26(5); 45(46),10; 50(51),13; 57(58),9;
71(72),7
A: *to remove from* [τι ἀπό τινος] Ps 50(51),13;
to make an end to, to cease [τι] Ps 45(46),10; P:
to be removed, to be cancelled Ps 9(10),26(5); *to
be killed, to be destroyed* Ps 57(58),9

ἀντανακλάομαι   V 0-0-0-0-1-1
Wis 17,18
to be reflected, to be echoed (of sound)

ἀντανίσταμαι   V 0-0-0-0-1-1
Bar 3,19
to rise up against [ἀντί τινος]

ἀνταποδίδωμι⁺   V 9-13-24-21-23-90
Gn 44,4; 50,15; Lv 18,25; Dt 32,6.35
to give back, to repay, to render in return [τι] Gn
44,4; *to recompense* [τι] Lv 18,25; *to pay back, to
reward* [abs.] 2 Sm 3,39; ἀνταπόδομα
ἀνταποδίδωμί τί τινι *to repay sth to sb* Gn
50,15
Cf. CAIRD 1972, 117 (Dt 32,35)

ἀνταπόδομα,-ατος⁺   N3N 1-3-6-4-8-22
Gn 50,15; Jgsᴬ 9,16; 14,4; 2 Chr 32,25; Is 1,23
repayment, requital, recompense Gn 50,15;
reward Jgsᴬ 9,16; neol.
Cf. HARL 1986, 317

ἀνταπόδοσις,-εως⁺   N3F 0-3-6-6-0-15
Jgsᴮ 9,16; 16,28; 2 Sm 19,37; Is 34,8; 61,2
*giving back in return, rendering, requiting,
repayment, recompense* Jgsᴮ 16,28; *retribution* Is
61,2; *reward* Ps 18(19),12; *Ps 68(69),23
ἀνταπόδοσιν -◊ שָׁלוֹם *recompense* for MT שְׁלוֹמִים
those at ease?; *Ps 137(138),8 ἀνταποδώσεις
-◊ גמל *you will recompense* for MT גמר ◊ *he will
fulfill, he will finish*
Cf. CAIRD 1972, 117

ἀνταποθνῄσκω   V 1-0-0-0-0-1
Ex 22,2
to die or *to be killed in requital*
Cf. LE BOULLUEC 1989, 223-224

ἀνταποκρίνομαι⁺   V 0-1-0-2-0-3
Jgsᴬ 5,29; Jb 16,8; 32,12
to answer again; neol.

ἀνταπόκρισις,-εως   N3F 0-0-0-2-0-2
Jb 13,22; 34,36
answer; neol.

ἀνταποστέλλω   V 0-1-0-0-0-1
1 Kgs 21(20),10
to send back; neol.?

ἀνταποτίνω   V 0-1-0-0-0-1
1 Sm 24,20
to requite to, to repay to [τί τινι]
Cf. WALTERS 1973, 31

ἀντάω
(→ ἀπ-, κατ-, συν-, ὑπ-)

ἀντεῖπον⁺   V 1-1-1-5-1-9
Gn 24,50; Jos 17,14; Is 10,14; Jb 9,3; 23,13
aor. of ἀντιλέγω

ἀντερείδομαι   V 0-0-0-0-1-1
Wis 15,9

to stand firm, to resist pressure, to offer resistance [τινι]; *Wis 15,9 ἀντερείδεται *he resists* corr.? ἀντερίζεται *he rivals with*

Cf. LARCHER 1985, 867

ἀντερῶ V 1-0-0-1-1-3
Gn 44,16; Jb 20,2; Jdt 12,14
fut. of ἀντιλέγω

ἀντέχω⁺ V 1-0-9-6-4-20
Dt 32,41; Is 48,2; 56,2.4.6
A: *to hold out against, to withstand* [τινι] 4 Mc 7,4; M: *to cleave to* [τινος] Prv 4,6; *to cleave to, to worship* [τινι] Is 48,2; *to resist, to keep guard* [abs.] Neh 4,10; ἀνθέξεται κρίματος ἡ χείρ μου *my hand shall take hold of judgement* Dt 32,41

Cf. HELBING 1928, 130

ἀντηχέω V 0-0-0-0-1-1
Wis 18,10
to sound responsively, to resound

ἀντί⁺ P 78-131-94-26-62-391
Gn 2,21; 4,25; 9,6; 22,13.18
[τινος]: *in the presence of* (of pers.) Nm 32,14; *instead, in the place of* Gn 2,21; *in return for, for* Gn 29,27; ἀνθ' ὧν *because* Gn 22,18; ἀνθ' οὗ *because* Ez 39,29; ἀντὶ τούτου *therefore* 2 Sm 19,22; ἀνθ' ὧν ὅτι ἦτε *instead of being as you were* Dt 28, 62; ὁ ἀντ' αὐτοῦ *his successor* Ex 29,30

Cf. SCHREINER 1972, 171-176; SPICQ 1978, 96-99

ἀντιβάλλω⁺ V 0-0-0-0-1-1
2 Mc 11,13
to think over, to weigh up [τι πρός τινα]

Cf. SPICQ 1978, 100-101

ἀντίγραφον,-ου N2N 0-0-0-8-13-21
Est 3,13a.14; 4,8; 8,12a.13
copy (of a writing)

ἀντιγράφω V 0-0-0-0-3-3
1 Ezr 2,19; 1 Mc 8,22; 12,23
to write back, to write in reply [τι] 1 Ezr 2,19; *to copy, to transcribe* [τι] 1 Mc 8,22

ἀντιδίδωμι V 0-0-1-1-0-2
Ez 27,15; Dnᴸˣˣ 1,16
to give in return, to repay [τι] Ez 27,15; *to give for, to give instead of* [abs.] Dnᴸˣˣ 1,16

ἀντιδικέω V 0-2-0-0-0-2
Jgsᴬ 6,31; 12,2
to be an ἀντίδικος, *to dispute, to go to law* [abs.] Jgsᴬ 12,2; *to oppose* [τινα] Jgsᴬ 6,31

ἀντίδικος,-ος,-ον⁺ A 0-1-4-2-2-9
1 Sm 2,10; Is 41,11; Jer 27(50),34; 28(51),36;

Hos 5,11
opponent, adversary 1 Sm 2,10; ὁ ἀντίδικος *the opponent, the defendant* (in a lawsuit) Prv 18,17; ἡ ἀντίδικος *the adversary* Jer 28(51),36
→ TWNT

ἀντιδοξέω V 0-0-0-1-0-1
Est 4,17b
to be of a contrary opinion [τινι]; neol.?

Cf. HELBING 1928, 314

ἀντίζηλος,-ου N2M 1-0-0-0-2-3
Lv 18,18; Sir 26,6; 37,11
rival, adversary Lv 18,18; *in rivalry with, being jealous* [ἐπί τινι] (as adj.) Sir 26,6

Cf. HARLÉ 1988, 162

ἀντίθετος,-ος,-ον A 0-0-0-2-0-2
Jb 32,3; Est 3,13d
opposed, antithetic Jb 32,3; *in conflict with, inconsistent with* [τινι] Est 3,13d

ἀντικαθίζω V 0-1-0-0-0-1
2 Kgs 17,26
to place instead of, to substitute [τινα]

ἀντικαθίστημι⁺ V 1-1-0-0-0-2
Dt 31,21; Jos 5,7
A: *to raise up instead of* [τινα ἀντί τινος] Jos 5,7; M: *to stand up against, to confront* [intrans.] (as in court of justice) Dt 31,21

Cf. SPICQ 1978, 102

ἀντικαταλλάσσομαι V 0-0-0-0-2-2
3 Mc 2,32; Sir 46,12
M: *to exchange for, to pay* [τι περί τινος] 3 Mc 2,32; P: *to be transferred to* [ἐπί τινι] Sir 46,12

ἀντίκειμαι⁺ V 2-1-5-3-4-15
Ex 23,22(bis); 2 Sm 8,10; Is 41,11; 45,16
to be unfavourable, to be against [τινι] Is 51,19; *to resist, to be an adversary* [τινι] Ex 23,22

Cf. HELBING 1928, 314; LEE 1983, 82; SPICQ 1978, 102

ἀντικρίνομαι V 0-0-0-2-0-2
Jb 9,32; 11,3
to contend, to struggle against [τινι]; neol.

ἀντικρυς⁺ P 0-0-0-0-1-1
3 Mc 5,16
opposite, before [τινος]

Cf. SOLLAMO 1979, 318-319

ἀντιλαμβάνομαι⁺ V 2-8-15-15-14-54
Gn 48,17; Lv 25,35; 1 Kgs 9,9.11; 1 Chr 22,17
to lay hold of, to take hold of [τινος] Gn 48,17; *to gain* [τινος] 1 Mc 2,48; *to help, to support* [τινος] Lv 25,35; [τινι] 1 Chr 22,17; [τινα] Ez 16,49; [abs.] Is 59,16; *to take part in, to devote oneself to* [τινος] 1 Kgs 9,9, see also Mi 6,6; *Ps

106(107),17 ἀντελάβετο αὐτῶν -ם/יאיל he helped them for MT אולים fools, see also Ps 21(22),1; *Prv 11,28 ὁ δὲ ἀντιλαμβανόμενος δικαίων -ומעלה צריקים but he who helps the righteous for MT וכעלה צריקים but the righteous will flourish?; *Ps 138(139),13 ἀντελάβου μου -תסמכני you have helped me for MT תסכני you kept me hidden
Cf. HELBING 1928, 126-127; MARGOLIS 1972, 75-76; WALTERS 1973, 339-340; →TWNT

ἀντιλάμπω V-0-0-0-0-1-1
2 Mc 1,32
to reflect light, to shine back, to light up in turn

ἀντιλέγω V 0-0-4-1-4-9
Is 22,22; 50,5; 65,2; Hos 4,4; Est 8,8
to speak against, to gainsay, to contradict [τινι] Sir 4,25; to declare in opposition, to answer [τί τινι] Gn 24,50; to speak in opposition [abs.] Is 22,22

ἀντιλήμπτωρ,-ορος N3M 0-1-0-16-3-20
2 Sm 22,3; Ps 3,4; 17(18),3; 41(42),10; 45(46),8
helper, protector; neol.
Cf. MONTEVECCHI 1957, 52

ἀντίλημψις,-εως+ N 0-0-0-6-11-17
Ps 21(22),1.20; 82(83),9; 83(84),6; 88(89),19
help, aid, succour, defence 1 Ezr 8,27; hold, managing 2 Mc 11,26; *Ps 21(22),1 τῆς ἀντιλήμψεως -אֱיָלְת? of the aid for MT אֱיָלְת doe, hind; *Ps 107(108),9 ἀντίλημψις -מעון help for MT מעוז fortress
Cf. MARGOLIS 1972, 76

ἀντιλογία,-ας+ N1F 11-1-0-8-0-20
Ex 18,16; Nm 20,13; 27,14; Dt 1,12; 17,8
controversy Ex 18,16; contradiction, argument Dt 1,12; lawsuit 2 Sm 14,4
Cf. HORSLEY 1982, 78; LE BOULLUEC 1989, 196

ἀντιμαρτυρέω V 0-0-0-0-1-1
2 Mc 7,6
to witness against [κατά τινος]

ἀντίον,-ου N2N 0-3-0-0-0-3
2 Sm 21,19; 1 Chr 11,23; Chr 20,5
upper crossbeam of the loom, heddle-rod
Cf. CAIRD 1972, 117; SHIPP 1979, 83

ἀντιόομαι
(- ἐν-)

ἀντίπαλος,-ος,-ον A 0-0-0-0-2-2
2 Mc 14,17; 3 Mc 1,5
antagonist, rival, adversary

ἀντιπαραβάλλω V 0-0-0-0-1-1
Sir 23,12
to compare with [τί τινι]

ἀντιπαράγω V 0-0-0-0-1-1
1 Mc 13,20
to lead an army against, to march against [τινι]

ἀντιπαραγωγή,-ῆς N1F 0-0-0-1-0-1
Est 3,13e
opposition, hostility; neol.?

ἀντιπαρατάσσω V 0-0-0-0-1-1
1 Ezr 2,21
to stand in array against [τινι] (metaph.)

ἀντιπαρέρχομαι+ V 0-0-0-0-1-1
Wis 16,10
to come up and help against an enemy
Cf. LARCHER 1985, 906

ἀντιπίπτω+ V 3-0-0-0-0-3
Ex 26,5.17; Nm 27,14
to resist to [+inf.] Nm 27,14; to correspond [τινι] Ex 26,5; neol.?
Cf. LEE 1969, 239; WEVERS 1990, 414.421

ἀντιποιέομαι V 1-0-0-1-1-3
Lv 24,19; DnTh 4,35(32); 1 Mc 15,3
M: to lay claim to in turn, to usurp [τινος] 1 Mc 15,3; to withstand, to resist [τινι] DnTh 4,35(32); P: to be done to one in turn [τινι] Lv 24,19

ἀντιπολεμέω V 0-0-1-0-0-1
Is 41,12
to wage war against [τινα]

ἀντιπολιτεύομαι V 0-0-0-0-1-1
4 Mc 4,1
to be a political opponent [πρός τινα]

ἀντιπράττω V 0-0-0-0-1-1
2 Mc 14,29
to act against, to seek to counteract [τινι]

ἀντιπρόσωπος,-ος,-ον A 2-2-2-0-0-6
Gn 15,10; Ex 26,5; 2 Sm 10,9; 1 Chr 19,10; Ez 42,3
facing, opposite [τινι] (of things) Gn 15,10; facing (of pers.) 1 Chr 19,10; ἀντιπρόσωπον the front 2 Sm 10,9

ἀντίπτωμα,-ατος N3N 0-0-0-0-2-2
Sir 31,29; 32,20
accident, conflict, occasion or means for stumbling and falling Sir 31,29; ὁδὸς ἀντιπτώματος a way full of obstacles Sir 32,20; neol.

ἀντίρρησις,-εως N3F 0-0-0-1-0-1
Eccl 8,11
controversy, contradiction; neol.?

ἀντιρρητορεύω V 0-0-0-0-1-1
4 Mc 6,1
to speak against, to answer [τινι]; neol.

ἀντιστήριγμα,-ατος					N3N 0-0-1-1-0-2
Ez 30,6; Ps 17(18),19
support Ez 30,6; *support* (metaph.) Ps 17(18),19
ἀντιστηρίζω					V 0-0-2-1-0-3
Is 48,2; 50,10; Ps 36(37),24
M: *to lean for support upon* [ἐπί τινι] Is 48,2;
ἀντιστηρίζω χεῖρα *to offer resistance, to
withold, to support* Ps 36(37),24
ἀντιτάσσομαι⁺					V 0-2-2-4-0-8
1 Kgs 11,34(bis); Hos 1,6(bis); Prv 3,15
to oppose, to resist [τινι] Est 3,14; *Hos 1,6
ἀντιτασσόμενος ἀντιτάξομαι -נשׁא אשׂא / נשׂא or
שׂה *I shall certainly oppose* for MT נשׂא אשׂא *I
shall certainly take away* (semit.), see also 1 Kgs
11,34
Cf. CAIRD 1972, 117 (Prv 3,15)
ἀντιτίθημι					V 1-0-0-0-1-2
Lv 14,42; 4 Mc 3,16
to set against so as to contrast or *compare* [τί
τινι] 4 Mc 3,16; *to set instead of* [τι ἀντί τινος]
Lv 14,42
ἀντιφιλοσοφέω					V 0-0-0-0-1-1
4 Mc 8,15
to reason against [τινι]; neol.
ἀντιφωνέω					V 0-0-0-0-1-1
1 Mc 12,18
to answer by letter [τινι]
ἀντίψυχος,-ος,-ον					A 0-0-0-0-2-2
4 Mc 6,29; 17,21
giving one's life in recompense for another's 4 Mc
6,29; ἀντίψυχον *atonement, recompense* 4 Mc
17,21; neol.
ἀντλέω⁺					V 5-0-1-0-0-6
Gn 24,13.20; Ex 2,16.17.19
to draw water Gn 24,13
Cf. SPICQ 1982, 44
(ἀν-, ἐξ-, κατ-, περι-)
ἀντοφθαλμέω⁺					V 0-0-0-0-1-1
Wis 12,14
to look in the face, to meet face to face [τινι];
neol.
Cf. HELBING 1928, 314
ἄντρον,-ου					N2N 0-1-0-0-0-1
1 Kgs 16,18
cave or *fortified place*
Cf. CAIRD 1972, 117-118
ἀντρώδης,-ης,-ες					A 0-0-0-0-1-1
2 Mc 2,5
cave-like
ἄνυδρος,-ος,-ον⁺					A 1-0-11-10-2-24

Dt 32,10; Is 35,7; 41,19; 43,19.20
waterless, without water 2 Mc 1,19; *dry* Ps
62(63),2; (ἡ) ἄνυδρος *dry land* Jb 30,3; *desert* Ps
77(78),17
ἀνυπέρβλητος,-ος,-ον					A 0-0-0-0-1-1
Jdt 16,13
not to be surpassed, invincible
ἀνυπερθέτως					D 0-0-0-0-2-2
3 Mc 5,20.42
forthwith, without delay
ἀνυπόδετος,-ος,-ον					A 0-1-4-0-0-5
2 Sm 15,30; Is 20,2.3.4; Mi 1,8
barefoot(ed)
ἀνυπόκριτος,-ος,-ον⁺					A 0-0-0-0-2-2
Wis 5,18; 18,15
irrevocable, without hypocrisy, unfeigned
Cf. LARCHER 1984, 389-390; SPICQ 1978, 105.107; 1982,
656-657
ἀνυπομόνητος,-ος,-ον					A 1-0-0-0-0-1
Ex 18,18
unbearable Ex 18,18
ἀνυπονόητος,-ος,-ον					A 0-0-0-0-1-1
Sir 11,5
unexpected, never thought of (of pers.)
Cf. TOV 1977, 193
ἀνυπόστατος,-ος,-ον					A 0-0-0-1-3-4
Ps 123(124),5; 2 Mc 1,13; 8,5; Od 12,5
not to be withstood, irresistible 2 Mc 1,13;
overwhelming Ps 123(124),5
ἀνυψόω					V 0-1-0-5-24-30
1 Sm 2,7; Ps 112(113),7; Dnᴸˣˣ 4,22(19); 5,0.2
A: *to raise up, to lift up, to exalt* [abs.] (of God)
1 Sm 2,7; [τινα] Ps 112(113),7; *to raise up, to set
up* [τι] Ezr 4,12; *to lift up from* [ἀπό τινος] Sir
33,9; *to extol* [τι] Sir 13,23; *to increase* [τι] Sir
20,28; P: *to become tall* Dnᴸˣˣ 4,22(19);
ἀνυψόομαι ἀπὸ τοῦ οἴνου *to be inebriated, to
be in high spirits* Dnᴸˣˣ 5,0, cpr. Dnᴸˣˣ 5,2;
ἀνυψόω τὸ κέρας *to raise up the horn, to give
strength* (semit.) Sir 47,11; neol.
Cf. LUST 1993 (Dnᴸˣˣ 5,2)
ἀνύω					V 0-0-0-0-1-1
4 Mc 9,12
to achieve, to accomplish
(→ δι-)
ἄνω⁺					D 7-15-5-4-6-37
Ex 20,4; Dt 4,39; 5,8; 28,43(bis)
upward(s) (with verbs implying motion) Jgsᴮ
7,13; *above* (with verbs implying rest) Ex 20,4;
upper (as adj.) Jos 15,19; ἄνω ἄνω *very high* Dt

28,43; ἕως ἄνω *exceedingly* 2 Chr 26,8; ἀνωτέρω
upper 1 Kgs 10,22a; see ἀνώτατος and
ἀνώτερος

ἄνωθεν⁺ D 12-2-5-1-2-22
Gn 6,16; 27,39; 49,25; Ex 25,21.22
from above, from on high Gn 6,16; *above, on*
high Ex 25,21; *anew* Wis 19,6; *above* [τινος] Ex
25,22
Cf. LARCHER 1985, 1055 (Wis 19,6)

ἀνώνυμος,-ος,-ον A 0-0-0-0-1-1
Wis 14,27
not to be named or *nameless*
Cf. GILBERT 1973, 134-135

ἀνώτατος,-η,-ον A 0-0-0-0-1-1
Tob^BA 8,3
utmost; τὰ ἀνώτατα Αἰγύπτου *the south of*
Egypt

ἀνώτερος,-α,-ον⁺ A 1-0-2-2-0-5
Lv 11,21; Ez 41,7(bis); Neh 3,25.28
upper Neh 3,25; ἀνώτερόν τινος *above* (comp.
of ἄνω) Lv 11,21

ἀνωφελής,-ής,-ές⁺ A 0-0-2-1-2-5
Is 44,10; Jer 2,8; Prv 28,3; Wis 1,11; PSal 16,8
unprofitable (of things) Prv 28,3; *useless* (of
pers.) Jer 2,8

ἀξία,-ας N1F 0-0-0-0-2-2
Sir 10,28; 38,17
reputation, dignity

ἀξίνη,-ης⁺ N1F 1-4-2-1-0-8
Dt 19,5; Jgs 9,48; 1 Sm 13,20.21
axe

ἀξιόπιστος,-η,-ον A 0-0-0-2-1-3
Prv 27,6; 28,20; 2 Mc 15,11
trustworthy Prv 27,6; *worthy to be believed,*
convincing 2 Mc 15,11

ἄξιος,-α,-ον⁺ A 2-2-1-6-30-41
Gn 23,9; Dt 25,2; 1 Chr 21,22.24; Mal 2,13
worthy of [τινος] Est 7,4; *worthy, good* [abs.] (of
pers.) 2 Mc 15,21; *good, just* [abs.] (of money)
Gn 23,9; *deserved, due* [abs.] Wis 19,4; *sufficient*
for [τινος] 2 Mc 8,33; *worthy of, deserving*
[τινος] (in moral sense) Dt 25,2; [+inf.] Wis
18,4; αὐτοὶ ἄξιοι ἑαυτοῦ *worthy of himself* Wis
3,5; *Jb 11,6 ἄξια -שוה a deserved recompense
(for) for MT ישׁה he forgets
Cf. LARCHER 1983, 282 (Wis 3,5); →NIDNTT

ἀξιόω⁺ V 2-0-3-19-31-55
Gn 31,28; Nm 22,16; Is 33,7; Jer 7,16; 11,14
A: *to think* or *to deem worthy* [τινά τινος] 2 Mc
9,15; *to require, to entreat* [τινα] 1 Ezr 4,46; *to*

pray, to beseech one that [τινα +inf.] 1 Mc
11,28; [τινα ὅπως +subj.] Tob^S 10,8; [τινα
+subj.] Nm 22,16; [+inf.] Est 8,3; *to approve*
[+inf.] 4 Mc 5,17; P: *to be permitted* [+inf.] Gn
31,28; *to be thought worthy* LtJ 43; ἀξιόω
ἀξίωμα *to say a prayer, to present a petition*
Dn^LXX 6,6
Cf. HELBING 1928, 41-42; LEE 1983, 68-70 (Nm 22,16; Gn
31,27-28)
(→ κατ-, προσ-)

ἀξίωμα,-ατος N 1-0-0-8-2-11
Ex 21,22; Ps 118(119),170; Est 5,3.7; 7,2
judicial assessment Ex 21,22; *request, petition*
1 Ezr 8,4; *dignity, rank* 2 Mc 4,31
Cf. LE BOULLUEC 1989, 220; WEVERS 1990, 334

ἀξίως⁺ D 0-0-0-0-3-3
Wis 7,15; 16,1; Sir 14,11
in a manner fitting of [τινος] Wis 7,15; *fittingly*
Wis 16,1; *(as is) due* Sir 14,11

ἀξονέω
(→ ἐπ-)

ἄξων,-ονος N3M 1-0-0-3-2-6
Ex 14,25; Prv 2,9.18; 9,12; 4 Mc 9,20
axle Ex 14,25; *course, path* (metaph.) Prv 2,9
Cf. LE BOULLUEC 1989, 169

ἀοίδιμος,-ος,-ον A 0-0-0-0-1-1
4 Mc 10,1
sung of, famous in song, praiseworthy

ἀοίκητος,-ος,-ον A 1-2-1-5-2-11
Dt 13,17; Jos 8,28; 13,3; Hos 13,5; Jb 8,14
uninhabited, uninhabitable

ἄοκνος,-ος,-ον A 0-0-0-1-0-1
Prv 6,11a
without hesitation, resolute

ἀορασία,-ας N1F 2-2-0-0-2-6
Gn 19,11; Dt 28,28; 2 Kgs 6,18(bis); 2 Mc 10,30
inability to see, blindness; neol.?
Cf. HARL 1986, 180-181

ἀόρατος,-ος,-ον⁺ A 1-0-1-0-1-3
Gn 1,2; Is 45,3; 2 Mc 9,5
invisible Gn 1,2; *unseen* Is 45,3
Cf. SCHMITT 1974, 150-151 (Gn 1,2)

ἀπαγγελία,-ας N1F 0-0-0-1-0-1
Ru 2,11
report

ἀπαγγέλλω⁺ V 25-139-15-43-32-254
Gn 12,18; 14,13; 21,26; 24,28.49
to bring news, to announce, to report [τινί τι]
Gn 12,18; [abs.] Gn 14,13; *to tell of* [τι] Neh
2,18; *to report to, to relate to* [τινι] (of a speaker

or a writer) 2 Chr 34,18; *to explain, to interpret*
[τί τινι] Gn 41,8; *1 Sm 14,9 ἀπαγγείλωμεν
-הגירנו *we will tell you, we will send you word* for
MT הגיענו *we will touch you, we will come to you*
Cf.KILPATRICK 1963, 134-135

ἀπαγορεύω V 0-1-1-2-3-7
1 Kgs 11,2; Zech 11,12; Jb 9,14; 10,3; 4 Mc 1,34
A: *to forbid (to)* [τινι] 4 Mc 1,34; *to renounce, to
disown, to give up* [τι] Jb 10,3; M: *to refuse* [τι]
Zech 11,12; P: *to be forbidden* 4 Mc 1,33; *Jb
6,14 ἀπείπατο -מאס (mercy) has renounced*
(me), given (me) up for MT למס ?

ἀπάγχομαι⁺ V 0-1-0-0-3-4
2 Sm 17,23; Tob^BA 3,10; Tob^S 3,10(bis)
to hang oneself, to strangle oneself

ἀπάγω⁺ V 8-15-1-11-17-52
Gn 31,18.26; 39,22; 40,3; 42,16
to lead away, to carry off [τι] Gn 31,18; [τινα]
Gn 31,26; *to lead away, to bring back* [τινα]
1 Sm 6,7; *to lead away, to execute* [τινα] Est
1,1ο; *to carry off to prison* [τινα] Gn 39,22; *to
lead one in* [τινά τι] Prv 16,29

ἀπαγωγή,-ῆς N1F 0-0-0-0-1-1
1 Ezr 8,24
leading into captivity, imprisonment
Cf. WALTERS 1973, 129-130.316

ἀπαδικέω V 1-0-0-0-0-1
Dt 24,14
to withhold wrongfully; neol.?

ἀπαιδευσία,-ας N1F 0-0-1-0-3-4
Hos 7,16; Sir 4,25; 21,24; 23,13
lack of education Sir 21,14; *stupidity* Sir 4,25

ἀπαίδευτος,-ος,-ον⁺ A 0-0-2-7-9-18
Is 26,11; Zph 2,1; Prv 5,23; 8,5; 15,12
uncultivated, foolish, impious
Cf. LARCHER 1985, 947

ἀπαίρω⁺ V 73-11-2-2-28-116
Gn 12,9; 13,11; 26,21.22; 33,17
to remove [abs.] 1 Mc 3,57; *to bring out* [τι] (of
the wind) Ps 77(78),26; *to lead away* [τινα] Ps
77(78),52; *to march away, to depart* [abs.] Gn
12,9

ἀπαιτέω⁺ V 2-0-4-2-2-10
Dt 15,2.3; Is 3,12; 9,3; 14,4
A: *to demand back, to demand to have returned*
[τι] Sir 14,16; *to demand (back) sth of sb* [τινά
τι] Dt 15,3; P: *to be demanded sth* [τι] Wis 15,8;
*Is 30,33 ἀπαιτηθήσῃ *you will be required* corr.
ἀπατηθήσῃ for MT פתה ◊ *you shall be deceived*;
*Is 3,12 ἀπαιτοῦντες -נשים ◊נשה *exactors* for MT

נשים *women*
Cf. OTTLEY 1906, 260 (Is 30,33)

ἀπαίτησις,-εως N3F 0-0-1-2-2-5
Zph 3,5; Neh 5,10; 10,32; 2 Mc 4,28; Sir 31,31
demanding back Zph 3,5; *claim, right to demand*
Neh 5,10; *Zph 3,5 ἐν ἀπαιτήσει -נשה ◊ב/שת?
by extortion for MT בשת *shame*, cpr. Is 3,12
ἀπαιτοῦντες

ἀπαλείφω V 1-3-1-1-1-7
Gn 6,1; 2 Kgs 21,13(ter); Is 44,22
to wipe off [τι] 2 Kgs 21,13; *to wipe off, to
expunge* [τι] (metaph.) Is 44,22; *to blot out*
[τινα] (metaph.) Gn 6,7; *to wipe out* [τι]
(metaph.) 2 Kgs 21,13

ἀπαλλάσσω⁺ V 1-1-4-7-4-17
Ex 19,22; 1 Sm 14,29; Is 10,7; Jer 39(32),31; Ez
44,10
A: *to put away from, to remove from* [τι ἀπό
τινος] Jb 3,10; *to put away from, to separate* [τι
ἀπό τινος] Jb 7,15; *to part from* [ἀπό τινος] Ex
19,22; *to remove, to make away with* [τι] 1 Sm
14,29; *to get off, to depart* [intrans.] Jb 9,12; *to
remove, to change* [intrans.] Is 10,7; P: *to be set
free* or *released from* [τινος] 4 Mc 9,16; *to be
removed from* [τινος] Jb 10,19; *to be free from*
[τινος] Wis 12,2; *Is 10,7 ἀπαλλάξει corr.
ἀπολέται *to destroy*, see also 1 Sm 14,29?
Cf. HELBING 1928, 178; WALTERS 1973, 130 (Ex 19,22-24;
Is 10,7); →TWNT

ἀπαλλοτριόω⁺ V 0-1-5-3-2-11
Jos 22,25; Jer 19,4; 27(50),8; Ez 14,5.7
A: *to alienate* [τινα] Jos 22,25; *to alienate from*
[τινά τινος] Sir 11,34; *to estrange, to profane* [τι]
(of the temple) Jer 19,4; P: *to be alienated* Hos
9,10; *to be alienated from* [τινος] 3 Mc 1,3
Cf. HELBING 1928, 159; HORSLEY 1983, 62

ἀπαλλοτρίωσις,-εως N3F 0-0-1-1-0-2
Jer 13,27; Jb 31,3
estrangement Jer 13,27; *exclusion* Jb 31,3

ἀπαλός,-ή,-όν⁺ A 5-2-1-0-1-9
Gn 18,7; 27,9; 33,13; Dt 28,54.56
soft (to the touch) Wis 15,7; *tender* Gn 18,7;
delicate (of pers.) Gn 33,13

ἀπαλότης,-ητος N3F 1-0-2-0-0-3
Dt 28,56; Ez 17,4.9
softness, tenderness Dt 28,56; *tender twig* Ez 17,4;
*Ez 17,9 τῆς ἀπαλότητος -ינקת *of tender twigs*
for MT ינתק *he shall tear up*

ἀπαλύνω V 0-1-0-2-0-3
2 Kgs 22,19; Ps 54(55),22; Jb 33,25

A: *to make tender* [τι] Jb 33,25; P: *to be softened* (metaph.) 2 Kgs 22,19

ἀπαμαυρόομαι V 0-0-1-0-0-1
Is 44,18
to be deprived of sight; neol.?

ἀπαμύνομαι V 0-0-0-0-1-1
4 Mc 14,19
to keep off, to repel [τινα]

ἀπαναίνομαι V 0-0-0-2-3-5
Ps 76(77),3; Jb 5,17; Sir 4,4; 6,23; 41,4
to reject, to disown [τι] Jb 5,17; *to refuse to*
[+inf.] Ps 76(77),3

ἀπαναισχυντέω V 0-0-1-0-0-1
Jer 3,3
to behave with effrontery, to become shameless

ἀπανίσταμαι V 0-0-0-0-1-1
Wis 1,5
to depart from [ἀπό τινος]

ἀπαντάω⁺ V 3-13-3-7-23-49
Gn 28,11; 33,8; 49,1; Jgs^A 8,21; 15,12
A: *to meet, to encounter* [τινι] Gn 33,8; [ἔν τινι]
(semit.) Jgs^A 15,12; *to present oneself* [abs.] 1 Ezr
9,4; *to arrive at, to come to* [τινι] Gn 28,11; *to
meet at* [εἴς τι] 1 Mc 10,56; *to fall upon sb* [εἴς
τινα] 1 Sm 22,17; *to deal with* [τινι] 2 Mc 7,39;
to enter into, to reply [τινι] Prv 26,18; *to come
upon one, to meet* or *to happen to one* [τινι] (of
things) 1 Sm 28,10; M: *to meet, to encounter*
[τινι] Hos 13,8; *to plead with, to entreat* [τινι]
Ru 1,16
Cf. HARL 1986, 223 (Gn 28,11); HELBING 1928, 227-229;
SHIPP 1979, 85

ἀπαντή,-ῆς N1F 0-25-0-0-0-25
Jgs^A 4,22; 2 Sm 10,5; 15,32; 16,1; 19,16
meeting with [τινος] Jgs^A 4,22; [τινι] 2 Sm 15,32;
neol.

ἀπάντημα,-ατος N3N 0-1-0-1-2-4
1 Kgs 5,18; Eccl 9,11; Tob^S 6,8(bis)
meeting Tob^S 6,8; *reply* 1 Kgs 5,18; *occurrence,
chance* (literal transl. of פֶּגַע) Eccl 9,11

ἀπάντησις,-εως⁺ N3F 0-29-4-2-9-44
Jgs^A 4,18; 11,31.34; 14,5; 15,14
meeting 1 Sm 13,15; *meeting with* [τινος] Jgs^A
11,31; [τινι] 1 Sm 4,1; *reply* Est 8,12i

ἀπάνωθεν D 0-5-0-1-0-6
Jgs^B 16,20; 2 Sm 11,20.24; 20,21; 1 Kgs 1,53
from above, from the top Jb 31,2; [τινος]: *from
above, from the top* 2 Sm 11,20; *from above*
1 Kgs 1,53; *from upon* Jgs^B 16,20; *from* 2 Sm
20,21; neol.

ἅπαξ⁺ D 7-31-2-7-7-54
Gn 18,32; Ex 30,10(bis); Lv 16,34; Nm 16,21
once, once only, once for all Dt 9,13; *once in (a
year)* [τινος] Ex 30,10; τὸ ἅπαξ *for once* Jgs
15,3; τὸ ἅπαξ τοῦτο *at this moment* 2 Sm 17,7;
ἅπαξ καὶ ἅπαξ for MT כפעם *formerly, at former
times* Jgs^B 16,20; ἔτι ἅπαξ *yet once* Gn 18,32
Cf. SPICQ 1978, 110-113

ἀπαραίτητος,-ος,-ον A 0-0-0-0-2-2
Wis 16,4.16
not to be averted by prayers, inevitable

ἀπαραλλάκτως D 0-0-0-1-0-1
Est 3,13c
unchangeable; neol.?

ἀπαραπόδιστος,-ος,-ον A 0-0-0-0-1-1
3 Mc 6,28
free from interference, uninterrupted; neol.

ἀπαρασήμαντος,-ος,-ον A 0-0-0-0-1-1
2 Mc 15,36
unnoticed, without solemnity; neol.

ἀπαρέσκω V 0-0-0-0-1-1
Sir 21,15
to displease [τινι]

ἀπαρνέομαι⁺ V 0-0-1-0-0-1
Is 31,7
to renounce, to reject [τι]

ἄπαρσις,-εως N3F 1-0-0-0-0-1
Nm 33,2
setting out, departure, removal; neol.?

ἀπαρτία,-ας N1F 5-0-1-0-3-9
Ex 40,36; Nm 10,12; 31,17.18; Dt 20,14
*what is moved, baggage, household utensils,
movable goods* Ex 40,36; *spoil* Nm 31,17; *Ez
25,4 ἐν τῇ ἀπαρτίᾳ -◊טרח? with their household*
for MT טירותיהם *their encampments*
Cf. WALTERS 1973, 43.285 (Nm 10,28); WEVERS 1990, 651

ἀπαρχή,-ῆς⁺ N1F 31-7-23-7-8-76
Ex 22,28; 23,19; 25,2(bis).3
offering Ex 25,3; *the first(offering)* Dt 26,10;
portion 1 Sm 10,4; ἀπαρχαί *first-offerings* Ex
23,19; *first-fruits* Ex 22,28; *Ez 20,31 ἐν ταῖς
ἀπαρχαῖς -בראשית with the first fruits* for MT
בשאת *by placing (offerings), by offering*
Cf. LE BOULLUEC 1989, 250; PRIJS 1948, 13.16; →NIDNTT;
TWNT

ἀπάρχομαι V 0-5-0-1-0-6
2 Chr 30,24(bis); 35,7.8.9
to offer (the first-fruits of) [τι] 2 Chr 30,24; *to
offer first-fruits* [abs.] 2 Chr 35,8

ἅπας, ἅπασα, ἅπαν⁺ A 5-9-20-6-38-78

Gn 19,4; Lv 6,15; 8,27; Dt 22,19.29
(quite) all, the whole Gn 19,4; *every* 3 Mc 4,5; ἐν
ἅπασι *in all things* 1 Kgs 2,26; οὐ τὸν ἅπαντα
χρόνον *never* Dt 22,19; εἰς τὸν ἅπαντα χρόνον
for evermore 1 Mc 15,8; *Prv 25,4 ἅπαν -כל *all,
entirely* for MT כלי *vessel*

ἀπασπάζομαι⁺   V 0-0-0-0-1-1
Tobˢ 10,12
to take leave of; neol.

ἀπατάω⁺   V 2-15-10-5-8-40
Gn 3,13; Ex 22,15; Jgs 14,15; 16,5
to divert, to cheat, to deceive [τινα] Gn 3,13;
[τινά τινι] Is 36,14; *to distract* [τι] Sir 30,2; *to
seduce* [τινα] Susᴸˣˣ 56
Cf. SPICQ 1978, 116-118; →NIDNTT
(→ ἐξ-)

ἀπάτη,-ης⁺   N1F 0-0-0-0-5-5
Jdt 9,3.10.13; 16,8; 4 Mc 18,8
deceit
Cf. SPICQ 1978, 116-118

ἀπάτησις,-εως   N3F 0-0-0-0-1-1
Jdt 10,4
beguiling, allurement, charm; neol.

ἀπαύγασμα,-ατος⁺   N3N 0-0-0-0-1-1
Wis 7,26
radiance, brightness, reflection; neol.
Cf. LARCHER 1984, 502-503

ἀπαυτομολέω   V 0-0-0-1-1-2
Prv 6,11; 4 Mc 12,16
to go of one's own accord, to desert [abs.] Prv
6,11; [τινος] 4 Mc 12,17
Cf. HELBING 1928, 182

ἀπεῖδον
aor. of ἀφοράω

ἀπείθεια,-ας⁺   N1F 0-0-0-0-4-4
4 Mc 8,9.18; 12,3; PSal 17,20
disobedience

ἀπειθέω⁺   V 10-3-18-4-14-49
Ex 23,21; Lv 26,15; Nm 11,20; 14,43; Dt 1,26
to be disobedient in, to refuse compliance in [τι]
Dt 9,7; *to disobey* [τινι] Ex 23,21; [τινος] Jos
5,6; *to rebel* [abs.] Is 33,2; δίδωμι νῶτον
ἀπειθοῦντα *to stubbornly turn aside* Neh 9,29;
Is 8,11 ἀπειθοῦσιν -סור they rebelled for MT
יסרני יסר *he instructed me*; *Jer 13,25 ἀπειθεῖν
ὑμᾶς -מרר (for) your rebellion* for MT מדיך
מרה *your portion*
Cf. HELBING 1928, 204; THIBAUT 1988, 336

ἀπειθής,-ής,-ές   A 2-0-3-0-2-7
Nm 20,10; Dt 21,18; Is 30,9; Jer 5,23; Zech 7,12

disobedient Nm 20,10; *unbelieving, ungodly* Sir
16,6; *rebellious* Sir 47,21

ἀπεικάζω   V 0-0-0-0-1-1
Wis 13,13
to form, to fashion, to copy from [τί τινι]
Cf. GILBERT 1973, 83

ἀπείκασμα,-ατος   N3N 0-0-0-0-1-1
Wis 13,10
representation, likeness
Cf. GILBERT 1973, 83

ἀπειλέω⁺   V 2-0-2-0-6-10
Gn 27,42; Nm 23,19; 66,14; Na 1,4; Jdt 8,16
A: *to threaten* [τινι] Gn 27,42; P: *to be terrified
by threats* Nm 23,19
Cf. THOMAS 1939/40, 252
(→ δι-)

ἀπειλή,-ῆς⁺   N1F 0-0-4-5-14-23
Is 50,2; 54,9; Hab 3,12; Zech 9,14; Jb 23,6
anger Is 54,9; *threat, threats* Prv 13,8; ἐν ἀπειλῇ
τινι χράομαι *to threaten sb* Jb 23,6
Cf. DRESCHER 1976, 308-310

ἄπειμι (εἶναι)⁺   V 0-0-1-2-4-7
Hos 5,3; Jb 6,13; Prv 25,10; Wis 9,6; 11,11
to be far from [ἀπό τινος] Jb 6,13; *to be far
away* [abs.] Prv 25,10; *to be absent* [abs.] (of
pers.) Wis 11,11

ἄπειμι (ἰέναι)⁺   V 1-0-0-0-3-4
Ex 33,8; 2 Mc 12,1; 13,22; 4 Mc 4,8
to go away, to depart; fut. of ἀπέρχομαι
Cf. LEE 1983, 127-128

ἀπεῖπον
aor. of ἀπαγορεύω

ἀπειράγαθος,-ος,-ον   A 0-0-0-1-0-1
Est 8,12d
*unacquainted with goodness, stranger to what is
good*; neol.

ἀπείργω   V 0-0-0-0-1-1
2 Mc 12,40
to keep away from [ἀπό τινος] 2 Mc 12,40

ἄπειρος,-ος,-ον⁺   A 1-0-2-0-1-4
Nm 14,23; Jer 2,6; Zech 11,15; Wis 13,18
inexperienced, ignorant Nm 14,23; *unskillful* Zech
11,15; *untried, untrodden* Jer 2,6

ἀπεκδίδομαι   V 0-0-0-0-1-1
Tobˢ 3,8
to be given in marriage to [τινι] (of women);
neol.?

ἀπέκτασις,-εως   N3F 0-0-0-1-0-1
Jb 36,29
spreading out; neol.

ἀπελαύνω⁺ V 0-1-1-0-1-3
1 Sm 6,8; Ez 34,12; Wis 17,8
to drive away from, to expel from [τί τινος] Wis
17,8; *to drive away from* [τι ἀπό τινος] Ez 34,12

ἀπελέγχω V 0-0-0-0-2-2
2 Mc 4,33; 4 Mc 2,11
to refute, to condemn

ἀπελέκητος,-ος,-ον V 0-7-0-0-0-7
1 Kgs 6,1a(5,31).36; 7,11(48).12(49); 10,11
unhewn, unwrought; neol.?

ἀπελευθερό ομαι V 1-0-0-0-0-1
Lv 19,20
to be set free, to be emancipated

ἀπελπίζω⁺ V 0-0-1-2-4-7
Is 29,19; Est 4,17z; Jdt 9,11; 2 Mc 9,18
A: *to despair* [abs.] Sir 22,21; [τι] 2 Mc 9,18; P:
to be despaired (of pers.) Jdt 9,11; *to be
despaired of* [τινος] Is 29,19
Cf. SPICQ 1978, 119-121

ἀπέναντι⁺ or ἀπενάντιον D 34-21-13-12-18-98
Gn 3,24; 21,16(bis); 23,19; 25,9
opposite, in front Dt 32,52; *against* Sir 37,4;
[τινος]: *opposite, over against* Gn 3,24; *before*
(place) Ex 14,2; *before, in the presence of* (pers.)
Ex 30,36; ἀπενάντιόν τινος *from before* Ct 6,5
Cf. SOLLAMO 1979, 122.154-155.317-319

ἀπενεόομαι V 0-0-0-1-0-1
Dnᵀʰ 4,19(16)
to become mute

ἀπένθητος,-ος,-ον A 0-0-0-0-1-1
2 Mc 5,10
unlamented

ἀπέραντος,-ος,-ον⁺ A 0-0-0-1-1-2
Jb 36,26; 3 Mc 2,9
boundless, infinite 3 Mc 2,9; *countless, infinite* Jb
36,26
Cf. SPICQ 1978, 122

ἀπερείδομαι V 0-3-2-1-3-9
Jgsᴬ 6,37; 1 Kgs 14,28; 1 Chr 16,1; Ez 24,2; Am
5,19
to fix, to set upon [τι εἴς τι] 1 Kgs 14, 28; *to put
upon* [τι ἐπί τι] Am 5,19; *to put in* [τι ἔν τινι]
Jgsᴬ 6,37; *to direct oneself towards* [ἐπί τινα] Ez
24,2

ἀπερικάθαρτος,-ος,-ον A 1-0-0-0-0-1
Lv 19,23
unpurified, impure

ἀπερίσπαστος,-ος,-ον A 0-0-0-0-2-2
Wis 16,11; Sir 41,1
free from distractions Sir 41,1; *continually*

mindful of [τινος] Wis 16,11; neol.?
Cf. LARCHER 1985, 908-909; SPICQ 1978, 123

ἀπερίτμητος,-ος,-ον⁺ A 3-14-16-1-2-36
Gn 17,14; Ex 12,48; Lv 26,41; Jos 5,4.6
uncircumcised Gn 17,14; *uncircumcised, impure*
(metaph.) Lv 26,41; neol.
Cf. HARL 1986, 171; LEE 1983, 111.146

ἀπέρχομαι⁺ V 52-114-11-15-37-229
Gn 3,19; 14,11; 15,15; 18,33; 19,2
to go away, to depart Gn 14,11; *to go away from,
to depart from* [ἀπό τινος] Ex 4,26; [ἐκ τινος]
1 Sm 13,15; *to go away to* [πρός τινα] Gn 24,54;
to return to [εἴς τι] Gn 3,19; [κατά τινα] 1 Sm
26,11; *to depart from life* Sir 14,19; ἀπέρχομαι
ἐξ ὀφθαλμῶν τινος *to vanish before* Jgsᴬ 6,21;
ἀπέρχομαι εἰς εἰρήνην *to depart in peace* 1 Sm
20,13; *Jb 7,21 ἀπελεύσομαι -אשׁוב *I will depart
to* for MT אשׁכב *I will lay me down*
Cf. LEE 1983, 127

ἀπευθανατίζω V 0-0-0-0-1-1
2 Mc 6,28
to die well or *happily*; neol.
Cf. HELBING 1907, 123

ἀπεχθάνομαι V 0-0-0-0-1-1
3 Mc 2,30
to be hated

ἀπέχθεια,-ας N1F 0-0-0-0-1-1
3 Mc 4,1
hatred

ἀπεχθής,-ής,-ές A 0-0-0-0-2-2
2 Mc 5,23; 3 Mc 3,4
hateful, hostile 2 Mc 5,23; *hated* 3 Mc 3,4

ἀπεχθῶς D 0-0-0-0-2-2
3 Mc 5,3; Wis 19,15
hatefully Wis 19,15; ἀπεχθῶς ἔχω *to be hateful*
3 Mc 5,3

ἀπέχω⁺ D 5-2-12-12-11-42
Gn 43,23; 44,4; Nm 32,19; Dt 12,21; 18,22
A: *to be far off* [abs.] Gn 44,4; *to be far from*
[τινος] Dt 12,21; [ἀπό τινος] Ps 102(103),12;
[ἐκ τινος] Jl 1,13; *to receive in full* [τι] Gn
43,23; M: *to hold oneself off, to keep away from*
[τινος] Dt 18,22; *to hold oneself off* [ἀπό τινος]
Jb 1,8; *to abstain from* [+inf.] Prv 3,27; P: *to be
kept off* [ἀπό τινος] 1 Sm 21,5; *Jl 2,8 ἀφέξεται
-ירחקון ◊ רחק *he shall stand far from* for MT
ירחקון *he pushes*; *Mal 3,6 οὐκ ἀπέχεσθε -◊ כלא
ירחקון *you have not abstained (from)* for MT לא כליתם
◊ כלה *you are not consumed*
Cf. HELBING 1928, 179; LEE 1983, 61.62; SPICQ 1982, 46-

53

ἀπηλιώτης,-ου NlM 1-0-3-0-2-6
Ex 27,11; Jer 32(25),26; Ez 21,3.9; Jdt 7,18
east
Cf. BOGAERT 1981, 78-85; LE BOULLUEC 1989, 276-277;
WEVERS 1990, 434

ἀπήμαντος,-ος,-ον A 0-0-0-0-4-4
2 Mc 12,25; 3 Mc 6,6.8; Wis 7,22
unhurt 2 Mc 12,25; *invulnerable* or *unharming*
Wis 7,22
Cf. LARCHER 1984, 487

ἀπηνής,-ής,-ές A 0-0-0-0-2-2
Wis 17,17.18
rough, wild (of beasts) Wis 17,18; *hard* (of
sound) Wis 17,17

ἄπιος,-ου N2F 0-2-0-0-0-2
1 Chr 14,14.15
pear-tree

ἀπιστέω⁺ V 0-0-0-0-5-5
2 Mc 8,13; Wis 1,2; 10,7; 12,17; 18,13
A: *to disbelieve, to distrust* [τι] Wis 18,13; [τινι]
(of pers.) Wis 1,2; *to be incredulous* [abs.] Wis
10,7; M: *to disbelieve, to distrust* [τινι] Wis 12,17
Cf. HELBING 1928, 203; THIBAUT 1988, 76-77

ἀπιστία,-ας⁺ NlF 0-0-0-0-1-1
Wis 14,25
unfaithfulness

ἄπιστος,-ος,-ον⁺ A 0-0-2-1-0-3
Is 17,10(bis); Prv 17,6
unfaithful Prv 17,6; *Is 17,10 φύτευμα ἄπιστον
a spurious plant, weed corr.? φύτευμα πίστον
(haplogr.) -נטעי נאמנים *a cultivated plant* for MT
נטעי נעמנים *pleasant plants*

ἄπλαστος,-ος,-ον A 1-0-0-0-0-1
Gn 25,27
natural, unaffected, simple
Cf. HARL 1986, 63.209

ἄπλατος,-ος,-ον A 0-0-0-0-1-1
3 Mc 4,11
immense

ἀπληστεύομαι V 0-0-0-0-2-2
Sir 31,17; 37,29
to be insatiable [abs.] Sir 31,17; *to be insatiable
in* [ἔν τινι] Sir 37,29; neol.?

ἀπληστία,-ας NlF 0-0-0-0-2-2
Sir 37,30.31
insatiate desire, greediness

ἄπληστος,-ος,-ον A 0-0-0-4-1-5
Ps 100(101),5; Prv 23,3; 27,20; 28,25; Sir 31,20
insatiable Ps 100(101),5; *greedy* Prv 28,25

ἀπλοσύνη,-ης NlF 0-0-0-1-0-1
Jb 21,23
simplicity, frankness, sincerity; neol.
Cf. HELBING 1907, 117

ἀπλότης,-ητος⁺ N3F 0-2-0-0-5-7
2 Sm 15,11; 1 Chr 29,17; 1 Mc 2,37.60; 3 Mc
3,21
simplicity, sincerity, integrity, frankness 1 Chr
29,17; *simplicity, innocence* 2 Sm 15,11
Cf. AMSTUTZ 1968; ENGEL 1985, 133-134; HORSLEY 1989,
77; SPICQ 1978, 125-127; →TWNT

ἀπλοῦς,-ῆ,-οῦν⁺ A 0-0-0-1-0-1
Prv 11,25
simple, open, sincere
Cf. HORSLEY 1989, 77; SPICQ 1978, 125-127; →TWNT

ἀπλόω V 0-0-0-1-0-1
Jb 22,3
to make plain, to make perfect [τι]

ἀπλῶς⁺ D 0-0-0-1-2-3
Prv 10,9; 2 Mc 6,6; Wis 16,27
simply Wis 16,27; *in integrity, in sincerity* Prv
10,9; οὔτε ἀπλῶς *not at all* 2 Mc 6,6
Cf. HORSLEY 1989, 77

ἄπνους,-ους,-ουν A 0-0-0-0-1-1
Wis 15,5
without breathing, lifeless
Cf. GILBERT 1973, 193

ἀπό⁺ P 909-983-812-790-656-4150
Gn 2,2.3.7.16.17
[τινος]: *from, away from* (place) Gn 2,22; *away
from, far from* Gn 3,8; *from, of* (partitive) Gn
2,2; *from* (metaph.) Ex 1,12; *from, after* (time)
Ex 9,18; *beyond* 2 Sm 20,5; *from, by* (instr.) Lv
4,7; *from, by* (pers.) Gn 6,13; *from* (source) Gn
8,2; *from, by, because of, by reason of* Gn 9,11;
toward Gn 13,11; *before, because of* Nm 22,3; *of
a value of, worth* Est 1,7; ἀπὸ ἀνθρώπου ἔως
γυναικός *man and women* 1 Ezr 9,40; ἀπὸ
αἰῶνος *of old* Gn 6,4; ἀφ'οὗ *from the time, since*
Ex 4,10
Cf. GEHMAN 1972, 103; LE BOULLUEC 1989, 77.85-
86.87.155; SOLLAMO 42-43.89-90

ἀποβαίνω⁺ V 1-0-0-16-3-20
Ex 2,4; Jb 8,14; 9,20; 11,6; 13,5
to go away, to depart Jb 24,5; *to come to nothing*
Jb 27,18; *to issue, to happen* Ex 2,4; *to prove*
[+pred.] (of things) Jb 8,14; *to turn out, to prove
to be* [+pred.] (of pers.) Jb 9,20; *to turn into*
[εἰς τι] Jb 13,16; *to go up* (of a flame) Jb 18,5
Cf. HELBING 1928, 63-64; ORLINSKY 1937, 361-367

ἀποβάλλω⁺ V 1-0-1-1-2-5

Dt 26,5; Is 1,30; Prv 28,24; Tob^BA 11,8; Bel^LXX 17
A: *to throw away* [τι] Tob^BA 11,8; [τινα] Bel^LXX
17; *to throw away, to leave* [τι] (metaph.) Dt
26,5; *to shed, to cast* [τι] (leaves) Is 1,30; M: *to
cast off* [τινα] Prv 28,24

Cf. BEEK 1950, 197-199 (Dt 26,5)

ἀποβάπτω V 0-0-0-0-1-1

2 Mc 1,20
to draw

ἀποβιάζομαι V 0-0-0-1-0-1

Prv 22,22
to treat with violence, to rob [τινα]

Cf. HELBING 1928, 13; SPICQ 1978, 190 n.2

ἀποβλέπω⁺ V 0-1-3-3-1-8

Jgs^A 9,37; Hos 3,1; Mal 3,9(bis); Ps 9,29(10,8)
to look at, to turn attention to [ἐπί τινα] Hos
3,1; *to look upon, to watch* [εἰς τινα] Ps 9,29; *to
look away* Ct 6,1; *Mal 3,9 ἀποβλέποντες
ἀποβλέπετε you surely turn away your attention,
you surely disregard* or -◊ ראה *you surely do look
for* MT ◊ ארר *you are indeed accursed*

Cf. MURAOKA 1990, 45-46 (Mal 3,9); SPICQ 1978, 130-131

ἀπόβλημα,-ατος N3N 0-0-0-0-2-2

Wis 13,12.13
anything cast away, refuse; neol.

ἀπογαλακτίζω V 2-3-2-1-0-8

Gn 21,8(bis); 1 Sm 1,22.23(bis)
to wean from the mother's milk; neol.'?

ἀπογεύομαι V 0-0-0-0-5-5

4 Mc 4,26; 5,2.6; 6,15; 10,1
to take a taste of [τινος] 4 Mc 4,26; [abs.] 4 Mc
10,1

ἀπογινώσκω V 1-0-0-0-2-3

Dt 33,9; Jdt 9,11; 2 Mc 9,22
to give up as hopeless [τι] 2 Mc 9,22; ἀπ-
εγνωσμένοι *desperate men* Jdt 9,11

ἀπόγονος,-ου N2M 0-3-0-0-3-6

2 Sm 21,11.22; 1 Chr 20,6; Jdt 5,6; 4 Mc 18,1
offspring (mostly pl.)

ἀπογραφή,-ῆς⁺ N1F 0-0-0-1-5-6

Dn^LXX 10,21; 2 Mc 2,1; 3 Mc 2,32; 4,15.17
register, list 1 Ezr 8,30; *record* 2 Mc 2,1

ἀπογράφομαι⁺ V 0-1-0-1-4-6

Jgs^A 8,14; Prv 22,20; 3 Mc 2,29; 4,14; 6,34
M: *to register, to enroll for* [τί τινι] Prv 22,20; *to
register* [τινα] Jgs^A 8,14; P: *to be registered* 3 Mc
2,32

ἀποδείκνυμι⁺ V 0-0-0-5-7-12

Jb 33,21; Est 2,9; 3,13c; Dn^LXX 2,48; 4,37(34)

to appoint to, to assign to [τί τινι] Est 2,9; *to fix,
to prescribe* [τί τινι] Tob^S 3,8; *to prove, to
demonstrate* [τι] 4 Mc 1,8; *to appoint, to
proclaim, to create* [τινά τινα] Sus^Th 5; *to make,
to render* [τι +adj.] Jb 33,21

Cf. HELBING 1928, 59-60

ἀπόδειξις,-εως⁺ N3F 0-0-0-0-2-2

3 Mc 4,20; 4 Mc 3,19
showing forth, making known, exhibiting 4 Mc
3,19; *proof* 3 Mc 4,20

ἀποδειροτομέω V 0-0-0-0-1-1

4 Mc 15,20
to cut off the head

ἀποδεκατίζω V 0-0-0-0-1-1

Tob^S 1,7
to pay a tithe of [τι]; neol.

ἀποδεκατόω⁺ V 3-3-0-0-0-6

Gn 28,22; Dt 14,22; 26,12; 1 Sm 8,15.16
to tithe, to take a tenth of [τι] 1 Sm 8,15; *to pay
tithe of* [τι] Gn 28,22; *1 Sm 8,16 καὶ ἀπο-
δεκατώσει -ועשׂר and take the tenth for* MT ועשׂה
and make; neol.

Cf. HARL 1986, 224

ἀποδεσμεύω V 0-0-0-1-0-1

Prv 26,8
to bind [τι]

ἀπόδεσμος,-ου N2M 0-0-0-1-0-1

Ct 1,13
bundle

ἀποδέχομαι⁺ V 0-0-0-0-10-10

Tob^BA 7,16; 2 Mc 3,9.35; 4,22; 13,24
to accept [τι] 4 Mc 3,20; *to admit, to receive*
[τινα] 2 Mc 3,9; *to accept, to understand* [τι]
Tob^BA 7,16

ἀποδέω V 0-1-0-1-0-2

Jos 9,4; Prv 6,27
to bind [τι] Prv 6,27; *to patch* [τι] Jos 9,4

ἀποδιαστέλλω V 0-1-0-0-1-2

Jos 1,6; 2 Mc 6,5
A: *to divide* [τί τινι] Jos 1,6; P: *to be set apart,
to be forbidden* 2 Mc 6,5; neol.?

ἀποδιδράσκω V 10-13-2-4-8-37

Gn 16,6.8; 27,43; 28,2; 31,21
to run away Gn 27,43; *to run away from, to
escape from, to flee from* [ἀπό τινος] Gn 16,6; *to
flee away* (metaph.) Is 35,10

Cf. HELBING 1928, 32-33

ἀποδίδωμι⁺ V 75-33-19-41-52-220

Gn 20,7(bis).14; 25,31.33
A: *to give back, to restore, to return* [τινί τι] Gn

20,7; *to pay* [τι] Nm 5,7; *to recompense, to repay* [τι] Ex 20,5; *to render, to yield* [τι] Lv 26,4; *to render, to make* [τινα +pred.] Jb 22,25; *to deliver* [τί τινι] 1 Ezr 8,64; *to give as* [τινά τι] (sth due) Nm 8,13; M: *to sell* [τινα] Gn 37,27; ἀποδίδωμι λόγον *to render an account* 2 Chr 34,16; *Ps 54(55),21 ἐν τῷ ἀποδιδόναι -◊שַׁלֵּם *for retribution* for MT בִּשְׁלֹמֵי ◊שָׁלֵם *against those who are at peace with him, against his friends?*
Cf. HELBING 1928, 192; →NIDNTT

ἀποδιώκω   V 0-0-0-1-0-1
Lam 3,43
to chase away

ἀποδοκιμάζω⁺   V 0-0-7-1-2-10
Jer 6,30(bis); 7,29; 8,9; 14,19
to reject as unworthy or *unfit*

ἀπόδομα,-ατος   N3N 5-0-0-0-0-5
Nm 8,11.13.16.19.21
gift, offering; neol.

ἀπόδοσις,-εως   N3F 1-0-0-0-1-2
Dt 24,13; Sir 29,5
giving back, restitution, return

ἀποδοχεῖον,-ου   N2N 0-0-0-0-3-3
Sir 1,17; 39,17; 50,3
corr. ἀποδόχιον *storehouse, granary* Sir 1,17; *cistern* Sir 39,17; neol.?
Cf. WALTERS 1973, 47

ἀποδύρομαι   V 0-0-0-0-1-1
3 Mc 4,12
to lament bitterly [τι]

ἀποθαυμάζω   V 0-0-0-1-3-4
Dnᴸˣˣ 4,19(16); Sir 11,13; 40,7; 47,17
to marvel at [τινα] Sir 47,17; [ἐπί τινι] Sir 11,13; [εἴς τι] Sir 40,7; *to be astonished* Dnᴸˣˣ 4,19(16)

ἀποθερίζω   V 0-0-1-0-0-1
Hos 6,5
to cut off, to mow down [τινα] (metaph.)

ἀποθήκη,-ης⁺   N1F 4-5-2-0-1-12
Ex 16,23.32; Dt 28,5.17; 1 Chr 28,11
any place wherein to lay up a thing, store-room, barn Dt 28,5; *storage, store* Ex 16,23; *coffer, treasure* 1 Ezr 1,51
Cf. HUSSON 1983, 41; WEVERS 1990, 255

ἀποθησαυρίζω⁺   V 0-0-0-0-1-1
Sir 3,4
to store, to hoard up

ἀποθλίβω⁺   V 1-0-0-0-0-1
Nm 22,25
to press against, to crush [τι πρός τι]

ἀποθνήσκω⁺   V 182-208-65-28-117-600
Gn 2,17; 3,3.4; 5,5.8
to die Gn 2,17; *Jb 9,29 ἀπέθανον -◊גוע גוע *I have died* for MT אִינַע ◊יגע *I have laboured*; *Prv 24,9 ἀποθνῄσκει δέ -ומת *(the fool) also dies* for MT זמה ◊זמה *the divising of*
Cf. WALTERS 1973, 127.315.336

ἀποικεσία,-ας   N1F 0-3-0-4-1-8
2 Kgs 19,25; 24,15; 25,27; Ezr 6,16.19
captivity, exile 2 Kgs 24,15; *2 Kgs 19,25 ἀποικεσιῶν -◊נגלה *Jews in exile* for MT נלים *stone heaps*; neol.
Cf. WALTERS 1973, 277 (2 Kgs 19,25)

ἀποικία,-ας   N1F 0-1-17-9-4-31
Jgsᴮ 18,30; Jer 13,19; 30,19(49,3); 31(48),7; 35(28),4
colony Wis 12,7; *captivity, exile* Jer 36(29),1; *place of captivity* Ezr 1,11
Cf. LARCHER 1985, 712

ἀποικίζω   V 0-15-10-5-3-33
1 Sm 4,22; 2 Kgs 15,29; 16,9; 17,6.11
A: *to carry away, to send into exile* [τινα] 2 Kgs 15,29; P: *to be removed (far away)* 1 Sm 4,22

ἀποικισμός,-οῦ   N2M 0-0-4-0-2-6
Jer 26(46),19; 31(48),11; 50(43),11(bis); Bar 2,30
removal, captivity, exile

ἀποίχομαι   V 3-0-1-0-2-6
Gn 14,12; 26,31; 28,6; Hos 11,2; Jdt 6,13
to be gone away from [ἀπό τινος] Gn 26,31; *to be gone away, to have departed* [abs.] Gn 14,12
Cf. LEE 1983, 128

ἀποκαθαίρω   V 0-0-0-3-1-4
Jb 7,9; 9,30; Prv 15,27a(16,6); Tobˢ 12,9
A: *to cleanse, to purge* [τι] Tobˢ 12,9; M: *to clean oneself* Jb 9,30; P: *to be cleared away* Jb 7,9

ἀποκαθαρίζω   V 0-0-0-1-1-2
Jb 25,4; Tobᴮᴬ 12,9
to cleanse, to purge [τι] Tobᴮᴬ 12,9; *to purify from* [τινά τινος] Jb 25,4; neol.

ἀποκάθημαι   V 2-0-4-1-1-8
Lv 15,33; 20,18; Is 30,22; 64,5; Ez 22,10
to sit apart, to be removed, to be indisposed (of women in menstruation)
Cf. HARLÉ 1988, 150

ἀποκαθίστημι⁺   V 10-1-15-8-15-49
Gn 23,16; 29,3; 40,13.21; 41,13
to reestablish, to restore [τινα] Gn 40,13; *to return to* [τινί τι] Ps 15(16),5; *to bring back* [τινα] Jdt 6,7; *to pay* [τι] Gn 23,16; *to set again*

[τι] Gn 29,3; P: *to be brought back* 1 Ezr 1,29; ἀποκατέστην *to be restored* Lv 13,16; *to return* Ex 14,26; *1 Ezr 1,33 ἀπεκατέστησεν corr. ἀπέστησεν? -יסירהו *he removed, he dethroned*
→TWNT

ἀποκαίω V 0-0-0-0-1-1
4 Mc 15,20
to burn off

ἀποκακέω V 0-0-1-0-0-1
Jer 15,9
to sink under a weight of misery, to succumb to misfortune; neol.

ἀποκάλυμμα,-ατος N3N 0-1-0-0-0-1
Jgs^B 5,2
revelation; neol.

ἀποκαλύπτω⁺ V 35-18-24-22-12-111
Gn 8,13; Ex 20,26; Lv 18,6.7(bis)
A: *to uncover* [τι] Ex 20,26; *to uncover, to open* [τι] Gn 8,13; *to disclose, to reveal* [τι] Jos 2,20; *to reveal (mysteries)* [τι] Dn 2,29; P: *to be uncovered* 2 Sm 6,20; *to reveal oneself* 1 Sm 2,27; *to appear* Ct 4,1; ἔλεγχοι ἀποκεκαλυμμένοι *open reproofs* Prv 27,5; ἀποκαλύπτω τὸ ὠτίον *to uncover the ear, to inform* 1 Sm 9,15
Cf. BARR 1961, 230.256; GEHMAN 1972, 103; SPICQ 1982, 364-365; NIDNTT

ἀποκάλυψις,-εως⁺ N3F 0-1-0-0-3-4
1 Sm 20,30; Od 13,32; Sir 11,27; 22,22
uncovering 1 Sm 20,30; *discovering* Sir 11,27; *revelation* Sir 22,22
Cf. BARR 1961, 230.256; BICKERMAN 1976, 183 n.41; SPICQ 1982, 364-365

ἀπόκειμαι⁺ V 1-0-0-1-2-4
Gn 49,10; Jb 38,23; 2 Mc 12,45; 4 Mc 8,11
to be put away in store Gn 49,10; *to be reserved for* 2 Mc 12,45

ἀποκενόω V 0-1-0-0-2-3
Jgs^B 3,24; Sir 13,5.7
to exhaust [τινα] (metaph.) Sir 13,5; ἀποκενόω τοὺς πόδας *to relieve oneself* Jgs^B 3,24

ἀποκεντέω V 1-2-2-0-0-5
Nm 25,8; 1 Sm 31,4(bis); Ez 21,16; Zph 1,10
to pierce through Nm 25,8; *Zph 1,10 ἀποκεντοῦντων -הרנים *of the piercing* or *of the slaying* for MT הרנים *of the fishes*

ἀποκέντησις,-εως N3F 0-0-1-0-0-1
Hos 9,13
piercing

ἀποκεφαλίζω⁺ V 0-0-0-0-1-1
Ps 151,7

to behead [τινα]

ἀποκιδαρόω V 2-0-0-0-0-2
Lv 10,6; 21,10
to take the κίδαρις *(turban, tiara) off*; neol.
Cf. HELBING 1907, 124.128; LEE 1983, 52

ἀποκλαίομαι V 0-0-2-1-0-3
Jer 31(48),32; 38(31),15; Prv 26,24
to weep aloud Prv 26,24; *to bewail, to mourn for* Jer 38(31),15

ἀπόκλεισμα,-ατος N3N 0-0-1-0-0-1
Jer 36(29),26
guard-house, jail; neol.

ἀποκλείω⁺ V 1-23-2-3-10-39
Gn 19,10; Jgs^A 3,22.23.24; 9,51
to shut off from or *out of* [τινα ἔκ τινος] 1 Mc 5,47; *to shut out, to exclude* [τινα] Jgs^A 20,48; *to shut (up), to close* [τι] Gn 19,10; *to close in upon* [τι] Jgs 3,22; *to shut up, to deliver up* [τινα εἴς τι] 1 Sm 17,46
Cf. GEHMAN 1972, 107

ἀποκλίνω V 0-1-0-0-1-2
2 Sm 6,10; 1 Mc 5,35
to turn aside [τι] 2 Sm 6,10; [intrans.] 1 Mc 5,35

ἀποκλύζω V 0-1-0-0-0-1
2 Chr 4,6
to wash, to rinse

ἀποκνίζω V 2-2-2-0-1-7
Lv 1,15; 5,8; 1 Sm 9,24; 2 Kgs 6,6; Ez 17,4
to nip off, to snip off 2 Kgs 6,6; *to prune* 4 Mc 1,29; *to wring off* Lv 1,15

ἀποκομίζω V 0-0-0-1-1-2
Prv 26,16; 2 Mc 2,15
to bring back

ἀποκόπτω⁺ V 2-6-0-1-0-9
Dt 23,2; 25,12; Jgs^A 1,6.7; 5,22
to cut off, to hew Dt 25,12; ἀποκεκομμένος *eunuch* Dt 23,2
→TWNT

ἀποκοσμέω V 0-0-0-0-1-1
2 Mc 4,38
to remove from the world, to kill [τινα]

ἀπόκρημνος,-ος,-ον A 0-0-0-0-1-1
2 Mc 13,5
sheer, steep

ἀποκρίνομαι⁺ V 37-105-45-63-27-277
Gn 18,9.27; 23,5.10.14
to give answer, to reply Gn 18,9; *Sus^Lxx 48 ἀπεκρίνατε *you answered* corr. ἀπεκτείνατε *you decided to pronounce the death penalty*; *Zph 2,3 καὶ ἀποκρίνεσθε αὐτά -וענוה ◊ ענה׳

and answer it for MT ענה (-ι) / ענה‖ *(seek)*
humility; *1 Sm 12,3 ἀποκρίθητε -ענו / ענה‖
answer for MT עיני *my eyes*; *Lam 3,33 ἀπεκρίθη
-ענהᴵ *he answers* for MT ענה‖ *he afflicts*, see also
Ps 101(102),24; *Ps 87(88),1 ἀποκριθῆναι - ענה‖
to respond for MT / ענהᴵᴵᴵ *to sing*

Cf. ENGEL 1985, 118 (Sus 48); HELBING 1928, 221; LE
BOULLUEC 1989, 203.215; MOULTON 1910, 299-300;
THACKERAY 1909, 239

ἀπόκρισις,-εως⁺   N3F 1-0-0-9-3-13
Dt 1,22; Jb 15,2; 31,14; 32,4.5
decision, answer Ezr 7,12; *answer, report* Dt 1,22

ἀποκρυβή,-ῆς   N1F 0-0-0-1-0-1
Jb 24,15
concealment, covering; neol.

ἀποκρύπτω⁺   V 0-1-4-3-10-18
2 Kgs 4,27; Is 26,20; 40,27; Jer 39(32),17; Zph
3,5
A: *to hide* [τι] Sir 20,31; *to hide from, to keep
hidden from* [τι ἀπό τινος] 2 Kgs 4,27; [τί τινι]
Wis 6,22; M: *to hide* [τι] Wis 7,13; P: *to be
hidden* Zph 3,5; *to be hidden from* [τι] Ps
18(19),7; [ἀπό τινος] Is 40,27; *to hide oneself*
Prv 27,12; *Jer 39(32),17 ἀποκρυβῇ - כלא is
hidden for MT יפלא *is too difficult*, cpr. Jer
39(32),27

Cf. HELBING 1928, 42-43; WALTERS 1973, 262; ∕NIDNTT;
TWNT

ἀποκρυφή,-ῆς   N1F 0-1-1-1-0-3
2 Sm 22,12; Ps 17(18),12; Jb 22,14
hiding-place; neol.

ἀπόκρυφος,-ος,-ον⁺   A 1-0-2-10-12-25
Dt 27,15; Is 4,6; 45,3; Ps 9,29.30(10,8.9)
hidden, concealed Jb 39,28; *secret* Ps 9,29(10,8);
little known, obscure, hard to understand Sir
39,3; *hidden to* [τινι] Sir 42,9; ἐν ἀποκρύφῳ *in
secret* Dt 27,15; ἀπόκρυφον *hiding-place* Is 4,6
∕TWNT

ἀποκτείνω⁺   V 56-79-20-30-58-243
Gn 4,8.14.15.23.25
to kill, to slay [τινα] Gn 4,8; *to destroy* [τι]
(metaph.) Lam 2,4; *Ez 7,16 ἀποκτενῶ
-אמית / מות *I will slay* for MT המות / המה *moaning*

Cf. BOGAERT 1986, 36 (Ez 7,16); ENGEL 1985, 118

ἀποκυέω⁺   V 0-0-0-0-1-1
4 Mc 15,17
to bring forth [τι]

Cf. SPICQ 1978, 134-136

ἀποκυλίω⁺   V 3-0-0-0-1-4
Gn 29,8.10.3; Jdt 13,9

to roll away; neol.

Cf. HARL 1986, 224-225

ἀποκωλύω   V 0-7-0-1-3-11
1 Sm 6,10; 25,7.15.33.34
to keep off from [τι ἀπό τινος] 1 Kgs 21,7; *to
prevent from doing* [+inf.] 1 Sm 25,34; *to keep
off, to hinder* [τινα] 1 Sm 25,7; *to shut up* [τινα]
1 Sm 6,10

Cf. HELBING 1928, 160

ἀποκωφόομαι   V 0-0-3-0-0-3
Ez 3,26; 24,27; Mi 7,16
to become deaf; neol.

ἀπολακτίζομαι   V 1-0-0-0-1-2
Dt 32,15; Od 2,15
to be kicked

ἀπολαμβάνω⁺   V 1-0-1-0-4-6
Nm 34,14; Is 5,17; 2 Mc 4,46; 6,21; 8,6
to take, to regain [τι] (of places) 2 Mc 8,6; *to
receive* [τι] Nm 34,14; *to take aside* [τινα] 2 Mc
4,46; *Is 5,17 ἀπειλημμένων *of those that are
taken away* corr. ἀπηλειμμένων? (ἀπαλείφω)
-/ מחה *of those that were wiped out, destroyed* for
MT מחים *the fat ones*, cpr. Is 44,24

Cf. MARGOLIS 1972, 76; SEELIGMANN 1948, 11 (Is 5,17)

ἀπόλαυσις,-εως⁺   N3F 0-0-0-0-1-1
3 Mc 7,16
pleasure

Cf. SPICQ 1978, 137

ἀπολαύω   V 0-0-0-1-4-5
Prv 7,18; 4 Mc 5,9; 8,5; 16,18; Wis 2,6
to enjoy [τινος]

ἀπολέγομαι   V 0-0-1-0-0-1
Jon 4,8
to renounce, to give up [τι]

ἀπολείπω⁺   V 3-7-1-5-12-28
Gn 6,7; Ex 5,19; 12,10; Lv 22,30; Jgsᴬ 9,5
A: *to leave over of, to leave behind of* [ἀπό
τινος] Ex 12,10; *to desert, to abandon* [τινα] Jb
11,20; *to forsake* [τι] Sir 17,25; *to fail to
accomplish, to leave undone* [τι] Ex 5,19; *to
cease* [τινος] 2 Chr 16,5; *to leave off doing*
[+ptc.] 3 Mc 1,12; M: *to cease to* [+inf.] Prv
19,27; P: *to be left behind, to stay behind* Jgsᴬ
9,5; *to be deprived of* [τινος] 3 Mc 3,18

Cf. SPICQ 1978, 139; WEVERS 1990, 69

ἀπολεπίζω   V 0-0-0-0-2-2
Tobˢ 11,8.12
to peel [τι] Tobˢ 11,8; [abs.] Tobˢ 11,12

ἀπολήγω   V 0-0-0-1-0-1
Dnᴸˣˣ 5,26

to cease, to desist [abs.]
Cf. HELBING 1928, 170

ἀπολιθόομαι   V 1-0-0-0-1-2
Ex 15,16; Od 1,16
to become petrified
Cf. LE BOULLUEC 1989, 175-176

ἀπόλλυμι⁺   V 60-17-108-97-96-378
Gn 18,24.28(bis).29.30
A: *to destroy utterly, to kill* [τινα] Gn 18,24; *to
destroy* [τι] Gn 18,28; *to lose, to destroy*
(counsel) Dt 32,28; M: *to perish, to die* Ex 30,38;
to perish (metaph.) Ps 1,6; *to be destroyed* Ex
10,7; *to fail* Ps 141(142), 5; *to be lost* 1 Sm 9,3;
*Jb 5,15 ἀπόλοιντο -יגוע *let perish* for MT ישע *he
saves;* *Is 46,12 οἱ ἀπολωλεκότες τὴν καρδίαν
-אבירי לב- *the ones who lost their heart, the
senseless ones* for MT עבירי לב *the stubborn of
heart;* *Ez 26,2 ἀπόλωλε -דלות-? ◊ דלל *(is
humble?) is lost* for MT דלת ◊ דלות *the gates;*
*Prv 11,23 ἀπολεῖται -עברה- *passes away* for MT
עברה *anger;* *Est 9,2 ἀπώλοντο -שברו-? *they
perished* for MT שברו *they hoped*
Cf. DRIVER 1940, 174 (Prv 11,23); WALTERS 1973,
62.130.289

ἀπόλλω   V 0-0-0-0-1-1
4 Mc 6,14
late form of ἀπόλλυμι; *to destroy, to kill* [τινα];
neol.

ἀπολογέομαι⁺   V 0-0-2-0-1-3
Jer 12,1; 38(31),6; 2 Mc 13,26
to speak in defense, to plead [abs.] 2 Mc 13,26;
to defend oneself before [πρός τινα] Jer 12,1

ἀπολόγημα,-ατος   N3N 0-0-1-0-0-1
Jer 20,12
plea alleged in defense

ἀπολογία,-ας⁺   N1F 0-0-0-0-1-1
Wis 6,10
defense, reply

ἀπόλοιπον,-ου   N2N 0-0-10-0-0-10
Ez 41,9.11(bis).12.13
space left free, open space; neol.?

ἀπολούομαι⁺   V 0-0-0-1-0-1
Jb 9,30
to wash oneself

ἀπόλυσις,-εως   N3F 0-0-0-0-2-2
3 Mc 6,37.40
release, deliverance

ἀπολυτρόω   V 1-0-1-0-0-2
Ex 21,8; Zph 3,1
to release on payment of ransom

ἀπολύτρωσις,-εως⁺   N3F 0-0-0-1-0-1
Dnᴸˣˣ 4,34(31)
recovery, release, redemption
Cf. SPICQ 1982, 435

ἀπολύω⁺   V 3-0-0-1-31-35
Gn 15,2; Ex 33,11; Nm 20,29; Ps 33(34),1; 1 Ezr
9,36
A: *to acquit from* [τινος] 3 Mc 7,7; *to let go* [τι]
Sir 27,19; *to remove* [τι] Tobˢ 3,17; *to dismiss*
[τινα] 1 Ezr 9,36; *to discharge from* [τινά τινος]
2 Mc 4,47; M: *to return to* [εἰς τι] Ex 33,11; *to
depart, to die* Gn 15,2; P: *to be set free, to be
delivered* 1 Mc 10,43; *to be set free from, to be
delivered out of* [τινος] 2 Mc 6,22; (out of the
earth) [ἀπό τινος] Tob 3,13
Cf. HELBING 1928, 181

ἀπομαίνομαι   V 0-0-0-1-0-1
DnᴸˣˣΧ 12,4
to go mad; neol.

ἀπομαρτυρέω   V 0-0-0-0-1-1
2 Mc 12,30
to testify

ἀπομάσσομαι⁺   V 0-0-0-0-1-1
Tobˢ 7,16
to wipe off oneself [τι]

ἀπομάχομαι   V 0-0-0-0-1-1
2 Mc 12,27
to resist

ἀπομέμφομαι   V 0-0-0-1-0-1
Jb 33,27
to rebuke, to blame [τινι]; *Jb 33,27
ἀπομέμφεται -◊ יסר *he shall blame* for MT ישר
◊ שיר *he shall sing?* or שור *he shall repeat?*
Cf. HELBING 1928, 21

ἀπομερίζω   V 0-0-0-1-1-2
DnᴸˣˣΧ 11,39; 2 Mc 15,2
to divide DnᴸˣˣΧ 11,39; ἀπομερίζω δόξαν *to give
honour* 2 Mc 15,2

ἀπόμοιρα,-ας   N1F 0-0-1-0-0-1
Ez 45,20
portion; neol.?

ἀπονέμω⁺   V 1-0-0-0-2-3
Dt 4,19; 3 Mc 1,7; 3,16
to impart to, to assign to [τί τινι]

ἀπονίπτω⁺   V 0-1-0-2-0-3
1 Kgs 22,38; Prv 30,12.20
A: *to wash off* 1 Kgs 22,38; *to wash clean* (metaph.) Prv 30,12; M: *to wash oneself* Prv 30,20

ἀπονοέομαι   V 0-0-0-0-2-2
1 Ezr 4,26; 2 Mc 13,23

to have lost all sense

ἀπόνοια,-ας   N1F 0-0-0-0-3-3
2 Mc 6,29; 4 Mc 12,3; Sir 22,13
madness

ἄπονος,-ος,-ον   A 0-0-0-0-1-1
4 Mc 11,26
painless

ἀποξαίνω   V 0-0-0-0-1-1
4 Mc 6,6
to tear, to strip off; neol.

ἀποξενόω   V 0-0-0-1-1-2
Prv 27,8; 2 Mc 5,9
A: *to banish from* [τινος] 2 Mc 5,9; P: *to be far from home, to be a fugitive* Prv 27,8
Cf. CAIRD 1972, 118 (1 Kgs^A 14,5); HELBING 1928, 181

ἀποξηραίνω   V 0-3-1-1-0-5
Jos 4,23(bis); 5,1; Jon 4,7; Ps 36(37),2
A: *to dry up* Jos 4,23; P: *to wither (away)* Ps 36(37),2

ἀποξύω   V 3-0-0-0-0-3
Lv 14,41.42.43
to scrape (off)

ἀποπαρθενόω   V 0-0-0-0-1-1
Sir 20,4
to deflower, to violate [τινα]; neol.

ἀποπειράομαι   V 0-0-0-1-0-1
Prv 16,29
to make trial of [τινος]
Cf. KORN 1937, 7-8

ἀποπεμπτόω   V 2-0-0-0-0-2
Gn 41,34; 47,26
to give a fifth part of; neol.

ἀποπηδάω   V 0-0-3-1-0-4
Hos 7,13; Na 3,7; Ez 19,3; Prv 9,18a
to leap off Ezr 19,3; *to turn away from* [ἀπό τινος] Hos 7,13; *to hurry off* Prv 9,18a

ἀποπιάζω   V 0-1-0-0-0-1
Jgs^A 6,38
to squeeze tight; neol.?

ἀποπίπτω⁺   V 2-0-0-6-2-10
Lv 19,9; 23,22; Ps 5,11; 7,5; 36(37),2
to fall off [abs.] Lv 19,9; *to fall off from* [ἀπό τινος] Jb 24,24; *to miss, to fail* [abs.] Jb 29,24; [τινος] Jdt 11,6

ἀποπλανάω⁺   V 0-1-1-1-4-7
2 Chr 21,11; Jer 27(50),6; Prv 7,21; 2 Mc 2,2; Sir 4,19
A: *to lead astray* 2 Chr 21,11; P: *to go wrong, to wander from the truth* Sir 4,19

ἀποπλάνησις,-εως   N3F 1-0-0-0-1-2

Dt 29,18; Sir 34,11
wandering, error
Cf. HARL 1991, 253-254

ἀποπλύνω   V 0-0-3-0-0-3
Jer 2,22; 4,14; Ez 16,9
to wash away [abs.] Jer 2,22; [τι] Ez 16,9; *to cleanse from* [τι ἀπό τινος] Jer 4,14

ἀποπνέω   V 0-0-0-0-1-1
4 Mc 15,18
to expire, to die

ἀποπνίγω⁺   V 0-0-1-0-1-2
Na 2,13; Tob^BA 3,8
to choke, to throttle, to strangle

ἀποποιέομαι   V 0-0-0-6-0-6
Jb 8,20; 14,15; 15,4; 19,18; 36,5
to reject from oneself [τι] Jb 8,20; *to cast off from oneself* [τι] Jb 15,4; neol.?

ἀποπομπαῖος,-α,-ον   A 2-0-0-0-0-2
Lv 16,8.10
carrying away (evil) (of the scapegoat); *Lv 16,8 τῷ ἀποπομπαίῳ -◊ אזל *to the one who carries away* for MT לעזאזל/ *to Azazel*, see also Lv 16,10; neol.
Cf. HARLÉ 1988, 151-152

ἀποπομπή,-ῆς   N1F 1-0-0-0-0-1
Lv 16,10
sending away, elimination; neol.?
Cf. HARLÉ 1988, 153

ἀποπρατίζομαι   V 0-0-0-0-1-1
Tob^BA 1,7
to sell; neol.

ἀποπτύω   V 0-0-0-0-1-1
4 Mc 3,18
to abhor, to spurn

ἀπόπτωμα,-ατος   N3N 0-2-0-0-0-2
Jgs^B 20,6.10
error; neol.?

ἀπορΥίζομαι   V 0-0-0-0-1-1
2 Mc 5,17
to be angry; neol.

ἀπορέω⁺   V 2-0-5-1-6-14
Gn 32,8; Lv 25,47; Is 8,23; 24,19; 51,20
A: *to be at a loss how to* [+inf.] Wis 11,17; *to be at a loss for, to be in want for* [τινος] Prv 31,11; *to be in want, to be poor* [abs.] Wis 11,5; M/P: *to be at a loss, to be in doubt, to be puzzled* Gn 32,8; (metaph.) Is 24,19
Cf. HELBING 1928, 171

ἀπορία,-ας⁺   N1F 2-0-4-1-4-11
Lv 26,16; Dt 28,22; Is 5,30; 8,22; 24,19

embarassment, perplexity Lv 26,16; *distress, discomfort* Dt 28,22

ἀπορρέω   V 0-1-0-2-2-5
JgsᴬA 6,38; Ps 1,3; Jb 37,1; 1 Mc 9,7; 4 Mc 10,8
to flow from [κατά τινος] 4 Mc 10,8; *to drop from* [ἔκ τινος] Jgsᴬ 6,38; *to fall off* Ps 1,3; *to slip away, to decamp* 1 Mc 9,7; *to move from* [ἔκ τινος] Jb 37,1

ἀπορρήγνυμι   V 1-0-0-2-1-4
Lv 13,56; Jb 39,4; Eccl 4,12; 4 Mc 9,25
A: *to break forth, to break away* Jb 39,4; *to tear off* [τι] Lv 13,56; P: *to be broken* Eccl 4,12;
ἀπορρήγνυμι τὴν ψυχήν *to expire* 4 Mc 9,25

ἀπόρρητος,-ος,-ον   A 0-0-0-0-1-1
Sir 13,22
not to be spoken, forbidden

ἀπορρίπτω⁺   V 1-7-27-5-6-46
Ex 22,30; Jgs 2,19; 2 Sm 22,46; 1 Kgs 9,7
A: *to throw away, to put away* [τι] Ex 22,30; *to reject* [τι] Jer 9,18; *to abandon* [τι] Jgs 2,19; P: *to be cast (forth), to be cast out* 2 Sm 22,46; *Jer 8,14 ἀπέρριψεν ἡμᾶς - הרמנו ◊ רום *he cast us out* for MT הרמנו ◊ רמם *he doomed us, he made us perish,* see also Jer 28(51),6

ἀπόρροια,-ας   N1F 0-0-0-0-1-1
Wis 7,25
effluence, emanation
Cf. LARCHER 1983, 498-500

ἀπορρώξ,-ῶγος   N3F/M 0-0-0-0-2-2
2 Mc 14,45; 4 Mc 14,16
cliff, precipice

ἀποσάττω   V 1-0-0-0-0-1
Gn 24,32
to unsaddle, to unpack
Cf. HARL 1986, 64.201

ἀποσβέννυμι   V 0-0-1-1-2-4
Is 10,18; Prv 31,18; Sir 3,30; 43,21
A: *to extinguish, to quench* [τι] Sir 3,30; *to wither* [τι] Sir 43,21; P: *to be extinguished* Prv 31,18; *Is 10,18 ἀποσβεσθήσεται - יכבה ◊ כבה *shall be vanished, shall be consumed* for MT וכבוד/כבור *and the glory*

ἀποσείομαι   V 0-0-1-0-0-1
Is 33,15
to shake off; τὰς χεῖρας ἀποσειόμενος ἀπὸ δώρων *keeping one's hands from holding bribes* Is 33,11

ἀποσιωπάω   V 0-0-1-0-0-1
Jer 45(38),27
to cease speaking and be silent

ἀποσκαρίζω   V 0-1-0-0-0-1
Jgsᴬ 4,21
to struggle, to be convulsed

ἀποσκεδάννυμι   V 0-0-0-0-1-1
4 Mc 5,11
to scatter abroad, to disperse

ἀποσκευάζω   V 1-0-0-0-0-1
Lv 14,36
to remove furniture, to strip of furniture

ἀποσκευή,-ῆς   N1F 18-6-0-2-6-32
Gn 14,12; 15,14; 31,18; 34,29; 43,8
baggage, household Nm 16,27; (including pers. as well as inanimate objects) Gn 14,12; *a man's wife, children and other members of the household* Ex 10,24; *all persons apart from the full-grown men* or *apart from the men fit for military service* Ex 12,37; *impedimenta* Jdt 7,2
Cf. HARL 1986, 64; KIESLING 1927, 240-247; LE BOULLUEC 1989, 39; LEE 1983, 101-107

ἀποσκηνόω   V 1-0-0-0-1-2
Gn 13,18; PSal 7,1
to remove one's tent, to decamp
Cf. HARL 1986, 64

ἀποσκληρύνω   V 0-0-0-1-0-1
Jb 39,16
to deal cruelly with [τινα]

ἀποσκοπεύω   V 0-0-1-2-2-5
Hab 2,1; Lam 4,17(bis); Jdt 10,10; PSal 3,5
to look at [εἴς τι] Lam 4,17; *to keep watch, to look out for* [τινα] Jdt 10,10; neol.

ἀποσκοπέω   V 0-1-0-0-0-1
1 Chr 12,30
see ἀποσκοπεύω

ἀποσκορακίζω   V 0-0-1-1-1-3
Is 17,13; Ps 26(27),9; 1 Mc 11,55
to wish far away, to curse, to damn [τινα] Ps 26(27),9; *to discharge, to dismiss* [τινα] 1 Mc 11,55; neol.

ἀποσκορακισμός,-οῦ   N2M 0-0-1-0-0-1
Is 66,15
abjuration, renunciation, repudiation; neol.
Cf. CAIRD 1972, 118

ἀποσκυθίζω   V 0-0-0-0-1-1
4 Mc 10,7
to scalp

ἀποσοβέω   V 1-0-1-0-1-3
Dt 28,26; Jer 7,33; Sir 22,20
to scare away

ἀπόσπασμα,-ατος   N3N 0-0-1-1-0-2
Jer 26(46),20; Lam 4,7

a piece, that which is torn off Lam 4,7; *Jer 26(46),20 ἀπόσπασμα -◊ קרע *avulsion, destruction* for MT קרץ *biting* or *stinging insect*

Cf. ALBREKTSON 1963, 182

ἀποσπάω⁺   V 1-2-2-1-3-9

Lv 22,24; Jos 8,6; Jgs^B 16,9; Is 28,9; Jer 12,14
A: *to draw away from* [τι ἀπό τινος] Jos 8,6; *to detach, to break* [τι] Jgs^B 16,9; P: *to be dragged away, to be separated* Jb 41,9; ἀπεσπασμένος *cut, mutilated, eunuch* Lv 22,24

ἀποστάζω   V 0-0-0-4-0-4

Ct 4,11; Prv 5,3; 10,31.32
to fall drop by drop, to distil [τι] (metaph.) Prv 10,31; *to trickle* [intrans.] Prv 5,3

ἀπασταλάζω   V 0-0-2-0-0-2

Jl 4,18; Am 9,13
to drop, to let fall drop by drop [τι]; neol.

ἀποστασία,-ας⁺   N1F 0-2-1-0-1-4

Jos 22,22; 2 Chr 29,19; Jer 2,19; 1 Mc 2,15
revolt 1 Mc 2,15; *apostasy* Jos 22,22

··TWNT

ἀποστάσιον,-ου⁺   N2N 2-0-2-0-0-4

Dt 24,1.3; Is 50,1; Jer 3,8
abandonment; βιβλίον ἀποστασίου *a certificate of divorce*

ἀπόστασις,-εως   N3F 0-2-0-1-1-4

2 Chr 28,19; 33,19; Ezr 4,19; 1 Ezr 2,21
defection, revolt

ἀποστατέω   V 0-0-0-3-3-6

Ps 118(119),118; Neh 2,19; 6,6; 1 Mc 11,14; 13,16
to fall away from, to depart from [ἀπό τινος] Ps 118(119),118; *to revolt against* [ἐπί τινα] Neh 2,19

ἀποστάτης,-ου   N1M 1-2-1-3-4-11

Nm 14,9; Jos 22,16.19; Is 30,1; Jb 26,13
rebel 1 Ezr 2,17; *apostate* Nm 14,9; neol.?

ἀποστάτις,-ιδος   N3F 0-0-0-2-2-4

Ezr 4,12.15; 1 Ezr 2,14.17
rebel (fem. of ἀποστάτης); neol.

ἀποστέλλω⁺   V 94-283-97-64-153-691

Gn 8,7.8; 19,13; 20,2; 21,14
to send off, to send away [τινα] Gn 19,13; [τι] Ex 4,28; *to send off* or *away from* [ἀπό τινος] Gn 26,27; *to put forth* [τι] Jb 2,5; *to diffuse* [τι] 3 Mc 5,11; *Is 14,12 ὁ ἀποστέλλων -שׁולח *he who sends* for MT חולש *he who oppresses*; *Prv 26,13 ἀποστελλόμενος -שלוח *being sent* for MT שׁחל *young lion*; *Is 33,7 ἀποσταλήσονται -שלחו *they shall be sent* for MT שׁלום *of peace*

Cf. LEE 1983, 93-94; ··TWNT (with a discussion of ἀπόστολος in ms A in 1 Kgs 14,6)

ἀποστενόομαι   V 0-0-0-1-0-1

Est 5,1b
to be shrunken, to be anguished

ἀποστέργω   V 1-0-0-0-0-1

Dt 15,7
to empty of love, to harden

ἀποστερέω⁺   V 1-0-1-0-6-8

Ex 21,10; Mal 3,5; 4 Mc 8,23; Sir 4,1; 29,6
A: *to rob one of, to defraud one of* [τινά τινος] Sir 29,6; *to rob, to hold back* [τι] Ex 21,10; *to keep back* [τι] (of wages) Mal 3,5; P: *to be deprived of, to be robbed of* [τινος] Sir 29,7

Cf. HELBING 1928, 45

ἀποστολή,-ῆς⁺   N1F 1-1-1-3-5-11

Dt 22,7; 1 Kgs 5(9),14(16); Jer 39(32),36; Ps 77(78),49; Ct 4,13
sending away, sending off Dt 22,7; *shoot* Ct 4,13; *discharge* Eccl 8,8; *parting gift, reward* 1 Mc 2,18; *gift* 1 Ezr 9,51; *message* Ps 77(78),49; *exile, plague sent by the Lord* Jer 39(32),36, see also Bar 2,25

Cf. GEHMAN 1972, 107; PRIJS 1948, 39; TOV 1981, 67-68

ἀπόστρεβλόομαι   V 0-0-0-0-1-1

2 Mc 9,7
to be horribly tortured; neol.

ἀποστρέφω⁺   V 68-105-157-74-53-457

Gn 3,19; 14,16(bis); 15,16; 16,9
A: *to turn back, to bring back* [τι] Gn 14,16; *to turn away, to avert* [τι] Ex 3,6; *to turn away from* [τι ἀπό τινος] Ex 23,25 ; *to return* [intrans.] Gn 3,19; *to depart from* [ἀπό τινος] Ex 32,15; M: *to reject* [τι] 3 Mc 3,23; *to turn away from* [τινα] Am 1,3; [ἀπό τινος] Nm 32,15; *to return* Gn 15,16; ἀποστρέφω τὴν ἀποστροφήν (semit. for Hebr. שׁבית / שׁבות שׁוב) *to change the fortune* Ez 16,53; ἀποστρέφω ἀποστροφῇ (semit. for Hebr. אסתיר הסתר) *I will surely avert* Dt 31,18; *1 Kgs 13,11 καὶ ἐπέστρεψαν τὸ πρόσωπον -פנם ויסרו? *and they turned the face* for MT ויספרום *and they told them*; *1 Chr 4,22 ἀπέστρεψεν -ישׁיב *he changed* for MT ישׁבי ?; *Dn^LXX 11,26 ἀποστρέψουσιν αὐτόν -ישׁבוהו *they shall bring him back* for MT ישׁברוהו *they brake him*

Cf. HELBING 1928, 35; HOLLADAY 1958, 20-33; WALTERS 1973, 107-108; →TWNT

ἀποστροφή,-ῆς   N1F 4-1-10-0-4-19

Gn 3,16; 4,7; Dt 22,1; 31,18; 1 Sm 7,17
turning back Dt 22,1; *turning away from* Sir

18,24; *return* 1 Sm 7,17; *aversion, faithlessness*
Jer 5,6; *fortune?, captivity?* Ez 16,53; *Jer 6,19
ἀποστροφῆς αὐτῶν -משבותם *of their faithlessness*
for MT חשבותם/מ *of their (evil) thoughts*, see also
Jer 18,12; *Gn 3,16 ἡ ἀποστροφή σου -תשובך
your inclination for MT תשוקתך *your urge?*, see
also Gn 4,7; see ἀποστρέφω

Cf. HOLLADAY 1958, 20-33

ἀποστύφω   V 0-0-0-0-1-1
Tobˢ 11,8
to draw up, to contract

ἀποσυνάγω   V 0-4-0-0-0-4
2 Kgs 5,3.6.7.11
to recover from, to cure [τινα ἀπό τινος] 2 Kgs
5,3; *to recover, to cure* [τι] 2 Kgs 5,11; neol.

ἀποσυρίζω   V 0-0-1-0-0-1
Is 30,14
to whistle aloud; *Is 30,14 ἀποσυριεῖς corr.
ἀποσύρεις for MT חשף◊ *you shall draw, you
shall skim* (water)

ἀποσύρω   V 0-0-0-0-1-1
4 Mc 9,28
to tear away; see ἀποσυρίζω

ἀποσφάζω   V 0-0-0-0-1-1
4 Mc 2,19
to kill, to cut the throat of [τινα]

ἀποσφενδονάομαι   V 0-0-0-0-1-1
4 Mc 16,21
to be slung, to be cast; neol.?

ἀποσφράγισμα,-ατος   N3N 0-0-2-0-0-2
Jer 22,24; Ez 28,12
seal, signet, signet ring; neol.?

ἀποσχίζομαι   V 2-1-0-0-0-3
Nm 16,21.26; 2 Chr 26,21
to separate oneself from [ἔκ τινος] Nm 16,21;
[ἀπό τινος] Nm 16,26; *to be cut off* [ἀπό τινος]
2 Chr 26,21

ἀποτάσσω⁺   V 0-0-1-1-5-7
Jer 20,2; Eccl 2,20; 1 Ezr 6,26; 1 Mc 4,61; 6,50
A: *to detach* [τι] (a military garrison) 1 Mc 4,61;
M: *to renounce to, to give up* [τινι] Eccl 2,20; P:
to be detached, to be appointed 1 Ezr 6,26; *Jer
20,2 οἴκου ἀποτεταγμένου -בית מני *of the house
set apart* for MT בנימן *of Benjamin*

ἀποτείνω   V 1-0-0-0-0-1
Ex 8,24
to prolong, to continue with [+inf.]

ἀποτελέω⁺   V 0-0-0-0-1-1
2 Mc 15,39
to produce, to render

ἀποτέμνω   V 0-1-1-0-3-5
Jgsᴬ 5,26; Jer 43(36),23; 2 Mc 15,30; 4 Mc
15,20; Sir 25,26
to cut off [τι] Jer 43(36),23; *to decapitate* [τινα]
Jgsᴬ 5,26

ἀποτηγανίζω   V 0-0-1-0-0-1
Jer 36(29),22
to broil, to cook, to fry

ἀποτίθημι⁺   V 8-2-1-0-5-16
Ex 16,33.34; Lv 16,23; 24,12; Nm 15,34
A: *to put away* [τι] Lv 16,23; *to put aside* [τι] Ex
16,33; M: *to put, to keep (in prison)* [τινα] Lv
24,12; *to put off* [τι] (of a garment) 2 Mc 8,35;
*Jl 1,18 τί ἀποθήσομεν ἑαυτοῖς -מה נניחה בהם
נחה◊ *what shall we put aside for ourselves?* for
MT מה נאנחה בהמה◊ אנח *how the beasts groan*
(lit. *how are groaning the beasts*)

ἀποτίκτομαι   V 0-0-0-0-2-2
4 Mc 13,21; 14,16
to be born

ἀποτίναγμα,-ατος   N2N 0-1-0-0-0-1
Jgsᴬ 16,9
tow, cord; neol.

Cf. WALTERS 1973, 296

ἀποτινάσσω⁺   V 0-2-0-1-0-3
Jgsᴬ 16,20; 1 Sm 10,2; Lam 2,7
A: *to shake off, to cast off* [τι] Lam 2,7; M: *to
shake oneself* Jgsᴬ 16,20; ἀποτετίνακται τὸ
ῥῆμα τῶν ὄνων *he has got rid of the matter of
the asses* 1 Sm 10,2

ἀποτιννύω   V 1-0-0-1-1-3
Gn 31,39; Ps 68(69),5; Sir 20,12
to pay for [τι]; neol.

Cf. WALTERS 1973, 31

ἀποτίνω⁺   V 19-4-2-5-1-31
Ex 21,19.34.36.37; 22,3
to repay [τι ἀντί τινος] Ex 21,36; *to compensate,
to pay the damages* [τι] Ex 21,19; *to make
compensation* [abs.] Ex 22,5; *to pay* [τι] 2 Kgs
4,7; *to resolve* [τι] 2 Sm 15,7; *to exact repayment
from sb for sth* [παρά τινός τι] Jb 34,33;
ἀποτίνω ἀργύριον *to pay compensation* Ex
22,16

Cf. BICKERMAN 1976, 195.219-220; LE BOULLUEC 1989,
219.224-225; WEVERS 1990, 332.340.343.348

ἀποτομή,-ῆς   N1F 0-1-0-0-0-1
Jgsᴬ 5,26
instrument for cutting

ἀπότομος,-ος,-ον⁺   A 0-0-0-0-5-5
Wis 5,20; 6,5; 11,10; 12,9; 18,15

severe, relentless (of pers.) Wis 11,10; *severe* Wis
5,20; *sharp* Wis 6,6
Cf. LARCHER 1984, 391

ἀποτόμως⁺ D 0-0-0-0-1-1
Wis 5,22
severely, cruelly

ἀποτρέπω⁺ V 0-0-0-0-3-3
3 Mc 1,23; 4 Mc 16,12; Sir 20,29
to turn away, to turn back [τινα] 3 Mc 1,23; *to
turn away, to avert* [τι] Sir 20,29

ἀποτρέχω V 10-7-3-2-8-30
Gn 12,19; 24,51; 32,10; Ex 3,21; 10,24
to run off, to run away Ex 3,21; *to go free* Lv
25,41; *to depart* Gn 12,19; ἀποτρέχω τὴν ὁδόν
to go the way (of) (metaph.) Jos 23,14; πρὸς τὸ
ἀποτρέχειν ἐκ τοῦ ζῆν εἰμι *I am ready to
depart out of this life* Tobᴮᴬ 14,3
Cf. HARLÉ 1988, 202; LEE 1983, 86.125-128

ἀποτρίβω V 0-1-2-0-0-3
Jgsᴬ 5,26; Hos 8,5; Mi 7,11
A: *to rub off, to skin, to scalp* [τι] Jgsᴬ 5,26; M:
to reject [τι] (metaph.) Mi 7,11

ἀποτροπιάζομαι V 0-0-1-0-0-1
Ez 16,21
to avert evil by [ἔν τινι] (semit.); neol.?

ἀποτρυγάω V 0-0-1-0-0-1
Am 6,1
to pluck grapes or *fruit;* *Am 6,1 ἀπετρύγησαν
they have gathered or *plucked* (metaph.) corr.?
ἀπετρύπησαν for MT בקר they have pierced;
neol.?

ἀποτυγχάνω V 0-0-0-1-0-1
Jb 31,16
to miss, to notice the absence of [τι]

ἀποτυμπανίζω V 0-0-0-1-1-2
Dnᴸˣˣ 7,11; 3 Mc 3,27
to kill in a cruel way
Cf. OWEN 1929, 259-266

ἀποτυφλόω V 0-0-0-0-3-3
Tobˢ 2,10; Wis 2,21; Sir 20,29
A: *to make blind* [τινα] (metaph.) Wis 2,22; P:
to be blinded Tobˢ 2,10

ἀποτύφλωσις,-εως V 0-0-1-0-0-1
Zech 12,4
making blind, blindness; neol.

ἀποφαίνομαι V 0-0-0-2-2-4
Jb 27,5; 32,2; 2 Mc 6,23; 15,4
A: *to declare* [τινα +pred.] Jb 27,5; M: *to
declare* [abs.] 2 Mc 15,4; *to prove* [+ptc.] 2 Mc
6,22

ἀποφέρω⁺ V 2-2-6-12-12-34
Lv 20,19; Nm 17,11; 2 Sm 13,13; 2 Chr 36,7; Is
57,13
A: *to carry off, to carry away* [τι] Nm 17,11; *to
bring to as required* [τί τινι] 1 Ezr 1,13; *to bring*
[τι] Ezr 5,5; *to bear* [τι] Ez 32,30; M: *to carry
with one, to bear* [τι] Lv 20,19; *to carry away* [τι]
Jb 3,6

ἀποφεύγω⁺ V 0-0-0-0-1-1
Sir 22,22
to escape [abs.]

ἀποφθέγγομαι V 0-1-4-1-0-6
1 Chr 25,1; Ez 13,9.19; Mi 5,11; Zech 10,2
to utter, to speak, to prophesy Ps 58(59),8;
ἀποφθεγγόμενοι *soothsayers* Mi 5,11, see also
1 Chr 25,1; neol.?

ἀπόφθεγμα,-ατος V 1-0-1-0-1-3
Dt 32,2; Ez 13,19; Od 2,2
saying, prophecy Ez 13,19; *hymn* Dt 32,2

ἀποφράσσω V 0-0-0-1-1-2
Lam 3,8; 1 Mc 9,55
to block up, to stop up

ἀποφυσάω V 0-0-1-0-0-1
Hos 13,3
to blow away

ἀποχέω V 0-1-0-1-0-2
2 Kgs 4,4; Lam 4,21
to pour out

ἀποχύννω V 0-1-0-0-0-1
1 Kgs 22,35
later form of ἀποχέω; *to shed*

ἀποχωρέω⁺ V 0-0-1-0-2-3
Jer 26(46),5; 2 Mc 4,33; 3 Mc 2,33
to retire, to retreat Jer 26(46),5; *to withdraw* 2
Mc 4,33; *to dissent from* [ἐκ τινος] 3 Mc 2,33

ἀποχώρησις,-εως V 0-1-0-0-0-1
Jgsᴬ 3,24
privy
Cf. HUSSON 1983, 42-43

ἀποχωρίζω⁺ V 0-0-1-0-0-1
Ez 43,21
to separate

ἀποψύχω V 0-0-0-0-1-1
4 Mc 15,18
to expire, to die

ἄπρακτος,-ος,-ον Λ 0-0-0-0-3-3
Jdt 11,11; 2 Mc 12,18; 3 Mc 2,22
unsuccessful Jdt 11,11; *powerless* 3 Mc 2,22; *not
done, left undone* 2 Mc 12,18

ἀπρεπής,-ής,-ές Λ 0-0-0-0-1-1

4 Mc 6,17
unbecoming

ἀπρονοήτως D 0-0-0-0-1-1
3 Mc 1,14
thoughtlessly

ἀπρόπτωτος,-ος,-ον A 0-0-0-0-1-1
3 Mc 3,14
not precipitate; ἀπροπτώτῳ συμμαχίᾳ *by the help not lightly given*

ἀπροσδεής,-ής,-ές A 0-0-0-0-3-3
1 Mc 12,9; 2 Mc 14,35; 3 Mc 2,9
not in need of, without want of [τινος]; neol.

ἀπροσδόκητος,-ος,-ον A 0-0-0-0-4-4
3 Mc 3,8; 4,2; 5,33; Wis 17,14
unexpected, unlooked for

ἀπροσδοκήτως D 0-0-0-0-2-2
2 Mc 8,6; 12,37
without being noticed

ἀπρόσκοπος,-ος,-ον⁺ A 0-0-0-0-2-2
3 Mc 3,8; Sir 32,21
unobserved 3 Mc 3,8; *unexplored* Sir 32(35),21; neol.

ἄπταιστος,-ος,-ον⁺ A 0-0-0-0-1-1
3 Mc 6,39
intact

ἀπτόητος,-ος,-ον A 0-0-1-0-0-1
Jer 27(50),2
undaunted; *Jer 27(50),2 ἡ ἀπτόητος *the fearless one* corr.? ἡ πτοητός for MT חת ◊ חתת *the scared one*; neol.

ἅπτομαι⁺ V 52-20-18-31-11-132
Gn 3,3; 20,4.6; 26,11; 32,26
to grasp, to touch [τινος] Gn 3,3; [ἀπό τινος] Lv 5,3; [τι] Lv 15,10; *to reach* [τινος] Jb 20,6; *to attack, to take hold of* [τινα] 2 Sm 5,8; *to touch, to affect* [τινος] Jgs^ 20,41
Cf. HELBING 1928, 123-125; WALTERS 1973, 308 (Jb 6,7)
(→ ἐφ-, περι-, συν-)

ἅπτω⁺ V 0-0-0-0-2-2
Jdt 13,13; Tobˢ 8,13
to kindle, to set on fire
(→ ἀν-, ἀφ-, ἐξ-, ὑφ-)

ἄπυρος,-ος,-ον A 0-0-1-0-0-1
Is 13,12
unsmelted, natural (of gold)

ἀπωθέομαι⁺ V 0-7-27-31-8-73
Jgs^ 6,13; 1 Sm 12,22; 2 Kgs 4,27; 17,20; 21,14
M: *to thrust away, to push back* [τινα] 2 Kgs 4,27; *to repel, to drive back* [τινα] Jgs^ 6,13; *to reject* [τι] 2 Kgs 21,14; *to remove* [τι] Mi 2,6; P:

to be expelled, to be rejected Ps 87(88),6; *Ez 5,11 ἀπώσομαι -אגרע? *I will cut (you) off, I will reject you* for MT אגרע *I will diminish (you), I will shave (you)*; *Mi 4,7 τὴν ἀπωσμένην -◊הלאה? *the removed, expelled* for MT הנהלאה?; *Ez 19,5 ἀπῶσται -◊הלאה? *to be driven away* for MT נוחלה?

ἀπώλεια,-ας⁺ N1F 11-1-31-36-43-122
Ex 22,8; Lv 5,22.23; Nm 20,3; Dt 4,26
destruction, annihilation Nm 20,3; *loss* Ex 22,8; *thing lost* Lv 5,22(6,3); *Prv 13,1 ἐν ἀπωλείᾳ *for destruction, will be destroyed* corr.? ἐν ἀπειλῇ for MT נערה *threat, reproof*, cpr. Prv 13,8; 17,10; *Prv 13,15 ἐν ἀπωλείᾳ -אירם? *to destruction* for MT איתן *lasting*?; *Ez 26,21 ἀπώλειαν -כלהות ◊כלה? *(I will make you a) destruction* for MT בלהות *terror*, see also Ez 27,36; 28,19; *Dn^Th 8,25 καὶ ἐπὶ ἀπωλείας -ועל שר *and for the destruction* for MT ועל שר *and against the prince*
Cf. LE BOULLUEC 1989, 226; →TWNT

ἀπῶρυξ,-υγος N3F 0-0-1-0-0-1
Ez 17,6
shoot, layer of a vine

ἀπωσμός,-οῦ N2M 0-0-0-1-0-1
Lam 1,7
repulsion; *Lam 1,7 καὶ ἀπωσμῶν αὐτῆς -◊דרה or ומרודיה? *and her rejection* for MT רוד ◊ומרודיה *and her homelessness*; neol.
Cf. ALBREKTSON 1963, 60

ἀπωτέρω D 0-0-0-1-0-1
Dn^LXX 9,7
farther off

ἄρα⁺ X 3-0-7-23-5-38
Gn 18,3; 20,11; Nm 22,11; Is 56,3; Jer 4,10
always with inferential force; *mark you* (to draw attention) Ps 30(31),23; *then* (for conclusion, often after εἰ-cl.) Jb 40,14; *therefore* (conclusion in syllogism) Wis 6,20; *indeed* Is 56,3; *surely* Gn 20,11; εἰ ἄρα *if indeed* Gn 18,3; *Ps 57(58),2 ἄρα -אולם *indeed* for MT אלם *silence*?
Cf. CLARK 1972, 70-84

ἆρα⁺ X 2-0-1-1-1-5
Gn 18,13; 37,10; Jon 2,5; Jb 27,8; Od 6,5
interrogative particle implying anxiety or impatience; ἆρά γε *(shall I) then indeed (bear)* (each particle retains its force) Gn 18,13; (in exclamations) Jer 4,10

ἀρά,-ᾶς⁺ N1F 12-2-8-6-3-31
Gn 24,41; 26,28; Nm 5,21(bis).23
vow, oath Gn 26,28; *invocation of evil* Gn 24,41

Cf. HARL 1986, 67.213

αρααβ N 0-1-0-0-0-1
1 Chr 24,31
-הראב? for MT הראש the head, the chief
Cf. ALLEN 1974ᴵ, 163; 1974ᴵᴵ, 92

αραβωθ N 0-2-0-0-0-2
2 Sm 15,28; 17,16
=ערבות desert-plain; *2 Sm 15,28 ἐν ἀραβωθ =
qere בערבות in the desert-plains for MT ketib
בעברות at the passes

ἀράομαι V 4-7-0-0-0-11
Nm 22,6.11; 23,7.8; Jos 24,9
to curse [τινα] Nm 23,8; [τινι] Jos 24,9; to lay
an oath on sb [τινι] (implying a curse; semit.)
1 Sm 14,24; to swear [abs.] 1 Kgs 8,31
Cf. HELBING 1928, 70-71
(→ ἐπικατ-, κατ-)

ἀραρότως D 0-0-0-0-1-1
3 Mc 5,4
punctually

ἀράσσω
(→ κατ-)

αραφωθ N 0-1-0-0-0-1
2 Sm 17,19
=הרפות grains
Cf. LEE 1983, 109-110

ἀράχνη,-ης N1F 0-0-1-4-0-5
Is 59,5; Ps 38(39),12; 89(90),9; Jb 8,14; 27,18
spider Is 59,5; spider's web Jb 8,14

ἀργέω⁺ V 0-0-0-3-3-6
Eccl 12,3; Ezr 4,24(bis); 1 Ezr 2,26; 2 Mc 5,25
to be unemployed, to do nothing (of pers.) Eccl
12,3; to cease (of things) 1 Ezr 2,26; to keep
Sabbath 2 Mc 5,25; to be lazy Sir 33,28
(→ κατ-)

ἀργία,-ας N1F 1-0-1-1-2-5
Ex 21,19; Is 1,13; Eccl 10,18; Wis 13,13; Sir
33,28
inability to work Ex 21,19; idleness Eccl 10,18;
rest, leisure Wis 13,13; holyday Is 1,13
Cf. WEVERS 1990, 332; ZUNTZ 1956, 135

ἀργός,-ή,-όν⁺ A 0-1-0-0-3-4
1 Kgs 6,7; Wis 14,5; 15,15; Sir 37,11
idle, lazy Sir 37,11; idle, sterile Wis 14,5; slow
Wis 15,15; unworked, crude 1 Kgs 6,7
Cf. SPICQ 1978, 142; →TWNT

ἀργυρικός,-ός,-όν A 0-0-0-0-1-1
1 Ezr 8,24
of or in money; ἀργυρικὴ ζημία fine, monetary
penalty

ἀργύριον,-ου⁺ N2N 86-123-50-59-90-408
Gn 13,2; 23,9.13.15.16
money (coll. sg.) Gn 23,9; silver (= ἄργυρος) Gn
13,2; τὸ ἀργύριον the money, the cash Jgs 16,18;
ἀργύριον ἄξιον worthy prize, full prize 1 Chr
21,22; *Ezr 7,17 ἐν ἀργυρίῳ -בכספי/ב with money
for MT בכספיא/ב in Casiphia; *Jer 10,5 ἀργύριον
-כחם? silver for MT כתמר/כ like a scarecrow?
Cf. LEE 1983, 64

ἀργυροκοπέω V 0-0-1-0-0-1
Jer 6,29
to coin money; neol.

ἀργυροκόπος,-ου N2M 0-1-1-0-0-2
JgsᴮB 17,4; Jer 6,29
(silver)smith
Cf. HORSLEY 1987, 7-10

ἀργυρολόγητος,-ος,-ον A 0-0-0-0-1-1
2 Mc 11,3
subject to a levy in money; neol.

ἄργυρος,-ου N2M 1-0-2-9-2-14
Ex 27,11; Is 60,9; Ez 22,20; Prv 10,20; 17,3
silver

ἀργυροῦς,-ᾶ,-οῦν A 43-11-7-17-15-93
Gn 24,53; 44,2.5; Ex 3,22; 11,2
of silver, silver Gn 24,53; silver-plated 2 Kgs
12,14

ἀργυροχόος,-ου N2M 0-0-0-0-1-1
Wis 15,9
melter of silver, worker in silver; neol.

ἀργυρόω
(→ κατ-, περι-)

ἀργυρώματα,-ων N3N 0-0-0-0-3-3
Jdt 12,1; 15,11; 1 Mc 15,32
silver-plate

ἀργυρώνητος,-ος,-ον A 5-0-0-0-1-6
Gn 17,12.13.23.27; Ex 12,44
bought with silver, purchased
Cf. HARL 1986, 68

ἀρδαλόω V 0-0-0-0-1-1
Sir 22,1
to smear; ἠρδαλωμένος filthy

ἄρδην D 0-1-1-0-0-2
1 Kgs 7,31(45); Mal 3,23
utterly, entirely

ἄρδω
(→ ἐπ-)

ἀρεσκεία,-ας⁺ N1F 0-0-0-1-0-1
Prv 31,30
obsequiousness, desire to please
Cf. HARL 1991, 254; WALTERS 1973, 38

ἀρέσκω⁺   V 10-19-3-13-13-58
Gn 19,8; 20,15; 34,18; 41,37; Lv 10,20
to please [τινι] Gn 19,8; [ἐναντίον τινός] Gn
34,18; [ἐνώπιόν τινος] Jgsᴬ 10,15; *to please, to
satisfy* [τινι] Mal 3,4; *to seem good* Jgsᴬ 14,3; *to
approve oneself* 4 Mc 8,26; *Jb 31,10 ἀρέσαι *to
please* corr.? ἀλέσαι for MT תטחן *let her grind
(for another)*; *Prv 12,21 οὐκ ἀρέσει -לא נאוה *it
does not please* for MT לא יאנה *it does not befall*
-NIDNTT
(→ ἀπ-)

ἀρεστός,-ή,-όν⁺   A 10-0-4-6-15-35
Gn 3,6; 16,6; Ex 15,26; Lv 10,19; Dt 6,18
pleasing Dt 6,18; *pleasing to, pleasant to* [τινι]
Gn 3,6; *acceptable to, pleasing to* [τινι] Gn 16,6;
ὀπίσω τῶν ἀρεστῶν τῆς καρδίας *after the lusts
of their heart* Jer 9,13
Cf. DANIEL 1966, 193-194

ἀρεταλογία,-ας   N1F 0-0-0-0-1-1
Sir 36,13
celebration of divine ἀρεταί; neol.

ἀρετή,-ῆς⁺   N1F 0-0-6-2-25-33
Is 42,8.12; Is 43,21; 63,7; Hab 3,3
majesty, excellence Hab 3,3; *virtue* Wis 4,1;
distinction, fame Zech 6,13; ἀρεταί *praises (of
God)* Is 42,8
Cf. HATCH 1889, 40-41; →NIDNTT; TWNT

ἀρήγω   V 0-0-0-0-1-1
3 Mc 4,16
to aid
(→ ἐπ-)

ἀρήν, ἀρνός⁺   N3M 10-7-8-3-9-37
Gn 30,32.33.35; Ex 12,5; 23,19
lamb Ex 12,5; *sheep* Gn 30,32; *Is 5,17 ἄρνες
-גרים *lambs* for MT גרים *foreigners*; *Mi 5,6 ὡς
ἄρνες -כ/כרים *like lambs* for MT כ/רביבים *like
dewdrops*
Cf. HARLÉ 1988, 44

ἀρθρέμβολα,-ων   N2N 0-0-0-0-2-2
4 Mc 8,13; 10,5
instruments of torture 4 Mc 8,13; *of torture,
racking* (as adj.) 4 Mc 10,5; neol.

ἄρθρον,-ου   N2N 0-0-0-1-1-2
Jb 17,11; 4 Mc 9,17
joint 4 Mc 9,17; *joint, string* (metaph.) Jb 17,11

ἀρθόω
(→ ἐξ-)

αριηλ   N 0-1-3-0-0-4
1 Chr 11,22; Ez 43,15(bis).16
=אריאל *Ariel* (proper name of part of

Jerusalem?)

ἀριθμέω⁺   V 7-13-2-13-2-37
Gn 14,14; 15,5; 16,10; 32,13; 41,49
A: *to number, to count* Lv 23,15; P: *to be
numbered* Gn 16,10; *Gn 14,14 καὶ ἠρίθμησε
-וירק *and he counted, mustered* for MT וירק *and
he made suffer*?
Cf. QUAST 1990, 230-252; WALTERS 1973, 104
(→ δι-, ἐξ-, κατ-, παρ-, συν-)

ἀριθμητός,-ή,-όν   A 0-0-0-4-0-4
Jb 14,5; 15,20; 16,22; 36,27
numbered

ἀριθμός,-οῦ⁺   N2M 48-50-20-26-29-173
Gn 34,30; 41,49; Ex 12,4; 16,16; 23,26
number Ex 12,4; *amount, sum* Sir 51,28; *exact
number* Gn 41,49; *numbering, counting, census*
2 Chr 2,16; τινος οὐκ ἐστιν ἀριθμός *it is
indefinite* Ps 146(147),5; κατὰ ἀριθμὸν ψυχῶν
according to the numbers of persons Ex 12,14;
αὐτῶν οὐκ ἦν ἀριθμός *they could not be
counted, they were numerous* Jgs 6,5; ἀριθμῷ *few*
Nm 9,20, see also Ez 12,16; *Ez 20,37 ἐν
ἀριθμῷ -ב/משפר *according to (your) number* (i.e.
excluding others) for MT ב/מסרת *into the bond
(of the covenant)*?, cpr. 1 Chr 9,28; Lv 27,32;
*Jgsᴮ 11,33 ἐν ἀριθμῷ -◊מנין *in number* for MT
מנית *Minnith*; *Is 34,16 ἀριθμῷ -סֵפֶר (Aram.?
LH?) *in (full) number* for MT סֵפֶר *book*, cpr. Jer
40(33),13
Cf. MOULTON 1910, 297-298; THACKERAY 1909, 39;
ZIEGLER 1934, 122-123 (Is 34,16); →NIDNTT

ἀριστάω⁺   V 1-2-0-0-1-4
Gn 43,25; 1 Sm 14,25; 1 Kgs 13,7; Tobˢ 2,1
to take the ἄριστον, *to eat the midday meal, to
dine*

ἀριστεία,-ας   N1F 0-0-0-0-1-1
4 Mc 12,16
prowess

ἀριστερός,-ά,-όν⁺   A 17-27-7-8-6-65
Gn 13,9(bis); 14,15; 24,49; 48,13
left, on the left Lv 14,15; εἰς ἀριστερά *to the left*
Gn 13,9; ἐν ἀριστερᾷ (χειρί) τινος *on the left
(hand), to the north of* Gn 14,15

ἀριστεύω   V 0-0-0-0-1-1
4 Mc 2,18
to be superior

ἄριστον,-ου⁺   N2N 0-1-0-0-8-9
2 Sm 24,15; Tobˢ 2,1.4; 12,13; Susᵀʰ 14
dinner Tobˢ 2,1; ὥρα ἀρίστου *dinner time, noon*
2 Sm 24,15

ἄριστος,-η,-ον　　　　　　A 0-0-0-0-2-2
2 Mc 13,15; 4 Mc 7,1
sup. of ἀγαθός; *best, first-rate* 4 Mc 7,1; *valiant*
2 Mc 13,15

αριωθ　　　　　　N 0-1-0-0-0-1
2 Kgs 4,39
=ארת *herbs*

ἀρκεύθινος,-η,-ον　　　　　　A 0-3-0-0-0-3
1 Kgs 6,31.33; 2 Chr 2,7
of juniper, cedar, oleaster?; neol.

ἄρκευθος,-ου　　　　　　N2F 0-0-1-0-0-1
Hos 14,9
juniper-tree, cedar

ἀρκέω⁺　　　　　　V 3-3-0-2-4-12
Ex 12,4; Nm 11,22(bis); Jos 17,16; 1 Kgs 8,27
A: *to suffice, to be enough for* [τινι] Ex 12,4; P:
to be satisfied with [τινι] 2 Mc 5,15; ἀρκεῖ *it is
enough* Prv 30,16
Cf. WEVERS 1990, 169
(→ δι-, ἐξ-, ἐπ-)

ἄρκος,-ου　　　　　　N2F 0-7-4-3-3-17
Jgs 1,35; 1 Sm 17,34.36.37
bear; neol.

ἅρμα,-ατος⁺　　　　　　N3N 15-110-37-6-17-185
Gn 41,43; 46,29; 50,9; Ex 14,6.7
chariot Gn 41,43; (metaph.) 2 Kgs 13,14; *yoked
chariot* Zech 6,2; *team, chariot-horses* Gn 46,29;
*Hos 10,13 ἐν τοῖς ἅρμασί σου -ב/רכב/ך *in
your chariots* for MT ב/דרכ/ך *in your way*

ἁρματηλάτης,-ου　　　　　　N1M 0-0-0-0-1-1
2 Mc 9,4
charioteer

ἁρμόζω⁺　　　　　　V 0-2-1-3-3-9
2 Sm 6,5.14; Na 3,8; Prv 8,30; 17,7
A: *to adapt, to suit* [τινι] Prv 17,7; *to tune* [τι]
Ps 151,2; P: *to be suited to, to be adapted to*
[τινι] Prv 19,14; ἁρμόζων *fitting, suitable,
appropriate* 2 Mc 14,22; *Prv 8,30 ἁρμόζουσα
-אמוןᴵᴵ? *suiting to, being in harmony with* for MT
אמוןᴵ *master workman?*, cpr. Na 3,8; Ez 23,42;
*2 Sm 6,5 ἐν ὀργάνοις ἡρμοσμένοις -בכלי עז
on well-tuned instruments for MT בכל עצי *with
all (their) trees?*, cpr. 2 Sm 6,14; see ἁρμονία
(· ἐν-, ἐφ-, μεθ-)

ἁρμονία,-ας　　　　　　N1F 0-0-2-0-0-2
Ez 23,42; 37,7
joint Ez 37,7; *Ez 23,42 φωνὴν ἁρμονίας
קול ?אמון- *a sound of music* for MT קול המון *a
sound of a multitude*, cpr. Na 3,8; Prv 8,30

ἁρμόνιος,-ος,-ον　　　　　　A 0-0-0-0-1-1

Wis 16,20
fitting, harmonious, agreeing; neol.

ἁρμός,-οῦ⁺　　　　　　N2M 0-0-0-0-2-2
4 Mc 10,5; Sir 27,2
joint, socket 4 Mc 10,5; *joining* Sir 27,2

ἀρνέομαι⁺　　　　　　V 1-0-0-0-5-6
Gn 18,15; 4 Mc 8,7; 10,15; Wis 12,27; 16,16
to deny Gn 18,15; [+inf.] Wis 12,27; *to deny, to
disown, to forsake* [τι] 4 Mc 8,7
Cf. SPICQ 1982, 64-70
(→ ἀπ-, ἐξ-)

ἀρνίον,-ου⁺　　　　　　N2N 0-0-2-2-1-5
Jer 11,19; 27(50),45; Ps 113(114),4.6; PSal 8,23
a little lamb
Cf. WALTERS 1973, 46

ἀροτήρ,-ῆρος　　　　　　N3M 0-0-1-0-0-1
Is 61,5
ploughman

ἀροτρίασις,-εως　　　　　　N3F 1-0-0-0-0-1
Gn 45,6
ploughing, tillage; neol.
Cf. HARL 1986, 290

ἀροτριάω⁺　　　　　　V 1-2-8-2-2-15
Dt 22,10; JgsᴮB 14,18; 1 Kgs 19,19; Is 7,25(bis)
to plough Dt 22,10; *to devise* (metaph., semit.)
Sir 7,12; *Is 45,9 ὁ ἀροτριῶν ἀροτριάσει -◊חרש
shall the ploughman plough for MT חרש ◊ *the
vessel (with) the potter*
Cf. LEE 1983, 113

ἄροτρον,-ου⁺　　　　　　N2N 0-1-3-0-1-5
1 Chr 21,23; Is 2,4; Jl 4,10; Mi 4,3; Sir 38,25
plough 1 Chr 21,23; ἄροτρα *ploughshares* Mi 4,3

ἀροτρόπους,-ποδος　　　　　　N3M 0-1-0-0-0-1
JgsᴮB 3,31
ploughshare

ἄρουρα,-ας　　　　　　N1F 1-2-0-0-0-3
Gn 21,33; 1 Sm 22,6; 31,13
corn-land, field Gn 21,33; *land, field* 1 Sm 22,6
Cf. BARR 1968, 11-20; GEHMAN 1972, 107; HARL 1986,
191

ἁρπαγή,-ῆς⁺　　　　　　N1F 1-0-3-1-4-9
Lv 5,21; Is 3,14; 10,2; Na 2,13; Eccl 5,7
seizure, robbery Lv 5,21; *thing seized, booty* Na
2,13; *seizure* (metaph.) Eccl 5,7

ἅρπαγμα,-ατος　　　　　　N3N 1-0-13-2-2-18
Lv 5,23; Is 42,22; 61,8; Ez 18,7.12
booty, prey, spoil

ἁρπάζω⁺　　　　　　V 4-4-17-11-5-41
Gn 37,33; Lv 5,23; 19,13; Dt 28,31; JgsᴬA 21,21
to snatch away [τι ἔκ τινος] 2 Sm 23,21; *to carry*

off [τινα] Gn 37,33; *to seize* [τινα] Jgs 21,21; *to captivate, to ravish* [τι] Jdt 16,9
(· ἀν-, δι-, ἐξ-, συν-)

ἅρπαξ,-αγος⁺   A 1-0-0-0-0-1
Gn 49,27
robbing, rapacious

ἀρραβών,-ῶνος⁺   N3M 3-0-0-0-0-3
Gn 38,17.18.20
=ערבון *deposit*
Cf. HARL 1986, 265; WALTERS 1973, 163

ἀρρενωδῶς   D 0-0-0-0-1-1
2 Mc 10,35
bravely

ἄρρηκτος,-ος,-ον   A 0-0-0-0-1-1
3 Mc 4,9
not to be broken, hard

ἄρριζος,-ος,-ον   A 0-0-0-1-0-1
Jb 31,8
without roots, uprooted

ἀρρωστέω   V 0-13-0-0-1-14
2 Sm 12,15; 13,2.6; 1 Kgs 12,24; 17,17
to be unwell 2 Sm 12,15; ἀρρωστέω εἰς θάνατον
to be sick to death 2 Kgs 20,1

ἀρρώστημα,-ατος   N3N 0-0-0-0-5-5
Sir 10,10; 30,17; 31,2.22; 38,9
illness, sickness, disease

ἀρρωστία,-ας   N1F 0-7-0-5-2-14
1 Kgs 12,24(bis); 17,17; 2 Kgs 1,2; 8,8
sickness, disease

ἄρρωστος,-ος,-ον⁺   A 0-0-1-0-1-2
Mal 1,8; Sir 7,35
sick

ἀρσενικός,-ή,-όν   A 41-5-1-11-3-61
Gn 17,10.12; 34,15.22.25
male; neol.?
Cf. LEE 1983, 109-110

ἄρσην, ἄρσενος   N3M/N 40-6-5-1-5-57
or ἄρρην, ἄρρενος
Gn 1,27; 5,2; 6,19.20; Gn 7,2
male Gn 1,27; *Is 26,14 ἄρσεν - זכרᴵ *male* for
MT זכרᴵᴵ *memory*
Cf. LEE 1983, 109-110

ἄρσις,-εως   N3F 0-9-0-1-0-10
2 Sm 11,8; 19,43; 1 Kgs 2,35.46; 5,29
that which is lifted, burden 1 Kgs 5,15; *levy, forced labour* 1 Kgs 11,28; *portion, gift* (from the king) 2 Sm 11,8; *load* 2 Kgs 8,9

ἀρτάβη,-ης   N1F 0-0-1-0-2-3
Is 5,10; Bel 3
artaba (Persian measure, 6 ἀρτάβαι equal to the

Hebrew homer, ± 450 kg)

ἀρτάω
(··· δι-, ἐξ-)

ἀρτήρ,-ῆρος   N3M 0-0-0-1-0-1
Neh 4,11
that by which anything is carried, a device for carrying building material

ἄρτι⁺   D 0-0-0-2-10-12
Dnᴸˣˣ 9,22; 10,11; Jdt 9,1; 2 Mc 3,28; 9,5
just, a little afore (of the immediate past) 2 Mc 3,28; *now, at the same time* (of the immediate present) Jdt 9,1; *as soon as* 2 Mc 9,5
Cf. SHIPP 1979, 101-102; →TWNT (νῦν)

ἀρτίζω
(→ δι-, κατ-)

ἀρτίως   D 0-1-0-0-0-1
2 Sm 15,34
newly, just, recently

ἀρτοκοπικός,-ή,-όν   A 0-1-0-0-0-1
1 Chr 16,3
made by a baker; neol.
Cf. BATTAGLIA 1989

ἀρτός,-ή,-όν   A 2-0-0-0-0-2
Nm 4,27(bis)
that which is taken up, undertaken, burden; neol.

ἄρτος,-ου⁺   N2M 80-94-53-47-33-307
Gn 3,19; 14,18; 18,5; 21,14; 24,33
bread, cake Gn 14,18; *food* Is 65,25; ἐσθίω ἐκ τῶν ἄρτων τῶν ἐθνῶν *to adopt the way of life of the pagans* Tob 1,10; ἄρτοι ἐνώπιοι *bread put in the presence of the Lord* Ex 25,30; ἄρτοι τοῦ προσώπου 1 Sm 21,7; ἄρτοι τῆς πρόσθεως 1 Sm 21,7; ἄρτος ζυμίτης *leavened bread* Lv 7,13; *Ct 5,1 ἄρτον *bread* corr.? ἀγρόν יער (*woodland*) for MT יערᴵᴵ *honeycomb?*; *Jer 16,7 ἄρτος -לחם *bread* for MT להם/ל *for them*, see also Jgsᴬ 5,8
Cf. BATTAGLIA 1989; DANIEL 1966, 131-136; 141-153; HARL 1986, 68; LE BOULLUEC 1989, 260-261 (Ex 25,30); PELLETIER 1967, 364-367 (Ex 25,30); SHIPP 1979, 102-103; WEVERS 1990, 281.373.405.466.480.639; →NIDNTT

ἀρχαῖος,-α,-ον⁺   A 0-4-7-8-8-27
Jgsᴮ 5,21; 1 Sm 24,14; 1 Kgs 2,35; 5,10; Is 22,9
old, ancient (of things) 1 Sm 24,14; (of persons) 1 Kgs 2,35b; *former* Ps 43,1; *from the beginning, original* Ps 88(89),50; *old* (metaph.) Sir 9,10; τὸ ἀρχαῖον *original state* Is 23,17; ἐξ ἡμερῶν ἀρχαίων *from ancient times* Is 37,26; τὰ ἔσχατα καὶ τὰ ἀρχαῖα *the last and the first things* Ps 138(139),5; *Jgsᴮ 5,21 ἀρχαίων -קדמים *ancient*

for MT קרומים *Kedumim?*

··MM; NIDNTT

ἀρχή,-ῆς⁺   N1F 30-42-65-54-48-239
Gn 1,1.16(bis); 2,10; 10,10
often stereotyped rendition of √ראש; *beginning*
(temporal) Gn 1,1; *beginning* (of a process) Gn
41,21; *power, authority, office* (semit.?,
stereotyped rendition of ראש) Gn 41,21; *power,
principle of authority* Gn 1,16; *magistry, office* Gn
40,13; *government* Dt 17,18; *beginning* (local) Ez
21,26; *branch* (beginning of a river) Gn 2,10;
end, corner Ex 36,24; αἱ ἀρχαί *the heads* Ex
6,25 *authorities* (personification of invisible
powers); ἀπ' ἀρχῆς *of old* Hab 1,12; *at first, in a
distant time* Jos 24,2; τὴν ἀρχήν *in the beginning,
at first* (as adv.) Gn 13,4; ἀρχὴ τέκνων μου *the
first of my children* Gn 49,3; ἀπὸ κορυφῆς ὀρέων
ἀρχῆς *from the top of the ancient mountains* Dt
33,15; λάμβανω ἀρχὴν *to take a census, to take
the sum, to count* (semit., stereotyped transl. of
נשא ראש) Nm 1,2, cpr. Ex 30,12; Nm 1,49; 3,40;
4,2.22; 26,2; 31,26.49; 1 Chr 27,33; *Jer
28(51),58 ἐν ἀρχῆ בראש *in the beginning? in
(their) rule?* for MT אש ברי *for fire*, cpr. Na 1,6;
*Ez 21,19 ἐπ' ἀρχῆς ב/ראש *at the beginning* for
MT (ברה) ברא *selected'?; *Is 42,10 ἡ ἀρχὴ αὐτοῦ
תחלתו *his beginning* for MT תהלמו *his praises*;
*Ob 20 ἡ ἀρχὴ - החל ◊ חלל *beginning, first* for MT
החל חיל *the army*, cpr. Na 3,8; *Jer 30,18(49,2)
τὴν ἀρχὴν αὐτοῦ ראשיו *his dominion* for MT
ירשריו *those who possessed him*; *Jb 37,3 ἀρχὴ
αὐτοῦ - ◊ שור ישרהו *his dominion* for MT ישר◊ -? *he
directs it*

Cf. CARAGOUNIS 1986, 68-70; HARL 1986, 86.93; LE
BOULLUEC 1989, 342; TOV 1976, 530 (Gn 1,16); WALTERS
1973, 342; WEVERS 1990, 168.566.604; ·NDNTT; TWNT

ἀρχηγέτης,-ου   N1M 0-0-0-0-1-1
2 Mc 2,30
author, originator

ἀρχηγός,-οῦ⁺   N2M 9-9-6-4-4-32
Ex 6,14; Nm 10,4; 13,2.3; 14,4
chief, head Ex 6,14; *prince* Nm 10,4; *ruler* Nm
14,4; *guide* Jer 3,4; *beginning, origin* Mi 1,13

Cf. WEVERS 1990, 78; ·TWNT

ἀρχῆθεν   D 0-0-0-0-1-1
3 Mc 3,21
from of old

Cf. SHIPP 1979, 103

ἀρχιδεσμοφύλαξ,-ακος   N3M 3-0-0-0-0-3
Gn 39,21.22.23

chief gaoler, chief guard of the prison; neol.

ἀρχιδεσμώτης,-ου   N1M 1-0-0-0-0-1
Gn 40,4
see ἀρχιδεσμοφύλαξ; neol.

ἀρχιεράομαι   V 0-0-0-0-1-1
4 Mc 4,18
to be high-priest; neol.

Cf. HELBING 1907, 121

ἀρχιερατεύω   V 0-0-0-0-1-1
1 Mc 14,47
see ἀρχιεράομαι; neol.

Cf. HELBING 1907, 122

ἀρχιερεύς,-έως⁺   N3M 1-2-0-0-41-44
Lv 4,3; Jos 22,13; 24,33; 1 Ezr 5,40; 9,39
high-priest Lv 4,3; ἀρχιερεύς μέγας *high-priest*
1 Mc 13,42

Cf. HARLÉ 1988, 28; KILPATRICK 1969, 203-208; →TWNT

ἀρχιερωσύνη,-ης   N1F 0-0-0-0-13-13
1 Mc 7,21; 11,27.57; 14,38; 16,24
high-priesthood; neol.?

ἀρχιευνοῦχος,-ου   N2M 0-0-0-14-0-14
Dn^LXX 1,3.7.8.9.10
chief of the eunuchs; neol.

ἀρχιμάγειρος,-ου   N2M 4-7-10-2-0-23
Gn 37,36; 39,1; 41,10.12; 2 Kgs 25,8
chief of a royal guard lit. *chief cook* (in Egypt)
Gn 37,36; (in Babylon) 2 Kgs 25,8; neol.

Cf. HARL 1986, 263

ἀρχιοινοχοΐα,-ας   N1F 1-0-0-0-0-1
Gn 40,13
office of chief cup-bearer; neol.

ἀρχιοινοχόος,-ου   N2M 8-0-0-0-1-9
Gn 40,1.2.5.9.20
chief cup-bearer; neol.

ἀρχιπατριώτης,-ου   N1M 0-1-0-1-0-2
Jos 21,1; Dn^LXX 3,94
head of a family; neol.

ἀρχισιτοποιός,-οῦ   N2M 7-0-0-0-0-7
Gn 40,1.2.5.16.20
chief baker; neol.

ἀρχιστράτηγος,-ου   N2M 3-13-0-2-6-24
Gn 21,22.32; 26,26; Jos 5,14.15
commander-in-chief, chief captain; neol.

ἀρχισωματοφύλαξ,-ακος   N3M 0-1-0-1-0-2
1 Sm 28,2; Est 2,21
chief of the body-guard; neol.

Cf. BICKERMAN 1976, 127-128; MOOREN 1968, 171; VAN
'T DACK 1968, 263

ἀρχιτεκτονέω   V 3-0-0-0-0-3
Ex 31,4; 35,32; 37,21(38,23)

to be a commissioner of works, to be master workman
Cf. HELBING 1928, 118; WEVERS 1990, 507.588.619

ἀρχιτεκτονί α,-ας   N1F 2-0-0-0-0-2
Ex 35,32.35
architecture, workmanship
Cf. WEVERS 1990, 588.591

ἀρχιτέκτων,-ονος⁺   N3M 0-0-1-0-2-3
Is 3,3; 2 Mc 2,29; Sir 38,27
director of works, master-builder
Cf. SPICQ 1978, 149-151

ἀρχίφυλος,-ου   N2M 1-1-0-0-1-3
Dt 29,9; Jos 21,1; 1 Ezr 2,5
chief of a tribe; neol.

ἄρχω⁺   V 29-106-28-24-44-231
Gn 1,18.26.28; 2,3; 4,7
A: *to regulate* [τινος] Gn 1,18; *to rule* [τινος] Gn 1,26; [ἐπί τινος] Jgs 9,22; [ἔν τινι] 1 Sm 9,17; M: *to begin to do something* [+inf.] Gn 2,3; [τοῦ +inf.] 1 Chr 17,27; *to begin from someone* (in an enumeration) [ἀπό τινος] Gn 44,12; *2 Chr 35,25 αἱ ἄρχουσαι - השרות *the princesses, the female leaders* for MT השרות *the female singers of songs*, cpr. Jb 36,24; *Gn 18,27 ἠρξάμην - החלתי *I have begun* for MT הואלתי *I have decided, I have taken upon myself*; *Ps 76(77),11 ἠρξάμην - החלתי *I have begun* for MT חלותי *it is my grief*; *Mi 1,12 τίς ἤρξατο - מיהחל *for MT כיהחלה *for ?*; *Ez 13,6 καὶ ἤρξαντο - ויחלו *and they began* for MT ויחלו *and they expected*; *Hos 6,11 ἄρχου τρυγᾶν שית קצר *start harvesting* for MT שת קציר *a harvest has been appointed*; *Hos7,5 ἤρξαντο החלו *they started* for MT חלה *they make sick*, see also Mi 6,13
Cf. HELBING 1928, 113-114.118-119.167-168; →NIDNTT; TWNT

(→ ἀπ-, ἐν-, ἐξ-, ἐπ-, κατ-, προυπ-, ὑπ-)

ἄρχων,-οντος⁺   N3M 111-238-110-128-58-645
Gn 12,15; 14,7; 24,2; 25,16; 27,29
prince Gn 12,15; *chief, ruler* Gn 24,2; *overseer* Gn 47,4; *executor* (of commands) 1 Sm 22,14; *captain* 2 Sm 23,8; *governor* Neh 3,7; *guardian angel of nation* Dn 10,13; εἰμι εἰς ἄρχοντά τινι *to be head over* Jgs 10,18; χρίω τινὰ εἰς ἄρχοντα *to anoint sb to be ruler* 1 Sm 9,16; ἐντελέομαί τινι εἰς ἄρχοντα *to appoint sb to be a ruler* 1 Sm 13,14; δίδωμί τινα εἰς ἄρχοντά τινος *to make sb head of* 1 Kgs 12,24; ἄρχων τῶν ᾠδῶν *master of the bands (songs)* 1 Chr 15,22; *Lv 18,21 ἄρχοντι - מלך *leader* for MT מלך

Molech, cpr. Lv 20,2.3.4.5; *Jer 51(44),9 τῶν ἀρχόντων ὑμῶν - נשיכם *of your leaders* for MT נשיכם *of your wives* *Hos 12,12 ἄρχοντες - שרים *the chiefs* for MT שורים *bulls*; *1Sm 22,14 ἄρχων - שר *leader* for MT סר *he has turned aside*; *2 Chr 35,25 οἱ ἄρχοντες השרם *the princes, the leaders* for MT השרים *the singers of songs*; *Gn 14,7 τοὺς ἄρχοντας - שרי *the princes of* for MT שדה *field*, see also Neh 12,44; *JgsᴮB 5,8 ἀρχόντων - שרים *rulers* for MT שערים *gates*; *Hos 10,14 ἄρχων - שר *prince* for MT שד *he ravaged*
Cf. BICKERMAN 1976, 194 n.70; HARLÉ 1988, 162-163; KOENIG 1982, 161-172; LUST 1991, 193-208; RAURELL 1986, 85-89; →TWNT

ἄρωμα,-ατος⁺   N3N 0-8-0-8-1-17
2 Kgs 20,13; 1 Chr 9,29.30; 2 Chr 9,1.9
spice, aromatic herb (stereotyped rendering of בשם, *balsam*)

ἀσάλευτος,-ος,-ον⁺   A 3-0-0-0-0-3
Ex 13,16; Dt 6,8; 11,18
immovable, definitely fixed; ἔσται ἀσάλευτον πρὸ ὀφθαλμῶν σου *it shall be immovable before your eyes* (stereotyped rendering of טוטאפות *phylacteries*)
Cf. CLERMONT-GANNEAU 1905, 357-359; FREY 1952, 218-219; LE BOULLUEC 1989, 52-54; ·MM

ασαραμελ   N 0-0-0-0-1-1
1 Mc 14,27
=חצר עם אל? *court of God's people*
Cf. HOLLADAY 1989, 200

ασαρημωθ   N 0-0-1-0-0-1
Jer 38(31),40
=השרמות *Hasaremot?*

ἀσβόλη,-ης   N1F 0-0-0-1-0-1
Lam 4,8
soot; ὑπὲρ ἀσβόλην *blacker than soot*

ἀσέβεια,-ας⁺   N1F 5-1-46-16-5-73
Dt 9,4.5; 18,22; 19,16; 25,2
ungodliness, impiety Dt 9,5; *iniquity, wrong doing, injustice* Dt 19,16; ἀσέβειαι *crime, sin, wicked act* Am 1,3; *Prv 1,19 ἀσεβεία - עולה *by (their) sin* for MT בעליו *its masters, its possessors*; *Prv 28,3 ἐν ἀσεβείαις - רשע *by injustice* for MT רש *poor*
Cf. COX 1990, 119-130; ·NIDNTT; TWNT

ἀσεβέω⁺   V 4-1-12-11-9-37
Lv 20,12; Dt 17,13; Dt 18,20; Dt 25,2; 2 Sm 22,22
to be impious, to act profanely, to commit sacrilege Lv 20,12; *to sin against* [τινα] Prv 8,36;

to act wickedly against [εἴς τινα] 1 Ezr 1,24; [κατά τινος] Hos 8,1; *to sin before* [ἔναντί τινος] Jb 34,10; *to depart wickedly from* [ἀπό τινος] 2 Sm 22,22; [τι] (as cogn. acc.) *to sin in* (a way, a manner) Ez 16,27; ἀσεβέω λαλῆσαι *to speak impiously* (of prophets) Dt 18,20; ἀσεβέω νόμον *to transgress sinfully the law* Zph 3,4

Cf. COX 1990, 113-130; HARLÉ 1988, 174; HELBING 1928,12-13; WALTERS 1973,312; →NIDNTT; TWNT

ἀσέβημα,-ατος N3M 2-0-0-2-0-4
Lv 18,17; Dt 9,27; Lam 1,14; 4,22
impious or *profane act, sin*

ἀσεβής,-ής,-ές⁺ A 7-1-31-156-47-242
Gn 18,23(bis).25(bis); Ex 9,27
wicked, ungodly, sacrilegious, profane Gn 18,23; *Prv 21,30 πρὸς τὸν ἀσεβῆ (נגד ל/נֶגֶר יהוה- as verb) ? against the impious* or *the one behaving against the Lord* for MT ל/נֶגֶר יהוה *against the Lord;* *Is 24,8 ἀσεβῶν עוֹלִים- *of the evildoers* for MT עַלִּיזִם *of the jubilant;* *Is 26,19 ἀσεβῶν רְשָׁעִים- *the ungodly* for MT רְפָאִים *Rephaim*

LE BOULLUEC 1989, 84; →TWNT

ασεδεκ N 0-0-1-0-0-1
Is 19,18
=צֶדֶק *(city) of justice* for MT הַהֶרֶס *of destruction* (name of a town), cpr. Is 1,26

Cf. VAN DER KOOY 1981, 52-55

ἀσέλγεια,-ας⁺ N1F 0-0-0-0-2-2
3 Mc 2,26; Wis 14,26
licentiousness, insolence

ασελισι N 0-0-1-0-0-1
Jer 45(38),14
=הַשְּׁלִישִׁי *the third* (in rank)

ἄσημος,-ος,-ον⁺ A 1-0-0-1-1-3
Gn 30,42; Jb 42,11; 3 Mc 1,3
unmarked, without token Gn 30,42; *unimportant, obscure* (of a pers.) 3 Mc 1,3; *uncoined?* (of money) Jb 42,11

Cf. HALLEUX 1973, 370-380; HARL 1986, 233-235

ἄσηπτος,-ος,-ον A 15-0-1-0-0-16
Ex 25,5.10.13.28; 26,15
not liable to decay or *corruption* (of wood)

ασηρωθ N 6-1-0-0-0-7
Nm 11,35(bis); 12,16; 33,17.18
=חֲצֵרוֹת *villages* Dt 2,23 (also written as proper name e.g. Nm 11,35); *1 Chr 6,56 Ασηρωθ for MT עַשְׁתָּרוֹת *Astarte* (godess)

ἀσθένεια,-ας⁺ N1F 0-0-2-3-2-7
Jer 6,21; 18,23; Ps 15(16),4; Jb 37,7; Eccl 12,4
weakness Jb 37,7; *disease, sickness* 2 Mc 9,21;

stumbling block Jer 6,21

MATTIOLI 1983; →NIDNTT

ἀσθενέω⁺ V 0-14-26-24-13-77
JgsᴬA 16,7.11.17; Jgsᴮ 6,15; 16,17
to be weak, to be feeble Jgsᴮ 6,15; *to decline to* [εἴς τι] (of the day) Jgsᴮ 19,9; *to stumble, to fall* (metaph.) Hos 4,5; *to cause to fail* [τινα] (semit., rendering Hebr. hiphil) Mal 2,8; *to be too weak to, not to be able to* [+inf.] Is 28,20; ἠσθένησαν ταῖς διανοίαις αὐτῶν *their courage was abated* 1 Mc 11,49; *Hos 11,6 καὶ ἠσθένησεν -וחלתה◊חלה *it was weak* for MT וחלתה ◊חול *it shall rage*

Cf. WALTERS 1973, 118 (Mal 2,8); →NIDNTT; TWNT
(→ ἐξ-)

ἀσθενής,-ής,-ές⁺ A 2-4-2-10-5-23
Gn 29,17; Nm 13,18; Jgs 16,13; 1 Sm 2,10
weak Gn 29,17; *poor, helpless* Prv 21,13

ἀσθενόψυχος,-ος,-ον A 0-0-0-0-1-1
4 Mc 15,5
weak-minded; neol.

ἄσθμα,-ατος N3M 0-0-0-0-1-1
Wis 11,18
breath, vapour

ἀσθμαίνω V 0-0-0-0-1-1
Sir 31,19
to breathe hard, to gasp for breath
(→ ἐπ-)

ασιδα N 0-0-1-1-0-2
Jer 8,7; Jb 39,13
=חֲסִידָה *stork* or *heron*

ἀσίδηρος,-ος,-ον A 0-0-0-0-1-1
Wis 17,15
not made of iron, without iron bars

ἀσινής,-ής,-ές A 0-0-0-0-2-2
3 Mc 6,7; 7,20
unhurt, unharmed

ασιρ N 0-1-0-0-0-1
1 Chr 3,17
=אַסִּר; *1 Chr 3,17 Ιεχονια-ασιρ *Jechonia Asir* for MT יְכָנְיָה אַסִּר *Jeconiah, the prisoner*

ἀσιτέω V 0-0-0-1-1-2
Est 4,16; 1 Mc 3,17
to abstain from food, to fast

ἀσιτί D 0-0-0-1-0-1
Jb 24,6
without food; neol.

ἀσκέω⁺ V 0-0-0-0-1-1
2 Mc 15,4
to practise; ἀσκέω τὴν ἑβδομάδα *to keep the*

sabbath day
Cf. DRESSLER 1947; TWNT
(· ἐξ-)

ἄσκησις,-εως N3F 0-0-0-0-1-1
4 Mc 13,22
exercise, practice

ἀσκητής,-οῦ N1M 0-0-0-0-1-1
4 Mc 12,11
he who practises sth; ἀσκητής τῆς εὐσεβείας
doer of godliness, a pious man

ἀσκοπυτίνη,-ης N1F 0-0-0-0-1-1
Jdt 10,5
leathern canteen

ἀσκός,-οῦ⁺ N2M 3-6-2-5-0-16
Gn 21,14.15.19; Jos 9,4.13
bag (made from skin) Gn 21,14; ἀσκὸς οἴνου
wineskin Jos 9,4; *Jb 13,28 ἀσκῷ -כרקב like a
bag for MT כרקב like a rotten thing; *Ps 32(33),7
ὡς ἀσκόν -כנאר like a bag for MT כנד like a
dam, see also Ps 77(78),13

ᾆσμα,-ατος N3N 1-0-4-9-2-16
Nm 21,17; Is 5,1; 23,15.16; 26,1
song

ἀσμενίζω V 0-1-0-0-0-1
1 Sm 6,19
to be satisfied with, to be happy with [ἔν τινι];
neol.?

ἄσμενος,-η,-ον A 0-0-0-0-1-1
2 Mc 10,33
glad, eager

ἀσμένως⁺ D 0-0-0-0-3-3
2 Mc 4,12; 3 Mc 3,15; 5,21
gladly, readily

ἀσπάζομαι⁺ V 1-1-0-1-9-12
Ex 18,7; Jgsᴬ 18,15; Est 5,2; TobᴮᴬTob 5,10; Tobˢ
9,6
to embrace, to salute [τινα] Ex 18,7; [abs.] Sir
41,21
—TWNT
(· ἀπ-)

ἀσπάλαθος,-ου N2M 0-0-0-0-1-1
Sir 24,15
aspalathus, camel thorn

ἀσπάλαξ,-ακος N3M 1-0-0-0-0-1
Lv 11,30
a blind-rat, a mole

ἀσπιδίσκη,-ης N1F 5-0-0-0-1-6
Ex 28,13.14.29; 36,23.25(39,16.18)
small shield 1 Mc 4,57; boss, disk Ex 28,13; neol.
Cf. LE BOULLUEC 1989, 284

ἀσπίζω
(→ προ-, συν-, ὑπερ-)

ἀσπίς,-ίδος N3F 0-5-1-2-10-18
1 Sm 17,6.45; 1 Chr 5,18; 2 Chr 9,16(bis)
shield, armour

ἀσπίς,-ίδος⁺ N3F 1-0-6-5-1-13
Dt 32,33; Is 11,8(bis); 14,29; 30,6
asp, serpent Dt 32,33; *Ps 90(91),13 ἀσπίδα
-זחל serpent for MT שחל lion

ἀσταθής,-ής,-ές A 0-0-0-0-1-1
3 Mc 5,39
unsteady, unstable; neol.?

ἄστεγος,-ος,-ον A 0-0-1-2-0-3
Is 58,7; Prv 10,8; 26,28
without roof, unsheltered, houseless Is 58,7; ὁ
ἄστεγος χείλεσιν he who is unguarded in his
lips, he who is unable to keep his mouth shut Prv
10,8; στόμα ἄστεγον an unguarded mouth Prv
26,28

ἀστεῖος,-α,-ον⁺ A 2-2-0-0-3-7
Ex 2,2; Nm 22,32; Jgs 3,17; Jdt 11,23
pretty, graceful, charming Ex 2,2; handsome Jgs
3,17; good, honourable (morally) 2 Mc 6,23
Cf. ENGEL 1985, 91-92; SPICQ 1978, 152-153

ἀστείως D 0-0-0-0-1-1
2 Mc 12,43
honourably, honestly

ἄστεκτος,-ος,-ον A 0-0-0-0-1-1
Od 12,5
unendurable

ἀστήρ,-έρος⁺ N3M 6-3-5-7-2-23
Gn 1,16; 15,5; 22,17; 26,4; 37,9
star
→NIDNTT; TWNT

ἀστοχέω⁺ V 0-0-0-0-2-2
Sir 7,19; 8,9
to miss [τινος] (of things) Sir 8,9; to ignore
[τινος] (of pers.) Sir 7,19; neol.?
Cf. HELBING 1928, 143

ἀστράγαλος,-ου N2M 0-0-1-2-0-3
Zech 11,16; Dnᵀʰ 5,5.24
knuckle (of the hand) Dnᵀʰ 5,24; ἀστράγαλοι
the joints (of the anckle) Zech 11,16; the
knuckles (of the hand), fist Dnᵀʰ 5,5
Cf. CAIRD 1972, 118

ἀστραπή,-ῆς⁺ N1F 2-1-6-10-7-26
Ex 19,16; Dt 32,41; 2 Sm 22,15; Jer 10,13;
28(51),16
lightning Ex 19,16; gleaming, flashing Hab 3,11

ἀστράπτω⁺ V 0-0-0-1-1-2

Ps 143(144),6; Wis 11,18
to shoot (like lightning) [τι] Wis 11,18; ἀστράπτω
ἀτραπήν *to send lightning* (semit.) Ps 143(144),6
(→ δι-, ἐξ-, περι-)

ἀστρολόγος,-ου N2M 0-0-1-0-0-1
Is 47,13
astrologer

ἄστρον,-ου⁺ N2N 5-0-9-13-13-40
Ex 32,13; Nm 24,17; Dt 1,10; 10,22; 28,62
star

ἀστυγείτων,-ων,-ον A 0-0-0-0-1-1
2 Mc 6,8
neighboring

ἀσυλία,-ας N1F 0-0-0-0-1-1
2 Mc 3,12
right of sanctuary, inviolability
Cf. HORSLEY 1987, 168-169

ἄσυλος,-ος,-ον A 0-0-0-1-2-3
Prv 22,23; 2 Mc 4,33.34
safe from violence, inviolable Prv 22,23; ὁ
ἄσυλος τόπος *refuge, sanctuary* 2 Mc 4,33

ἀσύμφορος,-ος,-ον A 0-0-0-1-0-1
Prv 25,20
bad, inconvenient

ἀσύμφωνος,-ος,-ον⁺ A 0-0-0-0-2-2
Wis 18,10; Bel^LXX 15
not harmonious

ἀσύνετος,-ος,-ον⁺ A 1-0-0-3-9-13
Dt 32,21; Ps 75(76),6; 91(92),7; Jb 13,2; Od 2,21
without understanding, not intelligent, senseless Jb
13,2; *foolish, stupid* Wis 1,5; *Ps 75(76),6
ἀσύνετοι τῇ καρδίᾳ - עברי לב *the simple ones in
heart* for MT אבירי לב *the stouthearted*
Cf. LARCHER 1983, 176; →TWNT

ἀσυνθεσία,-ας N1F 0-0-1-3-0-4
Jer 3,7; Ezr 9,2.4; 10,6
transgression Ezr 9,2; *faithlessness* Jer 3,7; neol.

ἀσυνθετέω V 0-0-0-7-0-7
Ps 72(73),15; 77(78),57; 118(119),158; Ezr
10,2.10
to be faithless to (God) [τινι] Ezr 10,2; [ἔν τινι]
Neh 13,27; *Ps 118(119),158 ἀσυνθετοῦντας
being faithless vl. ἀσυνετοῦντας *acting foolish*;
neol.

ἀσύνθετος,-ος,-ον⁺ A 0-0-4-0-0-4
Jer 3,7.8.10.11
faithless

ἀσυρής,-ής,-ές A 0-0-0-0-1-1
Sir 23,13
lewd; neol.?

ἀσφάλεια,-ας⁺ N1F 2-0-3-4-11-20
Lv 26,5; Dt 12,10; Is 8,15; 18,4; 34,15
security, safety Lv 26,5; *steadfastness, stability* Ps
103(104),5; *Is 8,15(16) ἀσφαλείᾳ -צוּר *safe
place* (rock) for MT צוּר ◊ צרר *bind up*
Cf. SPICQ 1982, 71-73; →NIDNTT

ἀσφαλής,-ής,-ές⁺ A 0-0-0-3-4-7
Prv 3,18; 8,28; 15,7; Tob^S 5,17; Wis 4,3
safe Tob^S 5,17; *unfailing, trusty* Prv 3,18;
steadfast, immovable Prv 8,28
Cf. SPICQ 1982, 73-74; →NIDNTT

ἀσφαλίζομαι⁺ V 0-0-1-0-3-4
Is 41,10; Wis 4,17; 10,12; 13,15
to fasten with [τί τινι] Wis 13,15; *to set in safety,
to secure* [τινα] Wis 4,17; *to keep sb safe from*
[τινα ἀπό τινος] Wis 10,12; neol.?
Cf. SPICQ 1982, 74; →NIDNTT
(→ κατ-)

ἀσφαλτόπισσα,-ης N1F 1-0-0-0-0-1
Ex 2,3
bitumen (compound of asphalt and pitch); neol.
Cf. LE BOULLUEC 1989, 81

ἄσφαλτος,-ου N1F 3-0-0-0-0-3
Gn 6,14; 11,3; 14,10
pitch, tar, bitumen Gn 11,3; φρέατα ἀσφάλτου
bitumen-pits Gn 14,10

ἀσφαλτόω V 1-0-0-0-0-1
Gn 6,14
to smear with pitch, to cover with tar [τί τινι];
neol.

ἀσφαλῶς⁺ D 1-0-0-0-5-6
Gn 34,25; Tob^BA 6,4; 1 Mc 6,40; 3 Mc 7,6; Wis
18,6
securely 3 Mc 7,6 *steadfastly, unshaken in
purpose* Gn 34,25; *safely* Tob^BA 6,4; ἀσφαλῶς
εἰδώς *assuredly knowing* Wis 18,6
Cf. HORSLEY 1983, 9; SPICQ 1982, 74-75

ἀσχημονέω⁺ V 1-0-4-0-0-5
Dt 25,3; Ez 16,7.22.39; 23,29
to behave unseemly, to disgrace oneself

ἀσχημοσύνη,-ης⁺ N1F 37-0-2-2-3-44
Ex 20,26; 22,26; 28,42; Lv 18,6.7
stereotyped rendition עור / ערוה; *shame* Sir
26,8; *dishonour* Ezr 4,14; *looseness, impudence*
Sir 30,13; *shame* (euph. for *nakedness*) Ex
20,26; *disgrace* (euph. for *excrement*) Dt
23,13
Cf. LE BOULLUEC 1989, 293

ἀσχήμων,-ων,-ον⁺ A 2-0-0-0-3-5
Gn 34,7; Dt 24,1; 2 Mc 9,2; Wis 2,20; Sus^Th 63

shameful, unworthy Wis 2,20; ἄσχημον πρᾶγμα
sth shameful, dishonesty Sus[Th] 63; ἄσχημον
ποιέω *to do sth shameful* Gn 34,7

ἀσχολέομαι   V 0-0-0-0-1-1
Sir 39,1
to be occupied in [ἔν τινι]

ἀσχολία,-ας   N1F 0-0-0-0-2-2
3 Mc 5,34; Sir 40,1
occupation, engagement

ἀσωτία,-ας[+]   N1F 0-0-0-1-1-2
Prv 28,7; 2 Mc 6,4
luxury, debauchery, wastefulness
Cf. SPICQ 1978, 154-156; WALTERS 1973, 38-39

ἄσωτος,-ος,-ον[+]   A 0-0-0-1-0-1
Prv 7,11
luxurious, debauched, profligate

ἄτακτος,-ος,-ον[+]   A 0-0-0-0-1-1
3 Mc 1,19
undisciplined, disorderly
Cf. SPICQ 1978, 157-159

ἀταξία,-ας   N1F 0-0-0-0-1-1
Wis 14,26
disorder

ἀτάρ   C 0-0-0-2-0-2
Jb 6,21; 7,11
now

ἀταραξία,-ας   N1F 0-0-0-0-1-1
4 Mc 8,26
impassiveness, calmness; μετὰ ἀταραξίας
undisturbed

ἀτάραχος,-ος,-ον   A 0-0-0-2-1-3
Est 3,13; 8,12; 2 Mc 11,23
not disturbed, quiet

ἄταφος,-ος,-ον   A 0-0-0-0-1-1
2 Mc 5,10
unburied

ἄτε   X 0-0-0-0-1-1
3 Mc 1,29
since, in asmuch as (causal) [+gen. absol.]

ἀτείχιστος,-ος,-ον   A 1-0-0-1-0-2
Nm 13,19; Prv 25,28
unwalled, unfortified

ἀτεκνία,-ας   N1F 0-0-1-1-3-5
Is 47,9; Ps 34(35),12; 4 Mc 18,9; Wis 4,1; PSal
4,18
childlessness Wis 4,1; *bereavement* Ps 34(35),12

ἄτεκνος,-ος,-ον[+]   A 3-0-2-0-1-6
Gn 15,2; Lv 20,20.21; Is 49,21; Jer 18,21
without children

ἀτεκνόω   V 6-5-6-3-1-21

Gn 27,45; 31,38; 42,36; 43,14(bis)
A: *to make childless* [τινα] Gn 42,36; *to be
barren* Ct 4,2; P: *to be (made) childless* Hos
9,12; *to be made barren* (of the earth) 2 Kgs
2,19; *Ez 36,14 ἀτεκνώσεις -תשכלי *you will
make childless* for MT תכשלי *you will stumble*
Cf. HARL 1986, 241; LEE 1983, 45

ἀτέλεια,-ας   N1F 0-0-0-0-1-1
1 Mc 10,34
immunity of debts

ἀτέλεστος,-ος,-ον   A 0-0-0-0-2-2
Wis 3,16; 4,5
*unaccomplished, imperfect, immature, unable to
reach maturity* (of pers.) Wis 3,16; (of things)
Wis 4,5

ἀτελής,-ής,-ές   A 0-0-0-0-2-2
3 Mc 5,42; Wis 10,7
unripe, imperfect of growth Wis 10,7; *impious* (as
from one who is not initiated), *ineffectual* 3 Mc
5,42

ἀτενίζω[+]   V 0-0-0-0-3-3
1 Ezr 6,27; 3 Mc 2,26; Od 12,9
look intently [abs.] 1 Ezr 6,27; [εἴς τι] 3 Mc
2,26
Cf. DEPUYDT 1985, 40; SPICQ 1982, 79-80

ἄτερ[+]   P 0-0-0-0-1-1
2 Mc 12,15
without [τινος]

ἀτιμάζω[+]   V 3-3-9-10-8-33
Gn 16,4.5; Dt 27,16; 1 Sm 10,27; 17,42
to dishonour, to hold in no honour [τινα] Dt
27,16; [τι] Prv 30,17

ἀτίμητος,-ος,-ον   A 0-0-0-0-2-2
3 Mc 3,23; Wis 7,9
invaluable, priceless

ἀτιμία,-ας[+]   N1F 0-0-19-15-21-55
Is 10,16; 22,18; Jer 3,25; 6,15; 13,26
dishonour, disgrace Tob[S] 14,10; *Jb 40,13
ἀτιμίας ἔμπλησον - בוש? *with shame* for MT
חבש *bind*

ἄτιμος,-ος,-ον[+]   A 0-0-2-2-7-11
Is 3,5; 53,3; Jb 30,4.8; Wis 3,17
dishonoured, not honourable

ἀτιμόω   V 0-3-9-1-1-14
1 Sm 2,30; 15,9; 1 Chr 19,5; Jer 22,22.28
A: *to dishonour* [τι] Ez 16,59; P: *to suffer
dishonour* 1 Sm 2,30
(→ ἐξ-)

ἀτιμώρητος,-ος,-ον   A 0-0-0-4-0-4
Prv 11,21; 19,5.9; 28,20

unpunished

ἀτμίς,-ίδος⁺   N3F 2-0-3-0-6-11
Gn 19,28; Lv 16,13; Ez 8,11; Hos 13,3; Jl 3,3
smoke Gn 19,28; *thin smoke* Sir 22,24; *vapour*
Sir 43,4; *exhalation* (metaph.) Wis 7,25

ἀτοπία,-ας   N1F 0-0-0-0-1-1
Jdt 11,11
that which is not fit to be done, wickedness,
misdeed

ἄτοπος,-ος,-ον⁺   A 0-0-0-7-1-8
Jb 4,8; 11,11; 27,6; 34,12; 35,13
out of place, wrong Prv 30,20; *inappropriate* Jb
27,6; τὰ ἄτοπα (sc. ἔργα) *wicked deeds* Jb 4,8
Cf. COX 1990, 119-130

ἄτρακτος,-ου   N2M 0-0-0-1-0-1
Prv 31,19
spindle

ἀτραπός,-οῦ   N2M 0-1-0-2-2-5
Jgsᴮ 5,6; Jb 6,19; 24,13; Wis 5,10; Sir 5,9
by-way, path

ἄτρυγος,-ος,-ον   A 1-0-0-0-0-1
Ex 27,20
refined, pure (of oil)

ἄτρωτος,-ος,-ον   A 0-0-0-0-3-3
2 Mc 8,36; 10,30; 3 Mc 5,47
invulnerable 2 Mc 8,36; *unwounded* 2 Mc 10,30

ἀττάκης,-ου   N1M 1-0-0-0-0-1
Lv 11,22
kind of locust; neol.
Cf. WALTERS 1973, 64-65

ἀττέλεβος,-ου   N2M 0-0-1-0-0-1
Na 3,17
locust

ἀτυχέω   V 0-0-0-1-0-1
Prv 27,10
to be unfortunate

ἀτυχία,-ας   N1F 0-0-0-0-2-2
2 Mc 12,30; 14,14
failure, ill-luck

αὐγάζω⁺   V 7-0-0-0-0-7
Lv 13,24.25.26.28.38
to appear white or *bright*
(·· κατ-)

αὔγασμα,-ατος   N3N 2-0-0-0-1-3
Lv 13,38.39; Sir 43,11
bright (white) spot (on the skin) Lv 13,38;
brightness Sir 43,11; neol.

αὐγέω   V 0-0-0-1-0-1
Jb 29,3
to shine, glitter; neol.?

αὐγή,-ῆς⁺   N1F 0-0-1-0-1-2
Is 59,9; 2 Mc 12,9
brightness, bright light Is 59,9; *gleam* 2 Mc 12,9

αὐθάδεια,-ας   N1F 0-0-1-0-0-1
Is 24,8
wilfulness, stubbornness, insolence

αὐθάδης,-ης,-ες⁺   A 2-0-0-1-0-3
Gn 49,3.7; Prv 21,24
arrogant, stubborn
→TWNT

αὐθαιρέτως   D 0-0-0-0-3-3
2 Mc 6,19; 3 Mc 6,6; 7,10
of free choice, of one's own accord

αὐθέντης,-ου   N1M 0-0-0-0-1-1
Wis 12,6
murderer

αὐθεντία,-ας   N1F 0-0-0-0-1-1
3 Mc 2,29
restriction, status; neol.?

αὐθημερινός,-ή,-όν   A 0-0-0-1-0-1
Jb 7,1
ephemeral; μίσθιος αὐθημερινός *day-labourer*

αὐθημερόν   D 1-0-0-1-0-2
Dt 24,15; Prv 12,16
immediately, on the very (same) day

αὐθωρί   D 0-0-0-1-1-2
Dnᴸˣˣ 3,15; 3 Mc 3,25
immediately; neol.

αὐλαία,-ας   N1F 18-0-1-0-1-20
Ex 26,1.2(ter).3(bis)
curtain Ex 26,1; *door (of a tent)* Jdt 14,14

αὐλαῖος,-α,-ον   A 0-0-0-0-1-1
2 Mc 14,41
belonging to the courtyard

αὖλαξ,-ακος   N3F 1-0-0-3-2-6
Nm 22,24; Ps 64(65),11; Jb 31,38; 39,10; Sir 7,3
avenue (in a vineyard) Nm 22,24; *furrow* Jb
31,38

αὐλάρχης,ου   N1M 0-1-0-0-0-1
2 Sm 8,18
mayor of the palace, chief of the court (of the
temple?); neol.

αὐλαρχία,-ας   N1F 0-1-0-0-0-1
1 Kgs 2,46
function of chief of the (temple-)court; neol.

αὐλή,-ῆς⁺   N1F 33-27-72-37-16-185
Ex 27,9(bis).12.13.16
court of the tabernacle Ex 27,9; *court (garden)*
2 Sm 17,18; *court of a temple* 1 Kgs 6,36; *hall*
1 Kgs 6,37(7,12); *any dwelling, abode, chamber*

Neh 3,25; *court, palace* Est 1,1; * Ez 40,44 εἰς τὴν αὐλήν -ל/חצר *to the court* for MT ל/שער *to the gate*, cpr. LtJ 17; Est 2,19; 3,2.5; *Jer 30,23 (49,28) τῆς αὐλῆς -חצר *of the palace* for MT חצור *Hazor*, see also 30,25.28(49,30.33); *Is 34,13 αὐλή -חצר *a court* for MT חציר *grass*?; *Est 7,4 τῆς αὐλῆς -נשכה? *hall, court* for MT נזק *injury;* *2 Kgs 20,4 ἐν τῇ αὐλῇ -חצר *the palace* for MT העיר *the town*
Cf. HUSSON 1983, 45-54

αὐλίζομαι⁺   V 0-20-1-24-17-62
JgsᴮB 18,2; 19,4; Jgsᴬ 19,6.7.10
to lodge Jgsᴮ 18,2; *to lodge in* [τι] Jb 15,28; *to tarry* Tobᴮᴬ 4,14; *to make to dwell* (semit. rendering Hebr. hiphil) Jer 38(31),9
(→ συν-)

αὐλός,-οῦ⁺   N2M 0-3-7-0-3-13
1 Sm 10,5; 2 Sm 6,5; 1 Chr 28,12; Is 5,12; 30,29
pipe, flute

αὐλών,-ῶνος   N3M 0-5-0-0-6-11
1 Sm 17,3; 1 Chr 10,7; 12,16; 27,29; 2 Chr 20,26
valley

αὐξάνω⁺   V 23-7-4-2-4-40
Gn 1,22.28; 8,17; 9,1.7
A: *to increase, to cause to grow* [τινα] (semit. rendering Hebr. hiphil) Gn 17,6; P: *to grow* Gn 21,8; *to grow, to increase* Gn 1,22; *1 Chr 17,10 καὶ αὐξήσω σε -ואגדלך *I wil increase you* for MT נגד ◊ ואגד לך *I will declare to you*, cpr. 2 Sm 7,11; *Jgs 5,11 αὐξήσον -◊ פרה *increase* for MT פרזונו *his peasantry*
Cf. HARL 1986, 57.97; → NIDNTT; TWNT

αὐξήσις,-εως⁺   N3F 0-0-0-0-1-1
2 Mc 5,16
augmentation, amplification, increase
Cf. HORSLEY 1982, 78

αὔξω
(→ ἐπ-, συν-)

αὔρα,-ας   N1F 0-1-0-2-0-3
1 Kgs 19,12; Ps 106(107),29; Jb 4,16
breeze 3 Kgs 19,12; *breath, whisper* Jb 4,16

αὔριον⁺   D 19-32-1-6-6-64
Gn 30,33; Ex 8,6.19.25; 9,5
tomorrow Ex 8,29; *soon, at a future time* Dt 6,20; ἡ αὔριον (sc. ἡμέρα) *the morrow, the following day* Gn 30,33

αὐστηρία,-ας   N1F 0-0-0-0-1-1
2 Mc 14,30
harshness, roughness, sour behaviour

αὐστηρός,-ά,-όν⁺   A 0-0-0-0-1-1

2 Mc 14,30
harsh, rough, bitter

αὐτάρκεια,-ας   N1F 0-0-0-0-1-1
PSal 5,16
self-sufficiency, independence

αὐταρκέω   V 1-0-0-0-1-2
Dt 32,10; Od 2,10
to supply with necessaries [τινα]

αὐτάρκης,-ης,-ες⁺   A 0-0-0-1-5-6
Prv 30,8; 4 Mc 9,9; Sir 5,1; 11,24; 31,28
sufficient Prv 30,8; *sufficient in oneself, self-supporting* Sir 40,18; *measurably, without excess* Sir 34,28; *despotic* 4 Mc 9,9

αὐτίκα   D 0-0-0-0-2-2
4 Mc 1,12; 2,8
at once 4 Mc 1,12; *for example* 4 Mc 2,8

αὐτοδέσποτος,-ου   N2M 0-0-0-0-3-3
4 Mc 1,1.30; 13,1
absolute master of [τινος]; neol.

αὐτόθεν   D 0-0-0-0-1-1
Tobˢ 8,21
at once

αὐτόθι   D 0-1-0-0-7-8
Jos 5,8; 1 Ezr 8,41.61; Tobˢ 2,3; 2 Mc 3,24
there, on the spot

αὐτοκράτωρ,-ορος   N3M 0-0-0-0-5-5
4 Mc 1,7.13.30; 8,28; 16,1
absolute master of [τινος]

αὐτόματος,-η,-ον⁺   A 2-2-0-1-1-6
Lv 25,5.11; Jos 6,5; 2 Kgs 19,29; Jb 24,24
self-acting, spontaneously doing sth (of things)
Cf. SPICQ 1978, 162-165

αὐτομολέω   V 0-5-0-0-4-9
Jos 10,1.4; 1 Sm 20,30; 2 Sm 3,8; 10,19
to come of one's own accord, to change sides Jos 10,1; *to desert* Jdt 16,12; *to be rebellious* 1 Sm 20,30
(→ ἀπ-)

αὐτός,-ή,-όν⁺   R 6013-8089-4927-4921-5466-29416
Gn 1,9.11(bis).12(bis)
self (with name) 2 Mc 11,12; (with subst.) 4 Mc 17,17; (with pron.) 3 Mc 3,13; *he, she, it* (to emphasize a subject already known) Wis 6,7; (to refer with more or less emphasis to a subject) Ps 129,8; *him, her, it* (oblique cases used for third personal pron.) Gn 1,17; used pleonastically after a relative Gn 1,11; αὐτοῦ,-ῆς,-οῦ *of him, of her, of it* (used as lacking possessive pron.) Est 1,1e; καὶ αὐτός *even* 4 Mc 17,1; ὁ αὐτός *the same* 2 Mc 3,33; ἐπὶ τὸ αὐτό *at the same*

place, together 2 Sm 2,13; κατὰ τὸ αὐτό together
1 Kgs 3,18
Cf. SOLLAMO 1991, 75-85

αὐτοσχεδίως   D 0-0-0-0-1-1
Wis 2,2
randomly, accidentally, by chance
Cf. LARCHER 1983, 215

αὐτοῦ⁺   D 7-2-1-0-1-11
Gn 22,5; Ex 24,14; Nm 9,8; 22,8.19
(just) there, (just) here

αὐτόχθων,-ονος   N3M 11-1-2-0-0-14
Ex 12,19.48; Lv 16,29; 17,15; 19,34
indigenous, native Lv 16,29; *Jer 14,8 ὡς
αὐτόχθων -כאזרה like a native for MT כארה like
a traveller
Cf. HARLÉ 1988, 42

αὐχήν,-ένος   N3M 0-3-0-1-1-5
Jos 7,8.12; 2 Chr 29,6; Ps 128(129),4; 3 Mc 4,8
neck, throat Ps 128(129),4; μεταβάλλω αὐχένα
to flee Jos 7,8; δίδωμι αὐχένα to give the cold
shoulder, to turn one's back 2 Chr 29,6

αὐχμός,-οῦ   N2M 0-0-1-0-0-1
Jer 31(48),31
drought

αὐχμώδης,-ης,-ες   A 0-4-1-0-0-5
1 Sm 23,14.15.19; 26,1; Mi 4,8
dry, arid 1 Kgs 23,14; *Mi 4,8 αὐχμώδης -עפר?
dry dust for עפל hill

ἀφαγνίζω   V 10-0-0-0-0-10
Lv 14,49.52; Nm 6,2; 8,6.21
A: to purify [τι] Lv 14,49; M: to consecrate Nm
6,2

ἀφαίρεμα,-ατος   N3N 37-0-2-0-0-39
Ex 29,27.28(ter); 35,5
share or portion taken away as the choice part
(for sacrifice or consacration); neol.
Cf. HARLÉ 1988, 42; LE BOULLUEC 1989, 250

ἀφαίρεσις,-εως   N3F 0-0-0-0-2-2
3 Mc 1,1; Sir 41,23
taking away, removal Sir 41,21; seizure, capture
3 Mc 1,1

ἀφαιρέω⁺   V 46-22-49-26-25-168
Gn 21,25; 30,23; 31,9.16.31
A: to take away (as the choice part and as a
tribute) [τι] Ex 13,12; to remove (the hand) [τι]
Ex 33,23; M: to take away [τι] Gn 21,25; *Is 5,8
ἀφέλωνται -◊אסף? they will take away for MT
אפס none; *Is 38,14 ἀφείλατο μου
-◊עבר(hiphil)? he removed for MT ערבני◊ערב be
surety for me, cpr. Jb 11,7

Cf. HELBING 1928, 43-44

ἀφάλλομαι   V 0-0-2-0-1-3
Ez 44,10; Na 3,17;Sir 36,26
to jump Sir 36,26; to go down (of the sun) Na
3,17; to go away from, to abandon [ἀπό τινος]
Ez 44,10

ἀφανής,-ής,-ές⁺   A 0-0-0-1-3-4
Jb 24,20; 2 Mc 3,34; Sir 20,30; 41,14
unseen, invisible

ἀφανίζω⁺   V 7-8-39-29-9-92
Ex 8,5; 12,15; 21,29.36; Dt 7,2
to remove, to get rid of [τι] Ex 8,5; to destroy
[τινα] 2 Sm 22,38; to blot out (a name) [τι]
1 Sm 24,22; *Mi 6,15 καὶ ἀφανισθήσεται
-וישתקר and shall be abolished for MT וישתמר
and have been kept (6,1 ditogr.); *Ez 30,9
ἀφανίσαι -ל/החרים to destroy for MT ל/החריר to
terrify

ἀφανισμός,-οῦ⁺   N2M 1-5-42-5-6-59
Dt 7,2; 1 Kgs 9,7; 13,34; 2 Kgs 22,19; 2 Chr 29,8
extermination, destruction

ἀφάπτω   V 2-1-0-2-0-5
Dt 6,8; 11,18; Jgs^A 20,34; Prv 3,3; 6,21
A: to fasten from or upon [τι ἐπί τινος] Dt 6,8;
M: to let hang [τι ἐπί τινι] (metaph.) Prv 3,3;
ἀφῆπται αὐτῶν ἡ κακία evil is stuck upon them
Jgs^A 20,34

ἀφασία,-ας   N1F 0-0-0-0-1-1
2 Mc 14,17
speechlessness, silence (caused by fear)

ἀφεγγής,-ής,-ές   A 0-0-0-0-1-1
Wis 17,3
dark, obscure

ἄφεδρος,-ου   N2M 10-0-1-0-1-12
Lv 12,2.5; 15,19.20.25
menstruation

ἀφειδῶς   D 0-0-0-1-2-3
Prv 21,26; 2 Mc 5,6.12
unsparingly Prv 21,26; without mercy 2 Mc 5,6

ἄφεμα,-ατος   N3N 0-0-0-0-3-3
1 Mc 10,28; 13,37; 15,5
immunity (of tax), remission of tribute; neol.?

ἄφεσις,-εως⁺   N3F 31-1-10-3-5-50
Ex 18,2; 23,11; Lv 16,26; 25,10(bis)
channel issue (of water) Jl 1,20; remission, the
act of sending away (of pers.) Ex 18,2; release of
captivity 1 Ezr 4,62; cancellation (of a debt) Dt
15,3; letting go, release Lv 16,26; ἄφεσιν ποιέω
to let (the land) rest Ex 23,11; *Ez 47,3 = אפסים
ankless

Cf. SPICQ 1982, 83-84; WALTERS 1973, 178; →TWNT

ἀφεύκτως   D 0-0-0-0-1-1
·3 Mc 7,9
without any possibility of escape

ἀφή,-ῆς⁺   N1F 65-3-1-0-0-69
Lv 13,2.3(quater)
infection, plague Lv 13,2; *wound, stroke* Dt 17,8

ἀφηγέομαι   V 1-5-23-1-6-36
Ex 11,8; Jgs^A 1,1; 20,18(bis); Jgs^B 1,1
to be leader of, to lead [τινος] Ex 11,8; *to go first
(as leader)* Jgs 1,1; *to have a charge over* [τινος]
4 Mc 12,5; ἀφηγούμενος *leader* Ez 11,1; *Ez
22,25 ἀφηγούμενοι -נשאים *leaders* for MT נבאים
prophets; *Ez 12,10 ὁ ἀφηγούμενος -המשל *the
ruler* for MT המשא *burden*?

ἀφήγημα,-ατος   N3N 0-0-0-0-1-1
4 Mc 14,6
guiding, leading, command

ἀφθαρσία,-ας⁺   N1F 0-0-0-0-5-5
4 Mc 9,22; 17,12; Wis 2,23; 6,18.19
immortality Wis 2,23; *incorruption, integrity* Wis
6,19
Cf. REESE 1970, 63-69

ἄφθαρτος,-ος,-ον⁺   A 0-0-0-0-2-2
Wis 12,1; 18,4
incorruptible, incorrupt

ἄφθονος,-ος,-ον   A 0-0-0-0-2-2
3 Mc 5,2; 4 Mc 3,10
copious, bounteous

ἀφθόνως   D 0-0-0-0-1-1
Wis 7,13
abundantly, ungrudgingly

ἄφθορος,-ος,-ον   A 0-0-0-1-0-1
Est 2,2
uncorrupt, pure

ἀφιερόω   V 0-0-0-0-1-1
4 Mc 13,13
to consecrate [τινα]

ἀφίημι⁺   V 30-28-7-22-51-138
Gn 4,13; 18,26; 20,6; 35,18; 42,33
to acquit, to forgive [τινα] Gn 4,13; [τινί τι] Gn
50,17; *to leave unpunished, to spare* [τι] Gn
18,26; *to permit, to suffer* [τινα +inf.] Gn 20,6;
to leave [τινα] Gn 42,33; *to send away* Ex 22,4;
to remit (a debt) [τι] Dt 15,2; *to leave sb alone,
in peace* [τινα] 2 Kgs 4,27; *to set free* [τινα ἀπό
τινος] 2 Chr 10,4; *to take away* [τι ἀπό τινος]
2 Chr 10,10; *to neglect* [abs.] Prv 4,13; *to
abandon* [τι] Is 32,14; ἀφίημι τὴν ψυχήν *to die*
Gn 35,18; ἀφίημι φωνήν *to utter his voice* Gn

45,2; ἀφίημί τινα ἐλεύθερον *to set free* Jdt
16,23; ἀφίημί τι ἐν γραφῇ *to leave sth in writing*
Sir 39,32; ἀφίημι τοὺς υἱοὺς ἀπεριτμήτους *to
leave their children uncircumcised* 1 Mc 1,48;
ἀφίημί τινι ἀφέματα *to grant remission of
tribute* 1 Mc 10,28; ἀφειμένος *free* (left in
peace) 1 Mc 10,31
→TWNT

ἀφικνέομαι⁺   V 3-0-0-5-6-14
Gn 28,12; 38,1; 47,9; Jb 11,7; 13,27
to arrive at, to reach [εἴς τι] Gn 28,12; [πρός
τινα] Gn 38,1; [ἕως τινός] Jdt 1,14; [τινι] Prv
1,27; *Jb 16,20 ἀφίκοιτο -תמצא (Aram. תמשא)
you will arrive for MT מליצי *my scorners*

ἄφιξις,-εως⁺   N3F 0-0-0-0-1-1
3 Mc 7,18
arrival

ἀφίστημι⁺   V 21-76-28-46-58-229
Gn 12,8; 14,4; 19,9; 30,36; 31,40
A: *to remove, draw away from* [τινα ἀπό τινος]
Dt 7,4; [τι ἀπό τινος] Jer 16,9; *to send away* [τι]
1 Kgs 21,24; *to turn away* [τι] Ps 65(66),20; *to
cause to fall* [τινα] Si 19,2; M: *to depart
[intrans.]* Gn 12,8; *to depart from* [ἀπό τινος]
Gn 31,49; (metaph.) Nm 12,10; (of disease) Lv
13,58; *to stand back [intrans.]* Gn 19,9; *to keep
far from, to abstain from* [ἀπό τινος] Ex 23,7; *to
revolt [intrans.]* Gn 14,4; *to resign, to withdraw
from* [ἀπό τινος] Nm 8,25; *to reject* [τι ἀπό
τινος] Nm 14,31; ἀφίστημι ὁδὸν τριῶν ἡμερῶν
to set a distance of a three days' journey Gn
30,36; ἀφίστημι τὴν καρδίαν τινός *to change
the minds of* Nm 32,9
Cf. HELBING 1928, 179-181; LEE 1983, 35-36; →NIDNTT;
TWNT

ἄφνω⁺   D 0-1-3-2-4-10
Jos 10,9; Jer 4,20; 18,22; 28(51),8; Prv 1,27
unawares, of a sudden

ἀφοβία,-ας   N1F 0-0-0-1-0-1
Prv 15,16
fearlessness

ἄφοβος,-ος,-ον   A 0-0-0-2-2-4
Prv 3,24; 19,23; Wis 17,4; Sir 5,5
without fear, fearless Prv 3,24; *overconfident* Sir
5,5

ἀφόβως⁺   D 0-0-0-1-1-2
Prv 1,33; Od 9,74
fearless

ἀφόδευμα,-ατος   N3N 0-0-0-0-1-1
Tob^S 2,10

excrement; neol.

ἀφοδεύω   V 0-0-0-0-1-1
Tob[BA] 2,10
to discharge excrement

ἄφοδος,-ου   N2M 0-0-0-0-1-1
3 Mc 7,10
departure

ἀφόμοιον,-α   N2N 0-0-0-0-1-1
Sir prol.,29
copy; neol.

ἀφομοιόομαι[+]   V 0-0-0-0-4-4
LtJ 4(bis).62.70
to become or *to be made like* [τινι] LtJ 4
Cf. HELBING 1928, 254

ἀφοράω[+]   V 0-0-1-0-3-4
Jon 4,5; 3 Mc 6,8; 4 Mc 17,10.23
to look to sb (as to a model), to look up to [εἰς τινα]
Cf. SPICQ 1978, 170-172

ἀφόρητος,-ος,-ον   A 0-0-0-0-1-1
2 Mc 9,10
intolerable, unendurable

ἀφορία,-ας   N1F 0-0-1-0-0-1
Hag 2,17
barrenness, sterility

ἀφορίζω[+]   V 31-42-10-2-2-87
Gn 2,10; 10,5; Ex 19,12.23; 29,24
A: *to separate* [τινα] Ex 19,12; *to set apart* [τι]
Ex 45,1; *to grant as a special gift to* [τί τινι] Ps
67(68),10; M: *to mark off by boundaries* [τι] Ex
19,23; P: *to be separated* Ex 29,27; *to be set apart*
Ez 45,4; *to be divided from* [ἐκ τινος] Gn 10,5;
to divide oneself in [εἰς τι] Gn 2,10; ἀφορίζω τι
ἀφόρισμα *to separate as a separate offering, to
set aside as a wave-offering* Ex 29,26
Cf. LE BOULLUEC 1989, 44; →TWNT

ἀφόρισμα,-ατος   N3N 10-0-1-0-0-11
Ex 29,24.26.27; 36,37(39,30); Lv 10,14
the separate (or *special*) *offering, that which is set
apart, wave-offering* Ex 29,24; *that which is set
apart, enclosure* (of land) Nm 35,3; neol.
Cf. HARLÉ 1988,42; LE BOULLUEC 1989, 299-300; LEE
1983, 45; →TWNT

ἀφορισμός,-οῦ   N2M 0-0-3-0-0-3
Ez 20,31.40; 48,8
see ἀφόρισμα

ἀφορμή,-ῆς[+]   N1F 0-0-1-1-1-3
Ez 5,7; Prv 9,9; 3 Mc 3,2
occasion Prv 9,9; *starting-point, pretext* 3 Mc 3,2;
Ez 5,7 ἀφορμὴ ὑμῶν -מכורתכם? your origin for

MT המנכם (corr.? המרתכם) *your raging?*
→TWNT

ἀφορολόγητος,-ος,-ον   A 0-0-0-0-2-2
1 Ezr 4,50; 1 Mc 11,28
not subjected to tribute; neol.?

ἀφρονεύομαι   V 0-0-1-0-0-1
Jer 10,21
to act foolishly; neol.

ἀφρόνως   D 1-0-0-0-0-1
Gn 31,28
foolishly; neol.

ἀφροσύνη,-ης[+]   N1F 1-8-0-21-6-36
Dt 22,21; Jgs[A] 19,23.24; 20,6.10
folly, thoughtlessness Prv 5,5; *sinful foolishness*
Dt 22,21; *foolishness of the ungodly* Eccl 7,25
→NIDNTT; TWNT

ἄφρων,-ων,-ον[+]   A 0-1-3-109-20-133
2 Sm 13,13; Is 59,7; Jer 4,22; 17,11; Ps 13(14),1
crazy, foolish 2 Sm 13,13; *sinful* Is 59,7;
foolishness, rebellion against God Jer 4,22
→NIDNTT; TWNT

ἀφυλάκτως   D 0-0-1-0-0-1
Ez 7,22
unguardedly

ἀφυστερέω   V 0-0-0-1-1-2
Neh 9,20; Sir 14,14
to withhold from [τι ἀπό τινος] Neh 9,20; *to stay
away from* [ἀπό τινος] Sir 14,14; neol.?
Cf. HELBING 1928, 173

αφφουσωθ   N 0-2-0-0-0-2
2 Kgs 15,5; 2 Chr 26,21
=חפשית *exempt from duties*

αφφω   I 0-2-0-0-0-2
2 Kgs 2,14; 10,10
=אף הוא *he himself* 2 Kgs 2,14; =אפוא *then*
2 Kgs 10,10

ἄφωνος,-ος,-ον[+]   A 0-0-1-0-2-3
Is 53,7; 2 Mc 3,29; Wis 4,19
speechless Wis 4,19; *dumb* Is 53,7

ἀχανής,-ής,-ές   A 0-0-0-0-1-1
Wis 19,17
dense, thick; ἀχανὲς σκότος *dense, complete
darkness*

ἄχαρις,-ιτος   A 0-0-0-0-1-1
Sir 20,19
unpleasant, disagreeable

ἀχάριστος,-ος,-ον[+]   A 0-0-0-0-4-4
4 Mc 9,10; Wis 16,29; Sir 29,16.25
ungrateful

ἀχαρίστως   D 0-0-0-0-1-1

Sir 18,18
with bad grace, with an ill will; neol.?

ἀχάτης,-ου N1M 2-0-1-0-0-3
Ex 28,19; 36,19(39,12); Ez 28,13
agate

ἄχι N3N 2-0-1-0-1-4
Gn 41,2.18; Is 19,7; Sir 40,16
=אחו *grass, sedge weed* Gn 41,2; *grass, herbage* Is
19,2; neol.?

αχουχ N 0-2-0-0-0-2
2 Chr 25,18(bis)
=החוח *thistle*

ἀχρεῖος,-ος,-ον⁺ A 0-1-0-0-1-2
2 Sm 6,22; LtJ 15
vile, nothing worth (of pers.) 2 Sm 6,22; *nothing
worth* (of things) LtJ 15; neol.?

ἀχρειότης,-ητος N3F 0-0-0-0-2-2
Tob^BA 4,13(bis)
worthlessness, lewdness; neol.

ἀχρειόω⁺ V 0-1-1-4-1-7
2 Kgs 3,19; Jer 11,16; Ps 13(14),3; 52(53),4;
Dn^LXX 4,14(11)
A: *to damage* [τι] 2 Kgs 3,19; *to destroy* [τινα]
Dn^LXX 6,21; P: *to become useless* or *corrupted* Ps
13(14),3

ἄχρηστος,-ος,-ον⁺ A 0-0-1-0-9-10
Hos 8,8; 2 Mc 7,5; 3 Mc 3,29; Wis 2,11; 3,11

useless Wis 2,11; *without effect* Wis 3,11;
*(mutilated in all his members, and therefore)
unable to act* 2 Mc 7,5

ἄχρις⁺ or ἄχρι⁺ P 0-1-0-1-2-4
Jgs^B 11,33; Jb 32,11; 2 Mc 14,10.15
even to, as far as (of place) Jgs^B 11,33; ἄχρι
αἰῶνος *for ever* 2 Mc 14,15; *as long as* (as
conjunction) 2 Mc 14,10; ἄχρι οὗ [+subj.] *until*
Jb 32,11

ἄχυρον,-ου⁺ N2N 10-3-6-3-0-22
Gn 24,25.32; Ex 5,7(bis).10
chaff Jb 21,18; *straw* Gn 24,25

ἀψευδής,-ής,-ές⁺ A 0-0-0-0-1-1
Wis 7,17
truthful

ἄψυχος,-ος,-ον⁺ A 0-0-0-0-2-2
Wis 13,17; 14,29
inanimate
Cf. GILBERT 1973, 79-81.93

ἀωρία,-ας N1F 0-0-2-1-1-4
Is 59,9; Zph 1,15; Ps 118(119),147; 1 Ezr 1,14
night 1 Ezr 1,14; *midnight* Ps 118(119),147;
darkness (metaph.) Is 59,9

ἄωρος,-ος,-ον A 0-0-1-4-2-7
Is 65,20; Jb 22,16; Prv 10,6; 11,30; 13,2
untimely Jb 22,16; *unripe* Wis 4,5; ἄωρος *who
dies untimely* Is 65,20

βααλταμ N 0-0-0-3-0-3
Ezr 4,8.9.17
=בעל טעם chancellor

βαδδιν N 0-0-0-3-0-3
Dn^Th 10,5; 12,6.7
=ברין (Aram.? pl. of בד) for MT ברים fine linen

βαδίζω V 14-6-30-4-19-73
Gn 42,19; 44,25; Ex 4,18.19; 6,6
to walk Is 40,31; to go, to proceed Gn 42,19; to
sail (of a ship) Jon 1,3; βάδιζε go! (often
imper.) Ex 4,18; *Ex 6,6 βάδιζε -לכה go for MT
לכן therefore
Cf. SHIPP 1979, 122-124; WEVERS 1990, 75.307

βάδος,-ου N2M 0-0-0-2-0-2
Ezr 7,22(bis)
=בת (liquid) measure
Cf. WALTERS 1973, 331-332

βαθέως D 0-0-1-0-0-1
Is 29,15
profoundly
Cf. ZIEGLER 1934, 148

βαθμός,-οῦ⁺ N2M 0-6-0-0-1-7
1 Sm 5,5; 2 Kgs 20,9(bis).10(bis)
step, threshold 1 Sm 5,5; degree (on the dial)
2 Kgs 20,9
Cf. SPICQ 1978, 173

βάθος,-ους⁺ N3N 0-0-13-5-5-23
Is 7,11; 51,10; Ez 26,20; 31,14.18
depth Jb 28,11; bottom Ez 43,14; depth
(metaph.) Jdt 8,14; βάθη deep water Ps 68,3;
δίδωμι ρίζαν εἰς βάθος to strike deep roots
Wis 4,3; *Prv 18,3 εἰς βάθος -ב/אגם into a depth
for MT בא נם comes, also; *Jb 28,11 βάθη depth
-נבך ◊ מבכי? sources for MT מ/בכי from tears?

βαθύνω V 0-0-2-1-0-3
Jer 30,2.25(49,8.30); Ps 91(92),6
A: to dig deep Jer 30,2; P: to be deep (metaph.)
Ps 91,6

βαθύς,-εῖα,-ύ A 0-0-7-11-6-24
Is 30,33; 31,6; Jer 17,9; Ez 23,32; 27,34
deep Jb 11,8; profound 3 Mc 5,12; deep
(metaph.) Wis 16,11; inscrutable Jer 17,9;
βαθεῖαν βουλὴν βουλεύομαι to devise an
inscrutable counsel Is 31,6, cpr. 29,15; βαθεῖα
εἰρήνη secure peace 4 Mc 3,20; τὰ βαθέα the
secrets Dn^LXX2,22
Cf. MCKANE 1986, 397; ZIEGLER 1934, 148 (Is 31,6)

βαθύφωνος,-ος,-ον A 0-0-1-0-0-1
Is 33,19
of deep, i.e. guttural voice; neol.

Cf. CAIRD 1972, 119

βαθύχειλος,-ος,-ον A 0-0-1-0-0-1
Ez 3,5
obscure of speech; neol.

βαΐνη,-ης N1F 0-0-0-0-1-1
1 Mc 13,37
palm-rod; neol.
Cf. WALTERS 1973, 102.304

βαίνω V 1-0-0-0-3-4
Dt 28,56; 3 Mc 6,31; Wis 4,4; 18,16
to walk, to step Dt 28,56; to advance 3 Mc 6,31;
βέβηκα to stand Wis 18,16; ἐπισφαλῶς βεβηκώς
being without sure footing Wis 4,4
Cf. LUST 1990, 257-258
(→ ἀνα-, ἀπο-, δια-, ἐκ-, ἐμ-, ἐπι-, κατα-,
μετα-, παρα-, προ-, προσ-, προσανα-,
συνκατα-, συμ-, συνανα-, ὑπερ-)

βάϊς, βαίος⁺ N3F 0-0-0-0-1-1
1 Mc 13,51
palm-leaf; neol.
Cf. WALTERS 1973, 304

βακτηρία,-ας N1F 1-4-2-3-0-10
Ex 12,11; 1 Sm 17,40; 2 Kgs 4,29(bis).31
staff Ex 12,11; rod Jer 1,11

βακχούριον,-ου N2N 0-0-0-1-0-1
Neh 13,31
=בכורים firstfruits
Cf. WALTERS 1973, 162

βάλανος,-ου N2F 2-2-3-0-0-7
Gn 35,8(bis); Jgs 9,6; Is 2,13
acorn Is 6,13; tree which bears βάλανοι, oak Gn
35,8; bolt-pin, bar on doors Jer 30,26(50,31)

βαλλάντιον,-ου⁺ N2N 0-0-0-2-2-4
Jb 14,17; Prv 1,14; Tob^S 1,14; 8,2
bag, purse

βάλλω⁺ V 1-12-21-15-10-59
Nm 22,38; Jgs^A 20,16; Jgs^B 6,19; 7,12; 8,25
to throw [τι] Jgs^B 8,25; to cast (lots) [τι] 1 Chr
25,8; to put [τι] Nm 22,38; to aim at [εἴς τι] Jb
16,3; to pour [τι] Jgs^B 6,19; βεβλημένοι
scattered Jgs^B 7,12; βάλλω θάνατον εἰς κεφαλάς
τινων to bring death on the heads of Hab 3,13;
βάλλω κλῆρον ἐπί τινα to cast a lot over or
upon Sir 37,8; βάλλω κλῆρον ἕν τινι to cast a
lot with Prv 1,14; βάλλω τι ἕν κλήροις to divide
in lots Ez 48,29; βάλλω ρίζαν to strike root Jb
5,3; βάλλω χάρακα to lay the foundation, to
begin to form Is 29,3
Cf. SHIPP 1979, 129-130
(→ ἀμφι-, ἀνα-, ἀντι-, ἀντιπαρα-, ἀπο-, δια-,

διεκ-, διεμ-, εἰσ-, ἐκ-, ἐμ-, ἐνδια-, ἐπι-, κατα-, μετα-, παρα-, παρασυμ-, παρεμ-, περι-, προ-, προσ-, συμ-, ὑπερ-, ὑπο)

βαμα NF 0-10-0-0-0-10
1 Sm 9,12.13.14.19.25
=במה *high place* 2 Chr 1,13; in Ralph's edition most often written as a proper name (e.g. 1 Sm 9,12)

βάμμα,-ατος N3N 0-5-0-0-0-5
Jgs^ 5,30(bis); Jgs^B 5,30(ter)
dyed garment

βαπτίζομαι⁺ V 0-1-1-0-2-4
2 Kgs 5,14; Is 21,4; Jdt 12,7; Sir 34,25
to dip oneself 2 Kgs 5,14; *to wash* Jdt 12,7; ἡ ἀνομία με βαπτίζει *I am imbued with transgression* Is 21,4
Cf. DELLING 1970, 243-245; →TWNT

βαπτός,-ή,-όν A 0-0-1-0-0-1
Ez 23,15
bright-coloured

βάπτω⁺ V 10-3-0-5-0-18
Ex 12,22; Lv 4,6.17; 9,9; 11,32
to dip, to plunge
(→ ἀπο-)
Cf. WEVERS 1990, 180 (Ex 12,22); →TWNT

βαρ A 0-1-0-0-0-1
1 Sm 2,18
=בר for MT בר *piece of cloth*

βάραθρον,-ου N2N 0-0-1-0-0-1
Is 14,23
pit

βαρακηνιμ NF 0-2-0-0-0-2
Jgs 8,16
=ברקנים *sharp thorns*; see βαρκοννιμ

βάρβαρος,-ος,-ον⁺ A 0-0-1-1-5-7
Ez 21,36; Ps 113(114),1; 2 Mc 2,21; 4,25; 5,22
barbarous, foreign Ps 113,1; *Greek* (used by Jews) 2 Mc 2,21; *savage* 2 Mc 4,25
→TWNT

βαρβαρόομαι V 0-0-0-0-1-1
2 Mc 13,9
to become barbarous

βαρβάρως D 0-0-0-0-1-1
2 Mc 15,2
barbarously

βαρέω⁺ V 1-0-0-0-0-1
Ex 7,14
to weigh down, to depress; βεβάρηται ἡ καρδία *the heart is heavy, stubborn* Ex 7,14; see βαρύνω
Cf. THACKERAY 1909, 261; WEVERS 1990, 99 (Ex 7,14)

βαρέως⁺ D 1-0-1-0-4-6
Gn 31,35; Is 6,10; 2 Mc 11,1; 14,27; 3 Mc 3,1
with difficulty Is 6,10; βαρυτέρως *more heavily* 3 Mc 3,1; βαρέως φέρω *to be indignant* Gn 31,35; βαρέως φέρω ἐπί τινι *to take sth ill, to take displeasure at* 2 Mc 11,1
Cf. LEE 1983, 35 (Gn 31,35)

βάρις,-εως N3F 0-1-0-7-1-9
2 Chr 36,19; Ps 44(45),9; 47(48),4.14; Lam 2,5
large house, tower, palace 2 Chr 36,19; =בירה? *stronghold* Dn^Th 8,2
Cf. MUNNICH 78-80; WALTERS 1973, 186.304-305; WEBER 1950, 20-32; WILL 1987, 253-259

βαρκοννιμ NF 0-1-0-0-0-1
Jgs^ 8,7
=ברקנים *sharp thorns*; see βαρακηνιμ

βάρος,-ους⁺ N3N 0-1-0-0-3-4
Jgs^B 18,21; Jdt 7,4; 2 Mc 9,10; Sir 13,2
weight Jdt 7,4; *load, baggage* Jgs^B 18,21; *mass* 3 Mc 5,47; *oppressiveness* 2 Mc 9,10

βαρύγλωσσος,-ος,-ον A 0-0-1-0-0-1
Ez 3,5
grievous of tongue, speaking a foreign language; neol.

βαρυηχής,-ής,-ές A 0-0-0-0-1-1
3 Mc 5,48
deep-roaring

βαρυθυμέω V 1-1-0-0-1-3
Nm 16,15; 1 Kgs 11,25; PSal 2,9
to be indignant; neol.

βαρύθυμος,-ος,-ον A 0-0-0-0-1-1
3 Mc 6,20
heavy in spirit, indignant

βαρυκάρδιος,-ος,-ον A 0-0-0-1-0-1
Ps 4,3
heavy, slow of heart; *Ps 4,3 βαρυκάρδιοι ἵνα τι- כברי לב למה (be with) hardened heart. Why...* for MT כבודי ל/כלמה *my glory (turned) to shame*; neol.
Cf. CAIRD 1972, 119

βαρύνω V 5-19-9-5-12-50
Ex 5,9; 8,11.28; 9,7.34
A: *to make heavy* [τι] 1 Kgs 12,4; *to harden* [τι] Ex 8,28; P: *to be heavy* 1 Sm 5,3; *to be made heavy* Ex 5,9; *to be hardened, to be made stubborn* Ex 8,15; *to prevail against* [ἐπί τινα] Jos 19,48; *to be heavy with sleep* (of eyes, metaph.) 1 Sm 3,2; ὁ πόλεμος ἐβαρύνθη *the battle was heavy* (semit.?) Jgs^ 20,34; *Jb 35,16 βαρύνει -יכביד he makes weighty* (of words) for

MT יכביר *he multiplies* (of words)
Cf. KILPATRICK 1979, 291; LE BOULLUEC 1989, 38;
WEVERS 1990, 99.123
(- κατα-)

βαρύς,-εῖα,-ύ⁺   A 5-13-1-11-17-47
Gn 48,17; Ex 17,12; 18,18; Nm 11,14; 20,20
heavy Ex 17,12; *heavy with age, advanced* Jb
15,10; *heavy to bear, grievous* Gn 48,17; *heavy*
(metaph.) 3 Mc 5,47; *severe* (of fight) JgsᴮB 20,34;
severe, grievous (of pers.) Wis 2,14; *powerful,*
heavy-armed Nm 20,20; *heavy, great* 1 Sm 5,12
Cf. SPICQ 1978, 175-178

βαρυωπέομαι   V 1-0-0-0-0-1
Gn 48,10
to be dim-sighted; neol.
Cf. HARL 1986, 303

βασανίζω⁺   V 0-1-0-0-28-29
1 Sm 5,3; 2 Mc 1,28; 7,13.17; 9,6
A: *to torture* [τινα] 1 Sm 5,3; P: *to be tortured*
4 Mc 8,27
(- προ-)

βασανισμός,-οῦ⁺   N2M 0-0-0-0-2-2
4 Mc 9,6; 11,2
torture

βασανιστήρια,-ων   N2N 0-0-0-0-5-5
4 Mc 6,1; 8,1.12.19.25
instruments of torture 4 Mc 6,1; *tortures* (meton.)
4 Mc 8,1

βάσανος,-ου⁺   N2F 0-4-7-0-50-61
1 Sm 6,3.4.8.17; Ez 3,28
torture Wis 2,19; *touchstone used as a test,*
stumbling block Ez 3,20; *test* 1 Sm 6,3
Cf. CAIRD 1972, 119 (1 Sm 6,3.4.8.17); LEE 1967, 238-239;
→TWNT

βασιλεία,-ας⁺   N1F 13-114-33-200-86-446
Gn 10,10; 14,1; 20,9; Nm 21,18; 24,7
kingdom, dominion, reign Gn 10,10; οἱ ἐπὶ τῆς
βασιλείας σου *all who preside over your*
kingdom DnᵀʰTh 6,7; *1 Chr 4,23 ἐν τῇ βασιλείᾳ
αὐτοῦ -ב/מלכתו *in his kingdom* for MT במלאכתו/ב *for*
his work, in his service
Cf. SPICQ 1982, 88.92

βασίλειον,-ου   N2N 0-3-1-11-7-22
2 Sm 1,10; 1 Chr 28,4; 2 Chr 23,11; Na 2,7; Prv
18,19
royal dwelling, palace (sometimes pl.) 1 Chr 28,4;
tiara 2 Sm 1,10; *kingdom* 1 Ezr 4,40; *king's*
chamber Est 2,13

βασίλειος,-ος,-ον⁺   A 2-0-0-0-2-4
Ex 19,6; 23,22; Wis 18,15; 4 Mc 3,8

royal, of the kingdom
Cf. LE BOULLUEC 1989, 200 (Ex 19,6); SPICQ 1982, 93;
WEVERS 1990, 295 (Ex 19,6)

βασιλεύς,-έως⁺   N3M 103-1591-384-805-593-3476
Gn 14,1(quater).2
king Gn 14,1; (εἰς) βασιλέα τινά καθίστημι
to make king, to appoint as king 2 Chr 36,1; εἰς
βασιλέα τινά χρίω *to anoint to be king* 1 Sm
11,15; *Jgsᴬ^ 5,6 βασιλεῖς corr. βάσεις; *1 Kgs
11,5 τῷ βασιλεῖ αὐτῶν -ם/מלך *their king* for MT
מלכם *Milkom*, see also 1 Kgs 11,33
Cf. LUST 1991, 194-196; SPICQ 1982, 88.94-96; WALTERS
1973, 137 (Jgsᴬ^ 5,6)

βασιλεύω⁺   V 13-295-23-24-47-402
Gn 36,31(bis).32.33.34
A: *to be king, to rule, to reign* Gn 36,31; *to be*
king of, to rule over [ἐπί τινα] 2 Kgs 23,34;
[ἐπί τινος] 2 Kgs 11,3; [τινος] Jdt 1,1; *to*
appoint as king [τινα] (semit. rendering Hebr.
hiphil) Jgsᴮᴮ 9,6; P: *to be governed by a king* 1 Sm
27,5; βασιλεύω τισὶ βασιλέα *to make them a*
king (semit. rendering Hebr. hiphil) 1 Sm 8,22
Cf. CONYBEARE 1980, 76; HELBING 1928, 75-76.114
(→ παρα-)

βασιλικός,-ή,-όν⁺   A 2-1-0-17-25-45
Nm 20,17; 21,22; 2 Sm 14,26; Jb 18,14; Est 1,19
royal, kingly 2 Sm 14,26; *of* or *belonging to a*
king, king's Nm 20,17; βασιλικόν (sc.
πρόσταγμα) *royal decree* Est 1,19; τὸ
βασιλικόν (sc. ταμιεῖον) *king's treasury* Tobˢ
1,20; τὰ βασιλικά *property, revenues of the*
crown 1 Mc 10,43
Cf. SPICQ 1982, 88.93-94

βασιλίσκος,-ου   N2M 0-0-1-1-0-2
Is 59,5; Ps 90,13(91,13)
kind of serpent, basilisk

βασίλισσα,-ης⁺   N1F 0-8-6-29-0-43
1 Kgs 10,1.4.10.13; 2 Chr 9,1
queen 1 Kgs 10,1; *queen, princess* Ct 6,8(7)
Cf. SPICQ 1982, 88-92

βάσις,-εως⁺   N3F 59-2-5-1-3-70
Ex 26,19(ter).21(bis)
that with which one steps, foot Wis 13,18; *base,*
pedestal, foot Ex 26,19; *high place* Ez 16,31;
foundation Wis 4,3
Cf. LE BOULLUEC 1989, 277-278.370; WEVERS 1990,
428.627.629.647

βασκαίνω⁺   V 2-0-0-0-2-4
Dt 28,54.56; Sir 14,6.8
to turn a grudging eye upon [τινα] Dt 28,56; *to*

envy [τινα] Sir 14,6; [abs.] Sir 14,8
Cf. CAIRD 1972, 120; HELBING 1928, 95-96; SPICQ 1982,
105-109

βασκανία,-ας   N1F 0-0-0-0-3-3
4 Mc 1,26; 2,15; Wis 4,12
malign influence, witchcraft Wis 4,12; *envy* 4 Mc
1,26

βάσκανος,-ος,-ον   A 0-0-0-2-3-5
Prv 23,6; 28,22; Sir 14,3; 18,18; 37,11
grudging, envious Prv 23,6; ὁ βάσκανος *the
envious, an envious man* Sir 18,18
Cf. CAIRD 1972, 120; SPICQ 1982, 105-109

βάσταγμα,-ατος   N3N 0-1-4-2-0-7
2 Sm 15,33; Jer 17,21.22.24.27
burden

βαστάζω[+]   V 0-2-0-2-2-6
Jgs[B] 16,30; 2 Kgs 18,14; Ru 2,16(bis); Sir 6,25
to bear [τι] 2 Kgs 18,14; βαστάζοντες βαστάσ-
ατε *you must bear* (semit.) Ru 2,16; *Jgs[B] 16,30
ἐβάσταξεν -◊ נשא *lifted up* for MT ◊ נשה *to bow*
(– ἀνα-, συμ-)

βατεύω
(– ἐμ-)

βάτος,-ου[+]   N2M 6-0-0-1-0-7
Ex 3,2(ter).3.4
bramble
Cf. WALTERS 1973, 183.331

βάτραχος,-ου[+]   N2M 12-0-0-2-1-15
Ex 7,27.28.29; 8,1.2
frog

βαφή,-ῆς   N1F 0-1-0-0-1-2
Jgs[A] 5,30; Sir 31,26
dipping

βδέλλα,-ης   N1F 0-0-0-1-0-1
Prv 30,15
leech

βδέλυγμα,-ατος[+]   N3N 38-14-36-19-16-123
Gn 43,32; 46,34; Ex 8,22(bis); Lv 5,2
abomination, sth abominable (of idols and cultic
objects) Gn 43,32; τὸ βδέλυγμα (τῆς)
ἐρημώσεως *the abomination of desolation*
(semit.; sacrilegious object or rite causing the
desecration of a sacred place) Dn 12,11; *2 Kgs
17,32 τὰ βδελύγματα αὐτῶν שקוצי/הם/הם *their
abominations* for MT קצותם/מ/*from among them*
(LXX has a double transl.); *Lv 5,2
βδελυγμάτων -שקרץ *abomination* for MT שרץ
reptile; neol.
Cf. DANIEL 1966, 179; HARL 1986, 285-286; HARLÉ 1987,
100 (Lv 5,2); LEE 1983, 47; LUST 1992; –TWNT

βδελυγμός,-οῦ   N2M 0-1-1-0-0-2
1 Sm 25,31; Na 3,6
abomination; neol.

βδελυκτός,-ή,-όν[+]   A 0-0-0-1-1-2
Prv 17,15; 2 Mc 1,27
disgusting, abominable; neol.

βδελυρός,-ά,-όν   A 0-0-0-0-1-1
Sir 41,5
disgusting, loathsome, repulsive

βδελύσσω[+]   V 13-1-7-15-12-48
Gn 26,29; Ex 1,12; 5,21; Lv 11,11.13
A: *to make repulsive* or *abominable* [τι] Ex 5,21;
M: *feel a loathing at* [τι] Gn 26,29; [ἀπό τινος]
Ex 1,12; P: *to be abominated, to be abhorred* Lv
18,30; βδελύγματι βδελύσσομαι *to abominate*
Dt 7,26
Cf. CAIRD 1972, 120; CONYBEARE 1980, §84; DANIEL 1966,
179; HARL 1986, 213-214; HELBING 1928, 24-25; LE
BOULLUEC 1989, 77 (Ex 1,12); –TWNT

βέβαιος,-α,-ον[+]   A 0-0-0-1-4-5
Est 3,13; 3 Mc 5,31; 7,7; 4 Mc 17,4; Wis 7,23
firm, steadfast
Cf. HARL 1991, 248-249; SPICQ 1978, 182; –TWNT

βεβαιόω[+]   V 0-0-0-2-0-2
Ps 40(41),13; 118(119),28
to establish Ps 40,13; *to confirm* Ps 118,28
Cf. SPICQ 1978, 182

βεβαίως   D 1-0-0-0-1-2
Lv 25,30; 3 Mc 5,42
firmly 3 Mc 5,42; *surely* Lv 25,30

βεβαίωσις,-εως[+]   N3F 1-0-0-0-1-2
Lv 25,23; Wis 6,18
confirmation, assurance Wis 6,19; εἰς
βεβαίωσιν *in perpetuity* Lv 25,23
Cf. SPICQ 1978, 182

βέβηλος,-ος,-ον[+]   A 1-1-3-0-8-13
Lv 10,10; 1 Sm 21,6; Ez 21,30; 22,26; 44,23
profane Lv 10,10; *common, not holy* 1 Sm 21,5;
impure, unclean 1 Sm 21,6
Cf. KRAFT 1972, 164; SPICQ 1978, 186; –TWNT

βεβηλόω[+]   V 21-1-39-10-19-90
Ex 31,14; Lv 18,21; 19,8.12.29
to profane [τι] Ex 31,14; *to pollute, to defile* [τι]
Jdt 9,2; *Ps 9,26(10,5) βεβηλοῦνται -יחלו ◊ חלל
profaned for MT יחילו ◊ חיל *are persistent*; neol.
Cf. HARLÉ 1987, 178; SPICQ 1978, 186

βεβήλωσις,-εως   N3F 1-0-0-0-7-8
Lv 21,4; Jdt 4,3.12; 8,21; 3 Mc 1,29
profanation; neol.

βεδεκ   NN 0-9-0-0-0-9

2 Kgs 12,6(bis).7.8(bis)
=ברק *breach(es)*

βεθ N 0-1-0-0-0-1
1 Kgs 5,25
=בת *(liquid) measure*; see βάδος
Cf. WALTERS 1973, 331

βέλος,-ους⁺ N3N 2-9-5-19-8-43
Dt 32,23.42; 2 Sm 18,14; 22,15; 2 Kgs 9,24
missile, arrow, dart 2 Sm 18,14; *Jb 20,25 βέλος
-שלח *arrow* for MT שלף *he draws out?*
--TWNT

βελόστασις,-εως N3F 0-0-4-0-2-6
Jer 28(51),27; Ez 4,2; 17,17; 21,27; 1 Mc 6,20
engines of war

βέλτιστος,-η,-ον A 0-0-0-0-1-1
3 Mc 3,26
sup. of ἀγαθός; *best*

βελτίων,-ων,-ον Λ 1-2-9-1-3-16
Gn 29,19; Jgsᴬ 9,2; 18,19; Jer 33(26),13.14;
comp. of ἀγαθός; *better, more excellent* Gn
29,19; *fairer* Jb 42,15

βερσεχθαν N 0-1-0-0-0-1
1 Sm 6,8
=ב/ארגן *in a sack?*

βῆμα,-ατος⁺ N3N 1-0-0-1-4-6
Dt 2,5; 1 Ezr 9,42; Neh 8,4; 2 Mc 13,26; Sir
19,30
step, pace Sir 19,30; *step* (as a measure of
length) Dt 2,5; *raised place, tribune, pulpit* 1 Ezr
9,42; *judgement-seat* 2 Mc 13,26

βηρύλλιον,-ου N2N 2-0-1-0-0-3
Ex 28,20; 36,20(39,13); Ez 28,13
dim. of βήρυλλος; *beryl*

βήρυλλος,-ου⁺ N2F 0-0-0-0-1-1
Tobᴮᴬ 13,17
beryl

βία,-ας⁺ N1F 4-0-8-4-16-32
Ex 1,13.14(bis); 14,25; Is 17,13
force, violence Ex 1,13; *act of violence* Ezr 15,15;
βίᾳ *forcibly* Is 30,30; βίαν αὐτῶν οὐκ ἔφαγον
they ate nothing extorted from them Neh 5,4; *Is
63,1 βίᾳ -ב/רב? *by strife, by force* for MT ב/רב *in
the greatness (of his strength)*
Cf. HARL 1991, 250; LE BOULLUEC 1989, 77-78 (Ex 1,14)

βιάζομαι⁺ V 4-6-0-1-6-17
Gn 33,11; Ex 19,24; Dt 22,25.28; Jgsᴬ 13,15
to urge, to insist, to constrain [τινα] Gn 33,11;
to force [τινα] Ex 19,24; *to lay hands upon,
violate* [τινα] Est 7,8; *to break violently into* [τι]
2 Mc 14,41; *to constrain to* [+inf.] Ex 19,24

(-- ἀπο-, δια-, ἐκ-, κατα-, παρα-)
Cf. HELBING 1928, 13; SPICQ 1978, 189-194

βίαιος,-α,-ον⁺ A 1-0-3-2-6-12
Ex 14,21; Is 11,15; 58,6; 59,19; Ps 47(48),8
violent Ex 14,21; *forcible, constrained, hard* Is
58,6

βιαίως D 0-0-2-1-0-3
Is 30,30; Jer 18,14; Est 3,13
violently, by force

βιβάζω V 2-0-0-0-0-2
Lv 18,23; 20,16
A: *to put the female to the male* (of animals); P:
to have connexion with (an animal) (said of a
woman) Lv 18,23
(-- ἀνα-, δια-, ἐμ-, ἐπι-, κατα-, παρα-, προ-,
συμ-)

βιβλιαφόρος,-ου N2M 0-0-0-2-0-2
Est 3,13; 8,10
letter-carrier; neol.?

βιβλιοθήκη,-ης N1F 0-0-0-2-1-3
Est 2,23; Ezr 6,1; 2 Mc 2,13
library 2 Mc 2,13; *record-office, registry* Ezr 1,6

βιβλίον,-ου⁺ N2N 16-92-32-22-24-186
Ex 17,14; 24,7; Nm 5,23; 21,14; Dt 17,18
dim. of βίβλος; *paper, strip of* βίβλος Tob 7,14;
scroll, book Ex 17,14; *letter* 2 Sm 11,14; τὰ
βιβλία τὰ ἅγια *the sacred books, the Scriptures*
1 Mc 12,9; *Ezr 7,17 ἐν βιβλίῳ -א/ספרא=ב *with this
letter* for MT ב/כספא *with this money*
Cf. LEWIS 1989, 7 n.4; MAYSER 1970, 80; WEVERS 1990,
271.383; --TWNT

βιβλιοφυλάκιον,-ου N2N 0-0-0-0-2-2
1 Ezr 6,20.22
place to keep books in; τὰ βασιλικὰ
βιβλιοφυλάκια *royal archives* 1 Ezr 6,20

βίβλος,-ου⁺ N2F 4-1-1-8-15-29
Gn 2,4; 5,1; Ex 32,32.33; Jos 1,8
scroll, book Ex 32,32; *letter* Jer 36(29),1; ἡ ἱερὰ
βίβλος *the holy book* 2 Mc 8,23
--TWNT

βιβρώσκω V 19-5-11-3-5-43
Ex 12,46; 13,3; 21,28; 29,34; Lv 6,9
A: *to eat* Jos 5,12; P: *to be eaten* Ex 12,46; *to be
devoured* Is 51,8; ἄρτος βεβρωμένος *mouldy
bread* Jos 9,12
(-- κατα-)
Cf. WALTERS 1973, 73 (LIJ 11)

βῖκος,-ου N2M 0-0-2-0-0-2
Jer 19,1.10
jar

Cf. WALTERS 1973, 163

βίος,-ου⁺   N2M 0-0-0-24-45-69
Jb 7,1.6.16; 8,9; 9,25
life, existence Est 3,13b; *life, mode of life,*
manner of living 4 Mc 8,23; *lifetime* Jb 12,12;
livelihood, means of living Sir 31,4; μεταλλάττω
τὸν βίον *to die* 1 Ezr 1,29; διαλάττω τὸν βίον
to die 2 Mc 6,27; διὰ βίου *for life* 4 Mc 4,1

βιοτεύω   V 0-0-0-0-1-1
Sir prol.,35
to live

βιότης,-ητος   N3F 0-0-0-1-0-1
Prv 5,23
means of living, substance

βιόω⁺   V 0-0-0-3-4-7
Jb 29,18; Prv 7,2; 4 Mc 5,22; 17,18; 9,6
to live, to pass one's life
(- δια-, ἐπι-, κατα-, περι-, συμ-)

βιρα   NF 0-0-0-1-0-1
Neh 7,2
=בירה *palace*

βίωσις,-εως⁺   N3F 0-0-0-0-1-1
Sir prol 14
way of life; neol.

βλαβερός,-ά,-όν⁺   A 0-0-0-1-0-1
Prv 10,26
harmful
Cf. SPICQ 1978, 195

βλάβη,-ης   N1F 0-0-0-0-1-1
Wis 11,19
harm

βλάπτω⁺   V 0-0-0-1-6-7
Prv 25,20a; Tob 12,2; 2 Mc 12,22; 4 Mc 9,7
A: *to damage, to hurt* [τι] Prv 25,20a; [τινα]
4 Mc 9,7; [abs.] Wis 18,2; P: *to be hurt* 2 Mc
12,22; *to be hindered from* [τοῦ +μή +inf.] Wis
10,8; οὐ βλάπτομαι [+ptc.] *it is no harm to me*
to, it does not hurt me when Tob 12,2
Cf. HELBING 1928, 2-3
(- κατα-)

βλαστάνω⁺   V 3-2-2-1-2-10
Gn 1,11; Nm 17,23(bis); Jgs^B 16,22; 2 Sm 23,5
to bud, to blossom Nm 17,23; *to grow* Jgs^B 16,22;
to flourish (metaph.) 2 Sm 23,5; *to make to grow,*
to propagate, to produce [τι] (semit. Hebr.
hiphil) Gn 1,11
Cf. HELBING 1928, 78
(- ἀνα-, ἐκ-)

βλάστημα,-ατος   N3N 0-0-0-0-1-1
Sir 50,12

shoot

βλαστός,-οῦ⁺   N2M 4-2-3-2-1-12
Gn 40,10; 49,9; Ex 38,15(37,17); Nm 17,23;
1 Kgs 7,12(26)
shoot, bud Gn 40,10; *blossom* 1 Kgs 7,12;
offspring Jb 30,12; *Gn 49,9 βλαστοῦ -שֶׁרֶף
branch, freshly plucked for MT שֶׁרֶף *prey*
Cf. HARL 1986, 308 (Gn 49,9); LE BOULLUEC 1989, 365
(Ex 38,15); WALTERS 1973, 51.286 (Nm 17,23)

βλασφημέω⁺   V 0-3-1-1-4-9
2 Kgs 19,4.6.22; Is 52,5; Tob^S 1,18
to speak outrageously, to slander 2 Mc 10,34; *to*
speak impiously or *irreverently of God, to*
blaspheme 2 Kgs 19,4
Cf. HELBING 1928, 22; →TWNT

βλασφημία,-ας⁺   N1F 0-0-1-1-4-6
Ez 35,12; Dn^Th 3,96; 1 Mc 2,6; 2 Mc 8,4; 10,35
outrageous speech Ez 35,12; *irreverent speech* or
act against God, blasphemy 2 Mc 8,4
Cf. BICKERMAN 1986, 86-90; →TWNT

βλάσφημος,-ος,-ον⁺   A 0-0-0-1-0-6-7
Is 66,3; Tob^S 1,18; 2 Mc 9,28; 10,4.36
blasphemous 2 Mc 10,4; ὁ βλάσφημος
blasphemer 2 Mc 9,28

βλέπω⁺   V 9-31-51-19-23-133
Gn 45,12; 48,10; Ex 4,11; 23,8; Nm 21,20
to see, to perceive visually Gn 45,12; *to see, to*
behold [τι] 2 Kgs 9,17; [τινα] Tob 11,14; *to*
look (at), to face (towards) [κατά τι] (metaph.)
Nm 21,20; [παρά τι] Jos 18,14; [πρός τι] Ez
8,3; *to have the capacity of sight* Ex 4,11; ὁ
βλέπων *the seer, the clairvoyant* 1 Sm 9,9; τὰ
βλεπόμενα *the visible universe* Wis 13,7
Cf. DEPUYDT 1985, 36-37.42; LE BOULLUEC 1983, 234-235;
LEE 1983, 131-140.147-148; MURAOKA 1990, 36; WALTERS
1973, 197-202.335
(→ ἀνα-, ἀπο-, εἰσ-, ἐμ-, ἐπι-, κατα-, κατεμ-,
παρα-, περι-, προ-, ὑπο-)

βλέφαρα,-ων   N2N 0-0-1-6-1-8
Jer 9,17; Ps 10(11),4; 131(132),4; Prv 4,25;
6,4.25
eyelids

βλύζω
(→ ἐκ-)

βοάω⁺   V 13-67-31-17-27-155
Gn 4,10; 29,11; 39,14.15.18
to cry out (aloud) Gn 4,10; *to cry* (metaph.) Hos
7,14; *to roar* Is 5,29; *to call* [τι] Jgs^B 4,10; *1 Sm
11,7 ἐβόησαν *they cried out* corr.? ἔβησαν *they*
came out, or ἐβόησαν -יצעקו *they cried out* for

MT יצאו *they came out (to battle)*; *Jos 15,18
ἐβόησεν -תצוח *she cried* for MT תצנח *she came
down*

Cf. LEE 1983, 144; →TWNT

(→ ἀνα-, δια-, ἐκ-, ἐπι-, κατα-)

βοή,-ῆς⁺　　　　　　　　　　N1F 1-4-2-2-8-17
Ex 2,23; 1 Sm 4,14(bis); 9,16; 2 Chr 33,13
cry Ex 2,23; *cry of mourning* Jdt 14,16; *cry of joy*
3 Mc 7,16

βοήθεια,-ας⁺　　　　　　N1F 0-6-11-27-27-71
JgsᴬᵃA 5,23; Jgsᴮ 5,23(bis); 2 Sm 18,3; 1 Chr 12,17
help, aid Jgs 5,23; *auxiliary forces, allies* Jer 29,4;
ἡ βοήθειά μου παρὰ τοῦ κυρίου *my help from
the Lord* Ps 120,2; *Lam 3,56 εἰς τὴν βοήθειάν
μου -ל/תשועתי *to my help* for MT ל/שועתי *to my cry*;
*Jb 6,13 βοήθεια -תשועה *help* for MT תשיה *cry?*; *Is
8,20 εἰς βοήθειαν -◊ עור, עורר *as a help* for MT
עור ◊לתעורה *as a witness*

Cf. FLASHAR 1912, 242-244

βοηθέω⁺　　　　　　　　V 5-20-12-41-26-104
Gn 49,25; Dt 22,27; 28,29.31; 32,38
A: *to aid, to help* [τινι] Gn 49,25; *to come to
the rescue, to give aid* [abs.] 1 Chr 12,37; P: *to be
assisted, to receive help* Dnᵀʰ 11,34; *2 Chr 32,18
τοῦ βοηθῆσαι αὐτοῖς *to assist them* corr.? τοῦ
πτοηθῆναι αὐτοῖς -ל/ירא/ם *to frighten them*;
*1 Chr 12,34 βοηθῆσαι -ל/עזור *to help* for MT
ל/ערך *to order*; *Prv 18,19 βοηθούμενος -נושע
helped for MT נפשע *offended, suffering revolt?*

(→ ἐπι-)

βοηθήματα,-ων　　　　　　N3N 0-0-0-0-2-2
Wis 17,11; 2 Mc 15,8
assistance, succour

βοηθός,-οῦ⁺　　　　　　N2M 7-4-7-33-13-64
Gn 2,18.20; Ex 15,2; 18,4; Dt 33,7
helper, help

Cf. FLASHAR 1912, 242-244; LE BOULLUEC 1989, 172.193-
194 (Ex 15,2; 18,4); WEVERS 1990, 227 (Ex 15,2)

βόθρος,-ου　　　　　　　　N2M 0-2-11-6-3-22
Jos 8,29; 1 Sm 13,6; Ez 26,20(bis); 31,14
pit, trench 1 Sm 13,6; *Jos 8,29 εἰς τὸν βόθρον
-אל פתח *into the pit* for MT אל פתח *at the entrance*,
cpr. Zech 3,9; *Am 9,7 ἐκ βόθρου -מקור *from a
ditch* for MT מקיר *from Kir*

Cf. LIPINSKI 1970, 28-29

βόθυνος,-ου⁺　　　　　　N2M 0-3-9-0-0-12
2 Sm 18,17; 2 Kgs 3,16(bis); Is 24,17.18
hole Is 51,7; *trench* 2 Kgs 3,16; *pit* 2 Sm 18,17;
cave Jer 31,28; *Is 47,11 βόθυνος -שחת *pit* for MT
שחר/ה *charm against it?*

βοίδιον,-ου　　　　　　　N2N 0-0-1-0-0-1
Jer 27(50),11
dim. of βοῦς; *calf*

βόλβιτον,-ου　　　　　　N2N 0-0-4-0-1-5
Zph 1,17; Ez 4,12.15(bis); Sir 22,2
(cow-) dung, filth

βολή,-ῆς⁺　　　　　　　　N1F 1-0-0-0-2-3
Gn 21,16; 2 Mc 5,3; 3 Mc 5,26
throw 2 Mc 5,3; *shot* Gn 21,16; ἡλίου βολαί
sun-beams 3 Mc 5,26

βολίς,-ίδος　　　　　　　N3F 3-2-5-3-2-15
Ex 19,13; Nm 24,8; 33,55; Jos 23,13; 1 Sm 14,14
missile, javelin, dart, arrow Ex 19,13; *shaft*
(metaph.) Ez 5,16; βολίδες ἀστραπῶν *flashes of
lightning* Wis 5,21; *1 Sm 14,14 βολίσι -◊ חץ
arrows for MT חצי *half*; neol.

Cf. CAIRD 1972, 120

βολοκοπέω
(→ συμ-)

βομβέω　　　　　　　　　V 0-1-3-0-0-4
1 Chr 16,32; Jer 31(48),36(bis); 38,36(31,35)
to make a booming noise Jer 31(48),36; *to roar*
1 Chr 16,32

Cf. WALTERS 1973, 146

βόμβησις,-εως　　　　　　N3F 0-0-0-0-1-1
Bar 2,29
buzzing crowd; neol.

βοοζύγιον,-ου　　　　　　N2N 0-0-0-0-1-1
Sir 26,7
ox-yoke; neol.

βορά,-ᾶς　　　　　　　　N1F 0-0-0-4-1-5
Jb 4,11; 9,26; 38,39.41; 3 Mc 6,7
food

βόρβορος,-ου⁺　　　　　　N2M 0-0-2-0-0-2
Jer 45(38),6(bis)
mire, filth

βορρᾶς,-ᾶ or βορέας,-ου⁺　　N1M 15-36-82-29-4-166
Gn 13,14; 28,14; Ex 26,18.35; 37,9(38,11)
north wind Prv 25,23; *the north* Gn 13,14; ἐπὶ
(τὸν) βορρᾶν *northward* Jos 17,9; κατὰ βορρᾶν
Jos 19,27; *Dn 8,9 βορρᾶν -צפון *north* for MT צבי
glorious country; *2 Chr 14,9 κατὰ βορρᾶν -צפונה
northwards for MT צפתה *Zephathah*; *Ez 23,24
βορρᾶ -צפון *north* for MT חצן ?; *Prv 27,16
βορέας -צפונה *from the north* for MT צפן ◊ צפניה
who could keep her safe?

Cf. SHIPP 1979, 161-163; WEVERS 1990

βόσκημα,-ατος　　　　　　N3N 0-1-5-0-1-7
2 Chr 7,5; Is 7,25; 27,10; 32,14; 49,11
sheep 2 Chr 7,5; *pasture* Is 49,11; βοσκήματα

cattle 2 Mc 12,11

βόσκω⁺   V 5-1-20-2-0-28
Gn 29,7.9; 37,12.16; 41,2
A: *to feed* Gn 29,7; P: *to feed, to graze* (of cattle)
Is 11,6; *1 Kgs 12,16 βόσκε - רעה *feed* for MT
ראה *look,* cpr. Mi 5,4(3)
(→ κατα-, συμ-)

βοστρυχός,-οῦ   N2M 0-2-0-2-0-4
Jgs^A 16,14.19; Ct 5,2.11
lock of hair, curl

βοτάνη,-ης⁺   N1F 7-2-5-1-1-16
Gn 1,11.12; Ex 9,22.25; 10,12
pasture Jer 27(50),11; *herb, herbage* Gn 1,11

βοτρύδιον,-ου   N2N 0-0-1-0-0-1
Is 18,5
small cluster

βότρυς,-υος⁺   N3M 8-0-2-3-1-14
Gn 40,10; Nm 13,23(bis).24(bis)
bunch of grapes, cluster Gn 40,10; φάραγξ
βότρυος *valley of the cluster* Nm 13,24

βούβαλος,-ου   N2M 1-0-0-0-0-1
Dt 14,5
antelope

βούκεντρον,-ου   N2N 0-0-0-1-0-1
Eccl 12,11
ox-goad, pointed stick; neol.
Cf. WALTERS 1973, 334

βουκόλιον,-ου   N2N 8-8-3-1-3-23
Ex 13,12; Lv 22,19.21; 23,18; Dt 7,13
herd (of cattle) Ex 13,12; *1 Sm 8,16 τὰ
βουκόλια ὑμῶν-בקריכם *your herds* for MT בחוריכם
your young men
Cf. I.E BOULLUEC 1989, 158 (Ex 13,12); WEVERS 1990,
200 (Ex 13,12)

βουλευτήριον,-ου   N2N 0-0-0-0-4-4
1 Mc 8,15.19; 12,3; 4 Mc 15,25
council-room, senate(-house)

βουλευτής,-οῦ⁺   N1M 0-0-0-2-0-2
Jb 3,14; 12,17
councillor, counsellor

βουλευτικός,-ή,-όν   A 0-0-0-1-0-1
Prv 24,6
of a counsellor

βουλεύω⁺   V 2-15-25-15-29-86
Gn 50,20(bis); 2 Sm 16,23; 17,7.21
A: *to devise* [τι] Is 23,8; M: *to take counsel with
oneself, to deliberate* [abs.] Gn 50,20; *to resolve
on, to determine with oneself* [τι] 2 Sm 16,23; *to
advise* [τινι] 1 Kgs 12,6; *to resolve to do* [+inf.]
2 Chr 30,23; *to plot to* [+inf.] (in bad sense) Ezr

4,5; *to take counsel* [πρός τινα] 2 Kgs 6,8; [μετά
τινος] 1 Chr 13,1
Cf. WALTERS 1973, 109.242-243.343; →TWNT
(→ δια-, ἐπι-, συμ-)

βουλή,-ῆς⁺   N1F 3-24-49-56-45-177
Gn 49,6; Nm 16,2; Dt 32,28; Jgs^A 19,30; 20,7
counsel, advice Dt 32,28; *council* Nm 16,2; εἰς
βουλὴν εἶμι *to come to counsel* Gn 49,6;
τίθημι βουλήν *to take counsel* Jgs^A 19,30;
δίδωμι βουλήν *to give counsel* Jgs 20,7; φέρω
βουλήν *to deliberate* 2 Sm 16,20; *Prv 2,16 κακὴ
βουλή אשה זרה - עצה זרה? *(evil) counsel* for MT אשה זרה
(strange, evil) woman; *Prv 25,28 μετὰ βουλῆς
אין מעצה- *without counsel* for MT אין מעצר *without
limit*; *Is 41,21 βουλαὶ ὑμῶν -עצותיכם *your
counsels* for MT עצומותכם*your strong points, proofs*
Cf. COOK 1991, 344-345; WALTERS 1973, 242-243;
ZIEGLER 1934, 148; →TWNT

βούλημα,-ατος⁺   N3N 0-0-0-0-2-2
2 Mc 15,5; 4 Mc 8,18
intention 4 Mc 8,18; *will* 2 Mc 15,5
Cf. WALTERS 1973, 243

βούλομαι⁺   V 14-21-20-26-47-128
Gn 24,5; Ex 4,23; 7,27; 8,17; 9,2
to will [abs.] 1 Chr 10,4; *to will, to be willing*
[+inf.] Gn 24,5; *to consent to do* [+inf.] Ex
22,16; *to desire* [τι] 2 Sm 24,3; *to prefer, to be
for* [τινα] 2 Sm 20,11; *to wish sb sth* [τινί τι]
Ps 69,3; *to be disposed against* [ἐπί τινι] 2 Chr
25,16; ὁ βουλόμενος *anyone who likes* 1 Kgs
13,33; *Jb 30,14 ὡς βούλεται -כ/חפץ *as he will*
for MT כ/פרץ *as (by) a breach*; *Jb 37,10
βούληται -◊עצה *it pleases him* for MT מוצק *fast,
solid*
Cf. LEE 1983, 144.148; WALTERS 1973, 141.242-243;
WEVERS 1990, 53.106.146.148.257.593; →TWNT

βουνίζω   V 0-0-0-2-0-2
Ru 2,14.16
to heap up, to pile up; neol.

βουνός,-οῦ⁺   N2M 11-24-43-11-5-94
Gn 31,46(ter).48(bis)
hill Ex 17,9; *heap* Gn 31,46; *high place,
illegitimate place for sacrifice* Ps 77(78),58;
*2 Sm 17,9 βουνῶν *hills* corr.? βοθύνων for MT
פחתים *caves*; *2 Kgs 2,16 τῶν βουνῶν-הגבעות*the
hills* for MT הגיאות *the valleys*
Cf. HARL 1986, 80.238 (Gn 31,47); LEE 1983, 114; SHIPP
1979, 167-170

βοῦς, βοός⁺   N3M/F 98-40-17-23-7-185
Gn 18,7; 33,13; 41,3(bis).4

ox Ex 20,10; *cow* Gn 41,4; βόες *cattle* Lv 1,3

βούτομον,-ου   N2N 0-0-0-2-0-2
Jb 8,11; 40,21
sedge, reeds, rushes

βούτυρον,-ου   N2N 2-3-2-3-1-11
Gn 18,8; Dt 32,14; Jgs 5,25; 2 Sm 17,29
butter

βραβεύω⁺   V 0-0-0-0-1-1
Wis 10,12
to arbitrate for the benefit of, to decide on for [τί τινι]
Cf. LARCHER 1984, 633-634; →TWNT
(→ συμ-)

βραγχιάω   V 0-0-0-1-0-1
Ps 68(69),4
to have a sore throat

βραδέως   D 0-0-0-0-1-1
2 Mc 14,17
slowly

βραδύγλωσσος,-ος,-ον   A 1-0-0-0-0-1
Ex 4,10
slow of tongue; neol.
Cf. LE BOULLUEC 1989, 98-99

βραδύνω⁺   V 2-0-1-0-1-4
Gn 43,10; Dt 7,10; Sir 35,19; Is 46,13
to delay [τι] Is 46,13; *to loiter, to delay* [intrans.]
Gn 43,10

βράζω
(→ ἐκ-)

βράσσω
(→ ἀνα-)

βραχέως   D 0-0-0-0-4-4
2 Mc 5,17; 7,33; 13,11; 4 Mc 9,5
for a while 2 Mc 5,17; *a little* 2 Mc 13,11

βραχίων,-ονος⁺   N3M 33-11-36-33-16-129
Gn 24,18; 27,16; 49,24; Ex 6,1.6
arm Gn 24,18; *strength* Jb 35,9
Cf. HARLÉ 1988, 111 (Lv 7,32); LE BOULLUEC 1989, 111
(Ex 6,1).298-299 (Ex 29,22); WEVERS 1990, 475 (Ex 29,22);
→TWNT

βραχύς,-εῖα,-ύ⁺   A 3-4-1-5-5-18
Ex 18,22; Dt 26,5; 28,62; 1 Sm 14,29.43
short (of space) 2 Sm 16,1; *small* Dt 26,5; *few* Ps
104(105),12; *a little* Sm 14,43; βραχύ *a little* Ps
8,6; βραχύ *for a* (little) *while* Is 57,17; κατὰ
βραχύ *little by little* Wis 12,8; παρὰ βραχύ
almost Ps 93(94),17; τὰ βραχέα *the smaller
cases* Ex 18,22; βραχὺ τοῦ μέλιτος *small
quantity of honey* 1 Sm 14,29

βραχυτελής,-ής,-ές   A 0-0-0-0-1-1

Wis 15,9
ending shortly, brief; neol.

βρέφος,-ους⁺   N3N 0-0-0-0-5-5
1 Mc 1,61; 2 Mc 6,10; 3 Mc 5,49; 4 Mc 4,25; Sir
19,11
baby
Cf. HORSLEY 1987, 40-41

βρέχω⁺   V 3-0-9-3-1-16
Gn 2,5; 19,24; Ex 9,23; Is 5,6; 34,3
to drench (with tears) Ps 6,7; *to rain, to send rain*
Gn 2,5; *to rain, to send* [τι] Ex 9,23
(→ ἐπι-)
Cf. LEE 1983, 122

βρίθω   V 0-0-0-0-1-1
Wis 9,15
to weigh down [τι]
(→ ἐπι-)

βριμάομαι
(→ ἐμ-, προσεμ-)

βρόμος,-ου   N2M 0-0-1-2-1-4
Jb 6,7; 17,11; Wis 11,18; Jl 2,20
any loud voice, groaning Jb 17,11; *Jb 6,7
βρόμον *groaning* corr. βρῶμον *stink*, see also
Wis 11,18; Jl 2,20
Cf. MURAOKA 1991, 207; WALTERS 1973, 72-73

βροντάω   V 0-3-0-5-2-10
1 Sm 2,10; 7,10; 2 Sm 22,14; Ps 17(18),14;
28(29),3
to thunder

βροντή,-ῆς⁺   N1F 0-0-2-4-3-9
Is 29,6; Am 4,13; Ps 76(77),19; 103(104),7; Jb
26,14
thunder Ps 76(77),19; *Am 4,13 βροντήν -הרעם
the thunder for MT הרים *mountains*

βροτός,-οῦ   N2M 0-0-0-17-0-17
Jb 4,17; 9,2; 10,4.22; 11,12
mortal (man)

βροῦχος,-ου   N2M 1-2-6-1-0-10
Lv 11,22; 1 Kgs 8,37; 2 Chr 6,28; Ps
104(105),34; Jb 1,44
locust 1 Kgs 8,37; *Am 7,1 βροῦχος -ילק *locust*
for MT לקש *late grass*
Cf. LEE 1983, 42

βροχή,-ῆς⁺   N1F 0-0-0-2-0-2
Ps 67(68),10; 104(105),32
rain

βρόχος,-ου⁺   N2M 0-0-0-3-1-4
Prv 6,5; 7,21; 22,25; 3 Mc 4,8
snare Prv 6,5; *snare* (metaph.) Prv 7,21; *noose,
halter* 3 Mc 4,8

βρυγμός,-οῦ⁺   N2M 0-0-0-1-1-2
Prv 19,12; Sir 51,3
biting, Sir 51,3; *roaring* Prv 19,12
→TWNT

βρύχω⁺   V 0-0-0-5-0-5
Ps 34(35),16; 36(37),12; 111(112),10; Jb 16,9;
Lam 2,16
to gnash, to grind (the teeth) [τι]
→TWNT

βρῶμα,-ατος⁺   N3N 23-9-9-10-24-75
Gn 6,21; 14,11; 41,35(bis).36
that which is eaten, food, meat Gn 6,21;
βρώματα *provisions, victuals, food* Gn 14,11;
*LtJ 10 βρωμάτων - מאכל *food* for hypothetical
original מ/אכל *from the devourer,* cpr. Mal 3,11;
*Is 3,6 βρῶμα -מאכלה *food* for MT מכשלה *ruin*
Cf. MOORE 1977, 338; WALTERS 1973, 73; →TWNT

βρώσιμος,-ος,-ον⁺   A 1-0-1-1-0-3
Lv 19,23; Neh 9,25; Ez 47,12
eatable; ξύλον βρώσιμον *fruit-tree*

βρῶσις,-εως⁺   N3F 12-5-9-12-4-42
Gn 1,29.30; 2,9.16; 3,6
food Gn 1,29; *eating* Lv 19,7; *Hab 3,17 ἀπὸ
βρώσεως -מ/מאכלה *from the food, from the pasture*
for MT מ/מכלה *from the fold*
Cf. WALTERS 1973, 73

βρωτόν,-οῦ   N2N 0-1-0-1-1-3
Jgsᴮ 14,14; Jb 33,20; 1 Ezr 5,53
meat, food

βύβλινος,-η,-ον   A 0-0-1-0-0-1
Is 18,2
made of papyrus, paper
Cf. WALTERS 1973, 295.304 (Is 18,2)

βύβλος,-ου   N2F 0-1-0-0-1-2
2 Chr 17,9; 1 Ezr 1,31
see βίβλος
Cf. MAYSER 1970, 80

βυθίζω⁺   V 0-0-0-0-1-1
2 Mc 12,4

to sink, to drown [τινα]

βυθός,-οῦ⁺   N2M 1-0-0-5-1-7
Ex 15,5; Ps 67(68),23; 68(69),3.16; 106(107),24
depth, deep Ps 67(68),23; *bottom* Ex 15,5

βυθοτρεφής,-ής,-ές   A 0-0-0-0-1-1
3 Mc 6,8
living in the deep; neol.

βύρσα,-ης   N1F 2-0-0-2-0-4
Lv 8,17; 9,11; Jb 16,15; 40,31
hide, skin (of animals) Lv 8,17; *skin* (of men) Jb
16,15
Cf. HABERMANN 1986, 93-99

βύσσινος,-η,-ον⁺   A 3-3-2-8-1-17
Gn 41,42; Ex 28,39; 36,34(39,27); 1 Chr
15,27(bis)
(made) of fine linen Gn 41,42; τὰ βύσσινα
dressings of fine linen Est 1,6

βύσσος,-ου⁺   N2F 33-2-4-1-0-40
Ex 25,4; 26,1.31.36; 27,9
flax, linen made from it, fine linen

βύω   V 0-0-0-1-0-1
Ps 57(58),5
to stop; βύω τὰ ὦτα *to plug, to stop the ears*

βῶλαξ,-ακος   N3F 0-0-0-1-0-1
Jb 7,5
clod of earth

βῶλος,-ου   N2M 0-0-2-1-1-4
Ez 17,7.10; Jb 38,28; Sir 22,15
lump, drop Jb 38,28; *mass* Sir 22,15; *land* Ez
17,7

βωμός,-οῦ⁺   N2M 12-9-12-0-13-46
Ex 34,13; Nm 3,10; 23,1.2.4
(pagan, illegitimate) altar (as opposed to the
Israelite θυσιαστήριον, often =במה) Hos 10,8;
(legitimate, Israelite) altar Nm 3,10; *Jer
30(49),18 βωμοὶ αὐτῆς -במותיה *her altars* for MT
בנתיה *her daughters*
Cf. DANIEL 1966, 26-31.40-43 WALTERS 1973, 196

γαβης   N 0-1-0-0-0-1
1 Chr 4,9
artificial word, part of the personal name
Ἰγαβης, used in the interpretation of that
name; stands for Hebrew עצב *pain*, used in the
interpretation of יעבץ
Cf. SIMOTA 1968, 50-51

γαβιν   N 0-1-0-0-0-1
2 Kgs 25,12
=נבין (Aram.?) for MT יגבים *farmers*, cpr.
γεωργοί Jer 39(52),16

γαβις   N 0-0-0-1-0-1
Jb 28,18
=נביש *crystal*

γάζα,-ης⁺   N1F 0-0-1-5-0-6
Is 39,2; Est 4,7; Ezr 5,17; 6,1; 7,20
=גנזין (Persian loanword) *treasure* Ezr 6,1;
οἶκος τῆς γάζης *the treasure-house* Ezr 5,17

γαζαρηνοί,-ῶν   N2M 0-0-0-8-0-8
Dnᴸˣˣ 2,27; 5,7.8; Dnᵀʰ 2,27; 4,7(4)
=גזרין (גזר *to cut, to determine*) *diviners,
soothsayers*

γαζοφυλάκιον,-ου⁺   N2N 0-1-0-11-13-25
2 Kgs 23,11; Est 3,9; Ezr 10,6; Neh 3,30; 10,38
treasury
Cf. BICKERMAN 1980, 163

γαζοφύλαξ,-ακος   N3M 0-1-0-0-3-4
1 Chr 28,1; 1 Ezr 2,8; 8,19.45
treasurer

γαι   N 0-0-2-0-0-2
Ez 39,11.15
=גאי *valley*; see πολυάνδριον

γαῖα,-ας   N1F 0-1-1-5-0-7
2 Kgs 18,35; Ez 36,24; Ps 48(49),12; Ezr 3,3; 9,1
earth, land 2 Kgs 18,31; οἱ λαοὶ τῶν γαιῶν *the
peoples of the lands, the heathen* Ezr 9,1
Cf. CAIRD 1972, 120-121; WALTERS 1973, 59.288; ·TWNT

γαῖσος,-ου   N2M 0-2-0-0-1-3
Jos 8,18(bis); Jdt 9,7
spear, javelin

γάλα, γάλακτος⁺   N3N 22-5-9-8-5-49
Gn 18,8; 49,12; Ex 3,8.17; 13,5
milk Gn 18,8; *Ez 34,3 γάλα -חלב *milk* for MT חלב
fat
·TWNT

γαλακτίζω
(·· ἀπο-)

γαλαθηνός,-ή,-όν   A 0-1-1-0-1-3
1 Sm 7,9; Am 6,4; Sir 46,16
sucking, young

γαλακτοτροφία,-ας   N1F 0-0-0-0-1-1
4 Mc 16,7
nursing at the breast; neol.

γαλεάγρα,-ας   N1F 0-0-1-0-0-1
Ez 19,9
weasel-trap, cage for beasts; *cage* (used for
prisoners)

γαλῆ,-ῆς   N1F 1-0-0-0-0-1
Lv 11,29
weasel, marten

γαληνός,-ός,-όν   A 0-0-0-0-1-1
4 Mc 13,6
calm

γαμβρεύω   V 2-0-0-0-0-2
Gn 38,8; Dt 7,3
A: *to form connexions by marriage* [πρός τινα]
Dt 7,3; M: *to marry* [τινα] Gn 38,8; neol.
Cf. HARL 1986, 265; HELBING 1928, 251-252
(·· ἐπι-)

γαμβρός,-οῦ   N2M 18-12-0-1-1-32
Gn 19,12.14(bis); Ex 3,1; 4,18
son-in-law Gn 19,12; *father-in-law* Ex 3,1
Cf. HARL 1991, 244-245; SHIPP 1979, 185

γαμετή,-ῆς   N1F 0-0-0-0-1-1
4 Mc 2,11
married woman, wife
Cf. SHIPP 1979, 186-187

γαμέω⁺   V 0-0-0-1-3-4
Est 10,3c; 2 Mc 14,25(bis); 4 Mc 16,9
to marry, to take a wife [abs.] 2 Mc 14,25; [τινα]
Est 10,3c
Cf. KILPATRICK 1967, 139-140; →TWNT

γαμικός,-ή,-όν   A 0-0-0-0-1-1
3 Mc 4,6
of or *for marriage, bridal*

γάμος,-ου⁺   N2M 1-0-0-3-21-25
Gn 29,22; Est 1,5; 2,18; 9,22; Tobᴮᴬ 6,13
wedding (feast), marriage
Cf. HARL 1986, 70; ·· TWNT

γάρ⁺   X 294-32-190-371-642-1529
Gn 2,5; 3,5; 4,25; 7,4; 9,5
conjunction used to express cause, inference,
continuation, or to explain; *for, since, as* (cause)
Gn 2,5; *for* (explanation) Gn 9,5; γὰρ ... γὰρ ...
(introducing several arguments for the same
assertion) Sir 37,13; γὰρ ... γὰρ ... (one cl.
confirming another cl.) Jdt 7,27; with other
particles and conjunctions: ἰδοὺ γάρ *for, behold*
Jdt 5,23; καὶ γάρ *for* 2 Mc 1,19; οὔτε γάρ ...
οὔτε ... *for neither ... nor ...* Wis 12,13; *Jb 9,24

γάρ corr.? γῆ or γαῖ for MT ארץ *land* or *lands*
Cf. AEJMELAEUS 1982, 64-66; LE BOULLUEC 1989, 31

γαρεμ　　　　　　　　　　　　　　　N 0-1-0-0-0-1
2 Kgs 9,13
=גרם *bone*; ἐπὶ γαρεμ τῶν ἀναβαθμῶν *on the bare steps* (architectural term)
Cf. SIMOTA 1968, 51-52

γασβαρηνός,-οῦ　　　　　　　　N2M 0-0-0-1-0-1
Ezr 1,8
=גזבר *treasurer*
Cf.SIMOTA 1968, 54

γαστήρ, γαστρός⁺　　　　　　N3F 15-14-7-26-8-70
Gn 16,4.5.11; 25,21.23
belly, stomach, womb Nm 5,22; ἐν γαστρὶ ἔχω *to be pregnant* Gn 16,4; ἐν γαστρὶ λαμβάνω *to conceive* Gn 30,41
Cf. SPICQ 1982, 110-112

γαστριμαργία,-ας　　　　　　　N1F 0-0-0-0-1-1
4 Mc 1,3
gluttony

γαστρίμαργος,-ος,-ον　　　　　A 0-0-0-0-1-1
4 Mc 2,7
gluttonous

γαυρίαμα,-ατος　　　　　　　　N3N 0-0-0-1-4-5
Jb 4,10; Jdt 10,8; 15,9; Sir 43,1; 47,4
arrogance, exultation; neol.

γαυριάω　　　　　　　　　　　　V 0-0-0-3-1-4
Jb 3,14; 39,21.23; Jdt 9,7
to exalt, to exult Jdt 9,7; *Jb 3,14 οἳ ἠγαυριῶντο ἐπὶ ξίφεσιν -הרנים חרבות? *they gloried in their swords* for MT הבנים חרבות *they rebuilt ruins*
Cf. HELBING 1928, 261-262

γαυριόομαι　　　　　　　　　　V 1-0-0-0-0-1
Nm 23,24
to exalt; neol.

γαυρόομαι　　　　　　　　　　　V 0-0-0-0-3-3
3 Mc 3,11; 6,5; Wis 6,2
to exalt oneself, to glory
Cf. HELBING 1928, 261-262

γε⁺　　　　　　　　　　　X 4-72-2-76-13-167
Gn 18,13; 26,9; 37,10; Ex 35,34; Jos 9,4
enclitic particle that emphasizes the preceding or following word, and often cannot be translated; *at least, at any rate* (limitation) Jb 30,24; ἐγώ γε see ἔγωγε; after other particles: ἄρα γε *surely, then* Gn 26,9; καί γε *also* (intensification) Jgs 1,22; *even, surely* Jgsᴮ 6,39; *moreover* 2 Sm 14,6; *indeed* (explanation) 2 Kgs 8,1; *specifically* (or without transl.; specification)

Ezr 1,1; καί γε ... καί γε ... *and ... and ...* (enumeration) Eccl 9,11; after conjunctions: εἰ γε *really* Jb 16,4; εἰ δὲ μή γε (to heighten a contrast after condition cl.) Dnᴸˣˣ 3,15; ὅπου γε (to heighten the contrast after a relative cl.) 4 Mc 6,34; modifying the sentence of the following particle: γέ τοι 4 Mc 2,17

γεδδουρ　　　　　　　　　　　N 0-5-0-0-0-5
1 Sm 30,8.15(bis).23; 1 Chr 12,22
=גדור *troop, band*
Cf. SIMOTA 1968, 55-56

γεδωρ　　　　　　　　　　　　N 0-1-0-0-0-1
1 Chr 12,8
=גדור meaning uncertain; see γεδδουρ

γεῖσος,-ους　　　　　　　　　N3N 0-1-6-0-0-7
1 Kgs 7,46(9); Jer 52,22(ter); Ez 40,43
projecting part of the roof, cornice, border, ground-sill; neol.

γειτνιάω　　　　　　　　　　　V 0-0-0-0-2-2
2 Mc 9,25; Susᵀʰ 4
to be a neighbour, to be adjacent [τινι]

γείτων,-ονος⁺　　　　　　　N3F/M 2-1-3-9-1-16
Ex 3,22; 12,4; 2 Kgs 4,3; Jer 6,21; 12,14
neighbour

γειώρας,-ου　　　　　　　　　N1M 1-0-0-0-0-1
Ex 12,19
=גיורא (Aram.) *sojourner, proselyte*; see γιώρας; neol.
Cf. LEE 1983, 16; SIMOTA 1968, 56-57; WALTERS 1973, 33-34

γελάω⁺　　　　　　　　　　　V 5-0-1-6-5-17
Gn 17,17; 18,12.13.15(bis)
to laugh (most often ironically) Gn 17,7; *to laugh at sb* [ἐπί τινα] Ps 51(52),8; *Jb 19,7 γελῶ -אצחק *I laugh* for MT אצעק *I cry*
Cf. HELBING 1928, 259; →NIDNTT; TWNT
(→ ἐκ-, ἐπεγ-, ἐπι-, κατα-, προσ-, συγ-)

γελοιάζω　　　　　　　　　　V 1-0-0-0-0-1
Gn 19,14
to jest; neol.

γελοιασμός,-οῦ　　　　　　　N2M 0-0-1-0-0-1
Jer 31,(48)27
jesting; neol.?

γελοιαστής,-οῦ　　　　　　　N1M 0-0-0-1-0-1
Jb 31,5
jester, scorner; neol.?

γελοῖος,-α,-ον　　　　　　　A 0-0-0-0-3-3
4 Mc 1,5; 3,1; 6,34
ridiculous, absurd

γέλως, γέλωτος⁺　　　　　　N3M 1-0-6-8-5-20

Gn 21,6; Jer 20,7; 31(48),26.39; Am 7,9
laughter, derision Gn 21,6; *Am 7,9 βωμοὶ τοῦ
γέλωτος* -במות שׂחק *the highplaces of laughter, the
ridiculous highplaces* for MT במות ישׂחק *the
highplaces of Isaac*; *Mi 1,10 κατὰ γέλωτα (bis)
-◊חפר? *shame* for MT (בית ל)עפרה (*Bet-le-) Afra?*
and עפר *dust*
--NIDNTT; TWNT

γεμίζω⁺   V 1-0-0-0-1-2
Gn 45,17; 3 Mc 5,47
to load [τι] Gn 45,17; *to fill full of* [τί τινι]
3 Mc 5,47
Cf. LEE 1983, 62; HARL 1986, 291-292; HELBING 1928, 149
(→ ἐπι-)

γέμω⁺   V 1-0-1-2-2-6
Gn 37,25; Am 2,13; Ps 9,28(10,7); 13(14),3;
2 Mc 3,6
to be full of, to be laden with [τινος]
Cf. HELBING 1928, 148

γενεά,-ᾶς⁺   N1F 72-9-27-82-48-238
Gn 6,9; 7,1; 9,12; 15,16; 17,7
generation Gn 6,9; *family* Gn 31,3; *offspring* Ex
12,14; *age* 1 Mc 2,61; *Zph 3,9 εἰς γενεὰν
αὐτῆς* ב/דור/ה *for her generation?* for MT ברורה
pure

γενεαλογέω⁺   V 0-1-0-0-0-1
1 Chr 5,1
to trace a pedigree; οὐκ ἐγενεαλογήθη εἰς
πρωτοτόκια *he was not reckoned as first-born*

γενέθλιος,-ος,-ον   A 0-0-0-0-1-1
2 Mc 6,7
of or *belonging to one's birth*; γενέθλιος ἡμέρα
birthday

γένειον,-ου   N2N 0-0-0-0-2-2
4 Mc 9,28; 15,15
chin, beard

γενεσιάρχης,-ου   N1M 0-0-0-0-1-1
Wis 13,3
creator; neol.
Cf. LARCHER 1985, 761

γενεσιουργός,-οῦ   N2M 0-0-0-0-1-1
Wis 13,5
creator, author of existence; neol.
Cf. LARCHER 1985, 764-765

γένεσις,-εως⁺   N3F 20-11-4-4-17-56
Gn 2,4; 5,1; 6,9; 10,1.32
generation, offspring Gn 5,1; *nativity, birth* Gn
31,13; *family* Ex 6,25; βίβλος γενέσεως
οὐρανοῦ καὶ γῆς *book of the generation of
heaven and earth* (in the sense of active

generation, offspring, i.e. Adam and Eve; see
Gn 5,1) or *book of the origin (creation) of
heaven and earth* Gn 2,4; ἡμέρα γενέσεως
birthday Gn 40,20
Cf. HARL 1986, 32; LARCHER 1983, 201-203.299

γενετή,-ῆς⁺   N1F 1-0-0-0-0-1
Lv 25,47
birth

γενέτις, acc.-τιν   N3F 0-0-0-0-1-1
Wis 7,12
mother (fem. of γενέτης); neol.
Cf. LARCHER 1984, 458-459

γένημα,-ατος⁺   N3N 35-5-14-9-14-77
Gn 41,34; 47,24; 49,21; Ex 22,4; 23,10
that which is begotten or *born, offspring, product,
fruit* Gn 41,34; *Gn 49,21 γενήματι אמירי-
branches or אמרי *fawns* for MT אמרי *words*
Cf. LE BOULLUEC 1989, 224-225; LEE 1983, 99; WALTERS
1973, 115

γενικός,-ή,-όν   A 0-0-0-0-1-1
1 Ezr 5,39
belonging to or *connected with the* γένος; ἡ
γενικὴ γραφή *description of the kindred*

γενναῖος,-α,-ον   A 0-0-0-0-12-12
2 Mc 6,28; 7,21; 12,42; 3 Mc 2,32; 4 Mc 6,10
high-born, noble 2 Mc 12,42; *excellent* 2 Mc 6,28

γενναιότης,-ητος   N3F 0-0-0-0-2-2
2 Mc 6,31; 4 Mc 17,2
nobility

γενναίως   D 0-0-0-0-11-11
1 Mc 4,35; 2 Mc 6,28; 7,5.11; 8,16
nobly, bravely

γεννάω⁺   V 85-95-23-26-24-253
Gn 4,18(ter); 5,3.4
to bring forth, to create [τινα] Gn 4,18; *Ez
36,12 γεννήσω* -הולדתי *I will bring forth (men)* for
MT הלכתי *I will let (men) walk*
Cf. LE BOULLUEC 1989, 115; WALTERS 1973, 115-117;
WILLIAMSON 1985, 144-145 (Ezr 10,44); ZIEGLER 1965,
103-104; → TWNT
(→ ἐκ-)

γέννημα,-ατος⁺   N3N 0-2-0-0-1-3
Jgs 1,10; Sir 10,18
that which is begotten or *born, offspring, product,
fruit*; see γένημα
Cf. SHIPP 1979, 193

γέννησις,-εως⁺   N3F 0-1-0-0-1-2
1 Chr 4,8; Sir 22,3
engendering, producing, offspring; see γένεσις
Cf. ZIEGLER 1965, 104

γεννητός,-ή,-όν⁺   A 0-0-0-5-0-5
Jb 11,2.12; 14,1; 15,14; 25,4
born

γένος,-ους⁺   N3N 34-4-10-16-55-119
Gn 1,11(bis).12(bis).21
kind Gn 1,11; *race* Lv 21,17; *species* Gn 8,19;
nation Jer 38,1; *family* Gn 17,14; *Gn 40,17
γενῶν *kinds* corr.? γεννημάτων? *products* for
MT מאכל *food*
Cf. HARL 1986, 59

γεραιός,-ά,-όν   A 0-0-0-0-7-7
3 Mc 1,23; 3,27; 4,5; 4 Mc 6,2; 8,3
aged, old

γεραίρομαι⁺   V 0-0-0-0-1-1
3 Mc 5,17
to be honoured

γέρας,-αος   N3N 1-0-0-1-1-3
Nm 18,8; Wis 2,22; Est 3,13c
honour, reward, privilege Nm 18,8; δεύτερον τῶν
βασιλειῶν γέρας *the second post of honour in
the kingdom* Est 3,13c
Cf. LARCHER 1983, 266

γερουσία,-ας⁺   N1F 26-1-0-0-8-35
Ex 3,16.18; 4,29; 12,21; 24,9
council of elders, senate
Cf. BICKERMAN 1980, 48, n.15; DELCOR 1967, 159

γέρων,-οντος⁺   N3M 0-0-0-3-17-20
Jb 32,9; Prv 17,6; 31,23; 2 Mc 6,1; 4 Mc 5,31
old man

γεῦμα,-ατος   N3N 2-0-1-1-1-5
Ex 16,31; Nm 11,8; Jer 31(48),11; Jb 6,6; 2 Mc
13,18
taste Ex 16,31; *sample, indication* (metaph.)
2 Mc 13,18

γεῦσις,-εως   N3F 0-0-0-1-3-4
Dnᵀʰ 5,2; Wis 16,2.3.20
taste, tasting

γεύω⁺   V 1-6-1-5-6-19
Gn 25,30; 1 Sm 14,24.29.43(bis)
A: *to give a taste* [τινα] Gn 25,30; M: *to taste,
to eat* [abs.] 1 Sm 19,36; [τινος] 1 Sm 14,24;
[τι] 1 Sm 14,43; *to taste* [ἐκ τινος] Jb 20,18
Cf. HELBING 1928, 135; HORSLEY 1987, 41; →TWNT
(→ἀπο-)

γέφυρα,-ας   N1F 0-0-1-0-1-2
2 Mc 12,13; Is 37,25
bridge 2 Mc 12,13; τίθημι γέφυραν *to build a
bridge* Is 37,25

γεώδης,-ης,-ες   A 0-0-0-0-2-2
Wis 9,15; 15,13
earthy, earthly

γεωμετρία,-ας   N1F 0-0-1-0-0-1
Is 34,11
geometry; σπαρτίον γεωμετρίας *measuring line*

γεωμετρικός,-ή,-όν   A 0-0-1-0-0-1
Zech 2,5
of or *for geometry, geometrical*; σχοινίον
γεωμετρικόν *measuring line*

γεωργέω⁺   V 0-1-0-0-2-3
1 Chr 27,26; 1 Ezr 4,6; 1 Mc 14,8
to till, to plough, to cultivate [τι]

γεωργία,-ας   N1F 0-0-0-0-2-2
2 Mc 12,1; Sir 7,15
agriculture, farming

γεώργιον,-ου⁺   N2N 1-0-1-5-1-8
Gn 26,14; Jer 28(51),23; Prv 6,7; 9,12; 24,5
tilled land, field Gn 26,14; *farming* Jer 28(51),23;
crop Prv 24,5; *Prv 6,7 γεωργίου -◊ קציר *harvest*
for MT קצין *chief, ruler*

γεωργός,-ός,-όν⁺   A 2-1-6-0-1-10
Gn 9,20; 49,15; 2 Chr 26,10; Jer 14,4; 28(51),23
tilling the ground; ὁ γεωργός *farmer,
husbandman* Wis 17,16; ἄνθρωπος γεωργὸς γῆς
farmer Gn 9,20; ἀνὴρ γεωργός *farmer* Gn 49,15

γῆ,-ῆς⁺   N1F 983-572-805-450-344-3154
Gn 1,1.2.10.11(bis)
earth Gn 1,1; *land* Gn 12,1; *dust* 2 Sm 1,2; ἐπὶ
τὴν γῆν τὴν ἁγίαν *in the Holy land* Zech 2,16;
γῆ Ισραηλ for MT ארץ ישראל *Israel* 1 Sm 13,19;
*Dt 33,28 ἐπὶ γῆς *on the land* corr. ἐπὶ τῆς
πηγῆς *by the source?*, cpr. Gn 16,7; 24,13; *Hos
13,15 τὴν γῆν αὐτοῦ -ארצו *his land* for MT אוצר
treasure; *Is 41,24 ἐκ γῆς -מארץ *out of the earth*
for MT מאפס *nothing*; *Jer 9,20 εἰς τὴν γῆν ὑμῶν
-בארמותינו *into your* or *our land* for MT בארמנותינו
into our palaces; *Is 63,11 ἐκ τῆς γῆς *out of the
land* for MT מים *out of the sea* (*sea* understood
as *the North*?); *Zph 2,14 τῆς γῆς -גי *land,
valley* for MT גוי *people;* see Ez 32,5; *Hos 8,1
ὡς γῆ -כעפר *as dust* for MT שפר (-ך) *trumpet*
Cf. WALTERS 1973, 186-188; →TWNT

γηγενής,-ής,-ές   A 0-0-1-3-1-5
Jer 39(32),20; Ps 48(49),3; Prv 2,18; 9,18; Wis
7,1
earth-born, inhabitant of the earth, man Jer
39(22),20; *plebeian* Ps 48(49),3; οἱ γηγενεῖς for
MT רפאים *the dead, the shades?* Prv 2,18

γῆρας,-ως⁺   N3N 8-2-0-3-22-35
Gn 21,2.7; 25,8; 42,38; 44,22
old age

γηράσκω+   V 4-5-0-5-6-20
Gn 18,13; 24,26; 27,1.2; Jos 23,2
to grow old Sir 8,6; γεγήρακα *to be old* Gn
18,13; ἐγήρασα *to be old* 1 Sm 8,1
(→ κατα-, συγκατα-)

γηροβοσκέω   V 0-0-0-0-1-1
Tobˢ 14,13
to feed in old age, to cherish in old age [τινα]

γῆρος,-ους   N3N 2-2-1-4-1-10
Gn 15,15; 1 Kgs 11,4; 1 Chr 29,28; Is 46,4; Ps
70(71),9
not found in nom.; see γῆρας

γίγαρτον,-ου   N2N 1-0-0-0-0-1
Nm 6,4
grape-stone

γίγας,-αντος   N3M 8-11-11-4-7-41
Gn 6,4(bis); 10,8.9(bis)
giant, mighty one (mostly pl.)

γίνομαι+   V 431-618-398-337-390-2174
Gn 1,3(bis).5(bis).6
to be born, to be begotten Wis 7,3; *to be created*
Is 48,7; *to come about* Ex 10,22; *to happen to, to
be done to* [τινι] Tob 11,15; *to happen, to take
place* 2 Mc 1,32; *to become* Gn 4,6; *to be*
[+adv.] Tob 7,10; *to fall to, to belong to* [τινος]
Gn 30,42; *to fall to* [τινι] Gn 21,9; *to turn into*
[εἴς τι] Gn 20,12; μὴ γένοιτο (μοι) *far be it
(from me)* Gn 44,17; γίνομαι ἀνδρί *to be
married* Nm 30,7; ἐγενήθην τινὶ εἴς τινα *to
become* (e.g. *a king*) *for sb* Ru 4,13; ἐγενήθην
τινί *to be born to sb* Gn 10,21; οὐκ ἐγενήθη τὸ
πάσχα τοῦτο *no such passover had been cele-
brated* 2 Kgs 23,22; περὶ τὸ σάββατον γίνομαι
to celebrate the Sabbath 2 Mc 8,27; καὶ ἐγένετο
(semit.?; stereotyped rendition of ויהי) *and it
happened* Gn 4,8 and often; *Jer 15,11 γένοιτο
אמן- *amen, so be it* for MT אמר *he said*; *Mi 2,1
ἐγένοντο -היו *they were* for MT הוי *woe*, see also
Jer 30(37),7; *Is 2,1 γενόμενος -היה? *that
happened, came to pass* for MT חזה *(that Isaiah)
saw*; *Jos 16,1 καὶ ἐγένετο ויהי- *(and the
borders) were* for MT ויצא *and went forth*, see also
Jos 15,1; 17,1; 1 Sm 22,3; 1 Chr 14,17; Jb 18,1
Cf. HELBING 1928, 64; KRAFT 1972, 164; RENEHAN 1982,
48; WALTERS 1973, 115-117; → TWNT
(→ δια-, ἐμπαρα-, ἐπι-, ἐπιπαρα-, κατα-,
μετα-, παρα-, περι-, προ-, προσ-, συγ-,
συμπαρα-)

γινώσκω+   V 84-157-193-182-130-746
Gn 2,17; 3,5.7.22; 4,1

to come to know, to perceive [ὅτι +ind.] Ex
14,4; *to know* [τι] Gn 3,5; *to recognize* [τινα]
Hos 9,2; *to form a judgement, to think* [abs.]
1 Sm 23,23; *to acknowledge as true* [τινα] Hos
13,4; *to know carnally* [τινα] Gn 4,1; οὐχ ὑμῖν
γνῶναι *it is not your duty to know* Mi 3,1; *Mi
4,9 ἵνα τί ἔγνως κακά רע תרעי למה- *why did you
have to experience* (or *know*) *evil* for MT
רע תריעי למה *why did you cry aloud*; *Hos 12,1
ἔγνω αὐτούς ירעם- (*God*) *knows them* for MT
עם רד (*Judah*) *roams with (God)*?; *1 Sm 10,24
ἔγνωσαν -ירעו *they noticed* for MT ירעו ◇ רוע *they
shouted*; *Is 15,4 γνώσεται -ידע *shall know* for
MT ירעה *shall tremble*; *Ex 22,9 γνῷ -◇ ידע
(*nobody*) *knows* for MT ראה (*somebody*) *sees*, see
also Nm 11,25; Jgs 2,7; *Prv 15,14 γνώσεται -ידע
to know for MT רעה *to feed, to pasture*, see also
Jer 2,16; Hos 9,2; *Jer 15,12 εἰ γνωσθήσεται
-ירע ◇ה/יורע or ה/ירע *will (iron) be known?* for MT
ירע/ה רעע *will (iron) break*
Cf. HARL, 1986, 113; MURAOKA 1990, 26-27
(→ ἀνα-, ἀπο-, δια-, ἐπι-, κατα-, παρανα-,
προ-, συγ-)

γιώρας,-ου   N1M 0-0-1-0-0-1
Is 14,1
sojourner, resident alien; see γειώρας; neol.

γλαύξ, γλαυκός   N3F 3-0-0-0-0-3
Lv 11,16.19; Dt 14,15
owl

γλεύκος,-ους+   N3N 0-0-0-1-0-1
Jb 32,19
sweet new wine

γλυκάζω   V 0-0-1-0-0-1
Ez 3,3
to taste sweet; neol.

γλυκαίνω   V 1-0-0-4-8-13
Ex 15,25; Ps 54(55),15; Jb 20,12; 21,33; Prv
24,13
A: *to sweeten, to produce an effect of sweetness*
[τι] Ps 54(55),15; P: *to be sweetened, to taste
sweet* Ex 15,25; ἐν τοῖς χείλεσίν τινος
γλυκαίνω *to speak sweetly with one's lips* Sir
12,16

γλύκασμα,-ατος   N3N 0-0-0-2-2-4
1 Ezr 9,51; Prv 16,24; Neh 8,10; Sir 11,3
sweetness Prv 16,24; *sweet wine* Neh 8,10; neol.

γλυκασμός,-οῦ   N2M 0-0-2-1-0-3
Am 9,13; Jl 4,18; Ct 5,16
sweetness Ct 5,16; *sweet juice of grapes* Am 9,13;
neol.?

γλυκερός,-ά,-όν   A 0-0-0-1-0-1
Prv 9,17
sweet

γλυκύς,-εῖα,-ύ⁺   A 0-4-2-7-4-17
Jgs 14,14.18; Is 5,20
sweet Jgs 14,18; *pleasant, delightful* Prv 16,21

γλυκύτης,-ητος   N3F 0-2-0-0-1-3
Jgs 9,11; Wis 16,21
sweetness

γλύμμα,-ατος   N3N 1-0-2-0-2-5
Ex 28,11; Is 45,20; 60,18; Sir 38,27; 45,11
engraved figure, inscription Ex 28,11; *Is 60,18
γλύμμα *engraved figure* corr.? ἀγαλλίαμα
exultation for MT תהלה, cpr. Is 61,11

γλυπτός,-ή,-όν   A 9-30-17-6-3-65
Ex 34,13; Lv 26,1; Dt 4,16.23.25
carved, graven Lv 26,1; τὸ γλυπτόν *graven image*
Ex 34,13; τὰ γλυπτά *carved stones* Jgs 3,19
Cf. CAIRD 1972, 121

γλυφή,-ῆς   N1F 3-2-2-0-2-10
Ex 25,7; 28,21; 35,9; 2 Chr 2,6.13
carved work, carving Ex 28,21; εἰς τὴν γλυφήν
for engraving Ex 35,9, see also Ex 25,7
Cf. LE BOULLUEC 1989, 348

γλύφω   V 2-4-4-0-2-12
Ex 28,9; 39,6; 2 Chr 2,6.13; 3,5
to carve, to engrave
(→ δια-, ἐγ-)

γλῶσσα,-ης⁺   N1F 5-6-27-83-48-169
Gn 10,5.20.31; 11,7(bis)
tongue, language Ex 10,5; γλῶσσα χρυσῆ *golden
ingot, bar of gold* Jos 7,21; φαῦλοι γλώσσῃ *they
who speak evil* Sir 20,17; γλῶσσα τρίτη *slander*
(lit. *a third tongue*) Sir 28,15
→TWNT

γλωσσόκομον,-ου⁺   N2N 0-4-0-0-0-4
2 Chr 24,8.10.11(bis)
case, casket, ark
Cf. HARL 1987, 8.31-35; MEYERS 1971, 53; WALTERS 1973,
126

γλωσσότμητος,-ος,-ον   A 1-0-0-0-0-1
Lv 22,22; neol.
with the tongue cut out

γλωσσοτομέω   V 0-0-0-0-3-3
2 Mc 7,4; 4 Mc 10,19; 12,13
to cut out the tongue; neol.

γλωσσοχαριτέω   V 0-0-0-1-0-1
Prv 28,23
to flatter; neol.

γλωσσώδης,-ης,-ες   A 0-0-0-2-3-5

Ps 139(140),12; Prv 21,19; Sir 8,3; 9,18; 25,20
talkative, babbling; neol.

γνάθος,-ου   N2F 0-3-0-0-0-3
Jgsᴬ 4,21.22; 5,26
jaw

γναφεύς,-έως⁺   N3M 0-1-2-0-0-3
2 Kgs 18,17; Is 7,3; 36,2
fuller, cloth-carder, cloth-dresser

γνήσιος,-α,-ον⁺   A 0-0-0-0-2-2
3 Mc 3,19; Sir 7,18
belonging to the race, genuine, legitimate, real
3 Mc 3,19; *dear* Sir 7,18
Cf. DREW-BEAR 1972, 66; SPICQ 1978, 107-109.196-199

γνησίως⁺   D 0-0-0-0-2-2
2 Mc 14,8; 3 Mc 3,23
genuinely, truly

γνοφερός,-ά,-όν   A 0-0-0-1-0-1
Jb 10,21
dark; neol.

γνόφος,-ου⁺   N2M 5-4-8-8-1-26
Ex 10,22; 14,20; 20,21; 4,11; 5,22
darkness
Cf. HORSLEY 1987, 143; LE BOULLUEC 1989, 167-168.212-
213

γνοφόω   V 0-0-0-1-0-1
Lam 2,1
to darken [τινα]; neol.?

γνοφώδης,-ης,-ες   A 1-0-0-1-0-2
Ex 19,16; Prv 7,9
dark, gloomy; neol.

γνώμη,-ης⁺   N1F 0-0-0-25-9-34
Ps 82(93),4; Prv 2,16; 12,26; Dnᴸˣˣ 2,14; 6,5
will, decision, decree, judgement
→TWNT

γνωμονέω
(→ συγ-)

γνωρίζω⁺   V 1-9-8-45-5-68
Ex 21,36; 1 Sm 6,2; 10,8; 1 Sm 14,12; 16,3
A: *to make known, to point out* [τινί τι] 1 Sm
10,8; *to discover, to gain knowledge of, to become
acquainted with* [τι] Jb 34,25; *to declare, to
interpret* [τι] Dnᵀʰ 2,6.10.17; P: *to become known*
Ex 21,36; *Am 3,3 γνωρίσωσιν -נורעו ♢ ידע *to
know each other* for MT נוערו יער ♢ *to convene*
→TWNT
(→ ἀνα-)

γνώριμος,-ος,-ον   A 0-1-0-3-3-7
2 Sm 3,8; Prv 7,4; Ru 2,1; 3,2; 4 Mc 5,4
well-known 4 Mc 5,4; γνώριμος *acquaintance,
friend* Ru 3,2; ἀνὴρ γνώριμος *acquaintance,*

friend Ru 2,1
Cf. CAIRD 1972, 121

γνωριστής,-οῦ   N1M 0-1-0-0-0-1
2 Kgs 23,24
medium, familiar spirit (etym. transl. of ירדעני◊ ירע
to know)
Cf. CAIRD 1972, 121-122

γνῶσις,-εως⁺   N3F 1-6-8-33-19-67
Nm 11,23; 1 Sm 2,3; 1 Kgs 8,38.43(bis)
knowledge Nm 11,23; *Hos 10,12 γνώσεως -דעת.
(of) knowledge for MT ועת ו *and it is time*; *Prv
13,19 ἀπὸ γνώσεως -מדעת *(far) from knowledge* for
MT מרע *(away) from evil*, see also Eccl 8,6; 1 Chr
4,10
Cf. LARCHER 1983, 243-245; →TWNT

γνωστέος,-α,-ον   A 0-0-0-0-1-1
LtJ 1,51
knowable

γνώστης,-ου⁺   N1M 1-3-0-0-1-5
1 Sm 28,3.9; 2 Kgs 21,6; 2 Chr 35,19; Sus^Th 43
medium, familiar spirit

γνωστός,-ή,-όν⁺   A 2-2-3-10-8-25
Gn 2,9; Ex 33,16; 2 Kgs 10,11; 2 Chr 35,19a; Is
19,21
known Ex 33,16; ὁ γνωστός *acquaintance, friend*
Ps 87(88),9; γνωστόν *knowledge* Gn 2,9
Cf. HORSLEY 1987, 143

γνωστῶς   D 1-0-0-1-0-2
Ex 33,13; Prv 27,23
clearly, evidently (sc. to know)
Cf. LE BOULLUEC 1989, 333

γογγύζω⁺   V 7-2-2-3-2-16
Ex 17,3; Nm 11,1; 14,27(bis).29
to mutter, to murmur, to grumble
Cf. LE BOULLUEC 1989, 40-41; LEE 1983, 115; →TWNT
(→ δια-, κατα-)

γόγγυσις,-εως   N3F 1-0-0-0-0-1
Nm 14,27
murmuring, muttering, grumbling; neol.

γογγυσμός,-οῦ⁺   N2M 7-0-1-0-5-13
Ex 16,7.8(bis).9.12
murmuring, muttering, grumbling
Cf. HORSLEY 1987, 143; LE BOULLUEC 1989, 41; →TWNT

γοερός,-ά,-όν   A 0-0-0-0-1-1
3 Mc 5,25
mournful, distressful

γοητεία,-ας   N1F 0-0-0-0-1-1
2 Mc 12,24
trickery, witchcraft

γομορ   N 5-2-6-0-0-13

Ex 16,16.18.32.33.36
=המר or עמר *homer, dry measure, 10 ephah* or
±450 kg
Cf. SIMOTA 1968, 58-59

γόμος,-ου⁺   N2M 1-1-0-0-0-2
Ex 23,5; 2 Kgs 5,17
cargo, load
Cf. LEE 1983, 62; SHIPP 1979, 192-193

γομφιάζω   V 0-0-1-0-1-2
Ez 18,2; Sir 30,10
to grind one's teeth Sir 30,10; *to be set on edge*
Ez 18,2; neol.
Cf. CAIRD 1972, 122

γομφιασμός,-οῦ   N2M 0-0-1-0-0-1
Am 4,6
grinding of teeth; neol.
Cf. CAIRD 1972, 122

γονεῖς,-έων⁺   N3M 0-0-0-2-15-17
Prv 29,15; Est 2,7; Jdt 5,8; Tob 10,12
parents

γονορρυής,-ής,-ές   A 13-1-0-0-0-14
Lv 15,4(bis).6.7.8
discharge of seed or *blood, suffering from
gonnorhea*; neol.
Cf. HARLÉ 1988, 45-46.147

γόνος,-ου   N2M 1-0-0-0-1-2
Lv 15,3; 3 Mc 5,31
offspring, child 3 Mc 5,31; *seed* Lv 15,3

γόνυ,γόνατος⁺   N3N 3-16-4-8-7-38
Gn 30,3; 48,12; Dt 28,35; Jgs^A 4,21; 7,5
knee Gn 30,3; *2 Kgs 9,24 ἐπὶ τὰ γόνατα
αὐτοῦ -בברכו *on his knees* for MT ברכבו *on his
chariot*

γόος,-ου   N2M 0-0-0-0-4-4
3 Mc 1,18; 4,3.6; 5,49
weeping, wailing

γοῦν   X 0-0-0-0-5-5
2 Mc 5,21; 4 Mc 2,2.5.8; 3,6
therefore (=γε οὖν, emphatic)

γράμμα,-ατος⁺   N3N 2-9-3-9-4-27
Ex 36,37(39,30); Lv 19,28; Jos 15,15.16; Jos^BA
15,49
written character Ex 36,37; *letter* Est 4,3; *book*
Est 6,1; γράμματα στικτά *incisions, tattoo* Lv
19,28
→TWNT

γραμματεία,-ας   N1F 0-0-0-1-1-2
Ps 70(71),15; Sir 44,4
learning; neol.

γραμματεύς,-έως⁺   N3M 9-33-11-21-11-85

Ex 5,6.10.14.15.19
scribe (title of officials)
Cf. WALTERS 1973, 308-309
γραμματεύω   V 0-1-1-0-0-2
1 Chr 26,29; Jer 52,25
to be secretary, to hold the office of secretary
γραμματικός,-ή,-όν   A 0-0-1-3-0-4
Is 33,18; Dn^LXX 1,4.17; Dn^Th 1,17
knowing one's letters, scholarly Dn^LXX 1,4; ὁ
γραμματικός *teacher, scholar* Is 33,18
γραμματοεισαγωγεύς,-έως   N3M 4-0-0-0-0-4
Dt 1,15; 16,18; 29,9; 31,28
instructer, schoolmaster; neol.
Cf. CAIRD 1972, 122; LE BOULLUEC 1989, 197
γραπτόν,-οῦ   N2N 0-1-0-1-2-4
2 Chr 36,22; Ezr 1,1; 1 Ezr 2,1; 2 Mc 11,15
writing, book
γραφεῖον,-ου   N2N 0-0-0-1-0-1
Jb 19,24
stylus, pencil
γραφή,-ῆς⁺   N1F 3-8-1-26-13-51
Ex 32,16(bis); Dt 10,4; 1 Chr 15,15; 28,19
writing, written document, scripture, prescription
Ex 32,16; *1 Chr 15,15 κατὰ τὴν γραφήν -כתב/כ
according to the scripture for MT כתפם/ב *on their shoulders*
-TWNT
γραφικός,-ή,-όν   A 0-0-0-0-1-1
3 Mc 4,20
of or *for writing*; γραφικὸς κάλαμος *pen*
γραφίς,-ίδος   N3F 1-1-2-0-0-4
Ex 32,4; 1 Kgs 6,29; Is 8,1; Ez 23,14
pencil, stylus for writing Is 8,1; *engraving tool* Ex 32,4; *Ez 23,14 ἐν γραφίδι -שׁשׁר/ב ◊ שׁר *with a pointed tool* for MT שׁשׁר/ב *in vermilion, red paint*
Cf. LE BOULLUEC 1989, 318-319
γράφω⁺   V 35-92-39-62-76-304
Ex 24,4.12; 31,18; 32,15.32
to write Ex 24,4; *to describe* Prv 8,15; *to engrave* 1 Kgs 6,29; *to prescribe* Est 10,1; *to enroll, to record* 1 Mc 10,65
Cf. HELBING 1928, 223-224; →TWNT
(→ ἀνα-, ἀντι-, ἀπο-, δια-, ἐγ-, ἐκ-, ἐπι-, κατα-, προ-, προσ-, συγ-, ὑπο-)
γρηγορέω⁺   V 0-0-3-3-3-9
Jer 5,6; 38(31),28(bis); Lam 1,14; Dn^Th9,14
to be or *become fully awake, to watch* [abs.] Neh 7,3; *to watch over* [ἐπί τι] Jer 5,6; [ἐπί τινα] Jer 38,28; [ἐπί τινι] Bar 2,9
γρηγόρησις,-εως   N3F 0-0-0-2-2-4

Dn^Th 5,11.14; PSal 3,2; 16,4
wakefulness; neol.
γρύζω   V 1-1-0-0-1-3
Ex 11,7; Jos 10,21; Jdt 11,19
to murmur; γρύζω τῇ γλώσσῃ *to growl* (of dogs and men)
γρύψ, γρυπός   N3M 2-0-0-0-0-2
Lv 11,13; Dt 14,12
griffin
γυάω
(→ διεγ-, ἐγ-)
γυμνάζω⁺   V 0-0-0-0-1-1
2 Mc 10,15
to harass, to vex
γυμνασία,-ας⁺   N1F 0-0-0-0-1-1
4 Mc 11,20
exercise, contest
γυμνάσιον,-ου   N2N 0-0-0-0-4-4
1 Mc 1,14; 2 Mc 4,9.12; 4 Mc 4,20
(gymnastic) school, center for schooling in athletics and Greek culture
γυμνός,-ή,-όν⁺   A 5-2-15-10-4-36
Gn 2,25; 3,7.10.11; 27,16
naked, unclad, bare Gn 2,25; *unarmed* 2 Mc 11,12; *Am 4,3 γυμναί *naked* corr. γυναῖκες *women* for MT אשׁה *(every) woman*
γυμνότης,-ητος⁺   N3F 1-0-0-0-0-1
Dt 28,48
nakedness
γυμνόω   V 1-0-0-0-2-3
Gn 9,21; Jdt 9,1.2
to strip naked, to lay bare [τινα] Gn 9,21; *to lay aside* [τι] Jdt 9,1
γύμνωσις,-εως   N3F 3-0-0-0-0-3
Gn 9,22.23(bis)
stripping, exposure
γυναικεῖος,-α,-ον⁺   A 2-0-0-2-3-7
Gn 18,11; Dt 22,5; Est 2,11.17; Jdt 12,15
belonging to women, feminine Dt 22,5; τὰ γυναικεῖα *menses of women* Gn 18,11; τὸ γυναικεῖον *part of the house reserved for the women* Tob^BA 2,11
γυναικών,-ῶνος   N3M 0-0-0-4-0-4
Est 2,3.9.13.14
women's apartments, harem
γύναιον,-ου   N2N 0-0-0-1-0-1
Jb 24,21
weak woman
γυνή, γυναικός⁺   N3F 308-347-81-109-229-1074
Gn 2,22.23.24.25; 3,1

woman Gn 2,22; *wife, spouse* Gn 2,25; λαμβάνω
τινὰ εἰς γυναῖκα *to marry* Neh 6,18

γῦρος,-ου   N2M 0-0-1-1-1-3
Is 40,22; Jb 22,14; Sir 24,5
ring, circle of the horizon

γυρόω   V 0-0-0-1-1-2
Jb 26,10; Sir 43,12
to circle [τι] Sir 43,12; *to draw a circle* [abs.] Jb
26,10
Cf. CAIRD 1972, 122-123

γύψ, γυπός   N3M 2-0-0-4-0-6
Lv 11,14; Dt 14,13; Jb 5,7.23; 28,7
vulture

γωλαθ   N 0-1-0-0-0-1
2 Chr 4,12

=נלה *ball, small globe* (on the capitals of
columns)

γωληλα   N 0-0-0-1-0-1
Neh 2,13
=גיא לילה; *Neh 2,13 (ἐν πύλη (חנ) τοῦ γωληλα *(by
the gate of) Golela* for MT (בשער) הגיא לילה) *(by the
gate of) the valley by night*

γωνία,-ας⁺   N1F 3-10-9-10-1-33
Ex 26,23.24; 27,2; 1 Sm 14,38; 1 Kgs 7,20(34)
corner, angle Ex 26,23; *leader, chief* (of pers.)
1 Sm 14,38

γωνιαῖος,-α,-ον   A 0-0-0-1-0-1
Jb 38,6
on or *at the angle*; λίθος γωνιαῖος *corner stone*

δαβιρ   N 0-13-0-0-0-13
1 Kgs 6,5.16.19.21.23
=דביר shrine, backroom of the temple

δαδουχία,-ας   N1F 0-0-0-0-1-1
2 Mc 4,22
torch-bearing, torch light; neol.

δαιμόνιον,-ου⁺   N2N 1-0-3-3-17-24
Dt 32,17; Is 13,21; 34,14; 65,3(4); Ps 90(91),6
demon (esp. for heathen gods) Dt 32,17; *Ps
90(91),6 καὶ δαιμονίου -שׁד/ו and a demon for
MT ישׁוד that devastates
Cf. SEELIGMANN 1940, 389; →TWNT

δαίμων,-ονος⁺   N3M 0-0-1-0-0-1
Is 65,11
demon for MT גד a goddess of fate and luck
Cf. HORSLEY 1981, 17; OWEN 1931, 133-153; SEELIGMANN
1940, 389; →TWNT

δάκνω⁺   V 6-0-5-2-2-15
Gn 49,17; Nm 21,6.8(bis).9
to bite [τι] Gn 49,17; [τινα] Nm 21,6; [τινα]
(metaph.) Hab 2,7; to sting [τινα] (metaph., of
a substance) Tob^BA 11,8
(→ συν-)

δάκρυ, δάκρυος   N3N 0-1-9-12-13-35
2 Kgs 20,5; Is 25,8; 38,5; Jer 8,23; 9,17
tear, teardrop 2 Kgs 20,5; *Mi 2,6 see δακρύω
Cf. SHIPP 1979, 207

δάκρυον,-ου⁺   N2N
see δάκρυ

δακρύω⁺   V 0-0-2-1-6-9
Ez 27,35; Mi 2,6; Jb 3,24; 2 Mc 4,37; 3 Mc 4,4;
to weep, to shed tears Jb 3,24; to shed tears at
[τι] 3 Mc 4,3; *Mi 2,6 δακρύω and δάκρυ -◊ נטף
drip (tears), shed tears, weep for MT ◊ נטף drip
(words), preach (said of prophets), cpr. Ez
21,2.7; Am 7,16
Cf. DONAT 1911, 350-360; WILLIS 1970, 72-77 (Mi 2,6)

δακτυλήθρα,-ας   N1F 0-0-0-0-1-1
4 Mc 8,13
thumb-screw, torturing instrument

δακτύλιος,-ου⁺   N2M 27-0-1-9-8-45
Gn 38,18.25; 41,42; Ex 25,12(bis)
ring, signet Gn 38,18; σφραγίζω δακτυλίῳ to
seal with a ring Est 8,8
Cf. WEVERS 1990, 426.583.604-605

δάκτυλος,-ου⁺   N2M 17-5-4-12-4-42
Ex 8,15; 29,12; 31,18; Lv 4,6.17
finger Lv 4,6; finger's breadth (ca. 2 cm or 7/10
of an inch) 1 Kgs 7,15; οἱ δάκτυλοι τῶν ποδῶν
the toes 2 Sm 21,20; ὁ μικρὸς δάκτυλος little

finger 2 Chr 10,10
Cf. WEVERS 1990, 115 (Ex 8,19); →TWNT

δαλός,-οῦ   N2M 0-0-5-0-0-5
Is 7,4; Ez 24,9; Am 4,11; Zech 3,2; 12,6
fire-brand, burnt-out torch

δαμάζω⁺   V 0-0-0-3-0-3
Dn^LXX 2,40; Dn^Th 2,40(bis)
to subdue, to overpower [τι]
(→ κατα-)

δάμαλις,-εως⁺   N3F 22-8-8-1-2-41
Gn 15,9; Nm 7,17.23.29.35
young cow, heifer Gn 15,9; *Is 5,18 δαμάλεως
-עגלה of a young cow for MT עגלה chariot; *Jl
1,17 δαμάλεις -פרות heifers or פרדות -◊ פרד
mules for MT פרדות dried figs?

δανείζω or δανίζω⁺   V 8-0-2-6-7-23
Dt 15,6(bis).8.10; 28,12
A: to lend [τί τινι] Dt 15,8; [τινι] Dt 15,6; M:
to borrow [τι] Neh 5,4; [abs.] Dt 15,6
Cf. WALTERS 1973, 29-30; →KIESSLING
(→ ἐκ-)

δάνειον,-ου⁺   N2N 3-0-0-0-1-4
Dt 15,8.10; 24,11; 4 Mc 2,8
loan
Cf. WALTERS 1973, 29; →KIESSLING

δανεισμός,-οῦ   N2M 0-0-0-0-1-1
Sir 18,33
borrowing-money

δανειστής,-οῦ⁺   N1M 0-1-0-2-1-4
2 Kgs 4,1; Ps 108(109),11; Prv 29,13; Sir 29,28
money-lender, creditor
Cf. WALTERS 1973, 29

δάνος,-ους   N3N 0-0-0-0-1-1
Sir 29,4
loan
Cf. WALTERS 1973, 29

δαπανάω⁺   V 0-0-0-0-13-13
Jdt 11,12; 12,4; Tob 1,7; 1 Mc 14,32
to spend Tob 1,7; to consume, to use up Jdt
11,12
(→ κατα-)

δαπάνη,-ης⁺   N1F 0-0-0-2-7-9
Ezr 6,4.8; 1 Mc 3,30; 10,39.44
cost, expenditure 1 Mc 10,39; money for spending
Ezr 6,4
→KIESSLING

δαπάνημα,-ατος   N3N 0-0-0-0-3-3
1 Ezr 6,24; 2 Mc 3,3; 11.31
cost, expense 1 Ezr 6,24; δαπανήματα necessaries, supplies, food 2 Mc 11,31

→ KIESSLING

δάσος,-ους   N3N 0-1-1-0-0-2
2 Sm 18,9; Is 9,17
thicket, copse

δασύπους,-ποδος[+]   N3M 2-0-0-0-0-2
Lv 11,5; Dt 14,7
rough-foot, i.e. *hare*
Cf. BARTHÉLEMY 1978, 179-193

δασύς,-εῖα,-ύ   A 5-1-2-1-2-11
Gn 25,25; 27,11.23; Lv 23,40; Dt 12,2
hairy Gn 27,23; *rough, thick (with leaves)* Lv
23,40; *bushy, thick with trees* Od 4,3; *Hab 3,3
δασέος -פארה *thick with leaves* for MT פארן
Paran
Cf. HELBING 1907, 53

δαψιλεύομαι   V 0-1-0-0-0-1
1 Sm 10,2
to be anxious or *careworn for* [διά τινα]

δαψιλής,-ής,-ές   A 0-0-0-0-4-4
1 Mc 3,30; 3 Mc 5,2.31; Wis 11,7
abundant, plentiful

δέ[+]   X 1554-155-259-1620-1298-4887
Gn 1,2; 2,6.10.12.14
connecting particle in the second place, often it
cannot be translated Gn 2,12; *and* Gn 1,2; *but*
Gn 2,6; *rather* (after neg.) Wis 2,11; introducing
an apodosis after hypothetical or temporal
protasis 2 Mc 1,34; ... μέν ... δέ ... *on the one
hand ... on the other hand ...* Gn 38,22; δὲ καί
but also, but even 2 Mc 12,13; ἔτι δὲ καί *and
(even)* LtJ 40; καί ... δέ *and also, but also* Wis
7,3; in the fourth place Wis 16,8; in the fifth
place 1 Ezr 1,22
Cf. AEJMELAEUS 1982, 34-47.139.151-152

δεβραθα or **χεβραθα**   N 0-1-0-0-0-1
2 Kgs 5,19
=כברת *stretch, a short distance*; in LXX
understood as a nomen proprium *Debratha*

δέδοικα   V 0-0-1-7-0-8
Is 60,14; Jb 3,19.25; 7,2; 26,13
perf. with pres. sense; *to fear, to be anxious*
[intrans.] Jb 38,40; *to fear* [τινα] Jb 3,19; [τι] Jb
3,25; *Jb 26,13 δεδοίκασιν αὐτόν -שערה? (*the
barriers of heaven*) *fear him* for MT שפרה (*his
breath*) *has swept clean*?
Cf. HELBING 1928, 34

δέησις,-εως[+]   N3F 0-15-4-40-22-81
1 Kgs 8,28.30.38.45.52
entreaty, petition, supplication 1 Kgs 8,38; *want,
need* Sir 38,34; *prayer* Sir 35,13; *Jb 8,6 δεήσεως

ἐπακούσεταί σου -יעתר עליך *he will listen to
your supplication* for MT יעיר *he would rouse
himself for you, he will keep watch over you*; *Jb
16,20 δέησις -רנה *supplication* for MT רע *friend*?
Cf. BICKERMAN 1980, 318; ENGEL 1985, 106-107;
HORSLEY 1987, 86

δεῖ (impers.)[+]   V 4-5-2-10-21-50
Ex 16,22; 21,10; Lv 4,2; 5,17; Jos 18,4
one must, it is needful to [+inf.] 2 Kgs 4,13; *one
must* [τινα +inf.] Ru 4,5; *it is proper to* [+inf.]
Jos 18,4; *it is fit to* [+inf.] Is 50,4; *it must, it is
fated, it is doomed to* [+inf.] Dn[LXX] 2,28; [abs.
with inf. understood] Jb 15,3; δέον ἐστίν
[+inf.] *it ought to, it must* Sir prol.,3; οὐ δεῖ
[+inf.] *it is not right to* Lv 5,17; τὰ δέοντα *what
is needed, necessaries* Ex 16,22
Cf. FASCHER 1954, 244-252; HELBING 1907, 110; LE
BOULLUEC 1989, 185; →NIDNTT; TWNT

δειγματίζω
(→ παρα-)

δείκνυμι[+]   V 26-20-28-18-32-124
Gn 12,1; 41,25.28.39; 48,11
to bring to light, to show Ps 4,7; *to point out* Gn
12,1; *to make known, to explain* Ex 13,21; *to
display* 2 Kgs 16,14; *Ex 15,25 καὶ ἔδειξεν
αὐτῷ -ויראהו ◊ ראה (Sam.) *and he showed him* for
MT ויורהו ◊ ירה *and he taught him*, see also 1 Sm
12,23; Jb 34,32; *Dt 32,20 καὶ δείξω -ואראה
(hiphil) *and I will show* for MT אראה (qal) *I will
see*, see also Nm 24,17; 1 Kgs 13,12; Eccl 39,18;
Is 53,11; Jer 18,17; *Zech 8,12 δείξω -ארעה
◊ ירע *I will make known* for MT זרע *seed*
Cf. HELBING 1907, 107; WEVERS 1990, 239 (Ex 15,25);
→TWNT
(→ ἀνα-, ἀπο-, ἐν-, ἐπι-, κατα-, παρα-, παρεπι-,
προαπο-, ὑπο-)

δεικνύω[+]   V 1-1-1-0-1-4
Dt 1,33; 1 Kgs 13,12; Ez 40,4; Tob[BA] 13,8
see δείκνυμι

δειλαίνω   V 0-0-0-0-1-1
1 Mc 5,41
to be a coward, to be cowardly

δείλαιος,-α,-ον   A 0-0-2-0-3-5
Hos 7,13; Na 3,7; Bar 4,31.32(bis)
wretched, miserable (of pers.) Hos 7,13; *wretched*
(of city) Na 3,7

δειλανδρέω   V 0-0-0-0-3-3
2 Mc 8,13; 4 Mc 10,14; 13,10
to be cowardly; neol.
Cf. HELBING 1928, 34

δείλη,-ης   N1F 2-7-2-1-1-13
Gn 24,63; Ex 18,14; 1 Sm 20,5; 30,17; 2 Sm 1,12
late afternoon, evening 1 Sm 20,5; πρὸς δείλης
toward evening Gn 24,63; ἀπὸ πρωίθεν ἕως
δείλης *from morning till evening* Ex 18,14
Cf. WEVERS 1990, 283

δειλία,-ας⁺   N1F 1-0-0-3-5-9
Lv 26,36; Ps 54(55),5; 88(89),41; Prv 19,15;
1 Mc 4,32
timidity, cowardice Prv 19,25; *fear, terror* Ps
54(55),5
Cf. SPICQ 1978, 200-202

δειλιαίνω   V 1-0-0-0-0-1
Dt 20,8
to make afraid; neol.

δειλιάω⁺   V 3-3-2-5-4-17
Dt 1,21; 31,6.8; Jos 1,9; 8,1
to be afraid, to fear; neol.
Cf. HELBING 1928, 25; SPICQ 1978, 200-202

δειλινός,-ή,-όν⁺   A 4-2-0-0-3-9
Gn 3,8; Ex 29,39.41; Lv 6,13; 1 Kgs 18,29
of the afternoon, of the evening 2 Chr 31,3; τὸ
δειλινόν (as adv.) *in the evening* Ex 29,39; τὸ
δειλινόν *at evening* for MT לרוח היום *in the cool
of the day* Gn 3,8; τὸ δειλινόν *evening* 1 Kgs
18,29
Cf. LACHS 1978, 52-54; LE BOULLUEC 1985, 108; LEE
1983, 110; WEVERS 1990, 170.484

δειλόομαι   V 0-0-0-0-3-3
1 Mc 4,8; 4,21; 16,6
to be afraid
Cf. HELBING 1928, 34

δειλός,-ή,-όν⁺   A 1-4-0-0-7-12
Dt 20,8; Jgs 7,3; Jgsᴮ 9,4; 2 Chr 13,7
cowardly, fearful Dt 20,8; *miserable, wretched,
worthless* Wis 9,14; *Jgsᴮ 9,4 δειλούς -◊חפז
cowardly (men) for MT פחזים *reckless*
Cf. SPICQ 1978, 200-202

δειλόψυχος,-ος,-ον   A 0-0-0-0-2-2
4 Mc 8,16; 16,5
fainthearted; neol.

δεῖμα,-ατος   N3N 0-0-0-0-1-1
Wis 17,8
fear, terror

δειματόω
(→ ἐκ-)

δεινάζω   V 0-0-0-0-2-2
2 Mc 4,35; 13,25
to be in straits, to take offense, to be indignant
2 Mc 4,35; *to take offense at* [τι] 2 Mc 13,25;
neol.

δεινός,-ή,-όν⁺   A 0-1-0-3-12-16
2 Sm 1,9; Jb 2,13; 13,11; 33,15; 4 Mc 4,15
fearful, terrible, awful

δεινῶς⁺   D 0-0-0-2-2-4
Jb 10,16; 19,11; 4 Mc 12,2; Wis 17,3
terribly, dreadfully, horribly

δειπνέω⁺   V 0-0-0-2-2-4
Prv 23,1; Dnᴸˣˣ 11,27; Tobᴮᴬ 8,1; Tobˢ 7,9
to take the main meal, to dine
Cf. SPICQ 1978, 203
(→ περι-, συν-)

δεῖπνον,-ου⁺   N2N 0-0-0-6-1-7
Dnᴸˣˣ 1,8.13.15; Dn 1,16
meal 4 Mc 3,9; *food, provisions* Dn 1,16

δέκα⁺   M 71-157-36-29-33-326
Gn 5,10.14; 7,20; 14,14; 16,3
ten Gn 5,10; *Ez 40,49 δέκα -אשר *ten* for MT
אשר *which;* *Ez 45,15 ἀπὸ δέκα -מין אשר *(one)*
out of ten, tithe for MT מין המאתים *(one) out of
two hundred*

δεκάδαρχος,-ου   N2M 3-0-0-0-1-4
Ex 18,21.25; Dt 1,15; 1 Mc 3,55
commander of ten men

δεκαέξ   M 0-2-0-0-0-2
Josᴮᴬ 15,41
sixteen

δεκαμηνιαῖος,-α,-ον   A 0-0-0-0-1-1
Wis 7,2
consisting of ten months; neol.

δεκάμηνος,-ου   N2F 0-0-0-0-1-1
4 Mc 16,7
period of ten months

δεκάπηχυς,-εια,-υ   A 0-1-0-0-0-1
1 Kgs 7,47(10)
ten cubits long

δεκαπλασιάζω   .V 0-0-0-0-1-1
Bar 4,28
to multiply by ten; neol.

δεκαπλασίων,-ων,-ον   A 0-0-0-1-0-1
Dnᵀʰ 1,20
tenfold

δεκαπλασίως   D 0-0-0-1-0-1
Dnᴸˣˣ 1,20
tenfold

δέκατος,-η,-ον⁺   M 54-8-14-8-17-101
Gn 8,5; 14,20; 28,22; Ex 12,3; 16,36
tenth Gn 8,5; ἡ δεκάτη (ἡμέρα) τοῦ μηνός *tenth
day* Lv 23,27; δεκάτη (μερίς) τῆς γῆς Lv 27,30;
τὸ δέκατον *tenth part, tithe* Lv 23,13; *gift,*

offering Tob 1,6; δέκατόν τινος *tenth of* Ex 29,40; δέκατον δέκατον *a tenth at a time* (semit.) Nm 28,21

Cf. BAUMGARTEN 1984, 245-261; HORSLEY 1985, 65; WEVERS 1990, 484; →NIDNTT

δεκατόω⁺   V 0-0-0-1-0-1
Neh 10,38
to tithe, to receive tithes [abs.] (more often ἀποδεκατόω); neol.
(→ ἀπο-)

δεκάχορδος,-ος,-ον   A 0-0-0-3-0-3
Ps 32(33),2; 91(92),4; 143(144),9
ten-stringed

δεκτός,-ή,-όν⁺   A 13-0-7-11-3-34
Ex 28,38; Lv 1,3.4; 17,4; 19,5
received, accepted, acceptable Prv 10,24; *acceptable for* [τινι] Ex 28,38(34); neol.?

Cf. DANIEL 1966, 193; HARL 1991, 248; →TWNT

δέλτος,-ου   N2F 0-0-0-0-4-4
1 Mc 8,22; 14,18.26.48
writing-tablet
Cf. WALTERS 1973, 171-173

δελεχέω
(→ ἐν-)

δελεχίζω
(→ ἐν-)

δένδρον,-ου⁺   N2N 6-0-8-19-7-40
Gn 18,4.8; 23,17; Nm 13,20; Dt 12,2
tree Gn 18,4; *Is 16,9 τὰ δένδρα σου -אֲרָזָיִךְ *your cedars* for MT אֲרַוֵּךְ *I will water you*
Cf. ORLINSKY 1948, 384 (Jb 40,21.22)

δένδρος,-ους   N3N 1-0-0-0-0-1
Dt 22,6
tree

δενδροτομέω   V 0-0-0-0-1-1
4 Mc 2,14
to cut down trees

δεξαμενή,-ῆς   N1F 1-0-0-0-0-1
Ex 2,16
receptacle, trough (used to hold water or food for animals)

δεξιάζω   V 0-0-0-0-1-1
2 Mc 4,34
to greet with the right hand, to welcome [τινα]

δεξιός,-ά,-όν⁺   A 55-43-29-58-43-228
Gn 13,9(bis); 24,49; 48,13(bis)
right Gn 48,14; ἡ δεξιά *right hand* Gn 48,13; δίδωμι δεξιάν τινι *to give peace to sb* 1 Mc 11,50.62; καθίζω ἐκ δεξιῶν τινος *to sit at someone's right* i.e. *at the place of honor* (of

pers.) 1 Kgs 2,19; ἐκ δεξιῶν τινος *at the right of, south of* (of places, when facing the east) 1 Sm 23,19; *Ps 89(90),12 τὴν δεξιάν σου -יְמִינֶךָ ◊ יָמִין *your right hand* for MT יָמֵינוּ ◊ יוֹם *our days*

δέομαι⁺   V 14-13-5-27-37-96
Gn 19,18; 25,21; 43,20; 44,18; Ex 4,10
to pray [abs.] Gn 19,18; *to pray for* [περί τινος] (for pers.) Jdt 8,31; (for things) Sir 51,9; *to pray sb concerning* [τινος περί τι] Gn 25,21; *to pray to* [πρός τινα] Jb 8,5; *to supplicate, to beg, to beseech* [τινος] Dt 3,23; *to beseech for, to seek for* [τινος] Jb 17,1; *to entreat, to ask for sth* [τινος] Jb 9,15; *to want, to desire* [ἵνα +subj.] 1 Ezr 4,46; *to be in need* Wis 16,25; δέομαι περὶ τῶν ἁμαρτιῶν *to ask forgiveness* Sir 28,4; *Jb 34,20 δεῖσθαι -(שׁוּעַ) יָנוּעַ? *to cry (for help)* for MT עַם יְנֻעֲשׁוּ *the people are shaken?*

Cf. CIMOSA 1985, 43-52; HARLÉ 1988, 62; HELBING 1928, 171-173; KRAFT 1972, 165; LE BOULLUEC 1989, 327
(→ ἐν-, κατα-, προσ-)

δέος,-ους⁺   N3N 0-0-0-0-5-5
2 Mc 3,17.30; 12,22; 13,16; 15,23
fear, alarm
Cf. SHIPP 1979, 211-212

δέρμα,-ατος⁺   N3N 63-0-5-9-1-78
Gn 27,16; Ex 25,5(bis); 26,14(bis)
hide, skin

δερμάτινος,-η,-ον⁺   A 13-1-0-0-0-14
Gn 3,21; Lv 13,52.53.57.58
of skin, leathern

δέρρις,-εως⁺   N3F 17-3-4-2-0-26
Ex 26,7(bis).8(tris)
skin Zech 13,4; *(tent-)curtain (of goats' hair)* Ex 26,7

δέρω⁺   V 0-1-0-0-0-1
2 Chr 29,34
to flay, to skin
Cf. HORSLEY 1987, 66; SHIPP 1979, 212-213
(→ ἐκ-)

δέσις,-εως   N3F 0-0-0-0-1-1
Sir 45,11
setting (of precious stones)

δεσμεύω⁺   V 2-2-1-2-2-9
Gn 37,7; 49,11; Jgsᴮ 16,11; 1 Sm 24,12; Am 2,8
to bind [τινα] Jgsᴮ 16,11; *to bind, to tie together* [τι] (as corn in the sheaf) Gn 37,7; *to bind fast to* [τι πρός τι] Gn 49,11; *to bind up* [τι] (of wounds) Ps 146(147),3; *Am 2,8 δεσμεύοντες -חֹבְלִים ◊ חֶבֶל *binding* for MT חֲבֻלִים ◊ חֶבֶל" *(taken in) pledge*; *1 Sm 24,12 δεσμεύεις -צרר (part.)

(you) shut up, bind for MT צדה (part.) *(you) lay snares*

Cf. CAIRD 1972, 123 (1 Sm 24,12)

(- ἀπο-, κατα-)

δέσμη,-ης⁺   N1F 1-0-0-0-0-1
Ex 12,22
package, bundle
Cf. WALTERS 1973, 94

δέσμιος,-ος,-ον⁺   A 0-0-2-3-5-10
Zech 9,11.12; Eccl 4,14; Lam 3,34; 2 Mc 14,27
bound, captive 2 Mc 14,27; ὁ δέσμιος *prisoner*
Eccl 4,14
Cf. WALTERS 1973, 316 (Jb 3,18)

δεσμός,-οῦ⁺   N2M 6-7-15-10-14-52
Gn 42,27.35(bis); Lv 26,13; Nm 19,15
band, bond Lv 26,13; δεσμοί *bonds, chains* Prv
7,22; (τὰ) δεσμά *prison* Ezr 7,26; καταλαμβάνω
τινὰ ἐν δεσμοῖς *to take in bonds* 2 Chr 33,11;
ὅρκος δεσμοῦ *binding oath* Nm 30,14; ὁ δεσμὸς
τοῦ ἀργυρίου *bundle of money, bag of money*
Gn 42,27, see also Hag 1,6; *Hab 3,13 δεσμούς
- יסר.אסר? *bonds* for MT יסוד *foundation, base*;
*Jb 38,31 δεσμόν -מעדנות *chains* (here denoting
the stellar group the Pleiades) for MT מעדנות
sweets, dainties? or *reluctance*?; *Mal 3,20 ἐκ
δεσμῶν -מ/רבק מין and רבק (*let loose*) *from
bonds* for MT רבק מרבק *fatted* (through
binding)
Cf. WALTERS 1973, 129.316

δεσμοφύλαξ,-ακος⁺   N3M 1-0-0-0-0-1
Gn 40,3
jailer; neol.

δεσμωτήριον,-ου⁺   N2N 5-2-1-0-0-8
Gn 39,22(bis).23; 40,3.5
prison

δεσμώτης,-ου⁺   N1M 1-0-2-0-1-4
Gn 39,20; Jer 24,1; 36(29),2; Bar 1,9
prisoner, captive Bar 1,9; *Jer 24,1 τοὺς
δεσμώτας - סנר *the prisoners* for MT מסגר סגר
(piel) *someone who shuts up* or *closes, jailer,
locksmith*?
Cf. WAMBURG 1959, 458

δεσπόζω   V 0-1-0-5-11-17
1 Chr 29,11; Ps 21(22),29; 58(59),14; 65(66),7;
88(89),10
to be lord or *master* Ps 65(66),7; *to be lord of, to
be master of* [τινος] 1 Chr 29,11
Cf. HELBING 1928, 116-117

δεσποτεία,-ας   N1F 0-0-0-2-0-2
Ps 102(103),22; 144(145),13

dominion, absolute authority, sovereignty

δεσποτεύω   V 0-0-0-0-1-1
3 Mc 5,28
to be lord of, to be master [τι]; neol.?
Cf. HELBING 1928, 117

δεσπότης,-ου⁺   N1M 2-1-7-14-36-60
Gn 15,2.8; Jos 5,14; Is 1,24; 3,1
lord, master Jos 5,14; δέσποτα κύριε *master lord*
(semit.) Gn 15,8
Cf. BARDY 1910, 373-379; 1911, 458-459; FISCHER 1958-
1959, 132-138; GUILLAND 1959, 52-89; HARL 1986, 52.163;
HORSLEY 1987, 144; —TWNT

δεῦρο⁺   D 14-51-0-9-5-79
Gn 19,32; 24,31; 31,44; 37,13; Ex 3,10
hither 2 Mc 14,7; *come (on)* (as interjection) Gn
19,32; *go, you may go* 1 Kgs 1,53; δεῦρο
ἀποστέλλω σε *go, I send you* Ex 3,10; *Ct 4,8
δεῦρο -אתי אתה *come* for MT אתי *with me*;
*2 Sm 18,22 δεῦρο -לכה. הלך *go* for MT ל/כה
for you
Cf. AVALOS 1989, 165-176; CAIRD 1972, 123; EYNIKEL-
LUST 1991, 57-68

δεῦτε⁺   I 6-11-12-12-2-43
Gn 11,3.4.7; 37,20.27
come (now) (as interjection) Gn 11,7; *go* 2 Kgs
6,2; *Is 27,11 δεῦτε - אתה *come* for MT אותה *it*;
see δεῦρο

δευτερεύω   V 0-2-1-1-0-4
1 Chr 16,5; 2 Chr 35,24; Jer 52,24; Est 4,8;
to be second; neol.?
Cf. WALTERS 1973, 57.120.121.313-314

δευτέριος,-α.-ον   A 0-0-0-0-1-1
1 Ezr 1,29
second, secondary, second-best; neol.?
Cf. WALTERS 1973, 57.121

δευτερολογέω   V 0-0-0-0-1-1
2 Mc 13,22
to speak a second time; neol.

δευτερονόμιον,-ου   N2N 1-1-0-0-0-2
Dt 17,18; Jos 9,2c(8.32)
second or *repeated Law, the fifth book of the
Pentateuch*; neol.

δεύτερος,-α,-ον⁺   M 66-76-23-35-30-230
Gn 1,8; 2,13; 4,19; 7,11; 8,14
next Jdt 2,4; *second* Gn 1,8; *second of two, other*
Gn 32,9; δευτέρα σαββάτου (sc. ἡμέρα) *the
second day of the week* Ps 47(48),1
Cf. WALTERS 1973, 155-158 (1 Chr 25,9)

δευτερόω   V 1-5-1-1-5-13
Gn 41,32; 1 Sm 26,8; 2 Sm 20,10; 1 Kgs

18,34(bis)
to do sth a second time, to repeat [τι] Sir 7,14;
[abs.] 1 Kgs 18,34; *to give sb a second blow* [τινι]
1 Sm 26,8; *to smite, to slay* [τινα] 1 Kgs 21,20;
to occur twice Gn 41,32; *Jer 2,36 δευτερῶσαι
-שנה *to repeat* for MT שנה *to change*; neol.
Cf. CAIRD 1972, 123-124; WALTERS 1973, 120-121, 313-314

δευτέρωσις,-εως   N3F 0-2-0-0-1-3
2 Kgs 23,4; 25,18; Sir 41,26
second rate or *course* 2 Kgs 23,4; *retelling,
iteration* Sir 41,26; neol.
Cf. WALTERS 1973, 313-314

δέχομαι⁺   V 13-5-13-18-13-62
Gn 4,11; 33,10; 50,17; Ex 32,4; Lv 7,18
to receive [τι] Gn 4,11; *to accept* [τι] Lv 19,7; *to
take* [τι] Ezr 8,30; *to accept and forgive* [τι] (an
injustice) Gn 50,17; *to receive* [τινα] Dt 32,11; *to
welcome with, to receive with* [τινά τινι] Jdt 3,7;
τὸ οὖς δέχεταί τι *the ear receives, hears* Jb 4,12;
δέχομαι παιδείαν *to accept correction* Jer 2,30;
δέχομαι λόγους *to accept teaching* Jer 9,20;
*Prv 30,1 δεξάμενος αὐτούς -קח/ קח(ם) *accept
them* for MT (שא)ה/מ(קה)(י) *(Ja)keh of Ma(ssa)?*;
*Prv 9,9 τοῦ δέχεσθαι -/ לקח (verb) *to receive*
for MT / לקח (subst.) *teaching*
Cf. HARL 1986, 317 (Gn 50,17); HELBING 1928, 53; →TWNT
(→ ἀνα-, ἀπο-, δια-, εἰσ-, ἐκ-, ἐν-, ἐπι-, κατα-,
παρα-, προσ-, ὑπο-)

δέω⁺   V 2-33-13-11-10-69
Gn 38,28; 42,24; Jgsᴬ 15,10.12.13
to bind [τι] Gn 38,28; *to put in chains* [τινα] Gn
42,24
Cf. HORSLEY 1981, 49
(→ ἀπο-, δια-, ἐκ-, ἐν-, ἐπι-, κατα-, προσ-, συν-,
ὑπο-)

δή⁺   X 5-177-35-61-49-327
Gn 15,5; 18,4; 27,34.38; Dt 32,26
at this or *that point, now, then, already, at length*
(intensive particle)

δῆγμα,-ατος   N3N 0-0-1-0-2-3
Mi 5,4; Wis 16,5.9
bite, sting Wis 16,5; *Mi 5,4 δήγματα -נשׂיכי
bites, attacks? for MT נסיכי *princes, leaders*

δηλαιστός,-ά,-όν   A 0-0-1-0-0-1
Ez 5,15
wretched, miserable; neol.

δῆλος,-η,-ον⁺   A 2-2-1-0-3-8
Nm 27,21; Dt 33,8; 1 Sm 14,41; 28,6; Hos 3,4
visible, clear Nm 27,21; δῆλον (sc. ἐστί) ὅτι
[+ind.] *it is manifest that* 4 Mc 2,7; οἱ δῆλοι

symbols of revelation, manifestation (semit.,
transl. of the Urim, understood as deriving from
אור *to give light*) 1 Sm 28,6, see also Sir 33,3; (of
the Teraphim) Hos 3,4
Cf. CAIRD 1972, 124; GUINOT 1989, 23-48

δηλόω⁺   V 3-4-2-20-7-36
Ex 6,3; 33,12; Dt 33,10; Jos 4,7; 1 Sm 3,21
to make visible or *manifest* [τι] Jer 16,21; *to
show* [τινα] Ex 33,12; *to make known, to reveal*
[τι] Ex 6,3; *to explain* Jos 4,7
Cf. DRESCHER 1970, 139-142; LE BOULLUEC 1989, 332;
→NIDNTT
(→ προ-)

δήλωσις,-εως   N3F 2-0-0-2-1-5
Ex 28,30; Lv 8,8; Ps 118(119),130; Dnᴸˣˣ 2,27;
1 Ezr 5,40
revelation, manifestation Lv 8,8; *interpretation*
Dnᴸˣˣ 2,27; *symbol of revelation* (semit., transl.
of the Urim, understood as deriving from אור *to
give light*) Ex 28,30; see δῆλος
Cf. CAIRD 1972, 124; GUINOT 1989, 23-48; HARLÉ 1988,
113; LE BOULLUEC 1989, 288-289

δημαγωγία,-ας   N1F 0-0-0-0-1-1
1 Ezr 5,70
control or *leadership of the people* (in bad sense,
by various means of persuasion)

δημεύω   V 0-0-0-1-0-1
Dnᴸˣˣ 3,96
to seize as public property

δημέω
(→ ἀπο-)

δημηγορέω⁺   V 0-0-0-1-1-2
Prv 30,31; 4 Mc 5,15
to speak publicly 4 Mc 5,15; *Prv 30,31
δημηγορῶν -עמו אל קם? *standing over his people,
haranguing his people* for MT עמו אלקום?
δήμιος,-ου   N2M 0-0-0-0-2-2
2 Mc 5,8; 7,29
public executioner

δημιουργέω⁺   V 0-0-0-0-3-3
2 Mc 10,2; 4 Mc 7,8; Wis 15,13
A: *to work at, to fabricate, to create* [τι] Wis
15,13; P: *to be made* or *fabricated* 2 Mc 10,2
Cf. LARCHER 1985, 876

δημιουργός,-οῦ⁺   N2M 0-0-0-0-1-1
2 Mc 4,1
maker, producer
Cf. HORSLEY 1982, 151

δῆμος,-ου⁺   N2M 151-47-0-5-17-220
Nm 1,20.22.24(26).26(28).1,28(30)

tribe, family Nm 3,27; *people* Jdt 4,8; *multitude* Jdt 6,1

Cf. PASSONI DELL'ACQUA 1982, 197-214

δημόσιος,-α,-ον⁺   A 0-0-0-0-3-3
2 Mc 6,10; 3 Mc 2,27; 4,7
belonging to the people or *state;* δημοσίᾳ *publicly, in public* (as adv.)

δημοτελής,-ής,-ές   A 0-0-0-0-1-1
3 Mc 4,1
at the public cost

δημότης,-ου   N1M 0-0-0-0-1-1
Wis 18,11
one of the people, commoner

διά⁺   P 218-201-401-181-426-1427
Gn 4,1; 24,62; 26,6; 30, 35; 32,16
|τινος|: *through, throughout* (of time) 1 Mc 12,27; *after* 4 Mc 13,21; *through (the agency of)* (personal agent) Gn 4,1; *by* (originator of an action) 1 Ezr 6,13; |τινα|: *thanks to, with the aid of, on the account of* Gn 12,13; |τι|: *on the account of, because of, by reason of, for* Gn 7,7; *out of, because of* (with words denoting emotions) 2 Mc 5,21; *because* Gn 39,9; δι' αἰῶνος *for ever* Dt 5,29; δι' εὐθείας *by a straight path* Is 59,14; διὰ κενῆς *idly* Ps 30(31),7; διὰ μέσου τινός *through the midst of* Jdt 11,19; δι' ὀλίγων *in a few words* 2 Mc 6,17; δι' ὅλου *entirely* Ez 38,8; διὰ παντός *continually* Ex 27,20; διὰ τάχους *quickly* Ps 6,11; διὰ τέλους *continually* Is 62,6; διὰ χειρός τινος *by the hand of* 1 Kgs 10,13; διὰ τί *wherefore?* Ex 2,3; διὰ τοῦτο *therefore, on this account* Gn 10,9

Cf. SOLLAMO 1979, passim; ·TWNT

διαβάθρα,-ας   N1F 0-1-0-0-0-1
2 Sm 23,21
ladder; neol.?

Cf. HUSSON 1983, 318

διαβαίνω⁺   V 35-72-7-4-10-128
Gn 31,21.52(bis); 32,11.23
to step across, to pass over |τι| Gn 31,21; |διά τινος| Jos 3,17; *to cross over* |abs., πόταμον being omitted| Nm 32,7; *1 Sm 13,7 οἱ διαβαίνοντες - עברים *they that went over* for MT עברים *Hebrews*

Cf. HELBING 1928, 80

διαβάλλω⁺   V 0-0-0-3-2-5
Dn 3,8; Dnᵀʰ 6,25; 2 Mc 3,11; 4 Mc 4,1
to calumniate, to speak slanderously 4 Mc 4,1; *to accuse* |τινα| Dn 3,8; *to accuse about, to injure with* |ὑπέρ τινος| 4 Mc 4,1; *to misinform* |abs.|

2 Mc 3,11; *Nm 22,22 διαβαλεῖν -שׂטן *to accuse* for MT שׂטן *adversary*

διάβασις,-εως   N3F 1-10-2-0-1-14
Gn 32,23; Jos 2,7; 4,8; Jgs 3,28
crossing over, passage Jos 4,8; *place of crossing, ford* Jgsᴬ 3,28

Cf. DREW-BEAR 1972, 67

διάβημα,-ατος⁺   N3N 0-1-0-15-1-17
2 Sm 22,37; Ps 16(17),5(bis); 17(17),37; 36(37),23
a step (across); neol.

διαβιάζομαι   V 1-0-0-0-0-1
Nm 14,44
to use force (strengthened for βιάζομαι)

διαβιβάζω   V 3-4-0-0-1-8
Gn 32,24; Nm 32,5.30; Jos 7,7; 2 Sm 19,16
to carry over or *across, to transport* |τι| Gn 32,24; *to lead over* |τινά τι| Nm 32,5

Cf. HELBING 1928, 81

διαβιόω   V 1-0-0-0-0-1
Ex 21,21
to survive, to continue to live

διαβοάω   V 2-0-0-0-1-3
Gn 45,16; Lv 25,10; Jdt 10,18
A: *to proclaim, to publish* |τι| Lv 25,10; P: *to be the common talk, to be a by-word* Jdt 10,18

διαβολή,-ῆς⁺   N1F 1-0-0-1-8-10
Nm 22,32; Prv 6,24; 2 Mc 14,27; 3 Mc 6,7; Sir 19,15
false accusation, slander Sir 26,5; *quarrel, enmity* Sir 28,9; εἰς διαβολήν σου *to withstand you* Nm 22,32

διάβολος,-ου⁺   N2M 0-1-3-16-2-22
1 Chr 21,1; Zech 3,1.2(bis); Ps 108(109),6
enemy, adversary (frequently) Est 7,4; *menace, threat* 1 Mc 1,36; *Sâtân, the Devil* (exceptionally) 1 Chr 21,1, see also Wis 2,24

·NIDNTT; TWNT

διαβουλεύομαι   V 1-0-0-0-0-1
Gn 49,23
to devise (evil) plans

διαβουλία,-ας   N1F 0-0-0-1-0-1
Ps 5,11
deliberation, plotting, intrigue

Cf. HEDLEY 1933, 270

διαβούλιον,-ου   N2N 0-0-5-1-4-10
Ez 11,5; Hos 4,9; 5,4; 7,2; 11,6
counsel, deliberation Sir 17,6; *decree, intrigue, plotting* (in LXX mostly pejorative) Wis 1,9; neol.?

Cf. LARCHER 1983, 188

διαγγέλλω⁺ V 3-1-0-2-3-9
Ex 9,16; Lv 25,9(bis); Jos 6,10; Ps 2,7
to give notice by a messenger [τινι] 2 Mc 1,33; *to*
tell abroad, to proclaim [τι] Ex 9,16; *to declare*
[abs.] Sir 43,2
Cf. LE BOULLUEC 1989, 132

διάγγελμα,-ατος N3N 0-1-0-0-0-1
1 Kgs 5,1(7)
message, notice; *1 Kgs 5,1(7) πάντα τὰ
διαγγέλματα - כל הקרוא *everything called for* or
ordered for MT כל הקרב *all the guests;* neol.
Cf. CAIRD 1972, 124

διαγίνομαι⁺ V 0-0-0-0-1-1
2 Mc 11,26
to go through life, to live

διαγινώσκω⁺ V 3-0-0-1-5-9
Nm 33,56; Dt 2,7; 8,2; Prv 14,33; Jdt 11,12
to consider [+indir. question] Dt 2,7; *to discern*
exactly, to perceive, to know exactly [τι] Dt 8,2; *to*
determine [+inf.] Nm 33,56; τὸ διεγνωσμένον
that what is decreed 2 Mc 3,23

διαγλύφω V 1-1-2-0-0-4
Ex 28,11; 2 Chr 4,5; Ez 41,19.20
to carve, to engrave Ex 28,11; διαγεγλυμμένα
βλαστοὺς κρίνου *engraved with flowers of lilies*
2 Chr 4,5; neol.?

διάγνωσις,-εως⁺ N3F 0-0-0-0-1-1
Wis 3,18
discernment, distinguishing, decision; ἐν ἡμέρᾳ
διαγνώσεως *in the day of trial*
Cf. HORSLEY 1981, 48-49; 1987, 86; LARCHER 1983, 311

διαγογγύζω⁺ V 8-1-0-0-1-10
Ex 15,24; 16,2.7.8; Nu 14,2
to mutter, to murmur against [ἐπί τινα] Ex
15,24; [ἐπί τινι] Jos 9,18; [κατά τινος] Ex 16,7;
neol.
Cf. LE BOULLUEC 1989, 40

διαγορεύω V 0-0-0-0-2-2
1 Ezr 5,48; Susᴸˣˣ 60
to declare, to state explicitly Susᴸˣˣ 60; τὰ
διηγορευμένα *orders, instructions* 1 Ezr 5,49

διαγραφή,-ῆς N1F 0-0-1-0-0-1
Ez 43,12
prescribed plan, scheme

διαγράφω V 0-1-5-2-1-9
Jos 18,4; Ez 4,1; 8,10; 42,3; 43,11
to mark out by lines, to delineate Ez 4,1; *to mark*
out by lines, to draft, to carve Ct 8,9; *to describe*
Jos 18,4; *to pay* Est 3,9

διάγω V 0-7-4-4-7-22
2 Sm 12,31; 2 Kgs 16,3; 17,17; 21,6; 23,10
to carry over [τινα] 3 Mc 1,3; *to draw through, to*
make to pass through [τινα διά τινος] 2 Sm
12,31; *to bring through (the fire)* [τι διά τινος]
Zech 13,9; *to celebrate* [τι] 2 Mc 12,38; *to go*
through life, to live [abs.] Sir 38,27; *to keep* [τινα
+pred.] Jb 12,17; διάγω τὴν ἡμέραν *to spend*
the day, to pass the day 3 Mc 4,8; διάγω τὰ
σκέλη *to spread one's legs* Ez 16,25; *2 Chr 28,3
διῆγε- יעבר *he carries over* for MT יבער *he burns*

διαγωγή,-ῆς N1F 0-0-0-1-0-1
Est 3,13e
management; διαγωγὴ νόμων *code of laws, way*
of life

διαδέχομαι⁺ V 0-3-0-1-5-9
1 Chr 26,18(bis); 2 Chr 31,12; Est 10,3; 2 Mc
4,31
to succeed, to take one's place [τινα] 4 Mc 4,15;
to relieve guard 1 Chr 26,18; *to be next in rank,*
to be second in command Est 10,3; δια-
δεχόμενος *next* (as adj.) 2 Chr 31,12; *regent* (as
subst.) 2 Mc 4,31

διαδέω V 0-0-0-0-1-1
4 Mc 9,11
to bind

διάδηλος,-ος,-ον A 1-0-0-0-1-2
Gn 41,21; 3 Mc 2,5
distinguishable among others; διάδηλος
γίγνομαι *to become perceptible* Gn 41,21; *to*
become known, notorious 3 Mc 2,5

διάδημα,-ατος⁺ N3N 0-0-1-3-13-17
Is 62,3; Est 1,11; 2,17; 8,15; 1 Ezr 4,30
crown Is 62,3; *diadem, cloth headband worn as*
a symbol of power Est 8,15

διαδιδράσκω V 0-0-0-0-2-2
2 Mc 8,13; Sir 11,10
to run away, to flee
Cf. CAIRD 1972, 124

διαδίδωμι⁺ V 1-1-0-0-9-11
Gn 49,27; Jos 13,6; 2 Mc 4,39; 7,5; 3 Mc 2,27
A: *to pass on, to hand over* Jos 13,6; *to distribute*
Sir 39,14; P: *to be spread about* 4 Mc 4,22

διάδοχος,-ος,-ον⁺ A 0-3-0-0-4-7
1 Chr 18,17; 2 Chr 26,11; 28,7; 2 Mc 4,29; 14,26
succeeding Sir 46,1; ὁ διάδοχος *successor* 2 Mc
4,29; *deputy, court official* 1 Chr 18,17
Cf. DANIEL 1966, 110 (Sir 46,1)

διαδύομαι V 0-1-0-0-0-1
1 Sm 17,49

to slip through, to penetrate [διά τινος]

διαζάω   V 0-0-0-0-1-1
2 Mc 5,27
to live through

διάζομαι   V 0-1-1-0-0-2
Jgs^A 16,14; Is 19,10
to set the warp in the loom, to begin the web

διαθερμαίνω   V 1-3-0-0-0-4
Ex 16,21; 1 Sm 11,9.11; 2 Kgs 4,34
A: *to warm up* Ex 16,21; P: *to be heated, to be hot* 2 Kgs 4,34; ἕως ἡ ἡμέρα διεθερμάνθη *until the heat of the day* 1 Sm 11,11

διάθεσις,-εως   N3F 0-0-0-2-7-9
Ps 72(73),7; Est 8,12q; 2 Mc 5,23; 14,5; 3 Mc 2,28
arrangement 3 Mc 3,26; *disposition* 4 Mc 1,25; *state, condition* 2 Mc 5,23; διάθεσις καρδίας *intention* Ps 72(73),7
Cf. PELLETIER 1967, 175-186

διαθήκη,-ης^+   N1F 87-115-65-47-44-358
Gn 6,18; 9,9.11.12.13
treaty, covenant (stereotyped equivalent of ברית); see διατίθημι
Cf. DA FONSECA 1927, passim; 1928, 26-40.143-160; HARL 1986, 55.67; HELBING 1928, 241; HINDLEY 1961, 13-24; NORTON 1908; PENNA 1965, 149-180; SWETNAM 1966, 438-444; TOV 1976, 534.542; →MM; TWNT

διαθρύπτω   V 1-0-3-0-2-6
Lv 2,6; Is 58,7; Na 1,6; Hab 3,6; Od 4,6
A: *to break into pieces* [τι] Is 58,7; P: *to burst (through)* Hab 3,6; *to be broken into pieces* Sir 43,15; διαθρύπτω τι κλάσματα *to break sth into pieces* Lv 2,6
Cf. HELBING 1907, 96

διαίρεσις,-εως^+   N3F 0-30-0-2-2-34
Jos 19,51; Jgs^A 5,15; Jgs^B 5,16; 1 Chr 24,1; 26,1
dividing, distribution Jdt 9,4; *division* Jos 19,51

διαιρέω^+   V 11-16-4-8-6-45
Gn 4,7; 15,10(bis); 32,8; Ex 21,35
A: *to take apart, to divide* Gn 15,10; *to divide* Gn 4,7; *to separate* Nm 31,42; *to dispense* Sir 27,25; M: *to divide for oneself* Ex 21,35; ἀριθμοὶ μηνῶν αὐτοῦ διηρέθεσαν *his days were numbered* Jb 21,21; *Am 5,9 ὁ διαιρῶν- המפליג *who dispenses* for MT המבליג *who brightens up?*; *Gn 4,7 ἐὰν ὀρθῶς δὲ μὴ διέλῃς- אם לא תיטיב- לפתח חטאת רבץ *if you did not rightly divide* for MT לא אם תיטיב לפתח *if you did not act rightly, at the door*
Cf. HARL 1986, 114

δίαιτα,-ης^+   N1F 0-0-0-12-1-13

Jb 5,3.24; 8,6.22; 11,14
way of living, mode of life Jdt 12,15; *dwelling, abode* Jb 8,22; *Jb 20,25 ἐν διαίταις αὐτοῦ- ב/מררת/ו *in his dwelling place* for MT מ/מררת/ו *out of his liver*
Cf. HORSLEY 1987, 69

διαιτάω   V 0-0-0-1-1-2
Jb 30,7; 4 Mc 2,17
A: *to moderate, to regulate* 4 Mc 2,17; M/P: *to lead one's life, to live* Jb 30,7
(→ ἐκ-, μετα-)

διαιτέομαι   V 0-0-0-0-1-1
Jdt 8,16
to be turned by entreaty, to waver; neol.
Cf. HELBING 1907, 79

διακαθιζάνω   V 1-0-0-0-0-1
Dt 23,14
to sit down apart, to relieve oneself; neol.

διακαθίζω   V 0-1-0-0-0-1
2 Sm 11,1
to besiege

διακαίω   V 0-0-0-0-1-1
4 Mc 11,19
to burn through, to burn away [τι]

διακάμπτω   V 0-1-0-0-0-1
2 Kgs 4,34
to bend about, to turn about; neol.

διακαρτερέω   V 0-0-0-0-2-2
Jdt 7,30; 4 Mc 6,9
to endure to the end Jdt 7,30; *to bear patiently* 4 Mc 6,9

διακατέχω   V 0-0-0-0-1-1
Jdt 4,7
to keep, to occupy, to hold; neol.?

διάκειμαι   V 0-0-0-0-2-2
3 Mc 3,23; 4,10
to be fixed 3 Mc 4,10; *to be disposed in a certain manner, to be in a certain state* [+adv.] 3 Mc 3,23; serving as passive to διατίθημι

διάκενος,-ος,-ον   A 1-0-0-0-0-1
Nm 21,5
light, worthless

διακινδυνεύω   V 0-0-0-0-1-1
2 Mc 11,7
to run every risk, to make a desperate attempt

διακινέω   V 0-0-0-0-1-1
3 Mc 5,23
to move, to agitate

διακλάω   V 0-0-0-1-0-1
Lam 4,4

to break in two, to cut (a piece of bread)

διακλέπτομαι V 0-2-0-0-0-2
2 Sm 19,4(bis)
to steal away

διακολυμβάω V 0-0-0-0-1-1
1 Mc 9,48
to swim across; neol.?

διακομίζω V 0-2-0-0-8-10
Jos 4,3.8; 1 Ezr 2,11; 2 Mc 4,5; 9,29
A: *to carry over* or *across* [τινα] Jos 4,3; P: *to be carried, to be brought (over)* (of things) 1 Ezr 2,11; *to pass over, to cross, to go* (of pers.) 2 Mc 4,5

διακονία,-ας[+] N1F 0-0-0-0-1-1
1 Mc 11,58
service, table service, ustensils; χρυσώματα καὶ διακονία *golden vessels to be served in* (hendiadys)
Cf. ABEL 1949, 216

διάκονος,-ου[+] N2M 0-0-0-5-1-6
Prv 10,4; Est 1,10; 2,2; 6,3.5
court-servant Est 1,10; *torturer* 4 Mc 9,17
Cf. DANIEL 1966, 98; HORSLEY 1987, 239-243; →NIDNTT

διακοπή,-ῆς N1F 0-10-1-2-0-13
Jgs^A 5,17; Jgs 21,15; 2 Sm 5,20(bis)
breach Jgs 21,15; *narrow channel, passage* Jb 28,4; *deep wound* 2 Sm 6,8; *Mi 2,13 διὰ τῆς διακοπῆς -על ה/פרץ? *through the breach* for MT עלה הפרץ *the one who goes up (before them), breaks through*

διακόπτω V 1-7-4-1-4-17
Gn 38,29; 2 Sm 5,20(bis); 6,8; 1 Kgs 3,1
A: *to cut in two, to cut through, to divide* [τι] Ps 28(29),7; *to break open* [τι] 2 Mc 10,36; *to cut through* [abs.] 2 Kgs 3,26; *to break through* [τινα] 2 Sm 5,20; *to destroy, to devastate* [τι] Jdt 2,23; *to cut through into* [εἴς τι] Am 9,1; *to make a breach upon* [ἔν τινι] (of pers.) 1 Chr 15,3; P: *to be cut through* Gn 38,29; *to be broken up* (of a city) Jer 52,7; *to be killed* 2 Mc 10,30; *to be dispersed* (of water) 2 Sm 5,20; διακόπτω διακοπήν *to inflict a deep wound* (semit.) 2 Sm 6,8

διακόσιοι,-αι,-α M 22-28-4-25-12-91
Gn 5,3.6.22; 11,19.21
two hundred

διακοσμέω V 0-0-0-0-1-1
2 Mc 3,25
to adorn

διακόσμησις,-εως N3F 0-0-0-0-1-1

2 Mc 2,29
decoration, embellishment

διακούω[+] V 1-0-0-1-0-2
Dt 1,16; Jb 9,33
to hear a case (out or *to the end)* Dt 1,16
Cf. HELBING 1928, 157; LEE 1983, 60

διακρατέω V 0-0-0-0-2-2
1 Ezr 4,50; Jdt 6,12
to hold in possession [τι] 1 Ezr 4,50; *to hold back, to detain* [τι] Jdt 6,12; neol.?
Cf. HELBING 1928, 122

διακριβάζομαι V 0-0-0-0-1-1
Sir 51,19
to examine with precision, to be exact; neol.

διακριβόω V 0-0-0-0-1-1
2 Mc 2,28
to examine closely

διακρίνω[+] V 3-2-9-10-4-28
Ex 18,16; Lv 24,12; Dt 33,7; 1 Kgs 3,9; 1 Chr 26,29
A: *to distinguish* [τι] Jb 15,5; *to decide, to give judgement* [τι] Est 8,12i; [abs.] 1 Chr 26,29; *to judge* [τινα] Ex 18,16; P: *to bring an issue to decision, to plead with* [πρός τινα] Jl 4,2; διέκρινέ με ὥσπερ τὸ χρύσιον *he weighed my words as gold* Jb 23,10
Cf. HELBING 1928, 96.237

διάκρισις,-εως[+] N3F 0-0-0-1-0-1
Jb 37,16
separation, dissolution

διακυβερνάω V 0-0-0-0-2-2
3 Mc 6,2; Wis 14,3
to steer through, to govern 3 Mc 6,2; ἡ πρόνοια διακυβερνᾶ *the providence governs* Wis 14,3

διακύπτω V 0-4-2-5-0-11
Jgs^A 5,28; 2 Sm 6,16; 24,20; 2 Kgs 9,30; Ez 41,16
to bend (the head) in order to see Jgs^A 5,28; *to look out, to stoop out* 2 Sm 24,20; *Ez 41,16 διακύπτειν -השקיף *to look down*? *to recline*? for MT שחיף *veneer*?, cpr. 1 Kgs 6,4
Cf. NEIRYNCK 1982, 411-415

διακωλύω[+] V 0-0-0-0-2-2
Jdt 4,7; 12,7
to prevent, to hinder

διαλαμβάνω V 0-0-0-1-4-5
Est 3,13e; Jdt 8,14; 2 Mc 5,11; 6,29; 3 Mc 3,26
to comprehend Est 3,13e; *to perceive* Jdt 8,14; *to think* [+inf.] 2 Mc 5,11

διαλανθάνω V 0-1-0-0-0-1
2 Sm 4,6

to escape notice [abs.]

διαλέγομαι⁺   V 1-1-1-1-3-7
Ex 6,27; Jgsᴮ 8,1; Is 63,1; Est 5,2b; 1 Ezr 8,45
to converse with [τινι] Jgsᴮ 8,1; *to discourse, to
reason* [abs.] Sir 14,20; *to discuss* [τι] Is 63,1; οἱ
διαλεγόμενοι *negotiators* Ex 6,27
Cf. HELBING 1928, 246; →NIDNTT; TWNT

διαλείπω⁺   V 0-4-7-2-0-13
1 Sm 10,8; 13,8; 1 Kgs 15,21; 2 Chr 29,11; Is
5,14
to intermit, to allow an interval of [τι] 1 Sm 10,8;
to intermit, to cease [τινος] 1 Kgs 15,21; *to cease
from, to fail from* [ἀπό τινος] Jer 8,6; *to cease to*
[+ptc.] (often with neg.) Jer 17,8

διάλεκτος,-ου⁺   N2F 0-0-0-2-0-2
Est 9,26; Dnᴸˣˣ 1,4
language of a nation or *a region*
Cf. MUNTZ 1920, 85-94; →MM

διάλευκος,-ος,-ον   A 8-0-0-0-0-8
Gn 30,32.33.35(bis).39
speckled, with white spots
Cf. HARL 1986, 232

διάλημψις,-εως   N3F 0-0-0-0-1-1
2 Mc 3,32
judgement, opinion

διαλιμπάνω⁺   V 0-0-0-0-1-1
Tobᴮᴬ 10,7
to cease to [+ptc.]; neol.?

διαλλαγή,-ῆς   N1F 0-0-0-0-2-2
Sir 22,22; 27,21
reconciliation

διαλλάσσω⁺ or διαλλάττω   V 0-2-0-4-4-10
Jgsᴬ 19,3; 1 Sm 29,4; Jb 5,12; 12,20.24; 36,28
A: *to change, to alter* [τι] Jb 12,20; *to reconcile*
[τινά τινι] Jgsᴬ 19,3; P: *to leap out from* [ἀπό
τινος] Jb 36,28b; *to be reconciled* [τινι] 1 Sm
29,4; διαλλάττω τὸν βίον *to depart from this
life, to die* 2 Mc 6,27; χρώμασι διηλλαγμένοις
with diverse colours Wis 15,4; διαλλάσσοντα
βουλάς *frustrating the counsels* Jb 5,12
Cf. HELBING 1928, 246; HORSLEY 1981, 17

διάλλομαι   V 0-0-0-1-0-1
Ct 2,8
to leap across, to jump over

διαλογή,-ῆς   N1F 0-0-0-1-1-2
Ps 103(104),34; PSal 4,0
account, discourse

διαλογίζομαι⁺   V 0-1-0-8-3-12
2 Sm 19,20; Ps 9,23(10,2); 20(21),12; 34(35),20;
35(36),5

to devise, to consider [τι] Ps 20(21),12; *to think
on, to consider* [τι] Ps 118(119),59; [ὑπέρ τινος]
2 Mc 12,43; *to impute* [τι] 2 Sm 19,20; *to devise
against, to argue against* [κατά τινος] Ps
139(140),9
→NIDNTT; TWNT

διαλογισμός,-οῦ⁺   N2M 0-0-3-15-7-25
Is 59,7(bis); Jer 4,14; Ps 39(40),6; 55(56),6;
91(92),6
consideration, thought Ps 39(40),6; *debate,
discussion* Sir 9,15; *device* Lam 3,60

διαλοιδόρησις,-εως   N3F 0-0-0-0-1-1
Sir 27,15
railing, abuse; neol.

διάλυσις,-εως⁺   N3F 0-0-0-1-0-1
Neh 1,7
break-up; see διαλύω

διαλύω⁺   V 0-2-1-4-5-12
Jgsᴬ 15,14; 1 Kgs 19,11; Is 58,6; Jb 30,17; Prv
6,35
A: *to break up, to rend* [τι] 1 Kgs 19,11; *to untie*
[τι] Is 58,6; *to dissolve* [τι] (metaph.) Sir 22,20;
to end [τι] 3 Mc 1,2; *to relax* Jb 30,17; P: *to be
loosed* Jgsᴬ 15,14; *to be reconciled* Prv 6,35;
διάλυσει διαλύω πρός τινα *to break altogether
with* (semit.) Neh 1,7

διαμαρτάνω   V 1-1-0-0-0-2
Nm 15,22; Jgsᴬ 20,16
to fail utterly Nm 15,22; *to miss* Jgsᴬ 20,16

διαμαρτυρέομαι   V 3-1-0-1-0-5
Gn 43,3; Ex 19,23; 21,36; 1 Sm 21,3; Neh 9,26
to warn [τινι] Gn 43,3; *to testify against* [ἔν τινι]
Neh 9,26; *1 Sm 21,3 διαμεμαρτύρημαι העירתי
עור *I have warned* for MT יורעתי ירע *I made
known?*; see διαμαρτύρομαι
Cf. HELBING 1928, 225; WEVERS 1990, 286

διαμαρτυρία,-ας   N1F 1-0-0-0-1-2
Gn 43,3; 4 Mc 16,16
testifying, testimony

διαμαρτύρομαι⁺   V 10-2-1-2-0-15
Ex 18,20; 19,10.21; 21,29; Dt 4,26
to inform about [τινί τι] Ex 18,20; *to warn* [τινι]
Ex 19,10; *to call to witness against* [τί τινι] Dt
4,26; *to testify to* [τί τινι] Neh 9,34; *to testify, to
affirm solemnly* [πρός τινα] Zech 3,7(6); see
διαμαρτυρέομαι
Cf. LE BOULLUEC 1989, 201; →KIESSLING; NIDNTT

διαμασάομαι   V 0-0-0-0-1-1
Sir 31,16
to devour

διαμαχίζομαι   V 0-0-0-0-1-1
Sir 51,19
to strive for [ἔν τινι]; neol.
Cf. HELBING 1907, 123; 1928, 233

διαμάχομαι⁻   V 0-0-0-1-3-4
Dn^{LXX} 10,20; Sir 8,1.3; 38,28
to fight, to contend Sir 8,1; *to contend* (metaph.)
Sir 8,3; neol.
Cf. HELBING 1907, 88

διαμελίζω   V 0-0-0-1-0-1
Dn^{LXX} 3,96
to dismember; neol.?

διαμένω⁻   V 0-0-2-8-10-20
Jer 3,5; 39(32),14; Ps 5,6; 18(19),10; 60(61),8
to continue [intrans.] Ps 5,6; *to persevere* [ἔν
τινι] 3 Mc 3,11; *to live on* [intrans.] Ps
101(102),27; *to endure* [intrans.] Ps 18(19),10; *to
abide with* [μετά τινος] Sir 12,15; *Ps 71(72),17
διαμενεῖ - יכין *endure* for MT ינין *sprout forth?*
Cf. MARGOLIS 1972, 61

διαμερίζω⁻   V 3-5-4-6-2-20
Gn 10,25; 49,7; Dt 32,8; Jos 21,42a; Jgs^A 5,30
A: *to divide* Gn 10,25; *to distribute* 2 Sm 6,19;
M: *to divide, to part* Ps 21(22),19; *Ps 16(17),14
διαμέρισον αὐτούς -חלקם *divide them* for MT
חלקם *their part*

διαμερισμός,-οῦ⁻   N2M 0-0-3-0-0-3
Ez 48,29; Mi 7,12(bis)
division Ez 48,29; *Mi 7,12 διαμερισμόν - מנה
division for MT מין *from*

διαμετρέω   V 0-1-33-2-0-36
2 Sm 8,2; Ez 40,5.6.11.13
to measure out 2 Sm 8,2; *to measure* Ez 47,3; *to
divide* Sir 2,4; *Ez 41,26 διεμέτρησεν -תמד?
measured for MT תמרים *palm trees*

διαμέτρησις,-εως   N3F 0-2-3-0-0-5
2 Chr 3,3; 4,2; Jer 38(39),39; Ez 42,15; 45,3
measure, measuring out 2 Chr 3,3; *diameter*
2 Chr 4,2; neol.?

διαναπαύω   V 1-0-0-0-0-1
Gn 5,29
to allow to rest a while from [τινα ἀπό τινος]
Cf. HARL 1986, 124; HELBING 1928, 169

διανέμω⁻   V 1-0-0-0-0-1
Dt 29,25
to distribute

διανεύω⁻   V 0-0-0-1-1-2
Ps 34(35),19; Sir 27,22
to wink, to beckon (with the eyes); neol.?

διανήθω   V 6-0-0-0-0-6

Ex 28,8.33; 35,6; 36,10(39,3).12(39,5)
to spin out; διανενησμένον *spun*; neol.
Cf. CAIRD 1972, 124; LEE 1983, 48

διανθίζω   V 0-0-0-1-0-1
Est 1,6
to adorn with flowers; διηνθισμένος *decorated*;
neol.
Cf. HELBING 1907, 118

διανίσταμαι   V 2-0-0-0-1-3
Dt 6,7; 11,19; Jdt 12,15
to rise up, to arise [intrans.]

διανοέομαι   V 4-3-5-23-22-57
Gn 6,5.6; 8,21; Ex 31,4; 2 Sm 21,16
to have a mind, to intend, to purpose [+inf.]
2 Sm 21,16; *to have in mind* [τι] Gn 6,5; *to
ponder* [τι] Sir 21,17; *to understand* [τι] Sir 17,6;
to think [abs.] Gn 8,21; *to recollect oneself*
[intrans.] Gn 6,6; *Dn 9,24 διανοηθῆναι -להבין
to understand for MT להביא *to bring*

διανόημα,-ατος⁻   N3N 0-0-3-3-7-13
Is 55,9; Ez 14,3.4; Prv 14,14; 15,24
thought, notion Is 55,9; *Ez 14,3.4 τὰ
διανοήματα - עלילה *deeds, thoughts?* for MT
גלוליהם and גלולין *their or his idols*; *Prv 15,24
διανοήματα -מעלה *thought* for MT למעלה
upward; *Prv 14,14 τῶν διανοημάτων αὐτοῦ
-מעליו *his thoughts* for MT מעלי/עליו *from upon him,
from himself*

διανόησις,-εως   N3F 0-1-0-0-0-1
2 Chr 2,13
skill, cunning, contrivance

διάνοια,-ας⁺   N1F 24-3-7-10-25-69
Gn 8,21; 17,17; 24,15.45; 27,41
thought 1 Chr 29,18; *mind, heart* for MT לב Gn
17,17; *thinking faculty, understanding* Prv 2,10;
διάνοια ἀγαθή *sound mind* Prv 9,10; *Dn^{Th}
11,14 διάνοιαι -קרבים *minds, thoughts* for MT
רבים *many*, cpr. Jer 38(31),33; *Is 59,15
διάνοιαν -מדע *mind* for MT מרע/ *from evil*
Cf. HARL 1986, 61; LE BOULLUEC 1989, 67; →TWNT

διανοίγω⁺   V 11-4-11-8-2-36
Gn 3,5.7; Ex 13,2.12(bis)
A: *to lay open* Gn 3,5; *to reveal* Jb 38,32; M: *to
open so as to connect, to spread* Jb 29,19; τὸ
διανοῖγον μήτραν *the first-born* Ex 13,12; *Hab
3,14 διανοίξουσι - פצה *burst* for MT פוץ
scatter
Cf. WEVERS 1990, 195

διανυκτερεύω⁺   V 0-0-0-1-0-1
Jb 2,9c

to pass the night
διανύω⁺   V 0-0-0-0-1-1
2 Mc 12,17
to arrive [abs.]
διαξαίνω   V 0-0-0-0-1-1
Jdt 10,3
to card, to comb
διαπαρατηρέομαι   V 0-1-0-0-0-1
2 Sm 3,30
to lie in wait for continually; *2 Sm 3,30 διε-
παρετηροῦντο -ארבו they had lain in wait for MT
הרגו they killed; neol.
Cf. HELBING 1907, 77
διαπαρθενεύω   V 0-0-2-0-0-2
Ez 23,3.8
A: to deflower a maiden [τινα] Ez 23,8; P: to
loose one's virginity Ez 23,3
διαπαύω   V 1-0-1-0-0-2
Lv 2,13; Hos 5,13
to bring to an end, to cease [τι] Lv 2,13; to cease,
to leave [abs.] Hos 5,13
Cf. HELBING 1928, 169
διαπειλέομαι   V 0-0-1-0-2-3
Ez 3,17; 3 Mc 6,23; 7,6
to threaten violently [τινι] Ez 3,17; [abs.] 3 Mc
7,6
διαπειράζω   V 0-0-0-0-1-1
3 Mc 5,40
to tempt, to make trial of [τινα]; neol.
διαπείρω   V 0-0-0-0-1-1
4 Mc 11,19
to transfix, to pierce [τι]
διαπέμπω   V 0-0-0-1-5-6
Prv 16,28; 1 Ezr 1,24; Jdt 14,12; 2 Mc 3,37;
11,26
A: to send over [abs.] Jdt 14,12; M: to send
messages [abs.] 1 Ezr 1,24; to send off in different
directions, to spread [τι] Prv 16,28
διαπεράω⁺   V 1-0-1-0-7-9
Dt 30,13; Is 23,2; 1 Mc 3,37; 5,6.41
to go over or across [abs.] Dt 30,13; to go over,
to pass through, to traverse [τι] Is 23,2
διαπετάννυμι   V 0-14-1-7-1-23
2 Sm 17,19; 1 Kgs 6,27.32.35; 8,7
to open and spread out 2 Sm 17,19; to open
1 Kgs 8,22; to spread out Ps 104(105),39
διαπίπτω   V 6-2-4-2-4-18
Nm 5,21.22.27; Dt 2,14.15
to fall away to rot, to fall to pieces Jer 18,4; to
fall apart, to crumble to pieces Jb 14,18; to perish

Dt 2,14; to be lost 2 Mc 2,14; to breakdown, to
collapse (of people) Neh 8,10; to be useless, to
be in vain Jdt 6,9
διαπλατύνω   V 0-0-1-0-0-1
Ez 41,7
to dilate, to prolong, to lengthen
διαπληκτίζομαι   V 1-0-0-0-0-1
Ex 2,13
to spar, to fight, to come to blows; neol.
Cf. LE BOULLUEC 1989, 84
διαπνέω   V 0-0-0-3-0-3
Ct 2,17; 4,6.16
to blow through [τι] Ct 4,16; to dawn (of day) Ct
2,17
διαπονέω⁺   V 0-0-0-1-1-2
Eccl 10,9; 2 Mc 2,28
A: to work out, to elaborate, to labour 2 Mc 2,28;
P: to be worn out Eccl 10,9
διαπορεύομαι⁺   V 2-11-10-14-6-43
Nm 11,8; 31,23; Jos 15,3; Jgsᴬ 9,25; 1 Sm 12,2
to pass across or through [abs.] Nm 11,8; to go
through [τι] 2 Chr 7,21; to go through [διά τινος]
Nm 31,23; διαπορευόμενοι πόλιν ἐκ πόλεως
who went through from city to city 2 Chr 30,10;
*1 Sm 29,3 διαπορευόμενοι -העברים the passers-
by for MT העברים the Hebrews
Cf. HELBING 1928, 81
διάπρασις,-εως   N3F 1-0-0-0-0-1
Lv 25,33
sale to various purchasers
διαπράσσομαι   V 0-0-0-0-2-2
2 Mc 8,29; 10,38
to bring about, to accomplish [τι]
διαπρεπής,-ής,-ές   A 0-0-0-0-2-2
2 Mc 3,26; 10,29
distinguished, prominent, eminent, illustrious
διαπρίω⁺   V 0-1-0-0-0-1
1 Chr 20,3
to saw in pieces
διάπτωσις,-εως   N3F 0-0-2-0-0-2
Jer 19,6.14
fall, error; *Jer 19,6 Διάπτωσις Error proper
noun? for MT תפת Tofet, corr.? διάπτυσις for
talmudic תוף sth to be spat upon, sth despicable,
see also 19,14
Cf. WALTERS 1973, 179.329-330
διαπυρόομαι   V 0-0-0-1-1-2
Dnᴸˣˣ 3,46; 3 Mc 6,6
to be consumed with thirst
διάπυρος,-ος,-ον   A 0-0-0-0-1-1

4 Mc 3,15
extremely hot

διαριθμέομαι V 0-0-0-0-1-1
3 Mc 3,6
to count and classify; οὐδαμῶς τι διαριθμέομαι
to make no account of

διαρκέομαι V 0-0-0-0-1-1
3 Mc 2,26
to be content with, to be satisfied with [τινι]

διαρπαγή,-ῆς N1F 2-1-7-4-6-20
Nm 14,3.31; 2 Kgs 21,14; Is 5,5; 42,24
(act of) plundering Ezr 9,7; *booty, spoil* Nm 14,3;
*Ez 25,7 εἰς διαρπαγήν -לבז/ל *as spoil* for MT
לבז ?

διαρπάζω⁺ V 3-6-14-9-6-38
Gn 34,27.29; Dt 28,29; Jgsᴬ 21,23; Jgsᴮ 9,25
to spoil, to plunder Gn 34,27; *Is 5,17
διηρπασμένοι -כבשׂים *the spoiled, the oppressed*
for MT כבשׂים *lambs*

διαρραίνω V 0-0-0-1-0-1
Prv 7,17
to sprinkle with [τί τινι]; neol.

διαρρέω V 0-0-0-0-1-1
2 Mc 10,20
to flow through, to slip away

διαρρήσσω or **διαρρήγνυμι⁺** V 2-36-12-15-15-84
Gn 37,29.34; 44,13; Lv 10,6; 21,10; Nm 14,6; Jos
7,6
A: *to break through* [abs.] 2 Sm 23,16; *to break
through* [τι] Ps 2,3; *to rend* [τι] Gn 37,29; *to part*
[τι] (of water) Ps 73(74),15; *to crush* (of earth)
Ps 140(141),7; *to rend* [τι] (metaph.) 1 Sm 15,28;
P: *to burst, to rip up* Hos 14,1; *to be dashed to
pieces* 2 Chr 25,12; *to be bruised* Neh 9,21
Cf. HORSLEY 1982, 80

διαρριπτέω or **διαρρίπτω** V 0-0-1-1-0-2
Is 62,10; Jb 41,11
to cast through, to throw [τι]

διαρρυθμίζω V 0-0-0-0-1-1
2 Mc 7,22
to arrange in order [τι]; neol.?

διαρτάω V 1-0-0-0-0-1
Nm 23,19
to deceive, to mislead [τινα]

διαρτίζω V 0-0-0-2-0-2
Jb 33,6(bis)
to mould, to form; neol.

διασαλεύομαι V 0-0-1-0-0-1
Hab 2,16
to shake; *Hab 2,16 διασαλεύθητι -הרעל *shake*

for MT הערל *show uncircumcision, be uncircumcised*; neol.?

διασαφέω⁺ V 1-0-0-1-8-10
Dt 1,5; Dnᴸˣˣ 2,6; 1 Mc 12,8; 2 Mc 1,18.20
to make quite clear, to show plainly [τι] Dt 1,5;
to instruct plainly [τινα] 2 Mc 1,18
Cf. HELBING 1928, 222; →KIESSLING

διασάφησις,-εως N3F 1-0-0-2-0-3
Gn 40,8; Ezr 5,6; 7,11
explanation, interpretation Gn 40,8; *copy?,
translation?* Ezr 5,6; neol.?
Cf. HARL 1986, 270; LEE 1983, 47; PELLETIER 1962, 25;
ZUNTZ 1959, 112

διασείομαι⁺ V 0-0-0-0-1-1
3 Mc 7,21
to be shaken off from [τινος]
→NIDNTT

διασκεδάννυμι V 8-8-14-10-6-46
Gn 17,14; Ex 32,25(bis); Lv 26,15.44
A: *to scatter abroad* [τινα] Ex 32,25; *to turn
away from* [τινα ἀπό τινος] 2 Chr 16,3; *to reject*
[τι] 2 Sm 15,31; *to break* [τι] Gn 17,14; P: *to be
dispersed* Jb 38,24
Cf. LE BOULLUEC 1989, 325-326

διασκευάζομαι V 0-1-0-0-1-2
Jos 4,12; 1 Mc 6,33
to be equiped to [εἴς τι] 1 Mc 6,33;
διεσκευασμένος *equiped, armed* Jos 4,12;
neol.?

διασκευή,-ῆς N1F 1-0-0-0-1-2
Ex 31,7; 2 Mc 11,10
equipment, furniture Ex 31,7; ἐν διασκευῇ *in
armour, armed* 2 Mc 11,10; neol.?

διασκιρτάω V 0-0-0-0-1-1
Wis 19,9
to leap about; neol.

διασκορπίζω⁺ V 3-0-32-14-4-53
Nm 10,34(35); Dt 30,1.3; Jer 9,15; 10,21
A: *to scatter (abroad)* [τινα] Dt 30,1; *to scatter
(abroad)* [τι] Jb 37,11; *to scatter to and fro*
[τινα] Ps 58(59),15; P: *to be scattered* Nm 10,34;
*Jer 13,14 διασκορπιῶ αὐτούς -הפצתים *פוץ *I
will scatter them* for MT נפצתים ◊נפץ *I will shatter
them*, cpr. Jer 28(51),20.21.22; neol.
Cf. TOV 1976, 52.84; →TWNT

διασκορπισμός,-οῦ N2M 0-0-3-1-0-4
Jer 24,9; Ez 6,8; 13,20; Dnᵀʰ 12,7
dispersion, scattering, dispersal Ez 6,8; *Jer 24,9
εἰς διασκορπισμόν -◊זרע *זרע or זרה? *in dispersion*
for MT לזועה/ל (qere) *as a horror*, cpr. Dt 28,25

and διασπορά; neol.?

δίασμα,-ατος   N3N 0-4-0-0-0-4
Jgs 16,13.14
warp

διασπασμός,-οῦ   N2M 0-0-1-0-0-1
Jer 15,3
tearing in pieces; neol.?

διασπάω⁺   V 0-6-5-1-0-12
Jgs^A 14,6(bis); Jgs 16,9; Jgs^A 16.12
to tear asunder [τινα] Jgs^A 14,6; [τι] Jgs^A 14,6; *to tear asunder, to disentangle, to unravel* [τι] Jgs^A 16,9; *to break (through)* [τι] Jer 2,20; *to tear asunder, to break, to cancel* [τι] Is 58,6; *to tear down* [τινα] (metaph.) Jb 19,10

διασπείρω⁺   V 13-11-31-4-10-69
Gn 9,19; 10,18.32; 11,4.8
A: *to scatter, to spread about* [τινα] Gn 11,8; [τινα] (of wind, tempest) Is 41,16; P: *to be scattered* (of pers.) Gn 9,19; (of things) Gn 10,32; *to be extended (of war)* 1 Sm 14,23; *Ez 32,15 ὅταν διασπείρω *when I shall scatter* corr.? ὅταν διασπείρω -בהכיתי ◊ נכה *when I (shall) smite*; *Ezr 9,19 οἱ διεσπαρμένοι -הפזורים *who where dispersed* for MT הפרוזים *those living in the rural country*
Cf. SEELIGMANN 1948, 113 (Is 35,8); TOV 1976, 74.91

διασπορά,-ᾶς⁺   N1F 2-0-3-3-4-12
Dt 28,25; 30,4; Is 49,6; Jer 15,7; 41(34),17
scattering, dispersion (and humiliation of the Jews among the gentiles) Jdt 5,19; *the dispersed (and humiliated Jews among the gentiles)* Ps 146(147),2; *Dn^LXX 12,2 εἰς διασποράν -דרא Aram.? *to dispersion* for MT לדראון *to abhorrence, horror?* or εἰς διασποράν corr. εἰς διαφθοράν *to corruption*, cpr. Jer 13,14; *Jer 41(34),17 εἰς διασποράν -זרע ◊? (זרוע Aram. *sowing*) or -זרה ◊? *in dispersion* for MT לזועה/ל (qere) *as a horror*, see also Dt 28,25, cpr. Jer 15,7; 24,9; *Jer 15,7 ἐν διασπορᾷ -זרה ◊? *in dispersion* for MT במזרה/ב *(winnow) with a pitchfork*, cpr. Dt 28,25; Jer 41(34),17; *Dt 28,25 ἐν διασπορᾷ -זרע ◊ (זרוע Aram. sowing) *in dispersion* for MT לזועה/ל *as a horror*, see also Jer 41(34),17; cpr. Jer 15,7; 24,9; see διασκορπισμός; neol.
Cf. ALFRINK 1959, 367-368 (Dn 12,2); SEELIGMANN 1948, 112-113; → TWNT

διάσταλσις,-εως   N3F 0-0-0-0-1-1
2 Mc 13,25
arrangement, pact; neol.?

διάστασις,-εως   N3F 0-0-0-0-1-1
3 Mc 3,7
contrast, difference

διαστέλλω⁺   V 18-9-16-8-7-58
Gn 25,23; 30,28.35.40; Lv 5,4
A: *to put asunder from, to separate from* [τινα ἔκ τινος] Nm 8,14; *to set aside* [τι] Lv 16,26; *to separate out* [abs.] Mi 5,7; *to separate, to distinguish* [τι] (animals) Gn 30,35; *to draw aside (a curtain)* Jdt 14,15; *to split up, to divide (people)* [τινα] Sus^LXX 48; *to define precisely* [τι] Gn 30,28; *to define, to teach* [abs.] Neh 8,8; *to discharge (a vow)* [τι] Lv 22,21; *to pay (for food)* [τινι εἴς τι] Mal 3,11; *to assign, to appoint* [τι] Sir 16,26; *to give charge* [τινι] Ezr 8,24; *to assign, to appoint* [τι] Sir 16,26; M: *to command (expressly), to give express orders to* [τινι] Jdt 11,12; *to warn* [τινι] Ez 3,21; P: *to be separated from* [ἔκ τινος] Gn 25,23; *to be sent away* Na 1,12; *to be set apart* Lv 16,26; *to be divided, to be structured* [τινι] (in architecture) Jer 22,14; διαστέλλω ἀνὰ μέσον τινός *to distinguish between* Lv 11,47; *to intrude, to come between, to separate* 2 Kgs 2,11; τὰ διεσταλμένα *the agreements* 2 Mc 14,28; ὅρασις διαστέλλουσα *distinct vision* 1 Sm 3,1; διαστέλλω τοῖς χείλεσι *to pronounce, to make an explicit statement* Lv 5,4; *Jgs 1,19 διεστείλατο -הבדיל *he set apart* for MT ברזל *iron*; *Hos 13,15 διαστελεῖ -יפריד? *he will divide* for MT יפריא *he shall be fruitful*; *Ez 24,14 οὐ διαστελῶ -לא אפרק? *I will not make distinctions?* for MT לא אפרע *I will not neglect it?*, cpr. 1 Sm 3,1
Cf. CAIRD 1972, 124-125; HARL 1986, 208-209 (Gn 25,23); HELBING 1928, 165.210; → KIESSLING

διάστημα,-ατος⁺   N3N 1-2-10-0-3-16
Gn 32,17; 1 Kgs 6,6; 7,46(9); Ez 41,6.8
space Ez 41,6 and elsewhere in Ez 40-48, as a transl. of several technical terms in connection with the architecture of the temple; *interval* 3 Mc 4,17
Cf. HORSLEY 1987, 86; 1989, 88

διαστολή,-ῆς⁺   N1F 3-0-0-0-2-5
Ex 8,19; Nm 19,2; 30,7; 1 Mc 8,7; PSal 4,4
command, injunction, order Nm 19,2; *distinction, discrimination* PSal 4,4; διαστολὴ χειλέων *explicit (verbal) statement, utterance* Nm 30,7; *1 Mc 8,7 διαστολὴν καὶ ... *a detailed list and ...* corr.? διασταλῆναι *to be barred (from)*; *Ex 8,19 δίδωμι διαστολὴν ἀνὰ μέσον -שים פלת בין

to put a division between, to distinguish between for MT בין פרת שׁים *to set redemption between'?*
Cf. CAIRD 1972, 124-125; GOLDSTEIN 1976, 353; HORSLEY 1982, 80; LE BOULLUEC 1989, 34.127-8

διαστράπτω V 0-0-0-0-1-1
Wis 16,22
to flash like lightening

διαστρέφω⁺ V 5-4-9-11-9-38
Ex 5,4; 23,6; Nm 15,39; 32,7; Dt 32,5
A: *to turn, to carry around* [τι] Jb 37,12; *to divert from, to turn from* [τινα ἀπό τινος] Ex 5,4; *to distort, to pervert* [τι] Ex 23,6; M: *to turn back* Nm 15,39; P: *to be distorted, to be twisted* (metaph.) Prv 4,27; γεννεὰ διεστραμμένη *perverse generation* Dt 32,5
Cf. ENGEL 1985, 95.124-125 (Sus^LXX 9.56); HELBING 1928, 165; WEVERS 1990, 61.360

διαστροφή,-ῆς N1F 0-0-0-1-0-1
Prv 2,14
perversion

διαστρώννυμι V 0-1-0-0-0-1
1 Sm 9,25
to spread; *1 Sm 9,25 καὶ διέστρωσαν -וירברו *and they spread (a bed)* for MT וירבר *and he said*; neol.?

διασυρίζω V 0-0-0-2-0-2
Dn^LXX 3,50; Dn^Th 3,50(23)
to whistle; neol.

διασφαγή,-ῆς N1F 0-0-0-1-0-1
Neh 4,1
breach, gap; neol.?

διασφάλλομαι V 0-0-0-0-1-1
3 Mc 5,12
to be disappointed of [τινος]

διασχίζω V 0-0-0-1-1-2
Ps 34(35),15; Wis 18,23
A: *to part, to separate* or *to sever, to cut off* [τι] Wis 18,23; P: *to be separated, to be parted* Ps 34(35),15
Cf. LARCHER 1985, 1035 (Wis 18,23)

διασῴζω⁺ V 5-31-10-12-19-77
Gn 19,19; 35,3; Nm 10,9; 21,29; Dt 20,4
A: *to preserve (through), to save* [τινα] Gn 35,3; *to preserve, to maintain, to keep safe* [τι] LtJ 58; P: *to come safe through* [ἀπό τινος] Nm 10,9; *to come safe to* [εἰς τι] Gn 19,19; *to escape from* [τινος] Jgs 12,4; ἐν τῷ ἐλαχίστῳ διασωθέντι *in his youngest surviving son* Jos 6,26(25); *Prv 10,5 διεσώθη -אנר (pual) *he was collected (from), he was saved (from)* for MT אנר (qal) *he collected,*

he gathered

διαταγή,-ῆς⁺ N1F 0-0-0-1-0-1
Ezr 4,11
command, ordinance; neol.?
→KIESSLING

διάταγμα,-ατος⁺ N3N 0-0-0-2-1-3
Est 3,13d; Ezr 7,11; Wis 11,7
ordinance, commandment; neol.?
→KIESSLING

διάταξις,-εως⁺ N3F 0-3-1-1-2-7
1 Kgs 6,1(38); 2 Chr 31,16.17; Ez 43,10; Ps 118(119),91
disposition, arrangement, plan 1 Kgs 6,1(38); *command* Ps 118(119),91; *deployment* Jdt 1,4

διατάσσω⁺ V 0-7-6-2-10-25
Jgs 5,9; Jgs^B 3,23; 1 Sm 13,11; 1 Kgs 11,18
A: *to appoint, to assign* [τί τινι] 1 Kgs 11,18; *to set* [abs.] Ez 21,25(20); *to draw up, to set in array* [τινα] 2 Mc 12,20; *to make arrangements, to purpose* [abs.] 1 Sm 13,11; M: *to arrange for oneself* [τι] 4 Mc 8,3; P: *to be appointed, to be constituted* 2 Chr 5,11; οἱ διατεταγμένοι *the appointed* Jgs^B 3,23; διατεταγμένοι *set in array* 2 Mc 5,3
·KIESSLING

διατείνω V 0-0-2-2-1-5
Is 21,15; 40,22; Ps 84(85),6; 139(140),6; Wis 8,1
to stretch out [τι] Ps 139(140),6; *to continue, to extend* [τι] Ps 84(85),6; *to reach, to extend as far as* [intrans.] Wis 8,1; τὰ τοξεύματα τὰ διατεταμένα *bent bows* Is 21,15
Cf. LARCHER 1984, 515-516

διατελέω⁺ V 1-0-2-1-1-5
Dt 9,7; Jer 20,7.18; Est 8,12l; 2 Mc 5,27
to continue doing or *being* [+ptc.] Dt 9,7; *to continue* [intrans.] Jer 20,18; προσκυνούμενος διατελέω ὑπό τινος *to continue to be reverenced by* Est 8,12l

διατήκομαι V 0-0-1-0-0-1
Hab 3,6
to melt away

διατηρέω⁺ V 11-0-1-3-9-24
Gn 17,9.10; 37,11; Ex 2,9; 9,1
to take care of [τινα] Ex 2,9; *to maintain* [τι] Gn 17,9; *to preserve* [τινα] Ex 9,16; *to keep sth in such a state* [τι +pred.] 2 Mc 14,36
Cf. HORSLEY 1983, 65; LE BOULLUEC 1989, 82

διατήρησις,-εως N3F 5-0-0-0-0-5
Ex 16,33.34; Nm 17,25; 18,8; 19,9
preservation, reserve; neol.

Cf. LE BOULLUEC 1989, 188

διατίθημι⁺   V 17-39-17-8-6-87
Gn 9,17; 15,18; 21,27.32; 26,28
A: *to treat, to dispose one so or so* [τινα +adv.]
2 Mc 9,28; M: *to treat, to dispose one so or so*
[τινα +adv.] 4 Mc 8,9; *to establish (a law)* [τι]
Wis 18,9; stereotyped equivalent of כרת in the
expression διατίθημι διαθήκην for MT כרת ברית
*to establish (a covenant), to conclude (an
agreement)* Gn 9,17; *Ps 83(84),6(7) διέθετο
-ערך *he arranged, he planned* for MT עברי
passing through; *Ez 16,30 διαθῶ- מול אמלה אמול *I
circumcise (you as a sign of the covenant)* for MT
אמלה אמל *feverish*
Cf. HARL 1986, 55; HELBING 1928, 241-242; →TWNT

διατίλλω   V 0-0-0-1-0-1
Jb 16,12
to pluck

διατόνιον,-ου   N2N 1-0-0-0-0-1
Ex 35,11
traverse, beam; neol.?
Cf. LE BOULLUEC 1989, 269.348

διατρέπω   V 0-1-0-4-0-5
Jgs^B 18,7; Jb 31,34; Est 7,8; Dn^LXX 1,10.13
A: *to pervert* [τι] Jgs^B 18,7; P: *to be overawed by*
[τι] Jb 31,34; διατετραμμένος *perverse, changed
for the worse* Dn^LXX 1,10; *Est 7,8 Αμαν
διετράπη τῷ προσώπω- פני המן חפרו- *the face of
Haman was confounded* for MT פני המן חפו *the
face of Haman was covered*

διατρέφω   V 3-7-0-6-1-17
Gn 7,3; 50,20.21; Jos 14,10; Ru 4,15
A: *to support, to maintain* [τι] Gn 7,3; *to breed
up, to feed* [τινα] 1 Kgs 17,4; P: *to be sustained
continually, to be fed* Gn 50,20; *to be nourished*
Jdt 5,10

διατρέχω   V 1-1-1-0-1-4
Ex 9,2; 1 Kgs 18,26; Na 2,5; Wis 3,7
to run across, to run over (metaph.) Ex 9,23;
ἀστραπαὶ διατρέχουσαι *flashing lightnings* Na
2,5

διατριβή,-ης⁺   N1F 1-0-1-3-0-5
Lv 13,46; Jer 30,28(49,33); Prv 12,11; 14,24;
31,27;
way of life, passing of time Prv 14,24; *place of
stay, haunt* Lv 13,46
Cf. PELLETIER 1967, 175-186

διατρίβω⁺   V 1-0-1-0-4-6
Lv 14,8; Jer 42(35),7; Tob^BA 11,8.12; 2 Mc 14,23
to spend [τι] (time) Lv 14,8; *to rub hard* [abs.]

Tob^BA 11,8; *to pass time* [abs.] Jdt 10,2

διατροφή,-ῆς⁺   N1F 0-0-0-0-1-1
1 Mc 6,49
sustenance and support

διατυπόω   V 0-0-0-0-1-1
Wis 19,6
to form, to fashion; neol.?

διαφαίνομαι   V 0-0-0-0-1-1
Wis 17,6
to glow, to shine through

διαφανής,-ής,-ές   A 1-0-1-1-0-3
Ex 30,34; Is 3,22; Est 1,6
translucent, transparent

διαφαύσκω   V 1-4-0-0-1-6
Gn 44,3; Jgs^A 19,26; Jgs^B 16,2; 1 Sm 14,36; 2 Sm
2,32
to show light through, to dawn

διαφέρω⁺   V 0-0-0-8-9-17
Prv 20,2; 27,14; Est 3,13c; Dn^LXX 7,3.23
A: *to carry over* or *across* [τι] 1 Ezr 5,53; *to
differ from* [τινος] Prv 20,2; *to excel in* [τινι] Est
3,13c; P: *to be spread abroad* Wis 18,10; *to be at
variance with, to quarrel, to fall out with* [τινι]
2 Mc 3,4; *to be separated* Wis 18,2
Cf. HELBING 1928, 177.238; LARCHER 1985, 987.1008

διαφεύγω⁺   V 1-5-3-1-5-15
Dt 2,36; Jos 8,22; 10,28.30.33
to get away from, to escape [τινα] Dt 2,36; [τι]
2 Mc 7,31; *to escape* [abs.] Jos 8,22; *to escape
safely* [abs.] Prv 19,5; *to escape from* [ἔκ τινος]
(place) 1 Mc 15,21
Cf. HELBING 1928, 27-29

διαφθείρω⁺   V 0-32-20-24-7-83
Jgs 2,19; Jgs^A 6,4.5; 20,21
A: *to destroy utterly* [τι] Jgs^A 6,4; *to do away
with, to kill* [τινα] Jgs^A 20,21; *to break* [τι] (a
covenant) Mal 2,8; *to ruin* [τι] (inheritance) Ru
4,6; *to corrupt* [τι] Ez 23,11; *to corrupt, to seduce*
[τινα] (a woman) Ez 16,52; P: *to be spoiled, to
be desiccated* Jgs^B 16,7; *to be consumed* Wis
16,27; *to perish* Wis 16,5; *to be corrupted* Mal
1,14; διέφθειρα *I became corrupt* Jgs 2,19
→NIDNTT; TWNT

διαφθορά,-ᾶς⁺   N1F 0-0-9-13-1-23
Jer 13,14; 15,3(7); 28(51),8; Ez 19,4.8
destruction, corruption (stereotyped equivalent of
שחת *decay, pit, grave*) Ps 15(16),10; *Zph 3,6 ἐν
διαφθορᾷ -ב/שחת *with destruction* for MT בשת
shame
→NIDNTT; TWNT

διαφλέγω V 0-0-0-1-0-1
Ps 82(83),15
to burn up; neol.

διαφορά,-ᾶς⁺ N1F 0-0-0-0-4-4
1 Ezr 4,39; 1 Mc 3,18; Wis 7,20; Sir Prol.,26
difference, diversity

διαφορέω V 0-0-1-0-0-1
Jer 37(30),16
to tear to pieces; neol.

διαφόρημα,-ατος N3N 0-0-1-0-0-1
Jer 37(30),16
thing torn to pieces, prey

διάφορος,-ος,-ον⁺ A 2-0-0-3-7-12
Lv 19,19; Dt 22,9; Dn^Th 7,7.19 Ezr 8,27
different Dn^Th 7,7; *various* Ezr 8,27; τὸ διάφορον
money 2 Mc 1,35
Cf. BICKERMAN 1980, 163-166; ·KIESSLING; MM

διαφόρως D 0-0-0-1-0-1
Dn^LXX 7,7
differently

διαφυλάσσω⁺ V 5-1-3-6-15-30
Gn 28,15.20; Lv 19,20; Dt 7,12; 32,10
to watch closely, to guard carefully, to preserve
|τινα| (often of providential care) Gn 28,15; *to
maintain, to keep* |τι| Dt 7,12; *to reserve* Jdt
11,13; *to keep* |τι| (a feast) 2 Mc 6,6; *to keep sth
or sb in a certain state* |τι +pred.] 2 Mc 3,15;
|τινα +pred.] 2 Mc 10,30

διαφωνέω V 2-3-1-0-1-7
Ex 24,11; Nm 31,49; Jos 23,14; 1 Sm 30,19;
1 Kgs 8,56
to be missing, to fail to answer roll-calls Nm
31,49; *to be lost, to perish* Ez 37,11; *to fail, to be
found wanting* 1 Kgs 8,56; neol.?
Cf. CAIRD 1972, 125; HORSLEY 1982, 9; LE BOULLUEC
1989, 247; LEE 1983, 82; MILLIGAN 1980, 62

διαφώσκω V 0-1-0-0-0-1
Jgs^B 19,26
to dawn

διαφωτίζω V 0-0-0-1-0-1
Nch 8,3
to dawn, to rise (of the sun)

διαχέω V 14-1-4-4-3-26
Lv 13,22.23.27.28.32
P: *to be spread, to be diffused* (of disease) Lv
13,22; *to be scattered* (of pers.) 1 Sm 30,16; *to be
dissolved* Wis 2,3; *to be poured out* Ez 30,16; *to
run through* Zech 1,17; διαχέω τὰς ὁδούς *to
scatter one's ways, to wander from the right path*
Jer 3,13; *Ez 30,16 διαχυθήσεται -נפצו? פוץ

shall be poured out for MT נף צרי (*in*) *Nof*
(*=Memphis) there shall be oppressors*, cpr. Zech
1,17

διαχρίομαι V 2-0-0-0-0-2
Lv 2,4; 7,12
to be spread with, to be sprinkled with (oil) [ἔν
τινι]

διάχρυσος,-ος,-ον A 0-0-0-1-1-2
Ps 44(45),10; 2 Mc 5,2
interwoven with gold; neol.?

διάχυσις,-εως N3F 3-0-0-0-0-3
Lv 13,27.35; 14,48
diffusion, spreading

διαχωρίζω⁺ V 11-4-1-1-10-27
Gn 1,4.6.7.14.18
A: *to separate* |τι| Gn 30,32; *to separate from*
|τινα ἀπό τινος| Sus 51; |τί τινος| 1 Mc 12,36;
to distinguish |τινα| Sir 33,11; *to decide for sb
that* |τινι +inf.] 2 Chr 25,10; P: *to be separated*
Sus^LXX 52; *to be separated from* |ἀπό τινος| Gn
13,11; *to be divided* (of more pers.) 2 Sm 1,23;
to set oneself apart from, to go away from |ἀπό
τινος| Gn 13,9; *to go away, to depart* Sir 12,9; *to
be distinguished* Sir 33,8; διαχωρίζω ἀνὰ μέσον
τινός *to divide between* Gn 1,4; *Nm 32,12 ὁ
διακεχωρισμένος -הנזיר? set apart for MT הקנזי
the Kennizite* Nm 32,12; *Jgs^B 13,9 διεχώρισε
-מפלא (Aram.) *separating* for MT מפלא (Hebr.)
acting wonderfully
Cf. HELBING 1928, 164

διάψαλμα,-ατος N3N 0-0-3-73-5-81
Hab 3,3.9.13; Ps 2,2; 3,3
*leading motif, verse expressing a central idea in a
Psalm*? stereotyped rendering of סלה; neol.
Cf. STIEB 1939, 102-110

διαψεύδομαι V 0-1-0-0-2-3
2 Kgs 4,16; 1 Mc 13,19; 3 Mc 5,12
M: *to deceive* |τινα| 2 Kgs 4,16; διαψευσμένος
cheated out of, deceived in |τινος| 3 Mc 5,12
Cf. HELBING 1928, 105-106

διαψιθυρίζω V 0-0-0-0-1-1
Sir 12,18
to whisper
Cf. CAIRD 1972, 125

δίγλωσσος,-ος,-ον A 0-0-0-1-4-5
Prv 11,13; Sir 5,9.14.15; 28,13
double-tongued, deceitful

διγομία,-ας N1F 0-1-0-0-0-1
Jgs^B 5,16
double burden, load; *Jgs^B 5,16 τῆς διγομιάς

-המשאתים *double burden* for MT המשפתים *the sheepfolds*? neol.

διδακτός,-ή,-όν⁺   A 0-0-1-0-2-3
Is 54,13; 1 Mc 4,7; PSal 17,32
taught, instructed

διδασκαλία,-ας⁺   N1F 0-0-1-1-2-4
Is 29,13; Prv 2,17; Sir 24,33; 39,8
teaching, instruction

διδάσκαλος,-ου⁺   N2M 0-0-0-1-1-2
Est 6,1; 2 Mc 1,10
teacher, master
·NIDNTT; TWNT

διδάσκω⁺   V 10-9-13-50-25-107
Dt 4,1.10.14; 5,31; 6,1
A: *to instruct* [τινα] (in how to live according to the law) 1 Ezr 8,23; *to teach* [τινα] Dt 4,10; [τί τινα] Dt 5,31; [τινα +inf.] Dt 4,1; *to communicate skills* (rare) 2 Sm 22,35; P: *to be taught, to learn* Wis 6,10; *Jb 33,4 διδάσκουσά με חוה/ תחוני *teaches me* for MT תחיני /חיה *gives me life*; *Dn^LXX 11,4 διδάξει מלמר *teaches* for MT מ/לבד *beside*; *Dn^Th 12,4 διδαχθῶσιν *are taught* corr.? διαχθῶσι (διάγειν) for MT ישטטו *run to and fro*
Cf. HELBING 1928, 38; ·NIDNTT; TWNT
(·ἐκ-)

διδαχή,-ῆς⁺   N1F 0-0-0-1-0-1
Ps 59(60),1
teaching, instruction

δίδραχμον,-ου⁺   N2N 22-2-0-2-0-26
Gn 20,14.16; 23,15.16; Ex 21,32
coin of two drachmas, half-shekel
Cf. HARLÉ 1988, 211; WEVERS 1990, 388,495

διδράσκω
(·ἀπο-, δια-)

διδυμεύω   V 0-0-0-2-0-2
Ct 4,2; 6,6
to bear twins; neol.

δίδυμος,-η,-ον⁺   Λ 3-1-0-2-0-6
Gn 25,24; 38,27; Dt 25,11; Jos 8,29; Ct 4,5
forked Jos 8,29; *twin* Ct 4,5; τὰ δίδυμα *twins* Gn 25,24; *testicles* Dt 25,11

διδύσκω
(·ἐκ-, ἐν-)

δίδωμι⁺   V 467-541-391-364-368-2131
Gn 1,29; 3,6.12(bis); 4,12
to give [τινα] Gn 29,26; [τί τινι] Gn 1,29; *to give into* [τι εἴς τι] Gn 27,17; [τινα εἴς τι] Gn 16,5; *to grant* (of gods) [τί τινι] Gn 30,18; *to offer* [τί τινι] Ex 10,25; *to give to* [+inf.] 2 Chr

28,15; *to give (a daughter) for a wife* [τινα] Gn 34,9; *to make sb as* [τινα +pred.] 2 Chr 25,16; [τινα εἴς τινα] Gn 17,20; *to appoint, to establish* [τινα] Ex 31,6; *to put* [τι] Ex 8,19; *to place* [abs.] Gn 9,2; *to grant, to allow* [τινα +inf.] Gn 31,7; τιμὴν δίδωμί τινι *to pay (a price) to* Nm 20,19; δίδωμι ἀνταπόκρισιν *to give an answer* Jb 13,22; δίδωμι ἀπόκρισιν Jb 3,24; δίδωμι σημεῖόν τινι *to give a sign* Ex 7,9; [ἐπί τι] *to set a mark* Ez 9,4; δίδωμι ἰσχύν *to strengthen* Ez 30,21; δίδωμι φωνήν *to utter a voice* Ps 76(77),18; δίδωμί τι εἰς ἀφανισμόν *to bring to nought* Jdt 4,1; δίδωμί τινα εἰς σωτηρίαν *to put in safety* 2 Chr 12,7; δίδωμι λόγον κατά τινος *to bring a charge against sb* 1 Sm 22,15; τίς δώσει (semit., lit. transl. of מי יתן) *would that* (expressing a wish) Dt 5,29; *1 Chr 9,2 οἱ δεδομένοι -הנתנים/נתנים *the appointed ones*? for MT הנתינים *the Nethinim* (ministers of the Temple); *Ez 13,11 δώσω -אתנה *I will give* or *send* for MT אתה/ אתנה *you*; *1 Kgs 6,5 ἔδωκεν -יתן *he set* for MT יבן *he built*; *Dn 9,27 δοθήσεται -תתן/ נתן *shall be put* for MT תתך /נתך *is poured out*; *Jgs 5,11 δώσουσιν -יתנו/ נתן *to give* for MT תנה/ יתנו *to repeat* (deeds, triumphs)
Cf. HELBING 1928, 51-53.191-193; LE BOULLUEC 1989, 127; ·KIESSLING
(·ἀνα-, ἀνταπο-, ἀντι-, ἀπο-, δια-, ἐκ-, ἐν-, ἐπι-, καταπρο-, μετα-, παρα-, προ-, προσ-)

διεγγυάω   V 0-0-0-1-0-1
Nch 5,3
to mortgage one's property

διεγείρω⁺   V 0-0-0-1-4-5
Est 1,1l; Jdt 1,4; 2 Mc 7,21; 15,10; 3 Mc 5,15
A: *to make up, to stir up* [τι] 2 Mc 7,21; [τινα] 2 Mc 15,10; P: *to awake* Est 1,1l; *to be raised up, to be built up* Jdt 1,4

διεκβάλλω   V 0-9-0-0-0-9
Jos 15,4.7.8.9(bis)
to issue at, to terminate at [εἴς τι] Jos 15,9; [ἐπί τι] Jos 15,17; [ἕως τινός] Jos 15,4; [κατά τινος] Jos 15,11; neol.?

διεκβολή,-ῆς   N1F 0-0-6-0-0-6
Jer 12,12; Ez 47,8.11; 48,30; Ob 14
passage Jer 12,12; *way out, city gate* Ez 48,30; *estuary*? Ez 47,8; *Ez 47,11 ἐν τῇ διεκβολῇ -יצא ב/צאתו *in the estuary*?, *at the outlet*? for MT בצה/ בצאתו *its swamp(s)*; neol.?

διεκκύπτω   V 0-0-0-0-1-1

2 Mc 3,19
to peep out, to lean out; neol.

διελαύνω V 0-2-0-0-0-2
Jgs^A 4,21; 5,26
to thrust through [τι] Jgs^A 5,26; *to ride through, to go through* [intrans.] Jgs^A 4,21

διελέγχομαι V 0-0-2-0-0-2
Is 1,18; Mi 6,2
to discuss, to argue a case

διεμβάλλω V 5-0-0-0-0-5
Ex 40,18; Nm 4,6.8.11.14
to put in through, to insert [τι]; neol.

διεμπίμπλημι V 0-0-0-0-1-1
2 Mc 4,40
to fill completely; neol.

διεξάγω V 0-0-1-1-3-5
Hab 1,4; Est 3,13b; 2 Mc 10,12; 14,30; Sir 3,17
to bring to an end, to accomplish [τι] Sir 3,17; *to manage, to treat* [τι] Est 3,13b; *to treat* [τι +adv.] 2 Mc 10,12; διεξάγομαι εἰς τέλος *to be brought to an end, to proceed effectually* Hab 1,4

διέξειμι V 0-0-0-0-1-1
4 Mc 3,13
to go through; impft. of διεξέρχομαι

διεξέρχομαι V 0-2-1-1-0-4
Jgs^B 4,21; 2 Sm 2,23; Ez 12,5; Jb 20,25
to go through, to pass through Jgs^B 4,21; *to pierce* 2 Sm 2,23

διεξοδεύω V 0-0-0-1-0-1
Dn^LXX 3,48
to have a way out, to break a way

διέξοδος,-ου⁺ N2F 5-19-0-6-1-31
Nm 34,4.5.8.9.12
going out, going forth, issue Ps 143(144),14; *spring* 2 Kgs 2,21; *stream* (of water) Ps 106(107),33; διέξοδοι *places of egress* Jgs^B 5,17; διέξοδοι τοῦ θανάτου *escape from death, issues from death* Ps 67(68),21; ἔσται ἡ διέξοδος *the termination shall be* (of a border) Nm 34,4

διέπω V 0-0-0-0-2-2
Wis 9,3; 12,15
to manage, to order

διερεθίζω V 0-0-0-0-1-1
4 Mc 9,19
to stimulate

διερευνάω V 0-0-0-0-2-2
Wis 6,3; 13,7
to search

διερμηνεύω⁺ V 0-0-0-0-1-1
2 Mc 1,36

to interprete, to expound, to explicate
Cf. SPICQ 1978, 205

διέρχομαι⁺ V 14-55-34-23-26-152
Gn 4,8; 15,17; 22,5; 41,46; Ex 12,12
to go through, to pass through [abs.] Gn 4,8; *to pass through* [τι] Gn 41,46; *to go abroad, to spread* (of reports) 2 Chr 30,5; *to pass through, to shoot through one* (of pain) Jdt 6,6; *to pass through and reach, to arrive at* [εἴς τι] Am 6,2; *to pass, to elapse* (of time) Ex 14,20; *to extend* (of borders) Jos 18,14; *to go through* [διά τινος] (metaph.) Lv 26,6; σίδηρον διῆλθεν ἡ ψυχὴ αὐτοῦ *his soul passed into iron, he spent his life in jail* Ps 104(105),18; *Jgs^A 5,16 διελθεῖν *to go through* corr.? διελεῖν for MT פלג (Hebr.) *to separate*, or διελθεῖν - פלג (Aram.) *to go away, to cross over*, cpr. Prv 28,10
Cf. HELBING 1928, 81; SCHREINER 1957, 110

διίεσις,-εως N3F 0-0-0-0-1-1
Wis 12,20
deliberation, release
Cf. LARCHER 1985, 733

διεστραμμένως D 0-0-0-0-1-1
Sir 4,17
perversely

διετηρίς,-ίδος N3F 0-1-0-0-0-1
2 Sm 13,23
space of two years; neol.

διετής,-ής,-ές⁺ A 0-0-0-0-1-1
2 Mc 10,3
of or lasting two years

διευλαβέομαι V 1-0-0-1-1-3
Dt 28,60; Jb 6,16; 2 Mc 9,29
to reverence [τινα] 2 Mc 9,29; διευλαβέομαί τι ἀπὸ προσώπου τινός *to fear sth from sb* (semit.) Dt 28,60
Cf. HELBING 1928, 25-26

διηγέομαι⁺ V 11-9-8-23-13-64
Gn 24,66; 29,13; 37,9; 40,8.9
to set out in detail, to describe, to tell [τι] Gn 24,66; διηγέομαι εἰς τὰ ὦτα *to relate to* Ex 10,2; διηγέομαι τὴν ἀγωγήν *to pass one's life* Est 10,3; *Ps 118(119),85 διηγήσαντο -קראו? *they told me* for MT כרו *they have dug*
Cf. WEVERS 1990, 145; →NIDNTT

διήγημα,-ατος N3N 1-1-1-0-3-6
Dt 28,37; 2 Chr 7,20; Ez 17,2; 2 Mc 2,24; Sir 8,8
tale, discourse; neol.?

διήγησις,-εως⁺ N3F 0-2-1-0-9-12
Jgs^A 7,15; Jgs^B 5,14; Hab 2,6; 2 Mc 2,32; 6,17

tale, discourse, talk
→MM; NIDNTT

διηθέω V 0-0-0-1-0-1
Jb 28,1
to filter, to refine by washing (of gold)

διήκω V 0-0-0-0-1-1
Wis 7,24
to extend, to pass through, to pervade

διηλόω V 0-2-0-0-0-2
Jgsᴮ 5,26(bis)
to drive a nail through, to nail fast; neol.

διηνεκῶς D 0-0-0-1-3-4
Est 3,13d; 3 Mc 3,11.22; 4,16
continually, constantly

διηχέομαι V 0-0-0-0-1-1
2 Mc 8,7
to be spread, to be widely heard

δίθυμος,-ος,-ον A 0-0-0-1-0-1
Prv 26,20
at variance; neol.

διίημι V 1-0-0-0-1-2
Dt 32,11; Od 2,11
to spread [τι] (of wings)

διικνέομαι⁺ V 1-0-0-0-0-1
Ex 26,28
to go through
Cf. WALTERS 1973, 93

διιπτάομαι V 0-0-0-0-1-1
Wis 5,11
to fly through

διίστημι⁺ V 1-1-2-2-5-11
Ex 15,8; 2 Kgs 2,14; Is 59,2; Ez 5,1; Prv 17,9
A: *to set apart, to separate* [τινα] Prv 17,9; [τι]
Tobˢ 7,12; *to set apart, to disperse* [τι] Sir 28,44;
M: *to resolve, to constitute* [τι] 2 Mc 8,10;
διέστην *to separate, to make way, to open* Ex
15,8; *to differ, to be different from* [τινος] 3 Mc
2,32; διέστηκά τινος Est 8,12k; διίστημι ἀνὰ
μέσον τινός *to separate between* Is 59,2
Cf. GOLDSTEIN 1983, 328; HELBING 1928, 164

δικάζω V 0-15-3-4-3-25
Jgs 6,31(bis); Jgsᴮ 6,32
A: *to judge* [τινα] 1 Sm 7,6; *to pass judgement
on, to condemn* [τινα] Ps 34(35),1; M: *to plead
one's cause, to go to law* Jgs 6,31; [ἔν τινι]
(semit.) Jgsᴮ 6,32; δικάζω τὴν δίκην τινός *to
plead one's cause* Ps 42(43),1; δικάζω ἀνὰ
μέσον τινός *to judge between* 1 Sm 24,13;
δικάζω τινὶ ἐκ χειρός τινος *to rescue out of
one's hands* 1 Sm 24,16; *Mi 7,2 δικάζονται

ריב יריבו ◊ ריב *they sue (each other)* for MT יארבו
◊ ארב *they lie in wait*
Cf. HELBING 1928, 96.237
(→ ἐκ-, κατα-)

δικαιοκρίτης,-ου N1M 0-0-0-0-1-1
2 Mc 12,41
righteous judge; neol.

δικαιολογία,-ας N1F 0-0-0-0-1-1
2 Mc 4,44
plea in justification, speech in defence

δίκαιος,-α,ον⁺ A 27-10-56-221-121-435
Gn 6,9; 7,1; 18,23(bis).24
just, righteous Gn 6,9; ὁ δίκαιος *the righteous,
just* Gn 18,23; τὸ δίκαιον *righteousness* Jb
34,10; τὰ δίκαια *legal* or *civil rights* Wis 19,16;
αἷμα δικαίος *innocent blood* Jl 4,19; *2 Sm 2,2
δίκαιος -צריק *righteous* for MT צור *rock*, cpr. Dt
32,4.30; Ps 18(19),32; 2 Sm 22,32 (where LXX
also replaces צור); *Jb 36,10 τοῦ δικαίου -מי/ישר
of the righteous for MT מוסר *warning*
Cf. HILL 1967, 104-110; KILPATRICK 1942, 34-36;
LARCHER 1983, 239-240; 1985, 723-724; SPICQ 1982, 122-
128; →NIDNTT; TWNT

δικαιοσύνη,-ης⁺ N1F 18-18-95-139-81-351
Gn 15,6; 18,19; 19,19; 20,5.13
virtue of righteousness Wis 8,7; *justice* Gn 18,19
Cf. CAIRD 1972, 125; FIEDLER 1970, 120-143; GOODING
1981, 204-212; HORSLEY 1987, 144-145; MURAOKA 1984,
441-448; OLLEY 1978; SNAITH 1944, 161-173; SPICQ 1982,
128-139; →NIDNTT; TWNT

δικαιόω⁺ V 4-3-16-7-21-51
Gn 38,26; 44,16; Ex 23,7; Dt 25,1; 2 Sm 15,4
A: *to pronounce and treat as righteous, to justify,
to vindicate, to acquit* [τινα] Ex 23,7; *to do
justice to sb* [τινα] 2 Sm 15,4; P: *to be justified*
Jb 33,32; *to be shown to be righteous* Is 42,21;
δικαιόω τὴν δίκην τινός *to deem right one's
cause* Mi 7,9; see δικαιοσύνη
Cf. MURAOKA 1984, 441-448, esp. 444; →NIDNTT; TWNT

δικαίωμα,-ατος⁺ N3N 42-22-22-39-15-140
Gn 26,5; Ex 15,25.26; 21,1.9
ordinance, decree Gn 26,5; *justification, legal
right* 2 Sm 19,29; *justice* 1 Kgs 3,28; τὰ
δικαιώματα *righteous deeds* Bar 2,19; *custom*
(semit. for MT משפט) 1 Sm 27,11; *rightful due*
(semit. for MT משפט) 1 Sm 2,23; *Hos 13,1
δικαιώματα -תרת? or תורות? *precepts* for MT
רתת *trembling*
Cf. LE BOULLUEC 1989, 43; MURAOKA 1991, 210; SPICQ
1982, 146-148; TOV 1976, 539-540; 1990, 83-97; →NIDNTT;

TWNT
δικαίως⁺ D 3-0-0-2-7-12
Gn 27,36; Dt 1,16; 16,20; Prv 28,18; 31,9
rightly, justly

δικαίωσις,-εως⁺ N3F 1-0-0-0-2-3
Lv 24,22; Sir 10,29; PSal 3,3
justification, judgement of what is right; see
δικαιοσύνη
Cf. Spicq 1982, 148-149

δικαστήριον,-ου N2N 0-1-0-0-0-1
Jgs^A 6,32
court of justice; *Jgs^A 6,32 δικαστήριον τοῦ
Βααλ -◊ ריב *court of justice* and בעל *Baal* for MT
ירבעל *Jerubaal*

δικαστής,-οῦ⁺ N1M 1-6-1-0-5-13
Ex 2,14; Jos 9,2d(8,33); 23,2; 24,1; 1 Sm 8,1
judge
Cf. Spicq 1982, 149-151

δικέω
(→ ἀντι-, ἐκ-)

δίκη,-ης⁺ N1F 4-0-6-9-20-39
Ex 21,20; Lv 26,25; Dt 32,41.43; Ez 25,12
right Ps 139(140),13; *justice* 4 Mc 8,22;
judgement Jl 4,14; *cause* Ps 42(43),1; *vengeance*
Est 8,12d; *penalty* Hos 13,14; δίκην τινός *in the
way of* (as adv.) Wis 12,24; δίκην ἀποδίδωμί
τινι *to take vengeance to* Dt 32,41; ἐκδικέω
δίκην (semit. for MT נקם נקם) *to execute
vengeance* Lv 26,25; *Hos 13,14 ἡ δίκη σου
-רברך *your cause* (cpr. Ex 18,16)? for MT רבריך
your plagues
Cf. Spicq 1982, 120-122; Walters 1973, 35 (Hos 13,14)

δίκτυον,-ου⁺ N2N 0-9-8-5-0-22
1 Kgs 7,5(17)(ter); 7,27(41).28(42)
net 1 Kgs 7,5; *lattice* Ct 2,9

δικτυόομαι V 0-1-0-0-0-1
1 Kgs 7,6(18)
to be formed in net-work; neol.

δικτυωτός,-ή,-όν A 2-2-1-0-0-5
Ex 27,4; 38,24(4); Jgs^A 5,28; 2 Kgs 1,2; Ez 41,16
made in net-fashion Ex 27,4; *latticed, trellised* Ez
41,16; τὸ δικτυωτόν *lattice-window* 2 Kgs 1,2;
neol.?
Cf. Le Boulluec 1989, 275; Lee 1983, 112

διμερής,-ής,-ές A 0-0-0-1-0-1
Dn^LXX 2,41
bipartite, in two parts

δίμετρον,-ου N2N 0-3-0-0-0-3
2 Kgs 7,1.16.18
double measure

δίνη,-ης N1F 0-0-0-2-0-2
Jb 28,10; 37,9
whirlwind Jb 37,9; *Jb 28,10 δίνας -בצורות
◊ בצר? *whirlpools* for MT בצורות/ב *in the rocks*

διό⁺ C 0-1-0-8-19-28
Jos 5,6; Ps 115(116),1; Jb 9,22; 32,6.10
therefore, on which account

διοδεύω⁺ V 2-0-8-2-8-20
Gn 12,6; 13,17; Is 59,8; Jer 2,6; 9,11
*to travel through, to march through, to pass
through* [τι] Gn 12,6; [διά τινος] Jer 27(50),13
Cf. Harl 1986, 153; Helbing 1928, 82; Horsley 1981,
45; 1987, 146

δίοδος,-ου N2F 1-0-4-1-5-11
Dt 13,17; Is 11,16; Jer 2,28; 7,34; 14,16
way through, passage Jdt 5,1; *street* Jer 2,28

διοικέω V 0-0-0-1-4-5
Dn^LXX 3,1; Wis 8,1.14; 12,18; 15,1
to manage, to control, to administer [τι] Wis 8,1;
to control, to order, to govern [τινα] Wis 12,18
Cf. Gilbert 1973, 175-177

διοίκησις,-εως N3F 0-0-0-0-2-2
Tob 1,21
internal (financial) administration

διοικητής,-οῦ N1M 0-0-0-2-2-4
Dn^LXX 3,2; Ezr 8,36; Tob 1,22
administrator, steward

διοικοδομέω V 0-0-0-1-0-1
Neh 2,17
to build across, to wall off

διόλλυμι V 0-0-0-0-2-2
Wis 11,19; 17,9
A: *to destroy utterly* [abs.] Wis 11,19; P: *to die, to
perish utterly* Wis 17,10

διόλου C 0-0-0-0-1-1
Bel^Th 12
continually; see διά

διόπερ⁺ C 0-0-0-0-6-6
Jdt 8,17; 2 Mc 5,20; 6,16.27; 7,8
therefore

διοράω V 0-0-0-1-0-1
Jb 6,19
to distinguish

διοργίζομαι V 0-0-0-0-2-2
3 Mc 3,1; 4,13
to be very angry [abs.] 3 Mc 4,13; *to be very angry
at* [τινι] 3 Mc 3,1; neol.?

διορθόω V 0-0-5-1-1-7
Prv 15,29b(16,9); Wis 9,18; Is 16,5; 62,7; Jer 7,3
to make straight [τι] Prv 15,29b; *to establish, to*

set right [τι] Is 16,5; to restore to order [τινα]
Wis 9,12; to correct [τι] Jer 7,3

διορθωτής,-οῦ   N1M 0-0-0-0-1-1
Wis 7,15
corrector; neol.
Cf. LARCHER 1984, 465-466

διορίζω   V 2-4-8-1-0-15
Ex 26,33; Lv 20,24; Jos 5,6; Jos^BA 15,47
to draw a boundary through, to separate [abs.] Ex
26,33; to separate [τινα] Lv 20,24; [τι] Is 45,18;
to determine [+inf.] Jos 5,6; ἡ θάλασσα
διορίζει the sea is the boundary Jos^BA 15,47; τὸν
ποταμὸν τὸν διορίζοντα διά τινος the river that
flowed through 2 Chr 32,4; *Ez 41,12 τὸ
διορίζον -◊ בין partition for MT ה/בנין the
building, see also Ez 41,13(MT הבניה).15;
42,1.5.10

διόρυγμα,-ατος   N3N 1-0-2-0-0-3
Ex 22,1; Jer 2,34; Zph 2,14
digging through, house-breaking Ex 22,1; breach,
hole Zph 2,14

διορύσσω^+   V 0-0-3-1-0-4
Ez 12,5.7.12; Jb 24,16
to dig through [τι] Jb 24,16; [abs.] Ez 12,5

διότι^+   C 15-21-262-12-31-341
Gn 26,22; 29,32; Ex 4,26; Lv 22,20; 25,23
because, since, for the reason that Lv 25,23;
wherefore Hos 8,6; *Jgs^B 5,28 διότι because corr.
διὰ τί for MT מרוע why, cpr. Jgs^A 5,28; *Mal
1,10 διότι כי because for MT מי who; oh that
there were one

δίπηχυς,-υς,-υ   A 1-0-0-0-0-1
Nm 11,31
two cubits high

διπλασιάζω   V 0-0-2-0-0-2
Ez 21,19(14); 43,2
to double; διπλασιάζω ῥομφαίαν to sharpen the
sword on both sides Ez 21,19(14); *Ez 43,2 ὡς
φωνὴ διπλασιαζόντων πολλῶν- כקול שנים רבים?
like the sound of many people redoubling (their
voices) or -כקול מ/מרבים like the voice of the
increasing numbers (of angelic beings) for MT
כקול מים רבים like the sound of many waters
Cf. LUST 1986, 212-214

διπλασιασμός,-οῦ   N2M 0-0-0-1-0-1
Jb 42,10
double, doubling

διπλάσιος,-α,-ον   A 0-0-0-0-2-2
Sir 12,5; 26,1
double, twofold

διπλοΐς,-ίδος   N3F 0-6-0-2-1-9
1 Sm 2,19; 15,27; 24,5.6.12
double cloak; neol.?

διπλοῦς,-ῆ,-οῦν^+   A 18-1-3-2-3-27
Gn 23,9.17.19; 25,9; 43,15
double, twofold Gn 23,9; *Ex 25,4 διπλοῦν -שָׁנִי
second, double for MT שָׁנִי scarlet, see also Ex
35,6; *Gn 23,9 τὸ διπλοῦν -ה/מכפלה \ פלה the
double (etym. transl.) for MT המכפלה Machpelah
Cf. LARCHER 1984, 251-347; LE BOULLUEC 1989, 251.347

διπλόω
(→ περι-)

δίς^+   M 5-2-2-1-7-17
Gn 41,32; 43,10; Lv 12,5; Nm 20,11; Dt 9,13
twice, doubly

δίσκος,-ου   N2M 0-0-0-0-1-1
2 Mc 4,14
discus

δισμύριοι,-αι,-α   M 0-0-0-0-6-6
2 Mc 5,24; 8,9.30; 10,17.23
twenty thousand

δισσός,-ή,-όν   A 2-0-1-3-2-8
Gn 43,12; 45,22; Prv 20,10.23; 31,22
double Gn 43,12; two Gn 45,22; *Prv 31,22(21)
δισσάς -שנים two, double for MT שָׁנִים (ם) scarlet
Cf. HARL 1986, 295 (Gn 45,22)

δισσῶς   D 0-0-0-0-1-1
Sir 23,11
double, in two ways

δίστομος,-ος,-ον^+   A 0-2-0-2-1-5
Jgs 3,16; Ps 149,6; Prv 5,4; Sir 21,3
two-edged
Cf. SPICQ 1982, 152-153

δισχίλιοι,-αι,-α^+   M 8-10-1-14-17-50
Nm 4,36.40; 7,85; 35,4.5
two thousand Nm 4,36; δισχίλιος two thousand
(with coll. nouns, e.g. ἵππος) Is 36,8

διτάλαντον,-ου   N2N 0-1-0-0-0-1
2 Kgs 5,23
two talents

διυλίζω^+   V 0-0-1-0-0-1
Am 6,61
to strain; *Am 6,6 διυλισμένον οἶνον -מזקק ייו?
strained, clarified wine for MT מ/זרקי יין wine
from bowls; neol.?

διυφαίνω   V 1-0-0-0-0-1
Ex 36,30(39,23)
to (inter)weave [τι]; neol.
Cf. LE BOULLUEC 1989, 68

διφθέρα,-ας   N1F 1-0-0-0-0-1

Ex 39,20(34)
skin, leather
Cf. LIEBERMAN 1950, 205, n.23

δίφραξ,-ακος   N3F 0-0-0-0-1-1
2 Mc 14,21
seat, chair

διφρεύω   V 0-0-0-0-1-1
LtJ 30
to drive a chariot or *to sit*

δίφρος,-ου   N2M 0-6-0-2-3-11
JgsᴬA 3,24; 1 Sm 1,9; 4,13.18; 28,23
seat, couch, stool

δίχα   D 0-0-0-0-1-1
Sir 47,21
in two, divided

διχηλέω   V 11-0-0-0-0-11
Lv 11,3.4(bis).5.6
to divide (the hoof) [τι]
Cf. HELBING 1907, 121

διχομηνία,-ας   N1F 0-0-0-0-1-1
Sir 39,12
full moon

διχοστασία,-ας⁺   N1F 0-0-0-0-1-1
1 Mc 3,29
sedition, dissension

διχοτομέω⁺   V 1-0-0-0-0-1
Ex 29,17
to cut (in two)
Cf. LE BOULLUEC 1989, 297; SPICQ 1982, 154-156; →TWNT

διχοτόμημα,-ατος   N3N 5-0-2-0-0-7
Gn 15,11.17; Ex 29,17; Lv 1,8; Ez 24,4
divided part, divided piece; neol.
Cf. HELBING 1907, 115

δίψα,-ης   N1F 1-1-3-4-7-16
Dt 8,15; 2 Chr 32,11; Is 5,13; 41,17; Am 8,11
thirst

διψάω⁺   V 1-4-17-10-6-38
Ex 17,3; Jgs 4,19; 15,18
to thirst, to be thirsty Jgs 4,19; *to be parched* or
dry Is 35,6; *to thirst after* or *for* [πρός τινα] Ps
41(42),2; [τινι] Ex 17,3; *Jb 18,9 διψῶντας
-צמא that thirst for MT צמים a snare
Cf. SHIPP 1979, 219; →TWNT

δίψος,-ους⁺   N3N 3-3-5-2-3-16
Ex 17,3; Dt 28,48; 32,10; Jgs 15,18
thirst

διψώδης,-ης,-ες   A 0-0-0-1-0-1
Prv 9,12
thirsty; τὸ διψῶδες *thirst*

διωγμός,-ου⁺   N2M 0-0-0-2-1-3

Prv 11,19; Lam 3,19; 2 Mc 12,23
persecution Prv 11,19; *Lam 3,19 ἐκ διωγμοῦ
μου -מ/רוד/י ◊רדה? *because of my persecution*
for MT מרוד/י *my homelessness*?
Cf. ALBREKTSON 1963, 60.139-140

διωθέομαι   V 0-0-1-0-0-1
Ez 34,21
to push from oneself, to push away

διώκω⁺   V 14-24-27-15-32-112
Gn 14,15; 31,23; Ex 15,9; Lv 26,7.8
to pursue, to chase [τινα] 2 Sm 21,5; [ὀπίσω
τινός] (of pers.) Gn 31,23; *to pursue, to seek
after* [τι] Prv 15,9; [ὀπίσω τινός] (of things) Jgs
4,16; *to follow* [τι] Ezr 9,4; *to run, to flee*
[intrans.] Hab 2,2; ὁ διώκων *the prosecutor,
pursuer* Ps 7,2; *Ez 25,13 διωκόμενοι -ירדנה
◊נרד *being pursued* for MT ורדנה and to
Dedan; *Is 30,28 καὶ διώξεται -וינס ◊נוס *it shall
pursue* for MT רסן *a bridle*; *Prv 21,6 διώκει
-רדף *pursues* for MT נרף *fleeting*?; *Lv 26,17
διώκοντος -רדף *pursuing* for MT רדה *dominating*
Cf. HARLÉ 1988, 207 (Lv 26,17); →TWNT
(→ ἀπο-, ἐκ-, ἐπι-, κατα-, μετα-, συν-)

διώροφος,-ος,-ον   A 1-0-0-0-0-1
Gn 6,16
with two stories, with two floors; neol.

διῶρυξ,-υγος   N3F 2-0-5-0-2-9
Ex 7,19; 8,1; Is 19,6; 27,12; 33,21
canal, channel, brook

διωστήρ,-ῆρος   N3M 5-0-0-0-0-5
Ex 38,4(37,5).10(37,14).11(37,15); 39,14(35);
40,20
pole running through rings, stave (for carrying the
ark)
Cf. LE BOULLUEC 1989, 256.364

δόγμα,-ατος⁺   N3N 0-0-0-13-5-18
3 Mc 1,3; 4 Mc 4,23.24.26; 10,2
decree, ordinance
Cf. HORSLEY 1987, 146; →TWNT

δογματίζω   V 0-0-0-3-4-7
Dnᴸˣˣ 6,13; Dnᵀʰ 2,13; 3,10.12.96(29)
to ordain, to decree; neol.?

δοκέω⁺   V 6-2-1-20-34-64
Gn 19,14; 38,15; Ex 25,2; 35,21.22
to think that [τινα +inf.] Gn 38,15; *to seem*
[+inf.] Gn 19,14; δοκεῖ τινι *it seems good, it is
a pleasure* Ex 25,2; τὸ δεδογμένον *decision,
decree* 3 Mc 5,40; *Jb 20,22 δοκῇ -◊ספק (Aram.)
he seems, supposes for MT שפק his plenty
→TWNT

δοκιμάζω⁺   V 0-1-10-12-13-36

Jgs^A 7,4; Jer 6,27(bis); 9,6; 11,20

A: *to assay, to test, to prove* [τι] Wis 2,19; [τινα] Ps 25(26),2; *to put to a test, to make trial of* [τινα] Ps 65(66),10; *to verify* [τινα] Sir 31,10; *to discern* [τι] Jb 34,3; *to approve* [τι] 2 Mc 4,3; *Jer 6,27 δεδοκιμασμένους -מבצר ◊ בצר? tried* for MT מבצר *fortification*; *Prv 17,3 ὥσπερ δοκιμάζεται -כ/צרף as (silver and gold) are tried* for MT מצרף *crucible*; *Ps 67(68),31 δεδοκιμασμένους -◊ צרף tested, proved* for MT רצץ ב/רצי? *crushing*

Cf. SPICQ 1982, 157-161

(→ ἀπο-)

δοκιμασία,-ας⁺   N1F 0-0-0-0-2-2

Sir 6,21; PSal 16,14

test, trial

Cf. SPICQ 1982, 161-162

δοκιμαστός,-ή,-όν   A 0-0-1-0-0-1

Jer 6,27

approved

δοκίμιον,-ου⁺   N2N 0-0-0-2-0-2

Ps 11(12),7; Prv 27,21

test, means of testing

Cf. WALTERS 1973, 49-50; →MM

δόκιμος,-ος,-ον⁺   A 1-4-1-0-0-6

Gn 23,16; 1 Kgs 10,18; 1 Chr 28,18; 29,4; 2 Chr 9,17

approved Gn 23,16; *good, excellent* Zech 11,13; χρυσίον δόκιμον *pure gold* 1 Kgs 10,18

Cf. SPICQ 1982, 162-164; WALTERS 1973, 57

δοκός,-οῦ⁺   N2M/F 1-5-0-1-3-10

Gn 19,8; 1 Kgs 6,15.16; 2 Kgs 6,2.5

balk, beam

δόκωσις,-εως   N3F 0-0-0-1-0-1

Eccl 10,18

roofing; neol.

δόλιος,-α,-ον⁺   A 0-0-3-20-5-27

Jer 9,3.7; Zph 3,13; Ps 5,7; 11(12),3

deceitful, treacherous, crafty Ps 5,7; *false* Prv 11,1

δολιότης,-ητος   N3F 1-0-0-4-1-6

Nm 25,18; Ps 37(38),13; 49(50),19; 54(54),24; 72(73),18

deceit, subtlety; neol.

δολιόω⁺   V 1-0-0-3-0-4

Nm 25,18; Ps 5,10; 13(14),3; 104(105),25

to deal treacherously with [τινα] Nm 25,18; *to be treacherous* Ps 5,10; M: *to deal treacherously with* [ἔν τινι] Ps 104(105),25; neol.

δολίως   D 0-0-0-1-0-1

Jer 9,4(3)

treacherously, craftily

δόλος,-ου⁺   N2M 5-1-8-23-22-59

Gn 27,35; 34,13; Ex 21,14; Lv 19,16; Dt 27,24

deceit, craft, treachery Ex 21,14; μετὰ δόλου διδόμενος *dishonestly given* Prv 26,23; *Ez 35,5 δόλῳ -עול? with deceit, treacherously* for MT על *to, for*

δολόω⁺   V 0-0-0-2-0-2

Ps 14(15),3; 35(36),3

to beguile, to ensnare

δόμα,-ατος⁺   N3N 14-8-8-11-17-58

Gn 25,6; 47,22; Ex 28,38; Lv 7,30; 23,38

gift Gn 25,6; *Mal 1,3 δόματα gifts* corr. δώματα -תנאות ◊ תנא Arab. *dwellings* for MT תנות *jackals*; *Hos 10,6 ἐν δόματι -ב/אתנה? as a gift* for MT בשנה (hapax) ?

Cf. DANIEL 1966, 139.212; HARLÉ 1988, 42.111; MURAOKA 1991, 211; WALTERS 1973, 209 (Gn 47,22)

δόμος,-ου   N2M 0-0-0-2-2-4

Ezr 6,4(bis); 1 Ezr 6,24(bis)

course, layer (of stones or bricks in a building)

δόξα,-ης⁺   N1F 32-28-115-122-156-453

Gn 31,1.16; 45,13; Ex 15,7.11

subjective sense: *the opinion which others have of one, estimation, repute* (of pers.) Is 11,3; *opinion, glory* Eccl 10,1; objective sense (semit.): *richess, honour, glory* Gn 31,1; *magnificence* (of a building) 1 Ezr 6,10; *brightness, splendor* (of the appearance of the Lord) Ez 10,4; δόξαι *glorious works* Ex 15,11; *2 Chr 30,8 δότε δόξαν give glory* corr.? δότε δεξιάν for MT חנו יד *give a hand, yield yourselves*, cpr. Is 62,8; *Dn^LXX 12,13 ἐπὶ τὴν δόξαν σου -לגרלך in your glory* for MT כברי -לגרלך *for your lot*; *Lam 2,11 ἡ δόξα μου -כבור ◊ my glory* for MT כְּבֵרִי *my insides, my gall*

Cf. BROCKINGTON 1951, 23-32; CAIRD 1968, 265-277; FORSTER 1929-30, 311-316; LE BOULLUEC 1989, 174.-281.330; MOHRMANN 1954, 321-328; OWEN 1932, 132-150.265-279; RAURELL 1979; 1980; 1982; 1984; 1985; SPICQ 1982, 166-181; →NIDNTT; TWNT

δοξάζω⁺   V 10-12-19-37-65-143

Ex 15,1.2.6.11.21

A: *to magnify, to extol* [τινα] 1 Sm 2,29; M: *to display one's greatness* or *glory* [intrans.] Is 33,10; *to shine* [intrans.] Ex 34,29; P: *to be distinguished, to be held in honour, to be magnified* Ex 15,1

Cf. CAIRD 1968, 265-277; HELBING 1928, 20; LE BOULLUEC 1989, 345; LEDOGAR 1967, 44-49; SPICQ 1982,

81-184; WEVERS 1990, 228 (Ex 15,2); →NIDNTT; TWNT
(→ ἐν-, παρα-)

δόξασμα,-ατος N3N 0-0-1-1-0-2
Is 46,13; Lam 2,1
glory (semit.)

δοξαστός,-ή,-όν A 1-0-0-0-0-1
Dt 26,19
glorified, glorious

δοξικός,-ή,-όν A 0-0-0-0-1-1
2 Mc 8,35
glorious; neol.

δοξολογέω V 0-0-0-0-1-1
Od 14,7
to glorify, to praise; neol.

δορά,-ᾶς N1F 1-0-1-0-1-3
Gn 25,25; Mi 2,8; 4 Mc 9,28
skin (when removed), hide
Cf. BICKERMAN 1980, 95; RUDOLPH 1975, 58 (Mi 2,8)

δορατοφόρος,-ου N2M 0-1-0-0-0-1
1 Chr 12,25
spear-bearer

δοριάλωτος,-ος,-ον A 0-0-0-0-3-3
2 Mc 5,11; 10,24; 3 Mc 1,5
captive of the spear, taken by war 2 Mc 5,11;
captive (of pers.) 3 Mc 1,5

δορκάδιον,-ου N2N 0-0-1-0-0-1
Is 13,14
fawn, little gazelle; neol.?
·KIESSLING

δορκάς,-άδος N3F 4-4-0-5-1-14
Dt 12,15.22; 14,5; 15,22; 2 Sm 2,18
deer, gazelle

δόρκων,-ωνος N3M 0-0-0-1-0-1
Ct 2,17
roe

δόρυ, δορατος N3N 0-41-2-4-7-54
1 Sm 13,19.22; 17,7(bis).45
spear

δορυφορία,-ας N1F 0-0-0-0-1-1
2 Mc 3,28
guard kept over, body-guard

δορυφόρος,-ου N2M 0-0-0-0-11-11
2 Mc 3,24; 4 Mc 5,2; 6,1.8.23
spear-bearer 4 Mc 5,2; *guard* 2 Mc 3,24

δόσις,-εως N3F 3-0-0-2-18-23
Gn 47,22(ter); Prv 21,14; 25,14
gift 1 Ezr 2,4; *portion* Gn 47,22
Cf. WALTERS 1973, 209 (Gn 47,22)

δότης,-ου N1M 0-0-0-1-0-1
Prv 22,8a

giver, dispenser; neol.

δοτός,-ή,-όν A 0-1-0-0-0-1
1 Sm 1,11
granted; neol.

δουλεία,-ας N1F 13-10-5-14-3-45
Gn 30,26; Ex 6,6; 13,3.14; 20,2
slavery, bondage Ex 6,6; *service* Ezr 6,18; *service,
labour, toil* Ps 103(104),14; *service for hire* 1 Kgs
5,20; *Est 7,4 δουλείαν - עבד *slavery* for MT
◊ אבד *annihilation, to be annihilated*; *1 Sm
14,40 εἰς δουλείαν - ל/עבד *to slavery* for MT
ל/עבד *on one side*
Cf. DANIEL 1966, 56-64.112-115

δουλεύω V 25-63-35-19-16-158
Gn 14,4; 15,14; 25,23; 27,29.40
to be a slave 2 Mc 1,27; *to serve* [τινι] Gn 14,4;
to serve against [ἐπί τινα] Ez 29,18; *1 Sm 2,24
δουλεύειν -◊ עבד *to serve* for MT ◊ עבר *to cause
(a rumour) to circulate*, see also Ps 80(81),7
Cf. DANIEL 1966, 56-58.61-75.102-104.111-117;
HILHORST 1989, 179-181; LE BOULLUEC 1989, 242;
→NIDNTT; TWNT

δούλη,-ης N1F 2-28-5-6-11-52
Ex 21,7; Lv 25,44; Jgs^A 19,19; Ru 2,13; 3,9
bondwoman, bondmaid, servant

δοῦλος,-η,-ον A 0-0-0-1-1-2
Ps 118(119),91; Wis 15,7
subject, subservient Wis 15,7; τὸ δοῦλον *servant,
slave* Ps 118(119),91

δοῦλος,-ου N2M 3-221-29-95-35-383
Lv 25,44; 26,13; Dt 32,36; Jos 9,23; 24,30(29)
servant, slave Lv 25,44; *1 Sm 13,3 δοῦλοι
-עברים *servants, slaves* for MT עברים *Hebrews*,
see also 1 Sm 14,21; *Jon 1,9 δοῦλος Κυρίου
-עברי/*servant of the Lord* (abbrev.) for MT עברי
Hebrew
Cf. BICKERMAN 1986, 148-151; DANIEL 1966, 56.61-62.71.
99.104.112 etc.; KRAFT 1972, 37-39.176-178; SPICQ 1978,
211-217; →NIDNTT; TWNT

δουλόω V 1-0-0-1-4-6
Gn 15,13; Prv 27,81; Mc 8,11; 4 Mc 3,2; 13,2
A: *to enslave* [τινα] Gn 15,13; M: *to make
subject to oneself, to enslave* [τινα] Wis 19,14; P:
to be enslaved 4 Mc 3,2
(→ κατα-)

δοχή,-ῆς N1F 2-0-0-7-1-10
Gn 21,8; 26,30; Est 1,3; 5,4.5
reception, entertainment, feast
Cf. HARL 1968, 68.189; LEE 1983, 82-83

δράγμα,-ατος N3N 10-1-2-5-1-19

Gn 37,7(ter); 41,47; Lv 23,10
handful Lv 23,10; *as many stalks of corn as the*
reaper can grasp in his left hand, sheaf Gn 37,7;
ἐποίησεν ἡ γῆ δράγματα *the land produced*
plenty Gn 41,47
Cf. HARLÉ 1988, 43

δράκος,-ους   N3N 0-0-0-0-1-1
3 Mc 5,2
handful; see δράγμα, δράξ; neol.
Cf. WALTERS 1973, 290

δράκων,-οντος⁺   N3M 4-0-10-14-13-41
Ex 7,9.10.12; Dt 32,33; Is 27,1
dragon, serpent
Cf. LE BOULLUEC 1989, 36; →TWNT

δράμα,-ατος   N3N 0-0-0-0-1-1
4 Mc 6,17
drama, play; ὑποκρίνομαι δρᾶμα *to play the*
part (metaph.)

δράξ, δρακός   N3F 3-1-3-2-0-9
Lv 2,2; 5,12; 6,8; 1 Kgs 17,12; Is 40,12
handful Lv 2,2; *hand* Ez 10,2
Cf. WALTERS 1973, 290

δραπέτης,-ου   N1M 0-0-0-0-1-1
2 Mc 8,35
runaway slave

δράσσομαι⁺   V 3-0-0-1-4-8
Lv 2,2; 5,12; Nm 5,26; Ps 2,12; Jdt 13,7 4,41
to grasp, to lay hold of [τινος] Jdt 13,7; *to take*
(by handfuls) [τι] Lv 2,2; *Ps 2,12 δράξασθε -נשׂוֹ
or נשׂאו *to accept* for MT נשׁקוּ *kiss*
Cf. DUBARLE 1955, 510-511; HELBING 1928, 128

δραχμή,-ῆς⁺   N1F 2-0-0-0-6-8
Gn 24,22; Ex 39,3(38,26); Tob 5,15; 2 Mc 4,19
drachm (a weight) Gn 24,22; *drachma* (silver
coin) 2 Mc 4,19

δράω   V 0-0-0-0-3-3
4 Mc 11,4; Wis 14,10; 15,6
to do, to accomplish

δρεπανηφόρος,-ος,-ον   A 0-0-0-0-1-1
2 Mc 13,2
bearing a scythe or sickle or hook

δρέπανον,-ου⁺   N2N 2-2-8-0-0-12
Dt 16,9; 23,25(26); 1 Sm 13,20.21; Is 2,4
sickle Dt 16,9; *pruning knife* Is 18,5; *Zech 5,1.2
δρέπανον -מגל *a sickle* for MT מגלה *a scroll*
Cf. WALTERS 1973, 189-190.334 (1 Sm 13,20.21)

δρομεύς,-έως   N3M 0-0-1-4-0-5
Am 2,14; Jb 9,25; Prv 6,11(bis); 24,34
runner

δρόμος,-ου⁺   N2M 0-2-2-1-4-9

2 Sm 18,27(bis); Jer 8,6; 23,10; Eccl 9,11
running, course, race

δροσίζω   V 0-0-0-0-1-1
3 Mc 6,6
to bedew, to sprinkle all over

δρόσος,-ου   N2F 7-12-8-20-7-54
Gn 27,28.39; Ex 16,13; Nm 11,9; Dt 32,2
dew

δρυμός,-οῦ   N2M 1-18-31-10-5-65
Dt 19,5; Jos 17,15.18(bis); Jgs^A 4,16
thicket Ps 73(74),6; *Jer 27,32 δρυμῷ -יער *thicket*
for MT עיר *city*, see also Is 27,9
Cf. LEFORT 1935, 414-415

δρῦς, δρυός   N3F 5-12-4-0-0-21
Gn 12,6; 13,18; 14,13; 18,1; Dt 11,30
oak Gn 12,6; *Jer 2,34 δρυΐ -אֵלָה *oak* for MT
אֵלֶּה *them*

δυάζω
(→ συν-)

δύναμαι⁺   V 65-61-52-72-82-332
Gn 13,6.16; 15,5; 19,19.22
to be able Gn 30,8; [+inf.] Gn 13,16; *to dare*
[+inf.] Ex 7,18; *to bear* [τι] 1 Kgs 8,64; δύναμαι
πρός τινα *to resist sb, to prevail over sb* Jer
45(38),5; δύναμαί τινι Ps 128(129),2; *Hos
11,4 δυνήσομαι αὐτῷ -לוֹ אוּכַל ◊ יכל *I shall*
prevail over him for MT לא : אוּכִיל *I fed. Not...*;
*Jgs^A 18,7 δυναμένους -◊ יכל *they that were able*
for MT מכלים ◊ כלה *making ashamed, perverting*
→TWNT

δύναμις,-εως⁺   N3F 76-150-63-112-189-590
Gn 21,22.32; 26,26; Ex 6,26; 7,4
power, might, strength Dt 6,5; *ability* Dt 16,17;
outward power, influence, authority Jos 4,24;
force for war, army, host Gn 21,22; *power,*
heavenly host 2 Chr 18,18; *power, personal*
supernatural spirit or angel 4 Mc 5,13; υἱοὶ
δυνάμεων *mighty men* 1 Sm 10,26; *Jb 40,10
δύναμιν -גבורה *power* for MT גבה *height,*
eminence; *2 Sm 23,36 ἀπὸ δυνάμεως -מ/צָבָא *of*
the army for MT מ/צבה *from Zobah*; *Jb 11,6
δύναμιν for MT -עלם ◊ *power* for MT תעלמות
◊ עלם^II *secrets*, see also 28,11; *Dn^Th 8,9 τὴν
δύναμιν -צבא *the host* for MT צבי *the fairest (of*
all lands); *Ct 2,7 δυνάμεσι -צבאות ◊ צבא *the*
powers, the hosts for MT צבאות ◊ צביא *gazelle*, see
also Ct 3,5
Cf. LARCHER 1983, 171-172; TOV 1976, 531-532; WEVERS
1990, 132; →NIDNTT; TWNT

δυναμόω⁺   V 0-0-0-4-0-4

Ps 51(52),9; 67(68),29; Eccl 10,10; Dnᵀʰ 9,27
A: *to strengthen* [τι] Ps 67(68),29; P: *to
strengthen oneself in* [ἐπί τινι] Ps 51(52),9;
neol.?
(⸱ ὑπερ-)

δυναστεία,-ας   N1F 1-15-6-23-11-56
Ex 6,6; Jgsᴬ 5,31; 1 Kgs 15,23; 16,5.27
lordship, domination Ex 6,6; *(exercise of) power*
Sir 3,20; δυναστείαι *mighty deeds*
Cf. Le Boulluec 1989, 112

δυναστεύματα,-ων   N3N 0-1-0-0-0-1
1 Kgs 2,46c
possessions; neol.
Cf. Tov 1984, 98

δυναστεύω   V 0-2-1-8-4-15
2 Kgs 10,13; 1 Chr 16,21; Jer 13,18; Ez 22,25;
Prv 19,10
to rule (over) [τινος] 3 Mc 2,7; *to overpower, to
dominate, to oppress* [τινα] 1 Chr 16,21; *to hold
authority, to exercise power* Est 8,12g; ὁ
δυναστεύων *noble, official* Jer 13,18; ἡ
δυναστεύουση *queen* 2 Kgs 10,13
Cf. Helbing 1928, 117
(⸱ κατα-)

δυνάστης,-ου⁺   N1M 3-4-5-29-33-74
Gn 49,24; 50,4; Lv 19,15; Jgsᴬ 5,9; 1 Sm 2,8
mighty one Jb 5,15; *lord, master* Jdt 9,3; *prince*
Prv 8,15; *Am 6,7 δυναστῶν -גדלים *princes* for
MT נלים *exiles*; *Jb 36,22 δυνάστης -מרא?
(Aram.) *master, powerful* for MT מורה *teacher*;
*Jb 29,12 δυνάστου -מ/שׁוע ◊ שׁועᴵᴵ *of the
oppressor* for MT משׁוע ◊ שׁועᴵ *who cried*, see also
Ps 71(72),12; *Prv 8,3 δυναστῶν -שׂרים *princes*
for MT שׁערים *gates* (double transl.)
Cf. Harl 1986, 52.313; ⸱⸱TWNT

δυνατός,-ή,-όν⁺   A 12-96-10-27-40-185
Gn 26,16; 32,29; 47,5; Ex 8,22; 17,9
strong, mighty Gn 32,29; *able* Gn 47,5; *able to*
[+inf.] Nm 22,38; *possible* Ex 8,22; δυνατόν
ἐστι *it is possible* 2 Mc 3,6; *Mal 1,14 ὃς ἦν
δυνατός -יכל *the one who had the power* for
MT נכל *the cheat*; *1 Chr 24,4 τῶν δυνατῶν
-הגבורים *the mighty ones* for MT הגברים *the men*

δυνατῶς   D 0-1-0-0-1-2
1 Chr 26,8; Wis 6,6
strongly, mightily

δύνω⁺   V 0-3-0-1-0-4
2 Sm 2,24; 1 Kgs 22,36; 2 Chr 18,34; Eccl 1,5
to sink, to go down (of the sun) 2 Sm 2,24;
δύνοντος τοῦ ἡλίου *at sunset* 1 Kgs 22,36; see

δύω

δύο⁺   M 240-213-62-73-106-694
Gn 1,16; 2,24.25; 3,7; 4,19
two Gn 1,16; *Hab 3,2 δύο -שָׁנִים *two* for MT
שָׁנִים *years*
Cf. Helbing 1907, 53

δύρομαι
(→ ἀπο-)

δυσάθλιος,-ος,-ον   A 0-0-0-0-1-1
3 Mc 4,4
most miserable

δυσαίακτος,-ος,-ον   A 0-0-0-0-1-1
3 Mc 6,31
most mournful; neol.

δυσάλυκτος,-ος,-ον   A 0-0-0-0-1-1
Wis 17,16
hard to escape

δυσβάστακτος,-ος,-ον⁺   A 0-0-0-1-0-1
Prv 27,3
cumbersome, intolerable; neol.

δυσδιήγητος,-ος,-ον   A 0-0-0-0-1-1
Wis 17,1
hard to explain or *describe*; neol.

δυσημερία,-ας   N1F 0-0-0-0-1-1
2 Mc 5,6
unlucky day

δύσις,-εως⁺   N3F 0-0-0-1-0-1
Ps 103(104),19
setting (of sun or stars)

δυσκατάπαυστος,-ος,-ον   A 0-0-0-0-1-1
3 Mc 5,7
hard to check

δυσκλεής,-ής,-ές   A 0-0-0-0-2-2
3 Mc 3,23.25
infamous

δυσκολία,-ας   N1F 0-0-0-1-0-1
Jb 34,30
discontent

δύσκολος,-ος,-ον⁺   A 0-0-1-0-0-1
Jer 30,2(49,8)
troublesome, harassing; τὰ δύσκολα *troubles*
Cf. Shipp 1979, 223-224; Spicq 1978, 218-220; ⸱⸱MM

δύσκωφος,-ος,-ον⁺   A 1-0-0-0-0-1
Ex 4,11
very hard of hearing

δυσμαί,-ῶν⁺   N1F 16-18-9-9-10-62
Gn 15,12.17; Ex 17,12; 22,25; Nm 22,1
setting (of the sun) Gn 15,12; *quarter of sunset,
west* Nm 22,1; *Jgsᴬ 20,33 ἀπὸ δυσμῶν τῆς
Γαβαα -נבע ממערב *from the west of Gabaa*

(Gibeah) for MT מ/מערה נבע *from the vicinity?*
of Gibeah; *Nm 22,1 δυσμαί- מערב- *the west* for
MT ערבות *the plains, the wilderness,* see also Nm
33,48.49.50; 36,13; Dt 1,1; 11,30; Jos 5,9; 2 Sm
2,29; 4,7; Ps 67,5; Is 51,3; Am 6,14; *Ez 27,9
ἐπὶ δυσμὰς δυσμῶν *uttermost west -*ערב to go
down, to become evening for MT לערב מערבך
ערב *to exchange merchandise*
Cf. HARL 1986, 65

δυσμένεια,-ας   N1F 0-0-0-0-5-5
2 Mc 6,29; 12,3; 14,39; 3 Mc 3,19; 7,4
ill-will, enmity

δυσμενής,-ής,-ές   A 0-0-0-2-3-5
Est 3,13d.g; 3 Mc 3,2.7.25
ill-disposed, hostile

δυσμενῶς   D 0-0-0-0-1-1
2 Mc 14,11
maliciously

δυσνοέω   V 0-0-0-1-1-2
Est 3,13c; 3 Mc 3,24
to be ill-affected, to be ill-disposed [τινι]; neol.
Cf. HELBING 1928, 213

δυσπέτημα,-ατος   N3N 0-0-0-0-1-1
2 Mc 5,20
misfortune; neol.?

δυσπολιόρκητος,-ος,-ον   A 0-0-0-0-1-1
2 Mc 12,21
hard to take by siege

δυσπρόσιτος,-ος,-ον   A 0-0-0-0-1-1
2 Mc 12,21
difficult of access or *attack*

δυσσέβεια,-ας   N1F 0-0-0-0-2-2
1 Ezr 1,40; 2 Mc 8,33
impiety, ungodliness

δυσσεβέω   V 0-0-0-0-1-1
2 Mc 6,13
to be ungodly or *impious, to act wickedly*

δυσσέβημα,-ατος   N3N 0-0-0-0-2-2
1 Ezr 1,49; 2 Mc 12,3
impious act; neol.?
Cf. HELBING 1907, 115

δυσσεβής,-ής,-ές   A 0-0-0-0-7-7
2 Mc 3,11; 8,14; 9,9; 15,33; 3 Mc 3,1
ungodly, wicked, impious

δυστοκέω   V 1-0-0-0-0-1
Gn 35,16
to suffer in childbirth

δυσφημέω⁺   V 0-0-0-0-1-1
1 Mc 7,41
to use bad words, to blaspheme

δυσφημία,-ας⁺   N1F 0-0-0-0-2-2
1 Mc 7,38; 3 Mc 2,26
blasphemy, slander

δύσφημος,-ος,-ον   A 0-0-0-0-2-2
2 Mc 13,11; 15,32
slanderous, blasphemous

δυσφορέω   V 0-0-0-0-2-2
2 Mc 4,35; 13,25
to be angry, to be grieved

δυσφόρως   D 0-0-0-0-2-2
2 Mc 14,28; 3 Mc 3,8
grievously

δυσχέρεια,-ας   N1F 0-0-0-0-2-2
2 Mc 2,24; 9,21
annoyance, difficulty

δυσχερής,-ής,-ές   A 0-0-0-0-4-4
2 Mc 6,3; 9,7.24; 14,45
grievous, annoying

δύσχρηστος,-ος,-ον   A 0-0-1-0-1-2
Is 3,10; Wis 2,12
inconvenient, burdensome

δυσώδης,-ης,-ες   A 0-0-0-0-1-1
4 Mc 6,25
ill-smelling, stinking

δύω   V 4-4-7-2-9-26
Gn 28,11; Ex 15,10; Dt 23,12; Jgs^A 14,18; 19,14
A: *to cause to sink, to withdraw* [τι] (of light) Jl
2,10; M: *to go into* [εἴς τι] (metaph.) Jon 2,6; *to
enter, to make one's way into* [εἴς τι] Is 29,4; *to
sink, to set* (of the sun) Gn 28,11; *to sink* (of
pers.) Ex 15,10; see δύνω
(- δια-, εἰσ-, ἐκ-, ἐν-, ἐπι-, κατα-, περι-, ὑπο-)

δώδεκα⁺   M 31-41-8-8-12-100
Gn 5,8; 14,4; 17,20; 25,16; 35,22
twelve

δωδεκαετής,-ής,-ές   A 0-0-0-1-0-1
1 Ezr 5,41
twelve years old
Cf. ENGEL 1985, 33-35

δωδεκάμηνος,-ου   N2F 0-0-0-0-1-1
Dn^Th 4,29(26)
period of twelve months, year
Cf. CLARYSSE 1990, 38-39

δωδέκατος,-η,-ον⁺   M 1-8-5-9-3-26
Nm 7,78; 2 Kgs 8,25; 17,1; 25,27; 1 Chr 24,12
twelfth

δῶμα,-ατος⁺   N3N 1-16-7-4-1-29
Dt 22,8; Jos 2,6(bis).8; Jgs^A 9,51
housetop, roof, dwellings Dt 22,8; *2 Chr 28,4
δωμάτων -גנות *roofs* for MT גבעות *high places*

Cf. SHIPP 1979, 225; HUSSON 1983, 63-65

δωρεά,-ᾶς⁺   N1F 4-5-4-12-10-35

Gn 29,15; Ex 21,2.11; Nm 11,5; 1 Sm 19,5
gift, present 1 Ezr 3,5; *privilege* 3 Mc 1,7; δωρεάν
(as adv.) *freely, for nothing* Gn 29,15; *without a
cause* Ps 108(109),3

→KIESSLING

δωρέομαι⁺   V 2-0-0-2-4-8

Gn 30,20; Lv 7,15(5); Prv 4,2; Est 8,1; 1 Ezr 1,7
M: *to give to, to present to* [τί τινι] Gn 30,20;
[τινά τινι] Sir 7,25; *to offer* Lv 7,15(5); P: *to be
given to* [εἴς τι] 1 Ezr 8,13

Cf. DANIEL 1966, 122; HELBING 1928, 193

δώρημα,-ατος⁺   N3N 0-0-0-0-1-1

Sir 34,18
gift, present

δωροδέκτης,-ου   N1M 0-0-0-1-0-1

Jb 15,34

one who takes bribes; neol.

δωροκοπέω   V 0-0-0-0-2-2

3 Mc 4,19; Sir 35,11
to bribe; neol.

δωρολήμπτης,-ου   N1M 0-0-0-1-0-1

Prv 15,27
receiver of bribes; neol.

δῶρον,-ου⁺   N2N 103-27-16-19-13-178

Gn 4,4; 24,53; 30,20; 32,14.19
gift, present Gn 24,53; *votive gift, offering* Gn 4,4;
bribe Is 1,23; *Jer 28,59 δώρων -מנחה *tribute, gift*
for MT מנוחה *resting place, court*; *Is 8,20 δῶρα
-שחר *gift* for MT שַׁחַר *dawn*; *Jgs^ 9,31 μετὰ
δώρων -ב/תרומה *with a gift* for MT ב/תרמה
(hapax) *with a ruse?*; *Jb 20,6 δῶρα - שי *gifts* for
MT שיא/ו *his height*

Cf.DANIEL 1966, 120-130.138-140.209-213.222-223; HARL.
1988, 33.86.182; WELCH 1918-19, 277-278

ἔα⁺   I 0-0-0-3-0-3
Jb 15,16; 19,5; 25,6
alas Jb 19,5; ἔα δέ *let alone* Jb 15,16
Cf. KATZ 1946, 168-169

ἐάν⁺   C 556-215-186-215-171-1343
Gn 2,19; 4,7; 6,17; 15,14; 18,24
[+subj.]: *if (perhaps* or *by chance)* Gn 18,24;
ἐὰν μή *if not* Gn 24,8; ἐάν for ἄν (in Hellenistic
and late Greek after relative pronouns and
conjunctions): ὃς ἐάν *whosoever* Gn 15,14;
ἡνίκα ἐάν *whensoever* Gn 24,41; ὅθεν ἐάν
whencesoever Ex 5,11; ὅπου ἐάν *wheresoever* Ru
1,16; πλὴν ἐάν *provided only* 1 Kgs 8,25; ὃν
τρόπον ἐάν *as if* Is 17,5; ὡς ἐάν *whosoever* Jgs
7,5
Cf. AEJMELAEUS 1982, 75-78; GHEDINI 1935, 234-263;
STERENBERG 1908; WEVERS 1991, 53

ἐάνπερ   C 0-0-0-0-1-1
2 Mc 3,38
if indeed [+subj.]

ἔαρ, ἔαρος   N3N 2-0-1-1-1-5
Gn 8,22; Nm 13,20; Zech 14,8; Ps 73(74),17;
Wis 2,7
spring

ἑαυτοῦ,-ῆς,-οῦ   R 108-153-74-161-166-662
Gn 1,29.30; 3,7; 4,19.23
also dat. and acc.; *of himself, of herself, of itself*
Gn 1,29; *each of his own* Ex 18,23
Cf. LE BOULLUEC 1989, 110; WEVERS 1990, 289 (Ex
18,23)

ἐάω⁺   V 3-4-1-10-12-30
Gn 38,16; Ex 32,10; Dt 9,14; Jos 19,47a; Jgsᴬ
11,37
to suffer, to permit, to allow [τινα +inf.] Gn
38,16; *to let alone* [τινα] Ex 32,10; οὐκ ἐάω *to
forbid, to prevent* Jos 19,47a
Cf. LE BOULLUEC 1989, 321

ἑβδομάς,-άδος   N3F 9-1-0-13-9-32
Ex 34,22; Lv 23,15.16; 25,8; Nm 28,26
the number seven 4 Mc 14,8; *period of seven
days, week* Ex 34,22; *sabbath* 4 Mc 2,8; *period of
seven years, year-week* Dn 9,24

ἑβδομήκοντα⁺   M 40-35-9-22-16-122
Gn 5,12; 11,17.24.26; 12,4
seventy Gn 5,12; *Gn 11,24 ἑβδομήκοντα
-שבעים *seventy (nine)* for MT עשרים *twenty
(nine)*; *1 Sm 9,22 ἑβδομήκοντα -שבעים *seventy*
for MT שלשים *thirty?*, see also 1 Sm 11,8; 2 Sm
6,1

ἑβδομηκοντάκις⁺   M 1-0-0-0-0-1

Gn 4,24
seventy times

ἑβδομηκοστός,-ή,-όν   M 0-0-1-0-6-7
Zech 1,12; 1 Mc 13,41.51; 14,1.27
seventieth

ἕβδομος,-η,-ον⁺   M 63-32-11-10-16-132
Gn 2,2.3; 7,11; 8,4(bis)
seventh Gn 2,2; τὰ ἕβδομα *seven years' work* Gn
29,27

ἐγγαστρίμυθος,-ος,-ον   A 4-8-3-0-0-15
Lv 19,31; 20,6.27; Dt 18,11; 1 Sm 28,3
ventriloquizing 1 Sm 28,7; ὁ ἐγγαστρίμυθος
ventriloquist Lv 19,31; *familiar spirit* (of such a
pers.) 1 Sm 28,8
Cf. HARLÉ 1988, 172

ἐγγίζω⁺   V 40-18-46-25-29-158
Gn 12,11; 18,23; 19,9; 27,21.22
to bring near, to bring up to [τινα πρός τινα] Gn
48,10; *to approach* [τινι] Gn 27,21; [πρός τινα]
Ex 19,21; [εἴς τι] Jb 33,22; [ἕως τινός] Sir
37,30(33); *to be next of kin* [τινι] Lv 21,3; *to be
on the point of ...* [+inf.] Gn 12,11; *Hos 12,7
ἔγγιζε *draw near (to your God)* corr.? ἔλπιζε
for MT קוה *hope, wait (for your God)*, cpr. Ez
36,8; *Is 8,15 ἐγγιοῦσιν -נגשׁו *they draw near* for
MT נוקשׁו *they shall be spared*
Cf. CARAGOUNIS 1989, 13-15; CIMOSA 1985, 72-73;
FERNANDEZ MARCOS 1980, 357-360; HELBING 1928, 230-
232; WALTERS 1973, 112; →NIDNTT; TWNT
(→ προσ-, συν-)

ἐγγίων,-ων,-ον   A 0-1-0-2-0-3
1 Kgs 20(21), 2; Ru 3,12; Neh 13,4
nearer

ἐγγλύφω   V 0-0-0-1-1-2
Jb 19,24; 1 Mc 13,29
to carve

ἔγγραπτος,-ος,-ον   A 0-0-0-1-0-1
Ps 149,9
inscribed (sc. in the Scripture)

ἐγγράφω⁺   V 1-0-0-1-1-3
Ex 36(39),21; Dnᴸˣˣ 12,1; 1 Mc 13,40
to write down, to inscribe Ex 36(39),21; *to enroll*
1 Mc 13,40

ἐγγυάομαι   V 0-0-0-5-4-9
Prv 6,1.3; 17,18; 19,28; 28,17
to give surety for [τινα] Prv 6,1; *to betroth* [τινι]
Tobˢ 6,13; *to secure* [abs.] Sir 8,13

ἐγγύη,-ης   N1F 0-0-0-2-2-4
Prv 17,18; 22,26; Sir 29,19
surety, security

Cf. SPICQ 1982, 185-190

ἐγγύθεν D 0-2-1-0-0-3
Jos 6,13; 9,16; Ez 7,5
from close by, from near at hand Jos 6,13;
[τινος] Jos 9,16
Cf. SPICQ 1982, 185-190

ἔγγυος,-ος,-ον⁺ A 0-0-0-0-5-5
2 Mc 10,28; Sir 29,15(bis).16(bis)
reliable 2 Mc 10,28; ὁ ἔγγυος *giver of security or*
pledge (=ἐγγυητής) Sir 29,15

ἐγγύς⁺ D 12-4-17-14-12-59
Gn 19,20; 45,10; Ex 13,17; 32,27; Lv 21,2
near, near at hand Gn 19,20; *close (relative)* Tob
3,15; ἐγγύς τινος *near by* 1 Mc 4,18; οἱ ἐγγύς
who were near Est 9,20; ὁ ἔγγιστα *neighbour* Ex
32,27; *Jb 13,18 ἐγγύς εἰμι -קרבתי *I am near*
for MT ערכתי *I have drawn up*
Cf. LE BOULLUEC 1989, 159.326; nidntt

ἐγγύτατος,-η,-ον A 0-0-0-2-0-2
Jb 6,15; 19,15
nearest of kin [τινος]

ἐγείρω⁺ V 3-10-10-18-16-57
Gn 41,4.7; 49,9; Jgs 2,16
A: *to awaken, to rouse, to stir up* [τινα] Gn 49,9;
to raise (up) [τινα] Jgs 2,16; *to set up, to erect*
[τι] 1 Ezr 5,43; P: *to rouse oneself* Gn 41,4;
ἐγρήγορα *to be awake* Jer 1,12; *Ez 38,14
ἐγερθήσῃ -תער *you will stir yourself* for MT תדע
will you (not) know?; *Prv 28,2 ἐγείρονται -שרו
(*quarrels*) *arise* for MT שריה *its princes*
(ἀν-, δι-, ἐξ-, ἐπ-, συν-)

ἔγερσις,-εως⁺ N3F 0-1-0-1-1-3
Jgsᴬ 7,19; Ps 138(139),2; 1 Ezr 5,59
awaking Jgsᴬ 7,19; *raising* 1 Ezr 5,59

ἐγκάθετος,-ος,-ον⁺ A 0-0-0-2-0-2
Jb 19,12; 31,9
laid waiting Jb 31,9; *set in ambush* Jb 19,12

ἐγκάθημαι V 16-3-3-1-1-24
Gn 49,17; Ex 23,31.33; 34,12.15
to lie in wait Gn 49,17; *to lie* Ez 29,3; *to dwell*
Ex 23,31; *to encamp* Nm 22,5
Cf. TOV 1984 (A), 69 (Gn 49,17)

ἐγκαθίζω V 0-2-1-0-2-5
Jos 8,9; 1 Kgs 20(21),10; Ez 35,5; 1 Mc 10,52;
Sir 8,11
to set [τινα] 1 Kgs 20(21),10; *to sit in or upon*
[ἐπί τινος] 1 Mc 10,52; *to lie in wait* [intrans.]
Jos 8,9
Cf. HELBING 1928, 269

ἐγκαίνια,-ων⁺ N2N 0-0-0-5-0-5

Dnᵀʰ 3,2; Ezr 6,16.17; Neh 12,27(bis)
feast of renovation or *consecration*; neol.

ἐγκαινίζω⁺ V 2-4-3-1-5-15
Dt 20,5(bis); 1 Sm 11,14; 1 Kgs 8,63; 2 Chr 7,5
to renew, to restore 1 Sm 11,14; *to inaugurate, to*
consecrate Dt 20,5; *Is 41,1 ἐγκαινίζεσθε
-החרישו *renew, be renewed* for MT החרישו *be*
silent, see also Is 45,16; *Is 16,11 ἐνεκαίνισας
-חרשת *you have renewed* for MT חרש (*Kir*)*heres*;
neol.
Cf. SPICQ 1982, 185-190; →TWNT

ἐγκαινισμός,-οῦ N2M 3-1-0-4-5-13
Nm 7,10.11.84; 2 Chr 7,9; Ps 29(30),1
consecration, dedication; neol.

ἐγκαίνωσις,-εως N3F 1-0-0-0-0-1
Nm 7,88
consecration, dedication; neol.

ἐγκαίω V 0-0-0-0-1-1
2 Mc 2,29
to paint in encaustic (i.e. with colours mixed
with wax)

ἐγκαλέω⁺ V 1-0-1-1-3-6
Ex 22,8; Zech 1,4; Prv 19,5; 2 Mc 5,8; Wis 12,12
to call in (a debt) [τι] Ex 22,8; *to accuse* (abs.)
Prv 19,5; *to bring a charge against* [τινι] Zech
1,4; P: *to be accused before* [πρός τινα] 2 Mc 5,8
Cf. LE BOULLUEC 1989, 226 (Ex 22,8); HELBING 1928,
269; PRIJS 1948, 3

ἔγκαρπος,-ος,-ον A 0-0-1-0-0-1
Jer 38(31),12
fruitful

ἐγκαρτερέω V 0-0-0-0-1-1
4 Mc 14,9
to persevere, to hold out

ἔγκατα,-ων N2N 0-0-0-4-2-6
Ps 50(51),12; 108(109),18; Jb 21,24; 41,7; Tobˢ
6,4
inwards, entrails Ps 50(51),12; *the inside of the*
body Sir 21,14; *Jb 41,7 ἔγκατα -גוה (*his*) *insides*
for MT גאוה *pride*

ἐγκατάλειμμα,-ατος N3N 2-0-1-4-0-7
Dt 28,5.17; Jer 11,23; Ps 36(37),37.38
remnant, residue Jer 11,23; *Dt 28,5.17
ἐγκαταλείμματα -שאר *remnant, surplus* for
MT משארת?
Cf. CAIRD 1972, 126 (Dt 28,5.17); TOV 1984 (A), 68

ἐγκαταλείπω⁺ V 12-55-49-42-29-187
Gn 24,27; 28,15; Lv 26,43; Nm 10,31; Dt 4,31
A: *to leave behind, to desert, to forsake* Gn
28,15; P: *to be left behind* Lv 26,43; *Is 17,9

ἐγκαταλελειμμέναι -עזובות deserted for MT מעזו
of his strength; *Is 17,9 ὅν τρόπον ἐγκατέλιπον
-כ/עזובו for MT כעזובה like the deserted; *Hos
11,9 ἐγκαταλίπω -יאזוב? I will abandon for MT
אשוב I will again (destroy)
Cf. SPICQ 1988, 223-226

ἐγκαταλιμπάνω   V 0-0-0-1-0-1
Ps 118(119),53
to forsake

ἐγκαταπαίζω   V 0-0-0-2-0-2
Jb 40,19; 41,25
to mock at [τινα]; neol.

ἐγκαυχάομαι⁺   V 0-0-0-4-0-4
Ps 51(52),3; 73(74),4; 96(97),7; 105(106),47
to pride oneself in, to glory in [ἔν τινι] Ps
51(52),3; to exult Ps 73(74),4; neol.?
Cf. CAIRD 1972, 126; HELBING 1928, 260-261; TWNT

ἔγκειμαι   V 2-0-0-1-0-3
Gn 8,21; 34,19; Est 9,3
to be involved with [τινι] Gn 34,19; to weigh
upon [τινι] Est 9,3; to be inclined to [ἐπί τι] Gn
8,21
Cf. HELBING 1928, 269-270

ἐγκεντρίζω⁺   V 0-0-0-0-1-1
Wis 16,11
to goad, to spur on
Cf. CAIRD 1972, 126

ἐγκηδεύω   V 0-0-0-0-1-1
4 Mc 17,9
to bury (in); neol.?

ἐγκισσάω   V 4-0-0-0-0-4
Gn 30,39.41(bis); 31,10
to conceive; neol.
Cf. CAIRD 1972, 126-127; HARL 1986, 233

ἐγκλείω   V 0-0-1-0-0-1
Ez 3,24
to shut in, to shut up

ἔγκληρος,-ος,-ον   A 1-0-0-0-0-1
Dt 4,20
having a share of inheritance

ἐγκλοιόομαι   V 0-0-0-1-0-1
Prv 6,21
to enclose as with a collar; neol.

ἐγκοίλια,-ων   N2N 2-0-0-0-0-2
Lv 1,9.13
entrails

ἐγκοιλότερος,-α,-ον   A 2-0-0-0-0-2
Lv 13,30.31
comp. of ἔγκοιλος; deeper, beneath, lower

ἐγκολαπτός,-ός,-όν   A 0-2-0-0-0-2

1 Kgs 6,29.32
engraved, sculptured

ἐγκολάπτω   V 0-2-0-0-0-2
1 Kgs 6,32.35
to cut or carve upon

ἐγκολλάομαι   V 0-0-1-0-0-1
Zech 14,5
to be joined [ἔως τινός]
Cf. LEE 1969, 239

ἔγκοπος,-ος,-ον   A 0-0-1-2-0-3
Is 43,23; Jb 19,2; Eccl 1,8
wearied, weary Is 43,23; ἔγκοπον ποιέω to make
weary Jb 19,2

ἐγκοσμέομαι   V 0-0-0-0-1-1
4 Mc 6,2
to be adorned

ἐγκοτέω   V 1-0-0-1-0-2
Gn 27,41; Ps 54(55),4
to be angry with [τινι]

ἐγκότημα,-ατος   N3N 0-0-1-0-0-1
Jer 31(48),39
anger, hatred

ἐγκράτεια,-ας⁺   N1F 0-0-0-0-1-1
4 Mc 5,34
self-control
Cf. SPICQ 1978, 61-63

ἐγκρατεύομαι⁺   V 1-1-0-0-0-2
Gn 43,31; 1 Sm 13,12
to exercise self-control, to restrain oneself Gn
43,31; to force oneself 1 Sm 13,12
Cf. CAIRD 1972, 127 (1 Sm 13,12)

ἐγκρατέω   V 1-0-0-0-0-1
Ex 9,2
to exercise control over [τινος]

ἐγκρατής,-ής,-ές⁺   A 0-0-0-0-10-10
2 Mc 8,30; 10,15.17; 13,13; Wis 8,21
having possession of [τινος] Sir 15,1; master of
oneself, self-controlled Sir 26,15; ἐγκρατής
γίγνομαι [τνος] to seize, to take possession of
2 Mc 8,30

ἐγκρίς,-ίδος   N3F 2-0-0-0-0-2
Ex 16,31; Nm 11,8
a cake made with oil and honey

ἐγκρούω   V 0-3-0-0-0-3
Jgsᴬ 4,21; Jgs 16,13
to knock, to hammer in

ἐγκρύπτω⁺   V 0-2-3-1-1-7
Jos 7,21.22; Ez 4,12; Hos 13,12; Am 9,3
to hide, to conceal in Jos 7,21; ἐγκρύπτω
(ἐγκρυφίαν) to bake a cake Ez 4,12; see

ἐγκρυφίας
Cf. HARL 1986, 174
ἐγκρυφίας,-ου N1M 3-3-2-0-0-8
Gn 18,6; Ex 12,39; Nm 11,8; 1 Kgs 17,12.13
cake baked hidden in the ashes; see ἐγκρύπτω

ἐγκτάομαι V 1-0-0-0-0-1
Gn 34,10
to acquire possessions in (a foreign land)

ἔγκτησις,-εως N3F 1-0-0-0-0-1
Lv 25,16
estate, property, possession

ἔγκτητος,-ος,-ον A 3-0-0-0-0-3
Lv 14,34; 22,11; Nm 31,9
possessed (in a foreign country), acquired; neol.

ἐγκύκλιος,-ος,-ον A 0-0-0-1-0-1
DnᴸˣˣΧ 4,37b
circular; ἐγκύκλιος ἐπιστολή circular letter,
encyclical letter

ἐγκυλίομαι V 0-0-0-1-2-3
Prv 7,18; Sir 23,12; 37,3
to be involved in [τινι] (metaph.) Prv 7,18; [ἔν
τινι] Sir 23,12; [+inf.] Sir 37,3
Cf. HELBING 1928, 270

ἔγκυος,-ος,-ον⁺ A 0-0-0-0-1-1
Sir 42,10
pregnant

ἐγκύπτω V 0-0-0-0-1-1
Belᴸˣˣ 40
to stoop down

ἐγκωμιάζω V 0-0-0-5-0-5
Prv 12,8; 27,2.21; 28,4; 29,2
to praise, to laud, to extol [τι] Prv 12,8; *Prv 29,2
ἐγκωμιαζομένων -ברכות/ב when (the righteous)
are praised for MT רבות/ב when (the righteous)
become numerous

ἐγκώμιον,-ου N2N 0-0-0-2-0-2
Prv 10,7; Est 2,23
eulogy

ἐγρήγορος,-ος,-ον A 0-0-0-1-0-1
Lam 4,14
watchful; *Lam 4,14 ἐγρήγοροι -עירים?
watchmen for MT עורים blind; neol.

ἐγχάσκω V 0-0-0-0-1-1
1 Ezr 4,19
to gape

ἐγχειρέω V 0-1-3-0-0-4
2 Chr 23,18; Jer 18,22; 28(51),12; 30(49),10
to take in hand, to undertake, to attempt [τι] Jer
18,22; to make an attempt or a beginning [abs.]
Jer 28(51),12; to lay hands on, to attack [τινι]

(metaph.) Jer 30(49),10; to commit [τι] 2 Chr
23,18
(→ κατ-)

ἐγχείρημα,-ατος N3N 0-0-2-0-0-2
Jer 23,20; 37(30),24
undertaking, attempt

ἐγχειρίδιον,-ου N2N 1-0-4-0-1-6
Ex 20,25; Jer 27(50),42; Ez 21,8.9.10
dagger Ez 21,8; hand-knife, tool for flint-
knapping Ex 20,25
Cf. CAIRD 1972, 127

ἐγχέω V 2-3-2-0-0-7
Ex 24,6; Nm 35,33; Jgsᴬ 6,19; 2 Kgs 4,41; 2 Chr
36,5d
to pour in [τι εἴς τι] Ex 24,6; to pour out for [τί
τινι] 2 Kgs 4,41

ἐγχρίω⁺ V 0-0-1-0-4-5
Jer 4,30; Tob 6,9; Tobᴮᴬ 11,8; Tobˢ 2,10
to anoint Tob 6,9; ἐγχρίω τοὺς ὀφθαλμούς τινι
to paint the eyes with Jer 4,30

ἐγχρονίζω V 0-0-0-3-0-3
Prv 9,18a; 10,28; 23,30
to delay in [ἔν τινι] Prv 9,18; to be long about,
to delay [ἔν τινι] (metaph.) Prv 23,30; to
continue in [τινι] Prv 10,28
Cf. HELBING 1928, 270

ἐγχώριος,-ος,-ον A 5-1-0-0-2-8
Gn 34,1; Ex 12,49; Lv 18,26; 24,22; Nm 15,29
in or of that country 1 Ezr 6,24; ὁ ἐγχώριος
inhabitant, native Gn 34,1
Cf. LE BOULLUEC 1989, 155

ἐγώ⁺ R 1824-2459-2672-3782-1792-12529
Gn 2,23(bis); 3,12(bis).13
acc. ἐμέ, με; gen. ἐμοῦ, μου; dat. ἐμοῖ, μοι; I
Gn 2,23; ἐγώ εἰμί used as personal pronoun for
אנכי I (semit.) Jgs 6,18; Jgsᴮ 5,13(bis); *Ps
101(102),24 μοι -אלי (tell) me for MT אלי my
God; *Jb 17,16 μετ'ἐμοῦ -ידי/ב or בׇי/ב at my
side, with me for MT ברי the bars (of Sheol); *Jb
30,14 μοι -אתי? against me for MT יאתיו they
come; *Jgsᴬ 11,36 εἰ ἐν ἐμοί -בי/ה could (you)
for me? for MT אבי my father (double transl.)
Cf. BARTHELEMY 1963, 69-78; THACKERAY 1923, 23.26;
→NIDNTT; TWNT

ἔγωγε R 0-0-0-0-2-2
4 Mc 8,10; 16,6
I (strengthened form: I at least, I for my part)

ἐδαφίζω⁺ V 0-0-5-1-0-6
Is 3,26; Ez 31,12; Hos 10,14; 14,1; Na 3,10
to dash to the ground [τινα] Hos 10,14; to level

with the ground [τινα] Is 3,26

ἔδαφος,-ους⁺						N3N 1-3-8-3-9-24
Nm 5,17; 1 Kgs 6,15.16.30; Is 25,12
floor Nm 5,17; *bottom* Dnᵀʰ 6,25; *pavement* Sir
20,18; *ground* Jdt 5,18

ἔδεσμα,-ατος						N3N 6-1-0-3-6-16
Gn 27,4.7.9.14.17
prime meat, delicacies Gn 27,4; *select food* Sir
29,22; *1 Sm 15,9 ἐδεσμάτων -שמנים? *(of the fat
animals,) of the prime meat* for MT משנים *of the
second* or *the double portions*?; *Ps 54(55),15
ἐδέσματα -סעורה (late Hebrew) *food* for MT
סור *council*
Cf. HARL 1986, 215 (Gn 27,5)

ἔδρα,-ας						N1F 1-6-0-0-0-7
Dt 28,27; 1 Sm 5,3.9(bis).12
hind parts, buttocks? or (better) *seat, abode,
residence, locality*? 1 Sm 5,9; πατάσσω εἰς τὰς
ἔδρας αὐτῶν *to strike them (with an army) in
their localities (Ashdod and its coast)* (Vetus
Latina *et percussit illos in domibus eorum, in
Azotum et regiones eius*) 1 Sm 5,3; ἐποίησαν
ἑαυτοῖς ἔδρας *they made themselves (images
of) the* ἔδραι 1 Sm 5,9
Cf. LUST 1992

ἑδράζω						V 0-0-0-1-2-3
Prv 8,25; Wis 4,3; Sir 22,17
A: *to establish, to lay* Wis 4,3; P: *to be settled, to
be created* Prv 8,25; *to be settled* (metaph.) Sir
22,17

ἑδρεύω
(→ ἐν-, παρ-, προσ-, συν-)

ἑδριάζω
(→ συν-)

ἕζομαι
(→ καθ-)

ἐθελοκωφέω						V 0-0-0-0-1-1
Sir 19,27
to affect deafness, to pretend not to hear; neol.

ἐθίζω⁺						V 0-0-0-0-2-2
2 Mc 14,30; Sir 23,9
to accustom to [τινι] Sir 23,9; εἰθισμένος *usual*
2 Mc 14,30
(→ συν-)

ἐθισμός,-οῦ						N2M 1-1-0-0-4-6
Gn 31,35; 1 Kgs 18,28; Jdt 13,10; 2 Mc 4,11;
12,38
custom, habit 1 Kgs 18,28; τὰ κατ' ἐθισμὸν τῶν
γυναικῶν *the things according to the custom of
women, menstruation* Gn 31,35

ἐθνάρχης,-ου⁺						N1M 0-0-0-0-3-3
1 Mc 14,47; 15,1.2
ethnarch (title of official)
Cf. SMALLWOOD 1976, 4

ἐθνηδόν						D 0-0-0-0-1-1
4 Mc 2,19
as a whole nation; neol.

ἐθνοπάτωρ,-ορος					N3M 0-0-0-0-1-1
4 Mc 16,20
father of the nation, father of our nation; neol.

ἐθνόπληθος,-ους					N3M 0-0-0-0-1-1
4 Mc 7,11
nation, people, crowd composed of the nation or
people or *countrymen*; neol.

ἔθνος,-ους⁺					N3N 151-78-348-157-269-1003
Gn 10,5(bis).20.31.32
stereotyped rendition of גוי; *nation, people* Gn
10,5; *non-Jews, Gentiles* Ps 2,1; *the Jewish nation*
(spoken of by Gentiles) 2 Mc 11,25; *Prv 26,3
ἔθνει -לגוי/גו *for a nation* for MT לגו/גו *for the back*;
*Na 3,3 ἔθνεσιν αὐτῆς -ל/גוי-גויה *to her nations*
for MT גו/לגויה ◊ גו *to her corpses*; *Prv 30,31 ἔθνει
-עם *nation* for MT עם *with*; *Is 33,8 ἐθνῶν -עמים
peoples for MT ערים *cities*; *Nm 24,7 ἐθνῶν
-עמים *nations* for MT מים *water*; see λαός
Cf. HARL 1986, 47.58-59; MONSENGWO-PASINYA 1980,
366; NESTLE 1895, 288-290; →TWNT

ἔθος,-ους⁺						N3N 0-0-0-0-6-6
1 Mc 10,89; 2 Mc 11,25; 13,4; 4 Mc 18,5; Wis
14,16
custom, habit 2 Mc 11,25; πάτρια ἔθη *habits of
the fathers, manner of life of the fathers* 4 Mc
18,5; ἔθος ἐστι [+inf.] *it's customary to* 1 Mc
10,89; (τὸ ἀσεβὲς) ἔθος *(impious) custom* (as
opposed to νόμος *law*) Wis 14,16
→NIDNTT

εἰ⁺						X 119-243-122-170-151-805
Gn 4,14; 8,7.8; 13,9(bis)
if [+ind.] (to express a condition thought of as
real or to denote assumptions relating to what
has already happened) Gn 4,14; [+subj.] Jgs
11,9; *that* (after verbs of emotion) 2 Mc 14,28;
certainly not (in aposiopesis) Gn 14,23; *whether*
[+dir. question] Am 3,3; *whether* [+indir.
question] 2 Kgs 1,2; *not* (after an oath in a
sense practically equivalent to a negative) Ps
94(95),11; εἰ μή *verily* (in oaths equivalent to a
positive) 1 Kgs 21,23; εἰ ... ἤ ... *whether... or...*
Gn 27,21; εἰ δὲ μή *if not, otherwise* (after
affirm. cl.) Gn 30,1; (after neg. cl.) Jb 32,22; εἰ

πως *if perhaps, if somehow* 1 Kgs 21,31; εἰ μήν
surely Ez 33,27
Cf. COLEMAN 1927, 159-167; CONYBEARE 1981, §§99-103;
STERENBERG 1908

εἰδέχθεια,-ας   N1F 0-0-0-0-1-1
Wis 16,3
odious or *ugly look*; neol.

εἴδησις,-εως   N3F 0-0-0-0-1-1
Sir 42,18
knowledge

εἶδον
aor. of ὁράω
Cf. WALTERS 1973, 197-204
(→ προσ-)

εἶδος,-ους⁺   N3N 22-10-9-8-10-59
Gn 29,17; 32,31(bis).32; 39,6
appearance Gn 29,17; *form, shape* Gn 41,2;
visible form (of God) Gn 32,31; *pattern* Ex 26,30;
kind Jer 15,3; ἀγαθὸς τῷ εἴδει *handsome* 1 Sm
16,18; καλὴ τῷ εἴδει *beautiful* 2 Sm 13,1
Cf. HARL 1986, 53.244; →NIDNTT

εἰδώλιον,-ου⁺   N2N 0-0-0-1-4-5
DnᴸˣˣX 1,2; 1 Ezr 2,7; 1 Mc 1,47; 10,83; BelᴸˣX 10
idol's temple; neol.
Cf. WALTERS 1973, 56

εἰδωλόθυτος,-ος,-ον⁺   A 0-0-0-0-1-1
4 Mc 5,2
sacrificed to idols; εἰδωλόθυτα *meats offered to
idols*; neol.
Cf. HORSLEY 1982, 36-37

εἴδωλον,-ου⁺   N2N 12-21-31-8-19-91
Gn 31,19.34.35; Ex 20,4; Lv 19,4
image of god, idol Gn 31,19; *Is 41,28 ἀπὸ τῶν
εἰδώλων -מ/אלהים *from the idols* for MT מ/אלה
from them
Cf. LE BOULLUEC 1989, 205-206; → NIDNTT; TWNT

εἴθε   I 0-0-0-1-2-3
Jb 9,33; 2 Mc 4,22; 15,13
would that (he were) [+ind. hist. tense] (for
unattained wish) Jb 9,33; [+inf.] 2 Mc 15,13

εἰκάζω   V 0-0-1-0-3-4
Jer 26(46),23; Wis 8,8; 9,16; 19,18
to conjecture, to guess
(→ ἀπ-)

εἰκάς,-άδος   N3F 5-1-7-4-11-28
Gn 7,11; 8,4.14; Ex 12,18; Nm 10,11
the twentieth day of the month Nm 10,11;
ἑβδόμη καὶ εἰκάδι *on the twenty-seventh day*
Gn 7,11

εἰκεύομαι

(→ ἐπι-)

εἰκῆ⁺   D 0-0-0-1-0-1
Prv 28,25
at random, rashly
Cf. HORSLEY 1982, 81

εἰκονίζω
(→ ἐξ-)

εἰκοσαετής,-ής,-ές   A 22-5-0-1-1-29
Ex 30,14; 39(38),3; Lv 27,3; Nm 1,3.18
of twenty years, twenty years old

εἴκοσι⁺   M 46-137-37-42-32-294
Gn 6,3; 11,25; 18,31(bis); 23,1
twenty

εἰκοστός,-ή,-όν   M 0-18-3-5-0-26
1 Kgs 15,8.9; 16,6; 2 Kgs 12,7; 13,1
twentieth

εἰκότως   D 0-0-0-0-1-1
4 Mc 9,2
with good reason

εἴκω⁺   V 0-0-0-0-2-2
4 Mc 1,6; Wis 18,25
to give way to [τινι] 4 Mc 1,6; *to withdraw from*
Wis 18,25
Cf. LARCHER 1985, 1040
(→ συν-, ὑπ-)

εἰκών,-όνος⁺   N3F 6-2-6-33-9-56
Gn 1,26.27; 5,1.3; 9,6
image Gn 1,26; *imitation* or *reproduction of an
archetype* Wis 7,26; *image of god, idol* 2 Kgs
11,18; *Hos 13,2 κατ' εἰκόνα -ב/תמונה *according
to the image* or כ/תבנית *according to the likeness*
for MT כ/תבונם *according to their craft, skilfully*
Cf. HARL 1986, 95-96; KOONCE 1988, 108-110; LARCHER
1983, 268-269; 1984, 504-505; →NIDNTT

εἰλέω or εἴλεω   V 0-1-1-0-0-2
2 Kgs 2,8; Is 11,5
A: *to roll up tight* 2 Kgs 2,8; P: *to be enclosed, to
be covered* Is 11,5
(→ ἀν-, ἀπ-, ἐν-, κατ-)

εἰλικρινής,-ής,-ές⁺   A 0-0-0-0-1-1
Wis 7,25
pure
Cf. SPICQ 1982, 211-214

εἰμί (εἶναι)⁺   V 1730-1486-1362-1167-1202-6947
Gn 1,2.6.7.14.15
to be, to exist Gn 1,7; *to be* [+pred.] Gn 1,2; *to
be* [+adv.] Jb 9,2; *to be occupied with* [τινος]
2 Chr 30,17; *to have* [τινι] Jb 1,12; ἔστι
(impers.) *it is possible* Wis 5,10; εἰμι ὁ ὤν *I am
the one who is, I am the being* Ex 3,14; εἰμι

πρός τινος *to become attached to* Gn 29,34;
ἔσομαί τινος *to be about to* 2 Sm 10,11; ἐγώ
εἰμι see ἐγώ; *Jer 1,6 ὁ ὤν -◊ היה *the being* for
MT אהה *Ah*

Cf. AERTS 1965, 52-209; LE BOULLUEC 1989, 92; HORSLEY
1989, 56; KILPATRICK 1963, 133; →NIDNTT

(→ ἀπ-, διέξ-, εἰσ-, ἔν-, ἔξ-, ἔπ-, πάρ-, συμπάρ-,
συμπρόσ-, σύν-)

εἵνεκεν⁺   P 6-1-1-1-0-9
Gn 18,5; 19,8; 22,16; 38,26; Nm 10,31
see εἵνεκα

εἴπερ⁺   C 0-0-0-0-2-2
Jdt 6,9; Susᵀʰ 54
if really, if indeed

εἶπον⁺   V 1031-1850-732-492-503-4608
Gn 1,3.6.9.11.14
aor. of λέγω

(→ ἀντ-, ἀπ-, κατ-, προσ-, συν-)

εἴργω   V 0-0-0-0-3-3
1 Ezr 5,69.71; 3 Mc 3,18
to hinder, to prevent from [τινος]

(→ ἀπ-)

εἰρηνεύω⁺   V 0-4-0-6-9-19
1 Kgs 22,45; 2 Chr 14,4.5; 20,30; Jb 3,26
to live in prosperity Jb 5,24; *to live in community,
to live together with* [τινι] Jb 5,23; *to bring peace
to, to reconcile* [abs.] 2 Chr 14,5(4); *to keep
peace, to live peaceably* 1 Kgs 22,45

Cf. VAN LEEUWEN 1940, 13-117

εἰρήνη,-ης⁺   N1F 7-92-80-46-69-294
Gn 15,15; 26,29; Ex 18,23; Lv 26,6; Nm 6,26
peace 1 Mc 12,22; *peace-treaty* Ezr 5,7; stereotyped rendering of שׁלום (semit.): *prosperity, wel-
fare* (of pers.) Jgs 6,23; *prosperity* (of land) Lv
26,6; *eternal rest* Wis 3,3; εἰρήνη *all is well*
2 Kgs 5,22; ὁ ἄνθρωπος τῆς εἰρήνης μου *my
friend* Ps 40(41),10, cpr. Jer 20,10; 54(38),20;
ἐρωτάω τινὰ (τὰ) εἰς εἰρήνην *to greet a person,
to inquire after his health* Jgsᴮ 18,15; ἐπερωτάω
εἰς εἰρήνην τοῦ πολέμου *to ask how the war is
going* 2 Sm 11,7; *Ps 75(76),3 εἰρήνη -שׁלום (in)
peace* for MT שׁלם *Salem*; *Mi 2,8 εἰρήνης -שׁלום
his peace for MT שׁלמה *a garment*; *Ez 34,29
εἰρήνης -שׁלום *of peace* for MT לשׁם/ל *of name*

Cf. GEHMAN 1972 (A), 107-108; GOETTSBERGER 1906,
246; LARCHER 1983, 277-278; SANTI AMANTINI 1979-80,
467-495; SPICQ 1982, 215-230; TOV 1987, 151; VAN
LEEUWEN 1940, 13-117; →NIDNTT; TWNT

εἰρηνικός,-ή,-όν⁺   A 11-15-6-4-13-49
Gn 34,21; 37,4; 42,11.19.31

peaceful 1 Chr 12,39; *peaceable* Gn 34,21;
εἰρηνικὰς (sc. θυσίας) *peace- (offerings)* 1 Sm
11,15; *Mi 7,3 εἰρηνικούς -שׁלום *peaceful* for
MT שׁלום *retribution*

Cf. DANIEL 1966, 289-295; HARL 1986, 259-260.279;
→TWNT

εἰρηνικῶς   D 0-0-0-0-4-4
1 Mc 5,25; 7,29.33; 2 Mc 10,12
peaceably

εἰρηνοποιέω⁺   V 0-0-0-1-0-1
Prv 10,10
to make peace, to promote well-being; neol.

Cf. SPICQ 1982, 229-230; →TWNT

εἱρκτή,-ῆς   N1F 0-0-0-0-1-1
Wis 17,15
prison

εἴρω

(→ ἐν-)

εἰρωνεία,-ας   N1F 0-0-0-0-1-1
2 Mc 13,3
feigning, hypocrisy, dissimulation

εἷς, μία, ἕν⁺   M 388-277-130-123-134-1052
Gn 1,5.9; 2,11.21.24
one 2 Chr 9,13; *first* Gn 1,5; *one, the same* Gn
1,9; *one, a, an* (indefinite) Gn 21,15; εἷς
ἕκαστος *each one* 4 Mc 4,26; οὐ μίαν οὐδὲ
δύο *not once nor twice* 2 Kgs 6,10; εἷς ... εἷς ...
the one ... the other ... Neh 4,11; *1 Chr 24,6 εἷς
-אחד *one* for MT אחז *seized by, pointed to*; *Am
7,1 εἷς -אחד *one* for MT אחר *after*, see also Gn
22,13; Ez 10,11; *Ps 108(109),13 μιᾷ -אחד *one*
for MT אחר *an other*, see also Gn 43,14

εἰς⁵   P 1198-2033-1435-1297-1475-7438
Gn 1,9(bis).14(ter)
[τι, τινα]: *into, to* Gn 1,9; *in* Nm 35,33; *for*
(time) Ex 14,13; *to the number of* 1 Sm 15,29; *by*
(distributive) 1 Sm 10,21; *towards, in regard to*
4 Mc 11,8; *for* (purpose) Gn 1,14; *to* (forming a
pred. with εἶναι and γίγνεσθαι) Ex 2,10;
[τινος]: *to* (mostly of proper names) 1 Kgs 2,6;
Mal 2,31 εἰς -בער (go) after for MT בת
daughter

Cf. SOISALON-SOININEN 1982, 190-200

εἰσάγω⁺   V 48-28-42-25-15-158
Gn 6,19; 7,2; 8,9; 12,15; 29,13
to bring in, to introduce [τινα] Gn 47,7; *to bring
in* [τι] Ex 23,10; *to lead in(to), to bring in, to
introduce* [τι εἴς τι] Gn 6,19; [τινα ἐπί τι] Ez
8,7; [τι πρός τι] 3 Mc 5,2; [τι πρός τινα] Gn
7,2; [τινι] Gn 39,14; *to put in* [τι εἴς τι] Ex

25,14; *to carry into* [τινα εἴς τι] Eccl 8,10;
εἰσάγω τινά ἐν ἀρᾷ *to bind with an oath* Ez
17,13; *Ez 27,15 εἰσαγομένοις -באים/ה? *to
those who brought in* for MT הובנים *ebony*

εἰσακούω⁺   V 64-37-49-76-23-249
Gn 21,17; 34,17.24; 42,21.22
to hearken, to give ear to [τινος] Ps 4,2; *to hear*
[τι] Jb 34,28
Cf. COX 1981, 251-258; HELBING 1982, 153-154; SPICQ
1982, 231-245; →TWNT

εἰσβάλλω   V 0-0-0-0-2-2
2 Mc 13,13; 14,43
to throw oneself into, to enter [εἴς τι] 2 Mc
13,13; [ἔσω τινός] 2 Mc 14,43

εἰσβλέπω   V 0-0-1-2-0-3
Is 37,17; Jb 6,28; 21,5
to look at or *upon* [abs.] Is 37,17; [εἴς τι] Jb
6,28; [εἴς τινα] Jb 21,5

εἰσδέχομαι⁺   V 0-0-15-0-4-19
Jer 23,3; Ez 11,17; 20,34.41; 22,19
to receive [τινα] Wis 19,16; *to receive into* [τινα
πρός τινα] Hab 2,5; *to gather* [τινα] Ez 11,17
··NIDNTT

εἰσδύω   V 0-0-1-0-1-2
Jer 4,29; 1 Mc 6,46
to crawl (under) [ὑπό τι] 1 Mc 6,46; *to go into,
to enter* [εἴς τι] Jer 4,29

εἴσειμι   V 2-1-0-0-3-6
Ex 28,29.35; 1 Sm 16,6; 2 Mc 3,14; 3 Mc 1,11
to enter, to go into 1 Sm 16,6; [εἴς τι] Ex 28,29;
impft. and fut. of εἰσέρχομαι

εἰσέρχομαι⁺   V 162-247-120-95-76-700
Gn 6,18.20; 7,1.7.9
to go in(to), to enter Gn 7,16; [εἴς τι] Gn 6,18;
[κατά τι] Jos 1,11; [τι] 1 Kgs 22,25; [ἔν τινι]
Jgsᴮ 11,18; *to come in to, to visit* [πρός τινα] Gn
6,20; [ἐπί τινα] Gn 34,27; [εἴς τινα] Dt 33,7;
to enter into [ἔν τινι] (metaph.) Neh 10,30;
*2 Kgs 3,24 καὶ εἰσῆλθον εἰσπορευόμενοι
-ויבא בא *and they went in* for MT בה ויבו?; *Jer
37(30),20 καὶ εἰσελεύσονται -ובאו *and they
went* for MT ויהיו *and they were*; *Na 2,12
εἰσελθεῖν -לבוא/ל *to enter* for MT לביא *lion*
Cf. HARL 1986, 70; HELBING 1928, 83; →TWNT

εἰσκυκλέομαι   V 0-0-0-0-1-1
2 Mc 2,24
to plunge into [τινι]

εἰσκύπτω   V 0-1-0-0-0-1
1 Sm 13,18
to overlook [ἐπί τι] (of a road); neol.?

εἰσοδιάζομαι   V 0-2-0-0-0-2
2 Kgs 12,5; 2 Chr 34,14
to come in (of revenue); neol.?

εἰσόδιον,-ου   N2N 0-0-0-1-0-1
Dnᵀʰ 11,13
entrance, entering

εἴσοδος,-ου⁺   N2F 1-25-12-4-10-52
Gn 30,27; Jos 13,5; Jgsᴬ 1,24.25; Jgsᴮ 1,14
place of entrance Jgs 1,24; *entrance hall,
vestibule* 2 Kgs 23,11; *entering, entrance* 1 Sm
29,6; *that which comes in, influx* Is 66,11; ἐπὶ
τῆς εἰσόδου *on the way* 1 Mc 5,46
Cf. HUSSON 1983, 65-72; →TWNT

εἰσοράω   V 0-0-0-0-1-1
Jdt 4,13
to look upon [τι]

εἰσπέμπω   V 0-0-0-0-1-1
2 Mc 13,20
to send in

εἰσπηδάω⁺   V 0-0-1-0-1-2
Am 5,19; Susᵀʰ 27
to rush in

εἰσπλέω   V 0-0-0-0-2-2
2 Mc 14,1; 4 Mc 13,6
to sail in, to enter

εἰσπορεύομαι⁺   V 55-42-35-14-23-169
Gn 6,4; 7,16; 23,10.18; Ex 1,1
to go in(to), to enter Gn 6,4; *2 Kgs 3,24
εἰσπορευόμενοι -בא *going in* for MT בה *through*
or *in it*; see εἰσέρχομαι
Cf. LEE 1983, 86-88; →TWNT

εἰσσπάομαι   V 1-0-0-0-0-1
Gn 19,10
to draw into oneself [τινα εἴς τι]; neol.

εἰστρέχω⁺   V 0-0-0-0-1-1
2 Mc 5,26
to run in [εἴς τι]

εἰσφέρω⁺   V 25-44-10-9-8-96
Gn 27,10.18.25.33; 37,32
A: *to carry in, to bring in* Gn 27,10; *to gather in*
Dt 28,38; P: *to be brought in* Lv 6,23

εἰσφορά,-ᾶς   N1F 4-0-0-0-0-4
Ex 30,13.14.15.16
contribution, offering
Cf. LE BOULLUEC 1989, 308

εἶτα⁺   D 0-0-0-13-5-18
Jb 5,24; 11,6; 12,2; 13,22; 14,15
then, and then, so then Jb 5,24; *furthermore,
then, next* (transition-word) Wis 14,22

εἴτε⁺   C 0-0-0-1-3-4

Jb 9,21; Sir 41,4(ter)
even if Jb 9,21; εἴτε ... εἴτε ... *whether ... or ...*
Sir 41,4

εἴτοι   C 0-0-0-2-0-2
Ru 3,10(bis)
εἴτοι ... εἴτοι ... *whether ... or ...*

εἴωθα⁺   V 1-0-0-0-3-4
Nm 24,1; 4 Mc 1,12; Sir 37,14; Sus^{l.XX} 13
pft. used as pres.; *to be in the habit of, to be
wont* [+inf.] Sir 37,14; κατὰ τὸ εἰωθός
according to the custom Nm 24,1

ἐκ or ἐξ⁺   P 904-1070-685-520-644-3823
Gn 2,6.9.10.19.23
[τινος]: *out of, forth, from* (motion) Gn 2,6; *out
of* (separation with a group; as partitive gen.)
Jgs^B 15,2; *of* (origin) Ex 2,1; *by* (cause, means)
Nm 1,2; *out of* (material out of which sth is
made) Wis 15,8; *according to, in accordance with*
1 Mc 8,30; *for* (price) LtJ 24; *since, from* (time)
1 Ezr 2,26; *after* (time) Gn 39,10; *on* Gn 6,16;
ἐκ περισσοῦ *extremely* Dn^{Th} 3,22; ἐκ δυνάμεως
εἰς δύναμιν *from strength to strength* (for
special emphasis) Ps 83(84),8; κρίσιν ἐκ τῶν
ἐχθρῶν *judgement on the enemies* (semit.) Is
1,24
Cf. GEHMAN 1972 (A), 95

ἕκαστος,-η,-ον⁺   R 80-74-94-24-84-356
Gn 10,5; 11,7; 13,11; 34,25; 37,19
each Gn 10,5; εἷς ἕκαστος *each one* 4 Mc 4,26;
καθ᾽ ἑκάστην ἡμέραν *every single day* Ex 5,8
Cf. MURAOKA 1990, 19-20

ἑκάτερος,-α,-ον   R 1-0-3-0-10-14
Gn 40,5; Ez 1,11.12; 37,7; Tob^S 5,3
each (of two)

ἑκατέρωθεν   D 0-0-0-0-2-2
4 Mc 6,3; 9,11
on each side, on either hand

ἑκατόν⁺   M 70-74-21-42-42-249
Gn 5,9.12.15.18.21
a hundred Gn 5,9; *Ex 27,18 (ἐφ᾽) ἑκατόν
-ב/מאה (*in*) *a hundred* for MT ב/אמה *in cubits*
Cf. LE BOULLUEC 1989, 279

ἑκατονταετής,-ής,-ές⁺   A 1-0-0-0-0-1
Gn 17,17
a hundred years old

ἑκατονταπλασίων,-ων,-ον⁺   A 0-1-0-0-0-1
2 Sm 24,3
a hundredfold

ἑκατονταπλασίως   D 0-1-0-0-0-1
1 Chr 21,3

a hundred times as much or *many*

ἑκατοντάρχης,-ου⁺   N1M 0-2-0-0-0-2
2 Kgs 11,10.15
leader of a hundred

ἑκατόνταρχος,-ου⁺   N2M 7-14-0-0-1-22
Ex 18,21.25; Nm 31,14.48.52
leader of a hundred, centurion

ἑκατοντάς,-άδος   N3F 0-3-0-0-0-3
1 Sm 29,2; 2 Sm 18,4; 1 Chr 28,1
a hundred

ἑκατοστεύω   V 1-0-0-0-0-1
Gn 26,12
to bear a hundredfold; neol.
Cf. HARL 1986, 213

ἑκατοστός,-ή,-όν   M 0-0-0-0-29-29
1 Mc 1,10.20.54; 2,70; 3,37
hundredth

ἐκβαίνω⁺   V 0-3-1-0-6-10
Jos 4,16.17.18; Is 24,18; Jdt 5,8
to step out of [ἔκ τινος] Is 24,18; *to go out of, to
depart from* [ἔκ τινος] Jos 4,16; *to leave* [ἔκ
τινος] Jdt 5,8; *to disembark* [abs.] 1 Mc 15,4; *to
come out, to turn out* [+pred.] (as a result) Sir
30,8; *to be fulfilled* [abs.] 1 Mc 4,27

ἐκβάλλω⁺   V 29-25-12-16-19-101
Gn 3,24; 4,14; 21,10; Ex 2,17; 6,1
to cast out of, to drive out of Ex 6,1; *to divorce*
Lv 21,7; *Ps 16(17),11 ἐκβάλλοντές με -אשרוני
◊אשר (Aram.) *casting me out* for MT אשרינו *our
steps*; *Ps 108(109),10 ἐκβληθήτωσαν -ינרשו *let
them be cast out* for MT ודרשו/ו *and they seek*;
*Jb 24,12 ἐξεβάλλοντο -◊קיא *they who casted
forth* for MT ינאקו *they groan*
→TWNT

ἔκβασις,-εως⁺   N3F 0-0-0-0-3-3
Wis 2,17; 8,8; 11,14
end, end of life Wis 2,17; *event, result* Wis 11,14;
event Wis 8,8

ἐκβιάζω   V 0-1-0-2-2-5
Jgs^B 14,15; Ps 37(38),13; Prv 16,26; Wis 14,19;
Sus^{l.XX} 19
A: *to do violence to, to force* [τινα] Jgs^B 14,15;
M: *to press upon* [τι] Ps 37(38),13; *to force out,
to dislodge, to expel* [τι] Prv 16,26; *to use
violence against, to rape* [τινα] Sus^{l.XX} 19
Cf. HELBING 1928, 13; LARCHER 1985, 819-820 (Wis
16,19)

ἐκβλαστάνω   V 1-0-1-1-0-3
Nm 17,20; Is 55,10; Jb 38,27
to shoot, to sprout Nm 17,5(20); *to cause to*

grow, to produce Jb 38,27

ἐκβλύζω V 0-0-0-1-0-1
Prv 3,10
to gush out

ἐκβοάω V 0-1-0-0-0-1
2 Kgs 4,36
to cry out

ἐκβολή,-ῆς⁺ N1F 1-0-1-0-0-2
Ex 11,1; Jon 1,5
throwing out Ex 11,1; *jettisoning* Jon 1,5

ἔκβολος,-ος,-ον A 0-0-0-0-1-1
Jdt 11,11
frustrated

ἐκβράζω V 0-0-0-2-2-4
Neh 13,28(bis); 2 Mc 1,12; 5,8
to expel, to drive away

ἐκβρασμός,-οῦ N2M 0-0-1-0-0-1
Na 2,11
trembling, shaking; neol.

ἐκγελάω V 0-0-0-5-1-6
Ps 2,4; 36(37),13; 58(59),9; Neh 2,19; 3,33
to laugh at, to jeer at [τινα] Neh 2,19; [ἐπί τινι]
Neh 3,33

ἐκγεννάω V 0-0-0-1-0-1
Ps 109(110),3
to beget [τινα]; neol.

ἔκγονος,-ος,-ον⁺ A 12-2-8-6-5-33
Gn 48,6; Dt 7,13; 28,4.11(bis)
born of, spring from, young Is 11,8; ἔκγονον
generation Prv 30,11; οἱ ἔκγονοι *descendants*
2 Mc 1,20; τὰ ἔκγονα *offspring* Gn 48,6; τὰ
ἔκγονα τῆς κοιλίας σου *the spring of your body*
Dt 7,13

ἐκγράφω V 0-0-0-1-0-1
Prv 25,1
to write out

ἐκδανείζω V 2-0-0-0-0-2
Ex 22,24; Dt 23,20
to lend (out) at interest
Cf. LEE 1983, 93

ἐκδειματόομαι V 0-0-0-0-1-1
Wis 17,6
to be greatly terrified

ἐκδέρω V 1-1-2-0-0-4
Lv 1,6; 2 Chr 35,11; Mi 2,8; 3,3
to strip off the skin from, to flay

ἐκδέχομαι⁺ V 2-0-6-1-7-16
Gn 43,9; 44,32; Is 57,1; Hos 8,7; 9,6
to receive [τι] Sir 18,14; *to receive from, to gather*
[τινα] Mi 2,12; *to await* [τι] Hos 8,7; *to take or*

understand in a certain sense [τι] 3 Mc 3,22; *to
be surety for* [τινα] Gn 43,9; ἐκδεκτέος
admitted, accepted LtJ 1,56
Cf. HARL 1986, 283; LEE 1983, 59-60; →NIDNTT

ἐκδέω V 0-1-0-0-1-2
Jos 2,18; 2 Mc 15,35
to bind so as to hang from, to fasten to or *on* [τι
εἴς τι] Jos 2,18; [τι ἔκ τινος] 2 Mc 15,35

ἔκδηλος,-ος,-ον⁺ A 0-0-0-0-2-2
3 Mc 3,19; 6,5
conspicuous; ἔκδηλον καθίστημί τι *to make
clear, to show clearly* 3 Mc 3,19; ἔκδηλον
δείκνυμί τι 3 Mc 6,5

ἐκδημία,-ας N1F 0-0-0-0-1-1
3 Mc 4,11
going or *being abroad*
Cf. SPICQ 1982, 246-248

ἐκδιαιτάω V 0-0-0-0-2-2
4 Mc 4,19; 18,5
A: *to make to change one's habits*; P: *to change
one's mode of life from* [τινος] 4 Mc 18,5

ἐκδιδάσκω V 0-0-0-0-3-3
4 Mc 5,23.24; Wis 8,7
to teach thoroughly [τινα] Wis 8,7; [τί τινα]
4 Mc 5,23

ἐκδιδύσκω V 0-2-1-1-0-4
1 Sm 31,8; 2 Sm 23,10; Hos 7,1; Neh 4,17
A: *to strip, to despoil* [τινα] 1 Sm 31,8; [abs.]
Hos 7,1; P: *to be put off* [τι]; see ἐκδύω; neol.

ἐκδίδωμι V 2-5-0-1-11-19
Ex 2,21; Lv 21,3; Jgs 1,14; JgsᴬA 1,15
A: *to give up, to surrender* [τι] Jdt 7,13; *to give
up, to deliver* [τινά τινι] Jdt 2,10; *to put out, to
publish* [τι] Sir prol.,33; *to bring out* [τι] 1 Ezr
1,30; *to pay out to* [τινι] 2 Kgs 12,12(11); *to
produce, to make* [τι] Sir 38,26; M: *to hand over,
to deliver* [τι] Jdt 7,26; [τινα] Jgs 1,14; *to give in
marriage* [τινα] (of daughter) Ex 2,21;
ἐκδίδομαι εἰς ἀπώλειαν *to perish* Dnᴸˣˣ 2,18
Cf. AEJMELAEUS 1991, 26 (Ex 2,21); HELBING 1928, 191-
193
(→ ἀπ-)

ἐκδιηγέομαι⁺ V 0-0-2-2-10-14
Ez 12,16; Hab 1,5; Ps 117(118),17; Jb 12,8; Sir
1,24
to tell (in detail)

ἐκδικάζω V 2-0-0-0-4-6
Lv 19,18; Dt 32,43; 1 Mc 2,67; 9,42; 2 Mc 6,15
to avenge

ἐκδικέω⁺ V 9-10-48-1-21-89

Gn 4,15.24; Ex 7,4; 21,20.21
to avenge [τι] Lv 26,25; [ἐπί τι] Jer 28(51),52;
to avenge, to punish [τινα] Ex 21,20; [ἔκ τινος]
Dt 18,19; [ἐπί τινα] Zph 1,8; *to exact vengeance*
for [τι] 2 Kgs 9,7; ἐκδικούμενα παραλύω *to pay*
penalties, to suffer vengeance Gn 4,15; *Jer
27(50),21 ἐκδίκησον -פקד *avenge* for MT פקד
Pekod (pers. name); *Ez 19,12 ἐξεδικήθη -◊ פקד
she was avenged for MT ◊ פרק *they were torn off*
Cf. HELBING 1928, 37-38; LE BOULLUEC 1989, 219;
WALTERS 1987, 111 (Tob 3,3); →NIDNTT; TWNT

ἐκδίκησις,-εως⁺　　　　　N3F 5-7-37-7-26-82
Ex 12,12; Nm 31,2.3; 33,4; Dt 32,35
vengeance Ex 7,4; ἐκδίκησιν ποιέω ἔν τινι *to*
avenge, to execute vengeance Ex 12,12; neol.?
Cf. HARL 1991, 252; LE BOULLUEC 1989, 35; →TWNT

ἐκδικητής,-οῦ　　　　　N1M 0-0-0-1-0-1
Ps 8,3
avenger, vindicator; neol.?
→TWNT

ἔκδικος,-ος,-ον⁺　　　　　A 0-0-0-0-3-3
4 Mc 15,29; Wis 12,12; Sir 30,6
avenging, maintaining the right Wis 12,12;
ἔκδικος *avenger* 4 Mc 15,29

ἐκδιώκω⁺　　　　　V 1-2-3-9-1-16
Dt 6,19; 1 Chr 8,13; 12,16; Jer 27(50),44;
30,13(49,19)
to chase away Dt 6,19; *to banish* 1 Chr 8,13; *to*
attack, to persecute Ps 68(69),5; *Ps 43(44),17
ἐκδιώκοντος *persecutor* corr. ἐκδικοῦντος for
MT נקם מתנקם ◊ *avenger*

ἔκδοτος,-ος,-ον⁺　　　　　A 0-0-0-0-1-1
Belᵀʰ 22
given up, delivered

ἐκδύω or ἐκδύνω⁺　　　　　V 5-3-7-7-6-28
Gn 37,23; Lv 6,4; 16,23; Nm 20,26.28
A: *to take off, to strip off* [τινά τι] Gn 37,23; *to*
escape [ἔκ τινος] Prv 11,8; M: *to strip oneself*
off, to put off [τι] Lv 6,4; *Jb 30,13 ἐξέδυσαν
γάρ μου -מעילי *they have stripped me off* for MT
יעילו *they help*; see ἐκδιδύσκω
Cf. HELBING 1928, 46

ἐκεῖ⁺　　　　　D 205-279-166-65-83-798
Gn 2,8.11.12; 11,2.7
there, in that place Gn 2,8; *thither* Gn 19,20; *Ez
28,25 ἐκεῖ -שם *there* for MT בם *among them*;
*Ps 49(50),23 ἐκεῖ -שם *there* for MT שם *he puts*,
see also Jer 13,16; *Dt 28,37 ἐκεῖ -שָׁמָּה *there*
for MT שַׁמָּה *horror, desolation*
Cf. SHIPP 1979, 228

ἐκεῖθεν⁺　　　　　D 48-65-20-2-15-150
Gn 2,10; 10,14; 11,8.9; 12,8
thence, from that place

ἐκεῖνος,-η,-ον⁺　　　　　R 164-209-166-85-115-739
Gn 2,12; 6,4(ter).21
that (... *there*) Gn 2,12; *that person, that thing*
Gn 6,21; μετ᾽ ἐκεῖνο *afterwards* Gn 6,4; ἀπ᾽
ἐκείνου *from that time* 1 Ezr 6,19; οὗτοι ...
ἐκεῖνοι ... *the nearer* ... *the more remote* ...,
those ... *the others* ... Wis 11,10; *1 Sm 20,19
ἐκεῖνο -הלאז? *that* for MT האזל?
Cf. MURAOKA 1990, 39

ἐκεῖσε⁺　　　　　D 0-0-0-1-0-1
Jb 39,29
there

ἐκζέω　　　　　V 2-2-1-1-0-6
Gn 49,4; Ex 16,20; 1 Sm 5,6; 6,1; Ez 47,9
to burst forth, to boil out, to be effervescent Jb
30,27; *to bring forth swarms of* 1 Sm 6,1

ἐκζητέω⁺　　　　　V 14-25-31-44-18-132
Gn 9,5(ter); 42,22; Ex 18,15
to seek out [τινα] 1 Sm 20,16; *to require, to*
demand on account of [τι] Gn 9,5; *to seek* [τι]
Lv 10,16; *to search* [τι] Jos 2,22; *to search, to*
weigh, to observe [τι] Ps 118(119),94; neol.?

ἐκζητητής,-οῦ　　　　　N1M 0-0-0-0-1-1
Bar 3,23
searcher out, inquisitor [τινος]; neol.

ἐκθαμβέω⁺　　　　　V 0-0-0-0-1-1
Sir 30,9
to amaze, to astonish

ἔκθαμβος,-ος,-ον⁺　　　　　A 0-0-0-1-0-1
Dnᵀʰ 7,7
terrible

ἐκθαυμάζω⁺　　　　　V 0-0-0-0-2-2
Sir 27,23; 43,18
to marvel at [τι] Sir 43,18; [ἐπί τινος] Sir 27,23

ἔκθεμα,-ατος　　　　　N3N 0-0-1-1-0-2
Ez 16,24; Est 8,17
public notice, proclamation, edict Est 8,17;
direction-notice (to a brothel) Ez 16,24

ἐκθερίζω　　　　　V 3-0-0-0-0-3
Lv 19,9(bis); 25,5
to reap or *mow completely*

ἔκθεσις,-εως　　　　　N3F 0-0-0-1-1-2
Dnᴸˣˣ 1,5; Wis 11,14
exposure (of children) Wis 11,14; *leftover* Dnᴸˣˣ
1,5
→KIESSLING

ἔκθεσμος,-ος,-ον　　　　　A 0-0-0-0-1-1

4 Mc 5,14
lawless, unlawful; neol.

ἐκθηλάζω   V 0-0-1-0-0-1
Is 66,11
to suck the breast; neol.

ἐκθλιβή,-ῆς   N1F 0-0-1-0-0-1
Mi 7,2
oppression; neol.

ἐκθλίβω   V 2-9-5-7-1-24
Gn 40,11; Lv 22,24; Jos 19,47; Jgs 1,34;
to squeeze, to press [τι] Gn 40,11; *to force* [τινα]
Jgs 1,34; *to afflict* [τινα] Jgs 2,15; *Mi 7,2
ἐκθλίβουσιν -יצורו *afflict, to subject to hardship*
for MT יצורו *hunt*

ἔκθυμος,-ος,-ον   A 0-0-0-0-3-3
2 Mc 7,3.39; 14,27
ardent, angry; neol.

ἐκκαθαίρω⁺   V 1-2-0-0-0-3
Dt 26,13; Jos 17,15; Jgsᴮ 7,4
to purge Jgsᴮ 7,4; *to clear away* Dt 26,13
·TWNT

ἐκκαθαρίζω   V 1-2-1-0-1-5
Dt 32,43; Jos 17,18; Jgsᴮ 20,13; Is 4,4; Od 2,43
to purge Dt 32,43; *to clear away* Jgsᴮ 20,13; neol.

ἐκκαίδεκα   M 1-7-0-0-0-8
Nm 31,40; 1 Kgs 12,24a; 2 Kgs 13,10; 14,21; 15,2
sixteen

ἐκκαιδέκατος,-η,-ον   M 0-3-0-0-0-3
1 Chr 24,14; 25,23; 2 Chr 29,17
sixteenth

ἐκκαίω⁺   V 5-10-8-19-14-56
Ex 22,5; Nm 11,1.3; Dt 29,19; 32,22
A: *to burn out* [τι] Dnᵀʰ 3,19; *to light up, to
kindle* [τι] Ex 22,6(5); *to burn down (a city)* [τι]
Prv 29,8; *to inflame (of anger)* 2 Kgs 20,21; P: *to
be kindled* Nm 11,1; (metaph.) Dt 29,19;
ἐκκαίω ὀπίσω τινός *to kindle a fire after sb, to
pursue with fierce enmity* (semit.) 1 Kgs
20(21),21; *Jb 3,17 ἐξέκαυσαν *they have burnt
out* corr.? ἐξέπαυσαν for MT חדלו *cease*; *Ps
117(118),12 ἐξεκαύθησαν -בערו? *they burst into
flame* for MT דעכו *they were extinguished*
Cf. LEE 1961, 235-236; MARGOLIS 1972 (A), 67

ἐκκαλέομαι   V 2-0-0-0-0-2
Gn 19,5; Dt 20,10
to call out [τινα]

ἐκκαλύπτω   V 0-0-0-1-0-1
Prv 26,26
to disclose, to reveal

ἐκκενόω   V 1-3-6-5-1-16

Gn 24,20; Jgsᴮ 20,31.32; 2 Chr 24,11; Is 51,17
to empty out, to clear out Gn 24,20; *to unsheath*
Ez 5,2

ἐκκεντέω⁺   V 1-4-2-0-2-9
Nm 22,29; Jos 16,10; Jgs 9,54; 1 Chr 10,4
to pierce, to stab Nm 22,29; *to massacre* Jos
16,10
→TWNT

ἐκκήρυκτος,-ος,-ον   A 0-0-1-0-0-1
Jer 22,30
banished, cast away; neol.

ἐκκινέω   V 0-1-0-0-0-1
2 Kgs 6,11
to disturb

ἐκκλάω⁺   V 1-0-0-0-0-1
Lv 1,17
to break off

ἐκκλησία,-ας⁺   N1F 9-45-2-24-23-103
Dt 4,10; 9,10; 18,16; 23,2.3
assembly (in political sense) Jdt 6,16; *assembly of
people* Sir 26,5; alternating with συναγωγή,
stereotyped rendition of קהל: *assembly of the
Israelites* Dt 4,10; *assembly of the returned exiles*
Ezr 10,8; *the cultic assembly of the people of
Israel* 2 Chr 6,3; ἐκκλησία κυρίου *the assembly
of the Lord* Dt 23,2; ἐκκλησία πονηρευομένων
assembly of evil doers Ps 25(26),5; *1 Sm 19,20
ἐκκλησίαν -קהלת *assembly of* for MT להיקת?
Cf. BARR 1961, 119-129; MURPHY 1958, 381-390; SCHMIDT
1927, 258-319; →TWNT; NIDNTT

ἐκκλησιάζω   V 5-7-1-1-0-14
Lv 8,3; Nm 20,8; Dt 4,10; 31,12.28
A: *to summon to an assembly, to convene* Lv 8,3;
P: *to assemble* Jer 33,9
(→ ἐξ-)

ἐκκλησιαστής,-οῦ   N1M 0-0-0-1-0-1
member of the ἐκκλησία?, *preacher*? (name or
epithet of the author of the Book called after
him)
Cf. WALTERS 1973, 85

ἔκκλητον,-ου   N2N 0-0-0-0-1-1
Sir 42,11
by-word

ἐκκλίνω⁺   V 23-53-16-51-17-160
Gn 18,5; 19,2.3; 38,16; Ex 10,6
*to bend out of the regular line, to bend outwards
or away* [τι] Gn 38,16; *to pervert (judgements)*
[τι] 1 Sm 8,3; *to turn away* [intrans.] Ex 10,6; *to
avoid, to shun* [τι] Prv 5,12; *to turn away or
aside towards* [πρός τινα] Gn 18,5; *to visit* [πρός

τινα] Gn 19,3; *Jb 29,11 ἐξέκλινε -עיט ⟨תעיטני turn aside for MT תעידני ⟨עוד bear witness;
*1 Sm 25,14 καὶ ἐξέκλινεν -נטה ⟨ויט he turned aside for MT ויעט but he hurled; *Jb 40,2 ἐκκλίνει -סור ⟨יסור shall he turn aside, pervert for MT יסור ⟨יסר shall he contend; *Prv 10,25 ἐκκλίνας -סור ⟨יסור turn aside for MT יסור be established

Cf. HELBING 1928, 35-36

ἐκκλύζω   V 1-0-0-0-0-1
Lv 6,21
to wash out

ἐκκόλαμμα,-ατος   N3N 1-0-0-0-0-1
Ex 36,13(39,6)
anything engraven; neol.

Cf. LE BOULLUEC 1989, 354

ἐκκολάπτω   V 1-0-0-0-0-1
Ex 36,13(39,6)
to hew, to carve out

ἐκκομιδή,-ῆς   N1F 0-0-0-0-1-1
2 Mc 3,7
transport

ἐκκόπτω⁺   V 9-11-10-11-10-51
Gn 32,9; 36,35; Ex 21,27; 34,13; Nm 16,14
to cut out, to knock out Nm 16,14; *to cut down, to fell* Dt 20,19; *to cut off, to make an end to* Jb 19,10; *to destroy* 2 Chr 14,14(13); *Zech 12,11 ἐκκοπτομένου -גרע ⟨מנרע cut out* for MT מגרון Megiddo

Cf. HELBING 1928, 128; HORSLEY 1983, 66

ἐκκρέμαμαι⁺   V 1-0-0-0-0-1
Gn 44,30
to depend upon [ἔκ τινος]

ἐκκρούομαι   V 1-0-0-0-0-1
Dt 19,5
to be knocked out; ἡ χεὶρ αὐτοῦ ἐκκρουσθῇ *his hand swings out*

Cf. LEE 1969, 239

ἐκκύπτω   V 0-0-1-3-2-6
Jer 6,1; Ps 101(102),20; Ct 2,9; 6,10; 1 Mc 4,19
to peep through or *out of* [διά τινος] Ct 2,9; *to proceed from* [ἀπό τινος] (metaph.) Jer 6,1

ἐκλαλέω⁺   V 0-0-0-0-1-1
Jdt 11,9
to blurt out, to blab

ἐκλαμβάνω   V 0-0-0-2-0-2
Jb 3,5; 22,22
to receive Jb 22,22; *to seize* Jb 3,5

Cf. MARGOLIS 1972, 76

ἐκλαμπρος,-ος,-ον   A 0-0-0-0-1-1

Wis 17,5
very bright; neol.

ἐκλάμπω⁺   V 0-1-1-1-4-7
2 Sm 22,29; Ez 43,2; Dnᵀʰ 12,3; Sir 26,17; 43,4
to shine or *beam forth* Sir 26,17; *to flash forth* [τι] (as cogn. acc.) Sir 43,4

ἐκλαμψις,-εως   N3F 0-0-0-0-1-1
2 Mc 5,3
shining forth, brightness

ἐκλατομέω   V 2-0-0-0-0-2
Nm 21,18; Dt 6,11
to hew in stone Nm 21,18; *to hew, to hollow out* Dt 6,11; neol.?

ἐκλέγω⁺   V 34-55-22-18-12-141
Gn 6,2; 13,11; Nm 16,5.7; 17,20
A: *to elect, to choose* Ez 20,38; M: *to elect, to choose* Gn 6,2; P: *to be chosen* 1 Chr 16,41; ἐκλεξάσθωσαν ἑαυτοῖς *let them choose for themselves* 1 Kgs 18,23; *1 Sm 17,8 ἐξελέξατο -בחרו *choose* for MT ברו ?

→TWNT; NIDNTT

ἐκλείπω⁺   V 29-24-65-48-34-200
Gn 8,13.13; 11,6; 18,11; 21,15
to forsake, to desert Jgsᴮ 5,6; *to die* Gn 49,33; *to faint* Gn 25,29; *to cease* Gn 18,11; *to fail* Gn 25,8; *to remain, to be left* 2 Kgs 7,13; *Is 38,12(11) ἐξέλιπεν -חדל (verb) *ceased, failed* for MT חדל (subst.) *world*?; *Prv 24,31 ἐκλελειμμένος -חדלים *ceased, destitute* for MT חדלים *thorns*, see also Zph 2,9

Cf. HELBING 1928, 97-98; LE BOULLUEC 1989, 161-162;
→NIDNTT

ἐκλείχω   V 2-2-0-0-2-6
Nm 22,4(bis); 1 Kgs 18,38; 22,38; Jdt 7,4
to lick up

ἐκλειψις,-εως   N3F 1-0-3-2-1-7
Dt 28,48; Is 17,4; Ez 5,16; Zph 1,2; Prv 14,28
abandonment Dt 28,48; *failing* Prv 14,28; *extinction (of a nation)* Ez 5,16

ἐκλεκτός,-ή,-όν⁺   A 11-20-31-24-13-99
Gn 23,6; 41,2.4.5.7
picked out, select Jgs 20,34; *choice, pure* Ex 30,23; *chosen of God, elect* Is 43,20; *Prv 17,3 ἐκλεκταί -בחר *choice* for MT בחן ⟨(the Lord) probes*, see also Is 28,16; *2 Sm 8,8 ἐκλεκτῶν -בחרי *the chosen* for MT ברתי *Berotai*; *Jer 10,17 ἐν ἐκλεκτοῖς -במבחר *in choice* (sc. vessels) for MT במצור *under siege*

→TWNT; NIDNTT

ἐκλευκαίνομαι   V 0-0-0-1-0-1

DnTh 12,10
to become quite white
ἔκλευκος,-ος,-ον A 1-0-0-0-0-1
Lv 13,24
quite white
ἐκλικμάω V 0-0-0-0-2-2
Jdt 2,27; Wis 5,23
to winnow, to sift, to empty; neol.
ἐκλιμία,-ας N1F 1-0-0-0-0-1
Dt 28,20
exceeding hunger, faintness; neol.
ἐκλιμπάνω V 0-0-1-0-0-1
Zech 11,16
to cease, to perish
ἐκλογή,-ῆς⁺ N 0-0-0-0-2-2
PSal 9,4; 18,5
choice, election, selection
ἐκλογίζομαι V 0-2-0-0-0-2
2 Kgs 12,16; 22,7
to ask an account of [τινά τι]
ἐκλογιστής,-οῦ N1M 0-0-0-0-1-1
TobBA 1,22
accountant (high position in the administration);
neol.?
ἐκλογιστία,-ας N1F 0-0-0-0-2-2
Tob 1,21
reckoning, accounts; neol.
ἐκλοχίζω V 0-0-0-1-0-1
Ct 5,10
to pick out of a cohort or *troop*; neol.
ἔκλυσις,-εως N3F 0-0-3-2-1-6
Is 21,3; Jer 29(47),3; Ez 23,33; Est 5,1d.2b
feebleness, faintness
ἐκλύτρωσις,-εως N3F 1-0-0-0-0-1
Nm 3,49
redemption; neol.
ἐκλύω⁺ V 4-14-10-8-9-45
Gn 27,40; 49,24(bis); Dt 20,3; Jos 10,6
A: *to unloose, to unstring* [τι] Gn 27,40; *to
weaken* Ezr 4,4; *to break up, to depart* [intrans.]
2 Mc 13,16; P: *to be faint, to fail* (physically)
1 Sm 14,28; (morally) Prv 6,3; ὁ ἐκλύειν με
μέλλων *he who is about to unloose me, my
redeemer* Jb 19,25; *Gn 49,24 ἐξελύθη -יפוצו?
they slacked for MT יפזו *they grew strong*? or *they
were agile*?
Cf. SPICQ 1978, 228-229; →NIDNTT
ἐκμαρτυρέω V 0-0-0-0-1-1
2 Mc 3,36
to bear witness to [τί τινι]

ἐκμάσσω⁺ V 0-0-0-0-3-3
Sir 12,11; LtJ 11.23
to wipe off or *away*
ἐκμελετάω V 0-0-0-0-1-1
2 Mc 15,12
*to get to know, to study, to learn perfectly, to
practise*
ἐκμελίζω V 0-0-0-0-3-3
4 Mc 10,5.8; 11,10
to dismember; neol.
ἐκμετρέω V 1-0-1-0-0-2
Dt 21,2; Hos 2,1
to measure (out) Hos 2,1; *to measure a distance*
Dt 21,2
ἐκμιαίνομαι V 3-0-0-0-0-3
Lv 18,20.23; 19,31
to defile, to pollute oneself, to copulate with
[πρός τι] Lv 18,23; [ἔν τινι] Lv 19,31
ἐκμυελίζω V 1-0-0-0-0-1
Nm 24,8
to suck the marrow out of, to deprive of strength;
neol.
ἐκμυκτηρίζω⁺ V 0-0-0-3-1-4
Ps 2,4; 21(22),8; 34(35),16; 1 Ezr 1,49
to hold in derision, to mock [τινα] Ps 2,4; [abs.]
1 Ezr 1,49; neol.
→TWNT
ἐκνεύω⁺ V 0-6-1-0-1-8
JgsA 4,18(ter); 18,26; 2 Kgs 2,24
to turn (aside)
ἐκνήφω⁺ V 1-1-3-0-1-6
Gn 9,24; 1 Sm 25,37; Jl 1,5; Hab 2,7.19
to sleep off a drunken fit, to sober up Hab 2,7; *to
sober up from* [ἀπό τινος] Gn 9,24; [ἔκ τινος] Jl
1,5; *to make an end to, to carry off* [τι] Sir 31,2;
neol.?
→TWNT
ἔκνηψις,-εως N3F 0-0-0-2-0-2
Lam 2,18; 3,49
sobering up, rest; neol.
ἑκουσιάζομαι V 0-2-0-6-1-9
JgsB 5,2.9; Ezr 2,68; 3,5; 7,13
to offer willingly, to be willing [abs] JgsB 5,2; *to
offer willingly to* [τί τινι] Ezr 3,5; *to volunteer to
do* [+inf.] Neh 11,2; ὁ ἑκουσιαζόμενος τῷ
νόμῳ *he who is voluntarily devoted to the law*
1 Mc 2,42; neol.
ἑκουσιασμός,-οῦ N2M 0-0-0-1-0-1
Ezr 7,16
free-will offering; neol.

Cf. HARLÉ 1988, 109; →TWNT

ἑκούσιος,-α,-ον⁺   A 5-0-0-8-2-15
Lv 7,16; 23,38; Nm 15,3; 29,39; Dt 12,6
voluntary Lv 7,16; τὰ ἑκούσια *voluntary acts,*
free will offering Nm 29,39; καθ' ἑκούσιον
voluntarily Nm 15,3
Cf. HARLÉ 1988, 109

ἑκουσίως⁺   D 1-0-0-1-3-5
Ex 36,2; Ps 53(54),8; 2 Mc 14,3; 4 Mc 5,23; 8,25
willingly Ps 53(54),8; ἑκουσίως βούλομαι *to*
freely will Ex 36,2

ἐκπαιδεύω   V 0-0-0-1-0-1
Dnᴸˣˣ 1,5
to bring up from childhood

ἐκπαίζω   V 0-0-0-0-1-1
1 Ezr 1,49
to laugh to scorn, to mock at [τινα]; neol.?

ἐκπειράζω⁺   V 4-0-0-1-0-5
Dt 6,16(bis); 8,2.16; Ps 77(78),18
to tempt, to put to the test; neol.

ἐκπέμπω⁺   V 3-3-0-1-2-9
Gn 24,54.56.59; 1 Sm 20,20; 24,20
to send forth, to dispatch Gn 24,59; *to conduct*
across [τινά τι] 2 Sm 19,32

ἐκπεράω   V 1-0-0-0-0-1
Nm 11,31
to carry out or *away*

ἐκπεριπορεύομαι   V 0-1-0-0-0-1
Jos 15,3
to make a detour; neol.

ἐκπετάζω or **ἐκπετάννυμι**   V 2-0-7-5-5-19
Ex 9,29.33; Is 54,3; 65,2; Ez 12,13
to spread out, to stretch out; neol.

ἐκπέτομαι   V 0-0-0-0-1-1
Sir 43,14
to fly out, to fly away

ἐκπηδάω⁺   V 1-2-0-1-5-9
Dt 33,22; 1 Kgs 21(20),39(bis); Est 4,1; Jdt 14,17
A: *to escape* 1 Kgs 21(20),39; M: *to leap out, to*
run out of [ἔκ τινος] Dt 33,22

ἐκπιάζω or **ἐκπιέζω**   V 0-3-2-1-0-6
Jgsᴮ 6,38; 18,7; 1 Sm 12,3; Ez 22,29; Zph 3,19
to squeeze out Jgsᴮ 6,38; *to force out* Prv 30,33;
to oppress 1 Sm 12,3; *to exort* Jgsᴮ 18,7

ἐκπικραίνω   V 1-0-0-0-1-2
Dt 32,16; Od 2,16
to embitter

ἐκπίνω   V 0-0-2-1-2-5
Is 51,17; Zech 9,15; Jb 6,4; Bel 15
A: *to drink (out), to quaff* Is 51,17; M: *to swal-*

low down (metaph.) Zech 9,15

ἐκπίπτω⁺   V 1-1-4-7-2-15
Dt 19,5; 2 Kgs 6,5; Is 6,13; 14,12; 28,4
to fall out of [ἀπό τινος] Is 6,13; *to fall from, to*
fall off [ἀπό τινος] Dt 19,5; [ἔκ τινος] Is 14,12;
to fall away Jb 15,30; *to fail* Sir 34,7; *to go forth,*
to go out (metaph.) 2 Mc 6,8
→TWNT

ἐκπληρόω⁺   V 0-0-0-0-3-3
2 Mc 8,10; 3 Mc 1,2.22
to make up, to defray 2 Mc 8,10; *to carry out*
3 Mc 1,2

ἐκπλήρωσις,-εως⁺   N3F 0-0-0-0-1-1
2 Mc 6,14
filling up the measure

ἐκπλήσσομαι⁺   V 0-0-0-1-4-5
Eccl 7,16; 2 Mc 7,12; 4 Mc 8,4; 17,16; Wis 13,4
M: *to marvel at, to be amazed at* [τι] 2 Mc 7,12;
P: *to be astonished* Wis 13,4; *to be confounded*
Eccl 7,16

ἐκπλύνω   V 0-0-1-0-0-1
Is 4,4
to wash out or *away*

ἐκποιέω   V 0-2-2-0-3-7
1 Kgs 21(20),10; 2 Chr 7,7; Ez 46,7.11; Sir 18,4
to procure Ez 46,7; *to permit* [τινι +inf.] Sir
18,4; *to be sufficient* [intrans.] 2 Chr 7,7

ἐκπολεμέω   V 3-7-0-0-4-14
Ex 1,10; Dt 20,10.19; Jos 9,2; 10,4
to go to war against [τινα] Dt 20,10; *to fight for*
[τινι] Jos 23,3

ἐκπολιορκέω   V 0-2-0-0-0-2
Jos 7,3; 10,5
to force a besieged town to surrender

ἐκπολιτεύω   V 0-0-0-0-1-1
4 Mc 4,19
to change the constitution of a state, to cause it
to degenerate; neol.

ἐκπορεύομαι⁺   V 49-49-38-20-16-172
Gn 2,10; 24,11.13.15.45
to go out, to go forth Gn 24,15; *to proceed out of*
[ἔκ τινος] (of water) Gn 2,10; (metaph.) Prv
3,16a; *to go out to* [+inf.] Gn 24,13; τὰ
ἐκπορευόμενα *the words* Dt 23,23(24); *Dnᵀʰ
11,30 οἱ ἐκπορευόμενοι -◊צא *those going forth*
for MT ציים *ships*
Cf. LEE 1983, 91-92; →TWNT

ἐκπορθέω   V 0-0-0-1-2-3
Jb 12,5(6); 4 Mc 17,24; 18,4
to pillage 4 Mc 17,24; *Jb 12,5(6) ἐκπορθεῖσθαι

-ישׁללו‎ to be plundered for MT ישׁליו‎ are at peace?

ἐκπορνεύω⁺   V 14-9-23-0-1-47

Gn 38,24; Ex 34,15.16(bis); Lv 17,7

to commit fornication, to play the harlot [abs.]
Gn 38,24; to prostitute, to cause to commit
fornication [τινα] 2 Chr 21,11; to go a whoring
after [ὀπίσω τινός] Ex 34,15; neol.

Cf. HARL 1986, 266; HELBING 1928, 78; →TWNT

ἐκπρεπής,-ής,-ές   A 0-1-0-0-2-3

1 Kgs 8,53a(13); 2 Mc 3,26; 3 Mc 3,17

pre-eminent, remarkable 2 Mc 3,26; extraordinary
3 Mc 3,17

ἐκπρίω   V 0-0-0-1-1-2

Prv 24,11; Wis 13,11

A: to saw off [τι] Wis 13,11; M: [τινα] Prv 24,11

ἐκπυρόω   V 0-0-0-0-2-2

2 Mc 7,3.4

to heat, to warm exceedingly

ἐκρέω   V 1-0-1-0-1-3

Dt 28,40; Is 64,5; 1 Mc 9,6

to fall off (of leaves) Is 64,5; to shed (fruit) Dt
28,40; to disappear 1 Mc 9,6

ἔκρηγμα,-ατος   N3N 0-0-1-0-0-1

Ez 30,16

rupture, bursting

ἐκρήγνυμαι   V 0-0-0-1-0-1

Jb 18,14

to break off

ἐκριζόω⁺   V 0-1-2-3-5-11

JgsᴮB 5,14; Jer 1,10; Zph 2,4; Dnᴸˣˣ
4,14(11).26(23)

to root out

ἐκριζωτής,-οῦ   N1M 0-0-0-0-1-1

4 Mc 3,5

rooter out, destroyer; neol.

ἐκρίπτω   V 0-5-2-2-3-12

Jgs 15,9; Jgsᴮ 6,13; 9,17; 15,15

A: to cast forth, to cast out Jgsᴮ 6,13; P: to be
spread abroad Jgs 15,9

ἔκρυσις,-εως   N3F 0-0-1-0-0-1

Ez 40,39

outflow, drain

ἐκσαρκίζομαι   V 0-0-1-0-0-1

Ez 24,4

to have the flesh stripped off; neol.

ἐκσιφωνίζομαι   V 0-0-0-1-0-1

Jb 5,5

to be drained, to be exhausted; neol.

ἐκσοβέομαι   V 0-0-0-0-1-1

Wis 17,9

to be scared (away)

ἐκσπάω   V 0-5-12-4-0-21

Jgs 3,22; Jgsᴬ 16,14; 20,32; 1 Sm 17,35

to draw out, to draw forth Ez 21,5; to remove Ez
11,9; to pull off, to pluck Jer 22,24

ἐκσπερματίζω   V 1-0-0-0-0-1

Nm 5,28

to conceive (of a woman); neol.

ἐκσπονδυλίζομαι   V 0-0-0-0-1-1

4 Mc 11,18

to break the vertebrae; neol.?

ἔκστασις,-εως⁺   N3F 5-9-7-7-1-29

Gn 2,21; 15,12; 27,33; Nm 13,32; Dt 28,28

illusion Dt 28,28; terror 2 Chr 14,14(13); dismay
1 Sm 14,15; entrancement, astonishment Gn
27,33; torpor Gn 15,12; ecstasy Ps 30(31),23;
*Hab 3,14 ἐν ἐκστάσει with astonishment corr.?
ἐν ἐκστάσει with an extension, with a stick for
MT מטהו‎ ◊ מטה ב/מטיו‎ with his shafts; *Ps 67(68),28 ἐν
ἐκστάσει -◊ רדם‎ in ecstasy for MT רדם‎ ◊ רדה ◊ רֹדֵם‎
their ruler?

Cf. HARL 1986, 165 (Gn 2,21; 15,12); →TWNT

ἐκστρατεύω   V 0-0-0-1-0-1

Prv 30,27

to march out

ἐκστρέφω⁺   V 1-0-3-0-1-5

Dt 32,20; Ez 13,20; Am 6,12; Zech 11,16; Od
2,20

to turn inside out, to dislocate [τι] Zech 11,16; to
change, to pervert [τι] Am 6,12; ἐξεστραμμένος
perverse Dt 32,20; *Ez 13,20 ἐκστρέφετε -◊ צרד‎?
you turn aside, pervert for MT מצדרות‎ ◊ צור‎ you
are hunting

ἐκσυρίζω   V 0-0-0-0-1-1

Sir 22,1

to hiss out or off

ἐκσύρω   V 0-1-0-0-0-1

Jgsᴮ 5,21

to sweep away

ἐκταράσσω⁺   V 0-0-0-2-3-5

Ps 17(18),5; 87(88),17; Wis 17,3.4; 18,17

A: to throw into confusion [τινα] Wis 18,17; to
agitate [τινι] Ps 87(88),17; P: to be greatly
troubled Wis 17,3

ἔκτασις,-εως   N3F 0-1-1-0-0-2

Jgsᴬ 16,14; Ez 17,3

stretching out, extension

ἐκτάσσω   V 1-1-0-2-1-5

Nm 32,27; 2 Kgs 25,19; Dn 1,10; 2 Mc 15,20

to draw out in battle-order [τι] (of the army)

2 Mc 15,20; *to keep muster-roll of* [τινα] 2 Kgs
25,19; *to order* [τι] Dn 1,10

ἐκτείνω⁺ V 28-31-35-25-22-141
Gn 3,22; 8,9; 14,22; 19,10; 22,10
to stretch out or *forth* Gn 3,22; *to spread out* Jdt
4,11; *to deploy* Jgsᴮ 20,37
Cf. CAIRD 1972, 127

ἐκτελέω⁺ V 0-1-0-1-2-4
2 Chr 4,5; Dnᵀʰ 3,40(23); 2 Mc 15,9; Od 7,40
to finish, to accomplish, to bring to an end Dnᵀʰ
3,40(23); *2 Chr 4,5 ἐξετέλεσεν -יכל‎? כלה‎ *he
finished* for MT יכיל‎ כול‎ *it held*

ἐκτέμνω V 0-0-1-0-6-7
Is 38,12; Tobˢ 2,12; 2 Mc 15,33; 4 Mc 10,17.21
to cut out 2 Mc 15,33; *to cut off* Is 38,12

ἐκτένεια,-ας⁺ N1F 0-0-0-0-2-2
Jdt 4,9(bis)
zeal, assiduousness; see ἐκτενία
Cf. SPICQ 1978, 230-234; WALTERS 1972, 45

ἐκτενής,-ής,-ές⁺ A 0-0-0-0-2-2
3 Mc 3,10; 5,29
assiduous 3 Mc 3,10; *strained* 3 Mc 5,29
Cf. SPICQ 1978, 230-234

ἐκτενία,-ας N1F 0-0-0-0-2-2
2 Mc 14,38; 3 Mc 6,41
zeal, assiduousness; see ἐκτένεια

ἐκτενῶς⁺ D 0-0-2-0-2-4
Jl 1,14; Jon 3,8; Jdt 4,12; 3 Mc 5,9
earnestly, zealously
Cf. SPICQ 1972, 230-234

ἐκτήκω V 1-0-0-5-2-8
Lv 26,16; Ps 38(39),12; 118(119),139.158;
138(139),21
A: *to cause to melt* or *pine* or *waste away* [τι] Ps
38(39),12; P: *to melt* or *to pine* or *to waste away*
Ps 118(119),158

ἐκτίθημι⁺ V 0-0-0-13-2-15
Jb 36,15; Est 3,14; 4,3.8; 8,12
A: *to make manifest* Jb 36,15; *to publish* Est
3,14; *to expose* Wis 18,5; *to set forth* 2 Mc 11,36;
M: *to publish* Dnᵀʰ 3,96(29)

ἐκτίκτω V 0-0-1-0-0-1
Is 55,10
to bring forth

ἐκτίλλω V 0-0-3-6-3-12
Jer 24,6; 49(42),10; 51,34(45,4); Ps 51(52),7;
Eccl 3,2
to pluck up Jer 51,34(45,4); *to pluck* Dnᵀʰ 7,4

ἐκτιναγμός,-οῦ N2M 0-0-1-0-0-1
Na 2,11

shaking out, violent shaking; neol.?

ἐκτινάσσω⁺ V 1-5-4-13-2-25
Ex 14,2; Jgs 7,19; Jgsᴮ 16,20; 2 Sm 22,33
to shake out Neh 5,13; *to expel* Ps 126(127),4; *to
shake off* Ex 14,27; ἐκτετιναγμένος *outcast* Neh
5,13; *2 Sm 22,33 καὶ ἐξετίναξεν -נער‎/ ויער‎
and he has shaken out (cleared) (my way) for
MT ויתר‎ ◊ נתר‎ *and he has set free (his way)*; *Neh
4,10(16) ἐκτετιναγμένων -נערי‎ נער‎ᴴ *that had
been driven forth* for MT נערי‎ *servants, men*, see
also Neh 5,15
Cf. LE BOULLUEC 1989, 170; ··NIDNTT

ἐκτίνω V 0-0-0-1-0-1
Jb 2,4
to pay (off)

ἐκτοκίζω V 3-0-0-0-0-3
Dt 23,20.21(bis)
to exact interest; neol.?
Cf. LEE 1983, 92

ἐκτομίας,-ου N1M 1-0-0-0-0-1
Lv 22,24
one that is castrated

ἐκτοπίζω V 0-0-0-0-1-1
2 Mc 8,13
to take (oneself) off, to remove oneself

ἕκτος,-η,-ον⁺ M 11-13-7-2-5-38
Gn 1,31; 2,2; 30,19; Ex 16,5.22
sixth

ἐκτός⁺ P 1-13-1-5-6-26
Ex 9,33; Jgsᴬ 3,31; Jgsᴮ 5,28; 8,26; 20,15
[τινος]: *out of* Ex 9,33; *beyond* 1 Chr 29,3;
outside of, free from Prv 24,22a(29,27); *except*
Jgsᴮ 20,17; *besides* Jgsᴮ 8,26; οἱ ἐκτός *those
without learning, the laity* Sir prol.,5

ἐκτρέπω⁺ V 0-0-1-0-0-1
Am 5,8
to turn, to change
Cf. SPICQ 1978, 235-236

ἐκτρέφω⁺ V 3-6-6-4-8-27
Gn 45,7.11; 47,17; 2 Sm 12,3; 1 Kgs 11,20
to bring up from childhood, to rear 1 Kgs 11,20;
to nourish Ez 31,4; *Prv 23,24 ἐκτρέφει -יגדל‎ *he
brings up* for MT יגול‎ or יגיל‎ (qere) *he will exult*

ἐκτρέχω V 0-2-0-0-0-2
Jgsᴬ 13,10; 1 Kgs 18,16
to run out, to run forth

ἐκτριβή,-ῆς N1F 1-0-0-0-0-1
Dt 4,26
destruction; neol.

ἐκτρίβω V 25-5-6-4-12-52

Gn 19,13.14.29; 34,30; 41,36

to rub out, to destroy Gn 19,13; *JgsᴬᴬÃ 8,12
ἐξέτριψεν -החריב *he destroyed* for MT החריד *he
terrified*; *Jb 30,23 ἐκτρίψει -ישברני *(death) will
destroy me* for MT תשיבני *you (Jahweh) will turn
me back (to death)?*

ἔκτριψις,-εως　　　　　　　　　N3F 1-0-0-0-0-1
Nm 15,31
destruction

ἐκτρυγάω　　　　　　　　　V 1-0-0-0-0-1
Lv 25,5
to gather in the vintage
Cf. LEE 1983, 93

ἐκτρώγω　　　　　　　　　V 0-0-1-0-0-1
Mi 7,4
to eat up, to devour; *Mi 7,4 ἐκτρώγων -חרק
devouring for MT חרק *a brier, thorn*

ἔκτρωμα,-ατος⁺　　　　　　　　　N3N 1-0-0-2-0-3
Nm 12,12; Jb 3,16; Eccl 6,3
untimely birth
Cf. SPICQ 1972, 237-239

ἐκτυπόω　　　　　　　　　V 4-0-0-0-0-4
Ex 25,33(32).34(33); 28,36(32); 36,37(39,30)
to model or *work in relief* Ex 28,36(32);
ἐκτετυπωμένοι καρυίσκους *fashioned like
almonds* Ex 25,33(32)

ἐκτύπωμα,-ατος　　　　　　　　　N3N 1-0-0-0-1-2
Ex 28,36; Sir 45,12
figure in relief

ἐκτύπωσις,-εως　　　　　　　　　N3F 0-1-0-0-0-1
1 Kgs 6,35
modelling in relief

ἐκτυφλόω　　　　　　　　　V 3-1-4-0-1-9
Ex 21,26; 23,8; Dt 16,19; 2 Kgs 25,7; Is 56,10
A: *to make quite blind* Ex 21,26; P: *to be blinded*
Zech 11,17

ἐκφαίνω　　　　　　　　　V 0-0-0-3-11-14
Dnᴸˣˣ 2,19.30.47; 3 Mc 4,1; Sir 8,19
A: *to bring to light, to disclose, to reveal* Sir 8,19;
to declare Sir 14,7; P: *to appear plainly* Dnᴸˣˣ
2,30

ἐκφαυλίζω　　　　　　　　　V 0-0-0-0-1-1
Jdt 14,5
to depreciate, to disparage; neol.

ἐκφέρω⁺　　　　　　　　　V 23-18-19-19-8-87
Gn 1,8.12; 2,24; 14,18; 24,53
to carry out of Ex 12,39; *to carry away, to carry
off* Ex 12,46; *to bear, to bring forth* Gn 1,12; *to
exact* 2 Kgs 15,20

ἐκφεύγω⁺　　　　　　　　　V 0-2-1-4-17-24

Jgs 6,11; Is 66,7; Jb 15,30; Prv 10,19
to escape [abs.] Sir 16,13; [τι] Tob 13,2; *to
escape from, to flee away from* [ἀπό τινος] Jgsᴮ
6,11; [ἔκ τινος] Jgsᴬ 6,11

ἐκφλέγομαι　　　　　　　　　V 0-0-0-0-1-1
4 Mc 16,3
to be set on fire

ἐκφοβέω⁺　　　　　　　　　V 1-0-6-2-5-14
Lv 26,6; Ez 32,27; 34,28; 39,26; Mi 4,4
to alarm, to frighten [τινα] Lv 26,6; *to frighten
with* [τινά τινι] Jb 7,14; *Ez 32,27 ἐξεφόβησαν
-חתתו *they terrified* for MT חתית *terror*

ἔκφοβος,-ος,-ον⁺　　　　　　　　　A 1-0-0-0-1-2
Dt 9,19; 1 Mc 13,2
terrified, in dread, affraid

ἐκφορά,-ᾶς　　　　　　　　　N1F 0-3-0-0-0-3
2 Chr 16,14; 21,19(bis)
carrying out, funeral

ἐκφορίον,-ου　　　　　　　　　N2N 2-1-2-0-0-5
Lv 25,19; Dt 28,33; Jgsᴬ 6,4; Hag 1,10; Mal 3,10
that which the earth produces

ἐκφυγή,-ῆς　　　　　　　　　N1F 0-0-0-0-1-1
3 Mc 4,19
escape; neol.

ἐκφύρομαι　　　　　　　　　V 0-0-1-0-0-1
Jer 3,2
to be defiled; neol.

ἐκφυσάω　　　　　　　　　V 0-0-4-0-2-6
Ez 22,20.21; Hag 1,9; Mal 1,13; 4 Mc 5,32
to kindle, to blow into a flame [τι] 4 Mc 5,32; *to
blow away* [τι] Hag 1,9

ἐκφωνέω　　　　　　　　　V 0-0-0-3-0-3
Dnᴸˣˣ 2,20.27.47
to cry out

ἐκχέω⁺　　　　　　　　　V 25-19-44-30-23-141
Gn 9,6(bis); 37,22; 38,9; Ex 4,9
A: *to pour out* or *forth* Ex 4,9; *to pour away, to
spill* Gn 38,9; *to bring forth* Ps 34(35),3; *to shed*
Gn 9,6; P: *to come forth* Jgs 20,37; *to be poured
out* or *forth* Dt 19,10
→NIDNTT; TWNT

ἐκχολάω　　　　　　　　　V 0-0-0-0-1-1
3 Mc 3,1
to be angry, to be incensed; neol.

ἔκχυσις,-εως　　　　　　　　　N3F 1-1-0-0-1-3
Lv 4,12; 1 Kgs 18,28; Sir 27,15
outflow, pouring out

ἐκχωρέω⁺　　　　　　　　　V 1-1-1-0-3-6
Nm 17,10; Jgsᴮ 7,3; Am 7,12; 1 Ezr 4,44.57
to depart Nm 17,10; *to move* Am 7,12; *to remove*

1 Ezr 4,44

ἐκψύχω⁺   V 0-1-1-0-0-2
Jgsᴬ 4,21; Ez 21,12
to faint, to lose consciousness, to swoon
Cf. SPICQ 1982, 249

ἑκών,-οῦσα,-όν⁺   A 1-0-0-1-0-2
Ex 21,13; Jb 36,19
willingly
Cf. LE BOULLUEC 1989, 217

ἐλαία,-ας⁺   N1F 4-9-12-5-4-34
Gn 8,11; Dt 8,8; 28,40(bis); Jgsᴬ 9,8
olive-tree Jgs 9,8; *olive* Mi 6,15
--NIDNTT

ἐλάϊνος,-η,-ον   A 1-0-0-0-0-1
Lv 24,2
of olives

ἐλαιολογέω   V 1-0-0-0-0-1
Dt 24,20
to pick olives; neol.

ἔλαιον,-ου⁺   N2N 109-27-30-24-10-200
Gn 28,18; 35,14; Ex 27,20(bis); 29,2
(olive-)oil
·NIDNTT

ἐλαιών,-ῶνος⁺   N3M 2-4-2-1-0-9
Ex 23,11; Dt 6,11; Jos 24,13; 1 Sm 8,14; 2 Kgs
5,26
olive-grove
Cf. LE BOULLUEC 1989, 236; LEE 1983, 108; →NIDNTT

ἔλασμα,-ατος   N3N 0-0-1-0-0-1
Hab 2,19
metal beaten out, metal-plate; neol.

ἐλάτη,-ης   N1F 1-0-1-1-0-3
Gn 21,15; Ct 5,11; Ez 31,8
silver fir Gn 21,15; *(like a) waving palm* Ct 5,11

ἐλάτινος,-η,-ον   A 0-0-1-0-0-1
Ez 27,5(6)
made of fir or *pine-wood*

ἐλατός,-ή,-όν   A 2-4-0-1-1-8
Nm 10,2; 17,3; 1 Kgs 10,16.17; 2 Chr 9,15
beaten 1 Kgs 10,16; *of beaten work* Nm 10,2

ἐλαττονέω⁺ or ἐλασσονέω   V 2-2-0-1-2-7
Ex 16,18; 30,15; 1 Kgs 11,22; 17,14; Prv 11,24
A: *to receive less, to have back* Ex 16,18; *to give
less, to diminish* Ex 30,15; M: *to lack, to want*
[τινι] 1 Kgs 11,22; *to loose of* [abs.] 2 Mc 13,19;
to receive less, to have lack Prv 11,24
Cf. LE BOULLUEC 1989, 308; SPICQ 1972, 241 n.2

ἐλαττονόω or ἐλασσονόω   V 4-1-0-1-3-9
Gn 8,3.5; 18,28; Lv 25,16; 1 Kgs 17,16
A: *to diminish* Lv 25,16; P: *to be diminished* Gn

8,3; *Prv 14,34 ἐλασσονοῦσι -חסר *diminish* for
MT חסר\| *shame;* neol.

ἐλαττόω or ἐλασσόω⁺   V 2-3-3-3-17-28
Nm 26,54; 33,54; 1 Sm 2,5; 21,16; 2 Sm 3,29
A: *to make less* or *smaller, to diminish, to reduce
in amount* [τι] Nm 26,54; *to lower, to degrade*
[τινα] Ps 8,6; P: *to suffer loss, to be depreciated*
Sir 32,24; *to be in want of* [τινος] 1 Sm 21,16;
[τινι] 2 Sm 3,29; *Ez 24,10 καὶ ἐλαττωθῇ
-והרקה ◊ריק *and be diminished* for MT והרקה *and
mix as an anointment;* *1 Sm 2,5 ἠλαττώθησαν
-נשברו or נחנסרו or נשברו *they are reduced* for MT נשכרו
they hire themselves out
Cf. HELBING 1928, 176-177

ἐλάττωμα,-ατος   N3N 0-0-0-0-2-2
2 Mc 11,13; Sir 19,28
loss, defect

ἐλάττων or ἐλάσσων,-ων,-ον⁺   A 10-0-0-4-6-20
Gn 1,16; 25,23; 27,6; Ex 16,17.18
comp. of ὀλίγος; *smaller, less* Gn 1,16; *fewer*
Nm 26,54; *younger* Gn 27,6

ἐλάττωσις,-εως   N3F 0-0-0-0-7-7
Tobᴮᴬ 4,13; Sir 20,3.9.11; 28,8; 31,4
defect, loss

ἐλαύνω⁺   V 1-1-2-0-4-8
Ex 25,12; 1 Kgs 9,27; Is 33,21; 41,7; 2 Mc 9,4
to drive, to set in motion [τι] Sir 38,25; *to drive*
[intrans.] 2 Mc 9,4; *to row* 1 Kgs 9,27; *to drive to
extremities, to persecute* [τινα] Wis 16,18; *to
plague, to vex* [τινα] Wis 17,14; *to forge* [τι] Ex
25,12(11); πλοῖον ἐλαῦνον *vessel with oars* Is
33,21
Cf. LE BOULLUEC 1989, 255
(→ ἀπ-, δι-, ἐξ-, περι-, συν-)

ἔλαφος,-ου   N2M/F 4-3-3-10-0-20
Dt 12,15.22; 14,5; 15,22; 2 Sm 22,34
deer, hart, hind Dt 12,15; *Prv 7,23 ὡς ἔλαφος
-כאיל *like a deer* for MT אויל *a fool*

ἐλαφρός,-ά,-όν⁺   A 1-0-1-3-0-5
Ex 18,26; Ez 1,7; Jb 7,6; 9,25; 24,18
light in weight Ez 1,7; *light to bear, minor* Ex
18,26; *light in moving, nimble* Jb 24,18

ἐλάχιστος,-η,-ον⁺   A 0-4-2-3-6-15
Jos 6,26(bis); 1 Sm 9,21; 2 Kgs 18,24; Is 60,22
sup. of ὀλίγος; *smallest, least* 1 Sm 9,21;
meanest Wis 6,6; *youngest* Jos 6,26; *Jb 18,7
ἐλάχιστοι -צערי *meanest* for MT צערי *steps*

ἐλεάω⁺   V 0-0-0-6-5-11
Ps 36(37),26; 114(115),5; Prv 13,9; 14,31; 21,26
to have pity on, to show mercy to [τινα] Prv

14,31; *to feel pity* [abs.] Tob 13,2

ἐλεγμός,-οῦ⁺   N2M 7-1-1-3-9-21
Lv 19,17; Nm 5,18.19.23.24
refuting, reproving; neol.
-NIDNTT

ἔλεγξις,-εως⁺   N3F 0-0-0-2-0-2
Jb 21,4; 23,2
refuting, reproving; neol.

ἔλεγχος,-ου⁺   N 0-0-3-20-8-31
Ez 13,14; Hos 5,9; Hab 2,1; Ps 72(73),14; Jb
6,26
rebuttal or *refutation, rebuke*; *Ez 13,14 μετ'
ἐλέγχων* -בתוכחת ◊ יכח *with rebukes* for MT
בתוכה *in its midst*
-NIDNTT

ἐλέγχω⁺   V 5-4-10-30-16-65
Gn 21,25; 31,37.42; Lv 5,24; 19,17
to reprove, to reproach Gn 21,25; *to decide* Gn
31,37; P: *to be ashamed of* [τινος] or *to become
a reprover of* [τινος]? Wis 1,5
Cf. HARLÉ 1988, 103; LARCHER 1983, 176-178 (Wis 1,5);
-NIDNTT; TWNT
(·ἀπ-, δι-, ἐξ-)

ἐλεεινός,-ή,-όν⁺   A 0-0-0-3-0-3
Dnᴸˣˣ 9,23; 10,11.19
having received mercy

ἐλεέω⁺   V 11-4-47-32-45-139
Gn 33,5.11; 43,29; Ex 23,3; 33,19
to have pity on, to show mercy to [τινα] Gn 33,5;
to feel pity [abs.] Jer 6,23
Cf. SPICQ 1982, 254-258; →twnt
(·κατ-)

ἐλεημοποιός,-ός,-όν   A 0-0-0-0-1-1
Tobˢ 9,6
giving alms; neol.

ἐλεημοσύνη,-ης⁺   N1F 3-0-4-12-51-70
Gn 47,29; Dt 6,25; 24,13; Is 1,27; 28,17
pity, mercy Gn 47,29; *charity, alms* Tob 4,7
Cf. BICKERMAN 1976, 183, n.41; HARL 1986, 301; LEE
1983, 108; -TWNT

ἐλεήμων,-ων,-ον⁺   A 2-1-3-12-11-29
Ex 22,26; 34,6; 2 Chr 30,9; Jer 3,12; Jl 2,13
pityful, merciful Ex 22,26; *Prv 20,6 ἐλεήμων
-*חסד *merciful* for MT חסדו *his mercy*; *Prv 28,22
ἐλεήμων -*חסיד *merciful* for MT חסר *want*

ἐλεόπολις,-εως   N3F 0-0-0-0-2-2
1 Mc 13,43.44
corr. ἐλέπολις *siege engine*
Cf. WALTERS 1973, 122

ἔλεος,-ου   N2M 0-0-6-5-5-16

see ἔλεος,-ους
Cf. SPICQ 1982, 252-254; -TWNT

ἔλεος,-ους⁺   N3N 15-45-31-153-94-338
Gn 19,19; 24,12.14.44.49
pity, mercy, compassion Gn 19,19; ἔλεος ποιέω
ἔν τινι *to deal mercifully with* Gn 40,14; [ἐπί
τινα] Tobˢ 7,12; [μετά τινος] Gn 24,12; [τινι]
Gn 24,14; *Ps 83(84),12 ἔλεον corr.? ἥλιου *sun*
for MT שמש *(sun shaped) shield*
Cf. GRIBOMONT-THIBAUT 1959, 83-85; LE BOULLUEC
1989, 338

ἐλευθερία,-ας⁺   N1F 1-0-0-0-6-7
Lv 19,20; 1 Ezr 4,49.53; 1 Mc 14,26; 3 Mc 3,28
freedom, liberty
→NIDNTT

ἐλεύθερος,-α,-ον⁺   A 8-2-4-4-10-28
Ex 21,2.5.26.27; Dt 15,12
free Ex 21,2; *honorable, noble* Eccl 10,17;
ἐλεύθερα *free woman* 1 Mc 2,11
Cf. VYCICHL 1983, 42; -NIDNTT

ἐλευθερόω⁺   V 0-0-0-1-2-3
Prv 25,10; 2 Mc 1,27; 2,22
to set free
-NIDNTT
(— ἀπ-)

ἐλεφαντάρχης,-ου   N1M 0-0-0-0-3-3
2 Mc 14,12; 3 Mc 5,4.45
master of the elephants

ἐλεφάντινος,-η,-ον⁺   A 0-4-3-3-0-10
1 Kgs 10,18; 22,39; 2 Chr 9,17.21; Ez 27,15
of ivory

ἐλέφας,-αντος   N3M 0-0-1-0-16-17
Ez 27,6; 1 Mc 1,17; 3,34; 6,30.34
elephant 1 Mc 3,34; *ivory* Ez 27,6

ἑλικτός,-ή,-όν   A 1-1-0-0-0-2
Lv 6,14; 1 Kgs 6,8
rolled (bread) Lv 6,14; *winding* (staircase) 1 Kgs
6,8

ἕλιξ,-ικος   N3F 1-0-0-0-0-1
Gn 49,11
tendril, branch (of the vine)

ἑλίσσομαι⁺   V 0-0-1-1-0-2
Is 34,4; Jb 18,8
to be entangled Jb 18,8; *to be rolled up* Is 3,4
(- ἐξ-)

ἕλκος,-ους⁺   N3N 12-1-0-1-0-14
Ex 9,9.10.11(bis); Lv 13,18
festering wound, sore, ulcer
Cf. LE BOULLUEC 1989, 131

ἕλκω   V 1-8-6-12-8-35

Dt 21,3; Jgsᴮ 5,14; 20,2.15.17

to draw [τι] Dt 21,3; *to draw, to pull* [τινα] Jer
38,3; *to draw (a sword)* [τι] Jgsᴮ 20,2; *to draw, to
scribe* [intrans.] (of pen) Jgsᴮ 5,14; *to draw in, to
breathe* [τι] Ps 118(119),131; *to excite* [τι] Eccl
2,3; *to draw* [τι] (metaph.) Jb 28,18; ἕλκω τι εἰς
τέλος *to bring to an end* Jb 20,28

(· ἐξ-, ἐφ-, παρ-, συν-)

ἐλλείπω　　　　　　　　　　　　　V 0-0-0-0-1-1
Sir 42,2
to fall short, to fail

ἐλλιπής,-ής,-ές　　　　　　　　　A 0-0-0-0-2-2
Sir 14,10; PSal 4,17
defective, wanting

ελλουλιμ　　　　　　　　　　　N 0-1-0-0-0-1
Jgsᴮ 9,27
=הלולים *festival exultation*
Cf. SIMOTAS 1968, 63

ελμωνι　　　　　　　　　　　A 0-1-0-0-0-1
2 Kgs 6,8
=אלמני (פלני) *such and such*
Cf. SIMOTAS 1968, 63

ἕλος,-ους　　　　　　　　　N3N 4-0-6-0-2-12
Ex 2,3.5; 7,19; 8,1; Is 19,6
marsh-meadow, marshy ground

ἐλπίζω⁺　　　　　　　　V 1-7-15-75-19-117
Gn 4,26; Jgs 20,36; Jgsᴮ 9,26; 2 Kgs 18,5
to hope for, to look for, to expect Is 38,18; *to
deem, to suppose* [+inf. pres.] Gn 4,26; *to hope
in, to trust in* [ἔν τινι] 2 Kgs 18,5; [πρός τι] Jgsᴮ
20,36; [ἐπί τι] Jgsᴬ 20,36; [ἐπί τινι] Ps
25(26),1; *Gn 4,26 ἤλπισεν-הוחל יחל *he hoped
for* MT הוחל ◊ חלל *be begun, one began*, cpr.
ἐνάρχομαι and Prv 13,12
Cf. FRAADE 1984, 5-10; MARCOS 1980, 357-360; →TWNT
(· ἀπ-, ἐπ-)

ἐλπίς,-ίδος⁺　　　　　　　N3F 1-7-29-43-36-116
Dt 24,15; Jgsᴬ 18,7(bis).9; Jgsᴮ 18,7
hope, expectation 2 Chr 35,26; *object of hope, a
hope* Ps 13(14),6; τὴν ἐλπίδα ἔχω *to trust* Jer
17,5
Cf. GRIBOMONT-THIBAUT 1959, 79-82; HORSLEY 1982, 77;
LARCHER 1983, 279-280.297; VAN MENXEL 1983; →NIDNTT;
TWNT

ελωαι　　　　　　　　　　　N 0-1-0-0-0-1
1 Sm 1,11
=אלוהי *my God*
Cf. SIMOTAS 1968, 64

ἐμαυτοῦ,-ῆς,-οῦ⁺　　　　　R 11-7-15-13-13-59
Gn 12,19; 22,16; 27,12; 30,30; 31,39

also dat. and acc.; *of me, of myself* Gn 12,19;
*Gn 30,30 ἐμαυτῷ οἶκον -לי בית- *for me a house*
for MT לביתי *for my house*

ἐμβαίνω⁺　　　　　　　　　V 0-0-2-0-2-4
Jon 1,3; Na 3,14; 1 Mc 15,37; 2 Mc 12,3
to embark [εἰς τι] Jon 1,3; *to step into, to enter
upon* [εἰς τι] Na 3,14

ἐμβάλλω⁺　　　　　　　V 31-6-17-25-10-89
Gn 31,34; 37,22; 39,20; 40,15; 43,22
A: *to cast* or *throw in(to)* Gn 37,22; *to lay* or *put
in(to)* Ex 2,3; *to set* Jer 34(27),8; P: *to be cast
in(to)* Dnᵀʰ 3,6; *Jer 11,19 ἐμβάλωμεν -נשיתה *let
us put in* for MT נשחיתה *let us cut, destroy*
Cf. HELBING 1928, 270

ἐμβατεύω⁺　　　　　　　　V 0-2-0-0-5-7
Jos 19,49.51; 1 Mc 12,25; 13,20; 14,31
to step in or *on* [εἰς τι] 2 Mc 2,30; *to enter on,
to come into possession of* [τι] Jos 19,49; *to enter
into a subject, to go into detail* [abs.] 2 Mc 2,30
Cf. HELBING 1928, 83

ἐμβιβάζω⁺　　　　　　　　　V 0-0-0-1-0-1
Prv 4,11
to set on, to put on [τινι]
Cf. HELBING 1928, 271

ἐμβίωσις,-εως　　　　　　　N3F 0-0-0-0-3-3
3 Mc 3,23; Sir 34,22; 38,14
maintenance of life Sir 38,14; *way of living* 3 Mc
3,23; neol.

ἐμβλέπω⁺　　　　　　　　V 0-3-9-2-9-23
Jgsᴬ 16,27; 1 Sm 16,7; 1 Kgs 8,8; Is 5,12.30
A: *to look in the face, to look at* [abs.] Jb 2,10;
to consider, to look into [τι] Is 5,12; P: *to appear*
1 Kgs 8,8
Cf. HELBING 1928, 271

ἐμβολή,-ῆς　　　　　　　　　N1F 0-0-0-0-1-1
3 Mc 4,7
putting aboard

ἐμβριμάομαι⁺　　　　　　　　V 0-0-0-1-0-1
Dnᴸˣˣ 11,30
to admonish urgently, to rebuke

ἐμβρίμημα,-ατος　　　　　　　N3N 0-0-0-1-0-1
Lam 2,6
indignation; neol.

ἔμετος,-ου　　　　　　　　　N2M 0-0-0-1-0-1
Prv 26,11
vomiting

ἐμέω⁺　　　　　　　　　　V 0-0-1-0-1-2
Is 19,14; Sir 31,21
to vomit
(· ἐξ-)

ἐμμανής,-ής,-ές   A 0-0-0-0-1-1
Wis 14,23
frantic, raving
ἐμμελέτημα,-ατος   N3N 0-0-0-0-1-1
Wis 13,10
exercise, practice
ἐμμένω⁺   V 3-0-8-2-8-21
Nm 23,19; Dt 19,15; 27,26; Is 7,7; 8,10
to abide by, to stand by, to cleave to, to be true to
[τινι] Jer 51(44),25; [ἔν τινι] Dt 27,26; *to remain fixed, to stand fast* (of things) Is 8,10
Cf. HELBING 1928, 271; MARGOLIS 1972 (A), 62; →NIDNTT;
TWNT
ἐμμολύνομαι   V 0-0-0-1-0-1
Prv 24,9
to be polluted by or *with* [τινι]; neol.
ἔμμονος,-ος,-ον   A 3-0-0-0-1-4
Lv 13,51.52; 14,44; Sir 30,17
chronic (of a disease)
Cf. MARGOLIS 1972 (A), 62
ἐμός,-ή,-όν⁺   R 16-8-16-58-14-112
Gn 22,18; 24,41; 26,5; 31,31.43
mine, of me Gn 22,18; τὰ ἐμά *my possessions*
Gn 31,31
ἔμπαιγμα,-ατος   N3N 0-0-1-0-1-2
Is 66,4; Wis 17,7
jest, mocking, delusion; neol.
ἐμπαιγμός,-οῦ⁺   N2M 0-0-1-1-6-8
Ez 22,4; Ps 37(38),8; 2 Mc 7,7; 3 Mc 5,22; Wis 12,25
mockery, mocking; neol.
Cf. HARL 1984, 89-105
ἐμπαίζω⁺   V 4-9-7-3-6-29
Gn 39,14.17; Ex 10,2; Nm 22,29; Jgsᴬ 16,25
to mock at, to make sport of [τινι] Gn 39,14; *to abuse* [τινι] Jgsᴬ 19,25; [ἔν τινι] Jgsᴮ 19,25; *Na 2,4 ἐμπαίζοντας -מתלעבים? sporting* for MT מתלעים *clad in scarlet*; *Is 33,4 ἐμπαίξουσιν -שחקו *they will mock* for MT שוקק *leaping*; *Zech 12,3 ἐμπαίζων ἐμπαίξεται -ישרקו שרוק *they will utterly mock* for MT ישרטו שרוט *they shall grievously hurt themselves*
Cf. HARL 1986, 269; HELBING 1928, 271-272; →TWNT
ἐμπαίκτης,-ου⁺   N1M 0-0-1-0-0-1
Is 3,4
mocker, deceiver; neol.
ἐμπαραγίνομαι   V 0-0-0-1-0-1
Prv 6,11
to come in upon [τινι]; neol.
Cf. HELBING 1928, 272

ἐμπειρέω   V 0-0-0-0-3-3
Tob 5,6; Tobˢ 5,4
to be experienced in, to have knowledge of
[τινος]; neol.
Cf. HELBING 1928, 144
ἐμπειρία,-ας   N1F 0-0-0-0-1-1
Wis 13,13
experience
ἔμπειρος,-ος,-ον   A 0-0-0-0-2-2
Tobᴮᴬ 5,5; PSal 15,9
acquainted with [τινος]
ἐμπεριπατέω⁺   V 2-2-0-3-1-8
Lv 26,12; Dt 23,15; Jgsᴬ 18,9; 2 Sm 7,6; Jb 1,7
to walk about in [ἔν τινι] Dt 23,15; *to tarry among* [ἔν τινι] (metaph.) Lv 26,12; *to walk about upon* [τι] Jb 1,7; neol.?
Cf. HELBING 1928, 84.272; →TWNT
ἐμπήγνυμι   V 0-4-0-6-0-10
Jgs 3,21; 1 Sm 26,7; 2 Sm 18,14; Ps 9,16
A: *to fix in, to plant in* [τι εἴς τι] (of sharp things) Jgsᴬ 3,21; P: *to be fixed in, to be stuck in, to stick in* [τινι] Ps 37(38),3; [εἴς τι] Lam 2,9; [abs.] Ps 68(69),15; *to be caught in, to be stuck in* [ἔν τινι] Ps 9,16; ἐμπεπηγὸς εἴς τι *stuck in, fixed in* 1 Sm 26,7; *Ps 31(32),4 ἐν τῷ ἐμπαγῆναι -חרב/ב (verb understood as a denominative derived from חרב *sword*) *while (a thorn) was fastened* for MT חרבני/ב? (hapax)
Cf. HELBING 1928, 272
ἐμπηδάω   V 0-0-0-0-1-1
1 Mc 9,48
to leap into
ἐμπίμπλημι⁺   V 22-6-52-38-29-147
Gn 42,25; Ex 15,9; 28,3.41; 31,3
A: *to fill quite full* [τι] Nm 14,21; *to fill full of* [τί τινος] Gn 42,25; *to satisfy* [τι] Ex 15,9; *to fulfill, to accomplish* [τι] Ez 24,13; P: *to be filled with* [τινος] Dt 34,9; *to be satiated* Lv 26,26; ἐμπίμπλημι τὰς χεῖρας *to fill the hands, to consecrate* Ex 28,41, see also Nm 7,88; Ez 43,26; ἐμπέπλησται ἀνὰ μέσον μου καὶ τοῦ θανάτου *(the space) is filled up between me and death* or *I am close to death* 1 Sm 20,3; *Ez 28,13 ἐνέπλησας -מלאת *you filled* for MT מלאכת *works in* (gold)
Cf. HELBING 1928, 144-148; LE BOULLUEC 1989, 44; →TWNT
ἐμπίμπρημι⁺   V 2-27-6-1-12-48
Nm 31,10; Dt 13,17; Jos 6,24; 8,19; 11,9
A: *to kindle, to set on fire* Nm 31,10; P: *to be set*

on fire Neh 1,3; *1 Kgs 18,10 ἐνέπρησε (τὴν
βασιλείαν) he set fire (to the kingdom) corr.?
ἐνέπλησε -השביע he completed for MT השביע he
took an oath (of the nation)

ἐμπίπτω⁺ V 2-11-5-13-22-53
Gn 14,10; Ex 21,33; Jgs 15,18 Jgsᴮ 18,1
to fall in or on [abs.] Gn 14,10; to fall in [εἴς τι]
Ps 7,15; (metaph.) Prv 17,16a; [ἔν τινι]
(metaph.) Jgs 15,18; [τινι] (metaph.) Jgs 18,1; to
fall into the hands of [τινι] (of pers.) 2 Mc
12,24; to fall on [τινι] (of diseases) Prv 17,12; to
fall upon, to attack [τινι] Am 5,19; to press upon
Sir 13,10; to desert to [πρός τινα] 2 Kgs 25,11;
ἐμπίπτω εἰς χεῖράς τινος to fall into sb hands
2 Sm 24,14; ἐμπίπτω εἰς ἀρρωστίαν to fall sick
1 Mc 6,8; οἱ ἐμπίπτοντες those who fall in their
way 2 Mc 5,12
Cf. HELBING 1928, 273-274; SPICQ 1978, 243-244

ἐμπιστεύω V 1-4-1-0-18-24
Dt 1,32; Jgsᴮ 11,20; 2 Chr 20,20(ter)
to trust in, to give credence to [τινι] Dt 1,32; [ἔν
τινι] 2 Chr 20,20; [ἐπί τινι] 3 Mc 2,7

ἐμπλάσσω V 0-0-0-0-1-1
Tobˢ 11,8
to plaster up

ἐμπλατύνω V 4-0-2-1-0-7
Ex 23,18; Dt 12,20; 19,8; 33,20; Am 1,13
to widen, to extend Ex 23,18; to enlarge Prv 18,16

ἐμπλέκομαι⁺ V 0-0-0-1-1-2
Prv 28,18; 2 Mc 15,17
to be entagled in [τινι] (metaph.) Prv 28,18;
[μετά τινος] (metaph.) 2 Mc 15,17

ἐμπληθύνομαι V 0-0-0-0-1-1
3 Mc 5,42
to be filled with [τινος]

ἐμπλόκιον,-ου N2N 5-0-2-0-0-7
Ex 35,22; 36,22(39,15).24(39,17).25(39,18); Nm
31,50
hair-clasp Ex 35,22; ἔργον ἐμπλοκίου wreathed
work Ex 36,22(39,15); τὰ ἐμπλόκια wreaths Ex
36,24(39,17)
Cf. LE BOULLUEC 1989, 349-350.356

ἔμπνευσις,-εως N3F 0-0-0-1-0-1
Ps 17(18),16
breathing on; neol.
Cf. CAIRD 1972, 128

ἐμπνέω⁺ V 1-9-0-0-1-11
Dt 20,16; Jos 10,28.30.35.37
to breathe, to live, to be alive [abs.] Dt 20,16; to
breathe of, to be laden with (life) [τινος] Jos

10,40; to breathe into, to infuse into [τι] Wis
15,11; ἐμπνέον living creature Jos 10,37
→TWNT

ἔμπνους,-ους,-ουν A 0-0-0-0-2-2
2 Mc 7,5; 14,45
with breath in one, alive

ἐμποδίζω V 0-1-0-1-5-7
Jgsᴮ 5,22; Ezr 4,4; 1 Mc 9,55; Sir 12,5; 18,22
A: to hinder, to thwart Sir 32(35),3; to hinder, to
hold back Sir 12,5; to hinder from [+inf.] Ezr
4,4; P: to be put in bonds Jgsᴮ 5,22; to be
hindered 1 Mc 9,55

ἐμποδιστικός,-ή,-όν A 0-0-0-0-2-2
4 Mc 1,4(bis)
hampering, impeding, trammelling, being a
hindrance

ἐμποδοστατέω V 0-1-0-0-0-1
Jgsᴬ 11,35
to be in the way of [τι]

ἐμποδοστάτης,-ου N1M 0-1-0-0-0-1
1 Chr 2,7
one who is in the way, troubler; neol.

ἐμποιέομαι V 1-0-0-0-1-2
Ex 9,17; 1 Ezr 5,38
to lay claim to [τινος]
Cf. LE BOULLUEC 1989, 132

ἐμπολάω V 0-0-1-0-0-1
Am 8,5
to traffic

ἔμπονος,-ος,-ον A 0-0-0-0-1-1
3 Mc 1,28
vehement

ἐμπορεύομαι⁺ V 3-2-4-2-0-11
Gn 34,10.21; 42,34; 2 Chr 1,16; 9,14
to travel for traffic or business [abs.] Gn 34,10; to
be a merchant, to traffic, to trade [abs.] 2 Chr
9,14; to trade in a place [τι] Gn 34,21; to traffic
for [τι] Prv 3,14; to trade with sb in sth [τινι ἔν
τινι] Ez 27,13; [τινα ἔν τινι] Ez 27,21
Cf. HELBING 1928, 85.274; WALTERS 1973, 85-86

ἐμπορία,-ας⁺ N1F 0-0-11-0-0-11
Is 23,18(bis); Is 45,14; Ez 27,13.15
market, trade, business Is 23,18; merchandise Na
3,16

ἐμπόριον,-ου⁺ N2N 1-0-2-0-0-3
Dt 33,19; Is 23,17; Ez 27,3
mart; *Is 23,17 καὶ ἔσται ἐμπόριον -◊ זון and
he shall be the mart (for) for MT וזנתה ◊ זנה and
she shall play the harlot, commit fornication
(with); *Ez 27,3 τῷ ἐμπορίῳ -רְכֻלּת to the

market (of) for MT וּכְלָת *the merchant* (of)
Cf. SEELIGMANN 1948, 54

ἔμπορος,-ου⁺   N2M 2-3-14-0-6-25
Gn 23,16; 37,28; 1 Kgs 10,15.28; 2 Chr 1,16
merchant, trader

ἐμπορπάω   V 0-0-0-0-1-1
3 Mc 7,5
to fasten with a brooch or *pin, to buckle*;
ἐμπεπορπημένοι ὠμότητα *they buckled
themselves with cruelty*

ἐμπορπόομαι   V 0-0-0-0-1-1
1 Mc 14,44
to wear; ἐπορπόομαι πορπήν *to wear a buckle*;
see ἐμπορπάω

ἔμπροσθεν⁺   D 11-81-22-24-24-162
Gn 24,7; 32,4.17; 33,3.14
before 2 Kgs 21,11; *before, in front of* [τινος] Gn
24,7; τὰ ἔμπροσθεν *the former things* Is 41,26
Cf. SOLLAMO 1975, 773-782; 1979, 34-36.88.98-99.319-325

ἐμπρόσθιος,-ος,-ον   A 1-1-0-0-1-3
Ex 28,14; 1 Sm 5,4; 2 Mc 3,25
fore, in front

ἔμπτυσμα,-ατος   N3N 0-0-1-0-0-1
Is 50,6
spitting on; neol.

ἐμπτύω⁺   V 2-0-0-0-0-2
Nm 12,14; Dt 25,9
A: *to spit upon* [εἴς τι] Nm 12,14; M: Dt 25,9

ἐμπυρίζω   V 2-13-6-7-24-52
Lv 10,6.16; Jos 8,28; Jgsᴬ 14,15; 15,5
A: *to set on fire, to burn* Jos 8,28; P: *to be burnt*
Lv 10,6; neol.?
Cf. LEE 1983, 113

ἐμπυρισμός,-οῦ   N2M 3-3-0-1-0-7
Lv 10,6; Nm 11,3; Dt 9,22; Jos 6,24; 1 Kgs 8,37
burning
Cf. LEE 1969, 239; 1983, 100-101

ἐμπυριστής,-οῦ   N1M 0-0-0-0-1-1
4 Mc 7,11
one who sets on fire

ἔμπυρος,-ος,-ον   A 0-0-2-0-0-2
Ez 23,37; Am 4,2
feverish (of a plague, pest) Am 4,2; τά ἔμπυρα
burnt-offerings Ez 23,37

ἐμφαίνω   V 0-0-0-1-1-2
Ps 79(80),2; 2 Mc 3,16
A: *to exhibit, to display* Sir 24,32; *to indicate*
2 Mc 3,16; M/P: *to become visible, to be
manifested* Ps 79(80),2

ἐμφανής,-ής,-ές⁺   A 1-0-3-0-3-7

Ex 2,14; Is 2,2; 65,1; Mi 4,1; Wis 6,22
manifest, visible
Cf. HORSLEY 1987, 148; →NIDNTT

ἐμφανίζω⁺   V 1-0-1-1-7-10
Ex 33,13; Is 3,9; Est 2,22; 1 Mc 4,20; 2 Mc 3,7
A: *to show forth, to exhibit, to manifest* Ex 33,13;
to make clear Is 3,9; *to declare, to explain* Est
2,22; P: *to become visible to, to be manifested to*
[τινι] Wis 1,2
Cf. HELBING 1928, 222-223; →NIDNTT

ἐμφανισμός,-οῦ   N2M 0-0-0-0-1-1
2 Mc 3,9
information, disclosure

ἐμφανῶς   D 0-0-1-1-0-2
Zph 1,9; Ps 49(50),2
openly, visibly, manifestly Ps 49(50),2; *Zph 1,9
ἐμφανῶς corr.? ἐφαλλομένους
Cf. WALTERS 1973, 137 (Zph 1,9)

ἔμφασις,-εως   N3F 0-0-0-0-1-1
2 Mc 3,8
outward appearance, impression

ἐμφέρομαι   V 0-0-0-0-1-1
2 Mc 15,17
to rush in

ἔμφοβος,-ος,-ον⁺   A 0-0-0-0-1-1
Sir 19,24
terrified, frightened

ἐμφραγμός,-οῦ   N2M 0-0-0-0-1-1
Sir 27,14
stoppage, barrier; ἡ μάχη αὐτῶν ἐμφραγμὸς
(ὠτίων) *(their noisy quarrel) makes one stop
(one's ears)*; neol.

ἐμφράσσω   V 2-5-5-7-4-23
Gn 26,15.18; 2 Kgs 3,19.25; 2 Chr 32,3
to bar a passage, to stop up, to block up 2 Chr
32,30; *to stop* Jb 5,16; *Mi 4,14 ἐμφραχθήσεται
- ◊ נדר *she shall be hedged in* for MT נדר ◊ *you
administer incisions to yourself*?

ἐμφυσάω⁺   V 1-1-3-1-3-9
Gn 2,7; 1 Kgs 17,21; Ez 21,36; 37,9; Na 2,2
to blow in, to breathe in(to) Wis 15,11; *to breathe
upon* [τινι] Jb 4,21; [εἴς τινα] Ez 37,9; *Na
2,1(2) ἐμφυσῶν *breathing (into your face)*
imitating the sound of MT מפיץ *disperser*
Cf. HELBING 1928, 274; →TWNT

ἐμφυσιόω   V 0-0-0-0-2-2
1 Ezr 9,48.55
A: *to inspire, to put meaning into* [τι] 1 Ezr 9,48;
P: *to be inspired* 1 Ezr 9,55

ἔμφυτος,-ος,-ον⁺   A 0-0-0-0-1-1

Wis 12,10
inborn, natural

ἐν⁺   P 2199-4208-2659-2684-2526-14276

Gn 1,1.6.11.12.14

[τινι]: *in* (place) Gn 9,21; *on* Ex 25,40; *in* (of books) 2 Mc 2,4; *at* 1 Ezr 4,29; *in the number of, among* Jos 3,5; *amongst, in* Sir 16,6; *in the presence of, before* Jdt 6,2; *towards* Gn 40,14; *into* Tob^BA 5,5; *in* (state) 3 Mc 5,8; *with* (instrument) 1 Ezr 1,52; *by* (means) Sir 4,24; *in, with* (of clothes) 1 Mc 6,35; *with* (of pers. accompanying sb) 1 Mc 4,6; *with* (of things carried with) Gn 32,11; *in* (point of time) Bar 1,2; *in the course of* Gn 6,4; *because of, on account of* 1 Mc 16,3; *for* (periphrasis for gen. of prize) 1 Chr 21,24; ἐν τοῖς Ραγουήλου *in the house of Raguel* Tob^S 6,11; ἐν δωρεᾷ *as a gift* 2 Mc 4,30; ὄμνυμι ἔν τινι *to swear by* Jgs 21,7; ἐν τῷ κινῆσαι αὐτούς *while they were moving* Gn 11,2; *Zph 3,19 ἔν σοὶ ἕνεκεν σοῦ -אתך למענך (*I will do things*) *to you for your sake* for MT את כל מעניך (*I will do things*) *to all your oppressors*

Cf. KRAFT 1972, 165; MILLIGAN 1980, 120; SOISALON-SOININEN 1982, 190-200; THACKERAY 1909, 25; →TWNT

ἐναγκαλίζομαι⁺   V 0-0-0-2-0-2
Prv 6,10; 24,33
to take in one's arms

ἐναγκάλισμα,-ατος   N3N 0-0-0-0-1-1
4 Mc 13,21
that which embraces; neol.

ἐναγωνίζομαι   V 0-0-0-0-1-1
4 Mc 16,16
to take part in the strife, to fight

ἐναθλέω   V 0-0-0-0-1-1
4 Mc 17,13
to struggle bravely in

ἐνακούω   V 0-0-1-0-2-3
Na 1,12; 1 Ezr 4,3.10
A: *to obey* [abs.] 1 Ezr 4,10; *to do, to fulfil* [τι] 1 Ezr 4,3; P: *to be heared* [τι] Na 1,12

ἐναλλαγή,-ῆς   N1F 0-0-0-0-1-1
Wis 14,26
change, inversion
Cf. GILBERT 1973, 167; LARCHER 1985, 824

ἐναλλάξ   D 1-0-0-0-0-1
Gn 48,14
crosswise

ἐνάλλομαι   V 0-0-0-4-2-6
Jb 6,27; 16,4.10(9); 19,5; 1 Mc 3,23

to leap upon [εἰς τι] 4 Mc 6,8; *to attack* Jb 16,10; *to insult* [ἐπί τινι] Jb 6,27
Cf. HELBING 1928, 274

ἔναντι⁺   P 172-27-6-22-36-263
Ex 6,12; 28,12.29.38; 29,10
in the presence of, before [τινος]
Cf. SOLLAMO, 1975, 773-782

ἐναντίον⁺   D 193-92-38-71-38-432
Gn 6,8.11.13; 7,1; 10,9
[τινος]: *opposite, facing* Ez 33,31; *in the presence of* Gn 6,8; *before, in the sight of* Gn 10,9; *against* (in hostile sense) Nm 14,27; τοὐναντίον *on the other hand* 3 Mc 3,22; εὐαρεστέω ἐναντίον τινός *to be well-pleasing before* Gn 17,1; *Am 3,10 ἐναντίον αὐτῆς -נכחה *in front (of her)* for MT נכחה *that which is right*
Cf. LE BOULLUEC 1989, 95.131.139.260-261; SOLLAMO 1975, 773-782; 1979, 21-28; WIKENHAUSEN 1910, 263-270

ἐναντιόομαι⁺   V 0-0-0-1-7-8
Prv 20,8; 1 Ezr 1,25; 8,51; 3 Mc 3,1.7
to set oneself against, to oppose, to withstand [abs.] Prv 20,8; [τινι] 1 Ezr 1,25; *to be adverse to* [τινι] Wis 2,12; τὰ ἐναντιωθησόμενα *things that are repugnant* 4 Mc 5,26

ἐναντίος,-α,-ον⁺   A 4-38-7-12-11-72
Ex 14,2.9; 36,25(39,18); Nm 2,2; Jos 8,11
opposite, contrary, adverse [τινι] Prv 14,7; *opposing, facing* (in hostile sense) Jos 8,11; ἐξ ἐναντίας τινός (mostly in LXX) *opposite* 1 Sm 10,10
Cf. SOLLAMO 1979, 29.121

ἐναπερείδομαι   V 0-0-0-0-1-1
2 Mc 9,4
to vent upon; neol.

ἐναποθνήσκω   V 0-1-0-0-2-3
1 Sm 25,37; 4 Mc 6,30; 11,1
to die in

ἐναποσφραγίζω   V 0-0-0-0-1-1
4 Mc 15,4
to impress in or *on*

ἐνάρετος,-ος,-ον   A 0-0-0-0-1-1
4 Mc 11,5
virtuous

ἐναρίθμιος,-ος,-ον   A 0-0-0-0-1-1
Sir 38,29
in the number, making up the number

ἐναρμόζομαι   V 0-0-0-0-2-2
Jdt 16,1; 4 Mc 9,26
to fit, to adapt [τί τινι]

ἐνάρχομαι⁺   V 5-2-0-1-3-11

Ex 12,18; Nm 9,5; Dt 2,24.25.31
to begin Ex 12,18; *to make a beginning of* [τινος]
Jos 10,24; *Prv 13,12 ἐναρχόμενος -תחלת
beginning for MT תוחלת *hope*, cpr. Gn 4,26 and
ἐλπίζω
Cf. LEE 1983, 70-71

ἐνατενίζω V 0-0-0-0-1-1
3 Mc 5,30
to look fixedly on [intrans.]

ἔνατος,-η,-ον⁺ M 3-13-9-1-5-31
Lv 23,32; 25,22; Nm 7,60; 2 Kgs 15,13.17
ninth

ἐναφίημι V 0-0-1-0-0-1
Ez 21,22
to discharge

ἐνδεής,-ής,-ές⁺ A 4-0-2-16-2-24
Dt 15,4.7.11; 24,14; Is 41,17
wanting or *lacking in, in need of* [τινος] Prv 7,7;
in want, in need [abs.] Prv 13,25; ὁ ἐνδεής *a
poor, a needy one* Is 41,17

ἔνδεια,-ας N1F 2-0-4-8-6-20
Dt 28,20.57; Is 25,4; Ez 4,16; 12,19
want, lack Dt 28,57; *deficiency, defect* Prv 6,11;
need, want Prv 14,23; *want of means, poverty* Jb
30,3

ἐνδείκνυμαι⁺ V 3-4-0-2-5-14
Gn 50,15.17; Ex 9,16; Jos 7,15.16
M: *to show forth oneself, to show what is one's
own* Ex 9,16; *to display, to exhibit* Gn 50,15; P:
to be marked, to be pointed out, to be shown Jos
7,15

ἐνδείκτης,-ου N1M 0-0-0-0-1-1
2 Mc 4,1
informer, complainant; neol.?

ἕνδεκα⁺ M 6-7-1-0-2-16
Gn 32,23; 37,9; Ex 26,7.8; Nm 29,20
eleven

ἑνδέκατος,-η,-ον⁺ M 3-10-8-0-1-22
Gn 8,5; Nm 7,72; Dt 1,3; 1 Kgs 6,1(38)(bis)
eleventh

ἐνδελεχέω V 0-0-0-0-1-1
Sir 30,1
to continue; ἐνδελεχέω μάστιγάς τινι *to let feel
the rod*; neol.

ἐνδελεχής,-ής,-ές A 0-0-0-0-2-2
1 Ezr 6,23; Sir 17,19
continuous, perpetual

ἐνδελεχίζω V 0-0-0-0-8-8
Sir 9,4; 12,3; 20,19.24.25
to persevere, to continue

ἐνδελεχισμός,-οῦ N2M 5-0-0-5-3-13
Ex 29,38.42; 30,8; Nm 28,6.23
continuity, persistency Sir 7,13; stereotyped
rendition of תמיר: (τοῦ) ἐνδελεχισμοῦ
perpetual, daily (sc. sacrifice) Ex 29,38; neol.
Cf. DANIEL 1966, 242.252-267; LUST 1992 (B)

ἐνδελεχῶς D 3-0-0-4-6-13
Ex 29,38; Lv 24,3; Nm 28,3; Dnᴸˣˣ 6,17.21
continually

ἐνδέομαι V 2-0-0-1-0-3
Dt 8,9; 15,8; Prv 28,27
to be in want, to lack

ἔνδεσμος,-ου N2M 0-2-1-2-0-5
1 Kgs 6,10(bis); Ez 13,11; Prv 7,20(bis)
bonding 1 Kgs 6,10; *bond* 3 Mc 3,25; ἔνδεσμος
ἀργυρίου *purse* Prv 7,20

ἐνδέχομαι⁺ V 0-0-0-1-1-2
Dnᴸˣˣ 2,11; 2 Mc 11,18
to admit of, to be possible that [+inf.] (impers.)
Dnᴸˣˣ 2,11; ἐνδεχόμενος *possible, so far as
possible* 2 Mc 11,18

ἐνδεχομένως D 0-0-0-0-1-1
2 Mc 13,26
to the best of his ability

ἐνδέω V 1-2-1-0-1-5
Ex 12,34; 1 Sm 25,29; 2 Chr 9,18; Ez 28,13; Sir
22,16
A: *to bind in* or *on* or *to* [τι ἔν τινι] Ex 12,34;
to rivet [τι ἔν τινι] 2 Chr 9,18; M: *to bind to
oneself* [τι] Ez 28,13
Cf. HELBING 1928, 274

ἐνδιαβάλλω V 1-0-0-5-0-6
Nm 22,22; Ps 37(38),21; 70(71),13; 108(109),4.20
to accuse falsely, to calumniate Ps 108(109),4; *to
divert from a course* or *purpose* Nm 22,22
Cf. CAIRD 1972, 128

ἐνδιατρίβω V 0-0-0-1-0-1
Prv 23,16
to linger on; *Prv 23,16 ἐνδιατρίψει corr.
ἐνδιαθρύψει for MT תעלוזנה *to exult at*

ἐνδιδύσκω⁺ V 0-2-0-1-1-4
2 Sm 1,24; 13,18; Prv 31,21; Sir 50,11
A: *to put on* [τινά τι] 2 Sm 1,24; M: *to put on
oneself, to clothe* [τι] 2 Sm 13,18

ἐνδίδωμι V 2-0-1-1-0-4
Gn 8,3(bis); Ez 3,11; Prv 10,30
to subside Gn 8,3; *to fail* Prv 10,30

ἐνδογενής,-ής,-ές A 1-0-0-0-0-1
Lv 18,9
born in the house

ἔνδοθεν   D 1-0-0-0-2-3
Nm 18,7; 4 Mc 18,2; Wis 17,12
from within Wis 17,12; *within* [τινος] Nm 18,7
ἔνδον   D 4-0-0-0-7-11
Lv 11,33(bis); Dt 21,12; 22,2; 2 Mc 6,4
within, inside Lv 11,33; τὰ ἔνδον *the inner parts*
2 Mc 9,5; οἱ ἔνδον *those who are within* 2 Mc
10,34

ἐνδοξάζομαι⁺   V 4-1-4-1-1-11
Ex 14,4.17.18; 33,16; 2 Kgs 14,10
to be glorified [ἔν τινι] Ex 14,4; *to be glorious, to
show oneself glorious* Ez 38,23; neol.
Cf. CAIRD 1972, 128-129

ἔνδοξος,-ος,-ον⁺   A 4-12-18-12-19-65
Gn 34,19; Ex 34,10; Nm 23,21; Dt 10,21; Jos 4,4
held in esteem or *honour, of high repute* Gn
34,19; *notable, glorious* Ex 34,10; *Nm 23,21
ἔνδοξα- נוראת *glory* for MT תרועת *shout*
→TWNT

ἐνδόξως   D 2-0-0-2-14-18
Ex 15,1.21; Dnᴸˣˣ 4,37b(34)(bis); Tobᴮᴬ 12,7
honourably, gloriously

ἐνδόσθια,-ων   N2N 7-0-0-0-1-8
Ex 12,9; 29,17; Lv 4,8(bis); 7,3
inwards, entrails; neol.

ἔνδυμα,-ατος⁺   N3N 0-3-2-6-3-14
2 Sm 1,24; 20,8; 2 Kgs 10,22; Is 63,2; Zph 1,8
garment

ἔνδυσις,-εως⁺   N3F 0-0-0-2-0-2
Est 5,1a; Jb 41,5
dressing, dress

ἐνδύω⁺   V 26-14-30-28-20-118
Gn 3,21; 27,15; 38,19; 41,42; Ex 28,41
A: *to put on* [τι] Lv 16,23; *to enter* [τινα] 2 Chr
24,20; *to put on, to clothe in* [τί τινα] Gn 41,42;
to clothe [τινα] Gn 3,21; M: *to put on* [τι] Lv
6,4; *to clothe oneself in* [τι] (metaph.) Ps
103(104),1; P: *to be clothed in, to have on* [τι]
2 Chr 5,12
Cf. PRIJS 1948, 28-29 (Ps 64(65),14)

ἐνέδρα,-ας⁺   N1F 0-2-0-1-0-3
Jos 8,7.9; Ps 9,29(10,8)
lying in wait, ambush

ἐνεδρεύω⁺   V 1-14-0-8-11-34
Dt 19,11; Jos 8,4; Jgsᴬ 9,32.34.43
to lie in wait for, to lay snares for [τινα] Dt
19,11; *to lay* or *set an ambush* [abs.] Jos 8,4;
*1 Sm 15,5 καὶ ἐνήδρευσεν- ויארב *and he laid
in wait* for MT וירב *he fought*; *Jb 24,11
ἐνήδρευσαν- יצורו *they have laid in wait* for MT

יצהירו *they have pressed oil*? or *they rest at noon*?
ἔνεδρον,-ου   N2N 2-29-1-1-8-41
Nm 35,20.22; Jos 8,2.12.14
ambush Nm 35,20; *Jb 25,3 ἔνεδρα παρ' αὐτοῦ
-ארבו *his ambush* for MT ארהו *his light*

ἐνειλέω⁺   V 0-1-0-0-0-1
1 Sm 21,10
to wrap in, to enwrap

ἔνειμι⁺ (εἶναι)   V 0-1-0-3-4-8
1 Kgs 10,17; Jb 27,3; 34,13; Prv 14,23; 1 Mc 5,5
to be in 1 Kgs 10,17; *to be present* 1 Mc 5,5; ἔνι
it is possible (equivalent for ἔνεστι) 4 Mc 4,22;
τὰ ἐνόντα πάντα *all things possible* Jb 34,13
Cf. WALTERS 1973, 111.112

ἐνείρω   V 0-0-0-1-0-1
Jb 10,11
to thread

ἕνεκα, ἕνεκεν or εἵνεκεν⁺   P 34-14-41-33-16-138
Gn 2,24; 12,13; 16,14; 18,5.24
on account of, for [τινος] Gn 12,13; *because*
[τοῦ +inf.] Am 6,1; ἕνεκα τούτου *for this
reason* Gn 2,24; οὗ εἵνεκεν [+ind.] *because* Is
61,1; *Lam 3,44 εἵνεκεν -בעבור *on account of*
for MT מעבור *from passing through*

ἐνενήκοντα⁺   M 5-2-4-9-3-23
Gn 5,9.17; 17,1.17.24
ninety

ἐνενηκονταετής,-ής,-ές   M 0-0-0-0-1-1
2 Mc 6,24
ninety years old

ἐνεξουσιάζομαι   V 0-0-0-0-2-2
Sir 20,8; 47,19
M: *to stand on one's rights* Sir 20,8; P: *to be
brought into subjection* Sir 47,19
Cf. CAIRD 1972, 129

ἐνεός,-ά,-όν⁺   A 0-0-1-1-1-3
Is 56,10; Prv 17,28; LtJ 1,40
dumb, speechless

ἐνεργάζομαι   V 0-0-0-0-1-1
2 Mc 14,40
to make, to produce (in)

ἐνέργεια,-ας⁺   N1F 0-0-0-0-8-8
2 Mc 3,29; 3 Mc 4,21; 5,12.28; Wis 7,17
activity, operation, action
→TWNT

ἐνεργέω⁺   V 1-0-1-2-3-7
Nm 8,24; Is 41,4; Prv 21,6; 31,12; 1 Ezr 2,16
A: *to be in action* or *activity, to operate* Wis
15,11; *to produce, to work, to affect* [τι] Prv
31,12; P: *to be the object of action* 1 Ezr 2,16;

*Prv 21,6 ὁ ἐνεργῶν - פֹּעַל the one producing for MT פֹּעַל production
- ·TWNT

ἐνεργός,-ός,-όν   A 0-0-1-0-0-1
Ez 46,1
active, working

ἐνευλογέομαι⁺   V 5-1-0-1-1-8
Gn 12,3; 18,18; 22,18; 26,4; 28,14
M: to take a blessing to oneself, to bless oneself
Ps 9,24(10,3); P: to be blessed in [ἔν τινι] Gn 12,3; *1 Sm 2,29 ἐνευλογεῖσθαι - להברך to bless (themselves) for MT להבריא/כם fattening yourselves; neol.
Cf. HARL 1986, 56

ἐνευφραίνομαι   V 0-0-0-1-0-1
Prv 8,31
to rejoice; neol.

ἐνεχυράζω   V 5-0-1-3-1-10
Ex 22,25; Dt 24,6(bis).10.17
to take in pledge [τι]; neol.?
Cf. BICKERMAN 1976, 195 n.71; DAVID 1943, 79-86

ἐνεχύρασμα,-ατος   N3N 1-0-1-0-0-2
Ex 22,25; Ez 33,15
pledge

ἐνεχυρασμός,-οῦ   N2M 0-0-3-0-0-3
Ez 18,7.12.16
taking in pledge, pledge

ἐνέχυρον,-ου   N2N 4-0-0-0-0-4
Dt 24,10.11.12.13
pledge

ἐνέχω⁺   V 1-0-2-0-1-4
Gn 49,23; Ez 14,4.7; 3 Mc 6,10
A: to be vehemently against [τινι] Gn 49,23; P: to be held in, to be caught in, to be entangled in [τινι] 3 Mc 6,10; *Ez 14,4 (ἐν οἷς) ἐνέχεται -ריב ב/רב◊? (because of which) it is inculpated, stained for MT רבה ב/רב◊ because of the multitude, cpr. Ez 14,7 (without parallel in Hebr.)
Cf. SPICQ 1982, 273-275 (esp. 274); HELBING 1928, 274-275

ἐνῆλιξ,-ικος   N3M/F 0-0-0-0-1-1
4 Mc 18,9
one of age, in the prime of manhood

ἔνθα   D 0-6-0-0-4-10
2 Kgs 2,8(bis).14(bis); 5,25
there 2 Mc 12,27; then 4 Mc 6,25; ἔνθα καὶ ἔνθα hither and thither, to and fro 2 Kgs 2,8

ἐνθάδε⁺   D 0-0-0-0-1-1
3 Mc 6,25
here

ἔνθεμα,-ατος   N3N 0-0-0-1-0-1
Ct 4,9
ornament

ἐνθέμιον,-ου   N2N 2-0-0-0-0-2
Ex 38,16(37,23)(bis)
socket corr.? ανθέμιον artificial flowers; neol.
Cf. GOODING 1959, 56; LE BOULLUEC 1989, 366; WEVERS 1990, 625

ἔνθεν⁺   D 6-16-44-2-6-74
Ex 26,13(bis); 32,15(bis); 37,13(38,15)
from here; ἔνθεν καὶ ἔνθεν on this and on that, on each side Ex 26,13; up and down 2 Kgs 4,35

ἔνθεσμος,-ος,-ον   A 0-0-0-0-1-1
3 Mc 2,21
lawful; neol.

ἐνθουσιάζω   V 0-0-0-0-1-1
Sir 31,7
to be inspired or possessed by a god

ἐνθρονίζω   V 0-0-0-0-1-1
4 Mc 2,22
to enthrone, to place on a throne; cpr. Est 1,2 vl.; neol.?

ἐνθρύπτω   V 0-0-0-0-2-2
Bel^LXX 32; Bel^Th 33
to crumble (in); neol.

ἐνθυμέομαι⁺   V 2-2-1-2-14-21
Gn 6,6; Dt 21,11; Jos 6,18; 7,21; Is 10,7
to lay to heart, to ponder Gn 6,6; to think much of, to think deeply of [τινος] Dt 21,11; to form a plan [abs.] 1 Ezr 8,11; *Jos 6,18 ἐνθυμηθέντες -תחמרו? you set your mind upon for MT תחרימו you devote to destruction
Cf. HELBING 1928, 138

ἐνθύμημα,-ατος   N3N 0-1-22-1-4-28
1 Chr 28,9; Jer 3,17; 7,24; Ez 14,5.7
thought, piece of reasoning, argument 1 Chr 28,9; invention, device, imagination Ez 14,7; *Mal 2,16 τὰ ἐνθυμήματά σου your thoughts corr.? τὰ ἐνδύματά σου for MT לבושׁ (one's garment) your garments; *Ps 118(119),118 ἐνθύμημα (αὐτῶν) -תרעיתם (their) thought for MT תרמיתם their cunning

ἐνθύμιον,-ου   N2N 0-0-0-2-0-2
Ps 75(76),11(bis)
thought, concept

ἐνιαύσιος,-α,-ον   A 55-0-2-0-0-57
Ex 12,5; 29,38; Lv 9,3; 12,6; 14,10
of a year, one year old

ἐνιαυτός,-οῦ⁺   N2M 45-51-25-13-24-158
Gn 1,14; 17,21; 26,12; 47,17.28

year Gn 1,14; ἐνιαυτὸς ἡμερῶν *a full year* Lv
25,29 κατ' ἐνιαυτὸν *yearly* 2 Chr 27,5; *Ez 15,4
·κατ' ἐνιαυτόν -שׁנה *yearly* for MT שׁני *two*
Cf. THACKERY 1909, 39

ἐνίημι   V 0-0-0-0-2-2
4 Mc 4,10; Bar 2,20
to send in(to) [τι εἴς τινα] (metaph.) Bar 2,20;
to evoke, to inspire [τί τινι] 4 Mc 4,10
Cf. HELBING 1928, 275

ἔνιοι,-αι,-α   R 0-0-0-0-2-2
3 Mc 2,31; 3,4
some

ἐνίοτε   D 0-0-0-0-1-1
Sir 37,14
at times, sometimes

ἐνίσταμαι⁺   V 0-1-0-1-11-13
1 Kgs 12,24x; Est 3,13f; 1 Ezr 5,46; 9,6; 1 Mc
8,24
to begin [abs.] 1 Kgs 12,24; ἐνέστη *to be at
hand, to arise* 1 Mc 8,24; *to be, to exist* 2 Mc
4,43; ἐνείστηκά τινι *to be upon, to threaten*
1 Mc 12,44; ἐνεστώς *present* 2 Mc 3,17; *current*
(with subst. indicating a period of time) Est
3,13f
Cf. HELBING 1928, 275; → TWNT

ἐνισχύω⁺   V 8-22-14-12-8-64
Gn 12,10; 32,29; 33,14; 43,1; 47,4
to strengthen, to confirm [τινα] Jgs 3,12; *to
prevail on* or *among* [ἐπί τινος] Gn 12,10; *to be
strong* Sir 48,22; *Jer 6,1 ἐνισχύσατε -העזו ◊
עזז *strenghten yourselves* for MT העזו ◊ עוז *bring into
safety*; *Jgsᴬ 5,11 ἐνίσχυσαν -פרזו *they prevailed*
for MT פרזו *his peasantry*; *Hos 10,11
ἐνισχύσει -ישׂרד *will prevail* for MT ישׂרד *will
harrow*
Cf. WALTERS 1972, 128

ἐννακισχίλιοι,-αι,-α   M 0-0-0-0-2-2
2 Mc 8,24; 10,18
nine thousand

ἐννακόσιοι,-αι,-α   M 7-5-0-5-2-19
Gn 5,5.8.11.14.20
nine hundred

ἐννέα⁺   M 14-18-0-5-6-43
Gn 5,27; 11,19.24.25; 17,1
nine

ἐννεακαίδεκα   M 0-1-0-0-0-1
2 Sm 2,30
nineteen

ἐννεακαιδέκατος,-η,-ον   M 0-3-0-0-0-3
2 Kgs 25,8; 1 Chr 24,16; 25,26

nineteenth

ἐννέμομαι   V 0-0-0-0-1-1
3 Mc 3,25
to live amongst [σύν τινι]

ἔννευμα,-ατος   N3N 0-0-0-1-0-1
Prv 6,13
signal; ἔννευμα δακτύλων *wave of the hand;*
neol.

ἐννεύω⁺   V 0-0-0-2-0-2
Prv 6,13; 10,10
to make signs; ἐννεύω ὀφθαλμῷ *to wink with the
eye*

ἐννοέω   V 0-0-1-3-5-9
Is 41,20; Jb 1,5; Dnᴸˣˣ 11,33; Dnᵀʰ 9,23; Jdt 9,5
to have in one's thoughts, to consider Jb 1,5; *to
understand* Is 41,20; *to intend* Jdt 9,5

ἐννόημα,-ατος   N3N 0-0-0-0-1-1
Sir 21,11
notion, concept

ἔννοια,-ας⁺   N1F 0-0-0-12-2-14
Prv 1,4; 2,11; 3,21; 4,1; 5,2
act of thinking, reflection, cogitation Prv 1,4;
notion, conception, idea Wis 2,14
→ NIDNTT; TWNT

ἔννομος,-ος,-ον⁺   A 0-0-0-0-1-1
Sir prol.,10
ordained by law, lawful, legal

ἐννόμως   D 0-0-0-1-1-2
Prv 31,25(26); Sir 0,35
lawfully, legally

ἐννοσσεύω   V 0-0-1-1-0-2
Jer 22,23; Ps 103(104),17
to make a nest

ἐννοσσοποιέομαι   V 0-0-0-0-1-1
4 Mc 14,16
to make oneself a nest on [τι]; neol.

ἔννυχος,-ος,-ον   A 0-0-0-0-1-1
3 Mc 5,5
by night, at night

ἐνοικειόομαι   V 0-0-0-1-0-1
Est 8,1
to be related to [τινι]

ἐνοικέω⁺   V 1-4-28-1-6-40
Lv 26,32; Jgsᴬ 6,10; 2 Kgs 19,26; 22,16.19
to dwell in [ἔν τινι] Lv 26,32; *to inhabit* [τι] Is
65,21; οἱ ἐνοικοῦντες *the inhabitants* 2 Kgs
22,16

ἐνοικίζω   V 0-0-0-0-1-1
Sir 11,34
to house, to receive into one's house [τινα]

ἔνοικος,-ου   N2M 0-1-2-0-0-3
Jgs^A 5,23; Jer 31(48),9; 51(44),2
inhabitant

ἐνοπλίζομαι   V 8-1-0-0-1-10
Nm 31,5; 32,17.20.27.29
to arm oneself Nm 32,17; ἐνοπλισμένος armed
Nm 31,5

ἔνοπλος,-ος,-ον   A 0-1-0-0-4-5
1 Kgs 22,10; 2 Mc 14,22; 3 Mc 5,48; 6,21; 4 Mc
5,1
at arms, armed

ἐνοράω   V 1-0-0-0-0-1
Gn 20,10
to see (in a person), to remark on [τι]

ἐνόρκιον,-ου   N2N 1-0-0-0-0-1
Nm 5,21
oath

ἔνορκος,-ος,-ον   A 0-0-0-1-0-1
Neh 6,18
having sworn, bound by oath

ἐνόρκως   D 0-0-0-0-1-1
Tob^BA 8,20
having sworn, bound by oath

ἐνοχλέω^+   V 1-2-1-1-2-7
Gn 48,1; 1 Sm 19,14; 30,13; Mal 1,13; Dn^Th 6,3
A: to trouble, to annoy 1 Ezr 2,24; P: to be
unwell Gn 48,1
Cf. HORSLEY 1983, 67; 1987, 167; LEE 1983, 66

ἔνοχος,-ος,-ον^+   A 13-2-1-1-5-22
Gn 26,11; Ex 22,2; 34,7; Lv 20,9.11
liable to, subject to [τινος] Gn 26,11; liable to
action for [τινος] 2 Mc 13,6; guilty Ex 22,2; guilty
of [τινι] Dt 19,10
Cf. BICKERMAN 1986, 91-93; →NIDNTT

ἐνσείω   V 0-1-0-0-4-5
2 Kgs 8,12; 2 Mc 3,25; 12,15.37; 14,46
to dash to the ground 2 Kgs 8,12; to rush upon,
to attack [τινι] 2 Mc 12,15
Cf. HELBING 1928, 275

ἐνσιτέομαι   V 0-0-0-1-0-1
Jb 40,30
to feed upon [ἔν τινι]; *Jb 40,30 ἐνσιτοῦνται
יכרו/כרה^Ιthey feed upon for MT יכרו ◊ כרה^ΙΙ they
barter for, they bargain; neol.

ἐνσκολιεύομαι   V 0-0-0-1-0-1
Jb 40,24
to twist and turn; *Jb 40,24 ἐνσκολιευόμενος
corr.? ἐνσκώλοις בקמושים- with pointed stakes
for MT במוקשים with snares; neol.
Cf. CAIRD 1972, 129; WALTERS 1973,76

ἐντάλματα,-ων^+   N3N 0-0-2-2-0-4
Is 29,13; 55,11; Jb 23,11.12
orders, commands; neol.

ἐντάσσω   V 0-0-1-5-0-6
Am 7,8; Dn^Th 5,24.25; 6,11; 10,21
to insert in Am 7,8; to issue orders, to order Dn^Th
5,24

ἐνταῦθα   D 4-20-0-1-7-32
Gn 38,21; 48,9; Nm 23,1(bis); Jgs^A 4,20
here Gn 38,21; hither 1 Sm 10,22; at the very
time, then 3 Mc 2,21; ἐνταῦθα ... ἐνταῦθα on
one side ... on the other side 1 Sm 17,3

ἐνταφιάζω^+   V 2-0-0-0-0-2
Gn 50,2(bis)
to prepare for burial, to lay out, to embalm;
neol.?

ἐνταφιαστής,-οῦ   N1M 2-0-0-0-0-2
Gn 50,2(bis)
undertaker, embalmer; neol.?

ἐντείνω   V 0-2-9-9-2-22
1 Kgs 22,34; 2 Chr 18,33; Is 5,28; Jer 4,29; 9,2
to stretch tight, to bend [τι] (of a bow) 1 Kgs
22,34; *Ps 44(45),5 καὶ ἔντεινον והדרך ◊ דרך
and bend (the bow) for MT והדרך ◊ הדר and
your glory; *Hos 7,16 ἐντεταμένον רמה ◊ רום
bent, stretched for MT רמיה treacherous

ἐντέλλομαι^+   V 156-137-49-41-41-424
Gn 2,16; 3,11.17; 6,22; 7,5
to command, to charge, to demand [τινι] Gn
2,16; *Prv 5,2 ἐντέλλεται יצוו- will command
for MT ינצרו will keep
Cf. PELLETIER 1982, 236-242; →TWNT

ἔντερον,-ου   N2N 1-0-0-0-2-3
Gn 43,30; 2 Mc 14,46; Sir 31,20
τὰ ἔντερα gut, bowel 2 Mc 14,46; ἐπὶ ἐντέρῳ
μετρίῳ for moderation in eating Sir 31,20

ἐντεῦθεν^+   D 16-8-2-3-5-34
Gn 37,17; 42,15; 50,25; Ex 11,1; 13,3
hence Gn 37,17; thence Ex 11,1; henceforth,
thereupon 1 Ezr 4,22; ἐντεῦθεν καὶ ἐντεῦθεν
on this side ... on that side ... Nm 22,24

ἔντευξις,-εως^+   N3F 0-0-0-0-1-1
2 Mc 4,8
petition (to the king)
Cf. SPICQ 1978, 246-249

ἐντήκομαι   V 0-0-1-0-1-2
Ez 24,23; 4 Mc 8,26
to pine away in, to be absorbed by [ἔν τινι] Ez
24,23; ἐντέτηκά τινι to sink deep in (metaph.)
4 Mc 8,26

Cf. HELBING 1928, 275

ἐντίθημι   V 0-0-0-2-2-4
Prv 8,5; Ezr 5,8; 2 Mc 3,27; 3 Mc 5,28
A: *to put in* [τινα ἔις τι] 2 Mc 3,27; M: [τι ἐν
τινι] Ezr 5,8; τινος λήθην ἐντίθημι *to make
forget* 3 Mc 5,28; *Prv 8,5 ἔνθεσθε -הכינו
imbibe? take (heart)? for MT הבינו *understand*

ἔντιμος,-ος,-ον⁺   A 2-1-6-11-10-30
Nm 22,15; Dt 28,58; 1 Sm 26,21; Is 3,5; 13,12
honourable Nm 22,15; *valuable, highly valued* Is
28,16; ὁ ἔντιμος *noble* Neh 2,16

ἐντιμόομαι   V 0-2-0-0-0-2
2 Kgs 1,13.14
to be held in honour; neol.

ἐντίμως   D 1-0-0-0-6-7
Nm 22,17; Tob 12,6; Tob 14,5.13
honourably

ἐντιναγμός,-οῦ   N2M 0-0-0-0-1-1
Sir 22,13
shaking; neol.

ἐντινάσσω   V 0-0-0-0-3-3
1 Mc 2,36; 2 Mc 4,41; 11,11
to hurl against [τί τινι] 1 Mc 2,36; [τι εἴς τινα]
2 Mc 4,41; *to charge upon* [εἴς τινα] 2 Mc 11,11
Cf. HELBING 1928, 275

ἐντολή,-ῆς⁺   N1F 59-48-6-79-48-240
Gn 26,5; Ex 12,17; 15,26; 16,28; 24,12
stereotyped rendering of מצוה; *commandment of
God, law* Dt 26,13; ἐντολαί *orders, commands*
Gn 26,5; *2 Chr 34,22 ἐντολάς *commandments*
corr.? στολάς for MT בגדים *garments*; *Ex 12,17
τὴν ἐντολήν -המצוה *command* for MT המצות
unleavened bread
Cf. LIEBERMAN 1946, 67-72; PELLETIER 1982, 236-242;
→NIDNTT; TWNT

ἐντομίς,-ίδος   N3F 2-0-1-0-0-3
Lv 19,28; 21,5; Jer 16,6
incision, gash; neol.

ἐντός⁺   D 0-0-1-5-2-8
Is 16,11; Ps 38(39),4; 102(103),1; 108(109),22;
Ct 3,10
within, inside [τινος]

ἐντρέπομαι⁺   V 3-13-9-12-11-48
Ex 10,3; Lv 26,41; Nm 12,14; Jgsᴬ 3,30; 8,28
to reverence, to feel regard for [τινα] Ex 10,3; *to
feel shame on account of* [τινα] Jb 32,21; *to feel
shame, to be ashamed* [abs.] Lv 26,41
Cf. GEHMAN 1972 (A), 108; HELBING 1928, 33; LE
BOULLUEC 1989, 136

ἐντρεχής,-ής,-ές   A 0-0-0-0-1-1

Sir 31,22
skilful, ready

ἔντριτος,-ος,-ον   A 0-0-0-1-0-1
Eccl 4,12
of three strands, threefold; neol.

ἔντρομος,-ος,-ον⁺   A 0-0-0-3-2-5
Ps 17(18),8; 76(77),19; Dnᵀʰ 10,11; 1 Mc 13,2;
Wis 17,9
trembling; neol.?

ἐντροπή,-ῆς⁺   N1F 0-0-0-7-0-7
Ps 34(35),26; 43(44),16; 68(69),8.20; 70(71),13
shame Ps 68(69),8; *humiliation* Ps 34(35),26

ἐντρυφάω⁺   V 0-0-4-0-1-5
Is 55,2; 57,4; Jer 38(31),20; Hab 1,10; 4 Mc 8,8
to revel in, to delight in [ἐν τινι] Is 55,2; [τινι]
4 Mc 8,8; *to exult over* [ἐν τινι] Hab 1,10
Cf. HELBING 1928, 275-276

ἐντρύφημα,-ων   N3N 0-0-0-1-0-1
Eccl 2,8
thing to take pleasure in, delight; neol.?

ἐντυγχάνω⁺   V 0-0-0-1-12-13
Dnᴸˣˣ 6,13; 1 Mc 8,32; 10,61.63.64
to obtain an audience or *an interview with* [τινι]
Dnᴸˣˣ 6,13; *to converse with, to talk to* [τινι] Wis
16,28; *to turn to sb with a supplication* [τινι] Wis
8,20; *to appeal to sb* [τινι] 3 Mc 6,37; *to plead
against* [κατά τινος] 1 Mc 8,32; *to read* [τινι]
2 Mc 6,12; οἱ ἐντυγχάνοντες *accusers* 1 Mc
10,64; *change persons* 2 Mc 2,25
Cf. HELBING 1928, 142; SPICQ 1978, 245-249; →TWNT

ἐντυχία,-ας   N1F 0-0-0-0-1-1
3 Mc 6,40
petition; ἐντυχίαν ποιέομαι *to ask*
(= ἐντυχάνω); neol.?

ἔνυδρος,-ος,-ον   A 0-0-0-0-3-3
4 Mc 1,34; Wis 19,10.19
living in water Wis 19,10; *of water, watery* Wis
19,19

ἐνυπνιάζομαι⁺   V 9-2-7-2-0-20
Gn 28,12; 37,5.6.9.10
to dream [abs.] Gn 28,12; [τι] Gn 37,5

ἐνυπνιαστής,-οῦ   N1M 1-0-0-0-0-1
Gn 37,19
dreamer; neol.

ἐνύπνιον,-ου⁺   N2N 27-9-11-50-6-103
Gn 37,5.6.8.9(bis)
dream
Cf. BICKERMAN 1976, 183 n.42

ἐνυποτάσσομαι   V 0-0-0-0-1-1
Tobˢ 14,9

to be made subject to [τινι]; neol.

ἔνυστρον,-ου N2N 1-0-0-0-0-1
Dt 18,3
fourth stomach of ruminating animals; see
ἤνυστρον

ενφωθ N 0-1-0-0-0-1
Jgs^A 8,26
=הנשפות *the pendants*

ἐνώπιον⁺ P 46-248-52-126-86-558
Gn 11,28; 16,13.14; 24,51; 30,33
[τινος]: *before* Gn 30,33; *in the presence of* Ex
34,10

Cf. BICKERMAN 1976, 176-177; CIMOSA 1985, 74-76;
SOLLAMO 1975, 773-782; 1979

ἐνώπιος,-ος,-ον A 5-0-0-5-0-10
Gn 16,13; Ex 25,30; 33,11(bis); Prv 8,9
evident Prv 8,9; ἄρτοι ἐνώπιοι *bread of the
presence, bread put in the presence of the Lord*
Ex 25,30; λαλέω ἐνώπιος ἐνωπίῳ *to speak face
to face* (semit.) Ex 33,11

Cf. LE BOULLUEC 1989, 260-261

ἐνωτίζομαι⁺ V 3-2-10-18-3-36
Gn 4,23; Ex 15,26; Nm 23,18; Jgs 5,3
to give ear, to hearken to [τι] Gn 4,23; [τινι] Ex
15,26; [τινος] Ps 38,13

Cf. HELBING 1928, 157-158; →NIDNTT; TWNT

ἐνώτιον,-ου N2N 7-8-3-2-1-21
Gn 24,22.30.47; 35,4; Ex 32,2
ear-ring

ἐξ
see ἐκ

ἕξ⁺ M 43-43-19-17-12-134
Gn 16,16; 30,20; 31,41; 46,18.26
six

ἐξαγγέλλω⁺ V 0-0-0-9-3-12
Ps 9,15; 55(26),9; 70(71),15; 72(73),28; 78(79),13
to tell out, to proclaim, to make known

→TWNT

ἐξαγοράζω⁺ V 0-0-0-2-0-2
Dn 2,8
to gain time; neol.?

ἐξαγορεύω V 4-1-0-6-1-12
Lv 5,5; 16,21; 26,40; Nm 5,7; 1 Kgs 8,31
to confess

ἐξαγορία,-ας N1F 0-0-0-0-1-1
PSal 9,6
cure by confession

ἐξαγριαίνομαι V 0-0-0-1-0-1
Dn^Th 8,7
to be worked into a fury against, to be made or to

become savage against [πρός τινα]

ἐξάγω⁺ V 93-49-38-27-14-221
Gn 1,20.21.24; 8,17; 11,31
to lead out, to lead away, to bring out of [τινα
ἔκ τινος] Gn 11,31; *to cause to be released from*
[τινα ἔκ τινος] Gn 40,14; *to bring forth, to
produce* [τι] Gn 1,20

Cf. LE BOULLUEC 1989, 26; LEE 1983, 67

ἐξάδελφος,-ου N2M 0-0-0-0-4-4
Tob 1,22; 11,19
nephew; neol.

ἔξαιμος,-ος,-ον A 0-0-0-0-1-1
2 Mc 14,46
bloodless, drained of blood

ἐξαίρετος,-ος,-ον A 1-0-0-1-0-2
Gn 48,22; Jb 5,5
given as a special honour Gn 48,22; *excepted,
delivered out of* [ἔκ τινος] Jb 5,5

ἐξαιρέω⁺ V 13-46-34-42-20-155
Gn 32,12; 37,21.22; Ex 3,8; 18,4
A: *to take (out)* [τι] Jgs 14,9; *to remove* [τι] Lv
14,40; M: *to take away* [τι] Mi 7,3; *to set free, to
deliver, to rescue* [τινα] Gn 32,12; [τι] 2 Kgs
18,35; *to choose* Jb 36,21; P: *to be delivered* Eccl
7,26; *to be taken out, to be chosen* 2 Sm 14,6;
ἐξαιρέομαί τινα ἐκ χειρός τινος *to rescue out
of sb's hands* Gn 37,21

Cf. BUSCEMI 1979, 293-314; SPICQ 1982, 276-279

ἐξαίρω⁺ V 59-58-61-12-36-226
Gn 29,1; 35,5; 41,44; 49,33; Ex 13,20
A: *to lift up* [τι] Gn 29,1; *to rise from the ground*
[intrans.] Nm 2,9; *to arouse* [τινα] Ex 15,22; *to
extoll* [τι] Sir 37,7; *to pervert* [τι] Dt 16,19; *to
remove, to depart* [intrans.] Ex 13,20; *to remove,
to make away with, to get rid of* [τινα ἔκ τινος]
Dt 17,7; P: *to be carried* or *taken away* 1 Kgs
8,25; ἐξαροῦσιν αἱ παρεμβολαί *the camps will
move* Nm 10,5; πνεῦμα ἐξαῖρον *storm* Ez 1,4;
*Na 1,2 ἐξαίρων -נטל *he cuts off, he removes*
for MT נוטר *he is angry*; *Ez 20,39 ἐξάρατε -עברו
put away for MT עברו *serve*

Cf. LE BOULLUEC 1989, 167.292-293; MURAOKA 1990, 31-
32

ἐξαίσιος,-ος,-ον A 0-0-0-9-0-9
Jb 4,12; 5,9; 9,10.23; 18,12
extraordinary, remarkable Jb 4,12; *extraordinary,
marvellous* Jb 5,9; *portentous, disastrous* Jb
22,10; *Jb 9,23 ἐξαισίῳ corr.? ἐξαίφνης for
MT פתאם *sudden*

ἐξαίφνης⁺ D 0-0-7-2-1-10

Is 47,9(bis); Jer 6,26; 15,8; Mi 2,3
suddenly, all of a sudden, in an instant Is 47,9;
immediately Mi 2,3
Cf. SHIPP 1979, 240-241; SPICQ 1982, 11-12

ἑξάκις   M 0-2-0-1-0-3
Jos 6,15; 2 Kgs 13,19; Jb 5,19
six times

ἑξακισχίλιοι,-αι,-α   M 2-2-0-3-2-9
Nm 2,9; 3,34; 2 Kgs 5,5; 1 Chr 23,4; Jb 42,12
six thousand

ἐξακολουθέω⁺   V 0-0-3-3-2-8
Is 56,11; Jer 2,2; Am 2,4; Jb 31,9; Dn^LXX 3,41
to follow [τινι]

ἐξακονάω   V 0-0-1-0-0-1
Ez 21,16
to sharpen; neol.

ἐξακόσιοι,-αι,-α⁺   M 17-35-0-14-14-80
Gn 7,6; Ex 12,37; 14,7; Nm 1,25(27).37(25)
six hundred

ἐξακοσιοστός,-ή,-όν   M 2-0-0-0-0-2
Gn 7,11; 8,13
six hundredth

ἐξακριβάζομαι   V 1-0-0-2-0-3
Nm 23,10; Jb 28,3; Dn^LXX 7,19
to examine accurately; neol.?

ἐξάλειπτρον,-ου   N2N 0-0-0-1-0-1
Jb 41,23
unguent-box, pot of ointment

ἐξαλείφω⁺   V 16-8-7-8-13-52
Gn 7,4.23(bis); 9,15; Ex 17,14
to plaster, to cover Lv 14,42; *to wipe out, to
destroy* Gn 7,4

ἐξάλειψις,-εως   N3F 0-0-2-0-0-2
Ez 9,6; Mi 7,11
blotting out, destruction; neol.

ἐξαλλάσσω   V 1-0-0-0-1-2
Gn 45,22; Wis 2,15
M: *to be different* Wis 2,15; ἐξαλλάσσουσαι
στολαί *exceptional sets of clothing* Gn 45,22
Cf. HARL 1986, 292

ἐξαλλοιόω   V 0-0-0-0-1-1
3 Mc 3,21
to change, to alter

ἐξάλλομαι⁺   V 0-0-5-0-1-6
Is 55,12; Jl 2,5; Mi 2,12; Na 3,17; Hab 1,8
to leap out of, to leap forth from [ἔκ τινος] Mi
2,12; *to leap* Hab 1,8; *to leap up, to exult*
(metaph.) Is 55,12

ἔξαλλος,-ος,-ον   A 0-1-0-2-2-5
2 Sm 6,14; Est 3,8; Dn^LXX 11,36; 3 Mc 4,4; Wis

14,23
special, distinguishing; neol.?

ἐξαλλοτριόομαι   V 0-0-0-0-1-1
1 Mc 12,10
to be estranged

ἐξαμαρτάνω   V 0-26-2-4-3-35
Jgs^B 20,16; 1 Kgs 15,26.30.34; 16,2
to miss one's aim [abs.] Jgs^B 20,16; *to err, to sin,
to do wrong* [abs.] Neh 9,33; *to cause to fail* or
sin [τινα] (semit., rendering Hebr. hiphil) 1 Kgs
15,26
Cf. CONYBEARE 1980, 76; HELBING 1928, 79.215

ἑξάμηνος,-ου   N2F 0-2-0-0-0-2
2 Kgs 15,8; 1 Chr 3,4
a half-year, period of six months

ἐξαναλίσκω   V 17-1-5-1-3-27
Ex 32,12; 33,3.5; Lv 26,22.33
A: *to consume* [τι] Lv 26,22; *to destroy utterly*
[τινα] Ex 32,12; P: *to perish* Nm 17,27

ἐξανάστασις,-εως⁺   N3F 1-0-0-0-0-1
Gn 7,4
getting up, creature; πᾶσαν τὴν ἐξανάστασιν,
ἥν ἐποίησα *all the work that I caused to spring
up*
Cf. HARL 1986, 133; TOV 1984 (A), 68

ἐξανατέλλω⁺   V 1-0-0-4-0-5
Gn 2,9; Ps 103(104),14; 111(112),4; 131(132),17;
146(147),8
to cause to spring up [τι] Gn 2,9; *to spring up, to
come forth* (of light) Ps 111(112),4

ἐξανθέω   V 11-0-5-5-0-21
Ex 28,33; 36,31(39,24); Lv 13,12(bis).20
to put out flowers, to bloom, to flourish [intrans.]
Ex 28,33(29); *to bloom* [τι] Nm 17,23(8); *to
blossom, to flourish* (of land) Is 27,6; *to flourish*
(metaph.) Ps 131(132),18; (metaph., of pers.) Ps
91(92),14; *to burst out, to break out* (of diseases
and ulcers) Lv 13,12

ἐξανίστημι⁺   V 9-10-10-4-8-41
Gn 4,25; 18,16; 19,1.32.34
A: *to raise up* [τι] Is 61,4; *to raise up, to support*
[τινα] Jb 4,4; M: *to arise, to rise up* (of pers.)
Jos 8,7; *to rise up* (of things) Hos 10,14; *to arise,
to rise up* (of pers.) Gn 18,16; *to rise up against*
[ἐπί τινα] Ob 1,1; *to rise up* (of sentiments) Ez
7,10; ἀνίστημι σπέρμα *to raise up seed* Gn
4,25; *Ez 25,15 καὶ ἐξανέστησαν -◊םקר *they
raised up (vengeance)* for MT ◊םקנ *they took
vengeance*
Cf. HARL 1986, 133; →TWNT

ἐξαντλέω   V 0-0-1-1-0-2
Hag 2,16; Prv 20,5
to draw out, to empty out

ἐξαπατάω⁺   V 1-0-0-0-1-2
Ex 8,25; Susᵀʰ 56
to deceive [intrans.] Ex 8,25(29); [τινα] Susᵀʰ 56

ἐξάπινα⁺   D 4-2-1-4-4-15
Lv 21,4; Nm 4,20; 6,9; 35,22; Jos 11,7
suddenly (later form of ἐξαπίνης) Nm 4,20; *Lv
21,4 ἐξάπινα -בעגל(Aram.) or בלע (cpr. Nm
4,20) *unexpectedly* for MT בעל *husband*?; neol.

ἐξαπίνης   D 0-0-1-2-0-3
Is 47,11; Prv 6,15; 29,1
suddenly

ἐξαπόλλυμαι   V 0-0-0-0-1-1
Wis 10,6
to perish utterly
··MM

ἐξαπορέομαι⁺   V 0-0-0-1-0-1
Ps 87(88),16
*to be brought into despair, to be in great trouble
or difficulty*

ἐξαποστέλλω⁺   V 80-86-61-28-32-287
Gn 3,23; 8,10.12; 19,29; 25,6
to send forth Gn 8,10; *to send away, to dismiss*
Gn 45,1; *to divorce* Dt 24,4; *to allow to leave, to
release* Ex 4,23; *to expel* Gn 3,23; ἐξαποστέλλω
τι ἐν πυρί *to send into fire, to destroy utterly, to
get rid of by fire* 2 Kgs 8,12; ἐξαποστέλλω πῦρ
εἴς τι *to set fire to* Hos 8,14, cpr. Am 1,4.12
Cf. LEE 1983, 93-94; MURAOKA 1990,28-30; ·NIDNTT

ἐξαποστολή,-ῆς   N1F 0-0-0-0-1-1
3 Mc 4,4
sending away, expulsion

ἐξάπτω   V 2-1-1-2-3-9
Ex 30,8; Nm 8,3; Jgsᴬ 15,5; Ez 21,3; Prv 22,15
A: *to set fire to, to light, to kindle* [τι] Ex 30,8; *to
fasten to* [τινος] Prv 22,15; P: *to cling to, to
pursue at heel* Lam 4,19

ἔξαρθρος,-ος,-ον   A 0-0-0-0-1-1
4 Mc 9,13
dislocated

ἐξαρθρόω   V 0-0-0-0-1-1
4 Mc 10,5
to dislocate

ἐξαριθμέω   V 10-0-2-4-4-20
Gn 13,16(bis); 15,5; Lv 15,13.28
A: *to enumerate, to count, to number* Gn 13,16;
M: Lv 15,13
Cf. SKEHAN 1987, 139 (Sir 1,9)

ἐξαρκέω   V 1-0-0-0-0-1
Nm 11,23
to be sufficient, to suffice

ἐξαρνέομαι   V 0-0-0-0-1-1
4 Mc 5,35
to deny utterly

ἐξαρπάζω   V 0-0-0-0-1-1
1 Mc 7,29
to snatch away

ἔξαρσις,-εως   N3F 1-0-1-0-0-2
Nm 10,6; Jer 12,17
destruction Jer 12,17; *setting out* Nm 10,6

ἐξαρτάομαι   V 1-0-0-0-0-1
Ex 28,7
to be hung upon, to be attached to [ἐπί τινι]

ἐξάρχω   V 5-3-1-1-4-14
Ex 15,21; 32,18(ter); Nm 21,17
A: *to begin* [τινος] Ex 32,18; [κατά τι] Ex 32,18;
to begin, to lead [τινος] (in songs, hymns) Ex
15,21; *to begin to sing of* [τι] Nm 21,17; *to begin
to sing* [τι] Jdt 15,14; [abs.] 1 Sm 18,7; M: *to
begin to* [+inf.] 1 Mc 9,66
Cf. LE BOULLUEC 1989, 323-324

ἐξασθενέω   V 0-0-0-1-1-2
Ps 63(64),9; PSal 17,31
to be utterly weak

ἐξασκέω   V 0-0-0-0-2-2
4 Mc 5,23; 13,24
to train thoroughly, to practise

ἐξαστράπτω⁺   V 0-0-3-1-0-4
Ez 1,4.7; Na 3,3; Dnᴸˣˣ 10,6
to flash as with lightning; neol.

ἐξατιμόομαι   V 0-0-1-0-0-1
Ez 16,61
to be utterly dishonoured; neol.

ἐξαφίημι   V 0-0-0-0-1-1
2 Mc 12,24
to set free

ἐξεγείρω⁺   V 4-18-31-25-10-88
Gn 28,16; 41,21; Nm 10,34(35); 24,19; Jgsᴬ 5,12
A: *to awaken* [τινα] Sir 22,9; *to stir up, to raise
up* [τι] Ps 79(80),3; *to raise up* [τι] (of love) Ct
2,7; *to raise up against* [τι ἐπί τινα] 2 Sm 12,11;
(of weapons) 2 Sm 23,18; *to lift* [τι] (of sea) Jer
1,11; *to raise, to lift, to bring* [τι] Hab 3,13; *to
remove* [τι] 2 Sm 19,19; *to revive* [τι] Is 38,16; *to
raise from the dead* [τινα] Jb 5,11; P: *to be
awaked, to wake up* Gn 28,16; *to arise* Nm 24,19;
*Ez 21,21 ἐξεγεί ρηται - מערות עור? *is stirred or
is aroused* for MT מערות יער ◊ *set, ordered*; *Jer

28(51),38 ἐξηγέρθησαν -נערו ◊ עורו they rose up
for MT נערו -יִנְעֲרוּ◊ they shall growl; *Jgsᴬ 5,16
ἐξεγειρόντων -עירים ◊ עורו? the ones who arouse,
vigilantes for MT עדרים flocks
Cf. WALTERS 1973, 279, n.1

ἐξέγερσις,-εως   N3F 0-0-0-0-1-1
PSal 4,15
awakening

ἐξέδρα,-ας   N1F 0-0-21-0-0-21
Ez 40,44.45.46; 41,10.11
room, arcade furnished with recesses and seats
Cf. HUSSON 1983, 73-77; SETTIS 1973, 661-745

ἐξεικονίζομαι   V 2-0-0-0-0-2
Ex 21,22.23
to be fully shapen or formed (in the image of
God), cpr. Gn 1,26; 9,6; neol.
Cf. LE BOULLUEC 1989, 219; LE DÉAUT 1984, 184-185;
PRIJS 1948, 11-12

ἔξειμι⁺   V 1-0-0-0-2-3
Ex 28,35; 3 Mc 5,5.48
to go out, to come out; fut. of ἐξέρχομαι

ἐξεκκλησιάζω   V 2-12-3-0-2-19
Lv 8,4; Nm 20,10; Jgs 20,1; 2 Sm 20,14
A: to summon to an assembly, to convene [τι] Lv
8,3; P: to be called together Jos 18,1;
ἐξεκκλησίαζω νηστείαν to proclaim a fast Jer
43(36),9; *2 Sm 20,14 ἐξεκκλησιάσθησαν
יקהלו- (qere) they assembled for MT יקלהו
(ketib) they treated with contempt
Cf. WALTERS 1973, 85

ἐξελαύνω   V 1-0-2-0-0-3
Lv 14,40; Zech 9,8; 10,4
to drive out, to drive away

ἐξελέγχω   V 0-0-1-0-2-3
Mi 4,3; 4 Mc 2,13; Wis 12,17
to refute, to confute [τι] Wis 12,17; [τινα] 4 Mc
2,13
Cf. SPARKS 1972, 149-152, esp. 151 (Wis 4,20)

ἐξέλευσις,-εως   N3F 0-1-0-0-0-1
2 Sm 15,20
going out; neol.

ἐξελίσσομαι   V 0-1-0-0-0-1
1 Kgs 7,45(8)
to extend to [τινι]

ἐξέλκω⁺   V 1-1-0-3-1-6
Gn 37,28; Jgsᴬ 20,31; Jb 20,15; 36,20; Prv 30,33
to drag or draw out

ἐξεμέω   V 0-0-2-3-0-5
Jer 32(25),16.27; Jb 20,15; Prv 23,8; 25,16
to vomit (forth), to disgorge

ἐξεραυνάω   V 0-1-0-0-0-1
Jgsᴬ 18,2
see ἐξερευνάω

ἐξεργάζομαι   V 0-0-0-3-0-3
Ps 7,14; 30(31),20; Est 8,12r
to work out, to bring to completion [τι] Est 8,12r;
to prepare [τι] Ps 7,14

ἐξεργαστικός,-ή,-όν   A 0-0-0-0-1-1
2 Mc 2,31
able to accomplish; τὸ ἐξεργαστικόν working
out, full presentation

ἐξερεύγομαι   V 0-0-0-4-1-5
Ps 44(45),2; 118(119),171; 143(144),13;
144(145),7; Wis 19,10
to vomit forth [τι] (of a river) Wis 19,10; to
overflow with [τι] (metaph.) Ps 44(45),2

ἐξερευνάω   V 0-5-4-10-4-23
Jgs 5,14; Jgsᴬ 18,2; 1 Sm 23,23; 1 Chr 19,3
to search out, to examine [abs.] Dt 13,14; [τι]
1 Chr 19,3; [τινα] 1 Mc 9,26; to search out
among [τινα ἔν τινι] 1 Sm 23,23; *Jgs 5,14
ἐξερευνῶντες -חקר◊ searching out for MT ◊חקק
the commanders; *Ps 108(109),11 ἐξερευνησάτω
-יחפש or יבקש let (him) search out, scrutinize for
MT ינקש let him lay snares
Cf. WALTERS 1973, 206-209 (Jgs 5,14)

ἐξερεύνησις,-εως   N3F 0-0-0-1-0-1
Ps 63(64),7
investigation; neol.

ἐξερημόω   V 2-2-14-1-1-20
Lv 26,31.32; Jgsᴬ 16,24; 2 Kgs 19,24; Is 37,26
to make quite desolate, to devastate [τι] Lv
26,31; to dry up [τι] 2 Kgs 19,24

ἐξέρπω   V 0-0-0-1-0-1
Ps 104(105),30
to make to come forth, to produce [τι]
Cf. CAIRD 1972, 129-130; HELBING 1928, 78

ἐξέρχομαι⁺   V 176-260-124-66-116-742
Gn 4,16; 8,7.16.18.19
to go out of, to come out of [abs.] Gn 8,18; [τι]
Gn 44,4; [ἔκ τινος] (of things) Gn 8,16; (of
pers.) Gn 15,4; to go forth from [ἀπό τινος] Gn
4,16; to proceed from [ἔκ τινος] 1 Sm 2,3; to
come forth from [παρά τινος] (of ordinances)
Gn 24,50; to be risen (of the sun) Gn 19,23; to
go forth to [+ inf.] Gn 24,43; ἐξέρχομαι εἰς
συνάντησίν τινι to come forth to meet sb Ex
4,14; ἐξῆλθεν τὸ ἔτος ἐκεῖνο that year passed,
came to an end Gn 47,18; *Nm 24,7
ἐξελεύσεται -אזל◊? shall come out of for MT יזל

◊נזל shall flow; *Nm 24,24 ἐξελεύσεται יצאים?
-◊יצא shall come out of (cpr. Sam. Pent.) for MT
צים ships

ἔξεστιν⁺ V 0-0-0-3-5-8
Est 4,2; 8,12g; Ezr 4,14; 1 Mc 14,44; 3 Mc 1,11
it is allowed to, it is possible to [+ inf.] Est 8,12g;
[τινι +inf.] Ezr 4,14; ἦν ἐξόν τινι [+inf] it was
allowed to Est 4,2
→TWNT

ἐξετάζω⁺ V 1-0-0-2-9-12
Dt 19,18; Ps 10(11),4.5; Jdt 8,13; Wis 6,3
to examine well or closely, to scrutinize [abs.] (of
judges) Dt 19,18; to question [τινα] Sir 23,10;
ἐξετασθέ ος to be scrutinized 2 Mc 2,29

ἐξέτασις,-εως N3F 0-0-0-0-2-2
3 Mc 7,5; Wis 1,9
close examination, scrutiny, test

ἐξετασμός,-οῦ N2M 0-1-0-1-1-3
Jgs^B 5,16; Prv 1,32; Wis 4,6
close examination Prv 1,32; trial Wis 4,6
Cf. LARCHER 1985, 324

ἐξευμενίζομαι V 0-0-0-0-1-1
4 Mc 4,11
to propitiate, to appease; neol.?

ἐξεύρεσις,-εως N3F 0-0-1-0-1-2
Is 40,28; Bar 3,18
discovery

ἐξευρίσκω V 0-0-0-0-3-3
2 Mc 7,23; Bar 3,32.37
to find out, to discover

ἐξέχω V 2-3-2-3-0-10
Ex 38,15(37,18); Nm 21,13; 1 Kgs
7,15(28).16(29)(bis)
A: to project [abs.] Neh 3,27; to stand out, to
project from [ἔκ τινος] Ex 38,15(37,18); [ἀπό
τινος] Nm 21,13; M: to project from [τινος] Ez
42,6; [ἔκ τινος] Ez 42,5

ἐξηγέομαι⁺ V 1-3-0-3-2-9
Lv 14,57; Jgs 7,13; 2 Kgs 8,5; Jb 12,8
to tell at length, to relate in full Jgs 7,13; to
explain Jb 12,8; to order, to dictate Lv 14,57
Cf. SPICQ 1978, 256-258; →NIDNTT; TWNT

ἐξήγησις,-εως N3F 0-1-0-0-1-2
Jgs^B 7,15; Sir 21,16
statement, narrative
→NIDNTT

ἐξηγητής,-οῦ N1M 2-0-0-1-0-3
Gn 41,8.24; Prv 29,18
expounder, interpreter (of visions and prophecies)
Gn 41,8; *Prv 29,18 ἐξηγητής -חזה prophet, seer

or חזן (Aram.) superintendent for MT חזון vision
Cf. SPICQ 1978, 257-258; →NIDNTT

ἐξηγορία,-ας N1F 0-0-0-2-1-3
Jb 22,22; 33,26; PSal 9,6
utterance Jb 33,26; confession Jb 22,22; neol.

ἑξήκοντα⁺ M 24-20-3-22-14-83
Gn 5,15.18.20.21.23
sixty

ἑξηκονταετής,-ής,-ές A 2-0-0-0-0-2
Lv 27,3.7
sixty years old

ἑξηκοστός,-ή,-όν M 0-0-0-0-6-6
1 Mc 10,1.21.57.67; 11,19
sixtieth

ἐξηλιάζω V 0-3-0-0-0-3
2 Sm 21,6.9.13
to hang in the sun (as a form of torture); neol.

ἐξημερόω V 0-0-0-0-1-1
4 Mc 1,29
to soften, to humanize

ἑξῆς⁺ D 3-1-0-0-2-6
Ex 10,1; Dt 2,34; 3,6; Jgs^A 20,48; 2 Mc 7,8
one after another, in order, in a row Dt 2,34;
next, thereafter 2 Mc 7,8

ἐξηχέω⁺ V 0-0-1-0-2-3
Jl 4,14; 3 Mc 3,2; Sir 40,13
A: to sound forth Jl 4,14; P: to be uttered abroad
3 Mc 3,2

ἐξικνέομαι V 0-1-0-0-0-1
Jgs^B 5,15
to arrive at, to reach; *Jgs^B 5,15 ἐξικνούμενοι
corr. ἐξιχνιαζόμενοι or ἐξιχνευόμενοι חקרי-
searchings for MT חקקי resolutions, decisions see
also Jgs^A 5,16
Cf. SCHREINER 1961, 354

ἐξίλασις,-εως N3F 1-0-0-0-1-2
Nm 29,11; Od 4,17
propitiation, atonement, appeasement; neol.
→NIDNTT

ἐξιλάσκομαι V 72-7-14-5-10-108
Gn 32,21; Ex 30,10.15.16; 32,30
M: to propitiate Gn 32,21; to make atonement Ex
30,15; P: to be atoned for 1 Sm 3,14; to be
atoned for to [τινι] Dt 21,8; to be purged from
[ἀπό τινος] Nm 35,33
Cf. HARLÉ 1988, 32; →NIDNTT

ἐξίλασμα,-ατος N3N 0-1-0-1-0-2
1 Sm 12,3; Ps 48(49),8
ransom, propitiatory offering, bribe; neol.

ἐξιλασμός,-οῦ N2M 3-1-3-0-9-16

Ex 30,10; Lv 23,27.28; 1 Chr 28,11; Ez 7,25
appeasement, propitiation, atonement Ex 30,10;
*Ez 7,25 ἐξιλασμός -כפרת ◊ כפר appeasement
for MT קפרה *terror* (hapax); neol.
Cf. HARLÉ 1988, 32; →NIDNTT

ἐξιππάζομαι   V 0-0-1-0-0-1
Hab 1,8
to ride out or *away*; neol.

ἐξίπταμαι   V 0-0-0-1-0-1
Prv 7,10
to fly out or *away*

ἕξις,-εως⁺   N3F 0-2-2-4-5-13
Jgsᴬ 14,9; 1 Sm 16,7; Is 7,14; Hab 3,16; Prv 13,5
state, habit Sir 30,14; *trained habit, skill*
Sir prol.,11; *outward appearance* 1 Sm 16,7;
corpse Jgsᴬ 14,9

ἐξισάζομαι   V 0-0-0-0-1-1
Sir 32,9
to make oneself equal

ἐξισόομαι   V 2-0-0-0-0-2
Ex 37,16(38,18); 38,15(37,18)
to be (made) equal to [τινι]

ἐξιστάνω   V 0-0-0-0-1-1
3 Mc 1,25
to divert from [τινος]; neol.

ἐξίστημι⁺   V 8-21-29-7-9-74
Gn 27,33; 42,28; 43,33; 45,26; Ex 18,9
A: *to drive out of his senses, to amaze, to
confound* [τινα] Ex 23,27; M: *to be astonished*
1 Mc 15,32; *to be amazed at* [πρός τινα] Gn
43,33; [ἐπί τινι] Wis 5,2; ἐξέστην *to be amazed*
Gn 27,33; *to exult* Ex 18,9; *to be confused* Gn
45,26; ἐξέστηκα *to be confounded* 1 Sm 4,13;
ἐξεστώς *having lost consciousness* Jgsᴮ 4,21;
ἐξίστημι βουλήν *to subvert the counsel* Jb 5,13;
**Hos 5,8 ἐξέστη -◊ חרד is driven out of his
senses* for MT אחריך *after you*; *Jgsᴬ 5,4
ἐξεστάθη -נמושו or נמוגו *they are wavering* for MT
נשׁפו *the heavens dropped*
Cf. HARLÉ 1988, 121; LE BOULLUEC 1989, 194;
SCHREINER 1957, 117-118; SPICQ 1982, 280-285

ἐξιχνεύω   V 0-0-0-0-3-4
Sir 6,27; 18,4; 42,18
to fathom, to track out, to examine

ἐξιχνιάζω   V 0-3-0-8-5-16
Jgsᴬ 18,2; Jgsᴮ 18,2(bis); Ps 138(139),3; Jb 5,27
to explore, to trace, to track out, to search out;
see ἐξιχνεύω; neol.

ἐξιχνιασμός,-οῦ   N2M 0-1-0-0-0-1
Jgsᴬ 5,16

tracking out, searching; neol.

ἐξοδεύω   V 0-1-0-0-3-4
Jgsᴮ 5,27; 1 Ezr 4,23; 1 Mc 15,41; 2 Mc 12,19
A: *to march out* [abs.] 1 Ezr 4,23; P: *to depart
this life* Jgsᴮ 5,27; ἐξοδεύω τὰς ὁδούς τινος *to
go out by the way of* 1 Mc 15,41

ἐξοδία,-ας   N1F 2-2-1-0-0-5
Dt 16,3; 33,18; 2 Sm 3,22; 11,1; Mi 7,15
marching out, expedition
Cf. WALTERS 1973, 139

ἐξοδιάζω   V 0-1-0-0-0-1
2 Kgs 12,13
to pay in full, to spend

ἐξόδιον,-ου   N2N 3-1-0-2-0-7
Lv 23,36; Nm 29,35; Dt 16,8; 2 Chr 7,9
final day of a festival
Cf. GEHMAN 1972, 108; HARLÉ 1988, 191; WALTERS 1973,
39.283

ἔξοδος,-ου⁺   N2F 4-21-8-24-13-70
Ex 19,1; 23,16; Nm 33,38; 35,26; Jgsᴬ 5,4
going out 1 Sm 29,6; *way out, outlet* 1 Chr 5,16;
deliverance out of Egypt, exodus out of Egypt Ex
19,1; *end* 2 Chr 23,8; *issue* Prv 4,23; *street* 2 Sm
22,43; *Prv 8,35 ἔξοδοί μου -מצאי ◊ יצא *my ways
out (of difficulties)* for MT מצאי *he who
finds me*; *Prv 30,12 εξόδου αὐτοῦ -מצאותו◊ יצא
his way, way out, or ἔξοδος for MT מצאה/מ *of his
excrement, discharge from the bowel*
Cf. LE BOULLUEC 1989, 26; →NIDNTT

ἔξοικος,-ος,-ον   A 0-0-0-1-0-1
Jb 6,18
houseless; neol.

ἐξοκέλλω   V 0-0-0-1-0-1
Prv 7,21
to drive headlong, to compel

ἐξολέθρευμα,-ατος   N3N 0-1-0-0-0-1
1 Sm 15,21
destruction; neol.

ἐξολέθρευσις,-εως   N3F 0-0-1-1-1-3
Ez 9,1; Ps 108(109),13; 1 Mc 7,7
destruction

ἐξολεθρεύω⁺   V 53-86-46-24-12-221
Gn 17,14; Ex 8,20; 12,15.19; 30,33
A: *to destroy utterly* [τι] Lv 26,30; P: *to be utterly
destroyed* Gn 17,14; *1 Kgs 11,15 ἐν τῷ
ἐξολεθρεῦσαι -בהכות *while destroying* for MT
בהיות *while being*; neol.?
Cf. HARL 1986, 171; →TWNT

ἐξόλλυμι   V 0-0-0-3-1-4
Prv 10,31; 11,17; 15,27; Sir 5,7

A: *to destroy utterly* [τινα] Prv 15,27; M/P: *to perish utterly* Prv 10,31

ἐξομβρέω V 0-0-0-0-2-2
Sir 1,19; 10,13
to pour out like rain; neol.

ἐξόμνυμαι V 0-0-0-0-4-4
4 Mc 4,26; 5,34; 9,23; 10,3
to forswear, to renounce

ἐξομοιόομαι V 0-0-0-0-1-1
2 Mc 4,16
to become like, to be like

ἐξομολογέομαι⁺ V 1-17-2-79-38-137
Gn 29,35; 2 Sm 22,50; 1 Kgs 8,33.35; 1 Chr 16,4
to confess Dn^LXX 9,20; *to acknowledge, to admit*
2 Mc 7,37; *to make grateful acknowledgements,
to give thanks, to sing praises* (semit., stereotyped
rendition of ‏ירה ◊ הורה‎) Gn 29,35; *Ps 73(74),19
ψυχὴν ἐξομολογουμένην σοι -‏תורך◊ נפש‎
the soul that sings praise to you for MT
‏תורך נפש‎ *the soul of your dove*; neol.?
Cf. HELBING 1928, 243-244; LEDOGAR 1967, 29-56; TOV
1976, 543-544; 1990, 97-110; →NIDNTT; TWNT

ἐξομολόγησις,-εως N3F 0-3-2-10-11-26
Jos 7,19; 1 Chr 25,3; 2 Chr 20,22; Is 51,3; Jon
2,10
confession of gratitude, thanksgiving (semit., cpr.
ἐξομολογέομαι); neol.?
Cf. TOV 1990, 97-110

ἐξόπισθεν D 0-4-0-1-2-7
1 Kgs 19,21; 2 Kgs 17,21; 1 Chr 17,7; 19,10; Ps
77(78),71
behind, in rear 1 Chr 19,10; *behind* [τινος] 1 Kgs
19,21

ἐξοπλησία,-ας N1F 0-0-0-0-1-1
2 Mc 5,25
getting under arms
Cf. WALTERS 1973, 122-123

ἐξοπλίζω V 2-0-0-0-1-3
Nm 31,3; 32,20; 2 Mc 5,2
A: *to arm completely* Nm 31,3; M: *to arm oneself*
Nm 32,20; λόγχας ἐξοπλισμένοι *armed with
lances* 2 Mc 5,2

ἐξορκίζω⁺ V 1-1-0-0-0-2
Gn 24,3; Jgs^A 17,2
to conjure; neol.?
Cf. HELBING 1928, 72; →NIDNTT; TWNT

ἐξορμάω V 0-1-0-0-4-5
Jgs^A 7,3; 2 Mc 11,7; 3 Mc 1,1.18; 5,47
to set out (esp. in haste), *to rush* [intrans.]

ἐξορύσσω⁺ V 0-2-0-1-0-3

Jgs^A 16,21; 1 Sm 11,2; Prv 29,22
to dig out or *up* Prv 29,22; *to gouge out* Jgs^A
16,21

ἐξουδενέω⁺ V 0-2-2-1-2-7
2 Kgs 19,21; 2 Chr 36,16; Ez 21,15; 22,8; Jb 30,1
to set at naught, to disdain, to scorn 2 Kgs 19,21;
*Ez 21,15 ἐξουδένει ‏בזי- ◊ בזה‎ set at naught for
MT ‏בני‎ *my son*; see ἐξουδενόω, ἐξουθενέω;
neol.
Cf. OLOFSSON 1990, 22-23 (Ps 59(60),14)

ἐξουδένημα,-ατος N3N 0-0-0-2-0-2
Ps 21(22),7; Dn^Th 4,17(14)
object of contempt

ἐξουδενόω V 0-10-5-20-2-37
Jgs 9,38; 1 Sm 8,7; 15,23(bis)
to set at naught, to disdain, to scorn Jgs 9,38; *Ps
59(60),14 ἐξουδενώσει -‏יבוז‎? *he treats with
contempt* for MT ‏יבוס‎ *he treads down*, cpr. Ps
43(44),6; see ἐξουδενέω, ἐξουθενόω; neol.

ἐξουδένωμα,-ατος N3N 0-0-0-1-0-1
Ps 89(90),5
scorn, contempt; neol.

ἐξουδένωσις,-εως N3F 0-0-0-6-1-7
Ps 30(31),19; 106(107),40; 118(119),22;
122(123),3.4
contempt, scorn

ἐξουθενέω⁺ V 0-2-2-1-3-8
1 Sm 8,7; 10,19; Jer 6,14; Am 6,1; Prv 1,7
late form of ἐξουδενέω; *to disdain, to scorn, to
set at naught* 1 Sm 8,7; *Am 6,1 τοῖς
ἐξουθενοῦσι *those who disdain* corr.? τοῖς
ἐξευθηνοῦσι (ἐν?) for MT ‏השאננים‎ *those who
thrive (in?)*; neol.

ἐξουθενόω V 0-3-0-3-3-9
1 Sm 2,30; 8,7; 15,9; Ps 43(44),6; 50(51),19
late form of ἐξουθενόω; *to disdain, to set at
naught*; neol.

ἐξουσία,-ας⁺ N1F 0-1-0-39-39-79
2 Kgs 20,13; Ps 113(114),2; 135(136),8.9; Prv
17,14
power, authority 1 Ezr 4,28; *control over* [τινος]
Ps 135(136),8; *permission* [+inf.] 1 Mc 11,58;
office, magistracy Dn 3,2
Cf. HORSLEY 1982, 83-84; →NIDNTT; TWNT

ἐξουσιάζω⁺ V 0-2-0-19-2-23
Jgs^B 5,2.9; Eccl 2,19; 5,18; 6,2
A: *to exercise authority* Eccl 8,4; *to have power to*
[+inf.] 2 Ezr 7,24; *to give power to* [τινα] Eccl
5,18; [τινι] Eccl 6,2; M: *to exercise authority over*
[ἐπί τινα] Neh 5,15; neol.?

ἐξοχή,-ῆς⁺ N1F 0-0-0-1-0-1
Jb 39,28
prominence

ἐξόχως D 0-0-0-0-1-1
3 Mc 5,31
especially, above others

ἐξυβρίζω V 1-0-1-0-2-4
Gn 49,4; Ez 47,5; 2 Mc 1,28; PSal 1,6
to break out into insolence, to wax wanton 2 Mc
1,28; ἐξύβρισας ὡς ὕδωρ *you are insolent as*
water that overruns Gn 49,4, see also Ez 47,5

ἐξυμνέω V 0-0-0-0-1-1
PSal 6,4
to praise [τινι]

ἐξυπνίζομαι⁺ V 0-3-0-1-0-4
JgsᴮB 16,14.20; 1 Kgs 3,15; Jb 14,12
to wake up, to awake

ἔξυπνος,-ος,-ον⁺ A 0-0-0-0-1-1
1 Ezr 3,3
awakened out of sleep; neol.

ἐξυπνόω V 0-0-0-0-1-1
4 Mc 5,11
to wake out of, to awake from [ἀπό τινος]; neol.

ἐξυψόω V 0-0-0-1-1-2
DnᴸˣˣLXX 3,51; Sir 1,30
to exalt; neol.

ἔξω⁺ D 56-23-4-16-10-109
Gn 9,22; 15,5; 19,17; 24,11.29
out Gn 15,5; *outside* Gn 9,22; *out (of), outside*
[τινος] Gn 24,11; *Am 4,5 ἔξω מחוץ *(from)*
outside for MT מחמץ *from what is leavened*

ἔξωθεν⁺ D 10-8-22-1-8-49
Gn 6,14; 7,16; 20,18; Ex 25,11; 26,35
from without, abroad Jgs 12,9; [τινος]: *outside*
(of) Ex 26,35; *out of* Jer 44(37),21; ἔσωθεν καὶ
ἔξωθεν *(from) within and without* Gn 6,14

ἐξωθέω⁺ V 1-6-15-4-2-28
Dt 13,6; 2 Sm 14,13.14(bis); 15,14
to thrust out, to force out Dt 13,6; *to expel, to*
eject, to banish 2 Sm 14,13; *to put forth* 2 Sm
15,14

ἐξώσματα,-ων N3N 0-0-0-1-0-1
Lam 2,14
banishment; neol.

ἐξώτατος,-η,-ον A 0-1-0-0-0-1
1 Kgs 6,30
sup. of ἔξω; *outermost*

ἐξώτερος,-α,-ον⁺ A 1-1-18-0-0-20
Ex 26,4; 1 Kgs 6,29; Ez 10,5; 40,19.20
comp. of ἔξω; *outer*

ἐξωτέρω D 0-0-0-1-0-1
Jb 18,17
comp. of ἔξω; *more outside*

ἔοικα⁺ V 0-0-0-2-0-2
Jb 6,3.25
to be like; ὡς ἔοικε *as it seems*

ἑορτάζω⁺ V 8-1-5-2-0-16
Ex 5,1; 12,14(bis); 23,14; Lv 23,39
to keep a festival or *holiday* Ex 5,1; *to celebrate*
Ex 12,14; *Ps 75(76),11 ἑορτάσει (σοι) -תחגך
(it) shall celebrate (you) for MT תחגר *(you) shall*
gird

ἑόρτασμα,-ατος N3N 0-0-0-0-1-1
Wis 19,16
festival, holiday; neol.

ἑορτή,-ῆς⁺ N1F 34-23-24-16-27-124
Ex 10,9; 12,14; 13,6; 23,15.16
feast, festival, holiday Ex 10,9; *Jer 38(31),8 ἐν
ἑορτῇ -ב/מועד *to the feast* for MT בם עור *with*
them the blind
Cf. DANIEL 1966, 185.205; MURAOKA 1990, 9

ἐπαγγελία,-ας⁺ N1F 0-0-1-2-5-8
Am 9,6; Ps 55(56),9; Est 4,7; 1 Ezr 1,7; 1 Mc
10,15
announcement, promise
Cf. HORSLEY 1982, 147; →NIDNTT; TWNT

ἐπαγγέλλομαι⁺ V 0-0-0-2-11-13
Prv 13,12; Est 4,7; 1 Mc 11,28; 2 Mc 2,18; 4,8
to promise (unasked) Est 4,7; *to offer of one's*
free will 1 Mc 11,28; *to profess, to make*
profession of Wis 2,13

ἐπάγω⁺ V 25-19-59-22-26-151
Gn 6,17; 7,4; 8,1; 18,19; 20,9
A: *to bring (on)* Dt 23,14; *to bring upon* [τι ἐπί
τινα] Ex 32,34; [τι ἐπί τι] Gn 6,17; [τί τινι] Ex
15,26; [τινα πρός τινα] Jgsᴮ 4,7; [τι πρός τινα]
Jgsᴮ 4,7; *to bring into* [τι εἴς τι] Lv 26,36; *to lay*
on, to apply to [τι ἐπί τινα] Is 10,24; *to stretch*
upon [τι ἐπί τινος] Jb 38,5; M: *to bring upon* [τι
πρός τινα] Ex 28,43; [τί τινι] Jb 22,17; *1 Sm
15,23 ἐπάγουσιν -הפיצו? *bring on* for MT הפצר
stubbornness?; *1 Sm 5,6 ἐπήγαγεν -וישימם
(and) he brought (evil) (upon them) for MT
וישמם *he terrified them*
Cf. HELBING 1928, 276-277; LE BOULLUEC 1989, 328

ἐπαγωγή,-ῆς N1F 1-0-2-0-11-14
Dt 32,36; Is 10,4; 14,17; Od 2,36; Sir 2,2
distress, misery
Cf. CAIRD 1972, 130; WALTERS 1972, 129

ἐπαγωγός,-ός,-όν A 0-0-0-0-1-1

4 Mc 8,15
attractive, alluring

ἐπᾴδω or ἐπαείδω   V 1-0-1-2-0-4
Dt 18,11; Jer 8,17; Ps 57(58),6; Eccl 10,11
to sing as an incantation, to use charms or incantations

ἐπαινεστός,-ή,-όν   A 0-0-1-0-0-1
Ez 26,17
praiseworthy, laudable; renouned

ἐπαινέω⁺   V 1-0-0-17-10-28
Gn 12,15; Ps 9,24(10,3); 33(34),3; 43(44),9; 55(56),5
A: *to praise, to commend* [τινα] Gn 12,15; M: *to praise oneself* Ps 9,24(10,3); P: *to be praised* Ps 33(34),3; *Eccl 8,10 καὶ ἐπηνέθησαν וישתבחו *and they were praised* for MT וישתכחו *and they were forgotten*

ἔπαινος,-ου⁺   N2M 0-2-0-3-5-10
1 Chr 16,27; 2 Chr 21,20; Ps 21(22),4.26; 34(35),28
praise, approval, commendation
·TWNT

ἐπαίρω⁺   V 8-20-10-28-17-83
Gn 7,17; 13,10; Ex 7,20; 10,13; 14,16
A: *to lift up* Gn 7,17; *to raise* Jgs 2,4; *to exalt, to magnify* Ezr 4,19; *to stir up, to excite* 2 Kgs 14,10; P: *to be lifted up* Ps 23(24),7; *to be exalted* Ps 8,2; *to be roused, to be led on, to be excited* 1 Kgs 12,24; *Jer 29(47),6 καὶ ἐπάρθητι -ורמי *and be lifted up* for MT ורמי *and be still*; *2 Kgs 18,29 ἐπαιρέτω -ישיא *let (him) arouse* for MT ישיא *let (him) deceive*, see also 2 Kgs 19,10; Ob 3; *Ps 72(73),18 ἐπαρθῆναι -◊נשא *to be lifted up* for MT נשא ל/משואות◊ *to deceptions*
Cf. LE BOULLUEC 1989, 138; →TWNT

ἐπαισχύνομαι⁺   V 0-0-1-2-0-3
Is 1,29; Ps 118(119),6; Jb 34,19
to be ashamed at, to reverence [τι] Jb 34,19; *to be ashamed of* [ἐπί τινι] Is 1,29; [ἔν τινι] Ps 118(119),6

ἐπαιτέω⁺   V 0-0-0-1-1-2
Ps 108(109),10; Sir 40,28
to beg, to act as a beggar

ἐπαίτησις,-εως   N3F 0-0-0-0-2-2
Sir 40,28.30
begging; neol.

ἐπακολουθέω⁺   V 5-4-1-3-2-15
Lv 19,4.31; 20,6; Nm 14,24; Dt 12,30
to follow, to attend to [τινι]

ἐπακουστός,-ός,-όν   A 0-0-0-0-1-1

1 Ezr 4,12
obeyed

ἐπακούω⁺   V 9-33-15-34-9-100
Gn 16,11; 17,20; 21,17; 25,21; 30,6
to hear [τινος] Gn 21,17; *to give ear, to listen* [τινι] Gn 16,11; [τινος] Gn 17,20; [τινι] 1 Chr 5,20; *to obey* [τινος] Eccl 10,19; ἐπακούσεταί μοι *shall answer for me* Gn 30,33
Cf. BARR 1980, 67-72; COX 1981, 251-258; HARL 1986, 233 (Gn 30,33); HELBING 1928, 154-155; SPICQ 1982, 231-245

ἐπακρόασις,-εως   N3F 0-1-0-0-0-1
1 Sm 15,22
hearkening, obedience; neol.

ἐπαλγέστερος,-α,-ον   A 0-0-0-0-1-1
4 Mc 14,10
comp. of ἐπαλγής; *painful*

ἔπαλξις,-εως   N3F 0-1-3-1-2-7
1 Kgs 2,35f; Is 21,11; 54,12; Jer 27(50),15; Ct 8,9
defence 1 Kgs 2,35f; ἐπάλξεις *bulwarks, battlements* Ct 8,9; *Is 21,11 ἐπάλξεις -חילה *fortification* for MT לילה *night*

ἐπαμύνω   V 0-0-0-0-2-2
3 Mc 1,27; 4 Mc 14,19
A: *to come to aid, to succour* [τινι] 3 Mc 1,27; M: *to ward off* [τινα] 4 Mc 14,19

ἐπάν⁺   X 0-0-0-0-1-1
Bel^{LXX} 11
when

ἐπανάγω⁺   V 0-0-1-0-4-5
Zech 4,12; 2 Mc 9,21; 12,4; Sir 17,26; 26,28
A: *to bring up* [τι] Zech 4,12; *to return to* [ἐπί τινα] Sir 17,26; *to turn back from to* [ἀπό τινος ἐπί τι] Sir 26,28; P: *to go forth into the sea* 2 Mc 12,4

ἐπαναιρέομαι   V 0-0-0-0-2-2
2 Mc 14,2.13
to kill, to slay

ἐπανακαινίζω   V 0-0-0-1-0-1
Jb 10,17
to renew, to revive; neol.

ἐπαναπαύομαι⁺   V 2-5-2-0-1-10
Nm 11,25.26; Jgs^A 16,26; 2 Kgs 2,15; 5,18
to rest upon, to come to rest upon [ἐπί τινα] Nm 11,25; *to rely upon* [τινι] 1 Mc 8,11; neol.?
Cf. HELBING 1928, 277

ἐπανάστασις,-εως   N3F 0-1-0-0-0-1
2 Kgs 3,4
rising up

ἐπαναστρέφω   V 8-0-0-1-0-9
Gn 18,10; Ex 14,28; Lv 22,13; Nm 35,28; Dt 3,20

to return [intrans.]
Cf. HARL 1986, 175

ἐπανατρυγάω V 2-0-0-0-0-2
Lv 19,10; Dt 24,21
to glean after the crop; neol.
Cf. HARLÉ 1988, 165; PELLETIER 1954, 523-527

ἐπανδρόω V 0-0-0-0-1-1
2 Mc 15,17
to make manly; neol.

ἐπανέρχομαι[+] V 2-0-0-2-2-6
Gn 50,5; Lv 25,13; Jb 7,7; Prv 3,28; Tob^BA 6,17
to return

ἐπανήκω V 1-0-0-2-2-5
Lv 14,39; Prv 3,28; 7,20; Sir 4,18; 27,9
to return

ἐπανθέω V 0-0-0-1-0-1
Jb 14,7
to bloom, to be in flower

ἐπανίσταμαι[+] V 3-10-4-22-5-44
Dt 19,11; 22,26; 33,11; Jgs^A 9,18.43
to rise 1 Sm 4,15; *to rise up against* [ἐπί τινα]
Dt 19,11; [τινι] Dt 33,11
Cf. HELBING 1928, 277-278

ἐπάνοδος,-ου N2F 0-0-0-0-3-3
Sir 17,24; 22,21; 38,21
return

ἐπανορθόω V 0-0-0-0-2-2
2 Mc 2,22; 5,20
to set up again, to reset [τι] 2 Mc 5,20; *to restore*
[τι] 2 Mc 2,22

ἐπανόρθωσις,-εως[+] N3F 0-0-0-0-2-2
1 Ezr 8,52; 1 Mc 14,34
setting right, correcting, reparation
Cf. ROBERT 1960, 518; →TWNT

ἐπάνω[+] D 50-28-20-18-11-127
Gn 1,2(bis).7.29; 7,18
above, on the upper side or *part* Gn 40,17; *over*
[τινος] Gn 1,2; *above* [τινος] Gn 1,7; *upon*
[τινος] Gn 22,9; *before, in front of* [τινος] Gn
18,2; *above, more* Ex 30,14; *2 Sm 5,20 ἐπάνω
-ממעל (*from*) *upper* (*breaches*) for MT בבעל *to*
Baal (*of the Philistines*), see also Ez 25,9

ἐπάνωθεν D 3-26-3-2-0-34
Ex 25,20; 26,14; 38,5(37,6); Jgs^A 13,20; Jgs^B 3,21
above, on top Ex 25,20; *from above* Jb 18,16
Cf. GEHMAN 1972 (A), 95

ἐπαξονέω V 1-0-0-0-0-1
Nm 1,18
to enroll on tablets, to register; neol.

ἐπαοιδή,-ῆς N1F 1-0-1-0-0-2

Dt 18,11; Is 47,12
enchantment
Cf. WALTERS 1973, 69

ἐπαοιδός,-οῦ N2M 8-2-1-11-1-23
Ex 7,11.22; 8,3.14.15
enchanter, charmer; neol.?
Cf. LE BOULLUEC 1989, 36; WALTERS 1973, 69

ἐπαποστέλλω V 2-1-3-1-3-10
Ex 8,17; Dt 28,48; 1 Kgs 12,24k; Jer 9,15;
25,17(49,37)
to send after [τί τινι] Wis 11,15; *to send upon*
[τι ἐπί τινα] Jb 20,23; neol.

ἐπάρδω V 0-0-0-0-1-1
4 Mc 1,29
to water; neol.?

ἐπαρήγω V 0-0-0-0-1-1
2 Mc 13,17
to come to aid, to help [τινι]

ἐπαρκέω[+] V 0-0-0-0-2-2
1 Mc 8,26; 11,35
to supply

ἔπαρμα,-ατος N3N 0-0-0-1-0-1
Ezr 6,3
foundation
Cf. CAIRD 1972, 130; DREW-BEAR 1972, 197

ἔπαρσις,-εως N3N 0-1-3-2-0-6
2 Kgs 19,25; Ez 24,25(bis); Zech 12,7; Ps
140(141),2
lifting up Ps 140(141),2; *elation, pride* Zech 12,7;
ἐπάρσεις *heap of ruins* 2 Kgs 19,25; *Lam 3,47
ἔπαρσις -השאת *elation* for MT השאת *ruin*; *Ez
24,25 ἔπαρσις -משא *pride* for MT משוש *joy*

ἐπαρυστήρ,-ῆρος N3M 1-0-0-0-0-1
Ex 25,38
vessel for pouring oil (into a lamp), *funnel*; neol.
Cf. LE BOULLUEC 1989, 264

ἐπαρυστρίς,-ίδος N3F 2-1-2-0-0-5
Ex 38,17(37,23); Nm 4,9; 1 Kgs 7,35(49); Zech
4,2.12
vessel for pouring oil, funnel; neol.
Cf. WALTERS 1973, 103

ἔπαρχος,-ου N2M 0-0-0-8-9-17
Ezr 5,3(bis).6; 6,13; 8,36
governor

ἐπάρχω V 0-0-0-1-0-1
Est 3,13b
to rule over [τινος]

ἐπασθμαίνω V 0-0-0-0-1-1
4 Mc 6,11
to breathe hard, to pant in working; neol.

ἔπαυλις,-εως⁺   N3F 14-19-5-6-2-46
Gn 25,16; Ex 8,7.9; 14,2.9
dwelling Gn 25,16; *fold* Nm 32,16; *unwalled*
village Lv 25,31; *Jos 15,36 αἱ ἐπαύλεις αὐτῆς
-גררתיה *its villages* for MT גררתים *Gederothaim*
Cf. HARL 1986, 207; HARLÉ 1988, 201; HUSSON 1983, 77-
80; LE BOULLUEC 1989, 124.162

ἐπαύξω   V 0-0-0-0-1-1
3 Mc 2,25
to increase

ἐπαύριον⁺   D 11-11-1-0-2-25
Gn 19,34; Ex 9,6; 18,13; 32,6; Lv 23,11
on the next day, on the morrow Gn 19,34; *on the*
day after [τινος] Lv 23,15

ἐπαφίημι   V 0-0-1-3-0-4
Ez 16,42; Jb 10,1; 12,15; 39,11
to send upon [τι ἐπί τινα] Jb 10,1; *to let loose*
or in (upon) (words) [τι] Jb 12,15; *to discharge*
at [τί τινι] Jb 39,11; *to throw at* [τι ἐπί τινα]
(metaph.) Ez 16,42
Cf. HELBING 1928, 278

ἐπεγγελάω   V 0-0-0-0-1-1
4 Mc 5,27
to laugh at [τινι]

ἐπεγείρω⁺   V 0-6-10-0-2-18
1 Sm 3,12; 22,8; 2 Sm 18,31; 22,49; 1 Chr 5,26
A: *to awaken, to excite, to raise up against* [τι
ἐπί τινα] 1 Sm 3,12; *to stir up against* [τινα ἐπί
τινα] 1 Sm 22,8; M/P: *to rise up against* [ἐπί
τινα] 2 Sm 18,31; [τινι] 2 Sm 22,49; *Jer
29(47),7 ἐπεγερθῆναι -יערה *to be raised up* for
MT יערה *he has appointed it*?; *Na 1,8
ἐπεγειρομένους -מקימיו *those who rise up*
(against him) for MT מקומה *her place*?
Cf. HELBING 1928, 278

ἐπεί⁺   C 4-5-0-8-22-39
Gn 15,17; 46,30; Ex 2,3; Dt 2,16; Jos 4,1
when Gn 15,17; *since, for, as* Gn 46,30
Cf. AEJMELAEUS 1982, 79-80

ἐπείγω   V 0-0-0-1-2-3
Dnᴸˣˣ 3,22; 2 Mc 10,19; Belᵀʰ 30
to urge [τινα] Belᵀʰ 30; *to be pressing, to be*
urgent Dnᴸˣˣ 3,22
(-- κατ-)

ἐπειδή⁺   C 8-0-5-3-4-20
Gn 15,3; 18,31; 19,19; 23,13; 41,39
when Gn 50,4; *since, for, as* Gn 41,39
Cf. AEJMELAEUS 1982, 79-80

ἔπειμι⁺ (ἐπεῖναι)   V 2-2-0-0-1-5
Ex 8,18; 9,3; 1 Kgs 10,16; 2 Chr 9,15; 4 Mc 1,10

to be upon [ἐπί τινος] Ex 8,18; *to be set upon*
[ἐπί τι] 2 Chr 9,15; ἔπεστί μοι [+inf.] *it is right*
that I should 4 Mc 1,10

ἔπειμι (ἐπιέναι)   V 1-1-0-3-0-5
Dt 32,29; 1 Chr 20,1; Prv 3,28; 27,1; Od 2,29
to come upon; ἐπιών *following, succeeding, next*
Dt 32,29; ἡ ἐπιοῦσα (sc. ἡμέρα) *the next (day)*
Prv 3,28; fut. of ἐπέρχομαι

ἐπεισέρχομαι⁺   V 0-0-0-0-1-1
1 Mc 16,16
to rush in and attack

ἐπεισφέρω   V 0-2-0-0-0-2
Jgs 3,22
to bring in besides, to bring next

ἔπειτα⁺   D 0-0-1-0-1-2
Is 16,2; 4 Mc 6,3
thereupon, thereafter, then

ἐπέκεινα⁺   D 4-4-8-0-2-18
Gn 35,16; Lv 22,27; Nm 15,23; 32,19; 1 Sm 10,3
henceforth Lv 22,27; *on the other side of, over*
and beyond [τινος] Gn 35,16(21)

ἐπεκχέομαι   V 0-0-0-0-1-1
Jdt 15,4
to rush upon [τινι]; neol.?

ἐπελπίζω   V 0-1-0-7-0-8
2 Kgs 18,30; Ps 51(52),9; 118(119),43.49.74
to buoy up with hope [τινα] Ps 118(119),49; *to*
pin one's hope upon, to hope in [εἰς τι] Ps
118(119),74
Cf. HELBING 1928, 78

ἐπενδύτης,-ου⁺   N2M 0-1-0-0-0-1
2 Sm 13,18
robe, garment (worn over another)

ἐπεξέρχομαι   V 0-0-0-0-2-2
Jdt 13,20; Wis 14,31
to take vengeance for [τινι] Jdt 13,20; *to punish*
[τινα] Wis 14,31
Cf. HELBING 1928, 279

ἐπερείδομαι   V 0-0-0-2-0-2
Prv 3,18; Est 5,1a
to lean upon, to rest in or *upon* [ἐπί τι]
Cf. HELBING 1928, 279

ἐπέρχομαι⁺   V 11-13-26-40-22-112
Gn 42,21; Ex 10,1; Lv 11,34; 14,43; 16,9
to come upon [ἐπί τινα] Gn 42,21; *to come*
forward Jgsᴮ 20,33; *to go* or *come against, to*
attack [ἐπί τινα] 1 Sm 30,23; *to be at hand* Jdt
9,5; τὰ ἐπερχόμενα *the future* Is 42,23; *Jb
40,20 ἐπελθὼν -ל יבוא כי *when going up to* for
MT בול כי *for they bring food*? *tribute, spoil*?

Cf. HELBING 1928, 84.279; LEE 1983, 88-89

ἐπερωτάω⁺   V 10-31-14-9-11-75
Gn 24,23; 26,7; 38,21; 43,7; Nm 23,3
to ask sb [τινα] Gn 24,23; *to consult, to inquire
of* [ἔν τινι] Jgs^A 18,5; *to ask about, to inquire
about* [τινα εἴς τι] 2 Sm 11,7; *Pvr 17,28
ἐπερωτήσαντι -◊ חרש he asks for MT חרש◊מחריש
keeping silent

Cf. HELBING 1928, 40-41; → NIDNTT; TWNT

ἐπερώτημα,-ατος⁺   N3N 0-0-0-1-0-1
Dn^Th 4,17(14)
answer, decision

Cf. SPICQ 1978, 261-262; → TWNT

ἐπερώτησις,-εως   N3F 1-0-0-0-0-1
Gn 43,7
questioning

ἐπευθυμέω   V 0-0-0-0-1-1
Wis 18,6
to rejoice at [τινι]; neol.

ἐπευκτός,-ή,-όν   A 0-0-1-0-1-2
Jer 20,14; PSal 8,16
longed for; neol.

ἐπεύχομαι   V 1-1-0-0-0-2
Dt 10,8; 1 Chr 23,13
to pray

ἐπέχω⁺   V 2-6-1-3-11-23
Gn 8,10.12; Jgs^B 20,28; 1 Kgs 22,6.15
to hold, to refrain Jb 27,8; *to hold back, to keep
in check* Jer 6,11; *to stop from, to cease from*
[τινος] 2 Kgs 4,24; *to forbear* 1 Kgs 22,15; *to
wait* Gn 8,10; *to wait for* Jb 30,26; *to intend, to
purpose* [abs.] Sir 13,11

Cf. HELBING 1928, 279

ἐπήκοος,-ος,-ον   A 0-2-0-0-0-2
2 Chr 6,40; 7,15
listening, giving ear to, attentive [εἴς τι] 2 Chr
6,40; [τινι] 2 Chr 7,15

ἐπήλυτος,-ου   N2M 0-0-0-1-0-1
Jb 20,26
foreigner, immigrant, stranger, incomer; see
προσήλυτος

ἐπί⁺   P 1418-1780-1765-1228-1106-7297
Gn 1,11.12.15.17.20
[τινος]: *on, upon* (place) Gn 1,11; *above* Gn
1,20; *at, near* 1 Mc 1,55; *by, on the basis of* Dt
19,15; *about, concerning* Jer 35,8; *in the time of,
under* 1 Ezr 2,12; *in* (time) Gn 49,1; *at, on*
(time) Ex 8,28; *during* 4 Mc 15,19; *over* (of pers.,
authority) Ex 2,14; [τινι]: *against* 2 Mc 13,19; *at,
near, by* Wis 19,17; *over* (of power) Est 8,12e;

to, in addition to Tob 2,14; *on the basis of* Dt
17,6; *in* (metaph. with verbs of believing, hoping,
trusting) Wis 3,9; *at, because of, from, with*
(after verbs which express feelings, opinions) Jdt
11,16; *at, in, at the time of, during* Sir 22,10; [τι,
τινα]: *upon* Gn 22,12; *against* Ps 40,10; [τινα]:
over Gn 37,8; *on, upon, to, over* Jer 1,1; *to,
toward* Dt 30,10; *in, on, for, toward* Wis 12,2;
[τι]: *for* Ps 21,19; *for, over a period of* Wis 18,20;
ἐπ' ἐσχάτων *at the last* Dt 17,7; εἴναι ἐπί
τινος *to have charge of* Jdt 14,13; ἐπ' ἀληθείας
truly Tob 8,7; χάρις ἐπὶ χάριτι *grace upon grace*
Sir 26,15; θλῖψιν ἐπὶ θλῖψιν *affliction on
affliction* Is 28,10; ἐπ' ὀνόματί τινος *after the
name of* Ezr 17,63; ἐπὶ πλεῖον (of place)
further 2 Mc 10,27; (of time) *longer, too long*
Wis 8,12; ἐπὶ τὸ αὐτό *together* Dt 25,5; ἐπὶ
πολύ *to a great extent, carefully* 3 Mc 5,17; *Ps
9,36(10,18) ἐπὶ corr.? ἀπὸ, see also Jb 23,15
and often; *LtJ 1,14 ἐπί -על *on, over* for MT על
yoke; *Is 4,2 ἐπὶ τῆς γῆς -על פני הארץ *on the
earth* for MT פרי הארץ *the fruits of the earth*

ἐπιβάθρα,-ας   N1F 0-0-0-0-1-1
3 Mc 2,31
means of approach (metaph.); neol.?

ἐπιβαίνω⁺   V 8-18-17-10-8-61
Gn 24,61; Lv 15,9; Nm 22,22.30; Dt 1,36
to set foot on, to tread, to walk upon Dt 1,36; *to
enter into* Mi 1,3; *to assault* Prv 21,22; *to continue* Jos 15,6; *to mount on* Gn 24,61; *to use* or
to put one's weight on Dt 33,29; *Jb 6,21 ἐπέβητε -אתה הייתם *you have come* for MT
◊עתה הייתם *now you have become* or ἐπέβητε
corr. ἀπέβητε *you have become*, see also Jb
30,21; *Ps 75(76),7 ἐπιβεβηκότες τοὺς ἵππους
-רכבי סוס *riders on horses* for MT רכב וסוס *rider
and horse*

Cf. HELBING 1928, 85.280; ORLINSKY 1937, 361-367

ἐπιβάλλω⁺   V 34-5-10-6-19-74
Gn 2,21; 22,12; 39,7; 46,4; 48,14
A: *to throw upon, to cast upon* [τι ἐπί τινα] Gn
39,7; *to lay on* [τι ἐπί τινα] Gn 2,21; *to add to,
to contribute to* [τί τινι] Jb 27,12; M: *to put
upon oneself* Jos 7,6; P: *to be put upon* [ἐπί τι]
Jos 9,2b(8,31); *to be imposed upon* [τινι] Ex
21,30; ἐπιβάλλει τινί [+ inf.] *it falls to the
share of sb to* Tob 3,17

Cf. HELBING 1928, 280

ἐπίβασις,-εως   N3F 0-0-0-2-2-4
Ps 103(104),3; Ct 3,10; Wis 5,11; 15,15

means of approach, access Ps 103(104),3; steps
Ct 3,10

ἐπιβάτης,-ου   N1M 0-5-1-1-1-8
2 Kgs 7,14; 9,17.18.19; 18,23
rider, horseman 2 Kgs 9,17; soldier on board
ship, mariner Ez 27,29; ἐπιβάτης ἵππου
horseman 2 Kgs 9,18

ἐπιβιβάζω⁺   V 0-6-3-1-2-12
2 Sm 6,3; 1 Kgs 1,33; 2 Kgs 9,28; 13,16(bis)
to put upon [τι ἐπί τι] 2 Sm 6,3; [τινα ἐπί τι]
2 Kgs 9,28

ἐπιβιόω   V 0-0-0-0-1-1
4 Mc 6,20
to live over, to live after, to survive

ἐπιβλέπω⁺   V 7-34-28-26-19-114
Gn 19,26.28; Ex 14,24; Lv 26,9; Nm 12,10
to look upon, to look attentively [ἐπί τινα] Gn
19,28; to look well at, to observe [τινα] 1 Kgs
7,13; *1 Sm 2,29 ἐπέβλεψας -חביט you look
(contemptuously) at for MT תבעטו you kick at;
*1 Sm 7,2 ἐπέβλεψεν -ויבטו they looked for MT
וינהו they lamented
Cf. DANIEL 1966, 186; HELBING 1928, 282

ἐπίβλημα,-ατος⁺   N3N 0-0-1-0-0-1
Is 3,22
house-coat, "négligé"
Cf. CAIRD 1972, 130

ἐπιβοάω   V 0-0-0-0-2-2
4 Mc 6,4; Wis 14,1
A: to cry out 4 Mc 6,4; M: to invoke, to call
upon Wis 14,1

ἐπιβοηθέω   V 0-0-0-0-4-4
1 Mc 7,7; 2 Mc 8,8; 11,7; 13,10
to come to aid, to succour [τινι]

ἐπιβόλαιον,-ου   N2N 0-1-2-0-0-3
JgsᴮB 4,18; Ez 13,18.21
covering, wrapper, garment; neol.

ἐπιβολή,-ῆς   N1F 0-0-0-0-2-2
1 Ezr 8,22; 2 Mc 8,7
hostile attempt, assault 2 Mc 8,7; penalty, fine
1 Ezr 8,22

ἐπιβουλεύω   V 0-0-0-2-0-2
Prv 17,26; Est 8,12u
to plot against, to contrive against [τινι]
Cf. HELBING 1928, 282

ἐπιβουλή,-ῆς⁺   N1F 0-0-0-1-6-8
Est 2,22; 1 Ezr 5,70; 2 Mc 5,7; 3 Mc 1,2
plan formed against, plot

ἐπίβουλος,-ος,-ον   A 0-4-1-0-8-13
1 Sm 29,4; 2 Sm 2,16; 19,23; 1 Kgs 5,18; Hab 2,7

plotting against, treacherous 1 Sm 29,4; *Hab 2,7
ἐπίβουλοι -מענניך those plotting against you for
MT מועזיך those making you tremble; *2 Sm
2,16 ἐπιβούλων -הצרים? (field) of the ambushes
for MT הצרים (field) of the sword-edges or of the
rocks?

ἐπιβρέχω   V 0-0-0-1-0-1
Ps 10(11),6
to rain upon

ἐπιβρίθω   V 0-0-0-1-0-1
Jb 29,4
to press closely on

ἐπιγαμβρεύω⁺   V 1-5-0-1-2-9
Gn 34,9; 1 Sm 18,22.23.26.27
A: to become son-in-law to [τινι] 1 Sm 18,22; to
become father-in-law to [τινι] 1 Mc 10,56; M: to
intermarry [τινι] Gn 34,9; neol.
Cf. HARL 1986, 248; HELBING 1928, 251-252

ἐπιγαμία,-ας   N1F 0-1-0-0-0-1
Jos 23,12
intermarriage; ἐπιγαμίαν ποιέω πρός τινα to
intermarry

ἐπιγελάω   V 0-0-0-1-1-2
Prv 1,26; TobᴮA 2,8
to laugh at [abs.] TobᴮA 2,8; [τινι] Prv 1,26

ἐπιγεμίζω   V 0-0-0-1-0-1
Neh 13,15
to impose as a burden; neol.

ἐπιγίνομαι⁺   V 0-0-0-0-2-2
3 Mc 2,5; LtJ 1,47
to be born after, to come after

ἐπιγινώσκω⁺   V 16-5-46-27-51-145
Gn 27,23; 31,32(bis); 37,32.33
to recognize Gn 27,23; to observe Gn 31,32; to
acknowledge Hab 3,2; to find out, to discover Gn
37,32; to take notice of Gn 31,32; to show favour
to Dt 16,19; *Hag 2,19 ἐπιγνωσθήσεται -הירע
shall it be known for MT הזרע the seed?; *Zech
6,10 ἐπεγνωκότων -ירעים those understanding for
MT ירעיה Iedaiah?, see also Zech 6,14

ἐπιγνωμοσύνη,-ης   N1F 0-0-0-1-0-1
Prv 16,23
prudence; neol.

ἐπιγνώμων,-ων,-ον   A 0-0-0-4-0-4
Prv 12,26; 13,10; 17,27; 29,7
understanding, intelligent Prv 17,27; ἐπιγνώμων
τινός judge, arbiter Prv 12,26

ἐπίγνωσις,-εως⁺   N3F 0-1-3-1-2-7
1 Kgs 7,2(14); Hos 4,1.6; 6,6; Prv 2,5
knowledge

ἐπίγνωστος,-ος,-ον   A 0-0-0-1-0-1
Jb 18,19
known; neol.

ἐπιγονή,-ῆς   N1F 0-2-1-0-0-3
2 Chr 31,16.18; Am 7,1
offspring, breed 2 Chr 31,16; *Am 7,1 ἐπιγονή
-יצר offspring for MT יוצר forming

ἐπιγράφω⁺   V 2-0-1-2-0-5
Nm 17,17.18; Is 44,5; Prv 7,3; Dn^LXX 5,0
to write upon

ἐπιδεής,-ής,-ές   A 0-0-0-0-2-2
Sir 4,1; 31,4
needy

ἐπιδεικνύω or ἐπιδείκνυμι⁺   V 0-0-1-2-11-14
Is 37,26; Prv 12,17; Est 3,13d; Jdt 8,24; Tob^S
11,15
A: to display, to exhibit, to show, to point out Is
37,26; to prove 4 Mc 1,17; M: to show off LtJ 59;
to make a display of one's powers Jdt 8,24

ἐπίδειξις,-εως   N3F 0-0-0-0-1-1
4 Mc 13,10
showing forth

ἐπιδέκατον,-ου   N2N 12-4-3-0-0-19
Nm 18,21.24.26(ter)
tenth, tithe

ἐπιδέξιος,-ος,-ον   A 0-0-0-2-0-2
Prv 27,16; Ezr 5,8
prosperous Ezr 5,8; *Prv 27,16 ἐπιδέξιος -ימין^II
prosperous for MT ימינו ◊ ימין his right hand?

ἐπιδέχομαι⁺   V 0-0-0-0-21-21
1 Ezr 9,14; 1 Mc 1,42.63; 6,60; 9,31
to receive, to welcome Sir 36,21; to take on
oneself, to undertake 1 Ezr 9,14; to agree 1 Mc
1,42; to allow, to admit Sir 51,26

ἐπιδέω (-εδέησα)   V 6-0-2-2-6-16
Dt 2,7; 15,7.8.9.10
A: to be in need of Sir 33,32; M: to be in want of
Dt 15,7

ἐπιδέω (-έδησα)   V 0-1-1-0-0-2
Jgs^B 16,21; Jer 28(51),63
to bind on, to fasten on Jer 28(51),63; to bind
Jgs^B 16,21

ἐπίδηλος,-ος,-ον   A 0-0-0-0-1-1
2 Mc 15,35
seen clearly, manifest

ἐπιδιαιρέω   V 1-0-0-0-0-1
Gn 33,1
to divide, to distribute
Cf. HARL 1986, 244-245

ἐπιδίδωμι⁺   V 1-1-1-1-8-12

Gn 49,21; 1 Sm 14,13; Am 4,1; Est 9,11; Sir 6,32
to give (freely), to bestow Gn 49,21; to give into
the hands of, to deliver 2 Mc 11,17; to add (his
own blow) 1 Sm 14,13; ἐπιδίδωμι τὴν ψυχήν
μου to give my soul, to intend Sir 6,32; καρδίαν
ἐπιδίδωμι [+inf.] to give one's heart to, to apply
oneself to Sir 38,30

ἐπιδιπλόω   V 1-0-0-0-0-1
Ex 26,9
to double; neol.
Cf. LE BOULLUEC 1989, 267-268

ἐπιδιώκω   V 1-0-0-0-1-2
Gn 44,4; 3 Mc 2,7
to pursue after [τινα] 3 Mc 2,7; [ὀπίσω τινός]
Gn 44,4

ἐπίδοξος,-ος,-ον   A 0-0-0-2-0-2
Prv 6,8b; Dn^LXX 2,11
glorious

ἐπιδόξως   D 0-0-0-0-1-1
1 Ezr 9,45
gloriously, honourably

ἐπιδύνω or ἐπιδύω⁺   V 1-1-1-0-0-3
Dt 24,15; Jos 8,29; Jer 15,9
to go down

ἐπιείκεια,-ας⁺   N1F 0-0-0-3-8-11
Dn 3,42(23); Dn^LXX 4,27(24); 2 Mc 2,22; 10,4
equity Wis 12,18; reasonableness, fairness,
goodness Wis 2,19
Cf. SPICQ 1979, 263-267; →NIDNTT; TWNT

ἐπιεικεύ ομαι   V 0-0-0-1-0-1
Ezr 9,8
to deal mercifully with [τινι]; neol.

ἐπιεικής,-ής,-ές⁺   A 0-0-0-2-1-3
Ps 85(86),5; Est 8,12i; PSal 5,12
fair, good, reasonable Ps 85(86),5; equitable Est
8,12i
→TWNT

ἐπιεικῶς or ἐπιεικέως   D 0-2-0-1-1-4
1 Sm 12,11; 2 Kgs 6,3; Est 3,13b; 2 Mc 9,27
kindly, mildly 2 Mc 9,27; ἐπιεικέστερον (comp.)
with greater moderation Est 3,13b
Cf. WALTERS 1973, 123

ἐπιζάω   V 1-0-0-0-1-2
Gn 47,28; 4 Mc 18,9
to survive

ἐπιζεύγνυμι   V 0-0-0-0-1-1
2 Mc 2,32
to add to [τί τινι] (metaph.)

ἐπιζήμιον,-ου   N2N 1-0-0-0-0-1
Ex 21,22

fine, punishment

ἐπιζητέω⁺ V 0-9-3-1-5-18
Jgs^B 6,29; 1 Sm 20,1; 2 Sm 3,8; 2 Kgs 1,2.3
to seek (after) [τι] 1 Sm 20,1; *to enquire (of), to consult* [τι] 2 Kgs 1,3; *to request* [τι] 1 Mc 7,13; *to seek a charge (against)* [ἐπί τινα] 2 Sm 3,8

ἐπιθανάτιος,-ος,-ον⁺ A 0-0-0-0-1-1
Bel^LXX 31
condemned to death; neol.?

ἐπίθεμα,-ατος N3N 11-8-0-0-0-19
Ex 25,17; Lv 7,34; 8,29; 14,24; 23,15
cover Ex 25,17; *heave-offering?, deposit?* Lv 14,24; *capital (of a column)* 1 Kgs 7,16
Cf. HARLÉ 1988, 42; LE BOULLUEC 1989, 256-257

ἐπίθεσις,-εως⁺ N3F 0-1-1-0-3-5
2 Chr 25,27; Ez 23,11; 2 Mc 4,41; 5,5; 14,15
setting upon, attack 2 Mc 4,41; *deception, corruption* Ez 23,11; see ἐπιτίθημι
Cf. RABINOWITZ 1958, 77-82, esp. 82; SPICQ 1978, 268-269

ἐπιθεωρέω V 0-0-0-0-1-1
4 Mc 1,30
to consider (next in order)

ἐπιθυμέω⁺ V 13-7-9-11-15-55
Gn 31,30; 49,14; Ex 20,17(bis); 34,24
to set one's heart upon, to long for, to desire [τινα] Ex 20,17; [τινος] Ex 34,24; [+inf.] Gn 31,30; *Gn 49,14 ἐπεθύμησεν - חמר he desired for MT חמר ass; *Is 58,11 ἐπιθυμεῖ -צחה (your soul) desires for MT צחצחות scorched land?
Cf. HELBING 1928, 137-138 LE BOULLUEC 1989, 210-211; TOV 1981, 107; →NIDNTT; TWNT

ἐπιθύμημα,-ατος N3N 1-1-6-7-2-17
Nm 16,15; 1 Kgs 21(20),6; Is 27,2; 32,12; Ez 24,16
object of desire 1 Kgs 21(20),6; *desire* Is 27,2; ἀγρὸς ἐπιθυμήματος *pleasant field* (semit.) Is 32,12; *Nm 16,15 ἐπιθύμημα - חמור desire for MT חמור ass; *Is 27,2 ἐπιθύμημα - חמר desire for MT חמר wine

ἐπιθυμητής,-οῦ⁺ N2M 1-0-1-1-0-3
Nm 11,34; Ez 26,12; Prv 1,22
one who lusts Nm 11,34; *one who longs for, one who desires* Prv 1,22

ἐπιθυμητός,-ή,-όν A 0-3-5-6-3-17
2 Chr 20,25; 32,27; 36,10; Is 32,14; Jer 12,10
(to be) desired Jer 12,10; σκεύη ἐπιθυμητά *precious vessels* 2 Chr 20,25; οἶκοι ἐπιθυμητοί *pleasant houses* Is 32,14

ἐπιθυμία,-ας⁺ N1F 11-2-1-30-41-85
Gn 31,30; 49,6; Nm 11,4.34.35

desire, yearning Gn 31,30; *lust* Nm 11,34; *longing after, desire of, desire for* [τινος] 2 Chr 8,6
→NIDNTT; TWNT

ἐπιθύω V 0-3-1-0-2-6
1 Kgs 12,33; 13,1.2; Hos 2,15; 1 Ezr 5,66
to offer (up)on 1 Kgs 13,2; *to burn incense* 1 Kgs 12,33
Cf. KILPATRICK 1983, 151-153

ἐπικάθημαι V 0-1-0-0-3-4
2 Sm 16,2; 2 Mc 3,25; Sir 33,6; LtJ 1,70
to sit upon

ἐπικαθίζω⁺ V 2-5-1-0-0-8
Gn 31,34; Lv 15,20; 2 Sm 13,29; 22,11; 1 Kgs 1,38
to set upon [τινα ἔν τινι] 2 Kgs 10,16; *to sit down upon* [τινι] Gn 31,34; [ἐπί τι] Lv 15,20

ἐπικαινίζω V 0-0-0-0-1-1
1 Mc 10,44
to renew, to restore; neol.

ἐπίκαιρος,-ος,-ον A 0-0-0-0-4-4
2 Mc 8,6.31; 10,15; 14,22
opportune, commodious, convenient

ἐπικαλέομαι⁺ V 26-35-31-50-46-188
Gn 4,26; 12,8; 13,4; 21,33; 26,25
M: *to call in, (up)on* Gn 4,26; P: *to be called upon* Gn 48,16; *to be called by surname* 1 Sm 23,28; *Am 4,12 τοῦ ἐπικαλεῖσθαι -לקרא ◊ קרא *to call on* for MT לקראת ◊ קרא var. of קרה *to meet,* see also Ex 3,18; *Ps 74(75),2 ἐπικαλεσόμεθα τὸ ὄνομά σου -בשמך ונקרא *and we will call upon your name* for MT שמך וקרוב *and near is your name*
Cf. HARL 1986, 153; SPICQ 1982, 286-291; →NIDNTT; TWNT

ἐπικάλυμμα,-ατος⁺ N3N 2-1-0-1-0-4
Ex 26,14; 39,20(34); 2 Sm 17,19; Jb 19,29
cover, covering, veil Ex 26,14; ἀπὸ ἐπικαλύμματος *from deceit?* (metaph.), mss. ἀπὸ κρίματος *from judgement* Jb 19,29

ἐπικαλύπτω⁺ V 6-3-4-4-2-19
Gn 7,19.20; 8,2; Ex 14,26; Nm 4,11
to cover (over), to cover (up) Gn 7,19; *to put as a covering over* Nm 4,11

ἐπικαρπολογέομαι V 0-0-0-0-1-1
4 Mc 2,9
to glean; neol.

ἐπικαταλαμβάνω V 1-0-0-0-0-1
Nm 11,23
to overtake
Cf. MARGOLIS 1972, 76-77

ἐπικαταράομαι V 9-0-1-0-1-11

Nm 5,18.19.22.23.24
to bring curses Nm 5,19; *to call down curses upon*
Nm 22,17; *to curse* (of God) Mal 2,2; neol.

ἐπικατάρατος,-ος,-ον⁺   A 25-8-7-2-3-45
Gn 3,14.17; 4,11; 9,25; 27,29
accursed; neol.?

ἐπίκειμαι⁺   V 1-0-0-2-4-7
Ex 36,38(39,31); Jb 19,3; 21,27; 1 Ezr 5,69; 1 Mc
6,57
to be placed, to lie in, to lie on [ἐπί τι] Ex
36,40(39,31); *to be laid upon* [abs.] 2 Mc 1,21 *to
press upon, to attack* [τινι] Jb 19,3; *to press upon*
[abs.] 3 Mc 1,12; serving as pass. to ἐπιτίθημι

ἐπικερδής,-ής,-ές   A 0-0-0-0-1-1
Wis 15,12
profitable, advantageous

ἐπικίνδυνος,-ος,-ον   A 0-0-0-0-1-1
3 Mc 5,33
dangerous

ἐπικινέομαι   V 0-0-0-0-1-1
1 Ezr 8,69
to be moved at [ἐπί τινι]

ἐπίκλησις,-εως   N3F 0-0-0-0-2-2
2 Mc 8,15; 15,26
calling upon, invocation
Cf. CONNOLLY 1924, 337-364; TYRER 1924, 139-150

ἐπίκλητος,-ος,-ον   A 7-2-1-0-0-10
Nm 1,16; 26,9; 28,18.26; 29,1
called to Nm 1,16; *appointed, designated* Jos
20,9; *Nm 28,18 ἡ ἐπίκλητος -קרא *the called*
(part.) for MT מקרא (subst.) *convocation, festival,*
see also 28,26; 29,1.7.12; *Jgsᴬ 15,19 ἐπίκλητος
-הקרוא *(the well) of the one called* for MT הקורא
(the well) of the one who calls
Cf. WALTERS 1973, 244-246

ἐπικλίνω   V 1-1-0-0-0-2
Gn 24,14; 1 Kgs 8,58
to incline

ἐπικλύζω   V 1-0-1-0-2-4
Dt 11,4; Is 66,12; Jdt 2,8; 3 Mc 2,7
to overflow, to flood

ἐπικοιμάομαι   V 1-1-0-0-0-2
Dt 21,23; 1 Kgs 3,19
to overlay, to lay upon

ἐπικοινωνέω   V 0-0-0-0-2-2
4 Mc 4,3; Sir 26,6
to communicate with [τινι] Sir 26,6; *to belong to*
[τινι] 4 Mc 4,3

ἐπικοπή,-ῆς   N1F 1-0-0-0-0-1
Dt 28,25

slaughter

ἐπικοσμέω   V 0-0-0-1-0-1
Eccl 1,15
to add ornaments to, to decorate (after)

ἐπικουρία,-ας⁺   N1F 0-0-0-0-1-1
Wis 13,18
supplication
Cf. GILBERT 1973, 93; HORSLEY 1983, 67-68

ἐπικουφίζομαι   V 0-0-0-0-1-1
4 Mc 9,31
to lighten

ἐπικραταιόομαι   V 0-0-0-1-0-1
Eccl 4,12
to be added strength to, to be confirmed; neol.

ἐπικράτεια,-ας   N1F 0-0-0-0-4-4
4 Mc 1,31.34; 3,18; 6,32
mastery

ἐπικρατέω   V 4-0-1-5-20-30
Gn 7,18.19; 41,57; 47,20; Ez 29,7
to have power, to hold power [abs.] Gn 7,18; *to
rule over* [τινος] Ezr 4,20; *to prevail over, to get
the mastery of* [τινος] Gn 47,20
Cf. HELBING 1928, 122

ἐπικράτησις,-εως   N3F 0-0-0-1-0-1
Est 8,12o
mastering, dominion

ἐπικρεμάννυμι   V 0-0-2-0-0-2
Is 22,24; Hos 11,7
to be depended upon, to be adhered to [τινι] Is
22,24; [ἔκ τινος] Hos 11,7

ἐπικρίνω⁺   V 0-0-0-0-2-2
2 Mc 4,47; 3 Mc 4,2
to adjudge, to inflict [τινί τι]
Cf. KILPATRICK (A) 1983, 151-153

ἐπικροτέω   V 0-0-3-1-1-5
Is 55,12; Jer 5,31; Am 6,5; Prv 17,18; Sir 12,18
to clap, to applaud

ἐπικρούω   V 0-0-1-0-0-1
Jer 31(48),26
to clap, to applaud

ἐπίκτητος,-ος,-ον   A 0-0-0-0-1-1
2 Mc 6,23
acquired

ἐπικυλίω   V 0-1-0-0-0-1
Jos 10,27
to roll down upon

ἐπίκυφος,-ος,-ον   A 0-0-0-0-1-1
3 Mc 4,5
bent over, crooked; neol.

ἐπιλαμβάνομαι⁺   V 5-16-15-8-9-53

Gn 25,26; Ex 4,4(bis); Dt 9,17; 25,11

to take hold of, to lay hold of [τινος] Gn 25,26; *Jb 30,18 ἐπελάβετο -יתחפש has taken hold of* for MT יתחפש *is disfigured*

Cf. HELBING 1928, 127-128; →NIDNTT; TWNT

ἐπιλάμπω							V 0-0-1-0-1-2
Is 4,2; Wis 5,6
to shine upon

ἐπιλανθάνομαι⁺						V 17-4-32-52-16-121
Gn 27,45; 40,23; 41,30.51; Dt 4,9
to forget, to lose thought of Ps 9,32; [τινος] Gn 41,30; [τι] Dt 4,9; *to forget to do* [+ptc.] Jb 9,27

Cf. HELBING 1928, 110-111

ἐπιλέγω⁺							V 3-3-0-1-16-23
Ex 17,9; 18,25; Dt 21,5; Jos 8,3; 2 Sm 10,6
to pick out, to select Ex 17,9; *to remove* 1 Kgs 14,10

ἐπίλεκτος,-ος,-ον						A 2-2-8-1-4-17
Ex 15,4; 24,11; Jos 17,16.18; Ez 17,3
chosen Ex 24,11; *choice* Jos 17,16

ἐπιλημπτεύομαι						V 0-1-1-0-0-2
1 Sm 21,16; Jer 30,19(49,3)
to have an epileptic fit; neol.

ἐπίλημπτος,-ος,-ον						A 0-3-0-0-0-3
1 Sm 21,15.16; 2 Kgs 9,11
suffering from epilepsy

ἐπιλησμονή,-ῆς⁺						N1F 0-0-0-0-1-1
Sir 11,27
forgetfulness

ἐπιλογίζομαι						V 0-0-0-0-3-3
2 Mc 11,4; 4 Mc 3,6; 16,5
to reckon with, to consider

ἐπίλοιπος,-ος,-ον⁺					A 3-3-5-3-12-26
Lv 27,18; Dt 19,20; 21,21; Jgsᴬ 7,6; 21,16
still left, remaining Lv 27,18; τὸ ἐπίλοιπον *remnant* Jer 32(25),20

ἐπιλυπέω							V 0-0-0-0-3-3
2 Mc 4,37; 8,32; 3 Mc 7,9
to annoy, to trouble, to offend (besides)

ἐπιμαίνομαι						V 0-0-0-0-1-1
4 Mc 7,5
to be mad, to rage

ἐπιμαρτύρομαι						V 0-1-2-3-1-7
1 Kgs 2,42; Jer 39(32),25; Am 3,13; Neh 9,29.30
to bear witness, to depose

Cf. HELBING 1928, 223-227; →NIDNTT

ἐπιμέλεια,-ας⁺						N1F 0-0-0-5-5-10
Prv 3,8.22; 13,4; 28,25; Est 2,3
care, attention, diligence Prv 3,8; *public administration* 1 Mc 16,14

Cf. SPICQ 1978, 270-273

ἐπιμελέομαι or ἐπιμέλομαι⁺				V 1-0-0-1-3-5
Gn 44,21; Prv 27,25; 1 Ezr 6,26; 1 Mc 11,37; Sir 30,25
to take care of [τινος] Gn 44,21; *Prv 27,25 ἐπιμελοῦ -ראה see to* for MT נראה *appears*

Cf. HELBING 1928, 111; SPICQ 1978, 69-71.273-275

ἐπιμελῶς⁺							D 2-0-0-4-9-15
Gn 6,5; 8,21; Prv 13,24; Ezr 6,8.12
carefully

Cf. SPICQ 1978, 276

ἐπιμένω⁺							V 1-0-0-0-0-1
Ex 12,39
to stay on, to tarry

Cf. MARGOLIS 1972 (A), 62; --NIDNTT

ἐπιμήκης,-ης,-ες						A 0-0-0-0-1-1
Bar 3,24
far-stretching, extensive

ἐπιμίγνυμαι or ἐπιμείγνυμαι				V 0-0-1-1-2-4
Ez 16,37; Prv 14,10; 1 Ezr 8,67.84
to mingle with [εἴς τι] 1 Ezr 8,67; [τινι] 1 Ezr 8,84; *to consort with* [ἔν τινι] Ez 16,37

ἐπίμικτος,-ος,-ον						A 2-0-1-1-1-5
Ex 12,38; Nm 11,4; Ez 30,5; Neh 13,3; Jdt 2,20
mixed

ἐπιμιμνήσκομαι						V 0-0-0-0-1-1
1 Mc 10,46
to call to mind, to recollect, to remember [τινος]

ἐπιμίξ							D 0-0-0-0-1-1
Wis 14,25
mixedly, confusedly, cpr. Hos 4,2

Cf. GILBERT 1973, 165-166

ἐπιμονή,-ῆς							N1F 0-0-0-0-1-1
Sir 38,27
steadfastness

ἐπίμοχθος,-ος,-ον						A 0-0-0-0-1-1
Wis 15,7
laborious, tiring, toilsome

ἐπιμύλιον,-ου						N2N 1-1-0-0-0-2
Dt 24,6; Jgsᴮ 9,53
the upper millstone

ἐπινεύω⁺							V 0-0-0-1-4-5
Prv 26,24; 1 Mc 6,57; 2 Mc 4,10; 11,15; 14,20
to grant, to promise [abs.] 2 Mc 4,10; [τί τινι] Prv 26,24; *to consent to* [τινι] 2 Mc 14,20; [ἐπί τινι] 2 Mc 11,15

ἐπινεφής,-ής,-ές						A 0-0-0-0-1-1
2 Mc 1,22
clouded, dark

ἐπινίκια,-ων						N2N 0-0-0-0-2-2

1 Ezr 3,5; 2 Mc 8,33
feast for a victory 2 Mc 8,33; *tokens of victory*
1 Ezr 3,5

ἐπινοέω   V 0-0-0-1-3-4
Jb 4,18; 4 Mc 10,16; Wis 14,2.14
to think on or *of, to contrive* [τι] Wis 14,2; *to
note, to observe* [τι] Jb 4,18

ἐπίνοια,-ας⁺   N1F 0-0-1-0-7-8
Jer 20,10; 2 Mc 12,45; 4 Mc 17,2; Wis 6,16; 9,14
thought Wis 6,16; *invention, device* Wis 9,14

ἐπινυστάζω   V 0-0-0-1-0-1
Prv 6,4
to fall asleep; neol.

ἐπιξενόομαι   V 0-0-0-2-1-3
Prv 21,7; Est 8,12k; Sir 29,27
to be entertained as a guest
Cf. HELBING 1928, 253

ἐπιορκέω⁺   V 0-0-0-0-2-2
1 Ezr 1,46; Wis 14,28
to swear falsely, to perjure oneself
Cf. KILPATRICK 1983, 151-153; LARCHER 1985, 832.835

ἐπιορκία,-ας   N1F 0-0-0-0-1-1
Wis 14,25
false swearing, perjury

ἐπίορκος,-ος,-ον⁺   A 0-0-1-0-0-1
Zech 5,3
falsely sworn, perjured

ἐπιπαραγίνομαι   V 0-1-0-0-0-1
Jos 10,9
to arrive also, to come also up(on)

ἐπίπεμπτον,-ου   N2N 8-0-0-0-0-8
Lv 5,16; 22,14; 27,13.15.19
the fifth part
Cf.LEE 1969, 236

ἐπιπέμπω   V 0-0-0-1-2-3
Prv 6,19; 3 Mc 6,6; Wis 11,17
to send upon or *against, to let loose upon* [τι ἀνὰ
μέσον τινός] Prv 6,19; [τινά τινι] Wis 11,17

ἐπιπίπτω⁺   V 11-7-1-19-17-55
Gn 14,15; 15,12(bis); 45,14; 46,29
to fall upon or *over* [τινι] Gn 15,12; *to fall upon,
to attack* [ἐπί τινα] Gn 14,15; ἐπιπίπτω ἐπὶ
τὸν τράχηλόν τινος *to fall on one's neck* Gn
45,14
Cf. HELBING 1928, 283

ἐπίπληξις,-εως   N3F 0-0-0-0-1-1
2 Mc 7,33
blame, rebuke
Cf. CAIRD 1972, 131

ἐπιπληρόω   V 0-0-0-0-2-2

2 Mc 3,30; 6,4
to fill up

ἐπιποθέω⁺   V 2-0-1-7-2-12
Dt 13,9; 32,11; Jer 13,14; Ps 41(42),2(bis)
to desire (besides), to yearn after, to long for [τι]
Ps 118(119),131; [τινα] Sir 25,21; [ἐπί τινι] Dt
32,11; [ἐπί τι] Ps 41(42),1; [πρός τινα] Ps
41(42),1; *to feel want of* [τινος] Ps 118(119),20;
[ἐπί τι] Ps 61(62)11; *Dt 13,9 ἐπιποθήσεις
-תחמר you shall desire *for MT* תחמל *you shall feel
regret*, see also Jer 13,14
Cf. SPICQ 1957, 184-195

ἐπιπολάζω   V 0-1-0-0-0-1
2 Kgs 6,6
to come to the surface, to float on the surface

ἐπιπολαίως   D 0-0-0-0-1-1
3 Mc 2,31
on the surface

ἐπίπονος,-ος,-ον   A 0-0-0-0-2-2
3 Mc 5,47; Sir 7,15
laborious, hard

ἐπιπορεύομαι⁺   V 1-0-1-0-3-5
Lv 26,33; Ez 39,14; 2 Mc 2,28; 3 Mc 1,4; LtJ
1,61
to travel Ez 39,14; *to come upon* Lv 26,33
Cf. HELBING 1928, 84; LEE 1983, 88-89

ἐπιπροστίθημι   V 0-0-0-0-1-1
Sir prol.,10
to add besides

ἐπιρραίνω or ἐπιρραντίζω   V 1-0-0-0-1-2
Lv 6,20; 2 Mc 1,21
to sprinkle upon or *over, to besprinkle*

ἐπιρρέω   V 0-0-0-1-0-1
Jb 22,16
to overflow, to wash away

ἐπιρρίπτω⁺   V 2-4-4-3-1-14
Nm 35,20.22; Jos 10,11; 23,4; 2 Sm 20,12
to cast at, to throw upon [τί τινι] Jos 10,11; [τι
ἐπί τινα] Nm 35,20; *to add to* [τί τινι] Jos
23,4; *to bring* (metaph.) Am 8,3
Cf. HELBING 1928, 283

ἐπιρρωγολογέομαι   V 0-0-0-0-1-1
4 Mc 2,9
to glean grapes; neol.

ἐπιρρωννύομαι   V 0-0-0-0-1-1
2 Mc 11,9
to recover strength, to pluck up courage

ἐπίσαγμα,-ατος   N3N 1-0-0-0-0-1
Lv 15,9
pack-saddle

ἐπισάσσω   V 2-11-1-0-0-14
Gn 22,3; Nm 22,21; Jgs 19,10; 2 Sm 16,1
to pile a load on, to saddle

ἐπισείω⁺   V 0-5-0-0-1-6
Jgs 1,14; 1 Sm 26,19; 2 Sm 24,1; 1 Chr 21,1
to stir up 1 Sm 26,19; *to urge (on)* Jgs 1,14; *to terrify* 2 Mc 4,1
Cf. BICKERMAN 1980, 189

ἐπισημαίνω   V 0-0-0-1-1-2
Jb 14,17; 2 Mc 2,6
to mark

ἐπίσημος,-ος,-ον⁺   A 1-0-0-2-6-9
Gn 30,42; Est 5,4; 8,12; 1 Mc 11,37; 14,48
marked Gn 30,42; *notable, remarkable* 3 Mc 6,1; *conspicuous* 1 Mc 11,37; *significant* Est 5,4; see ἄσημος
→TWNT

ἐπισιτίζομαι   V 0-1-0-0-0-1
Jos 9,4
to furnish oneself with food or *provisions*; *Jos^BA 9,4 ἐπεσιτίσαντο* יצטירו- *provided with provisions* for MT יצטירו *acted like envoys*

ἐπισιτισμός,-οῦ⁺   N2M 3-9-0-1-2-15
Gn 42,25; 45,21; Ex 12,39; Jos 1,11; 9,5
stock or *store of provisions*

ἐπισκάζω   V 1-0-0-0-0-1
Gn 32,32
to limp upon [τινι]

ἐπισκεπάζω   V 0-0-0-2-0-2
Lam 3,43.44
to cover or *put over*

ἐπισκέπτομαι or ἐπισκεπέω⁺ V 58-40-28-18-24-168
Gn 21,1; 50,24.25; Ex 3,16; 4,31
to visit [τινα] Gn 21,1; *to look upon* or *at* [τινα] Ex 3,16; *to inspect, to examine* [abs.] Lv 13,36 [τι] Ex 3,16; *to consider* [τινα] Nm 1,3; *to number* [τινα] 1 Sm 15,4; *Nm 16,5 ἐπέσκεπται -בקר* (piel) *to visit* for MT בקר *morning*; *Neh 12,42 καὶ ἐπεσκέπησαν -ויפקרו and were numbered* for MT הפקיר *the leader*
Cf. GEHMAN 1972, 197-207; HARL 1986, 186; →NIDNTT; TWNT

ἐπισκευάζω⁺   V 1-6-0-0-1-8
Ex 30,7; 1 Sm 3,3; 2 Chr 24,4.12(bis)
to arrange Ex 30,7; *to repair* 2 Chr 24,4

ἐπίσκεψις,-εως   N3F 45-7-4-0-4-60
Ex 30,13.14; 39,3(38,26); Nm 1,21.23
numbering, census Nm 1,21; *inspection, visitation* 2 Mc 5,18
Cf. BICKERMAN 1980, 171; GEHMAN 1972, 197-207

ἐπισκιάζω⁺   V 1-0-0-3-0-4
Ex 40,35; Ps 90(91),4; 139(140),8; Prv 18,11
to throw a shade upon, to overshadow
Cf. HELBING 1928, 284; LE BOULLUEC 1989, 377; →TWNT

ἐπισκοπέω⁺   V 1-1-0-2-0-4
Dt 11,12; 2 Chr 34,12; Prv 19,23; Est 2,11
to look upon or *at, to inspect, to observe*
Cf. GROSSFELD 1984, 83-101; HARL 1986, 187; →NIDNTT; TWNT

ἐπισκοπή,-ῆς⁺   N1F 13-0-7-10-15-45
Gn 50,24.25; Ex 3,16; 13,19; 30,12
visitation (pos.) Nm 16,29; (neg.) Wis 14,11; *office* Ps 108(109),8; *numbering, census* Nm 14,29; *Jb 29,4 ἐπισκοπὴν -ב/סוד the visitation over* for MT ב/סוד *in the council?, in intimacy?*; neol.
Cf. GEHMAN 1972 (A), 197-207; GILBERT 1973, 138-141; LARCHER 1983, 257; →NIDNTT; TWNT

ἐπίσκοπος,-ου⁺   N2M 2-7-1-4-2-16
Nm 4,16; 31,14; Jgs 9,28; 2 Kgs 11,15
one who watches over, overseer, guardian Nm 4,16; *supervisor, inspector* Nm 31,14
Cf. GEHMAN 1972 (A), 197-207; LARCHER 1983, 182; →NIDNTT

ἐπισπάομαι⁺   V 1-0-2-0-8-11
Gn 39,12; Is 5,18; Na 3,14; Jdt 12,12; 1 Mc 14,1
to draw (in or *to), to call (in)*
Cf. LARCHER 1983, 196

ἐπίσπαστρον,-ου   N2N 1-0-0-0-0-1
Ex 26,36
that which is drawn over, curtain, hanging
Cf. LE BOULLUEC 1989, 273; PELLETIER 1984, 406

ἐπισπεύδω   V 0-0-0-2-1-3
Prv 6,18; Est 6,14; 1 Ezr 1,25
to hasten to [τινα ἐπί τι] Est 6,14; *to hasten to do* [+inf.] Prv 6,18; *to hasten onwards* [intrans.] 1 Ezr 1,25

ἐπισπλαγχνίζομαι   V 0-0-0-1-0-1
Prv 17,5
to have compassion; neol.

ἐπισπουδάζω   V 1-0-0-2-0-3
Gn 19,15; Prv 13,11; 20,9b(21)
to urge on, to further Gn 19,15; *Prv 13,11 ἐπισπουδαζομένη מבהל gotten hastily* for MT מ/הבל *from vanity*; neol.

ἐπισπουδαστής,-οῦ   N1M 0-0-1-0-0-1
Is 14,4
one who presses on a work; *Is 14,4 ἐπισπουδαστής -מרהבה? compeller* for MT דהב מ/רהבה◊? (Aram.) *golden?*; neol.

ἐπίσταμαι⁺   V 14-6-12-7-14-53
Gn 47,5; Ex 4,14; 9,30; Nm 20,14; 22,34
to know, to be able or *capable* 2 Chr 2,6; *to
know, to be versed in* or *acquainted with* Dt
28,33; *to know (for certain)* Gn 47,5;
ἐπιστάμενον *knowing* 2 Chr 2,11; *Prv 10,21
ἐπίσταται -ירעו *knows* for MT ירעו *they feed,
pasture*; *Prv 14,22 ἐπίστανται -ירעו *they know*
for MT יתעו *they err*
(→ συν-)

ἐπιστατέω   V 0-0-0-0-1-1
1 Ezr 7,2
to be in charge of, to have the care of [τινος]

ἐπιστάτης,-ου⁺   N1M 2-5-2-0-4-13
Ex 1,11; 5,14; 1 Kgs 2,35h(9,23); 5,30
one who is set over, chief, commander Ex 5,14;
clerk Ex 1,11; *overseer, superintendent* 2 Chr 2,1
Cf. GLOMBITZA 1958, 275-278; LE BOULLUEC 1989, 33

ἐπιστήμη,-ης   N1F 6-1-7-17-31-62
Ex 31,3; 35,31; 36,1.2; Nm 24,16
knowledge Ex 31,3; *skill, understanding* 1 Ezr 8,7
Cf. LARCHER 1984, 466-467

ἐπιστήμων,-ων,-ον⁺   A 3-0-1-3-7-14
Dt 1,13.15; 4,6; Is 5,21; Dnᴸˣˣ 1,4
knowing, wise, prudent Dt 1,13; *acquainted with,
skilled* or *versed in* [ἔν τινι] Dnᴸˣˣ 1,4

ἐπιστήριγμα,-ατος   N3N 0-1-0-0-0-1
2 Sm 22,19
support; neol.

ἐπιστηρίζω⁺   V 1-7-1-5-1-15
Gn 28,13; Jgsᴬ 16,26(bis).29(bis)
A: *to cause to rest on* Ps 37(38),2; P: *to be sup-
ported, to be established* Jgs 16,26; *Ps 31(32),8
ἐπιστηριῶ -אעצה *I will cause to rest, I will fix* for
MT אעצה *I will counsel*, cpr. Prv 16,30
Cf. HARL 1986, 223

ἐπιστοιβάζω   V 3-0-0-0-1-4
Lv 1,7.8.12; Sir 8,3
to pile up; neol.

ἐπιστολή,-ῆς⁺   N1F 0-2-3-18-38-61
2 Chr 30,1.6; Is 18,2; 39,1; Jer 36(29),1
letter
·NIDNTT

ἐπιστρατεία,-ας   N1F 0-0-0-0-1-1
3 Mc 3,14
march or *expedition against*; neol.?

ἐπιστρατεύω   V 0-0-4-0-2-6
Is 29,7.8; 31,4; Zech 14,12; 2 Mc 12,27
to march against, to make war upon [ἐπί τι] Is
29,8; [ἐπί τινα] Is 29,7

ἐπιστράτηγος,-ου   N2M 0-0-0-0-1-1
1 Mc 15,38
viceroy

ἐπιστρατοπεδεύω   V 0-0-0-0-1-1
Jdt 2,21
to encamp (over against); neol.?

ἐπιστρέφω⁺   V 32-207-113-114-68-534
Gn 8,12; 21,32; 24,49; 44,13; Ex 4,20
A: *to turn* [τινα] Nm 10,35; *to return* [intrans.]
Gn 8,12; *again* [+inf.] (semit., as periphrasis of
πάλιν) Dt 30,9; [καί +finite verb] 2 Chr 33,3;
M/P: *to turn oneself (round)* Ex 7,23; P: *to be
converted, to return* Dt 30,2; *Lam 2,8 καὶ
ἐπέστρεψε -והשיב *he has turned* or *again (he
has)* for MT חשב *he planned*, cpr. ibidem
ἀπέστρεψεν; *1 Sm 14,21 ἐπεστράφησαν καὶ
-גם סבבו *they turned also* for MT וגם סביב *round
about, (they) also*; *1 Kgs 13,11 ἐπέστρεψαν τὸ
πρόσωπον -פנים יסירו *they turned the face* for MT
יספרום *they told them*; *Dn 11,18 ἐπιστρέψει
-השיב *he shall return* for MT השבית *he shall put
an end*
Cf. AUBIN 1963; CIMOSA 1985, 739; GEHMAN 1972 (A),
96; HELBING 1928, 284; →NIDNTT; TWNT

ἐπιστροφή,-ῆς⁺   N1F 0-1-3-1-6-11
Jgsᴮ 8,9; Ez 42,11; 47,7.11; Ct 7,11
return Jgsᴮ 8,9; *attention (paid to)* Ct 7,11;
conversion Sir 18,21; *turning* Ez 42,11
→TWNT

ἐπισυνάγω⁺   V 2-3-8-5-30-48
Gn 6,16; 38,29; 1 Kgs 18,20; 2 Chr 5,6; 20,26
to gather together, to narrow 2 Mc 2,13; *to draw
back* Gn 38,29; *Gn 6,16 ἐπισυνάγων -צבר?
gathering together, narrowing for MT צהר *window*
or *roof*?
Cf. HARL 1986, 132.267; HELBING 1928, 285

ἐπισυναγωγή,-ῆς⁺   N1F 0-0-0-0-1-1
2 Mc 2,7
gathering together; συνάγω ἐπισυναγωγήν τινος
to gather sb together; neol.?
Cf. SPICQ 1978, 282-283; →TWNT

ἐπισυνέχω   V 0-0-0-0-1-1
1 Ezr 9,17
to take to oneself (a wife); neol.

ἐπισυνίστημι   V 6-0-3-0-1-10
Lv 19,16; 26,16; Nm 14,35; 16,19; 26,9
A: *to bring upon* [τι ἐπί τινα] Lv 26,16; M: *to
conspire against, to rise up against, to attack* [ἐπί
τινα] Nm 14,35
Cf. HELBING 1928, 285

ἐπισύστασις,-εως   N3F 2-0-0-0-1-3
Nm 17,5; 26,9; 1 Ezr 5,70
insurrection Nm 17,5; *rising against* [τινος] Nm
26,9; neol.?

ἐπισυστρέφω   V 1-0-0-0-1-2
Nm 17,7; 1 Mc 14,44
to collect together; neol.?

ἐπισφαλής,-ής,-ές⁺   A 0-0-0-0-1-1
Wis 9,14
prone to fall, unstable, precarious

ἐπισφαλῶς   D 0-0-0-0-1-1
Wis 4,4
unstable

ἐπισφραγίζω   V 0-0-0-1-1-2
Neh 10,1; Bel^LXX 11
to put a seal (on), to confirm, to ratify

ἐπισχύω⁺   V 0-0-0-0-2-2
1 Mc 6,6; Sir 29,1
to be or *grow strong* [intrans.]

ἐπιταγή,-ῆς⁺   N1F 0-0-0-1-6-7
Dn^LXX 3,16; 1 Ezr 1,16; 3 Mc 7,20; Wis 14,17;
18,15
command, commandment; neol.?
Cf. HORSLEY 1982, 86

ἐπίταγμα,-ατος   N3N 0-0-0-0-1-1
4 Mc 8,6
command

ἐπιταράσσομαι   V 0-0-0-0-1-1
2 Mc 9,24
to be troubled

ἐπίτασις,-εως   N3F 0-0-0-0-2-2
2 Mc 6,3; Wis 14,18
increase (in intensity or *force)*

ἐπιτάσσω⁺   V 1-0-1-11-25-38
Gn 49,33; Ez 24,18; Ps 106(107),29; Est 1,8;
3,12
to impose commands [τινι] Gn 49,33; *to order to*
[+inf.] 1 Ezr 2,23
Cf. HELBING 1928, 208-209

ἐπιτάφιον,-ου   N2N 0-0-0-0-1-1
4 Mc 17,8
tomb

ἐπιτείνω   V 0-0-0-1-6-7
Dn^LXX 7,6; 2 Mc 9,11; 4 Mc 3,11; 13,25; 15,23
A: *to stretch* [abs.] Dn^LXX 7,6; *to increase in
intensity* [τι] (metaph.) 4 Mc 13,25; [intrans.]
4 Mc 3,11; *to urge on, to incite* [+inf.] 4 Mc
15,23; M: *to increase oneself* Wis 16,24; P: *to be
spread over* [τινι] Wis 17,20; *to suffer more
intensely* 2 Mc 9,11

ἐπιτελέω⁺   V 2-3-1-3-21-30
Lv 6,15; Nm 23,23; Jgs^A 11,39; 20,10; 1 Sm 3,12
to complete, to finish, to accomplish
→TWNT

ἐπιτέμνω   V 0-0-0-0-2-2
2 Mc 2,23(bis)
to abridge, to shorten

ἐπιτερπής,-ής,-ές   A 0-0-0-0-1-1
2 Mc 15,39
pleasing, delightful

ἐπιτήδειος,-α,-ον⁺   A 0-1-0-0-8-9
1 Chr 28,2; 1 Mc 4,46; 10,19; 13,40; 14,34
useful, serviceable, necessary 1 Chr 28,2;
convenient, suitable 1 Mc 4,46

ἐπιτήδευμα,-ατος   N3N 3-6-33-12-4-58
Lv 18,3(bis); Dt 28,20; Jgs 2,19
pursuit, business Jdt 13,5; ἐπιτηδεύματα *habits,
ways of living* Lv 18,3; *Mi 2,9 ἐπιτηδεύματα
αὐτῶν -מ/עלליהם *(because of) their practices* for
MT מעל עלליה *from her young children*

ἐπιτηδεύω   V 0-0-2-1-2-5
Jer 2,33; Mal 2,11; Est 8,12m; 3 Mc 2,14; Wis
19,13
to pursue, to practise [τι] Wis 19,13; *to life one's
life with an eye to* [εἰς τινα] Mal 2,11; *to take
care to, to use to* [+ inf.] Est 8,12m

ἐπιτηρέω   V 0-0-0-0-1-1
Jdt 13,3
to look out, to watch for

ἐπιτίθημι⁺   V 153-52-20-16-29-270
Gn 9,23; 11,6; 21,14; 22,6.9
A: *to lay, to put, to place (up)on* [τι ἐπί τι]; M:
to lay, to put, to place (up)on [τι ἐπί τι] Gn
9,23; *to apply oneself to, to undertake* [τι] Gn
11,6; *to make an attempt upon, to attack* [τινι]
Gn 43,18; ἐπιτιθέμενοι ἐπιτίθεσθε *you are
plotting* (semit.) 2 Chr 23,13; ἐπιτίθεμαί τινι
ἐπίθεσιν *to concoct a conspiracy against sb*
(semit.) 2 Chr 25,27, cpr. 2 Chr 24,25.26
Cf. GEHMAN 1972, 108; HELBING 1928, 285-286; LE
BOULLUEC 1989, 195.297

ἐπιτιμάω⁺   V 1-0-2-5-3-11
Gn 37,10; Zech 3,2(bis); Ps 9,6; 67(68),31
to rebuke, to censure [τινι] Gn 37,10; [ἔν τινι]
Zech 3,2
Cf. HELBING 1928, 286; →TWNT

ἐπιτίμησις,-εως   N3F 0-1-0-6-2-9
2 Sm 22,16; Ps 17(18),16; 75(76),7; 79(80),17;
103(104),7
rebuke, censure, criticism

ἐπιτιμία,-ας⁺ N1F 0-0-0-0-1-1
Wis 3,10
punishment, penalty
Cf. LARCHER 1984, 295

ἐπιτίμιον,-ου N2N 0-0-0-0-1-1
Sir 9,5
punishment, penalty

ἐπίτιμος,-ος,-ον A 0-0-0-0-2-2
2 Mc 6,13; Sir 8,5
valuable

ἐπιτομή,-ῆς N1F 0-0-0-0-2-2
2 Mc 2,26.28
summary, epitome, abridgement

ἐπιτρέπω⁺ V 1-0-0-2-5-8
Gn 39,6; Jb 32,14; Est 9,14; 1 Mc 15,6; 4 Mc
4,17
to commit to, to entrust to [τι ἔις τι] Gn 39,6;
[τινι] 4 Mc 4,18; *to permit* [+inf.] Est 9,14; *to
command* [τινι +inf.] Jb 32,14

ἐπιτρέχω V 1-0-0-0-4-5
Gn 24,17; 1 Mc 6,45; 4 Mc 7,11; PSal 13,3; Susᵀʰ
19
to run (unto) Gn 24,17; [τινι] Susᵀʰ 19

ἐπιτροπή,-ῆς⁺ N1F 0-0-0-0-1-1
2 Mc 13,14
power to decide, decision, outcome

ἐπίτροπος,-ου⁺ N2M 0-0-0-0-3-3
2 Mc 11,1; 13,2; 14,2
trustee, guardian, protector

ἐπιτυγχάνω⁺ V 1-0-0-1-0-2
Gn 39,2; Prv 12,27
to be successful [abs.] Gn 39,2; *to attain to, to
reach, to gain* [τινος] Prv 12,27
Cf. HARL 1986, 267; HELBING 1928, 142

ἐπιτυχία,-ας N1F 0-0-0-0-1-1
Wis 13,19
success

ἐπιφαίνω⁺ V 3-0-4-8-10-25
Gn 35,7; Nm 6,25; Dt 33,2; Jer 36(29),14; Ez
17,6
A: *to show forth, to display* [τι] Ps 30(31),17; *to
shine upon* [intrans.] Ps 117(118),27; P: *to
appear* Gn 35,7
Cf. SPICQ 1978, 284-286; TOV 1990, 116; →NIDNTT

ἐπιφάνεια,-ας⁺ N1F 0-1-1-1-9-12
2 Sm 7,23; Am 5,22; Est 1,5c; 2 Mc 2,21; 3,24
intervention 2 Mc 5,4; *manifestation, appearance,
presences* 3 Mc 2,9; *Am 5,22 ἐπιφανείας
-מראיכם *your (their) appearances* for MT מריאיכם
your fatted beasts

Cf. CUSS 1974, 134-144; DANIEL 1966, 185.283-286;
LÜHRMANN 1971, 185-199; MOHRMANN 1953, 644-670, esp.
649-651; PAX 1955; SPICQ 1978, 286; →NIDNTT

ἐπιφανής,-ής,-ές⁺ A 0-2-6-1-4-13
Jgsᴬ 13,6; 1 Chr 17,21; Jl 2,11; 3,4; Hab 1,7
notable, distinguished, famous 1 Chr 17,21;
manifest, evident Prv 25,14; often rendering
Heb. נורא ◊ ירא *terrible* seen as a derivative of
ראה?: ἡ ἡμέρα τοῦ κυρίου ... ἐπιφανής σφόδρα
the day of the Lord is glorious Jl 2,11, cpr. Jl 3,4
Cf. SPICQ 1978, 287; TOV 1990, 110-118; →NIDNTT; TWNT

ἐπιφαύσκω⁺ V 0-0-0-3-0-3
Jb 25,5; 31,26; 41,10
A: *to shine out* Jb 31,26; M: Jb 41,10; *Jb 25,5
ἐπιφαύσκει - יהל ◊ הלל *is bright* for MT יאהיל
pitches his tent; neol.
→TWNT

ἐπιφέρω⁺ V 3-7-1-3-3-17
Gn 1,2; 7,18; 37,22; 1 Sm 22,17; 24,7
A: *to bring, to put, to lay upon* [τί τινι] Gn
37,22; *to give* [τί τινι] Jdt 8,8; P: *to rush (upon)*
or *(after)* [ἐπάνω τινός] Gn 1,2; *to be borne
(on)* [ἐπάνω τινός] Gn 7,18; *to attack, to assault*
[τινι] 2 Mc 12,35; *Jb 15,12 ἐπήνεγκαν - ירומון
(they) have set themselves on (sc. the eyes) for
MT ירזמון *they have flashed*?
Cf. HELBING 1928, 286-288

ἐπιφημίζω V 1-0-0-0-1-2
Dt 29,18; Wis 2,12
A: *to ascribe to, to assign to* [τί τινι] Wis 2,12;
M: *to utter words, to flatter oneself* Dt 29,18
Cf. LARCHER 1983, 242

ἐπιφυλλίζω V 0-0-0-3-0-3
Lam 1,22; 2,20; 3,51
to gather [abs.] (metaph.) Lam 1,22; *to gather
(images from outside inside)* (of the eye) Lam
3,51; neol.

ἐπιφυλλίς,-ίδος N3F 0-2-3-2-0-7
Jgs 8,2; Ob 5; Mi 7,1; Zph 3,7
gleaning Jgs 8,2; *Zph 3,7 ἐπιφυλλὶς αὐτῶν
-עוללותם *their gleanings* for MT עלילותם *their
deeds*?; neol.?

ἐπιφύομαι V 0-0-0-0-1-1
2 Mc 4,50
to adhere to, to cling to [τινι]

ἐπιφυτεύομαι V 0-0-0-0-1-1
4 Mc 15,6
to be planted [τι] (metaph.)

ἐπιφωνέω⁺ V 0-0-0-0-3-3
1 Ezr 9,47; 2 Mc 1,23; 3 Mc 7,13

to answer, to respond

ἐπιχαίρω								V 0-0-7-8-6-21

Ez 25,3.6.15; Hos 10,5; Ob 12

to rejoice (malignantly) [abs.] Mi 4,11; *to rejoice*
(malignantly) over or *at* or *against* [τινι] Ps
34(35),19; [ἐπί τινι] Sir 8,7; [ἐπί τινα] Ps
40(41),11; M: [ἐπί τι] Hos 10,5; [τινι] Sir 23,3

Cf. HELBING 1928, 258-259; WALTERS 1973, 106-107

ἐπιχαρής,-ής,-ές							A 0-0-1-1-0-2

Na 3,4; Jb 31,29

gratifying, agreeable Na 3,4; *rejoiced at* [τινι] Jb
31,29

ἐπίχαρμα,-ατος							N3N 1-0-0-0-4-5

Ex 32,25; Jdt 4,12; Sir 6,4; 18,31; 42,11

object of malicious joy

Cf. LE BOULLUEC 1989, 326

ἐπίχαρτος,-ος,-ον						A 0-0-0-1-0-1

Prv 11,3

that wherein one feels (malicious) joy

ἐπιχειρέω⁺								V 0-1-0-3-8-12

2 Chr 20,11; Est 8,12c; 9,25; Ezr 7,23; 1 Ezr 1,26

to make an attempt against [ἐπί τινα] 2 Chr
20,11; *to endeavour, to attempt to* [+inf.] 1 Ezr
1,26; *to attack* [εἴς τι] Ezr 7,23

Cf. HELBING 1928, 288-289

ἐπιχείρημα,-ατος							N3N 0-0-0-0-1-1

Sir 9,4

undertaking, attempt

ἐπίχειρον,-ου							N2N 0-0-2-0-1-3

Jer 31(48),25; 34(27),5; 2 Mc 15,33

arm Jer 31(48),25; ἐπίχειρα *reward* 2 Mc 15,33

ἐπιχέω⁺								V 13-6-1-1-1-22

Gn 28,18; 35,14; Ex 29,7; Lv 2,1.6

A: *to pour over* [τι ἐπί τι] Gn 28,18; *to pour*
in(to) [abs.] 2 Kgs 4,5; P: *to be poured over* [ἐπί
τι] Lv 11,38; *to be poured out* Jb 36,27;
(metaph.) Wis 17,14

ἐπιχορηγέω⁺							V 0-0-0-0-1-1

Sir 25,22

to provide for [τινι]

ἐπίχυσις,-εως							N3F 0-0-0-1-0-1

Jb 37,18

pouring (upon or *in)*

ἐπιχωρέω								V 0-0-0-0-2-2

2 Mc 4,9; 12,12

to permit

ἐπιχώρησις,-εως							N3F 0-0-0-1-0-1

Ezr 3,7

concession, permission; neol.?

ἐπιψάλλω								V 0-0-0-0-1-1

2 Mc 1,30

to sing

ἐπιψοφέω								V 0-0-1-0-0-1

Ez 25,6

to stamp (with the foot) (in the sense of
applause)

ἐπόζω								V 4-0-0-0-0-4

Ex 7,18.21; 16,20.24

to become stinking, to putrefy; neol.

ἐποίκιον,-ου							N2N 0-1-0-0-0-1

1 Chr 27,25

village, hamlet; neol.?

Cf. HUSSON 1983, 83-84

ἔπομαι								V 0-0-0-0-1-1

3 Mc 2,26

to follow, to obey [τινι]

(→ δι-, συν-)

ἐπονείδιστος,-ος,-ον						A 0-0-0-4-1-5

Prv 18,1; 19,26; 25,10; 27,11; 3 Mc 6,31

reproached, disgraceful, shameful

ἐπονομάζω							V 31-5-0-0-0-36

Gn 4,17.25.26; 5,2.3

to name Gn 4,17; *to call* Gn 4,25

Cf. HELBING 1928, 51

ἐποξύνω								V 0-0-0-0-1-1

2 Mc 9,7

to hasten [τι]; neol.

ἐπόπτης,-ου⁺							N1M 0-0-0-1-3-4

Est 5,1a; 2 Mc 3,39; 7,35; 3 Mc 2,21

overseer, watcher

ἐποπτικός,-ή,-όν							A 0-0-0-0-1-1

4 Mc 5,13

pertaining to an overseer or *watcher*

ἐποργίζομαι							V 0-0-0-1-1-2

Dnᴸˣˣ 11,40; 2 Mc 7,33

to be angry [abs.] 2 Mc 7,33; [τινι] Dnᴸˣˣ 11,40;
neol.

ἔπος,-ους⁺							N3N 0-0-0-0-1-1

Sir 44,5

word

ἐποτρύνω								V 0-0-0-0-2-2

4 Mc 5,14; 14,1

to stir up, to excite, to urge on

ἐπουράνιος,-ος,-ον⁺						A 0-0-0-1-4-5

Ps 67(68),15; 2 Mc 3,39; 3 Mc 6,28; 7,6; Od
14,11

heavenly

Cf. HORSLEY 1987, 149; →TWNT

ἔποψ,-οπος								N3M 2-0-1-0-0-3

Lv 11,19; Dt 14,17; Zech 5,9

hoopoe (bird)
ἑπτά⁺   M 154-87-27-45-64-377
Gn 4,15.24; 5,7.25; 7,2
seven

ἑπταετής,-ής,-ές   A 0-2-0-0-0-2
Jgs 6,25
of seven years

ἑπτακαίδεκα   M 0-3-0-0-1-4
2 Kgs 13,1; 1 Chr 7,11; 2 Chr 12,13; 1 Ezr 4,52
seventeen

ἑπτακαιδέκατος,-η,-ον   M 0-4-0-0-1-5
1 Kgs 22,52; 2 Kgs 16,1; 1 Chr 24,15; 25,24; Jdt
1,13
seventeenth

ἑπτάκις⁺   M 16-5-0-2-1-24
Gn 4,24; 33,3; Lv 4,6.17; 8,11
seven times

ἑπτακισχίλιοι,-αι,-α⁺   M 3-6-0-3-3-15
Nm 3,22; 31,36.43; 2 Kgs 24,16; 1 Chr 29,4
seven thousand

ἑπτακόσιοι,-αι,-α   M 16-14-0-11-6-47
Gn 5,4.7.10.13.16
seven hundred

ἑπτάμηνος,-ου   N2F 0-0-2-0-0-2
Ez 39,12.14
a space of seven months

ἑπταμήτωρ,-ορος   N3F 0-0-0-0-1-1
4 Mc 16,24
mother of seven children; neol.

ἑπταπλάσιος,-α,-ον   A 0-0-1-1-3-5
Is 30,26; Prv 6,31; Sir 20,12; 35,10; 40,8
sevenfold

ἑπταπλασίων,-ων,-ον⁺   A 0-1-0-1-0-2
2 Sm 12,6; Ps 78(79),12
sevenfold

ἑπταπλασίως   D 0-0-0-5-1-6
Ps 11(12),7; Dn 3,19; Dn^LXX 3,22.46
sevenfold

ἑπτάπυργος,-ος,-ον   A 0-0-0-0-1-1
4 Mc 13,7
seven-towered

ἐπωμίς,-ίδος   N3F 26-0-3-0-1-30
Ex 25,7; 28,4.6.7.8
stereotyped rendition of אפוד, homophone,
ephod Ex 29,5; *shoulder-piece* Ex 36,11(39,4);
ἐπωμίδες *leaves*? *side-walls*? (of a door) Ez 41,2
Cf. LE BOULLUEC 1989, 251-252

ἐπώνυμος,-ος,-ον   A 0-0-0-1-0-1
Est 8,12u
named after [τινος]

ἐπωρύομαι   V 0-0-1-0-0-1
Zech 11,8
to howl at [ἐπί τινα]; neol.?

ἐραστής,-οῦ   N1M 0-0-14-1-2-17
Jer 4,30; 22,20.22; Ez 16,33.36
lover, admirer

ἐράω   V 0-0-0-2-1-3
Prv 4,6; Est 2,17; 1 Ezr 4,24
to love [τινος]
Cf. CASANOVA 1982, 213-226; STEINMÜLLER 1951, 404-423;
SWINN 1990, 70

εργαβ   N 0-4-0-0-0-4
1 Sm 6,11.15; 20,19.41
=ארגז *saddle-back, coffer*?

ἐργάζομαι⁺   V 29-4-33-32-24-122
Gn 2,5.15; 3,23; 4,2.12
M: *to work, to labour* Gn 29,27; *to work at, to till*
Gn 2,5; *to work at, to make* Ex 36,8; *to do, to
perform* Nm 3,7; P: *to be cultivated* Ez 36,34; οἱ
ἐργαζόμενοι τὴν πόλιν *those who live in the
city* Ez 48,18; *Is 23,10 ἐργάζου עברי- *cultivate
for* MT עברי *pass through*
Cf. LINDHAGEN 1950, 5-26; →NIDNTT; TWNT
(→ ἐν-, ἐξ-, κατ-, περι-)

ἐργαλεῖον,-ου   N2N 4-0-0-0-0-4
Ex 27,19; 39,9(38,30).19(40).21(42)
tool, instrument
Cf. LE BOULLUEC 1989, 370

ἐργασία,-ας⁺   N1F 5-17-7-5-11-45
Gn 29,27; Ex 26,1; 39,1(38,24); Lv 13,51; Nm
31,20
work Gn 29,27; *production* Ex 39,1(38,24)
Cf. DANIEL 1966, 89-91

ἐργάσιμος,-ος,-ον   A 2-1-0-0-0-3
Lv 13,48.49; 1 Sm 20,19
to be worked, that which can be worked Lv
13,48; ἡ ἡμέρα ἡ ἐργασίμη *work-day* 1 Sm
20,19

ἐργατεία,-ας   N1F 0-0-0-0-1-1
Wis 7,16
labour, work, handicraft
Cf. LARCHER 1984, 466

ἐργατεύομαι   V 0-0-0-0-1-1
Tob^S 5,5
to work hard, to labour; neol.?

ἐργάτης,-ου⁺   N1M 0-0-0-0-4-4
1 Mc 3,6; Wis 17,16; Sir 19,1; 40,18
workman Wis 17,16; ἐργάτης τῆς ἀνομίας
evildoer 1 Mc 3,6

ἐργάτις,-ιδος   N3F 0-0-0-1-0-1

Prv 6,8
workwoman
ἐργέω
(- ἐν-, συν-)
ἐργοδιωκτέω					V 0-1-0-0-0-1
2 Chr 8,10
to be a taskmaster; neol.
ἐργοδιώκτης,-ου				N1M 4-2-0-0-1-7
Ex 3,7; 5,6.10.13; 1 Chr 23,4
taskmaster
Cf. LE BOULLUEC 1989, 90; LEE 1983, 96-97
ἐργολαβία,-ας					N1F 0-0-0-0-1-1
Sir 29,19
profitmaking
Cf. WALTERS 1973, 45
ἔργον,-ου⁺					N2N 147-84-68-134-157-590
Gn 2,2(bis).3; 3,17; 5,29
work Gn 2,2; *deed* Gn 20,9; *occupation* Gn
46,33; *Gn 3,17 ἐν τοῖς ἔργοις σου -בעבדך *in*
your works for MT בעבורך *because of you*; *Gn
8,21 διὰ τὰ ἔργα- בעבור *work* for MT בעבור
because of; *Na 2,14 ἔργα σου -מלאכתיך *your*
works for MT מלאכה *its messengers*; *1 Sm
14,47 ἔργον -מלאכה *work* for MT מלוכה *rule?*;
*Prv 22,8 ἔργων αὐτοῦ -עברתו *his works* for MT
עברתו *his fury*
Cf. DANIEL 1966, 56-61.76-78.80-91.102.104-
107.114.329.331-333; LE BOULLUEC 1989, 77.372; →NIDNTT;
TWNT
ἐρεθίζω⁺						V 1-0-0-4-2-7
Dt 21,20; Prv 19,7; 25,23; Dnᴸˣˣ 11,10.25
A: *to be quarrelsome* or *perverse* [abs.] Dt 21,20;
to provoke, to excite [τι] Prv 25,23; [τινα] 1 Mc
15,40; P: *to be provoked* Dnᴸˣˣ 11,10
Cf. SPICQ 1978, 288-291
(→ δι-)
ἐρεθισμός,-οῦ					N2M 2-0-0-0-1-3
Dt 28,22; 31,27; Sir 31,29
irritation Dt 28,22; *rebelliousness* Dt 31,27
ἐρεθιστής,-οῦ					N1M 1-0-0-0-0-1
Dt 21,18
rebellious or *perverse person*
ἐρείδω⁺						V 1-0-0-10-0-11
Gn 49,6; Jb 17,10; Prv 3,26; 4,4; 5,5
A: *to fix firmly, to plant* [τι] Prv 3,26; *to support,*
to uphold [τινα] Prv 29,23; *to become fixed in*
[εἴς τι] Prv 4,4; M: *to prop oneself with* [τινι]
Prv 11,16; *to stay upon* [ἐπί τινι] Prv 9,12a; τὰς
βραχίονας ἐρείδω εἴς τι *to strengthen the arm*
for Prv 31,17; τὰς χεῖρας ἐρείδω εἴς τι *to apply*

the hands to Prv 31,19; *Gn 49,6 ἐρίσαι -תחר
do (not) contend for MT תחר *do (not) be joined*
Cf. BARR 1974, 198-215; SOISALON-SOININEN 1975, 367-
369
(→ ἀντ-, ἀπ-, ἐναπ-, ἐπ-, ὑπ-)
ἔρεισμα,-ατος					N3N 0-0-0-1-0-1
Prv 14,26
support
ἐρεοῦς,-ᾶ,-οῦν					A 4-0-1-0-0-5
Lv 13,47.48.52.59; Ez 44,17
of wool, woollen
ἐρεύγομαι⁺						V 2-0-3-1-1-7
Ex 7,28; Lv 11,10; Hos 11,10; Am 3,4.8
to discharge (of water) [abs.] Lv 11,10; *to utter*
[τι] Ps 18(19),3; *to bellow, to roar* [abs.] Hos
11,10
(→ ἐξ-)
ἔρευνα,-ης					N1F 0-0-0-0-1-1
Wis 6,8
inquiry, search
ἐρευνάω						V 6-4-2-1-2-15
Gn 31,33(bis).35.37; 44,12
to search
→TWNT
(→ ἀν-, δι-, ἐξ-)
ἐρημία,-ας⁺					N1F 0-0-3-0-3-6
Is 60,12; Ez 35,4.9; 4 Mc 18,8; Wis 17,16
solitude, loneliness Is 60,12; *desolation* Ez 35,4
ἐρημικός,-ή,-όν					A 0-0-0-2-0-2
Ps 101(102),7; 119(120),4
of or *for solitude, living in a desert*
ἐρημίτης,-ου					N1M 0-0-0-1-0-1
Jb 11,12
(one) of the desert; neol.
ἔρημος,-ος,-η,-ον⁺				A 123-70-122-38-33-386
Gn 12,9; 13,1.3; 14,6; 16,7
desolate Ex 23,29; *destitute of, without* [τινος]
3 Mc 5,6; ἡ ἔρήμη (sc. χῶρα) *desert, wilderness*
Gn 12,9; *Gn 24,62 ἐρήμου -במדבר (*through)*
the desert for MT מבוא *from coming to*; *Is 35,2
τὰ ἔρημα -◇גלה? *the desert* for MT גילת ◇גיל *joy*
→NIDNTT; TWNT
ἐρημόω⁺						V 5-4-38-10-20-77
Gn 47,19(bis); Lv 26,22.30.43
A: *to desolate, to lay waste* [τι] (of places) Ps
78,7; *to waste* [τι] Sir 21,4 [τινα] 2 Kgs 19,17; *to*
desolate, to dry up [τι] Is 37,25; *to leave alone*
[τινα] Bar 4,16; P: *to be (made) desolate* (of
places) Gn 47,19; *to be deserted* Jer 3,2
→NIDNTT; TWNT

(→ ἐξ-)

ἐρήμωσις,-εως⁺   N3F 2-2-6-13-3-26
Lv 26,34.35; 2 Chr 30,7; 36,21; Jer 4,7
desolation
·NIDNTT

ἐρίζω⁺   V 1-3-0-0-2-6
Gn 26,35; 1 Sm 12,14.15; 2 Kgs 14,10; Sir 8,2
*to challenge [τινι] Gn 26,35; to strive, to wrangle,
to quarrel 2 Kgs 14,10; to strive with [μετά τινος]*
Sir 8,2; [τινι] 1 Sm 12,14; *to strive about [περί
τινος]* Sir 11,9
Cf. BARR 1974, 198-215; HELBING 1928, 237-238; SPICQ
1978, 288-291
(→ συν-)

ἐριθεύομαι   V 0-0-0-0-2-2
Tob 2,11
to serve, to work for hire

ἔριθος,-ου   N2F 0-0-1-0-1-2
Is 38,12; Od 11,12
one who spins, weaver

ἐρικτά,-ῶν   N2N 1-0-0-0-0-1
Lv 2,14
barley-broth

ἔριον,-ου⁺   N2N 1-2-4-4-0-11
Dt 22,11; Jgs 6,37; Is 1,18; 51.8
wool

ἔρις,-ιδος⁺   N3F 0-0-0-0-3-3
Sir 28,11; 40,4.9
quarrel, strife
Cf. SPICQ 1978, 288-291

ἐρίφιον,-ου⁺   N2N 0-0-0-0-2-2
Tob 2,13
kid; neol.?

ἔριφος,-ου⁺   N2M 8-13-6-1-5-33
Gn 27,9.16; 37,31; 38,17.20
kid

ἑρμηνεία,-ας⁺   N1F 0-0-0-1-2-3
Dnᴸˣˣ 5,0; Sir prol.,20; 47,17
explanation, interpretation Sir 47,17; *translation*
Dnᴸˣˣ 5,0
·TWNT

ἑρμηνευτής,-οῦ   N1M 1-0-0-0-0-1
Gn 42,23
interpreter
Cf. HARL 1986, 280; →TWNT

ἑρμηνεύω⁺   V 0-0-0-3-0-3
Jb 42,17b; Ezr 4,7
to interpret, to translate Ezr 4,7; *to describe* Jb
42,17b
(→ δι-, μεθ-)

→TWNT

ἑρπετόν,-οῦ⁺   N2N 31-1-6-2-4-44
Gn 1,20.21.24.25.26
creeping thing, reptile Gn 1,24; ζῷον ἑρπετόν
animal of the reptile kind, reptiloid Gn 1,21; *Is
16,1 ὡς ἑρπετά (ἐπὶ τὴν γῆν) -(כרמש לארץ) like
reptiles (on the land) for MT* כר משל ארץ
lamb(s) to the ruler of the land
Cf. HARL 1986, 94

ἕρπω   V 10-0-1-1-0-12
Gn 1,26.28.30; 6,20; Lv 11,29
to move slowly, to creep
(→ ἐξ-)

ἔρρω
(→ κατα-)

ἐρυθαίνω   V 0-0-0-0-1-1
Wis 13,14
to dye red or *scarlet*

ἐρύθημα,-ατος   N3N 0-0-1-0-0-1
Is 63,1
scarlet

ἐρυθριάω   V 0-0-0-1-1-2
Est 5,1b; Tobᴮᴬ 2,14
to blush, to colour up, to be abashed
(→ προσ-)

ἐρυθροδανόω   V 5-0-0-0-0-5
Ex 25,5; 26,14; 35,7.23; 39,20(34)
to dye with madder, to dye red

ἐρυθρός,-ή,-όν⁺   A 13-5-1-6-5-30
Ex 10,19; 13,18; 15,4.22; 23,31
red

ἐρυμνός,-ή,-όν   A 0-0-0-0-1-1
2 Mc 11,5
fenced, fortified, strong

ἐρυμνότης,-ητος   N3F 0-0-0-0-2-2
2 Mc 10,34; 12,14
strength, security

ἐρυσίβη,-ης   N1F 1-1-3-1-0-6
Dt 28,42; 1 Kgs 8,37; Hos 5,7; Jl 1,4; 2,25
blight, mildew
Cf. WALTERS 1973, 77

ἔρχομαι⁺   V 145-397-153-171-188-1054
Gn 10,19(bis).30; 11,31; 12,5
to come, to go Gn 14,5; *to come* Eccl 1,4; *to
come, to arrive at [εἴς τι]* Gn 10,19; [ἐπί τι] Gn
22,3; [πρός τι] Gn 34,20; [ἐπί τινα] (in hostile
sense) 2 Chr 14,10; *to go as far as [ἕως τινός]*
Dt 1,20; *to visit [πρός τινα]* Gn 24,30; [τινι]
Zech 9,9; *to come into [εἴς τι]* Wis 8,20; *to
appear* Dnᵀʰ 7,13; *to come* (metaph.) Gn 18,21;

to come to [+inf.] Gn 23,2; ἔρχομαι ὁδόν *to go*
a way Nm 21,1; ἔρχομαι εἰς μέσον τινός *to*
come in the midst of Neh 4,5; ἔρχομαι εἰς
συνάντησίν τινι *to meet sb* Gn 32,7; ἔρχομαι
εἰς βουλήν τινος *to come into the counsel of*
Gn 49,6; ἔρχομαι ἐν τῷ ἀριθμῷ *to be numbered*
Lv 27,32; ἔρχομαι ἐπὶ τὴν καρδίαν τοῦ
[+inf.] *to come in the heart to do* 1 Kgs 8,18;
ἐρχόμενος *coming, future* Jer 29(47),4; τὰ
ἐρχόμενα *what is to come* Est 8,12i; ἦλθεν ἡ
πόλις εἰς συνοχήν *the city was besieged* Jer
52,5; 2 Mc 6,17; ἐλευστέος *one must come*
2 Mc 6,17; *Hos 10,10 ἦλθεν באתי- *he (I) come*
for MT באותי *in my desire*; *1 Chr 2,24 ἦλθε
Χαλεβ בא כלב *came Chaleb* for MT בכלב *in*
Chaleb; *Am 6,3 οἱ ἐρχόμενοι corr. οἱ
εὐχόμενοι המנדים-? for MT המנדים *the ones*
putting off?; *Ct 2,10 ἐλθὲ ל-ך ◊ הלך *come* for
MT ל-ך *to you*; *Neh 2,19 ἦλθον יבאו- *they come*
for MT יבזו *they despised*

Cf. MURAOKA 1990, 34-35; →NIDNTT; TWNT

(→ ἀν-, ἀντιπαρ-, ἀπ-, δι-, διεξ-, εἰσ-, ἐξ-, ἐπ-,
ἐπαν-, ἐπεισ-, ἐπεξ-, κατ-, μετ-, παρ-, περι-,
προ-, προσ-, συν-, συνεισ-, συνεξ-, ὑπ-)

ἐρῶ
fut. of λέγω
(→ ἀντ-, προ-)

ἐρωδιός,-οῦ   N2M 2-0-0-1-0-3
Lv 11,19; Dt 14,16; Ps 103(104),17
heron

ἔρως,-ωτος   N3M 0-0-0-2-0-2
Prv 7,18; 30,16
love

Cf. BARR 1987, 3-18; SWINN 1990, 51-52

ἐρωτάω⁺   V 14-29-12-9-6-70
Gn 24,47.57; 32,18.30(bis)
A: *to ask* [abs.] Dt 13,15; [τινά τι] Ezr 5,10; *to*
ask about a thing [τι] Gn 32,30; [τινά τι] 1 Sm
30,21 *to question, to ask* [τινα] Gn 24,47; [+dir.
question introduced by λέγων] Gn 32,18; *to ask*
sb concerning sb [τινα περί τινος] Is 45,11; *to*
inquire of [διά τινος] 1 Sm 23,4; [ἔν τινι] 1 Chr
14,14; *to beg, to entreat* [τινά τι] 1 Sm 30,21; P:
to be asked 2 Sm 20,18; ἐρωτάω τινὰ λόγον *to*
ask sb a question Jer 45(38),14; ἐρωτάω τὸ
στόμα *to ask (advice)* Gn 24,57

Cf. HELBING 1928, 40-41; →NIDNTT; TWNT

(→ ἐπ-)

ἐρώτημα,-ατος   N3N 0-0-0-0-1-1
Sir 33,3

question

εσεφιν   N 0-2-0-0-0-2
1 Chr 26,15.17
=אספים *stores*

ἐσθής,-ῆτος⁺   N3F 0-0-0-0-4-4
1 Ezr 8,68.70; 2 Mc 8,35; 11,8
clothing, garment

ἔσθησις,-εως   N3F 0-0-0-0-2-2
2 Mc 3,33; 3 Mc 1,16
clothing, raiment

ἐσθίω⁺   V 264-145-115-93-69-686
Gn 2,16.17(bis); 3,1.2
to eat, to consume

Cf. HELBING 1928, 131-135; →NIDNTT; TWNT

(→ κατ-, συγκατ-, συν-)

ἔσοπτρον,-ου⁺   N2N 0-0-0-0-2-2
Wis 7,26; Sir 12,11
looking-glass, mirror

Cf. HORSLEY 1987, 149-150; SPICQ 1978, 292-295

ἑσπέρα,-ας⁺   N1F 71-22-9-20-7-129
Gn 1,5.8.13.19.23
evening Gn 1,5; (τὸ) πρὸς ἑσπέραν *towards*
evening Gn 8,11; ἑσπέρας *at eve* Gn 19,1; εἰς
τὸ ἑσπέρας *at evening* Gn 49,27; *Ezr 4,20
ἑσπέρας *west* corr.? πέραν for MT עבר *beyond*,
see mss.; *Ezr 4,20 ἑσπέρας *west* corr? πέραν
beyond; *Is 21,13 ἑσπέρας בערב- *in the evening*
for MT בערב *concerning Arabia*; *1 Sm 23,24
καθ' ἑσπέραν בערב- *in the evening* for MT
בערבה *in the Arabah*

ἑσπερινός,-ή,-όν   A 1-1-0-6-0-8
Lv 23,5; 2 Kgs 16,15; Ps 140(141),2; Prv 7,9;
DnᴸˣˣX 9,21
towards evening

Cf. HARLÉ 1988, 188

ἑστία,-ας   N1F 0-0-0-0-1-1
Tobˢ 2,12
home

Cf. HUSSON 1983, 86-87; SHIPP 1979, 249-250

ἑστιατορία,-ας   N1F 0-2-0-2-0-4
2 Kgs 25,30(bis); DnᴸˣX 5,1.23
allowance of food 2 Kgs 25,30; *feast* DnᴸˣX 5,1

ἐσχάρα,-ας   N1F 7-1-3-2-1-14
Ex 27,4(bis).5(bis); 30,3
grate, grating Ex 27,4; *hearth, fire-place* Prv
26,21; *Jb 41,11 ὡς ἐσχάραι כ/רודי- ? *as braziers*
for MT כירודי *sparks*

Cf. DANIEL 1966, 26

ἐσχαρίτης,-ου   N1M 0-1-0-0-0-1
2 Sm 6,19

that which is baked over the fire

ἐσχατίζω   V 0-1-0-0-1-2
Jgsᴬ 5,28; 1 Mc 5,53
to be last, to come too late; [abs.] 1 Mc 5,53;
[+inf.] Jgsᴬ 5,28; neol.

ἐσχατογήρως   D 0-0-0-0-2-2
Sir 41,2; 42,8
in extreme old age

ἔσχατος,-η,-ον⁺   A 21-22-37-42-32-154
Gn 33,2; 49,1; Ex 4,8; Lv 23,16; 27,18
local sense: *last* Gn 33,2; *farthest, uttermost,
extreme* Dt 34,2; temporal sense: *last* 2 Chr
16,11; *final* (day) in the rendering of the
stereotyped expression באחרית הימים Hos 3,5;
εἰς τὴν ἐσχάτην *at the last (time)* Eccl 1,11; ἀπ'
ἐσχάτου βορρᾶ *from the furthest north* Ez 38,6;
*Jb 8,13 τὰ ἔσχατα -אחרית *the ends* for MT
ארחות *paths*; *Jer 9,1 ἔσχατον -אחרון *most
remote (lodging)* for MT ארחים *(a lodging) of
travellers*; *1 Kgs 9,26 ἐσχάτης -סוף *farthest
(sea)* for MT סוף *(sea) of reeds*; *Jon 2,6 ἐσχάτη
-סוף *lowest (depth)* for MT סוף *(sea)weed*
Cf. LARCHER 1983, 250; LE BOULLUEC 1989, 97-98;
→NIDNTT; TWNT

ἔσω⁺   D 7-7-2-1-2-19
Gn 39,11; Ex 26,33; Lv 10,18; 16,2.12
to within, into 2 Chr 29,16; *within, inside* Gn
39,11; ἐσώτερόν τινος *within* Ex 26,33; τὸ ἔσω
inward parts 1 Kgs 6,15; τὰ ἔσω τῆς οἰκίας
household Jb 1,10

ἔσωθεν⁺   D 5-6-11-1-2-25
Gn 6,14; Ex 25,11; 36,26(39,19); 38(37),2; Lv
14,41
(from) within

ἐσώτατος,-η,-ον   A 0-2-0-1-0-3
1 Kgs 6,30; 7,36(50); Jb 28,18
innermost

ἐσώτερος,-α,-ον⁺   A 0-3-20-1-1-25
1 Kgs 6,29; 1 Chr 28,11; 2 Chr 23,20; Ez 8,3.16
inner

ἐτάζω   V 1-2-1-7-4-15
Gn 12,17; 1 Chr 28,9; 29,17; Jer 17,10; Ps 7,10
to visit, to try, to afflict Gn 12,17; *to examine, to
test* 1 Ezr 9,16
Cf. ENGEL 1985, 119
(→ ἀν-, ἐξ-)

ἑταίρα,-ας   N1F 0-2-0-1-2-5
Jgs 11,2; Prv 19,13; 2 Mc 6,4; Sir 41,22
courtesan

ἑταιρίζομαι   V 0-0-0-0-1-1

Sir 9,3
to be a courtesan

ἑταῖρος,-ου⁺   N2M 0-12-0-8-8-28
Jgsᴬ 14,11.20; Jgsᴮ 4,17;
2 Sm 13,3; 15,32
comrade, companion, friend
Cf. SPICQ 1978, 296-298; WALTERS 1973, 214-218;
→NIDNTT; TWNT

ἔτασις,-εως   N3F 0-0-0-3-0-3
Jb 10,17; 12,6; 31,14
trial, affliction; neol.

ἐτασμός,-οῦ   N2M 1-0-0-0-2-3
Gn 12,17; Jdt 8,27; 2 Mc 7,37
trial, affliction; neol.?
Cf. LEE 1983, 44-45

ἑτερόζυγος,-ος,-ον   A 1-0-0-0-0-1
Lv 19,19
*animal of a different kind, an animal yoked
differently*
Cf. SPICQ 1978, 299-300; →NIDNTT

ἑτεροκλινῶς   D 0-1-0-0-0-1
1 Chr 12,34
rebelliously

ἕτερος,-α,-ον⁺   A 68-41-47-42-60-258
Gn 4,25; 8,10.12; 17,21; 26,21
another Gn 4,25; *other* Dt 4,28; *one* or *the other
(of two)* 1 Kgs 3,22; γενεὰ ἑτέρα *the next
generation* Ps 47(48),13; *Ez 11,19 ἑτέραν -אחר
another for MT אחד *one*, see also Ez 17,7; *Jb
18,19 ἕτεροι -אחרים *aliens* for MT אחרנים
westerners; *Neh 2,1 ἕτερος -רע ◊ רעᴵᴵ *another* for
MT רע ◊ רעע *sad*; *Prv 24,21 ἑτέρῳ -על שניהם
either (of them) for MT שונים עם *with those who
change?*; *Is 44,24 ἕτερος -אחר *else* for MT אתי
with me; *Dnᴸˣˣ 8,8 ἕτερα -אחרות *other* for MT
חזות *visions*
Cf. SHIPP 1979, 251-252; WALTERS 1973, 215-218; →NIDNTT

ἑτέρωθεν   D 0-0-0-0-1-1
4 Mc 6,4
on the other side, opposite

ἔτι⁺   D 93-138-148-82-88-549
Gn 2,9.19; 7,4; 8,10.12
yet Gn 8,10; *still* Gn 18,29; *no longer* [+neg.] Gn
9,11; *Gn 49,27 ἔτι -עור *yet* for MT ארᴵᴵᴵ *prey*

ἑτοιμάζω⁺   V 11-49-26-47-40-173
Gn 24,14.31.44; 43,16.25
A: *to prepare* Gn 24,14; M: *to prepare oneself, to
make oneself ready* Jos 9,4; P: *to be prepared*
1 Sm 20,31; *Gn 24,14 ἡτοίμασας -הכנות? *you
have prepared* for MT הכחת *you have appointed?*;

*Jos 9,4 ἡτοιμάσαντο יצטירו- *they prepared for*
for MT יצטירו *they made provisions* (LXX double
transl.); *Jb 41,2 ἡτοίμασταί μοι יוערני- *it has
been prepared by me* for MT יוערנו *will stir him
up*
Cf. GEHMAN 1972, 109; 1972 (A), 99; HELBING 1928, 56;
→NIDNTT
(- · προ-)
ἑτοιμασία,-ας⁺   N1F 0-0-2-8-1-11
Na 2,4; Zech 5,11; Ps 9,38(10,17); 64,10(65);
88,15(89)
preparation Ps 64,10; *foundation, base* Ezr 2,68;
*Ps 9,38(10,17) ἑτοιμασίαν -כונה *preparation*
for MT תכין *you will confirm*
-NIDNTT
ἕτοιμος,-η/-ος,-ον⁺   A 7-13-6-11-23-60
Ex 15,17; 19,11.15; 34,2; Lv 16,21
prepared Ex 15,17; *ready* Ex 19,11
Cf. BISSOLI 1983, 53-56; HARL 1991, 248-249; →NIDNTT
ἑτοίμως⁺   D 0-0-0-5-0-5
Dn 3,15; Ezr 7,17.21.26
readily, willingly
··NIDNTT
ἔτος,-ους⁺   N3N 189-271-75-93-90-718
Gn 5,3.4.5.6.7
year Gn 5,3; εἰμι ἐτῶν *to be ... years old* Gn 7,6;
κατ' ἔτος *every year* 2 Mc 11,3 *Ps 89(90),5 ἔτη
-שָׁנָה *year(s)* for MT שָׁנָה *dream*
εὖ⁺   D 25-1-7-8-19-60
Gn 12,13.16; 32,10.13; 40,14
well, good Gn 12,16; *very* [+adv.] 2 Mc 8,30; εὖ
ποιέω τινά *to do good to* Gn 32,10; εὖ ποιέω
τινί Ex 1,20; εὖ γίγνομαί τινι *it prospers, it is
good to* Gn 12,13; see εὖγε
εὐαγγελία,-ας   N1F 0-5-0-0-0-5
2 Sm 18,20.22.25.27; 2 Kgs 7,9
good tidings; neol.
Cf. HORSLEY 1983, 13; →NIDNTT; TWNT
εὐαγγέλια,-ων⁺   N2N 0-1-0-0-0-1
2 Sm 4,10
good tidings, good news
Cf. HORSLEY 1983, 12-13; SPICQ 1982, 302-305; →NIDNTT;
TWNT
εὐαγγελίζω⁺   V 0-10-9-3-1-23
1 Sm 31,9; 2 Sm 1,20; 4,10; 18,19.20
A: *to preach* or *to proclaim (as glad tidings)*
1 Kgs 1,42; *to proclaim glad tidings* [τινι] 1 Sm
31,9; M: *to proclaim glad tidings* Ps 39(40),10;
[τινι] 1 Chr 10,9; P: *to receive good tidings* 2 Sm
18,31; *Jl 3,5 καὶ εὐαγγελιζόμενοι -ומבשרים

and the receivers of glad tidings for MT ובשרים
and among the survivors
Cf. HELBING 1928, 223; HORSLEY 1983, 12; SPICQ 1982,
296-302; →NIDNTT; TWNT
εὐάλωτος,-ος,-ον   A 0-0-0-1-0-1
Prv 30,28
easily taken or *caught*
εὐανδρία,-ας   N1F 0-0-0-0-2-2
2 Mc 8,7; 15,17
manliness
εὐαπάντητος,-ος,-ον   A 0-0-0-0-1-1
2 Mc 14,9
affable, courteous
εὐαρεστέω⁺   V 8-1-0-4-1-14
Gn 5,22.24; 6,9; 17,1; 24,40
to be well pleasing [abs.] Ps. 34(35),14; [τινι] Gn
5,22; [τινι] Jgsᴬ 10,16
Cf. DANIEL 1966, 94-95.198; →NIDNTT
εὐάρεστος,-ος,-ον⁺   A 0-0-0-0-2-2
Wis 4,10; 9,10
well-pleasing, acceptable
εὐάρμοστος,-ος,-ον   A 0-0-1-0-1-2
Ez 33,32; 4 Mc 14,3
harmonious
εὖγε⁺   D 0-0-4-10-0-14
Ez 6,11(bis); 26,2; 36,2; Ps 34(35),21
good, well done!
Cf. KRAFT 1972, 166
εὐγένεια,-ας   N1F 0-0-0-0-3-3
2 Mc 14,42; 4 Mc 8,4; Wis 8,3
nobility (of birth)
Cf. LARCHER 1984, 522
εὐγενής,-ής,-ές⁺   A 0-0-0-1-7-8
Jb 1,3; 2 Mc 10,13; 4 Mc 6,5; 9,13.24
well-born Jb 1,3; *noble* 4 Mc 9,24
εὐγενίζω   V 0-0-0-0-1-1
2 Mc 10,13
to ennoble, to exercise honourably
εὐγενῶς   D 0-0-0-0-6-6
2 Mc 14,42; 4 Mc 6,22.30; 9,22; 12,14
nobly, bravely
εὐγνωμοσύνη,-ης   N1F 0-0-0-1-0-1
Est 8,12f
considerateness, courtesy
εὐγνωστος,-ος,-ον   A 0-0-0-3-0-3
Prv 3,15; 5,6; 26,26
well-known, familiar Prv 3,15; *easy to discern* Prv
5,6
εὐδία,-ας⁺   N1F 0-0-0-0-1-1
Sir 3,15

fair weather
Cf. SPICQ 1978, 305

εὐδοκέω⁺   V 6-10-6-15-22-59
Gn 24,26.48; 33,10; Lv 26,34(bis)
A: *to consent* [abs.] Gn 24,26; *to be well-pleasing*
[abs.] 2 Chr 10,7; *to be content with, to find*
pleasure in [τινα] Gn 33,10; [ἔν τινι] Ps
43(44),4; [ἐπί τινι] Jdt 15,10; *to enjoy* [τι] Lv
26,34; *to consent, to approve* [τινι] 1 Ezr 4,39; *to*
consent, to agree [+inf.] Jgs 19,10; P: *to be*
favoured, to prosper 1 Chr 29,23; *Jgsᴮ 15,18
εὐδόκησας *you have been pleased to* corr.?
ἔδωκας for MT נתת *you have given*, cpr. Jgsᴬ
15,18; neol.?
Cf. HARL 1986, 67.201 (Gn 24,26); HELBING 1928, 262-
265; LEE 1983, 97; SPICQ 1982, 307-311; WALTERS 1973,
317; →NIDNTT; TWNT
(→ συν-)

εὐδοκία,-ας⁺   N1F 0-1-0-9-18-28
1 Chr 16,10; Ps 5,13; 18(19),15; 50(51),20;
68(69),14
goodwill, approval 1 Chr 16,10; *pleasure* Ps
144(145),16; *Ps 140(141),5 ἐν ταῖς εὐδοκίαις
αὐτῶν -◊רעה? *in their friendship?, in their*
goodwill? for MT ב/רעותיהם רע ◊ *against their evil*
deeds
Cf. DANIEL 1966, 194; SPICQ 198, 311-315; →NIDNTT; TWNT

εὐδοκιμέω   V 1-0-0-0-3-4
Gn 43,23; Sir 39,34; 40,25; 41,16
A: *to be genuine* (of money) Gn 43,23; P: *to be*
highly esteemed, to be popular Sir 39,34

εὐδόκιμος,-ος,-ον   A 0-0-0-0-1-1
3 Mc 3,5
of good repute, honoured, famous, glorious

εὐδράνεια,-ας   N1F 0-0-0-0-1-1
Wis 13,19
bodily strength and health; neol.
Cf. GILBERT 1973, 93

εὕδω
(→ καθ-, παρακαθ-)

εὐειδής,-ής,-ές   A 0-0-0-1-0-1
Dnᴸˣˣ 1,4
well-shaped, comely, beautiful

εὐεκτέω   V 0-0-0-1-0-1
Prv 17,22
to be in good health; εὐεκτεῖν ποιέω *to promote*
good health Prv 17,22

εὔελπις,-ιδος   A 0-0-0-1-2-3
Prv 19,18; 3 Mc 2,33; Wis 12,19
hopeful, cheerful

εὐεξία,-ας   N1F 0-0-0-0-1-1
Sir 30,15
good habit of body, good health

εὐεργεσία,-ας⁺   N1F 0-0-0-1-5-6
Ps 77(78),11; 2 Mc 6,13; 9,26; 4 Mc 8,17; Wis
16,11
good deed, benefit Ps 77(78),11; *well-doing,*
kindness Wis 16,11
Cf. SPICQ 1978, 307; →TWNT

εὐεργετέω⁺   V 0-0-0-4-6-10
Ps 12(13),6; 56(57),3; 114(116),7; Est 8,12c;
2 Mc 10,38
A: *to be a benefactor* Est 8,12c; *to do good*
services to, to show kindness to [τινα] Ps
12(13),6; P: *to be benefited* Wis 3,5
Cf. SPICQ 1978, 308-309; →TWNT

εὐεργέτημα,-ατος   N3N 0-0-0-0-1-1
2 Mc 5,20
service done, benefit, kindness

εὐεργέτης,-ου⁺   N1M 0-0-0-2-4-6
Est 8,12c.12n; 2 Mc 4,2; 3 Mc 3,19; 6,24
benefactor
Cf. NOCK 1972, 720-735; PASSONI DELL'ACQUA 1976, 177-
191; SPICQ 1978, 309-313

εὐεργετικός,-ή,-όν   A 0-0-0-0-1-1
Wis 7,23
beneficent

εὔζωνος,-ος,-ον   A 0-2-0-0-1-3
Jos 1,14; 4,13; Sir 36,26
well-equipped

εὐήθης,-ης,-ες   A 0-0-0-0-1-1
2 Mc 2,32
foolish

εὐήκοος,-ος,-ον   A 0-0-0-1-2-3
Prv 25,12; PSal 18,4; LtJ 1,59
obedient

εὐημερέω   V 0-0-0-0-3-3
2 Mc 8,35; 12,11; 13,16
to be successful, to have good luck

εὐημερία,-ας   N1F 0-0-0-0-5-5
2 Mc 5,6; 8,8; 10,28; 14,14; 3 Mc 3,11
prosperity, health and wealth

εὔηχος,-ος,-ον   A 0-0-0-2-0-2
Ps 150,5; Jb 30,7
euphonious, melodious, pleasing to the ear Ps
150,5; *Jb 30,7 εὐήχων -◊שיחᴵᴵ *euphonious* for
MT ◊שיחᴵ *shrub*

εὐθαλέω   V 0-0-0-1-0-1
Dnᵀʰ 4,4(1)
to bloom, to thrive

εὐθαλής,-ής,-ές   A 0-0-0-1-0-1
Dn^Th 4,21(18)
blooming, flourishing, thriving

εὐθαρσής,-ής,-ές   A 0-0-0-0-3-3
1 Ezr 8,27; 2 Mc 8,21; 3 Mc 1,7
of good courage, bold

εὐθαρσῶς   D 0-0-0-0-1-1
2 Mc 7,10
boldly

εὔθετος,-ος,-ον^+   A 0-0-0-1-1-2
Ps 31(32),6; Sus^Th 16
convenient, well-fitting

εὐθέως^+   D 0-1-0-1-12-14
Jos 6,11; Jb 5,3; 1 Ezr 1,28; 1 Mc 11,22; 2 Mc
3,8
straightaway, forthwith, immediately

εὐθηνέω   V 0-0-4-9-1-14
Jer 12,1; 17,8; Hos 10,1; Zech 7,7; Ps 67(68),18
to be prosperous Jb 21,9; *to thrive, to flourish* Ps
127(128),3; *Ps 67(68),17(18) εὐθηνούντων
-שאנים? *thriving ones* for MT שנא *highness*

εὐθηνία,-ας   N1F 6-0-1-5-0-12
Gn 41,29.31.34.47.48
prosperity, plenty; neol.?

εὐθής,-ής,-ές   A 0-27-1-8-2-38
Jgs^A 21,25; Jgs^B 17,6; 1 Sm 29,6; 2 Sm 1,18; 17,4
straightforward, right (of pers., in moral sense)
1 Sm 29,6; *right* 2 Sm 17,4; τὸ εὐθές *that which
is right* Jgs^B 17,6; ἐπὶ βιβλίου τοῦ εὐθοῦς *in the
Book of the Righteous* 2 Sm 1,18; see εὐθύς;
neol.

εὐθίκτως   D 0-0-0-0-1-1
2 Mc 15,38
touching the point, conveniently

εὔθραυστος,-ος,-ον   A 0-0-0-0-1-1
Wis 15,13
easily broken, brittle

εὔθυμος,-ος,-ον^+   A 0-0-0-0-1-1
2 Mc 11,26
cheerful
Cf. SPICQ 1972, 314-317

εὔθυνα,-ης   N1F 0-0-0-0-1-1
3 Mc 3,28
setting straight, chastisement

εὐθύνω^+   V 1-4-0-1-9-15
Nm 22,23; Jos 24,23; Jgs^B 14,7; 1 Sm 18,20.26
to guide straight, to direct [τινα] Nm 22,23; *to
make straight, to put straight* (metaph.) Sir 2,2; *to
chastise* [τινα] 3 Mc 2,17; ηὐθύνθη τὸ ῥῆμα ἐν
ὀφθαλμοῖς αὐτοῦ *it pleased him* 1 Sm 18,20

(→ κατ-)

εὐθύς,-εῖα,-ύ^+   A 2-13-12-35-8-70
Gn 33,12; Nm 23,3; Jos 8,14; Jgs^B 14,3; 21,25
straightaway, immediate, straight, direct Ps
106(107),7; *straightforward, frank, right* Jgs^B 14,3;
ἡ εὐθεῖα (sc. γραμμή) *straight line* Gn 33,12;
κατ'εὐθύ *on level ground* 1 Kgs 21(20),23

εὐθύς^+   D 3-0-2-1-0-6
Gn 15,4; 24,45; 38,29; Ez 23,40; 46,9
straightway, forthwith Jb 3,11; (καὶ) εὐθύς
behold Gn 38,29
Cf. TABACHOVITZ 1956, 29-32

εὐθύτης,-ητος^+   N3F 0-3-0-17-4-24
Jos 24,14; 1 Kgs 3,6; 9,4; Ps 9,9; 10(11),7
righteousness Jos 24,14; *uprightness* 1 Kgs 3,6

εὐιλατεύω   V 1-0-0-1-1-3
Dt 29,19; Ps 102(103),3; Jdt 16,15
to be merciful to [τινι]; neol.
Cf. HELBING 1928, 215

εὐίλατος,-ος,-ον   A 0-0-0-1-1-2
Ps 98(99),8; 1 Ezr 8,53
merciful (of God)

εὐκαιρία,-ας^+   N1F 0-0-0-3-2-5
Ps 9,10.22(10,1); 144(145),15; 1 Mc 11,42; Sir
38,24
good season, opportunity
Cf. SPICQ 1978, 318-319; →TWNT

εὔκαιρος,-ος,-ον^+   A 0-0-0-1-4-5
Ps 103(104),27; 2 Mc 14,29; 15,20; 3 Mc 4,11;
5,44
well-timed, seasonable Ps 103(104),27;
convenient, well-situated 2 Mc 15,20; τὸ
εὔκαιρον *good season* 2 Mc 14,29
Cf. SPICQ 1978, 319; →TWNT

εὐκαίρως^+   D 0-0-0-0-1-1
Sir 18,22
seasonably, opportunely
Cf. SPICQ 1978, 320

εὐκατάλλακτος,-ος,-ον   A 0-0-0-0-1-1
3 Mc 5,13
easily appeased, placable

εὐκαταφρόνητος,-ος,-ον   A 0-0-1-1-0-2
Jer 30,9(49,15); Dn^LXX 11,21
easy to be despised, contemptible

εὐκίνητος,-ος,-ον   A 0-0-0-0-2-2
Wis 7,22; 13,11
easily moved

εὐκλεής,-ής,-ές   A 0-0-1-0-1-2
Jer 31(48),17; Wis 3,15
famous, glorious

εὔκλεια,-ας   N1F 0-0-0-0-3-3
2 Mc 6,19; 3 Mc 2,31; Wis 8,18
glory, good repute

εὐκληματέω   V 0-0-1-0-0-1
Hos 10,1
to grow luxuriantly; neol.?

εὔκολος,-ος,-ον   A 0-1-0-0-0-1
2 Sm 15,3
easy (to understand)

εὐκοπία,-ας   N1F 0-0-0-0-1-1
2 Mc 2,25
ease, facility; neol.?

εὔκοπος,-ος,-ον⁺   A 0-0-0-0-2-2
1 Mc 3,18; Sir 22,15
easy; neol.?

εὐκοσμέω   V 0-0-0-0-1-1
1 Mc 8,15
to behave in a orderly fashion; neol.

εὐκοσμία,-ας   N1F 0-0-0-0-2-2
Sir 32,2; 45,7
orderly behaviour, good conduct, decency

εὔκυκλος,-ος,-ον   A 0-0-0-0-1-1
Wis 5,21
well-rounded, well drawn (of a bow in the sky)

εὐλάβεια,-ας⁺   N1F 0-1-0-1-1-3
Jos 22,24; Prv 28,14; Wis 17,8
caution, discretion concerning [τινος] Jos 22,24;
godly fear Wis 17,8
→NIDNTT; TWNT

εὐλαβέομαι⁺   V 2-2-12-5-17-38
Ex 3,6; Dt 2,4; 1 Sm 18,15.29; Is 51,12
to be afraid 1 Sm 18,15; *to be cautious that, to
be afraid that* [μή +subj.] 2 Mc 12,40; *to be
afraid that* [+inf.] Ex 3,6; *to beware of, to dread*
[τινα] Dt 2,4; *to reverence, to pay honour to, to
fear (God)* [τινα] Na 1,7; [ἀπό τινος] Zech 1,7
Cf. HELBING 1928, 25-26; KILPATRICK 1963, 133-134;
MARGOLIS 1972, 74; →NIDNTT; TWNT
(→ δι-, ὑπ-)

εὐλαβής,-ής,-ές⁺   A 1-0-1-0-0-2
Lv 15,31; Mi 7,2
keeping from [ἀπό τινος] Lv 15,31; *pious,
reverent* Mi 7,2
Cf. MARGOLIS 1972, 74

εὐλαβῶς   D 0-0-0-0-1-1
2 Mc 6,11
reverently, piously
→NIDNTT; TWNT

εὔλαλος,-ος,-ον   A 0-0-0-1-1-2
Jb 11,2; Sir 6,5

sweetly-speaking Sir 6,5; *eloquent* Jb 11,2

εὐλογέω⁺   V 119-72-23-166-136-516
Gn 1,22.28; 2,3; 5,2; 9,1
to bless, to praise Gn 1,22; *to curse* (euph.)
1 Kgs 20(21),10
Cf. BICKERMAN 1980, 315-317.322-323; HARL 1986, 56;
HELBING 1928, 17-20; HORSLEY 1987, 113.151; LEDOGAR
1967, 29-56; WALTERS 1973, 143; →NIDNTT; TWNT
(→ ἐν-)

εὐλογητός,-ή,-όν⁺   A 10-15-1-28-20-74
Gn 9,26; 12,2; 14,20; 24,27.31
blessed; neol.
Cf. BICKERMAN 1980, 315-317; →NIDNTT; TWNT

εὐλογία,-ας⁺   N1F 32-13-10-16-30-101
Gn 27,12.35.36(bis).38
(act of) blessing Gn 27,12; *gift, bounty* Jos 15,19;
blessing called down or *bestowed* Prv 10,22;
praise Sir 50,20(22); ποιέω μετά τινος εὐλογίαν
to make peace with 2 Kgs 18,31
→NIDNTT; TWNT

εὐλογιστία,-ας   N1F 0-0-0-0-4-4
4 Mc 5,22; 8,15; 13,5.7
caution, prudence, circumspection

εὐμαθῶς   D 0-0-0-0-1-1
Wis 13,11
skilfully

εὐμεγέθης,-ης,-ες   A 0-1-0-0-1-2
1 Sm 9,2; Bar 3,26
tall

εὐμελής,-ής,-ές   A 0-0-0-0-1-1
Wis 17,17
melodious

εὐμένεια,-ας   N1F 0-0-0-0-1-1
2 Mc 6,29
goodwill, favour

εὐμενής,-ής,-ές   A 0-0-0-0-2-2
2 Mc 12,31; 13,26
well-disposed

εὐμενῶς   D 0-0-0-0-1-1
Wis 6,16
favourably

εὐμετάβολος,-ος,-ον   A 0-0-0-1-0-1
Prv 17,20
easily changed, changeable

εὐμήκης,-ης,-ες   A 1-0-0-0-0-1
Dt 9,2
tall

εὐμορφία,-ας   N1F 0-0-0-0-2-2
4 Mc 8,10; Wis 7,10
beauty of form

εὔμορφος,-ος,-ον   A 0-0-0-0-1-1
Sir 9,8
shapely, fair of form, comely
Cf. SHIPP 1979, 256

εὐνοέω⁺   V 0-0-0-2-1-3
Est 8,12u; Dnᴸˣˣ 2,43; 3 Mc 7,11
to be well-inclined to, to be favourable to [τινι]

εὔνοια,-ας⁺   N1F 0-0-0-3-15-18
Est 2,23; 3,13c; 6,4; 1 Mc 11,33.53
goodwill, favour Sir prol.,13; εὔνοιαι
benevolences, gifts or *presents in token of
goodwill* 1 Mc 11,53
Cf. BICKERMAN 1980, 69; SPICQ 1982, 321

εὐνομία,-ας   N1F 0-0-0-0-4-4
4 Mc 3,20; 4,24; 7,9; 18,4
good order, observance of the law

εὔνους,-ους,-ουν   A 0-0-0-0-1-1
4 Mc 4,3
well-disposed to, kindly to [τινι]

εὐνοῦχος,-ου⁺   N1M 3-10-5-13-4-35
Gn 39,1; 40,2.7; 1 Sm 8,15; 1 Kgs 22,9
eunuch 1 Sm 8,15; *one who is by nature
incapable of begetting children* Wis 3,14;
chamberlain Gn 39,1
→TWNT

εὐοδία,-ας   N1F 0-0-0-1-6-7
Prv 25,15; 1 Ezr 8,6.50; Tob 4,6; Sir 10,5
good journey 1 Ezr 8,6; *success* Tob 4,6
Cf. DANIEL 1966, 197; HARL 1991, 246; WALTERS 1973,
73-74

εὔοδος,-ος,-ον   A 1-0-0-1-1-3
Nm 14,41; Prv 11,9; 1 Ezr 7,3
free from difficulty, easy

εὐοδόω⁺   V 10-21-6-15-29-81
Gn 24,12.21.27.40.42
A: *to help on the way, to lead prosperously* [τινα]
Gn 24,27; *to set on the way prosperously, to send
prosperously* [τινα] Jgs 4,8; *to help on the way, to
prosper* [abs.] (metaph.) 1 Chr 22,11; [τινι]
2 Chr 14,6; *to make prosperous* [τι] Gn 39,3; *to
give success in* [τινί τι] Tobᴮᴬ 7,12; *to give
succes in* [+inf.] 2 Mc 10,7; P: *to have a
prosperous journey* Dnᴸˣˣ 8,11; *to prosper, to be
successful* (of things) Jgsᴮ 18,5; εὐοδόω τὴν ὁδόν
to make prosperous the way Gn 24,21; εὐοδόω
ἐναντίον τινός *to guide happily towards, to let
have a felicitous encounter with* Gn 24,12;
*2 Chr 35,13 εὐοδώθη -◊ צלח *went on well* for MT
צלחת ◊ צלח *pans*
Cf. HARL 1986, 199-200; HELBING 1928, 94-95; →NIDNTT;

TWNT

εὐόδως   D 0-0-0-1-0-1
Prv 30,29
easily

εὔοπτος,-ος,-ον   A 0-0-0-0-1-1
LtJ 60
conspicuous

εὐπαθέω   V 0-0-0-2-0-2
Ps 91(92),15; Jb 21,23
to be prosperous, to live comfortably

εὐπάρυφον,-ου   N2N 0-0-1-0-0-1
Ez 23,12
a fine garment

εὐπείθεια,-ας   N1F 0-0-0-0-4-4
4 Mc 5,16; 9,2; 12,6; 15,9
ready obedience
Cf. SPICQ 1978, 323-324

εὐπειθέω   V 0-0-0-0-1-1
4 Mc 8,6
to be disposed to obey

εὐπορέω⁺   V 3-0-0-0-1-4
Lv 25,26.28.49; Wis 10,10
A: *to cause to thrive, to make sb thrive* [τινα]
Wis 10,10; P: *to prosper, to thrive* Lv 25,26
Cf. HELBING 1928, 79; SPICQ 1978, 328; WALTERS 1973,
119

εὐπραξία,-ας   N1F 0-0-0-0-2-2
3 Mc 3,5.6
well doing

εὐπρέπεια,-ας⁺   N1F 0-1-2-7-7-17
2 Sm 15,25; Jer 23,9; Ez 16,14; Ps 25(26),8;
49(50),2
goodly appearance, comeliness 2 Sm 15,25;
dignity Ps 92(93),1; *Jer 23,9 εὐπρεπείας -הדר
majesty for MT דברי *words*
Cf. DANIEL 1966, 261; SPICQ 1978, 320

εὐπρεπής,-ής,-ές   A 0-2-1-1-2-6
2 Sm 1,23; 23,1; Zech 10,3; Jb 18,15; Wis 7,29
good-looking, comely 2 Sm 1,23; *beautiful* 2 Sm
23,1

εὐπρεπῶς   D 0-0-0-0-2-2
1 Ezr 1,10; Wis 13,11
handsomely, elegantly

εὐπροσήγορος,-ος,-ον   A 0-0-0-0-1-1
Sir 6,5
affable, courteous

εὐπρόσωπος,-ος,-ον   A 1-0-0-0-0-1
Gn 12,11
pleasing to the eye, fair in outward show, specious

εὕρεμα,-ατος   N3N 0-0-3-0-4-7

Jer 45(38),2; 46(39),18; 51,35(45,5); Sir 20,9;
29,4
finding, that which is found unexpectedly, piece of
good luck, windfall Jer 45(38),2; *sum realised by*
a sale Sir 20,9

εὕρεσις,-εως   N3F 0-0-0-0-2-2
Wis 14,12; Sir 13,26
invention, conception

εὑρετής,-οῦ   N1M 0-0-0-1-1-2
Prv 16,20; 2 Mc 7,31
inventor, discoverer

εὑρετός,-ή,-όν   A 0-1-0-0-0-1
Jgs^B 9,6
found at, situated at; *Jgs^B 9,6 τῇ εὑρετῇ (τῆς
στάσεως) -(מצב)ב הנמצא (the pillar) found at*
for MT (מצב) *palisade* or *entrenchment*
(haplogr.)

εὑρίσκω⁺   V 117-157-57-148-134-613
Gn 2,20; 4,14.15; 5,24; 6,8
A: *to find* Gn 4,14; *to find out, to discover* Gn
26,19; *to befall* [τινα] Gn 44,34; *to acquire
wealth* [abs.] Lv 25,47; *to find sb in such a state*
[τινα +pred.] Hos 6,3; *to find that* [+ptc.] Est
8,12p; P: *to be found* Gn 18,29; [+pred.] (mostly
of pers.) Wis 8,11; *to be found that* [ὅτι +ind.]
1 Ezr 2,21; *to amount to, to stand at* [+pred.]
1 Chr 20,2; ἡ χείρ τινος εὑρίσκει τι *to afford,
to have* Lv 5,11; εὑρίσκω τῇ χειρί *to afford* Lv
14,32; *Dn^LXX 8,26 ηὑρέθη *is found* corr.?
ἐρρήθη, cpr. Dn^Th 8,26; *Am 2,16 εὑρήσει -ימצא
he shall find for MT אמיץ *the strong*; *Zech 12,5
εὑρήσομεν -נמצא *we shall find* for MT אמצה
strength; *Ps 72(73),10 εὑρεθήσονται -ימצאו *they
shall be found* for MT ימצו *they are drained*; *Ez
27,33 εὗρες -מצאת *acquired* for MT בצאת *when
coming forth*; *Hos 6,3 εὑρήσομεν αὐτόν
-נמצאו/נ *let us find him* for MT מוצאו/ע *his coming
out*
Cf. GEHMAN 1953, 147; LEE 1983, 51; →NIDNTT
(··· ἀν-, ἐξ-)

εὖρος,-ους   N3N 13-4-36-3-1-57
Ex 25,23; 26,2.8; 27,1.12
breadth, width

εὔρυθμος,-ος,-ον   A 0-0-0-1-0-1
Est 4,17s
harmonious, rhythmical

εὐρύς,-εῖα,-ύ   A 3-0-0-0-0-3
Ex 38,4(37,5).10(37,14).24(5)
wide, broad; εὐρεῖς *wide enough*
Cf. LE BOULLUEC 1989, 364

εὐρυχωρία,-ας   N1F 1-0-0-0-0-1
Gn 26,22
large open space, free room
Cf. HUSSON 1983, 295

εὐρύχωρος,-ος,-ον⁺   A 0-2-3-2-4-11
Jgs^A 18,10; 2 Chr 18,9; Is 30,23; 33,21; Hos 4,16
roomy, wide, spacious Ps 103(104),25; τὸ
εὐρύχωρον *open space* 2 Chr 18,9

εὔρωστος,-ος,-ον   A 0-0-0-0-1-1
Sir 30,15
stout, strong

εὐρώστως   D 0-0-0-0-4-4
2 Mc 10,17; 12,27.35; Wis 8,1
strongly, mightily

εὐρωτιάω   V 0-1-0-0-0-1
Jos 9,5
to be or *become mouldy*

εὐσέβεια,-ας⁺   N1F 0-0-2-2-54-58
Is 11,2; 33,6; Prv 1,7; 13,11; 1 Ezr 1,21
piety, godliness, religion (always towards God)
Cf. SPICQ 1981, 219-221; →NIDNTT; TWNT

εὐσεβέω⁺   V 0-0-0-0-5-5
4 Mc 9,6; 11,5.23; 18,1; Sus^LXX 63
to live, to act piously or *reverently* 4 Mc 9,6; *to
worship* [τινα] 4 Mc 11,5
Cf. HELBING 1928, 13

εὐσεβής,-ής,-ές⁺   A 0-0-4-2-28-34
Is 24,16; 26,7(bis); 32,8; Prv 12,12; 13,19
pious, religious Jdt 8,31; *holy, sacred* 4 Mc 6,31
Cf. SPICQ 1981, 219-221; →TWNT

εὔσημος,-ος,-ον⁺   A 0-0-0-1-0-1
Ps 80(81),4
conspicuous

εὐσήμως   D 0-0-0-1-0-1
Dn^LXX 2,19
clearly, distinctly

εὔσκιος,-ος,-ον   A 0-0-1-0-0-1
Jer 11,16
well-shaded, shadowy

εὔσπλαγχνος,-ος,-ον   A 0-0-0-0-1-1
Od 12,7
compassionate

εὐστάθεια,-ας   N1F 0-0-0-1-6-7
Est 3,13; 2 Mc 14,6; 3 Mc 3,26; 6,28; Wis 6,24
stability, tranquillity

εὐσταθέω   V 0-0-1-0-3-4
Jer 30,26(49,31); 2 Mc 12,2; 14,25; 3 Mc 7,4
to be steady, to be stable

εὐσταθής,-ής,-ές   A 0-0-0-1-1-2
Est 3,13; Sir 26,18

steady, quiet

εὔστοχος,-ος,-ον   A 0-0-0-0-1-1
Wis 5,21
well-aimed

εὐστόχως   D 0-2-0-0-0-2
1 Kgs 22,34; 2 Chr 18,33
with a good aim

εὐστροφία,-ας   N1F 0-0-0-1-0-1
Prv 14,35
suppleness, versatility

εὐσυναλλάκτως   D 0-0-0-1-0-1
Prv 25,10
peaceably

εὐσχημοσύνη,-ης[+]   N1F 0-0-0-0-1-1
4 Mc 6,2
gracefulness
Cf. SPICQ 1978, 334

εὐσχήμων,-ων,-ον[+]   A 0-0-0-1-0-1
Prv 11,25
graceful
Cf. SPICQ 1978, 335-336

εὐτακτέω   V 0-0-0-0-1-1
2 Mc 4,27
to be orderly

εὐτάκτως   D 0-0-0-1-1-2
Prv 30,27; 3 Mc 2,1
in an orderly manner

εὐταξία,-ας   N1F 0-0-0-0-2-2
2 Mc 4,37; 3 Mc 1,10
orderly behaviour 2 Mc 4,37; *good arrangement*
3 Mc 1,10

εὐτεκνία,-ας   N1F 0-0-0-0-1-1
4 Mc 18,9
blessing of children

εὐτελής,-ής,-ές   A 0-0-0-0-4-4
Wis 10,4; 11,15; 13,14; 15,10
worthless, of small value Wis 10,4; *vile* Wis 11,15

εὐτελῶς   D 0-0-0-0-1-1
2 Mc 15,38
poorly, meanly

εὔτηκτος,-ος,-ον   A 0-0-0-0-1-1
Wis 19,21
easily melted

εὐτολμία,-ας   N1F 0-0-0-0-1-1
2 Mc 13,18
courage, boldness

εὐτονία,-ας   N1F 0-0-0-1-0-1
Eccl 7,7
vigour; *Eccl 7,7 καρδίαν εὐτονίας αὐτοῦ
מתן ◊ את לב מתנו/ה- *his strong heart* for MT

את לב מתנה *a gift* (corrupts) *the heart*
Cf. DRIVER 1954, 229-230

εὔτονος,-ος,-ον   A 0-0-0-0-2-2
2 Mc 12,23; 4 Mc 7,10
vigorous

εὐτόνως[+]   D 0-1-0-0-0-1
Jos 6,8
vigorously, loudly

εὐτρεπίζω   V 0-0-0-0-1-1
4 Mc 5,32
to make ready, to prepare

εὐφημέω   V 0-0-0-0-1-1
1 Mc 5,64
to acclaim

εὔφθαρτος,-ος,-ον   A 0-0-0-0-1-1
Wis 19,21
easily destroyed, perishable

εὐφραίνω[+]   V 20-31-49-104-50-254
Lv 23,40; Dt 12,7.12.18; 14,26
A: *to cheer, to gladden* Jgs[B] 9,13; P: *to enjoy
oneself, to rejoice* Lv 23,40; εὐφραινόμενον
ποιέω *to make merry* Jer 38(31),13; *Ps
76,3(77,4) εὐφράνθην-אחדה *rejoiced* for MT
אהמיה *moan;* *Is 45,8 εὐφρανθήτω-הריעו- see
1QIs[a] *rejoice!* for MT הרעיפו *let descend;* *Is
28,22 εὐφρανθείητε -תעלצו *rejoice* for MT
תתלוצצו *be scornful;* *Jgs[A] 5,11 εὐφραινομένων
-משמחים *rejoicing* for MT משאבים *the wells;*
*Dn[LXX] 9,24 εὐφρᾶναι-לשמח *to rejoice* for MT
למשח *to anoint;* *Prv 22,18 εὐφρανοῦσι -ירנו
they will gladden for MT יכנו *they are held;* *Ez
23,41 εὐφραίνοντο -שמחו *they rejoiced* for MT
שמת *you have set*
Cf. HELBING 1928, 257-258; →NIDNTT; TWNT
(→ ἐν-)

εὐφροσύνη,-ης[+]   N1F 3-13-47-48-59-170
Gn 31,27; Nm 10,10; Dt 28,47; Jgs[A] 9,13; 2 Sm
6,12
mirth, merriment (also pl.) Gn 31,27;
ἐμπίμπλαμαι εὐφροσύνης *to be filled with joy*
Sir 4,12
Cf. HORSLEY 1987, 152-153; ROBERT 1958, 208; ROUSSEL
1927, 134-135; →NIDNTT; TWNT

εὔφρόσυνος,-ος,-ον   A 0-0-0-0-3-3
Jdt 14,9; 3 Mc 6,36; 7,19
cheery, merry

εὐφυής,-ής,-ές   A 0-0-0-0-3-3
1 Ezr 8,3; 2 Mc 4,32; Wis 8,19
naturally clever 1 Ezr 8,3; *convenient* 2 Mc 4,32
Cf. LARCHER 1983, 551-552; 1969, 270

εὔχαρις,-ις,-ι   A 0-0-0-0-1-1
Wis 14,20
charming, gracious; τὸ εὔχαρι *grace*
εὐχαριστέω⁺   V 0-0-0-0-6-6
Jdt 8,25; 2 Mc 1,11; 12,31; 3 Mc 7,16; Od 14,8
to be thankful, to return thanks Wis 18,2; [τινι]
Jdt 8,25
Cf. SCHERMANN 1910, 383-384; →TWNT
εὐχαριστία,-ας⁺   N1F 0-0-0-1-3-4
Est 8,12d; 2 Mc 2,27; Wis 16,28; Sir 37,11
thankfulness, gratitude Est 8,12d; *giving of thanks*
Wis 16,28
Cf. LARCHER 1984, 558; SCHERMANN 1910, 384
εὐχάριστος,-ος,-ον⁺   A 0-0-0-1-0-1
Prv 11,16
agreeable
εὐχερής,-ής,-ές   A 0-0-0-1-2-3
Prv 14,6; Jdt 7,10; 2 Mc 2,27
easy
εὐχερῶς   D 0-0-0-1-3-4
Prv 12,24; Jdt 4,7; 3 Mc 2,31; Wis 6,12
easily
εὐχή,-ῆς⁺   N1F 45-9-5-20-12-91
Gn 28,20; 31,13; Lv 7,16; 22,21.23
prayer Jb 16,18; *vow* Nm 6,2; *votive offering* Dt
12,17; *Jb 11,17 εὐχή -תפלה-*prayer* for MT תעפה
darkness; *Jer 11,15 εὐχαί -נדרים-*prayers* for MT
רבים *the many*
Cf. HARL 1986, 224; HARLÉ 1988, 109.187.211; SPICQ
1982, 332-334; →TWNT
εὔχομαι⁺   V 34-9-5-16-22-86
Gn 28,20; 31,13; Ex 8,4.5.24
to pray Ex 8,4; *to vow* [abs.] Nm 6,20; [τι] Gn
28,20; [τί τινι] Nm 21,2; [πρός τινα] Ex 8,24; *to
vow to* [+inf.] 1 Ezr 4,44
Cf. CIMOSA 1985, 29-42; HARLÉ 1988, 211; SPICQ 1982,
330-331
(→ ἐπ-, κατ-, προσ-)
εὐχρηστία,-ας   N1F 0-0-0-0-1-1
3 Mc 2,33
ready use
εὔχρηστος,-ος,-ον⁺   A 0-0-0-1-1-2
Prv 31,13; Wis 13,13
useful, serviceable
εὐψυχία,-ας   N1F 0-0-0-0-3-3
2 Mc 14,18; 4 Mc 6,11; 9,23
good courage, high spirit
Cf. SPICQ 1978, 337-338
εὔψυχος,-ος,-ον   A 0-0-0-1-1-2
Prv 30,31; 1 Mc 9,14

of good courage, stout of heart
Cf. SPICQ 1978, 337-338
εὐψύχως   D 0-0-0-0-2-2
2 Mc 7,20; 3 Mc 7,18
courageously
Cf. DREW-BEAR 1972, 198-199
εὐώδης,-ης,-ες   A 2-0-0-0-2-4
Ex 30,23(bis); 3 Mc 5,45; 7,16
sweet-smelling, fragrant
Cf. DANIEL 1966, 190-193
εὐωδία,-ας⁺   N1F 42-0-4-3-9-58
Gn 8,21; Ex 29,18.25.41; Lv 1,9
sweet smell Ezr 6,10; ὀσμὴ εὐωδίας *smell of
appeasement* (semit., rendering of ריח ניחוח;
metaph.) Gn 8,21
Cf. DANIEL 1966, 190-199; HARL 1991, 246; WALTERS
1973, 73; →TWNT
εὐωδιάζω   V 0-0-1-0-1-2
Zech 9,17; Sir 39,14
to emit a sweet fragrance Sir 39,14; εὐωδιάζων
οἶνος *'bouquet' wine* Zech 9,17; neol.
εὐώνυμος,-ος,-ον   A 3-7-5-2-2-19
Ex 14,22.29; Nm 20,17; Jos 13,3; 23,6
left, on the left hand (euph.)
εὐωχέομαι   V 0-0-0-0-2-2
Jdt 1,16; 3 Mc 6,40
to feed, to fare sumptuously, to feast Jdt 1,16; *to
feast upon* [τι] 3 Mc 6,40
εὐωχία,-ας   N1F 0-0-0-2-7-9
Est 4,17; 8,12u; 1 Ezr 3,20; 3 Mc 4,1.8; 5,3
good cheer, feasting
εφαδανω   V 0-0-0-1-0-1
Dnᵀʰ 11,45
=אפדנו *his state-tents*
ἐφάλλομαι⁺   V 0-3-0-0-0-3
1 Sm 10,6; 11,6; 16,13
to come upon [ἐπί τινα]; πνεῦμα κυρίου
ἐφάλλεται ἐπί τινα *the spirit of the Lord comes
upon*
Cf. WALTERS 1973, 137-138
ἐφαμαρτάνω   V 0-0-1-0-0-1
Jer 39(32),35
to seduce to sin; neol.
ἐφάπτομαι   V 0-0-2-0-1-3
Am 6,3; 9,5; 2 Mc 7,1
to lay hold of, to reach, to attain to [τινος] Am
6,3; *to taste* [ἀπό τινος] 2 Mc 7,1
ἐφαρμόζω   V 0-0-0-0-1-1
4 Mc 11,10
to apply

ἐφέλκω									V 1-1-0-0-3-5
Nm 9,19; Jos 24,29(31); 4 Mc 15,21; Wis 14,20;
LtJ 1,43
A: *to draw* Jos 24,29; M: *to draw to oneself, to
attract* 4 Mc 15,21; P: *to be drawn* Nm 9,19; *to
be attracted* Wis 14,20

ἐφέτιος,-α,-ον								A 1-0-0-0-1-2
Dt 15,18; Sir 37,11
annual Sir 37,11; *Dt 15,18 ἐφέτιον -בשנה
annual for MT משנה *duplicate*
Cf. WALTERS 1973, 57-58

ἐφηβεῖον,-ου								N2N 0-0-0-0-1-1
2 Mc 4,9
a place for the training of youth

ἔφηβος,-ου								N2M 0-0-0-0-1-1
2 Mc 4,12
ephebe, adolescent, young man

ἔφηλος,-ος,-ον								A 1-0-0-0-0-1
Lv 21,20
with a white speck on (the eyes)

ἐφημερία,-ας⁺								N1F 0-16-0-4-2-22
1 Chr 9,33; 23,6; 25,8; 26,12; 28,1
*division (of priests) for the daily service of the
temple* Neh 13,30; *daily service of the temple*
1 Ezr 1,15; neol.

ἐφθός,-ή,-όν								A 1-1-0-0-0-2
Nm 6,19; 1 Sm 2,15
boiled

ἐφικτός,-ή,-όν								A 0-0-0-0-1-1
2 Mc 15,38
easy to reach, accessible, attainable

ἔφιππος,-ος,-ον								A 0-0-0-0-3-3
2 Mc 11,8; 12,35; 4 Mc 4,10
on horseback, riding

ἐφίπταμαι									V 0-0-0-0-1-1
LtJ 1,21
to fly to(wards) [ἐπί τι]

ἔφισος,-η,-ον								A 0-0-0-0-2-2
Sir 9,10; 31,27
equal

ἐφίστημι⁺									V 12-13-26-17-16-84
Gn 24,43; Ex 1,11; 7,23; Lv 17,10; 20,3
A: *to set, to place* [τι] Lv 17,10; *to set over* [τινά
τινι] Ex 1,11; [τινα ἐπί τι] Nm 1,50; *to set up,
to establish* [τι] Jos 6,26; *to set against* [τι ἐπί
τινα] Lv 20,3; *to set up over* [τί τινι] Jos 7,26;
to fix, to apply [τι] Prv 22,17; *to make firm* [τι]
Sir 40,25; M: *to stand* Zech 1,10; *to stand near
or by* [ἐπί τινος] Nm 23,6; *to rest upon* [ἐπί
τινος] Nm 14,14; *to be set over* [ἐπί τινα] Ru

2,5; [τινι] Jdt 8,10; [ἐπί τινι] Jdt 10,6; *to attend
to* [πρός τι] Neh 8,13; *to come to, to appear
before* [τινι] Jdt 6,14; *to come upon suddenly* Is
63,5; *to spring upon, to occur* [τινι] Wis 6,8;
ἐφεστῶτες ἐπ᾽ αὐτόν *who wait upon him* Jgsᴮ
3,19; παγίς ἐφεσταμένη *a snare which has been
set* Jer 5,27; ἐφίστημι τὸν νοῦν ἐπί τινι *to fix
one's mind upon, to attend to* Ex 7,23; ἐφίστημι
τὴν χεῖρα ἐπί τι *to extend power over* 1 Chr
18,3
Cf. HELBING 1928, 287-288

ἐφοδεύω									V 1-0-0-0-3-4
Dt 1,22; Jdt 7,7; 1 Mc 16,14; 2 Mc 3,8
to visit as a spy, to spy out Dt 1,22; *to visit, to
inspect* 2 Mc 3,8
Cf. HELBING 1928, 85

ἐφοδιάζω									V 1-1-0-0-0-2
Dt 15,14; Jos 9,12
A: *to furnish with supplies for a journey* [τινα]
Dt 15,14; P: *to be supplied with* [τι] Jos 9,12

ἐφόδιον,-ου								N2N 1-0-0-0-0-1
Dt 15,14
supply (for a journey)

ἔφοδος,-ου								N2F 0-0-0-0-9-9
1 Mc 9,68; 11,44; 14,21; 2 Mc 5,1; 8,12
approach, coming, entrance 1 Mc 11,44; *attempt,
plan, method* 1 Mc 9,68

ἐφοράω⁺									V 3-1-5-13-7-29
Gn 4,4; 16,13; Ex 2,25; 1 Chr 17,17; Jer
31(48),19
to watch over Jb 21,16; *to oversee, to observe* Jb
28,24; *to look upon, to behold* Mi 7,10
Cf. HELBING 1928, 288

εφουδ									N 0-15-0-0-0-15
Jgsᴬ 8,27; 17,5; 18,14.17.18
=אפוד *ephod* (i.e. priestly garment); see εφωδ

ἐφύβριστος,-ος,-ον							A 0-0-0-0-1-1
Wis 17,7
wanton, insolent
Cf. CAIRD 1972, 131

εφωδ									N 0-4-0-0-0-4
Jgsᴮ 17,5; 18,14.18.20
=אפוד *ephod* (i.e. priestly garment)

εφωθ									N 0-1-0-0-0-1
Jgsᴮ 8,27
see εφωδ, εφουδ

ἐχθάνομαι
(→ ἀπ-)

ἐχθές⁺									D 0-10-0-2-3-15
1 Sm 19,7; 20,27; 21,6; 2 Sm 3,17; 5,2

yesterday
Cf. GEHMANN 1972, 105

ἔχθρα,-ας⁺ N1F 3-0-7-2-2-14
Gn 3,15; Nm 35,20.22; Is 63,10; Jer 9,7
hatred, enmity
·TWNT

ἐχθραίνω V 4-0-0-2-6-12
Nm 25,17.18; Dt 2,9.19; Ps 3,8
to be at enmity Sir 28,6; *to be at enmity with*
[τινι] Nm 25,17
Cf. HELBING 1928, 212

ἐχθρεύω V 2-0-0-0-1-3
Ex 23,22; Nm 33,55; 2 Mc 10,26
to be at enmity Nm 33,55; *to be at enmity with*
[τινι] Ex 23,22
Cf. HELBING 1928, 213

ἐχθρός,-ά,-όν⁺ A 58-92-39-158-109-456
Gn 14,20; 49,8; Ex 15,6.9; 23,4
hating, hostile Ps 60(61),3; ὁ ἐχθρός *enemy* Gn
14,20; *Jb 22,25 ἀπὸ ἐχθρῶν -מ/צרי *from*
enemies for MT בצרי *gold*; *Ez 35,5 ἐχθρῶν
-איבם *enemies* for MT אידם *trouble*
→NIDNTT; TWNT

ἐχῖνος,-ου N2M 0-0-5-0-0-5
Is 13,22; 14,23; 34,11.15; Zph 2,14
hedgehog

ἔχις,-εως N3M 0-0-0-0-1-1
Sir 39,30
viper

ἐχομένως D 0-0-0-0-1-1
2 Mc 7,15
thereupon, immediately afterwards

ἐχυράζω
(→ ἐν-)

ἔχω⁺ V 63-43-79-97-215-497
Gn 1,29.30; 7,22; 8,11; 16,4
A: *to have* Gn 1,29; *to possess* Gn 49,25; *to seize*
Jb 21,6; *to bear, to wear* Jer 27(50),42; *to be able*
to [+inf.] Gn 18,31; *to be* [+adv.] Gn 43,27; *to*
possess mentally, to understand [τι] Jer
45(38),19; *to belong to* [τινος] Prv 23,3; M: *to*
hold on by, to cling to [τινος] Dt 30,20; *to be*
close to [τινος] Gn 41,23; *to be connected with*
[ἔκ τινος] Ex 26,3; P: *to be held* Jb 19,20; ἔχων
with Sir 29,28; ἐχόμενός τινος *next to* Nm 2,12;
τῇ ἐχομένῃ (sc. ἡμέρᾳ) *the next day* 1 Chr 10,8
Cf. AERTS 1965; HELBING 1928, 128-130; HORSLEY 1989,
56; JOÜON 1936, 96-98; SOISALON-SOININEN 1978, 92-99;
·TWNT

(→ ἀν-, ἀντ-, ἀπ-, διακατ-, ἐν-, ἐξ-, ἐπ-,
ἐπισυν-, κατ-, μετ-, παρ-, περι-, προσ-,
προσεν-, συμμετ-, συν-, ὑπ-, ὑπερ-)

ἔψεμα or ἔψημα,-ατος N3N 3-3-1-0-2-9
Gn 25,29.30.34; 2 Kgs 4,38.39
anything boiled, pottage

ἕψω V 12-5-3-1-5-26
Gn 25,29; Ex 12,9; 16,23(bis); 23,19
to boil, to seethe Gn 25,29; *1 Sm 9,24 ἥψησεν
corr.? ὕψωσεν for MT ירם *he took up*

ἑωθινός,-ή,-όν A 1-0-2-1-4-8
Ex 14,24; Am 7,1; Jon 4,7; Ps 21(22),1; Jdt 12,5
in the morning, early

ἕωλος,-ος,-ον A 0-0-1-0-0-1
Ez 4,14
a day old

ἕως⁺ C 302-568-204-285-206-1565
Gn 3,19; 6,7(bis); 7,23; 8,5
till, until [+ind.] Wis 10,14; [ἄν +subj.] Gn
24,14; [+inf.] Gn 10,19; *as long as, while* [+ind.]
Jdt 5,17; [τινος]: *until* (time) Gn 3,19; *up to the*
point where, as far as, to (place) Is 48,20; (of
pers.) 2 Kgs 4,22; *to the sum of* (by numbers)
1 Ezr 8,19(21); [τι]: *till* (rarely) Jgsᴬ 19,25; ἀπό
τινος ἕως τινός *from ... to ...* Bar 1,19; ἕως εἴς
τι *until* Lv 23,14; ἕως τοῦ νῦν *until now* Gn
15,16; ἕως οὗ *until* Jgs 3,30; ἕως ὅτου *until*
1 Kgs 10,7; ἕως πότε *how long?* 1 Mc 6,22; ἕως
πρός τινα *as far as* Gn 38,1; ἕως ἄνω *to the*
brim 2 Chr 26,8; ἕως ἑπτάκις *as many as seven*
times 2 Kgs 4,35; ἕως τίνος *how long?* Ex 16,28;
ἕως τότε *until that time* Neh 2,16; *Jos 3,16 ἕως
-עד אשר *as far as* for MT עיר אשר *a city (that)*;
*Mi 1,14 ἕως -עד *as far as* for MT על *to*; *Ps
60(61),7 ἕως ἡμέρας corr? ὡς ἡμέρας -כימי *as*
the days for MT כמו *like*; *Mal 2,12 ἕως -עד *until*
for MT ער *protector*?
Cf. AEJMELAEUS 1982, 79-80; GILMORE 1890, 153-160;
HORSLEY 1987, 154; JEANSONNE 1988, 98; LUST 1978, 62-
69 (Dn 7,13); MURAOKA 1990, 20-21; →TWNT

ἕως, ἕω N3F 0-0-0-0-1-1
3 Mc 5,46
dawn, early morning

ἑωσφόρος,-ου N2M 0-1-1-5-0-7
1 Sm 30,17; Is 14,12; Ps 109(110),3; Jb 3,9; 11,17
morning star, morning 1 Sm 30,17; *Ps
109(110),3 πρὸ ἑωσφόρου -מ/שחר *before the*
morning star or before Lucifer for MT משחר?
Cf. TOURNAY 1960, 11-12

ζακχω   N 0-1-0-0-0-1
1 Chr 28,11
=גנזך (transposition?) *treasury*
ζάω⁺   V 144-113-93-102-102-554
Gn 1,20.24; 2,7.19; 3,20
to live Gn 1,20; *to pass one's life* Dt 12,1; *to
quicken, to give life* [τινα] (semit. rendering
Hebr. hiphil) Ps 118(119),37; ὕδωρ ζῶν *springing
or running water* Gn 21,19; τὸ ὄνομα αὐτῶν ζῇ
εἰς γενεάς *may their name live for ever* Sir
44,14; ζήτω ὁ βασιλεύς *long live the king* 1 Sm
10,24; βασιλεὺς εἰς τὸν αἰῶνα ζῆθι *King, live
for ever* Dnᴸˣˣ 3,9; ζωῇ ζήσεται *he shall surely
live* (semit. for MT חיו יחיה) Ez 3,21; *Eccl 7,14
ζῆθι -חיה *live* for MT היה *be*, see also Ps
118(119),149. 156; *Jb 8,17 ζήσεται -יחיה *he
shall live* for MT יחזה *he shall see?*
Cf. HELBING 1928, 76; KILPATRICK 1963, 132-133; 1977,
107-112, esp. 111; 1983, 146-151; LARCHER 1969, 292-
295.296; LEE 1980, 289-298; MARTINI 1980, 145-152;
→TWNT
(→ δια-, ἐπι-)
ζέα,-ας   N1F 0-0-1-0-0-1
Is 28,25
one-seeded wheat
ζεμα,-ατος   N3N 0-1-0-0-0-1
Jgsᴮ 20,6
=זמה *lewdness, loose conduct?*
ζευγίζω   V 0-0-0-0-1-1
1 Mc 1,15
to unite, to join; neol.?
ζεύγνυμι or ζευγνύω   V 2-6-0-0-1-9
Gn 46,29; Ex 14,6; 1 Sm 6,7.10; 2 Sm 20,8
to harness, to yoke Gn 46,29; *to bind fast* 2 Sm
20,8
(→ ἀνα-, ἐπι-, παρα-, συ-)
ζεῦγος,-ους⁺   N3N 1-10-1-3-0-15
Lv 5,11; Jgsᴬ 17,10; 19,3.10; Jgsᴮ 19,3
yoke 1 Kgs 19,21; *carriage drawn by a yoke of
beasts, chariot* 2 Kgs 9,25; *pair, couple* Lv 5,11;
suit (of clothes) Jgsᴬ 17,10
ζέω⁺   V 0-0-2-1-1-4
Ez 24,5(bis); Jb 32,19; 4 Mc 18,20
to boil, to seethe, to be fiery hot Ez 24,5; *to boil,
to seethe* (metaph. of rage) 4 Mc 18,20
(→ ἀνα-, ἐκ-)
ζῆλος,-ου⁺   N2M 3-1-16-10-9-39
Nm 25,11(bis); Dt 29,19; 2 Kgs 19,31; Is 9,6
fervour, zeal, jealousy
Cf. LARCHER 1984, 387.391.392; →TWNT

ζηλοτυπία,-ας   N1F 4-0-0-0-0-4
Nm 5,15.18.25.29
jealousy, rivalry, envy Nm 5,29; ἡ θυσία (τῆς)
ζηλοτυπίας *the sacrifice of jealousy* Nm 5,15;
neol.
ζηλόω⁺   V 10-7-8-7-17-49
Gn 26,14; 30,1; 37,11; Nm 5,14(bis)
to be jealous of, to envy [τινα] Gn 26,14; [τινι]
Nm 11,29; *to be jealous* [abs.] Dt 32,19; *to be
zealous for, to strive after* [τι] Sir 51,18; ζηλόω
τὸν ζῆλον *to admire the zeal* Jdt 9,4; *Is 11,11
ζηλῶσαι -ל/קנוא *to be zealous* for MT ל/קנות *to
recover*
(→ παρα-)
Cf. HARL 1991, 252; HELBING 1928, 95; →TWNT
ζήλωσις,-εως   N3F 3-0-0-0-1-4
Nm 5,14(bis).30; Wis 1,10
zeal, eagerness (of the Lord's ear) Wis 1,10;
jealousy Nm 5,14
ζηλωτής,-οῦ⁺   N1M 5-0-1-0-2-8
Ex 20,5; 34,14; Dt 4,24; 5,9; 6,15
zealot 2 Mc 4,2; ζηλωτὴς θεός (always in Ex and
Dt) *jealous* or *zealous God* Ex 20,5
Cf. LE BOULLUEC 1989, 206
ζηλωτός,-ή,-όν   A 2-0-0-0-0-2
Gn 49,22; Ex 34,14
jealous Ex 34,14; *enviable* (of pers.) Gn 49,22
Cf. CAQUOT 1980, 46 (Gn 49,22); LE BOULLUEC 1989, 340
ζημία,-ας⁺   N1F 0-1-0-2-2-5
2 Kgs 23,33; Prv 27,12; Ezr 7,26; 1 Ezr 8,24;
2 Mc 4,48
penalty, fine
Cf. SPICQ 1978, 339-342
ζημιόω⁺   V 2-0-0-4-1-7
Ex 21,22; Dt 22,19; Prv 17,26; 19,19; 21,11
A: *to punish* [τινα] Prv 17,26; *to fine with* [τινά
τινι] 1 Ezr 1,34; [τινά τι] Dt 22,19; P: *to
suffer* (financial) *loss* Ex 21,22; *to be punished*
Prv 21,11
Cf. SPICQ 1978, 339-342
ζητέω⁺   V 16-88-53-101-62-320
Gn 19,11; 37,15.16; 43,9.30
to seek (for) [τι] Gn 19,11; *to inquire* [τινα]
2 Sm 11,3; *to seek after, to desire* [τι] Jb 38,41;
to seek to [+inf.] Gn 43,30; *to seek* or *desire that*
[τινα +inf.] 2 Sm 3,17; ζητέω τὴν ψυχήν *to
seek sb's life* 2 Sm 4,8; *Jer 43(36),24 ἐζήτησαν
they sought (the Lord?) corr.? ἐξέστησαν for
MT פחדו *they were afraid*
(→ ἀνα-, ἐκ-, ἐπι-)

Cf. LEE 1981, 51; →NIDNTT

ζιβύνη,-ης N1F 0-0-2-0-0-2
Is 2,4; Jer 6,23
(hunting-)spear; neol.?

ζυγός or **ζυγόν,-οῦ⁺** N2M/N 6-7-29-11-13-66
Gn 27,40; Lv 19,35.36; 26,13; Nm 19,2
yoke Gn 27,40; (metaph.) Sir 40,1; ζυγά
balance, scales Lv 19,35; *Dn^Th 8,25 ζυγός -עול
yoke for MT על *on, by*
Cf. HORSLEY 1982, 87; 1989, 116; SHIPP 1989, 261-262;
→TWNT

ζυγόω V 0-1-1-0-0-2
1 Kgs 7,43(6); Ez 41,26
to yoke, to join together

ζῦθος,-ου N2M 0-0-1-0-0-1
Is 19,10
beer; *Is 19,10 ζῦθον -שכר *strong drink, beer* for
MT שכר *wages, reward*
Cf. THACKERAY 1909, xx; WALTERS 1973, 90.113

ζύμη,-ης⁺ N1F 10-0-0-0-0-10
Ex 12,15(bis).19; 13,3.7
leaven, yeast
Cf. HARLÉ 1988, 90; LE BOULLUEC 1989, 148; LEE 1981,
46

ζυμίτης,-ου N1M 1-0-0-0-0-1
Lv 7,13
leavened; ζυμίτης ἄρτος *leavened bread*

ζυμόομαι⁺ V 4-0-1-0-0-5
Ex 12,34.39; Lv 6,10; 23,17; Hos 7,4
to be leavened, to ferment

ζυμωτός,-ή,-όν A 4-0-0-0-0-4
Ex 12,19.20; 13,7; Lv 2,11
leavened, fermented; neol.
Cf. LE BOULLUEC 1989, 148

ζωγραφέω V 0-0-3-0-2-5
Is 49,16; Ez 23,14(bis); 2 Mc 2,29; 4 Mc 17,7
to paint Is 49,16; *to paint, to draw, to represent
as art* Ez 23,14
Cf. HORSLEY 1987, 203.209

ζωγραφία,-ας N1F 0-0-0-0-1-1
Sir 38,27
painting, drawing, representation

ζωγρεία,-ας N1F 2-0-0-0-0-2
Nm 21,35; Dt 2,34
taking alive

ζωγρέω⁺ V 3-5-0-0-0-8
Nm 31,15.18; Dt 20,16; Jos 2,13; 6,25
to take alive Nm 31,15; *to save* or *preserve alive*
Jos 2,13
Cf. SPICQ 1978, 343

ζωγρίας,-ου N1M 0-0-0-0-1-1
2 Mc 12,35
one taken alive; ζωγρίαν λαμβάνω τινά *to take
one alive*; neol.?
Cf. WALTERS 1973, 37

ζωή,-ῆς⁺ N1F 38-20-36-95-100-289
Gn 1,30; 2,7.9; 3,14.17
life, existence Gn 1,30; *living, property* Sir 4,1;
way of life Sir 29,24; *Ez 31,17 ζωῆς -חים *life* for
MT גוים *nations*; *Gn 3,20 Ζωή proper name *Zoe*
(etym. *life*) for MT חוה ◊ חיה? proper name *Eve*
(etym. *living*?)
Cf. HILL 1967, 171-175; HORSLEY 1981, 98-99; LARCHER
1969, 145.292-296; →TWNT

ζωμός,-οῦ N2M 0-4-1-0-0-5
Jgs 6,19.20; Is 65,4
soup, sauce, broth

ζώνη,-ης⁺ N1F 9-3-5-2-0-19
Ex 28,4.39.40; 29,9; 36,36(34,25)
girdle, belt Ex 28,4; *Dt 23,14 ζώνης σου -אזרך
your girdle for MT אזנך *your tool, equipment*?

ζώννυμι or **ζωννύω⁺** V 4-6-5-3-2-20
Ex 29,9; Lv 8,7.13; 16,4; Jgs^B 18,11
A: *to gird with* [τινά τινι] Is 3,24; [τί τινι]
2 Mc 10,25; [τινά τι] 1 Sm 17,39; *to gird* [τι]
Jb 38,3; M: *to gird oneself with* [τι] 1 Sm 25,13;
to gird upon [τι ἐπί τι] 1 Kgs 20(21),27; P: *to
be girt with* [τι] Jgs² 18,11; [τινι] 1 Mc 6,37; *to
have (one's loins) girt with sth* [τί τινι]
(metaph.) Is 11,5; *to be girt with sth upon (one's
loins)* [τι ἐπί τι] Ez 23,15; ζώννυμί τινα ταῖς
ζώναις *to gird with girdles* Ex 29,9; ζώννυμί
τινα τὴν ζώνην Lv 8,7; ζώννυμαι ζώνη *to gird
oneself with a girdle* Lv 16,4
(→ ἀνα-, περι-, συ-, ὑπο-)
Cf. HELBING 1928, 47

ζωογονέω⁺ V 5-7-0-0-1-13
Ex 1,17.18.22; Lv 11,47(bis)
to be viviparous, to produce alive Lv 11,47; *to
preserve alive* Ex 1,17
Cf. SPICQ 1978, 346-347

ζῷον,-ου⁺ N2N 1-0-13-5-19-38
Gn 1,21; Ez 1,5.13(bis).15
living being, animal Gn 1,21; *Jb 38,14 ζῷον
-חיתם ◊ חיה *living creature* for MT חותם *seal*; *Hab
3,2 (ἐν μέσῳ δύο) ζῴων -חים (בקרב שני) *(between
two) living creatures* for MT חייהו (בקרב שנים) *(in the
midst of the years) bring it to life*
Cf. MARGOLIS 1970, 413 (Hab 3,2)

ζωοποιέω⁺ V 0-2-0-4-0-6

JgsᴮB 21,14; 2 Kgs 5,7; Ps 70(71),20; Jb 36,6; Eccl
7,12

to make alive 2 Kgs 5,7; *to preserve alive* Jgsᴮ
21,14

ζωοποίησις,-εως   N3F 0-0-0-2-0-2
Ezr 9,8.9

making alive, quickening; neol.

ζωόω   V 0-0-0-2-0-2
Ps 79(80),19; 84(85),7

to make alive, to quicken

ζωπυρέω   V 0-4-0-0-0-4
2 Kgs 8,1.5(ter)

to quicken, to restore to life [τινα]
(→ ἀνα-)

ζώπυρον,-ου   N2N 0-0-0-0-1-1
4 Mc 8,13

spark, hot coal

ζῶσις,-εως   N3F 0-0-1-0-0-1
Is 22,12

girding on; neol.

ζωτικός,-ή,-όν   A 0-0-0-0-1-1
Wis 15,11

fit for giving or *maintaining life*

Cf. GILBERT 1973, 212-214; LARCHER 1985, 871-873

ἤ⁺   C 348-138-133-145-170-934
Gn 19,9.12(ter); 21,26
or Gn 24,21; *than, as* (after a comp.) Gn 19,9;
ἤ ... ἤ ... *either ... or ...* Gn 19,12; πρὶν ἤ *before*
Nm 11,33; ἀλλ᾽ ἤ *but, except* Is 42,19; *Is 10,15
ἤ -וא *or* for MT לא *not*; *Jer 11,15 ἤ -וא *or* for
MT אם *so that*
Cf. AEJMELAEUS 1982, 67; MARGOLIS 1909, 257-275;
MURAOKA 1990, 21-22

ἤ   D 1-1-2-37-0-41
Gn 22,17; Jgs 14,15; Is 45,23; Jer 7,17; Jb 6,13
surely, truly; ἤ μὴν *surely, verily* Gn 22,17

ἡγεμονία,-ας⁺   N1F 3-0-0-0-4-7
Gn 36,30; Nm 1,52; 2,17; 4 Mc 6,33; 13,4
district of a chief (mil.) Gn 36,30; *regiment,
company* (mil.) Nm 1,52; *authority, rule* 4 Mc
6,33
Cf. LEE 1983, 83

ἡγεμονικός,-ή,-όν   A 0-0-0-1-1-2
Ps 50(51),14; 4 Mc 8,7
authoritative

ἡγεμών,-όνος⁺   N3M 43-13-15-3-10-84
Gn 36,15(quinquies)
leader, chief Gn 36,15; *Ps 67(68),28 ἡγεμόνες
αὐτῶν -רוזניהם *their leaders* for MT רגמתם *their
shouting crowd*?

ἡγέομαι⁺   V 7-51-21-29-58-166
Gn 49,10.26; Ex 13,21; 23,23.27
to go before, to lead (the way) [τινος] Ex
13,21; *to have dominion over, to be the head of*
[τινος] Gn 49,26; (metaph.) Ex 23,27; *to rule*
[ἐπί τινος] Dt 1,15; *to think, to deem* [+inf.]
Jb 30,1; *to hold as, to regard as* [τι +pred.] Jb
41,23; [τινα +pred.] Wis 1,16; ἡγούμενος
ruler, leader, commander Gn 49,10; *leader over,
head of, chief of* [τινος] 1 Sm 15,17; [ἐπί
τινος] 1 Sm 22,2; [ἐπί τι] 2 Chr 6,5; *leader to*
[τινι] 1 Chr 12,28; *head of* [εἴς τι] 2 Chr
19,11; ἡγουμένη τινός *woman leading over*
Jdt 15,13; ἡγουμένη φαρμάκων *skilled in
sorcery* Na 3,4; καθίστημί τινα εἰς
ἡγούμενον *to make sb ruler* Jgs^A 11,11;
ἡγητέος *to be held, to be considered* Prv 26,23;
*Ps 103(104),17 ἡγεῖται αὐτῶν -ב/ראש/ם *is in
the lead, takes the lead among them* for MT
ב/רושים *in the fir trees*; *Jer 4,22 ἡγούμενοι -אילי
(the) rulers (of)* for MT אויל *foolish*; *Mi 2,9
ἡγούμενοι -נשיאי *leaders* for MT נשי *women*;
*Ez 21,2 ἡγούμενον -השרה *the chief* for MT השרה
the field

Cf. DELCOR 1967, 151-179, esp. 156; HELBING 1928, 67-
68.117; LE BOULLUEC 1989, 240-241 (Ex 23,27); SPICQ
1978, 348-352
(→ ἀφ-, δι-, ἐκδι-, ἐξ-, προ-, προκαθ-,
προσεξ-)

ἥγημα,-ατος   N3N 0-0-1-0-0-1
Ez 17,3
thought, purpose; neol.?

ἥγησις,-εως   N3F 0-1-0-0-1-2
Jgs^A 5,14(15); 1 Mc 9,31
command; neol.

ἡγορέω
(→ κατ-, παρ-, προ-)

ἡδέως⁺   D 0-0-0-3-8-11
Prv 3,24; 9,17; Est 1,10; Tob^AB 7,10.11
pleasantly, sweetly, with pleasure, gladly Prv
3,24; ἡδέως γίνομαι *to become merry* Tob
7,11
Cf. SPICQ 1978, 353

ἤδη⁺   D 6-0-1-14-43-64
Gn 27,36; 43,10; Ex 6,1; Nm 11,23; 17,12
already, by this time Gn 43,10; *forthwith,
immediately* Jb 15,21; *actually, now* Ex 6,1;
ἤδη καί *even* (ἤδη not translated) 3 Mc 1,26

ἥδομαι   V 0-0-0-0-3-3
4 Mc 8,4; Wis 6,21; Sir 37,4
to delight in, to rejoice in [ἐπί τινι] Wis 6,21;
[ἔν τινι] Sir 37,4
Cf. HELBING 1928, 259

ἡδονή,-ῆς⁺   N1F 1-0-0-1-13-15
Nm 11,8; Prv 17,1; 4 Mc 1,20.21.22
enjoyment, pleasure Prv 17,1; *pleasant taste,
flavour, sweetness* Nm 11,8; *sexual desire* Wis
7,2
→NIDNTT; TWNT

ἡδύνω   V 0-0-2-5-1-8
Jer 6,20; Hos 9,4; Ps 104(103),34; 140(141),6;
146(147),1
A: *to please, to gladden* [τι] Prv 13,19; [τινι]
Hos 9,4; *to make sweet* [τι] Sir 40,21; P: *to be
sweet* (of pers.) Ct 7,7; *to be sweet, to be
pleasant* (metaph.) Ps 103(104),34; *Jb 24,5
ἡδύνθη -ערב ◊ ערב^III *is sweet, is pleasant* for MT
ערבה *the desert place*

ἡδυπάθεια,-ας   N1F 0-0-0-0-2-2
4 Mc 2,2.4
pleasant living, luxury

ἡδύς,-εῖα,-ύ   A 0-0-3-4-8-15
Is 3,24; 44,16; Jer 38(31),26; Prv 12,11; 14,23
pleasant Ct 2,14; *sweet* Est 1,7; *well-pleased,*

glad Prv 12,11

Cf. KRAFT 1972, 166; SPICQ 1978, 353

ἥδυσμα,-ατος N3N 2-5-1-1-0-9
Ex 30,23.34; 1 Kgs 10,2.10(bis)
relish, seasoning Eccl 10,1; ἡδύσματα spices,
sweet herbs, aromatics Ex 30,23

Cf. LE BOULLUEC 1989, 311.313

ἡδυσμός,-οῦ N2M 1-0-0-0-0-1
Ex 30,34
sweet savour, sweetness; neol.

Cf. LE BOULLUEC 1989, 313

ἡδύφωνος,-ος,-ον A 0-0-1-0-0-1
Ez 33,32
sweet-voiced

ηδω N 0-0-0-1-0-1
Jb 36,30
=אירו his disaster for MT אורו his light

Cf. SIMOTAS 1968, 71

ἠθέω
(→ δι-)

ἠθολογέω V 0-0-0-0-1-1
4 Mc 15,4
to express characteristically; neol.

ἦθος,-ους⁺ N3N 0-0-0-0-7-7
4 Mc 1,29; 2,7.21; 5,24; 13,27
disposition, character Sir 20,26; τὰ ἤθη
manners, customs Sir prol.,35; bearings 4 Mc
5,24; τὸ ἦθος as usual (as adv.) 4 Mc 2,7

ἥκω⁺ V 21-40-124-37-22-244
Gn 6,13; 18,10; 41,30; 42,7.9
to have come, to be present Ps 125(126),6;
(metaph.) Gn 6,13; to come into, to reach [εἴς
τι] Ex 18,23; to come to [πρός τινα] Gn
18,10; to come upon [ἐπί τινα] 2 Chr 20,2;
(metaph.) Jb 4,5; to come to [+inf.] Jos 2,3;
ἥκω εἴς τι to be in such a state, to become Mi
7,12; ἥκω εἰς κρίσιν to enter into judgement
Is 3,14; ἥκω εἰς πόλεμον to come to war 1 Sm
29,9; ἥκω εἰς χεῖράς τινος to come in the
power of Prv 6,3; *Is 4,5 καὶ ἥξει -ובא or -ויבא
and he will come for MT וברא and he will create;
*2 Chr 35,21 ἥκω -אתה come for MT אתה you

Cf. MURAOKA 1990, 34-35; →TWNT

(→ ἀν-, δι-, ἐπαν-, καθ-, προ-, προσ-)

ἤλεκτρον,-ου N2N 0-0-3-0-0-3
Ez 1,4.27; 8,2
alloy of silver and gold

ἡλιάζομαι V 0-1-0-0-0-1
2 Sm 21,14
to be hung in the sun; see ἐξηλιάζω; neol.?

(→ ἐξ-)

ἡλικία,-ας⁺ N1F 0-0-1-1-20-22
Ez 13,18; Jb 29,18; 2 Mc 4,40; 5,24; 6,18
time of life, age Jb 29,18; prime of life,
manhood 2 Mc 5,24; size, stature, degree of
growth Ez 13,18; *Jb 29,18 ἡλικία μου -זקני
my old age for MT קני my nest

Cf. SHIPP 1979, 264

ἡλικιώτης,-ου N1M 0-0-0-0-1-1
4 Mc 11,14
equal in age, comrade

ἥλιος,-ου⁺ N2M 28-47-34-62-40-211
Gn 15,12.17; 19,23; 28,11; 32,32
sun Gn 15,17; day Neh 8,3; sunshine Ps
18(19),5; sun's heat Est 10,3c; ἀνατολαὶ
ἡλίου quarter of sunrise, east Nm 21,11;
ἡλίου δυσμαί sunset Gn 15,12; ὑπὸ τὸν
ἥλιον under the sun, on earth Eccl 1,3; *Ez
30,17 Ἡλίου πόλεως -און Heliopolis, On for
MT און sin, cpr. Gn 41,45; Ex 1,11

Cf. HARL 1986, 276

ἧλος,-ου⁺ N2M 0-5-2-1-0-8
Jos 23,13; 1 Kgs 7,36(50); 2 Kgs 12,14; 1 Chr
22,3; 2 Chr 3,9
nail

ἡλόω
(→ δι-, προσ-)

ἧμαι
(→ ἀποκάθ-, ἐγκάθ-, κάθ-, περικάθ-)

ἡμέρα,-ας⁺ N1F 566-660-498-442-400-2566
Gn 1,5(bis).8.13.14
day Gn 1,5; feast-day 1 Mc 7,49; ἡμέραι age
Gn 18,11; lifetime Gn 5,17; times, period Dt
4,32; τὴν ἡμέραν (as adv.) daily Ex 29,38;
καθ' ἡμέραν daily Nm 4,16; ἡμέραν καθ'
ἡμέραν 2 Chr 30,21; καθ' ἑκάστην ἡμέραν
Jb 1,4; τὸ τῆς ἡμέρας the daily portion Dn 1,5;
πρὸς ἡμέραν at day break Ex 14,27; ἡ ἡμέρα
τῶν σαββάτων Sabbath day 1 Mc 2,32; ἡ
σήμερον ἡμέρα today, this day 1 Mc 10,30; ἡ
ἐπερχομένη ἡμέρα the following day 3 Mc
5,2; μιᾶς ὑπὸ καιρὸν ἡμέρας within the space
of one day 2 Mc 7,20; μετὰ δύο ἔτη ἡμερῶν
after two years fully expired 1 Mc 1,29; ἡμέραν
καὶ νύκτα day and night Gn 8,22; *2 Chr
24,18 ἐν τῇ ἡμέρα ταύτη in that day corr.? ἐν
τῇ ἁμαρτία ταύτη for MT זאת אשמה/באשמת because
of this (their) sin; *Jer 31(48),16 ἡμέρα -עת
appointed time, day for MT איד calamity; *1 Sm
21,14 ἡμέρα -יום day for MT יד/ם their hand;

*Dt 32,35 ἐν ἡμέρᾳ ליום- in the day for MT לי
for me, cpr. Sam. Pent.; *Ps 72(73),10 καὶ
ἡμέραι ומי- and days for MT ומי and waters
of, see also Lam 5,4; *Mi 7,12 ἡμέρα יום- day
for MT ים sea

Cf. ALLEN 1974ᴵᴵ, 13 (2 Chr 24,18); LE BOULLUEC 1989,
181-182; →TWNT

ἥμερος,-α,-ον   A 0-0-0-1-3-4
Est 3,13b; 2 Mc 12,30; 4 Mc 2,14; 14,15
civilized, gentle 2 Mc 12,30; cultivated 4 Mc
2,13; tame 4 Mc 14,15

ἡμερόω   V 0-0-0-0-1-1
Wis 16,18
to make tame, to restrain (of a flame)
(→ ἐξ-)

ἡμέτερος,-α,-ον⁺   R 1-1-0-7-13-22
Gn 1,26; Jos 5,13; Ps 34(35),14; Prv 1,13; 4,4
our Prv 1,13; my (pluralis maiestatis) or our
Gn 1,26

Cf. BARTHÉLEMY 1978, 189-191; HARL 1986, 95; TOV
1984, 65-89

ἡμίεφθος,-ος,-ον   A 0-0-1-0-0-1
Is 51,20
half-boiled

ἡμιθανής,-ής,-ές⁺   A 0-0-0-0-1-1
4 Mc 4,11
half-dead

ἡμίθνητος,-ος,-ον   A 0-0-0-0-1-1
Wis 18,18
half-dead

ἡμίονος,-ου   N2M/F 2-14-2-3-3-24
Gn 12,16; 45,23; 1 Sm 21,8; 22,9; 2 Sm 13,29
mule

ἡμίσευμα,-ατος   N3N 4-0-0-0-0-4
Nm 31,36.42.43.47
a half; neol.?

ἡμισεύω   V 0-0-0-1-0-1
Ps 54(55),24
to halve; neol.

ἥμισυς,-εια,-υ⁺   A 32-61-14-21-14-142
Ex 24,6(bis); 25,10(ter)
half, the half of Jos 13,31; τὰς ἡμίσεις τῶν
ἁμαρτιῶν half of the sins (subst. in gen. and
giving its number and gender to ἥμισυς) Ez
16,51, see also 1 Mc 3,34; οἱ ἡμίσεις φυλῆς
the half tribe Jos 4,12; τὸ ἥμισυ the half Lv
6,13(20); the half of [τινος] Ex 24,6; δυὸ
πήχεων καὶ ἡμίσους two cubits and a half Ex
25,10(9); ἐν ἡμίσει τῆς νυκτός at midnight
JgsᴮB 16,3; ἥμισυ τῆς ἡμέρας middle of the day

Neh 8,3; ἥμισυ ἡμερῶν μου in the midst of my
days Ps 101(102),25; ἥμισυ [+comp.] half Jos
9,2d; [+verb] Neh 13,24; *1 Chr 4,31 ἥμισυ
Σωσιμ סוסים חצי-half of Sosim for MT סוסים חצר
Hazar Susim (horse-farm)

ἡνία,-ας   N1F 0-0-1-0-1-2
Na 2,4; 1 Mc 6,28
bridle, rein Na 2,4; οἱ ἐπὶ τῶν ἡνίῶν cavalry
commanders 1 Mc 6,28

Cf. MARGOLIS 1911, 314; WALTERS 1973, 156 (1 Chr
25,9)

ἡνίκα⁺   D 53-23-10-18-6-110
Gn 6,1; 12,11.14; 16,16; 17,24
at the time when Gn 6,1; ἡνίκα ἄν [+subj.]
when, whenever, whensoever, every time that
Prv 1,26; ἡνίκα ἐάν [+subj.] Gn 24,41;
ἡνίκα δ'ἄν [+ind. impf.] Ex 33,8; *Is 50,4
ἡνίκα δεῖ לעת- when it is time for, when it fits
for MT לעות to sustain?

Cf. AEJMELAEUS 1980, 79-81; LE BOULLUEC 1989, 32

ἡνίοχος,-ου   N2M 0-2-0-0-0-2
1 Kgs 22,34; 2 Chr 18,33
charioteer

ἤνυστρον,-ου   N2N 0-0-2-0-0-2
Mal 2,3(bis)
dung; see ἔνυστρον

ἧπαρ,-ατος   N3N 13-2-0-1-12-28
Gn 49,6; Ex 29,13.22; Lv 3,4.10
liver Ex 29,13; *Gn 49,6 τὰ ἥπατά μου כברי-
◊ כבד my insides for MT כבוד כברי- my honour;
*1 Sm 19,13 ἧπαρ כבר- liver for MT כביר quilt,
net?, see also 1 Sm 19,16

ἡπατοσκοπέω   V 0-0-1-0-0-1
Ez 21,26
to inspect the liver for soothsaying; neol.

ἤπερ⁺   C 0-0-0-0-3-3
Tobˢ 14,4; 2 Mc 14,42; 4 Mc 15,16
than, rather than

ἡπιότης,-ητος   N3F 0-0-0-1-0-1
Est 3,13b
gentleness

ἠρεμάζω   V 0-0-0-2-0-2
Ezr 9,3.4
to be still, to be prostrated (from grief); neol.

ἡσυχάζω⁺   V 2-16-7-17-6-48
Gn 4,7; Ex 24,14; Jgsᴬ 3,11.30; 5,31
to keep quiet, to be at rest Jgsᴮ 18,9;
ἡσυχάζεται there is quiet Jb 37,17

Cf. HELBING 1928, 78-79; LE BOULLUEC 1989, 248-249
(Ex 24,14); SPICQ 1978, 359-360

ἡσυχῇ   D 0-1-1-0-1-3
Jgs^A 4,21; Is 8,6; Sir 21,20
stilly, quietly Jgs^A 4,21; *little* Sir 21,20

ἡσυχία,-ας⁺   N1F 0-3-1-4-4-12
Jos 5,8; 1 Chr 4,40; 22,9; Ez 38,11; Jb 34,29
rest, quiet 1 Chr 4,40; *silence, stillness* Prv 7,9;
ἡσυχίαν ἔχω *to be at rest, to keep quiet, to be
inactive* Jos 5,8; ἡσυχίαν ἄγω *to keep quiet*
Prv 11,12
Cf. SPICQ 1978, 359-360

ἡσύχιος,-ος,-ον⁺   A 0-0-1-0-1-2
Is 66,2; PSal 12,5
quiet
Cf. SPICQ 1978, 359-360

ἥσυχος,-ος,-ον   A 0-0-0-0-2-2
Wis 18,14; Sir 25,20
quiet

ἤτοι⁺   X 0-0-0-0-1-1
Wis 11,18
ἤτοι ... ἤ ... *either ... or ...*

ἡττάω⁺   ·   V 0-0-12-2-2-16
Is 8,9(ter); 19,1; 20,5
A: *to overcome* [τινα] Is 54,17; P: *to be less or
weaker, to be inferior* Sir 19,24; *to be defeated
or overcome* Is 8,9; *to faint* Is 19,1
Cf. HELBING 1928, 177; WALTERS 1973, 256-261

ἥττημα,-ατος⁺   N3N 0-0-1-0-0-1
Is 31,8
overthrow, complete defeat, discomfiture
Cf. WALTERS 1973, 256

ἥττων or ἥσσων,-ων,-ον⁺   A 0-1-1-4-7-13

1 Sm 30,24; Is 23,8; Jb 5,4; 13,10; 20,10
comp. of κακός; *inferior* Jb 20,10; *vile* Jb 5,4;
less, fewer Wis 17,13; *weaker* LtJ 36; ἧττον (as
adv.) *less* Jb 13,10; οὐχ ἧττόν τινος *no fewer
than* 2 Mc 10,17; *Is 23,8 μὴ ἥσσων ἐστὶν
ה/מעטה- *is she inferior?* for MT ה/מעטירה *the
bestower of crowns*

ἠχέω⁺   V 1-5-8-4-5-23
Ex 19,16; 1 Sm 3,11; 4,5; 1 Kgs 1,41.45
to sound, to ring Ex 19,16; *to resound* (of the
earth) 1 Mc 4,5; *to sound, to roar* (of water)
Ps 45(46),4; *to tingle* (of ears) 1 Sm 3,11; *to
make noise* (of pers.) Ps 82(83),3; *to cause to
roar* [τι] Is 51,15; ἠχέω φωνήν *to let sound* Sir
45,9; *Jb 30,4 ἐπὶ ἠχοῦντι- שיח על ישיח ◊ *on the
sounding?* for MT שיח עלי *the leaves of the
bushes?*
(→ ἀντ-, δι-, ἐξ-, συν-)

ἦχος,-ου⁺   N2M 0-1-5-6-5-17
1 Sm 14,19; Is 13,21; Jer 28(51),42; 29(47),3;
Jl 4,14
sound 1 Sm 14,19; *Is 13,21 ἤχου =אחים?
howling (beast); *Ps 9,7 ἤχου -המה *noise* for MT
המה *of them*

ἦχος,-ους⁺   N3N 0-1-1-3-0-5
1 Sm 4,15(16); Jer 28(51),16; Ps 9,7; 64(65),8;
76(77),17
see ἦχος,-ου

ἠχώ, ἠχούς   N3F 0-0-0-1-2-3
Jb 4,13; Wis 17,18; Sir 47,9
(ringing) sound Jb 4,13; *echo* Wis 17,19

θααλα N 0-3-0-0-0-3
1 Kgs 18,32.35.38
=תעלה*water-course*, trench, later corr. θάλασσα
Cf. WALTERS 1973, 190

θαιηλαθα N 0-0-1-0-0-1
Ez 40,7
=חא לחא* (from) porch to porch*? for MT תאים
porches

θάλαμος,-ου N2M 0-0-0-0-1-1
3 Mc 1,18
bed-room, women's appartment

θάλασσα,-ης+ N1F 82-104-134-74-56-450
Gn 1,10.22.26.28; 9,2
sea Gn 1,10; κατὰ θάλασσαν *seawards, westwards* Gn 12,8; κατὰ θάλασσαν καὶ βορρᾶν
καὶ νότον *westwards and northwards and south-
wards* Dn^Th 8,4; *1Kgs 10,29 κατὰ θάλασσαν
-בים *by sea* for MT בידם *by their hand*; *Jer 22,20
εἰς τὸ πέρας τῆς θαλάσσης -ים מעבר *to the
extremity of the sea* for MT מעברים *from Abarim*
Cf. BOGAERT 1981, 79-85 (Ex 27,12); CAIRD 1972, 131;
GEHMAN 1972, 99; HARL 1986, 65; RAHLFS 1911, 285;
WALTERS 1973, 190-192

θαλάσσιος,-α,-ον A 0-0-0-0-1-1
1 Mc 4,23
of the sea

θαλλός,-οῦ N2M 0-0-0-0-1-1
2 Mc 14,4
(young) branch, bough

θάλλω V 1-0-0-3-1-5
Gn 40,10; Jb 8,11; Prv 15,13; 26,20; Sir 14,18
to sprout, to grow, to thrive [τι] Gn 40,10; [abs.]
Jb 8,11; *to increase, to rage* (of fire) Prv 26,20; *to
flourish* (of face) Prv 15,13; φύλλον θάλλον
green leaves Sir 14,18
(→ ἀνα-)

θαλπιωθ N 0-0-0-1-0-1
Ct 4,4
=תלפיות* courses of stones* (of buildings)

θάλπω+ V 1-2-0-1-0-4
Dt 22,6; 1 Kgs 1,2.4; Jb 39,14
to warm, to hatch [τι] Jb 39,14; [ἐπί τινος] Dt
22,6; *to cherish* [τινα] (metaph.) 1 Kgs 1,2
Cf. SPICQ 1978, 365-366

θαμβέω+ V 0-4-0-1-2-7
Jgs^A 9,4; 1 Sm 14,15; 2 Sm 22,5; 2 Kgs 7,15;
Dn^Th 8,17
A: *to amaze, to alarm* [τινα] 2 Sm 22,5; *to be
terror-struck* 1 Sm 14,15; P: *to be astounded, to
be astonished* 2 Kgs 7,15; *Jgs^A 9,4

θαμβουμένους -פחרים* afraid* for MT פחזים *insolent,
reckless*
→TWNT
(→ ἐκ-)

θάμβος,-ους or -ου+ N3N/2M 0-1-1-4-0-6
1 Sm 26,12; Ez 7,18; Ct 3,8; 6,4.10
stupor 1 Sm 26,12; *fear* Eccl 12,5; neol.
→TWNT

θανατηφόρος,-ος,-ον+ A 1-0-0-1-3-5
Nm 18,22; Jb 33,23; 4 Mc 8,18.26; 15,26
death-bringing, fatal

θάνατος,-ου+ N2M 50-65-62-79-106-362
Gn 2,17; 3,4; 21,16; 26,11; Ex 5,3
death Jb 15,34; *mortality* 2 Sm 24,13; *pestilence*
Ex 5,3; θάνατος νοσερός *grievous death* Jer
14,15; σκιὰ θανάτου *shadow of death* (folk
etym. of צל/מות) Ps 22(23),4; ὠδῖνες θανάτου
2 Sm 22,6, see ὠδίς; θανάτῳ ἀποθανεῖσθε for
MT מות תמות *you shall surely die* (semit.) Gn 2,17;
*Is 9,7 θάνατον -רבָר *death, pestilence* for MT רבָר
word, message; *Is 53,8 εἰς θάνατον -למות *to
death* for MT למו *to him*; *Hab 3,13 θάνατον
-(ב)מות)? *death* for MT מבית *from the house*
(metath.?); *Zech 5,3 ἕως θανάτου במות *with
death* for MT כמוה *according to it*
Cf. LARCHER 1969, 285-291; WEVERS 1990, 328; →TWAT
(צלמות); NIDNTT; TWNT

θανατόω+ V 29-103-7-11-11-161
Gn 38,10; Ex 14,11; 21,12.14.15
A: *to destroy, to kill, to slay* 2Chr 23,17; P: *to be
put to death* Ex 21,12

θανάτωσις,-εως N3F 0-1-0-0-0-1
1 Sm 26,16
slaughter; υἱοὶ θανατώσεως for mt בני מות *sons
of death, those who deserve to die* (semit.)

θαννουριμ N 0-0-0-1-0-1
Neh 3,11
=תנורים *furnaces*

θάπτω+ V 33-88-10-2-44-177
Gn 15,15; 23,4.6(bis).8
to bury
Cf. HARL 1986, 70.315; →NIDNTT

θαραφιν N 0-1-0-0-0-1
Jgs^B 17,5
=תרפין (Aram.?) for MT תרפים *idols*; see θεραφιν

θαρραλέος,-α,-ον A 0-0-0-0-1-1
4 Mc 13,13
brave, confident

θαρραλέως D 0-0-0-0-3-3
3 Mc 1,4.23; 4 Mc 3,14

bravely, manfully

θαρρέω⁺ or **θαρσέω⁺**   V 3-1-6-5-20-33
Gn 35,17; Ex 14,13; 20,20; 1 Kgs 17,13; Jl 2,21
to be courageous (always imper.) Gn 35,17; *to be
bold* Prv 1,21; *to be confident about* [ἐπί τινι]
Prv 31,11
Cf. SPICQ 1978, 367-371
(→ κατα-)

θαρσις   N 0-0-1-3-0-4
Ez 1,16; Ct 5,14; Dn 10,6
=שׁישׁ or תרשׁ תרסית *precious stone, beryl*

θάρσος,-ους⁺   N3N 0-1-0-2-1-4
2 Chr 16,8; Jb 4,4; 17,9; 1 Mc 4,35
courage, manliness
Cf. SPICQ 1978, 367-371

θαρσύνω   V 0-0-0-1-0-1
Est 4,17r
to encourage [τινα]
(→ παρα-)

θαῦμα,-ατος⁺   N3N 0-0-0-2-0-2
Jb 17,8; 18,20
wonder; θαῦμα ἔχει *stupor seizes*

θαυμάζω⁺   V 5-2-8-16-26-57
Gn 19,21; Lv 19,15; 26,32; Dt 10,17; 28,50
to wonder (at) [abs.] Jb 21,5; [τι] Dnᵀʰ 8,27;
[ἐπί τινι] Jb 41,1; *to be astonished at* [ἐπί
τινι] Lv 26,32; *to admire, to honour* [τι] Lv
19,15; *to have respect for* [τινα] Sir 7,29;
θαυμάζω τὸ πρόσωπόν τινος *to have respect for,
to comply with his request* Gn 19,21; *to show
favouritism* Dt 10,17; *Is 52,15 θαυμάσονται
-יחזו◊ חזה *they shall look up to, in admiration* for
MT יזה ◊ נזה *he shall spatter?*
Cf. HARL 1986, 181-182; HARLÉ 1988, 209; → NIDNTT; TWNT
(→ ἀπο-, ἐκ-)

θαυμάσιος,-α,-ον⁺   A 2-4-3-39-13-61
Ex 3,20; Dt 34,12; Jgs 6,13; 1 Chr 16,9
wonderful, marvellous Sir 48,14; (τὰ) θαυμάσια
wonders, miracles, wonderful deeds Dt 34,12
Cf. LE BOULLUEC 1989, 34

θαυμασμός,-οῦ   N2M 0-0-0-0-2-2
2 Mc 7,18; 4 Mc 6,13
astonishment, marvelling, admiration; neol.?

θαυμαστός,-ή,-όν⁺   A 4-4-4-16-15-43
Ex 15,11; 34,10; Dt 28,58.59; Josᴮᴬ 3,5
wonderful, marvellous Ps 8,2; *honourable* Is 3,3;
astonishing Dt 28,59; θαυμαστά *wonderful
things, wonders* Jos 3,5; θαυμαστά (adv.)
wonderfully, terribly Dnᵀʰ 8,24; *Ps 41(42),5
θαυμαστῆς -אדרם ◊ אדיר*wonderful* for MT אדרם

◊ררה? *I led them;* *Am 3,9 θαυμαστά -תצנהות◊ תמה
wonderful things for MT מהומות *tumults*

θαυμαστόω   V 0-2-0-5-0-7
2 Sm 1,26; 2 Chr 26,16; Ps 4,4; 15(16),3;
16(17),7
A (semit., Hebr. hiphil): *to treat wonderfully, to
magnify* [τινα] Ps 4,4; *to make marvellous* [τι]
Ps 15(16),3; P: *to be wonderful* 2 Sm 1,26

θαυμαστῶς   D 0-0-0-3-1-4
Ps 44(45),5; 75(76),5; Dnᴸˣˣ 8,24; Sir 43,8
wonderfully, terribly

θέα,-ας   N1F 0-0-2-0-0-2
Is 2,16; 27,11
sight Is 2,16; *Is 27,11 ἀπὸ θέας -מ/ראות? *from
(that) sight* for MT מאירות *making a fire*

θεάομαι⁺   V 0-1-0-0-8-9
2 Chr 22,6; Jdt 15,8; Tobᴮᴬ 2,2; 13,7.16
to see [τινα] 2 Chr 22,6; [τι] Tobᴮᴬ 2,2; *to gaze
at, to behold* [τι] Jdt 15,8
Cf. LEE 1983, 140

θεε   N 0-1-13-0-0-14
1 Kgs 14,28; Ez 40,7(bis).8.10
=תא *room*

θεεβουλαθω   N 0-0-0-1-0-1
Jb 37,12
=תהבולותו *his guidance*

θειμ   N 0-0-3-0-0-3
Ez 40,12.14.16
=תאים *rooms*

θεῖον,-ου⁺   N2N 2-0-3-2-1-8
Gn 19,24; Dt 29,22; Jb 18,15; Is 30,33; 34,9
brimstone, sulphur

θεῖος,-α,-ον⁺   A 2-0-0-4-28-34
Ex 31,3; 35,31; Jb 27,3; 33,4; Prv 2,17
divine, of God Ex 31,3; τὰ θεῖα *divine things*
4 Mc 1,17
→ MM

θειότης,-ητος⁺   N3F 0-0-0-0-1-1
Wis 18,9
divinity; ὁ τῆς θειότητος νόμος *the divine law*
Cf. LARCHER 1985, 1003

θεκελ   N 0-0-0-4-0-4
Dnᴸˣˣ 5,0(bis); Dnᵀʰ 5,25.27
=תקל (Aram.) *cryptic word written on the wall*

θέλημα,-ατος⁺   N2N 0-6-9-25-11-51
2 Sm 23,5; 1 Kgs 5,22.23.24; 9,11
will 1 Ezr 8,16; *desire* 2 Sm 23,5; *decree* Est 1,8;
ἔστιν θέλημα ἔν τινι *pleasure is in sth* Eccl
5,3
Cf. SEGALLO 1965, 121-143; → TWNT

θέλησις,-εως⁺   N3F 0-1-1-3-3-8
2 Chr 15,15; Ez 18,23; Ps 20(21),3; Prv 8,35;
Dn^LXX 11,45
will Tob 12,18; *desire* 2 Chr 15,15; *favour* Prv
8,35; *prayer* Ps 20(21),3; neol.
·TWNT

θελητής,-οῦ   N1M 0-2-1-0-1-4
2 Kgs 21,6; 23,24; Mi 7,18; 1 Mc 4,42
one who wills, who delights in [τινος] Mi 7,18;
2 Kgs 23,24 τοὺς θελητάς -אבה the willing,
those who have will-control over spirits for MT
אבות *mediums?, spirits of the dead (fathers)?*, see
also 2 Kgs 21,6
Cf. MONTGOMERY 1951, 522

θελητός,-ή,-όν⁺   A 0-1-1-0-0-2
1 Sm 15,22; Mal 3,12
wished for, desired; neol.

θέλω⁺   V 20-36-24-38-30-148
Gn 24,8; 37,35; 39,8; 48,19; Ex 2,7
to be willing, to will [intrans.] Is 1,19; *to please*
[intrans.] Ct 2,7; *to be willing to, to will, to wish
to* [+inf.] Gn 24,8; *to be pleased to* [+inf.] Jgs^B
13,23; *to will that* [τινα +inf.] Dt 2,30; *to will
that* [+ind. fut.] Ex 2,7; *to delight in, to have or
take pleasure in, to rejoice in* [τι] Dt 21,14; *to
wish for* [τινα] Ps 67(68),31; *to delight in, to
take* or *have pleasure in, to prefer* [ἔν τινι]
1 Sm 18,22; *to order* [intrans.] Est 1,8; οὐ θέλω
τι *to reject* Is 5,24; οὐ θέλω [+inf.] *to refuse to*
Nm 20,21; (μὴ) θελέ [+inf.] *do (not)* Sir 6,35;
θελήσεις εἰ μὴ ἐγεννήθης *you wish that you
had not been born* Sir 23,14
Cf. HARL 1991, 253; LEE 1983, 144; WALTERS 1973, 141;
·TWNT
(·· συν-)

θέμα,-ατος   N3N 3-3-0-0-2-8
Lv 24,6(bis).7; 1 Sm 6,8.11
treasure Tob^BA 4,9; *pile* Lv 24,6; *coffer* 1 Sm 6,8
Cf. DANIEL 1966, 147.160

θεματίζω
(· ἀνα-)

θεμέλιον or θεμέλιος,-ου⁺   N2N/M 1-4-26-9-8-48
Dt 32,22; 2 Sm 22,8.16; 1 Kgs 6,1a(5,31); 7,46(9)
foundation, wall Hos 8,14; *2 Kgs 16,18
θεμέλιον -מוסך* a base* for MT מיסך *covered way*;
*Na 1,10 ἕως θεμελίου αὐτῶν -ער יסדם *to their
foundation* for MT ער סירים *as thorns?*
→NIDNTT

θεμελιόω⁺   V 0-8-10-20-4-42
Jos 6,26(bis); 1 Kgs 6,1c(37); 7,47(10); 16,34

A: *to lay the foundation of, to found, to establish
on* [τι] Jb 38,4; *to begin* [τι] Ezr 7,9; P: *to be
built from the foundation* Sir 50,2; *to be piled*
2 Chr 31,7; τεθεμελιωμέ νον βασίλειον *well-
founded palace* Prv 18,19

θεμελίωσις,-εως   N3F 0-0-0-2-0-2
Ezr 3,11.12
foundation; neol.

θέμις, θέμιστος   N3F 0-0-0-0-2-2
2 Mc 6,20; 12,14
θέμις (ἐστί) [+inf.] *it is lawful to*

θεμιτός,-ή,-όν   A 0-0-0-0-1-1
Tob^BA 2,13
lawful

θεννουριμ   N 0-0-0-1-0-1
Neh 12,38
=תנורים *furnaces*

θεόκτιστος,-ος,-ον   A 0-0-0-0-1-1
2 Mc 6,23
established by God

θεομαχέω   V 0-0-0-0-1-1
2 Mc 7,19
to fight against God

θεός,-οῦ⁺   N2M 1037-851-511-898-687-3984
Gn 1,1.2.3.4(bis)
God Ps 131(132),2; *god* Ps 80(81),10; τὰ πρὸς
τὸν θεόν *the relations with God* Ex 4,26; ὁ θεός
ὁ θεός μου *o God, my God* (nom. for voc.) Ps
21(22),2; κύριος ὁ θεός *the Lord God* Gn 8,21;
(τὰς κέδρους) τοῦ θεοῦ *divine, beautiful
(cedars)* (gen. as adj.) Ps 79(80),11, cpr. Gn 1,2;
θεοί *gods, idols* Is 44,15; *Prv 30,3 θεός -אל* God*
for MT לא *not*, see also 1 Sm 2,3; *Ps 7,7 ὁ θεός
μου -אלי* my God* for MT אלי *for me*, see also Ps
83(84),8; Hos 11,7; Jer 27(50),29; *1 Sm 3,13
θεόν -אלהים* God* for MT להם *themselves?*; *Dt
33,12 ὁ θεός -עליון* God* for MT עליו *over him*; *Ps
74(75),6 κατὰ τοῦ θεοῦ -ב/צור* against the Rock,
against God* for MT ב/צואר *with (insolent) neck*
Cf. BARR 1961, 151.266; HARL 1986, 49-51; JOHNSON
1938, 48-51; KATZ 1950, 141-154; LE BOULLUEC 1989,
99-101.215.230-231; WALTERS 1973, 250-255; →NIDNTT;
TWNT

θεοσέβεια,-ας⁺   N1F 1-0-0-1-5-7
Gn 20,11; Jb 28,28; 4 Mc 7,6.22; 17,15
service of God, fear of God
Cf. HARL 1986, 185-187; SPICQ 1978, 375; →NIDNTT; TWNT

θεοσεβής,-ής,-ές⁺   A 1-0-0-3-3-7
Ex 18,21; Jb 1,1.8; 2,3; Jdt 11,17
fearing God, pious

Cf. LE BOULLUEC 1989, 197; SPICQ 1978, 375; →NIDNTT; TWNT

θεοτόκος,-ος,-ον   A 0-0-0-0-1-1
Od 9,0
mother of God; neol.
→RAC (Gottesgebärerin)

θεράπαινα,-ης   N1F 3-0-1-4-0-8
Ex 11,5; 21,26.27; Is 24,2; Jb 19,15
handmaid, maidservant Ex 11,5; *Jb 31,31 αἱ
θεράπαιναι μου -אמהתי *my handmaids* for MT מתי
the men of
Cf. KRAFT 1972, 176-178

θεραπεία,-ας⁺   N1F 1-0-2-3-0-6
Gn 45,16; Jl 1,14; 2,15; Est 2,12; 5,1
attendance, homeguard Gn 45,16; ἡμέραι τῆς
θεραπείας *days of purification, days of treatment
of the body* Est 2,12; τὰ ἱμάτια τῆς θεραπείας
humble dress Est 5,1; κηρύττω θεραπείαν *to
proclaim a solemn service* Jl 1,14
Cf. HARL 1986, 80.291; THACKERAY 1909, 36; WEINFELD
1980, 394-396, esp. 395 n. 9

θεραπεύω⁺   V 0-2-1-6-17-26
2 Sm 19,25; 2 Kgs 9,16; Is 54,17; Prv 14,19; 19,6
A: *to serve* [abs.] Est 1,1b; *to serve, to worship
(God)* [τινα] Jdt 11,17; *to serve, to attend upon
(people)* [τινα] 1 Ezr 1,4; *to attend upon* [τι]
Prv 14,19; *to dress (one's feet)* 2 Sm 19,25; *to
heal* [τινα] Tob 12,3; *to take care of (one's
health)* Sir 18,19; *to repair* [τι] 1 Ezr 2,14; P: *to
get healed, to be treated medically* 2 Kgs 9,16;
θεραπεύω πρόσωπόν τινος *to wait on the favour
of sb* Prv 19,6
Cf. DANIEL 1966, 107-108.112; →MM; TWNT

θεράπων,-οντος⁺   N3M 38-4-0-11-11-64
Gn 24,44; 50,17; Ex 4,10; 5,21; 7,9
servant Gn 24,44; *member of the staff* Ex 5,21;
religious servant Ex 33,11; *servant, healer* Prv
18,14
Cf. BARR 1961, 254; DANIEL 1966, 103-104; HARL 1986,
202; KRAFT 1972, 176-177; LE BOULLUEC 1989, 110.332;
·MM

θεραφιν   N 0-10-0-0-0-10
Jgsᴬ 17,5; 18,14.17.18.20
=תרפין (Aram.?) for MT תרפים *teraphim, idols*

θερίζω⁺   V 3-4-2-15-3-27
Lv 23,10.22; 23,22; 1 Sm 6,13; 8,12
to reap Lv 23,22; *to cut down* Jb 8,12; θερίζω
τὸν θερισμόν *to reap the harvest* Lv 23,10
Cf. WALTERS 1973, 333
(·ἀπο-, ἐκ-, προ-)

θερινός,-ή,-όν   A 0-3-1-1-0-5
Jgs 3,20; Jgsᴮ 3,24; Am 3,15; Dnᵀʰ 2,35
of summer, summer-

θερισμός,-οῦ⁺   N2M 12-10-5-5-3-35
Gn 8,22; 30,14; Ex 23,16; 34,22; Lv 19,9
mowing-time, harvest Gn 30,14; *harvest, crop* Jb
14,9
Cf. LE BOULLUEC 1989, 341-342; WALTERS 1973, 227.334;
WEVERS 1990, 366; →NIDNTT; TWNT

θεριστής,-οῦ⁺   N1M 0-0-0-0-2-2
Bel 33
reaper
Cf. WALTERS 1973, 333

θέριστρον,-ου   N2N 3-1-1-1-0-6
Gn 24,65; 38,14.19; 1 Sm 13,20; Is 3,23
light summer garment, veil Gn 24,65; *1 Sm
13,20 θέριστρον corr.? θεριστήριον for MT
מחרשה *reaping-hook, harvest tool*; neol.
Cf. WALTERS 1973, 333-334

θερμαίνω⁺   V 0-3-6-3-2-14
1 Sm 11,9; 1 Kgs 1,1.2; Is 44,15.16
P: *to be warmed* 1 Kgs 1,1; *to grow hot*
(metaph.) Ps 38(39),4; θερμαίνω κοπετόν *to
lament feverishly* Sir 38,17
(→ δια-, παρα-)

θερμασία,-ας   N1F 0-0-1-1-0-2
Jer 28(51),39; Dnᴸˣˣ 3,46
warmth, heat

θερμάστρεις,-ων   N3F 0-2-0-0-0-2
1 Kgs 7,26(40).31(45)
tongs, fire iron
Cf. CAIRD 1972, 131; WALTERS 1973, 103-104

θέρμη,-ης⁺   N1F 0-0-0-2-2-4
Jb 6,17; Ps 18(19),6; Eccl 4,11; Sir 18,28
heat

θερμός,-ή,-όν   A 0-2-1-1-2-6
Jos 9,12; 1 Sm 21,7; Jer 38(31),2; Ps 18(19),7; Jb
6,17
hot, warm Jos 9,12; *hot, hot-headed, furious* Sir
23,17; θερμόν (sc. ἀφόδευμα) *warm dung* Tobˢ
2,10; *Jer 38(31),2 θερμόν -חם *warm, still alive*
for MT חן *grace*
Cf. CAIRD 1972, 132

θερμότης,-ητος   N3F 0-0-0-0-1-1
Wis 2,4
heat

θέρος,-ους⁺   N3N 1-0-2-4-1-8
Gn 8,22; Jer 8,20; Zech 14,8; Ps 73(74),17; Prv
6,8
summer

θέσις,-εως   N3F 0-1-0-0-3-4
1 Kgs 11,36; 1 Ezr 1,3; Wis 7,19.29
setting 1 Ezr 1,3; *constellation* Wis 7,19; *1 Kgs
11,36 θέσις -נור? ◊ נור *adoption* for MT ניר *lamp*
Cf. WEVERS 1950, 315-316

θεσμός,-οῦ   N2M 0-0-0-2-3-5
Prv 1,8; 6,20; 3 Mc 6,36; 4 Mc 8,7; Wis 14,23
ordinance 3 Mc 6,36; *rule* Prv 1,8; *rite* Wis 14,23

θεωρέω+   V 0-4-0-36-35-75
Jos 8,20; Jgs^A 13,19.20; Jgs^B 16,27; Ps 21(22),8
to look at, to behold, to see [τι] Jos 8,20; [τινα]
Tob 1,17; [abs.] Jgs^A 13,19; *to see in a dream* or
in a vision Dn 7,2; *to gaze at* [τινα] 1 Ezr 4,19;
to consider [τι] Ps 65(66),18; [ὅτι +ind.] 2 Mc
9,23; [+indir. question] Tob^S 9,3-4; οἱ
θεωροῦντες *the spectators* 4 Mc 17,7; *Prv 16,2
θεωρῶ ν -מראה? *seeing, causing to see* for MT מאור
light
Cf. LEE 1983, 133-134.138.140
(→ ἐπι-)

θεωρητός,-ή,-όν   A 0-0-0-1-0-1
Dn^Th 8,5
notable, to be reached in a vision

θεωρία,-ας+   N1F 0-0-0-1-3-4
Dn^LXX 5,7; 2 Mc 5,26; 15,12; 3 Mc 5,24
sight 2 Mc 15,12; *spectacle* Dn^LXX 5,7
Cf. ZIEGLER 1962, 108

θεωρός,-οῦ   N2M 0-0-0-0-1-1
2 Mc 4,19
envoy
Cf. BERGMANS 1979, 128-129

θήκη,-ης+   N1F 1-0-2-0-0-3
Ex 25,27; Is 3,26; 6,13
case, chest Is 3,26; θῆκαι *sheaths (for the poles)*
Ex 25,27
Cf. LE BOULLUEC 1989, 305; SEELIGMAN 1948, 40 (Is
6,13); WEVERS 1990, 403

θηλάζω+   V 9-5-4-8-4-30
Gn 21,7; 32,16; Ex 2,7.9(bis)
to suckle Gn 21,7; *to suck* Dt 32,13; θηλάζω
μαστούς *to suck the breasts* Jb 3,12; θηλάζων
suckling Dt 32,25
(→ ἐκ-)

θηλυκός,-ή,-όν   A 2-0-0-0-0-2
Nm 5,3; Dt 4,16
female, of women
Cf. LEE 1983, 109-110

θηλυμανής,-ής,-ές   A 0-0-1-0-0-1
Jer 5,8
lusty, mad after women; ἵπποι θηλυμανεῖς

wanton horses

θῆλυς,-εια,-υ+   A 25-3-1-4-4-37
Gn 1,27; 5,2; 6,19.20; 7,2
female, she- Gn 1,27; θήλεια ἵππος *mare* 1 Kgs
10,26; θῆλυ *woman* Ex 1,16; (ἡ) θήλεια *woman*
Lv 15,33; ἀλέκτωρ ἐμπεριπατῶν θηλείαις *a
cock walking boldly among the hens* Prv 30,31;
*Am 6,12 ἐν θηλείαις בנקבים- *among the mares*
for MT בבקרים *with oxen*
Cf. LEE 1983, 109

θήρ, θηρός   N3M 0-0-0-1-5-6
Jb 5,23; 2 Mc 4,25; 3 Mc 5,31; 6,7; 4 Mc 9,28
beast Jb 5,23; *lion* 3 Mc 6,7; θὴρ ἄγριος *wild
animal* 3 Mc 5,31
Cf. WALTERS 1973, 46

θήρα,-ας+   N1F 11-0-7-6-4-28
Gn 25,28; 27,3.5.7.19
hunting Gn 25,30; *prey, game* Ex 22,13; *gin,
snare* Ps 34(35),8; *Hos 9,13 εἰς θήραν -לצור *for
a prey* for MT לצור *for a rock?*; *Ps 131(132),15
θήραν -ציר' *prey, game* for MT ציר^II *provision*;
*Hos 5,2 τὴν θύραν -שחת *snare, (pit)* for MT שחטה
slaughter, lewdness
Cf. WALTERS 1973, 182 (Ps 131(132),15)

θήρευμα,-ατος   N3N 1-0-1-1-0-3
Lv 17,13; Jer 37(30),17; Eccl 7,26
trap, spoil, prey Lv 17,13; θηρεύματα *gin, snare*
Eccl 7,26; *Jer 37,17 θήρευμα -(ם)ציר *prey* for
MT ציון *Zion*

θηρευτής,-οῦ   N1M 0-0-1-1-1-3
Jer 16,16; Ps 90(91),3; Sir 11,30
hunter Ps 90(91),3; πέρδιξ θηρευτής *a decoy
partridge* Sir 11,30

θηρεύω+   V 4-0-3-11-1-19
Gn 27,3.5.33; Lv 17,13; Jer 5,6
A: *to hunt (after), to chase, to catch* [τι] Gn
27,3; *to hunt, to seek after* [τι] (metaph.) Ps
58(59),4; *to hunt for* [τινα] Lam 4,18; P: *to be
hunted, to be caught* Eccl 9,12; οἱ θηρεύοντες
fowlers Ps 123(124),7; *Jb 18,7 θηρεύσαισαν
-יצרו *let them chase* for MT יצרו *they form, shape?*

θηριάλωτος,-ος,-ον   A 7-0-2-0-0-9
Gn 31,39; Ex 22,12.30; Lv 5,2; 7,24
caught by wild beasts; neol.
Cf. TOV 1987, 141

θηριόβρωτος,-ος,-ον   A 1-0-0-0-0-1
Gn 44,28
eaten or *torn by wild beasts*
Cf. HARL 1986, 289

θηρίον,-ου+   N2N 29-6-40-54-35-164

Gn 1,24.25.30; 2,19.20
wild animal, beast Gn 1,24; *monster* Dnᴸˣˣ 7,3;
*2 Sm 23,11 εἰς θηρία -לחיה/ל *towards the
animals* can be understood as proper name *to
Theria* for MT לחיה *to Lechi*
→NIDNTT

θηριόομαι   V 0-0-0-0-1-1
2 Mc 5,11
to become like a wild beast, to become brutal;
neol.?

θηριώδης,-ης,-ες   A 0-0-0-0-2-2
2 Mc 10,35; 4 Mc 12,13
savage (of pers.; neg.) 4 Mc 12,13; *fierce* (of
pers.; pos.) 2 Mc 10,35

θηριωδῶς   D 0-0-0-0-1-1
2 Mc 12,15
fiercely

θησαυρίζω⁺   V 0-1-3-5-6-15
2 Kgs 20,17; Am 3,10; Mi 6,10; Zech 9,3; Ps
38(39),7
to store (up), to lay up, to treasure [τι] 2 Kgs
20,17; *to lay up treasure* [abs.] Ps 38(39),7
(→ ἀπο-)

θησαύρισμα,-ατος   N3N 0-0-0-1-0-1
Prv 21,6
treasure

θησαυρός,-οῦ⁺   N2M 3-34-22-19-15-93
Gn 43,23; Dt 28,12; 32,34; Jos 6,19.24
treasure Gn 43,23; *treasury* Jos 6,19; *granary,
magazine* Neh 10,39; θησαυροί *secret, hidden
places* Ps 134(135),7; *Jgsᴮ 18,7 θησαυρούς -◊ אצר
treasures for MT עצר *oppression?*
Cf. BICKERMAN 1980, 163; →NIDNTT; TWNT

θησαυροφύλαξ,-ακος   N3M 0-0-0-1-0-1
Ezr 5,14
treasurer

θίασος,-ου   N2M 0-0-1-0-1-2
Jer 16,5; Wis 12,5
orgy Wis 12,5; *mourning feast* Jer 16,5
Cf. LARCHER 1985, 709 (Wis 12,5)

θίβις,-εως   N3F 3-0-0-0-0-3
Ex 2,3.5.6
=תבה? *basket*; neol.?
Cf. HARL 1987, 18.31-35; LEE 1983, 115; WALTERS 1973,
163

θιγγάνω⁺   V 1-0-0-0-0-1
Ex 19,12
to touch [τι]
Cf. WEVERS 1990, 299

θιμωνιά,-ᾶς   N1F 2-0-1-2-3-8

Ex 8,10(bis); Zph 2,8; Jb 5,26; Ct 7,3
corr. θημωνιά; *heap* Jb 5,26; θιμωνιὰς
θιμωνιάς *in heaps* (semit.) Ex 8,10
Cf. LE BOULLUEC 1989, 125; WALTERS 1973, 65-66.289-
290

θίς, θινός   N3M/F 2-0-0-1-1-4
Gn 49,26; Dt 12,2; Jb 15,7; Bar 5,7
dune, mound, hill
Cf. SHIPP 1979, 270-272

θλαδίας,-ου   N1M 2-0-0-0-0-2
Lv 22,24; Dt 23,2
who is castrated, eunuch Dt 23,2; *that is
castrated, that has broken testicles* Lv 22,24; neol.
Cf. HARLÉ 1988, 186

θλάσμα,-ατος   N3N 0-0-1-0-0-1
Am 6,11
breach, bruise

θλάω   V 0-5-3-2-1-11
Jgs 10,8; 1 Sm 12,4; 2 Sm 22,39; 2 Kgs 18,21
to crush, to bruise [τινα] (of pers.) 2 Sm 22,39;
to break (down) [τι] (of things) 2 Kgs 18,21; *to
oppress* [τινα] (metaph.) Jgs 10,8
(→ κατα-, συν-)

θλίβω⁺   V 10-22-11-40-18-101
Ex 3,9; 22,20; 23,9; Lv 19,33; 25,14
A: *to compress* Wis 15,7; *to afflict, to oppress, to
press upon* [τι τινα] (of pers.) Ex 3,9; [τινί
τινα] Dt 28,53; *to oppress, to vex* [τι] (of
places) Jgsᴬᴮ 4,3; *to lay siege unto* [τι] (of a city)
2 Mc 11,5; P: *to be afflicted* Ps 68(69),18; *to be
distressed* 1 Sm 28,15; ὁ θλίβων *oppressor* Lam
1,3; *persecutor* Ps 12(13),5; τῷ θλιβῆναι αὐτόν
by the fact he was hard pressed 2 Chr 28,22;
ἔθλιψαν ἀπ' αὐτῶν τὸ ὅριον *they forcibly took
from them the border* Jos 19,47a; *Jb 36,15
ἔθλιψαν -◊ לחץ *they afflicted* for MT ◊ חלץ *set free?*;
*Is 28,15 τεθλιμμένοι -◊ צור *oppressed* for MT
לצון *of scorn*
Cf. HORSLEY 1987, 155; LE BOULLUEC 1989, 32; WEVERS
1990, 351; →TWNT
(→ ἀπο-, ἐκ-, παρα-, προσ-, συν-)

θλιμμός,-οῦ   N2M 2-0-0-0-0-2
Ex 3,9; Dt 26,7
oppression, affliction (metaph.); neol.
Cf. LE BOULLUEC 1989, 91

θλῖψις,-εως⁺   N3F 10-18-35-45-26-134
Gn 35,3; 42,21(bis); Ex 4,31; Dt 28,53
oppression, affliction Gn 35,3; *anguish* Gn 42,21;
distress 1 Sm 24,20; *Mi 2,12 ἐν θλίψει -בצרה *in
trouble* for MT בצרה *in the fold*; *Na 2,2 ἐκ

θλίψεως -מ/צרה from *affliction* for MT מצורה *ramparts, fortification*; *Hos 7,12 τῆς θλίψεως αὐτῶν -צרתם? *of their affliction* for MT ערתם *their congregation*; *Is 28,10 θλίψιν -צר *affliction* for MT צו *precept*?, see also Is 28,13; *Jer 11,16 ἡ θλῖψις-הצתה *the affliction* for MT הצית *he sets fire* (double translation)

Cf. WALTERS 1973, 96; → NIDNTT; TWNT

θνησιμαῖον,-ου N2N 22-3-6-1-0-32
Lv 5,2(ter); 7,24; 11,8
carcass of an animal Lv 5,2; *dead body, carcass* (of a pers.) Dt 14,8; *animal which has died of itself* (opp. θηριάλωτος) Lv 17,15; neol.

Cf. HARLÉ 1988, 100 (Lv 17,15)

θνήσκω⁺ V 17-49-3-9-19-97
Gn 50,15; Ex 4,19; 12,30; 14,30; 21,35
to die Wis 18,18; θανοῦμαι *shall die* Prv 13,14; τέθνηκα *to be dead* Gn 50,15; ὁ τεθνηκώς *the deceased, the dead* Ru 4,5; οἱ τεθνηκότες *the dead* Nm 17,13; τεθνήξῃ πρὸ ὥρας *you will perish yourself prematurely* 4 Mc 12,4

Cf. WALTERS 1973, 127.315

(→ προσαπο-, ἀνταπο-, ἀπο-, ἐναπο-, προαπο-, συναπο-)

θνητός,-ή,-όν⁺ A 0-0-1-3-5-9
Is 51,12; Jb 30,23; Prv 3,13; 20,24; 2 Mc 9,12
mortal Wis 7,1; ὁ θνητός *mortal man* Jb 30,23; πᾶσα θνητὴ φύσις *every living being* 3 Mc 3,29

θοῖνα,-ης N1F 0-0-0-0-2-2
3 Mc 5,31; Wis 12,5
meal, feast

θολερός,-ά,-όν A 0-0-1-0-0-1
Hab 2,15
turbid, cloudy

θορυβέω⁺ V 0-2-1-2-2-7
Jgs 3,26; Na 2,4; Dnᴸˣˣ 8,17; Ezr 10,9
A: *to trouble* [τινα] Wis 18,19; P: *to be in trouble, to be confusion* Na 2,4; *to be bewildered with awe* Dnᴸˣˣ 8,17

θόρυβος,-ου⁺ N2M 0-0-4-3-3-10
Jer 30,18(49,2); Ez 7,4(7).11; Mi 7,12; Prv 1,27
noise (mostly of a crowd) Est 1,1; *murmur* Jdt 6,1; *tumult, confusion* Ezr 10,9; τίνι θόρυβος; *who has trouble?* Prv 23,29; βαρυηχὴς θόρυβος *deep-roaring crowd* 3 Mc 5,48

Cf. KRAFT 1972, 166 (Prv 23,29)

θραελ N 0-0-1-0-0-1
Ez 41,8
=תראל? (*unidentified*) *part of the temple* for MT ראיתי *I saw*

θράσος,-ους N3N 0-0-1-1-12-14
Est 3,13b; Jdt 16,10; 1 Mc 4,32; 2 Mc 5,18; 3 Mc 2,26
audacity, boldness, hardiness (in pos. sense) 3 Mc 2,4; *confidence* 3 Mc 2,2; *over-boldness, insolence* (in bad sense) Jdt 16,10; *audacious presumption* 2 Mc 5,18; θράσος ἰσχύος *confidence in strength* 1 Mc 4,32; θράσει *courageously* 1 Mc 6,45; *Ez 19,7 τῷ θράσει αὐτοῦ -◇אלם? (Aram. *to be strong*) *in his boldness* for MT אלמנותיו *their widows*

θρασυκάρδιος,-ος,-ον A 0-0-0-2-0-2
Prv 14,14; 21,4
bold-hearted, stout-hearted

θρασύνομαι V 0-0-0-0-2-2
3 Mc 1,22.26
to take courage

θρασύς,-εῖα,-ύ A 1-0-0-5-5-11
Nm 13,28; Prv 9,13; 13,17; 18,6; 21,24
mostly in neg. sense: over-bold, rash Prv 13,17; *bold, arrogant, insolent* (of pers.) Prv 9,13; *fierce* (of animals) Wis 11,17; *strong, bold* (in pos. sense) Nm 13,28;

θραῦσις,-εως N3F 4-5-0-2-1-12
Nm 17,12.13.14.15; 2 Sm 17,9
destruction, slaughter 2 Kgs 17,9; *plague* Nm 17,12

θραῦσμα,-ατος N3N 15-0-0-0-2-17
Lv 13,30.31(bis).32(bis)
destruction (of pers.) Jdt 13,5; *break, lesion* (in the skin), *patch where the hair has fallen out* (of leprosy) Lv 13,30

Cf. BARBER 1968, 72; HARLÉ 1988, 138

θραυσμός,-οῦ N2M 0-0-1-0-0-1
Na 2,11
breaking (metaph.); neol.

θραύω⁺ V 5-4-8-0-7-24
Ex 15,6; Nm 17,11; 24,17; Dt 20,3; 28,33
A: *to break* [τι] 2 Chr 20,37; *to strike* [τι] Is 2,10; *to shatter* [τινα] Ex 15,6; *to smite* [τινα] 2 Sm 12,15; *to break down* [τι] (metaph.) Jdt 9,10; P: *to enfeeble* (metaph.) Dt 20,3; ἐθραύσθην ἐπί τινα *to be grieved for* 1 Sm 20,34

θρεπτός,-ή,-όν A 0-0-0-1-0-1
Est 2,7
brought up; παῖς θρεπτή *foster-child*

Cf. CAMERON 1939, 27-62

θρηνέω⁺ V 0-5-17-2-6-30
Jgs 11,40; 2 Sm 1,17; 3,33; 2 Chr 35,25

to wail, to mourn [abs.] Mi 1,8; *to bewail, to mourn for* [τινα] Jgs 11,40; *to mourn over* [ἐπί τινα] 2 Sm 3,33; *to lament for* [ὑπέρ τινος] Ezr 1,30; θρηνέω θρῆνον ἐπί τινα *to lament with lamentations over, to utter a lamentation over* 2 Sm 1,17

→TWNT

θρήνημα,-ατος   N3N 0-0-1-0-0-1
Ez 27,32
lament

θρῆνος,-ου⁺   N2M 0-3-20-1-9-33
2 Sm 1,17; 2 Chr 35,25(bis); Is 14,4; Jer 7,29
lamentation 2 Sm 1,17; οἱ θρῆνοι *lamentations, wailings* 2 Chr 35,25

→TWNT

θρησκεία,-ας⁺   N1F 0-0-0-0-4-4
4 Mc 5,7.13; Wis 14,18.27
cult, service of idols
Cf. DANIEL 1966, 112; SPICQ 1978, 379-383

θρησκεύω   V 0-0-0-0-2-2
Wis 11,15; 14,17
to worship [τι]
Cf. DANIEL 1966, 112

θρίξ, τριχός⁺   N3F 23-8-2-11-7-51
Ex 25,4; 35,6.26(bis); 36,10(39,3)
(mostly of the head) *a single hair* Prv 23,7; *hair* (coll. sg.) Lv 13,3; *thread* Ex 36,10; τρίχες αἰγείαι *goats' hair* Ex 25,4; αἱ τρίχες *the hairs of a ram, wool* Nm 6,18; αἱ τρίχες τῶν ποδῶν *hairs of the feet* Is 7,20; πρὸς τρίχα *by a hair's breadth, exactly* Jgs 20,16; *Prv 23,7 τρίχα -שער *hair* (eating and drinking with him is as if one should swallow a hair) for MT שער *estimate?*
Cf. LE BOULLUEC 1989, 353 (Ex 36,10); MCKANE 1970, 384-385

θροέω⁺   V 0-0-0-1-0-1
Ct 5,4
to stir, to move; ἡ κοιλία μου ἐθροήθη ἐπ᾽ αὐτόν *my belly was moved for him, I was thrilled by him*

θρονίζω   V 0-0-0-1-0-1
Est 1,2
to enthrone [τινα]; neol.
(→ ἐν-)

θρόνος,-ου⁺   N2M 3-62-29-42-27-163
Gn 41,40; Ex 11,5; 12,29; Jgs 3,20
throne, seat Gn 41,40; *throne (of glory)* (metaph.) 1 Sm 2,8; *throne, judge's bench* Ps 9,5; *throne, kingdom* 1 Kgs 2,33; δίδωμί τινα ἐπὶ τοῦ θρόνου *to set sb upon the throne* 1 Kgs 3,6;

θρόνος κυρίου *the throne of the Lord* Jer 3,17; *Prv 12,23 θρόνος αἰσθήσεως -כסה דעת *a throne of wisdom* for MT כסה דעת *he conceals (his) wisdom*
→TWNT

θροῦς,θροῦ   N2M 0-0-0-0-2-2
1 Mc 9,39; Wis 1,10
noise Wis 1,10; *bustle, hubbub* 1 Mc 9,39

θρυλέω   V 0-0-0-1-2-3
Jb 31,30; 3 Mc 3,6.7
A: *to repeat over and over* [τι] 3 Mc 3,7; P: *to be common talk* 3 Mc 3,6; *Jb 31,30 θρυληθείην -למשל *let be a byword* for MT לשאל *to ask*

θρύλημα,-ατος   N3N 0-0-0-2-0-2
Jb 17,6; 30,9
byword; neol.

θρύπτω
(→ δια-, ἐν-)

θυγάτηρ, θυγατρός⁺   N3F 183-164-122-85-87-641
Gn 5,4.7.10.13.16
daughter Gn 5,4; *young (of animals)* Is 43,20; θυγατέρες *dependent villages* Jgs 1,27; θυγάτηρ Σιών *city of Sion* (personification) Ps 9,15; *Ez 16,30 τὴν θυγατέρα σου -לבתך ◊ בת *your daughter* for MT לבתך ◊ לב *your hearts*
→TWAT (בת)

θύελλα,-ης⁺   N1F 3-0-0-0-0-3
Ex 10,22; Dt 4,11; 5,22
hurricane, storm
Cf. WEVERS 1990, 156

θυία,-ας   N1F 1-0-0-0-0-1
Nm 11,8
mortar

θυίσκη,-ης   N1F 18-4-1-0-2-25
Ex 25,29; 38,12(37,16); Nm 4,7; 7,14.20
censer; neol.
Cf. WEVERS 1990, 404

θυλάκιον,-ου   N2N 0-0-0-0-2-2
Tob 9,5
dim. of θύλακος; *small bag, small sack*

θύλακος,-ου   N2M 0-1-0-0-0-1
2 Kgs 5,23
bag, sack

θῦμα,-ατος   N3N 5-4-4-2-0-15
Gn 43,16; Ex 29,28; 34,15.25; Dt 18,3
sacrifice, offering Ex 29,28; *victim* (esp. of animals) Ez 40,41; *animals slaughtered* (for food) Gn 43,16; θύω τὰ θύματα *to offer sacrifices* Dt 18,3

Cf. BICKERMAN 1980, 96-97

θυμέω
(→ ἐν-, ἐπι-, προ-)

θυμήρης,-ης,-ες   A 0-0-0-0-1-1
Wis 3,14
well-pleasing

θυμίαμα,-ατος⁺   N3N 45-10-9-5-12-81
Gn 37,25; 43,11; Ex 30,1.7.8
incense Gn 43,11; θυμιάματα *fragrant stuffs* or
spices, perfumes Gn 37,25; τὸ θυσιαστήριον
τῶν θυμιαμάτων *altar of incense offerings* 1 Chr
6,34; *Ex 23,18 θυμίαμα corr. θυσίασμα *victim*
Cf. DANIEL 1966, 156.177.205.217; LE BOULLUEC 1989, 45;
WEVERS 1990, 368.650; →NIDNTT

θυμιατήριον,-ου⁺   N2N 0-1-1-0-1-3
2 Chr 26,19; Ez 8,11; 4 Mc 7,11
censer

θυμιάω⁺   V 5-38-23-1-3-70
Ex 30,7(bis).8; 40,5.27
A: *to burn incense* [abs.] Ex 30,8; *to burn so as
to produce a sweet fragrance, to offer by way of
incense* [τι] 1 Sm 2,16; P: *to be burnt for a sweet
fragrance* 1 Sm 2,15; θυμιάζω θυμίαμα *to burn
incense* Ex 30,7; τεθυμιαμένη σμύρναν
perfumed with myrrh Ct 3,6
Cf. DANIEL 1966, 205

θυμός,-οῦ⁺   N2M 34-34-118-72-74-332
Gn 27,44; 49,6.7; Ex 11,8; 15,8
soul Prv 6,34; *spirit* Lv 26,24; *mind* 2 Kgs 24,3;
temper 2 Mc 4,25; *sorrow* Eccl 7,3; *anger, wrath*
Gn 27,44; *fury, rage* Is 51,17; *rage* (of animals)
Prv 20,2; *angry emotion* 4 Mc 2,20; *violence*
(metaph.) Jb 6,4; *poison* Jb 20,16; ὀργὴ θυμοῦ
anger of the heart Nm 12,9; θυμὸς ὀργῆς *fierce
anger* 1 Sm 28,18; ἐν θυμῷ *in a rage* 2 Kgs 5,12;
ὀργίζομαι θυμῷ *to be angry with all his heart,
to be very angry* Ex 22,23; ἐκστρέφω εἰς θυμὸν
κρίμα *to turn judgement into poison* Am 6,13;
*Zech 10,4 ἐν θυμῷ -מלחמה/מ in anger for MT מלחמה
(of) war*; *Jb 13,13 θημοῦ -המה anger for MT מה
what*
Cf. FLASHAR 1912, 263-264; HARLÉ 1988, 207-208

θυμόω   V 19-24-9-8-6-66
Gn 6,7; 30,2; 39,19; 44,18; Ex 4,14
A: *to make angry, to provoke* Hos 12,15; P: *to be
angry* 2 Sm 13,21; *to be angry with* [τινι] Gn
30,2; [εἴς τινα] Ex 32,10; [ἔν τινι] 2 Kgs
17,18; [ἐπί τι] Hos 11,7; [ἐπί τινα] Ex 4,14;
[ἐπί τινι] Dt 9,8; [κατά τινα] 4 Mc 2,17;
[πρός τινα] 2 Chr 26,19; *to be inflamed, to*

become aggressive Hos 7,5; *to be enraged with*
[τι] Is 37,29; *to be enraged* (metaph.) Is 13,13;
to seethe 2 Kgs 23,26; *to be indignant at* [ἐπί τι]
Dnᵀʰ 11,30; ἐθυμώθην ὀργῇ *to be very angry* Gn
39,19; *Ez 21,14 θυμώθητι *rage* corr.?
ἑτοιμάσθητι *be ready;* *Hos 11,7 θυμωθήσεται
-יחד ◊ חרה *he shall be angry* for MT יחד *all, together?*
Cf. LARCHER 1984, 394.473-474; WALTERS 1973, 326 (Ez
21,14)

θυμώδης,-ης,-ες   A 0-0-1-5-2-8
Jer 37(30),23; Prv 11,25; 15,18; 22,24; 29,22
passionate Prv 11,25; *furious, angry* Prv 29,22;
wrathful Jer 37(30),23; *Prv 31,4 θυμώδεις
εἰσίν -ל *they are prone to anger* for MT אל ל *it
is not for ...*

θύρα,-ας⁺   N1F 82-73-18-29-37-239
Gn 6,16; 18,1.2.10; 19,6
door Gn 19,6; *door* (of a furnace) Dnᵀʰ 3,93;
double or *folding doors, the valve* (of a gate) Jgs
9,35; *door* (metaph.) Ps 140(141),3; *sluices of
heaven* Ps 77(78),23; *mouth* Zech 11,1; *doorway*
2 Kgs 6,32; *the panel* (of the door) 1 Kgs 6,34;
αἱ θύραι τῆς πόλεως *city-gate* 1 Sm 21,14

θυρεός,-οῦ⁺   N2M 0-16-3-4-0-23
Jgsᴮ 5,8; 2 Sm 1,21(bis); 2 Kgs 19,32; 1 Chr 12,9
oblong shield (shaped like a door)

θυρεοφόρος,-ος,-ον   A 0-1-0-0-0-1
1 Chr 12,25
armed with the oblong shield; neol.?

θυρίς,-ίδος⁺   N3F 2-11-16-4-4-37
Gn 8,6; 26,8; Jos 2,15.18; Jgsᴬ 5,28
window Gn 8,6; θυρίδες κρυπταί *niches?,
windows wide within and narrow outside?* Ez
40,16, cpr. 1 Kgs 6,4
Cf. HUSSON 1983, 117-118; 1983 (A), 155-162

θυρόω   V 0-0-0-0-1-1
1 Mc 4,57
to furnish with (folding) doors [τι]

θύρσος,-ου   N2M 0-0-0-0-2-2
Jdt 15,12; 2 Mc 10,7
*branch, wand wreathed in ivy and vine-leaves
with a pine-cone at the top*

θύρωμα,-ατος   N3N 0-7-14-0-3-24
1 Kgs 6,31; 7,36(50).42(5)(bis); 1 Chr 22,3
doorway 1 Kgs 6,31; *panel* 1 Kgs 7,36(50); *door*
1 Chr 22,3
Cf. CAIRD 1972, 132

θυρωρός,-οῦ⁺   N2M 0-2-1-0-7-10
2 Sm 4,6; 2 Kgs 7,11; Ez 44,11; 1 Ezr 1,15; 5,28
porter

θυσία,-ας⁺   N1F 180-63-51-45-56-395
Gn 4,3.5; 31,54; 46,1; Ex 10,25
sacrifice Gn 4,3; *meat-offering* Lv 14,31; *victim*
Lv 17,5; *the act of offering* Nm 23,3; *sacrificial
food* 2 Mc 1,23; θυσίαι *offerings* Gn 4,5; θύω
θυσίαν *to offer a sacrifice* Gn 31,54; θυσιάζω
θυσίαν 2 Chr 33,16; *2 Sm 14,17 εἰς θυσίας
-למנחה/ל*for an offering?* for MT למנחה/ל*(set) at rest,*
see also Zech 9,1; *Jb 20,6 θυσία αὐτοῦ
-אשי/ אשה his sacrifice for MT ראש√ his head
Cf. BARR 1961, 152 n.1.155-156; DANIEL 1966, 203-246;
MURAOKA 1990, 46-47; O'CALLAGHAN 1980, 325-330;
→TWNT

θυσιάζω   V 3-17-4-6-12-42
Ex 22,19; Lv 7,16; 24,9; Jgsᴮ 2,5; 2 Sm 15,12
to sacrifice Ex 22,20; θυσιάζω θυσίασμα *to
offer a sacrifice* Ezr 6,3; θυσιάζω θυσίαν 2 Chr
33,16; τῶν μνημάτων τῶν θυσιαζόντων *of the
tombs of those who had sacrificed* 2 Chr 34,4;
θυσιάζων σωτηρίου *offering a peace-offering* Sir
35,1
Cf. DANIEL 1966, 161; LARCHER 1985, 1002; SHENKEL
1968, 17

θυσίασμα,-ατος   N3N 6-2-0-2-0-10
Ex 23,18; 29,18; Lv 2,13; Nm 18,9; Dt 12,6
victim Ex 23,18; *offering* Nm 18,9; neol.
Cf. DANIEL 1966, 156; LE BOULLUEC 1989, 45.297-298

θυσιαστήριον,-ου⁺   N2N 184-154-43-10-46-437

Gn 8,20(bis); 12,7.8; 13,4
altar (mostly of the true God; opp. βωμός) Gn
8,20; *Hos 4,19 ἐκ τῶν θυσιαστηρίων αὐτῶν
מ/זבחותם/מ/מזבחותם *because of their altars* for MT מ/זבחותם
because of their sacrifices
Cf. DANIEL 1966, 27-31.203.241-242.252.255.367; KLAUCK
1980, 274-277; MURAOKA 1990, 46

θύω⁺   V 40-52-18-10-17-137
Gn 31,54; 46,1; Ex 3,18; 5,3.8
to offer, to sacrifice Gn 31,54; *to slay, to
slaughter, to kill* Ex 12,21
Cf. DANIEL 1966, 166.203.221; KILPATRICK 1961, 130-132;
LE BOULLUEC 1989, 150; SHIPP 1979, 274; →NIDNTT
(→ ἐπι-)

θωδαθα   N 0-0-0-1-0-1
Neh 12,27
=תודות *hymns of praise*

θωρακίζω   V 0-0-0-0-3-3
1 Mc 4,7; 6,35.43
to arm with a corslet, to harness [τι] 1 Mc 4,7; *to
arm with* [τινι] 1 Mc 6,43

θωρακισμός,-οῦ   N2M 0-0-0-0-1-1
2 Mc 5,3
arming with breastplates; neol.

θώραξ,-ακος⁺   N3M 0-5-3-3-5-16
1 Sm 17,5(bis); 1 Kgs 22,34; 2 Chr 18,33; 26,14
breastplate 1 Sm 17,5; *Jb 41,5 θώρακος סרינו
breastplate for MT רסנו *his bridle*

ιααρ   N 0-1-0-0-0-1
1 Sm 14,25
=יער wood (rendered twice, the second time by
δρυμός)

ἴαμα,-ατος⁺   N3N 0-1-5-1-3-10
2 Chr 36,16; Is 26,19; 58,8; Jer 26(46),11;
37(30),17
remedy 2 Chr 36,16; healing Is 58,8; soothing
Eccl 10,4; ἰάματα medicines Jer 26(46),11

ιαμιβιν   N 0-1-0-0-0-1
2 Kgs 12,10
=-בימין for MT המזבח בימין the altar at the right side

ιαμιν   N 0-1-0-0-0-1
2 Kgs 25,14
=יעין for MT יעים shovels (for cleaning the altar)

ἰάομαι⁺   V 9-8-24-14-12-67
Gn 20,17; Ex 15,26; Lv 14,3.48; Nm 12,13
M: to heal Gn 20,17; to repair, to restore Hos
14,5; to quench 4 Mc 3,10; to soothe (of pain) Is
30,26; to purify 2 Kgs 2,21; to deliver 2 Chr 7,14;
to forgive 2 Chr 30,20; P: to be removed from
[ἀπό τινος] (of a disease) Lv 14,3; to be healed,
to recover 1 Sm 6,3; οἱ ἰώμενοι those who need
correction Prv 26,18; ὁ ἰώμενός σε your healer
Ex 15,26; *Jb 12,21 ἰάσατο -רפא he heals for MT
רפה he slackens, see also Prv 18,9; *Is 7,4(5)
ἰάσομαι -ארפא I will heal for MT אפרים? Ephraim
·TWNT

ἴασις,-εως⁺   N3F 0-0-9-9-10-28
Is 19,22; Jer 8,15.22; 14,19(bis)
healing, remedy Jdt 5,12; health Jb 18,14

ἴασπις,-ιδος⁺   N3F 2-0-2-0-0-4
Ex 28,18; 36,18(39,11); Is 54,12; Ez 28,13
jasper (precious stone)
Cf. WEVERS 1990, 453

ἰατής,-οῦ   N1M 0-0-0-1-0-1
Jb 13,4
healer

ἰατρεία,-ας   N1F 0-1-1-0-0-2
2 Chr 21,18; Jer 31(48),2
healing, recovery 2 Chr 21,18; *Jer 31(48),2
ἰατρεία Μωαβ -מואב חעלת healing of Moab for MT
מואב תהלת glory of Moab

ἰατρεῖα,-ων   N2N 1-0-0-0-0-1
Ex 21,19
expense of a cure, doctor's fee
Cf. LE BOULLUEC 1989, 219; PRIJS 1948, 10

ἰατρεύω   V 0-4-4-0-0-8
2 Kgs 8,29; 9,15; 2 Chr 22,6.9; Jer 28(51),9
A: to treat medically, to treat for healing Jer 28,9;

to heal Jer 40(33),6; P: to be healed 2 Kgs 8,29

ἰατρός,-οῦ⁺   N2M 0-1-2-3-8-14
2 Chr 16,12; Is 26,14; Jer 8,22; Ps 87(88),11; Jb
13,4
physician 2 Chr 16,12; healer Prv 14,30; *Ps
87(88),11 ἰατροί -רפאים healers for MT רפאים shades, ghosts, see also Is 26,14

ἶβις,-εως   N3F 2-0-1-0-0-3
Lv 11,17; Dt 14,16; Is 34,11
ibis Lv 11,17; ἴβεις ibises (an Egyptian bird,
incarnation of Thot) Is 34,11

ιγλααμ   V 0-1-0-0-0-1
1 Chr 8,7
=הגלם took them into exile

ἰγνύα,-ης   N1F 0-1-0-0-0-1
1 Kgs 18,21
the part behind the thigh and knee, ham;
χωλαίνω ἐπ' ἀμφοτέραις ταῖς ἰγνύαις to halt
on both feet 1 Kgs 18,21

ἰδέ⁺
imper. aor. of ὁράω
Cf. WALTERS 1973, 100.303.335

ἰδέα,-ας   N1F 1-0-0-3-4-8
Gn 5,3; Dnᵀʰ 1,13(bis).15; 2 Mc 3,16
form, appearance Gn 5,3; countenance Dnᵀʰ
1,13; ἰδέαι forms 4 Mc 1,14; ὁράω τὴν ἰδέαν
τινός to look sb in the face 2 Mc 3,16
Cf. HARL 1986, 121

ἰδιόγραφος,-ος,-ον   A 0-0-0-0-1-1
Ps 151,1
written with one's own hand, genuine

ἰδιοποιέομαι   V 0-1-0-0-0-1
2 Sm 15,6
to win over [τι]

ἴδιος,-α,-ον⁺   A 4-0-1-21-53-79
Gn 14,14; 15,13; 47,18; Dt 15,2; Ez 21,35
own, one's (own) Gn 14,14; peculiar, proper Wis
19,6; ἐκ τῶν ἰδίων out of his own house 1 Ezr
6,31; τὰ ἴδια your own (property) Prv 20,25; οἱ
ἴδιοι your own men 2 Mc 12,22; ἰδίᾳ privately
Jb 6,13; κατ' ἰδίαν private, apart 2 Mc 4,5;
λαβὼν ἰδίᾳ taking apart 2 Mc 4,34; *Prv 5,18
ἰδίᾳ -לבדך? your own for MT ברוך blessed
Cf. LARCHER 1985, 1054-1055; MILLIGAN 1980, 25; SPICQ
1982, 337

ἰδιότης,-ητος   N3F 0-0-0-0-1-1
3 Mc 7,17
specific character
Cf. LARCHER 1983, 268-270

ἰδιώτης,-ου⁺   N1F 0-0-0-1-0-1

Prv 6,8
private man
Cf. SPICQ 1978, 384

ἰδιωτικός,-ή,-όν A 0-0-0-0-2-2
4 Mc 4,3.6
private

ἰδού⁺ I 186-409-362-137-51-1145
Gn 1,29.31; 3,22; 6,13.17
lo, behold Gn 1,29; ἰδού ἐγώ *here am I* Gn
27,1; *Ex 18,6 ἰδού -הנה *behold* for MT אני *I*, cpr.
Gn 48,2; *Jb 3,3 ἰδού -הרי? *behold* for MT הרה
conceive; *Jgsᴮ 16,13 ἰδού -הנה *behold* for MT
עד הנה *until now*, cpr. Jgsᴬ 16,13 ἕως νῦν; *1 Sm
27,8 ἰδού -הנה *behold* for MT הנה *they*, see also
2 Sm 4,6; 2 Kgs 4,40; 2 Chr 8,9
Cf. LE BOULLUEC 1989, 117.167; LEE 1983, 51; WEVERS
1990, 30.32

ἰδρόω V 0-0-0-0-2-2
4 Mc 3,8; 6,11
to sweat

ἰδρύω V 0-0-0-0-1-1
4 Mc 17,3
to build a roof upon a house
(→ καθ-)

ἰδρώς,-ῶτος⁺ N3M 1-0-0-0-2-3
Gn 3,19; 2 Mc 2,26; 4 Mc 7,8
sweat

ἱέραξ,-ακος N3M 2-0-0-1-0-3
Lv 11,16; Dt 14,17; Jb 39,26
hawk, falcon

ἱερατεία,-ας⁺ N1F 9-2-1-4-1-17
Ex 29,9; 35,19; 39(41),18; 40,15; Nm 3,10
priesthood, priestly office Ex 29,9; ἱερατεία
λαοῦ *priesthood among the people* Sir 45,7
Cf. LE BOULLUEC 1989, 281; →TWNT

ἱεράτευμα,-ατος⁺ N3N 2-0-0-0-1-3
Ex 19,6; 23,22; 2 Mc 2,17
priesthood
Cf. LE BOULLUEC 1989, 200.281; WEVERS 1990, 295

ἱερατεύω⁺ V 16-4-2-0-4-26
Ex 28,1.3.4.41; 29,1
*to hold the office of a priest, to perform the
service of a priest* [abs.] Nm 16,10; *to minister as
priest, to minister in the priest's office* [τινι] Ex
28,1
Cf. HORSLEY 1987, 156; LE BOULLUEC 1989, 281; WEVERS
1990, 466.500

ἱερατικός,-ή,-όν A 0-0-0-0-3-3
1 Ezr 4,54; 5,44; 2 Mc 3,15
priestly

ἱερεία,-ας N1F 0-1-0-0-0-1
2 Kgs 10,20
sacrifice, (solemn) festival

ἱερεύς,-εως⁺ N3M 313-284-90-89-124-900
Gn 14,18; 41,45.50; 46,20; 47,22
priest (Israelite) Lv 1,5; (non-Israelite, pagan) 2
Kgs 10,19; ὁ ἱερεύς ὁ μέγας *high priest* Lv
21,10; *Am 3,12 ἱερεῖς corr.? ἔρες for MT ערש
bed
Cf. HARLÉ 1988, 28; LE BOULLUEC 1989, 281;
THACKERAY 1909, 37 (Am 3,12); →TWNT

ἱερόδουλος,-ου N2M 0-0-0-0-7-7
1 Ezr 1,3; 5,29.35; 8,5.22
servant of the temple, attending the Levites
(always rendering נתנים *Nethinim*) 1 Ezr 8,22;
*1 Ezr 1,3 τοῖς Λευίταις ἱεροδούλοις
-ללוים הנתנים *to the Levites, the servants of the
temple* for MT (2 Chr 35,3) ללוי המבונים *to the
Levites who were teaching*
Cf. OTTO 1949, 10-12

ἱερόν,-ου N2N
see ἱερός

ἱεροπρεπής,-ής,-ές⁺ A 0-0-0-0-2-2
4 Mc 9,25; 11,20
befitting a sacred thing, holy 4 Mc 11,20; *befitting
a sacred person, revered* 4 Mc 9,25
Cf. SPICQ 1978, 387-388

ἱερός,-ά,-όν⁺ A 0-4-3-3-106-116
Jos 6,8; 1 Chr 9,27; 29,4; 2 Chr 6,13; Ez 27,6
sacred, holy Jos 6,8; *pious* 4 Mc 7,4; ἡ ἱερά
βίβλος *the holy book* 2 Mc 8,23; τὸ ἱερόν
(pagan) sanctuary, temple Belᵀʰ 22; *the Jewish
temple* (mostly after the Maccabean revolt,
earlier: τὸ ἅγιον) 2 Mc 3,2; *Ez 27,6 τὰ ἱερά
σου -קרשך *your sacred ustensils* or *your temple(s)*
for MT קרשך *your deck*?
Cf. BARR 1961, 282-287; BICKERMAN 1980, 211; HORSLEY
1983, 64; 1987, 111; →TWNT

ἱεροστάτης,-ου N1M 0-0-0-0-1-1
1 Ezr 7,2
governor of the temple

ἱεροσυλέω⁺ V 0-0-0-0-1-1
2 Mc 9,2
to rob a (the) temple

ἱεροσύλημα,-ατος N3N 0-0-0-0-1-1
2 Mc 4,39
sacrilegious plunder; neol.

ἱεροσυλία,-ας N1F 0-0-0-0-1-1
2 Mc 13,6
temple-robbery, sacrilege

Cf. BICKERMAN 1980, 223 n. 89

ἱερόσυλος,-ου⁺   N2M 0-0-0-0-1-1
2 Mc 4,42
temple-robber

ἱερουργία,-ας   N1F 0-0-0-0-1-1
4 Mc 3,20
religious service
Cf. BICKERMAN 1980, 304 n. 56

ἱεροψάλτης,-ου   N1M 0-0-0-0-6-6
1 Ezr 1,15; 5,27.45; 8,5.22
singer in the temple, holy singer; neol.?
Cf. BICKERMAN 1980, 60-61

ἱερόψυχος,-ος,-ον   A 0-0-0-0-1-1
4 Mc 17,4
of pious soul

ἱερόω
(→ ἀν-, ἀφ-)

ἱέρωμα,-ατος   N3N 0-0-0-0-1-1
2 Mc 12,40
(small) idol, amulet
Cf. ROBERT 1981, 517-519

ἱερωσύνη,-ης   N1F 0-1-0-0-7-8
1 Chr 29,22; 1 Ezr 5,38; 1 Mc 2,54; 3,49; 7,9
priesthood 1 Chr 29,22; ἵστημί τινι τὴν
ἱερωσύνην *to make sb high-priest* 1 Mc 7,9
Cf. WALTERS 1973, 319

ἵημι
(→ ἀφ-, δι-, ἐν-, ἐναφ-, ἐξαφ-, ἐπαφ-, καθ-,
παρ-, προ-, προσ-, συν-)

ἴθι
imper. of εἶμι, inf. ἰέναι

ἱκανόομαι   V 5-4-3-1-1-14
Gn 32,11; Nm 16,7; Dt 1,6; 2,3; 3,26
to be sufficient Gn 32,11; *to be satisfied* Mal
3,10; *to be contented with* [ἔν τινι] Est 4,17ο;
ἱκανούσθω ὑμῖν *let it suffice you to* [+inf.] Dt
1,6; ἱκανούμενος χείλεσιν καὶ ὀδοῦσιν
suiting the lips and teeth, delicious Ct 7,10
Cf. SPICQ 1982, 345-350

ἱκανός,-ή,-όν⁺   A 9-3-8-7-19-46
Gn 30,15; 33,15; Ex 4,10; 12,4; 36,7
sufficient, adequate, suited Sir prol.,11; *well
suited* Ex 4,10; *sufficient, enough, many, great*
Hab 2,13; ἱκανὸν ὅτι *it's enough that* Gn
30,15; τὸ ἱκανόν *what's enough* or *sufficient* Prv
25,16; ἰσχύω τὸ ἱκανόν *to afford* Lv 5,7;
εὑρίσκω τὸ ἱκανόν *to afford* Lv 12,8; κλέπτω
τὰ ἱκανά *to steal just enough* Ob 1,5; οἱ ἱερεῖς
ἱκανοί *a sufficient number of priests* 2 Chr 30,3;
ἱκανός εἰμι ἐν τοῖς ἔτεσι *to be of a sufficient*

age 1 Mc 16,3; ἐφ' ἱκανόν *for a good space, far*
2 Mc 7,5; ὁ ἱκανός *the Mighty one*, (lit.) *he who
is sufficient, competent* Ru 1,20.21; ἀφ' ἱκανοῦ
as often as 2 Kgs 4,8; *Jer 31(48),30 ἱκανὸν
αὐτοῦ -ברין/ *enough for him* for MT ברין *his
boasting*
Cf. BERTRAM 1958, 20-31; HARL 1986, 229.240-241; LE
BOULLUEC 1989, 98; SPICQ 1982, 345-350; TOV 1976, 540;
ZORELL 1927, 215-219

ἱκανῶς   D 0-0-0-1-1-2
Jb 9,31; 3 Mc 1,4
sufficiently, fully Jb 9,31; *often* 3 Mc 1,4

ἱκετεία,-ας   N1F 0-0-0-0-7-7
2 Mc 3,18; 8,29; 10,25; 12,42; 3 Mc 5,25
supplication (unto) [τινος] 2 Mc 10,25; εἰς
ἱκετείαν τρέπομαι *to turn to supplication*
2 Mc 12,42; ἱκετείαν ποιέομαι *to supplicate*
2 Mc 8,29

ἱκετεύω   V 0-0-0-2-7-9
Ps 36(37),7; Jb 19,17; 2 Mc 11,6; 3 Mc 5,51; 6,14
to supplicate, to beseech, to entreat [abs.] 4 Mc
16,13; [τινα] Jb 19,17; *to beseech sb that* [τινα
+inf.] 2 Mc 11,6

ἱκετηρία,-ας   N1F 0-0-0-1-1-2
Jb 40,27; 2 Mc 9,18
supplication

ἱκέτης,-ου   N1M 0-0-1-1-2-4
Mal 3,14; Ps 73(74),23; Sir 4,4; 36,16
suppliant Mal 3,14; *Ps 73(74),23 τῶν ἱκετῶν
σου *of your suppliants* corr.? τῶν ἐχθρῶν σου
for MT צרריך *of your enemies*

ἱκμάς,-άδος⁺   N3F 0-0-1-1-0-2
Jer 17,8; Jb 26,14
moisture, moist place Jer 17,8; ἐπὶ ἱκμάδα
λόγου *at the least (at a drop) of his words* Jb
26,14

ἱκνέομαι
(→ ἀφ-, δι-, ἐξ-)

ἴκτερος,-ου   N2M 1-1-2-0-0-4
Lv 26,16; 2 Chr 6,28; Jer 37(30),6; Am 4,9
jaundice Lv 26,16; *blight* 2 Chr 6,28; *paleness* Jer
37(30),6

ἰκτίν,-ῖνος   N2M 2-0-0-0-0-2
Lv 11,14; Dt 14,13
kite, milvus regalis

ἱλαρός,-ά,-όν⁺   A 0-0-0-3-3-6
Prv 19,12; 22,8a; Est 5,1b; 3 Mc 6,35; Sir 13,26
cheerful, glad Est 5,1; τὸ ἱλαρόν *favour,
cheerfulness* Prv 19,12

→TWNT

ἱλαρότης,-ητος⁺   N3F 0-0-0-1-2-3
Prv 18,22; PSal 4,5; 16,12
cheerfulness, gaiety; neol.?

ἱλαρόω   V 0-0-0-0-3-3
Sir 7,24; 35,8; 43,22
to refresh [intrans.] Sir 43,22; ἱλαρόω τὸ
πρόσωπον *to gladden, to brighten the
countenance* Sir 7,24; neol.?

ἱλαρύνω   V 0-0-0-1-1-2
Ps 103(104),15; Sir 36,22
to cheer, to make cheerful, to gladden; neol.

ἱλαρῶς   D 0-0-0-1-0-1
Jb 22,26
cheerfully

ἱλάσκομαι⁺   V 2-4-0-6-0-12
Ex 32,14; Dt 21,8; 2 Kgs 5,18(bis); 24,4
M: *to pardon* [τι] Ps 64,4; P: *to be merciful, to
be propitious, to be favorably inclined* [abs.] Ex
32,14; [τινι] 2 Kgs 5,18
Cf. DODD 1930, 352-360; HELBING 1928, 24-25; HILL 1967,
23-36; HORSLEY 1983, 24-25; →NIDNTT; TWNT
(· ἐξ-)

ἱλασμός,-οῦ⁺   N2M 2-0-2-2-1-7
Lv 25,9; Nm 5,8; Ez 44,27; Am 8,14; Ps
129(130),4
expiation, atonement, propitiation, sin-offering Lv
25,9; *forgiveness* Ps 129(130),4
Cf. DANIEL 1966, 319.325; HARLÉ 1988, 32.198; HORSLEY
1983, 25; →NIDNTT; TWNT

ἱλαστήριον,-ου⁺   N2N 21-0-6-0-0-27
Ex 25,17.18.19.20(bis)
lid of the ark of the covenant Ex 25,17; *ledge?* Ez
43,14; *Am 9,1 ἱλαστήριον -כפרת *propitiatory* for
MT כפתור *capital of pillar*; neol.
Cf. DEISSMAN 1903, 193-212; HILL 1967, 23-36; LE
BOULLUEC 1989, 256-257 (Ex 25,16(17)); LEE 1983, 30.52;
MANSON 1945, 1-10; MORRIS 1955, 33-43; ·NIDNTT; TWNT

ἱλαστήριος,-α,-ον   A 0-0-0-0-1-1
4 Mc 17,22
propitiatory; ὁ ἱλαστήριος ὁ θάνατος *propitiary
death*

ἱλατεύω   V 0-0-0-1-0-1
Dnᴸˣˣ 9,19
to be gracious (of God); neol.

ἵλεως,-ως,-ων⁺   A 5-14-6-0-9-34
Gn 43,23; Ex 32,12; Nm 14,19.20; Dt 21,8
favorably inclined, propitious, gracious (of God)
Gn 43,23; *propitious, merciful, blameless* (of
things) 4 Mc 9,24; ἵλεως γίνομαί τινι *to be
merciful* to Dt 21,8; *2 Sm 20,20 ἵλεώς μοι

=חלילה? *far be it from me* [εἰ +ind. fut.], cpr.
[τοῦ +inf.] 2 Sm 23,17; 1 Chr 11,19; [+inf.]
1 Mc 2,21
Cf. KRAFT 1972, 167; LE BOULLUEC 1989, 321; →NIDNTT;
TWNT

ἴλη,-ης   N1F 0-0-0-0-1-1
2 Mc 5,3
troop (military term, used for cavalry)

ἰλύς,-ύος   N3F 0-0-0-2-0-2
Ps 39(40),3; 68(69),3
mud, mire
Cf. WALTERS 1973, 77-78.295-296

ἱμάντωσις,-εως   N3F 0-0-0-0-1-1
Sir 22,16
piece of timber used instead of a bond-stone;
neol.

ἱμάς,-άντος⁺   N3M 0-0-2-1-2-5
Is 5,18.27; Jb 39,10; 4 Mc 9,11; Sir 33,27
thong Is 5,18; *halter, rein* Sir 33,27; ἱμάντες
thongs Jb 39,10; *shoe-latches, shoe-straps* Is 5,27

ἱμάτιον,-ου⁺   N2N 93-52-30-23-23-221
Gn 9,23; 27,27; 28,20; 37,29.34
garment, raiment (an outer garment) Gn 9,23; τὰ
ἱμάτια *clothes* Gn 39,12; *Is 33,1 ἐπὶ ἱματίου
-ל/בגד *on a garment* for MT ל/בגד *to deal
treacherously*; *Is 14,19 ἱμάτιον -בגד *garment* for
MT פגר *carcass*; *Ct 4,10 ἱματίων σου -שמלתיך
your garments for MT שמניך *your ointments*, cpr.
4,11

ἱματιοφύλαξ,-ακος   N3M 0-1-0-0-0-1
2 Kgs 22,14
keeper of the wardrobe; neol.

ἱματισμός,-οῦ⁺   N2M 5-9-6-5-7-32
Gn 24,53; Ex 3,22; 11,2; 12,35; 21,10
clothing, apparel, raiment
Cf. LEE 1983, 101; WEVERS 1990, 39

ἵν   N 15-0-6-0-0-21
Ex 29,40(bis); 30,24; Lv 23,13; Nm 15,4
=הין *an Egyptian and Jewish liquid measure, a
hin* (about 9 l.)
Cf. HARLÉ 1988, 189; WEVERS 1990, 484

ἵνα⁺   C 179-91-63-133-149-615
Gn 3,3; 4,6(bis); 6,19; 11,7
that, in order that [+subj.] Gn 6,19; [+opt.]
(after hist. tenses) 4 Mc 17,1; [ἄν +subj.] 1 Chr
21,18; *that* [without verb] Jos 4,6; *(so) that*
(equivalent of ὥστε) Gn 22,14; *see that* (in
commands, introducing a principal sentence)
2 Mc 1,9; *so that* [without verb] Jos 4,6; ἵνα μή
[+subj.] *that not* Gn 3,3; ἵνα τί [+ind.] *to what*

end, why Gn 42,1; [τινι +inf.] Gn 27,46;
[+subj.] 2 Sm 13,26; *why, for what good* [abs.]
Gn 25,22

Cf. AEJMELAEUS 1982, 68-72; HORSLEY 1983, 148; 1989,
54; WEVERS 1990, 67.132.264.498; →TWNT

ἰνδάλματα,-ων   N3N 0-0-1-0-1-2
Jer 27(50),39; Wis 17,3
appearances, forms, apparitions; neol.

ἰξευτής,-οῦ   N1M 0-0-3-0-0-3
Am 3,5; 8,1.2
fowler, bird-catcher

ἰοβόλος,-ος,-ον   A 0-0-0-0-1-1
Wis 16,10
shedding venom, venomous (of animals)

ἰόομαι   V 0-0-0-0-2-2
Sir 12,10; 29,10
to become or *be rusty*

ἰός,-οῦ[+]   N2M 0-0-5-3-2-10
Ez 24,6(bis).11.12(bis)
poison, venom Ps 13,3; *rust, scum* LtJ 10
→NIDNTT; TWNT

ἰός,-οῦ   N2M 0-0-0-1-0-1
Lam 3,13
arrow

ἰουδαΐζω[+]   V 0-0-0-1-0-1
Est 8,17
to side with or *to imitate the Jews*; neol.

ἰππάζομαι   V 0-0-3-0-0-3
Jer 27(50),42; Ez 23,6.12
to ride
(→ ἐξ-)

ἰππάρχης,-ου   N1M 0-1-0-0-0-1
2 Sm 1,6
commander of cavalry, horse captain

ἰππασία,-ας   N1F 0-0-2-0-1-3
Jer 8,16; Hab 3,8; Od 4,8
horsemanship

ἰππεύς,-έως[+]   N3M 3-23-16-5-22-69
Gn 49,17; 50,9; Ex 14,9; 1 Sm 8,11; 13,5
horseman, driver, cavalry-man Gn 49,17; οἱ
ἰππεῖς *cavalry* 1 Es 8,51; ἱππεῖς τοξόται
archers on horseback Jdt 2,15; *Na 2,4 οἱ
ἰππεῖς -פרשים *horsemen* for MT ברשים *cypresses*

ἰππεύω   V 0-1-2-0-0-3
2 Kgs 9,16; Ez 23,23; Mi 1,13
to ride horses 2 Kgs 9,16; ἱππεύοντες *horsemen*
Mi 1,13

ἱππικός,-ή,-όν   A 0-0-0-0-2-2
1 Mc 15,38; 3 Mc 1,1
of horsemen, equestrian; δυνάμεις ἱππικαί

horsemen 1 Mc 15,38

ἱππόδρομος,-ου   N2M 2-0-0-0-3-5
Gn 48,7(bis); 3 Mc 4,11; 5,46; 6,16
chariot-road, (horse-)course Gn 48,7; *hippodrome*
3 Mc 4,11

Cf. HARL 1986, 303

ἵππος,-ου[+]   N2M/F 18-55-66-20-47-206
Gn 14,11.16.21; 47,17; 49,17
horse Gn 47,17; ἡ ἵππος *cavalry, horses* Ex
15,19; θήλειαι ἵπποι *mares* 1 Kgs 10,26; *Gn
14,11 ἵππον -רכש *cavalry* for MT ש(ו)רכ *goods*, see
also Gn 15,16.21

Cf. HARL 1986, 158; LEE 1983, 35; RUDOLPH 1971, 218
(Am 6,7); WEVERS 1990, 211.235; →TWNT

ἵπταμαι
(→ ἀν-, ἐξ-, ἐφ-, καθ-, περι-)

ιρ   N 0-0-0-3-0-3
Dn^Th 4,13(10).17(14).23(20)
=עיר (Aram.) *watcher, angel*

ἶρις,-εως[+]   N3F 1-0-0-0-0-1
Ex 30,24
iris (plant)
Cf. LE BOULLUEC 1989, 311; →NIDNTT; TWNT

ἰσάζω
(→ ἐξ-)

ισανα   N 0-0-0-1-0-1
Neh 12,39
=ישנה *old* Neh 13,39, see also Neh 3,6

ἰσάστερος,-ος,-ον   A 0-0-0-0-1-1
4 Mc 17,5
like a star, bright as a star

ἰσηγορέομαι   V 0-0-0-0-1-1
Sir 13,11
to speak as an equal; neol.

ἰσοδυναμέω   V 0-0-0-0-1-1
Sir prol.,21
to have equal power, to have the same force

ἰσοδύναμος,-ος,-ον   A 0-0-0-0-2-2
4 Mc 3,15; 5,20
of equal value [abs.] 4 Mc 5,20; [τινι] 4 Mc
3,15; neol.

ἰσόθεος,-ος,-ον   A 0-0-0-0-1-1
2 Mc 9,12
equal to God, godlike; ἰσόθεα φρονέω *to think
to be able to vie with God*

ἰσόμοιρος,-ος,-ον   A 0-0-0-0-1-1
2 Mc 8,30
sharing equally [τινι]

ἰσονομέω   V 0-0-0-0-1-1
4 Mc 5,24

to render equal rights, to render what is due

ἰσόομαι   V 0-0-0-3-0-3

Ps 88(89),7; Jb 28,17.19

to be equalled to [τινι] Jb 28,17; *to be compared to* [τινι] Ps 88(89),7

Cf. HELBING 1928, 255

(→ ἐξ-)

ἰσόπεδος,-ος,-ον   A 0-0-0-0-3-3

2 Mc 8,3; 9,14; 3 Mc 5,43

even, even with the ground 2 Mc 9,14; ἰσόπεδον τίθεμαι *to level* 3 Mc 5,43; ἰσόπεδος γίγνεται *to be made even with the ground* 2 Mc 8,3

ἰσοπολίτης,-ου   A 0-0-0-0-2-2

3 Mc 2,30; 4 Mc 13,9

enjoying equal political rights 3 Mc 2,30; ἰσοπολῖτις *for people enjoying equal political rights* (fem.) 4 Mc 13,9

Cf. RENEHAN 1975, 112

ἴσος,-η,-ον⁺   A 7-0-12-14-7-40

Ex 26,24(2); 30,34(bis); Lv 7,10

equal (to) [abs.] Wis 7,6; [τινι] Εχ 30,34; [τινος] Dt 13,7(6); ἴσα τινί *as, even as* (as adv.) Jb 5,14; τὸ ἴσον *equal portion* Lv 7,10; τίθημι ἴσον τί τινι *to level with* Is 51,23; ἴσον ἴσῳ *in equal parts* Ex 30,34; ἐξ ἴσου *in the same manner* Ex 26,24; *Ex 26,24 ἴσοι -תאמים *equal* for MT תמים *complete*

Cf. LE BOULLUEC 1989, 270-271 (Ex 26,24), 313; SPICQ 1982, 351.358; → NIDNTT

ἰσότης,-ητος⁺   N3F 0-0-1-1-1-3

Zech 4,7; Jb 36,29; PSal 17,41

equality PSal 17,41; *Zech 4,7 ἰσότητα -שות *equality, is the equal* for MT תשאות *shouts*, see also Jb 36,29

Cf. SPICQ 1982, 358-359; → NIDNTT; TWNT

ἰσόψυχος,-ος,-ον⁺   A 0-0-0-1-0-1

Ps 54(55),14

equal, peer

Cf. FRIDRICHSEN 1938, 42-49

ἰστάνω   V 0-0-1-0-0-1

Ez 17,14

to establish; ἰστάνω τὴν διαθήκην *to establish a covenant*

(→ ἐξ-)

ἵστημι⁺   V 133-206-111-206-117-773

Gn 6,18; 9,11; 12,8; 17,7.19

A: *to set (down), to set up, to cause to stand* [τι] Gn 35,14; *to set* [τι] Gn 21,28; *to pitch* [τι] (of a tent) Gn 12,8; *to establish* [τι] (of a covenant) Gn 6,18; [τι] (of an oath) Gn 26,3; *to confirm*

[τι] Nm 30,15; *to appoint sb to sth* [τινα εἰς τι] 1 Chr 25,1; *to make sb as* [τινα +pred.] Is 22,23; *to set up as* [τί τι] Gn 28,18; *to place in the balance, to weigh* [τι] 2 Sm 14,26; *to pay* [τι] 1 Kgs 21,39; *to build* [τι] Jb 20,19; M: *to stand* Gn 18,2; *to rest* Nm 9,17; *to stop, to stand still* 1 Sm 14,9; *to cease doing* [τοῦ +inf.] Gn 29,35; *to present oneself* Lv 18,23; ἑστηκώς *abiding* Am 6,5; ἵστημι τὰς εὐχάς τινι *to bind one's vows upon sb* Nm 30,15; στῆσον σεαυτόν *prepare yourself* Jer 38,21; *Jb 37,20 ἑστηκώς -עמר *standing* for MT אמר *he has spoken*; *2 Kgs 25,8 ἑστὼς ἐνώπιον -ל עמר *stood before* for MT ל עבר *servant of*; *1 Kgs 22,36 ἔστη -עמר *stood* for MT עבר *crossed over*, see also Jos 3,16; *Jer 39(32),12 ἑστηκότων -העמרים *the standing by* for MT הערים *the witnesses*; *Jb 39,26 ἕστηκεν -יעמר *remain steady* for MT יאבר *is clad with feathers*; *Jos 3,16 εἱστήκει -עמרו *stood* for MT עברו *crossed over*, see also 1 Kgs 22,36

Cf. HARL 1986, 55.153.177; HARLÉ 1988, 205; LE BOULLUEC 1989, 103.112.131.165

(→ ἀν-, ἀνθ-, ἀνταν-, ἀντικαθ-, ἀπαν-, ἀποκαθ-, ἀφ-, δι-, διαν-, ἐν-, ἐξ-, ἐξαν-, ἐπαν-, ἐπισυν-, εφ-, καθ-, καταν-, μεθ-, μεταν-, παρ-, παρακαθ-, παρεξ-, περι-, προ-, προσκαθ-, προυφ-, συμπαρ-, συν-, συναφ-, ὑφ-)

ἰστία,-ων   N2N 13-0-1-0-0-14

Ex 27,9.11.12.13.14

curtains Ex 27,9; *sails* Is 33,23

Cf. WEVERS 1990, 435.613

ἰστορέομαι⁺   V 0-0-0-0-3-3

1 Ezr 1,31(bis).40

to be recorded 1 Ezr 1,31; τὰ ἰστορούμενα *the stories* 1 Ezr 1,31

ἰστορία,-ας   N1F 0-0-0-1-6-7

Est 8,12g; 2 Mc 2,24.30.32(bis)

account, story

ἰστός,-οῦ   N2M 0-0-6-0-3-9

Is 30,17; 33,23; 38,12; 59,5.6

mast Is 33,23; *pole* Is 30,17; *spider's web* Is 59,5; *weaver's web* Tobˢ 2,12; *Is 38,12 ἰστός -ארג *web* for MT ארג *weaver*

ἰσχία,-ων   N2N 0-1-0-0-0-1

2 Sm 10,4

haunches

ἰσχνόφωνος,-ος,-ον   A 2-0-0-0-0-2

Ex 4,10; 6,30

weak-voiced

Cf. LE BOULLUEC 1989, 98-99.116; TOV 1977, 196

ἰσχυρός,-ά,-όν⁺   A 14-34-32-48-32-160
Gn 14,5; 41,31; 50,10; Ex 19,19; Nm 13,18
strong Gn 14,5; *powerful, mighty* Dt 2,10; ὁ
ἰσχυρός *the Mighty One* 2 Sm 22,31; *Gn 14,5
ἰσχυρά -עזוזים *strong* for MT זוזים/ה *the Zuzim*

ἰσχυρόω   V 0-0-1-0-0-1
Is 41,7
to strengthen [τι]

ἰσχυρῶς   D 1-1-0-2-0-4
Dt 12,23; Jgsᴮ 8,1; Prv 14,29; 31,17
strongly Prv 31,17; *very much, exceedingly* Dt
12,23; διαλέγομαι ἰσχυρῶς πρός τινα *to argue
sharply with* Jgsᴮ 8,1

ἰσχύς,-ύος⁺   N3F 25-58-94-106-75-358
Gn 4,12; 9,16; 15,6; 31,6; 49,3
strength Gn 4,12; *might, power* Jdt 13,19; *host*
2 Sm 24,2; *capability* Hos 8,7; *wealth, material
possessions* Hos 7,9; κατ' ἰσχύν *perforce* Ex
32,18; *Ct 2,7 ἰσχύσεσι -אילות *forces, strength* for
MT אילות *hinds, female deer*; *Is 47,5 ἰσχύς -גבורה
strength for MT גברת *lady*; *Hos 6,9 ἰσχύς σου
-כחך *your strength* for MT כחכי *ambushing*?; *2 Chr
3,17 Ἰσχύς -עז *strength* for MT בעז *Boaz*; *Jb 4,2
ἰσχὺν δέ -וערץ *but the force* for MT ועצר *but
retain*
Cf. GEHMAN 1972, 99; GRUNDMANN 1932; LE BOULLUEC
1989, 324; MURAOKA 1990, 41-42; WALTERS 1973, 331;
WEVERS 1990, 232

ἰσχυσις,-εως   N3F 0-0-0-1-0-1
Ct 2,7
see ἰσχύς

ἰσχύω⁺   V 13-23-24-16-30-106
Gn 31,29; Ex 1,9.12.20; Lv 5,7
to be strong Ex 1,9; *to have power over, to prevail
against* [ἐπί τινα] Est 4,17; [πρός τινα] Ps
12,5; *to be able to* [τι] Wis 16,20; *to condense*
[τι] Sir 43,15; *to have power to, to be able to*
[+inf.] Gn 31,29; οἱ ἰσχύοντες *the mighty men*
Is 1,24
Cf. LARCHER 1985, 925 (Wis 16,20); WEVERS 1990, 4

(→ ἐν-, ἐπ-, κατ-, συνεπ-, ὑπερ-)

ἴσως⁺   D 1-1-4-1-3-10
Gn 32,21; 1 Sm 25,21; Jer 5,4; 33(26),3; 43(36),3
perhaps

ἰταμία,-ας   N1F 0-0-2-0-0-2
Jer 30,10(49,16).20(49,4)
effrontery, temerity; neol.

ἰταμός,-ή,-όν   A 0-0-2-0-0-2
Jer 6,23; 27(50),42
bold, reckless

ἰτέα,-ας   N3F 1-0-1-1-0-3
Lv 23,40; Is 44,4; Ps 136(137),2
willow

ἰχθυηρός,-ά,-όν   A 0-0-0-2-0-2
Neh 3,3; 12,39
fishy; ἡ πύλη ἡ ἰχθυηρά *the fish-gate*

ἰχθύς,-ύος⁺   N3M 7-1-11-6-23-48
Gn 1,26.28; 9,2; Ex 7,18.21
fish

ἰχνευτής,-οῦ   N1M 0-0-0-0-1-1
Sir 14,22
tracer

ἰχνεύω   V 0-0-0-1-1-2
Prv 23,30; Sir 51,15
to track out [+indir. question] Prv 23,30; *to seek
after* [τι] Sir 51,15
(→ ἐξ-)

ἴχνος,-ους⁺   N3N 5-8-2-8-11-34
Gn 42,9.12; Dt 11,24; 28,35.65
track Jgsᴬ 5,28; *footstep* Ps 17(18),37; *mark* Gn
42,9; *trace* (metaph.) Wis 2,4; *hard sole of the
foot* Dt 11,24; *palm of the hand* 1 Sm 5,4
Cf. HARL 1986, 279; LEE 1983, 42

ἰχώρ,-ῶρος   N3M 0-0-0-2-1-3
Jb 2,8; 7,5; 4 Mc 9,20
discharge, eruption Jb 2,8; *juice, colourless liquid*
4 Mc 9,20; *Jb 7,5 ἀπὸ ἰχῶρος *from (my)
eruption* corr.? ἀπὸ χρωτός for MT עורי *from
(my) skin*
Cf. RENEHAN 1975, 113